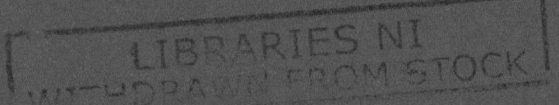

ANTIQUES
Handbook
& Price Guide

Judith Miller

CONTENTS

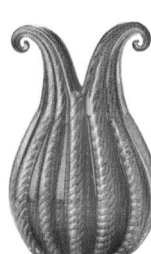

LIST OF CONSULTANTS

CERAMICS

John Axford
Woolley & Wallis
Salisbury, Wiltshire

Victoria Crake
Lyon & Turnbull
Edinburgh

Steven Moore
Anderson & Garland,
Newcastle upon Tyne

CLOCKS & BAROMETERS

Leighton Gillibrand
Dreweatts
Bristol

DECORATIVE ARTS

Michael Jeffrey
Woolley & Wallis
Salisbury, Wiltshire

John Mackie
Lyon & Turnbull
Edinburgh

FURNITURE

Lee Young
Lyon & Turnbull
Edinburgh

ORIENTAL

John Axford
Woolley & Wallis
Salisbury, Wiltshire

GLASS

Jeanette Hayhurst
Jeanette Hayhurst Fine Glass
Kensington Church Street, London W8 4HA

JEWELLERY

Trevor Kyle
Lyon &Turnbull
Edinburgh

Steven Miners
Cristobal
Church Street, London

MODERN

John Mackie
Lyon & Turnbull
Edinburgh

MUSIC BOXES

Stephen Kember
The Corn Exchange,
The Pantiles,
Tunbridge Wells, Kent

METALWARE

Colin Fraser
Lyon & Turnbull
Edinburgh

Rupert Slingsby
Woolley & Wallis
Salisbury, Wiltshire

HOW TO USE THIS BOOK

Page tab This appears on every page and identifies the main category heading as identified in the Contents List on pages 4-5.

Caption The description of the item illustrated, including when relevant, the period, the maker or factory, medium, the year it was made, dimensions and condition. Many captions have **footnotes**, which explain terminology or give identification or valuation information.

Essential Reference Gives key facts about the factory, maker or style, along with stylistic identification points, value tips and advice on fakes.

Running head Indicates the sub-category of the main heading.

Closer look Does exactly that. This is where we show identifying aspects of a factory or maker, point out rare colours or shapes, and explain why a particular piece is so desirable.

The object The antiques are shown in fulll colour. This is a vital aid to identification and valuation. With many objects, a slight colour variation can signify a large price differential.

Source code Every item has been specially photographed at an auction house, a dealer, an antiques market or a private collection. These are credited by code at the end of the caption, and can be checked against the Key to Illustrations on pages 632-633.

The price guide These price ranges give a ball park figure of what you should pay for a similar item. The great joy of antiques is that there is not a recommended retail price. The price ranges in this book are based on actual prices, either what a dealer will take or the full auction price.

INTRODUCTION

It is with great pride that I introduce the latest edition of the Antiques Handbook and Price Guide, packed as it is with thousands of antiques from every field of collecting and for every conceivable budget. Miller's continues to thrive on its international reputation as an authority on antiques and collectables. Old friends will welcome updated information on current trends and prices, while newcomers will, I trust, find an easy-to-use, approachable directory, from which to make a start in their chosen field.

Antique hunters and collectors have been around for many years, but few can say that the first decade of the 21st century has been easy. The recent global economic downturn have done much to shake up buyers and sellers alike, sending shockwaves through all areas of business, antiques being no exception. And, while it would be wrong to say that there have been no casualties – shops have, regrettably, closed and a number of dealers have gone out of business – the majority of sellers and auction houses do not give up easily, and many have found themselves adapting. In fact, according to reports from people in the trade the trends that have emerged over the last twelve months suggest that, although the antiques market may have changed, its fate is far from sealed, and there are many ways in which today's buyers and collectors can benefit, with a few insider tips.

For example, almost all fields of antique buying have seen excellent sales (even rising prices) at the top end of the market, yet falling or stagnant sales for mid-range and low-end items. While this may make top-end pieces prohibitively expensive for the masses – there is nothing new here – it does mean that many mid-range items can currently be bought for four-figure sums, making them incredible value for money. They also represent a good investment in the longer term, as prices for such items will inevitably rise again.

It is also important to consider the power of the collector in furthering and moving markets. This is, perhaps, clearly evident in the field of decorative arts, in which

A Regency rosewood, satinwood and brass inlaid sofa table. c1815 £8,000-12,000 FRE

the demand for pieces that exemplify, for example, Arts & Crafts furniture or Art Nouveau glassware or Art Deco ceramics, far outstrip the supply. The result is a healthy, buoyant market in which the best pieces that come up for sale are bid for by a number of keen collectors, and so realise a good price. Investing in such an area will always pay in the long run, particularly as pieces become increasingly rare.

Dealers are always looking for emerging markets, as this is where they stand to make good money if they get it right. A market in its infancy will have no shortage of available pieces at good prices. Only when demand starts to grow do prices rise as items get snapped up. Of course, there is some risk involved, as one can never be certain that demand will rise. However, two areas that have seen substantial growth in the last few years and that show no signs of abating are the Asian market, with renewed interest in China following the Olympic Games, and the Modern market, which continues to go from strength to strength.

Both areas still offer countless opportunities for buyers and collectors to make value-for-money purchases today that can become promising investments in the longer term. All of these trends and more are covered in this issue of the Antiques Handbook and Price Guide. And such is my enthusiasm for the subject that I hope you find, not only the information you are looking for, but also that something else might just catch your eye as you thumb through the pages – something to spark an interest in a different area to start you a new journey of discovery and wonder.

Judith Miller.

A Clarice Cliff square stepped bowl c1930 £800-1,000 L&T

PORCELAIN

While the early part of this year found sellers of European ceramics fearful of a media-hyped recession, and therefore reluctant to sell, there was fortunately little sign of such reticence among the buyers of porcelain, many of whom remain strong private collectors.

As is the case in many areas of antique buying and collecting, items of quality and/or rarity have continued to achieve good prices, and there has been no apparent marked change to the market in the last few years. The market leaders, Sèvres and Meissen, remain popular with collectors: sales for early 18th century examples from these factories have been strong throughout the year, although the uptake of later 18th century wares has been much slower. The same is true for other European factories, such as Limoges and Dresden. As well as looking for quality in a piece of porcelain, collectors are increasingly seeking specific subjects when it comes to design. In terms of Berlin plaques, for example, designs featuring attractive women are currently seen to be fetching a premium.

The market has been boosted this year in particular, with the dispersal of several private collections of varying size and significance. The most important of these was undoubtedly the recent Hoffmeister Collection of Meissen porcelain, sold by Bonhams in London in November 2009. This million-pound auction saw the sale of around a hundred lots of the very best in Meissen's history of production; the most prestigious lot – a pair of c.1732, turquoise-ground vases from the Japanese Palace in Dresden – sold for £102,000. The sale's success echoed the double-estimate prices Bonham's had achieved some six months previously for Meissen porcelain, demonstrating the resilience of quality European ceramics against an economic downturn.

An area that continues to do less well is that of British blue and white printed wares, which has been in steady decline for several years now. It is increasingly the case that buyers are looking for exceptional pieces in terms of condition and design – large platters with a rare pattern, for example. This is true for Worcester and Bow, where early pieces have performed well, while later wares are failing to sell for anything like the prices that have been reached in previous years. Conversely, a rare pink printed tea set was reported to have sold for £4,400 during the last twelve months, confirming the trend towards 'rare and exceptional'. Despite the sluggishness of blue and white wares, however, the year has generally been a very positive one for porcelain, which can only indicate a continued confidence among collectors.

Buyers of porcelain should always check the quality and provenance of a piece, as there are many fakes on the market, particularly of pieces from Sèvres and Meissen. As well as individual designs, factory marks have been forged, so relying on these may not always be enough to guarantee authenticity. Damage should be avoided, as this invariably lowers a piece's value. It is always best to buy from a reputable source that is happy to supply detailed receipts.

Clockwise from top right: rare Derby pierced basket c1750 £4,600 at Richard Winterton; Meissen milk jug c1730 £2,400 at Woolley & Wallis; Berlin plaque c1890 £4,000 at Freeman's; Meissen plate £1,700 at Lyon & Turnbull.

PORCELAIN

ESSENTIAL REFERENCE – BERLIN

- In 1763, Frederick the Great bought a bankrupt Berlin pottery factory (established 1761) and renamed it the Royal Porcelain Factory.
- Former Meissen employee, Carl Wilhelm Böhme (1720-89/95) was chief painter from 1761. The state-owned factory initially produced distinctive late Rococo style wares, made in creamy-toned porcelain, and embellished with trelliswork, pierced rims and flowers. The introduction of a new type of kaolin in 1770 led to a colder white tone to the porcelain, and at the same time the factory turned to a more severe Neo-classical style.
- Fine gilt wares in the Empire style, as developed at Sèvres, were made during the early 19thC, including dinner wares and vases painted with scenes framed by opulent gilt borders. Popular scenes included topographical views of famous buildings, such as Schinkel's theatre; Classical scenes; and portraits. Biscuit porcelain statuettes and busts were also made, sometimes after the marbles of J. G. Schadow.
- Successfully adapting to the growing middle class market in this period, the factory began to produce ornate display wares, notably cabinet cups and plates.
- From c1830 vases based on urns and kraters and decorated with Classical motifs, were a major part of production.
- Porcelain plaques in gilt frames were made from c1840. Framed blanks were sent to outside decorators to be painted with copies of Old Masters or sentimental subjects.
- Herman Seger (1839-93) was appointed as technical director in 1878, marking the end of the heavy Victorian style. He invented 'Seger-Porzellan', which was used for Chinese-shaped vases, decorated with rich flambé glazes in sange de boeuf, violet, green and yellow.
- Pieces are marked KPM for Königliche Porzellan-Manufaktur. The blue sceptre mark was used from 1763.
- In 1918 the factory was renamed Staatiliche Porzellan Manufaktur Berlin. It is still active.

A late 19thC KPM painted porcelain plaque of Judith, retailed by Shreve, Crump & Low, after the painting by August Riedel (German, 1799–1883), signed 'Sturm' or 'S. Flurm', with 'KPM', sceptre mark, in gilt wood frame.

In the second half of the 19thC, the Berlin porcelain factory was known for its elaborate, Neo-Classical porcelain and its plaques depicting paintings by popular artists such as Watteau.

Plaque 15in (38cm) high

£7,000-9,000   SK

A late 19thC KPM oval painted porcelain plaque, depicting the Penitent Magdalene after the painting by Correggio (1489-1534), the Virgin shown reading, her book propped up on a skull, in gilt wood frame.

Plaque 8.75in (22cm) wide

£900-1,200   SK

A late 19thC KPM painted porcelain plaque, decorated with a boy in Tyrolean dress, smoking a cigarette.

7in (18cm) high

£1,200-1,800   GORL

A KPM porcelain painted plaque, painted with a young woman in medieval costume, impressed 'KPM' and incised '9 3/4 - 7 3/8', old label with faint inscription pasted to the reverse.

c1870   *9.75in (25cm) high*

£2,000-2,500   TEN

A KPM Berlin porcelain plaque, of the young Queen Victoria, wearing a tiara, half length, impressed mark.

7in (18cm) high

£1,200-1,800   DUK

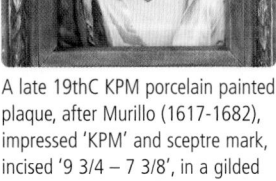

A late 19thC KPM porcelain painted plaque, after Murillo (1617-1682), impressed 'KPM' and sceptre mark, incised '9 3/4 – 7 3/8', in a gilded composition glazed frame.

Plaque 9.75in (25cm) high

£2,000-2,500   TEN

A late 19thC Berlin porcelain eight-piece cabaret set, painted with ornithological subjects, gilded borders, with coffee pot and tray.

£450-550   GORL

An early 20thC Berlin twin-handled potpourri vase and cover, painted with landscapes, with ringed lion-mask handles joined by gilded laurel garlands with Roman Emperor's profile medallion, pierced lid with gilded finial, sceptre mark.

A 13-piece Berlin KPM porcelain dessert service, decorated with raised gilt with acanthus leaves, centrally painted with fruits, marked with blue painted underglaze sceptre mark, orange printed orb, and 'KPM', some pieces with black Iron Cross.

c1880   *Dish 15in (38cm) wide*
£1,000-1,500   TEN

14in (35.5cm) high
£400-500   GORL

BOW

A pair of Bow white-glazed models of actors in Turkish dress, the man possibly David Garrick, with one hand on his hip, the woman in a fur-lined cloak, restoration.

c1752   *Tallest 8.25in (21cm) high*
£2,500-3,500   WW

A Bow model of Summer, personified as a young woman seated on piles of harvested corn, the outstretched hand broken and re-glued, minor chipping.

c1754   *5in (12.5cm) high*
£700-1,000   WW

A near pair of Bow figures of a sportsman and his companion, each holding a gun with a dog seated beside them, raised on Rococo moulded bases with applied flowers, restoration to both.

c1755   *5.25in (13.5cm) high*
£900-1,200   WW

A Bow figure of a Leventine lady, standing on a shaped flower-encrusted base, with gilt highlights to the garments, extensive restoration.

c1760   *6.5in (16.5cm) high*
£250-350   TEN

A Bow figure of a piping shepherd, with his dog at his feet and a bag over his shoulder, wearing a pink hat and floral sprigged coat and breeches, with red painted anchor and dagger marks.

c1770   *6in (15cm) high*
£350-450   L&T

An 18thC composite set of Bow busts, depicting the four seasons, comprising two men each on marbled plinths and two women on white plinths.

6in (15.5cm) high
£700-900   L&T

PORCELAIN

ESSENTIAL REFERENCE – A-MARK PORCELAIN

- There has been debate about 'A'-marked porcelain since 1937, when a 'curious teapot' and three cups were presented at a meeting of the English Ceramic Circle.
- Approximately 41 pieces are now known, most of which are cups. Nearly all have a British provenance.
- It is believed that these 'A'-marked wares represent the first production of porcelain in England, perhaps an early phase of experimental production by Bow. They are of similar type to the porcelain produced by the Heylyn and Frye patent of 1744 for Bow. Anton Gabszewicz has also compared the 'A'-mark porcelain to the 'drab' or 'mushroom' wares of early Bow.
- The pieces are extremely rare and desirable.

An 'A'-mark porcelain fluted coffee cup, painted with alternate panels of flowers and a bird with scrolls and ribbons, brown line rim above a black, speckled and gilt scrolling border, repairs.

3.5in (9cm) high

£15,000-20,000　　　　　　　　　WW

A Bow porcelain coffee can, of mildly waisted form with strap handle, painted in blue with a pine tree and pagodas in a landscape.
c1755　　　*2.25in (6cm) high*
£350-450　　　　　　BE

A Bow coffee can, painted in the famille rose palette with peony and lotus between iron-red borders, cracked.
c1755　　　*3in (7.5cm) high*
£250-350　　　　　　WW

A rare Bow mug, printed in brick red with scenes from Hubert Gravelot's 'Youthful Diversions' including 'Battledore and Shuttlecock' and 'Whip Top'.
c1755　　　*5in (12.5cm) high*
£7,000-9,000　　　　　WW

Two Bow bowls, printed in iron-red with 'The Singing Lesson' and other vignettes of figural groups.
c1760　　　*6in (15cm) diam*
£5,000-8,000　　　　　WW

A Bow large octagonal bowl, decorated in the Kakiemon palette, with birds, dragons and prunus branches, and a similar octagonal bowl, both damaged and restored.
10.5in (27cm) diam
£700-1,000　　　　　　WW

A rare Bow jug, printed in brick red with scenes from Hubert Gravelot's 'Youthful Diversions' including 'Battledore and Shuttlecock', and 'Marbles'.
c1755　　　*5in (12.5cm) high*
£8,000-10,000　　　　WW

A Caughley chestnut basket, printed in blue with the 'Pine Cone' pattern, the rope-twist handles issuing from applied leaves and flowers, printed 'C' mark, minor damages.

c1775   8.5in (21.5cm) wide

£500-700   WW

A Caughley heart-shaped dish, painted in the 'Weir' pattern with an Oriental landscape in blue, later polychrome decoration, '8' mark to inside of foot-rim, wear to the clobbered enamels and some peppering.

c1780-90   10.5in (27cm) wide

£50-100   WW

A late 18thC Caughley armorial soup plate, painted with the arms of Braithwaite, of Yorkshire and Westmorland, with a printed Fitzhugh border in blue, exhibition labels for Ironbridge 1999 and 2005.

7.75in (19.5cm) diam

£350-450   WW

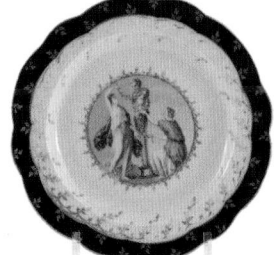

A Caughley plate, painted with two bacchantes adorning a term of Pan with garlands of flowers, after a painting by Angelica Kaufman (1741-1807), within a gilt foliate border on cobalt blue, wear to the gilding.

c1785   8in (20.5cm) diam

£250-350   WW

A Caughley plate, with ozier-moulded rim, painted with a central urn draped in floral garlands, a small chip to the rim.

c1790   8.75in (22cm) diam

£500-700   WW

A rare Caughley cup, decorated with a fruit print of an apple nestled in a border of flowers, the underside with a rare printed mark of a flower spray.

c1770-75   3.25in (8cm) high

£550-750   WW

A late 18thC Caughley teacup, painted with an armorial below a delicate gilt border, and a deep Caughley saucer with the 'Royal Lily' pattern in blue, gilded with the initials 'AR' and the title 'Jus Liberorum', 'S' mark to the saucer, wear.

Saucer 6in (15.5cm) diam

£400-500   WW

A rare Caughley two-handled cup, painted with a maiden, the reverse painted with a cottage in a landscape, and a Caughley saucer decorated with a child nursing a toy beside a crib, wear to the gilding.

In 1772, Thomas Turner moved from Worcester to the Caughley pottery (established in the 1750s), near Broseley, Shropshire. There he made Worcester-style transfer-printed porcelain called 'Salopian' ware, and introduced many Worcester shapes. The Chamberlain Worcester factory bought Caughley's porcelain blanks in 1780-95. Turner sold the Caughley works in 1799. It continued for 15 years before closing.

Cup 5.5in (14cm) wide

£1,000-1,500   WW

An unusual Caughley teapot and cover, the fluted form painted with sprays of flowers beneath border of overglaze blue and pink hatching, minor chipping.

c1785-95   8.25in (21cm) high

£350-450   WW

PORCELAIN

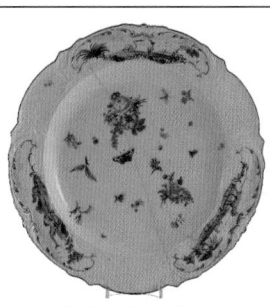

A large Chelsea plate, of Warren Hastings type, painted at the rim in the manner of Jefferyes Hamett O'Neale (1734-1801) between moulded diaper panels, red anchor mark, cracked in half and re-glued.

c1753   *14.5in (37cm) diam*

£500-600   **WW**

A large Chelsea scallop-edged dish, painted in the Kakiemon palette with the 'Hob in the Well' pattern, red anchor mark, damaged and restored.

c1752-55   *12.25in (31cm) diam*

£350-450   **WW**

ESSENTIAL REFERENCE – CHELSEA

● **The first successful British porcelain factory was founded at Chelsea c1744, by a Huguenot silversmith, Nicholas Sprimont (c1716-1771). Most periods are named after marks.**

● **The influence of British silverwares can be seen in early Chelsea pieces, from the Triangle Period (c1744-49).**

● **The Raised Anchor Period (c1749-52) saw a move away from the influence of silver, as wares became more robust. The glaze also changed, the addition of tin oxide giving it a more 'silky' feel. Popular decorative schemes included copies of Japanese Kakiemon wares and Meissen-style European landscapes.**

● **The introduction of innovative decorative styles, alongside further copies of Meissen, arrived with the Red Anchor period (c1752-56). Chelsea became famous for its dessert table settings and painted fruit and botanical decoration. It also made small 'toys' (tiny scent bottles) and figures by the Flemish modeller Josef Williams (c1715-1766).**

● **During the Gold Anchor period (c1756-69) the French factories of Vincennes and Sèvres became the dominant influences, with a strong Rococo style and increased gilding.**

● **The factory closed in 1769, but the owners of Derby porcelain factory (est. c1748) Heath and Duesbury, bought the works. This period is known as 'Chelsea-Derby'. It closed in 1784.**

A Chelsea scallop-edged dish, painted in the Kakiemon palette with the 'Lady in a Pavilion' pattern, minor restoration, wear to the enamels.

8.75in (22cm) diam

£900-1,200   **WW**

CLOSER LOOK – CHELSEA 'HANS SLOANE' PLATE

During the Red Anchor period, Chelsea became famous for its painted decoration of flowers, plants, fruit and animals. Good examples command high prices.

The decorative design is boldly applied to cover the whole plate asymmetrically.

The plate is decorated with Pink Siris, also known as the Silk Tree, which was introduced to London from China in 1745, only a decade before this plate was painted. There was a strong fascination with China in Europe during the 18thC.

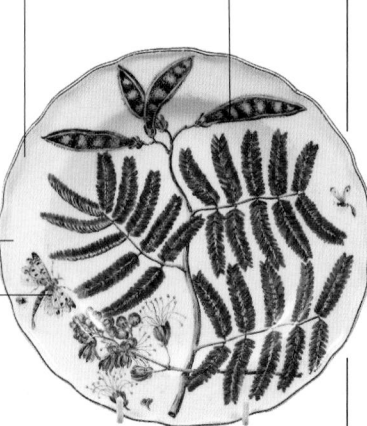

The delicately painted insects are a typical Chelsea feature. Small details such as these were often painted over imperfections to disguise faults.

A Chelsea 'Hans Sloane' plate, painted with a branch of Pink Siris (Albizia Julibrissia), flowers and insects, brown rim, with red anchor.

Chelsea's botanical designs were named after Hans Sloane, a noted scientist who, in 1713, bought four acres of Chelsea and leased it to the Society of Apothecaries to extend Chelsea Physic Garden, for £5 in perpetuity. The original Chelsea Physic Garden was founded in 1673.

c1755   *8in (20.5cm) high*

£3,500-4,500   **SWO**

A Chelsea porcelain bird and flower dessert plate, the rim panels alternately incised with waves and Oriental birds, red painted anchor mark and old label, also with circular green label inscribed 'IOM264'.

c1752-56   *8.5in (21.5cm) diam*

£350-450   **TEN**

A Chelsea fruit painted dessert plate, of shaped circular form with feather moulded rim picked out in iron-red and gilt, red painted anchor mark, old label of 'A J Filkins, Guaranteed Genuine' and inscribed 'Chelsea C. 1758'.

c1752-56   *8.5in (21.5cm) diam*

£1,000-1,300   **TEN**

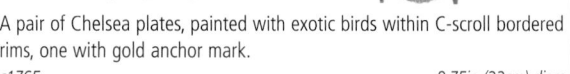

A pair of Chelsea plates, painted with exotic birds within C-scroll bordered rims, one with gold anchor mark.

c1765   *8.75in (22cm) diam*

£700-1,000   **DN**

A Chelsea gold anchor porcelain dessert plate, of bracketed circular form with solid gilt band to the slightly raised rim line, centrally painted in vivid enamel colours, anchor mark in gilt.

c1765   9.25in (23.5cm) diam

£450-550   TEN

A lobed Chelsea-Derby bowl, painted with colourful floral garlands within borders of mazarine blue and gilding, some wear to the gilding.

c1775   8.75in (22cm) diam

£250-350   WW

An early Chelsea fluted beaker, moulded with a spiralling pattern of flowering and fruiting branches, brightly painted with coloured enamels, a crack and small chips to the rim.

c1748-52   3in (7.5cm) high

£2,500-3,000   WW

A Chelsea spiral-lobed teabowl, with a moulded acanthus leaf border, the body painted with polychrome flower sprays and brown line rim, red anchor mark.

c1752-6   2.75in (7cm) high

£400-500   WW

A Chelsea fluted teabowl and saucer, with scalloped edges, finely painted with flower sprays, brown line rims, faint red anchor mark to the teabowl, minor faults.

c1755   Saucer 5in (13cm) diam

£1,200-1,800   WW

A Chelsea seal, modelled as hurdy-gurdy player, wearing a black cloth hat, a stone seal underneath with metal mount.

c1765   1.25in (3.5cm) high

£250-350   WW

CLOSER LOOK – 'GIRL IN A SWING' ÊTUI

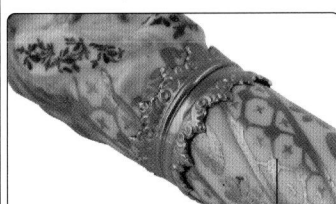

The rich Rococo-style gilt decoration and bright colours are typical of these pieces.

These decorative cases were popular during the 18th and 19thC. They were made to hold small items such as needles or perfume bottles.

Columbine was a popular female character from Commedia dell'arte', an improvised form of theatre that was frequently performed in the 18thC. A female servant, she was intelligent and flirtatious, recognisable here by her knowing and engaging gaze, and colourful costume.

Porcelain toys' were very fashionable and carefully treasured in their day, and their fine quality makes them highly desirable.

The figure is beautifully moulded, which is characteristic of 'Girl in a Swing' pieces.

A Chelsea êtui with gold or gilt metal mounts, the top modelled as a bust of Columbine, with a plumed veil, the spiral-moulded base decorated with a pattern of gilt motifs.

The origin of manufacture of these toys' is much debated. Originally attributed to the Chelsea factory, experts have since suggested they were made at a rival factory in London, set up by Charles Gouyn (died 1785), called the Girl in a Swing' factory, after an item attributed to it, now in the V&A museum, London. Gouyn was a jeweller based in St James's, London, and also a partner in the Chelsea factory until some time before March 1749. The Girl in a Swing' wares are made of a glassy paste similar to Chelsea's but with a greater percentage of lead. They also have some modelling differences that help to identify them, although the pieces are unmarked. The main items of production seem to have been toys such as perfume bottles, êtuis and patch boxes, but figures and other wares may also have been made.

c1760   5in (13cm) high

£5,000-6,000   WW

A Chelsea seal, with gold mounts, modelled as a putti and dog, the seal underneath carved with an eagle and the motto 'Suivez Raison' for the Browne family.

c1765-70   1.25in (3cm) h

£650-850   WW

A rare Chelsea fish tureen, cover and stand, modelled as a plaice with gaping mouth, the handle formed as seaweed, unmarked, damages and restoration.

c1752-58   11in (28cm) wide

£1,500-2,000   WW

A Chelsea Derby 'Time Clipping The Wings of Cupid' group, the scrolled base with a map of the world and crown, bow and arrows, with large firing crack under base.

c1760   12.5in (32cm) high

£600-800   SWO

PORCELAIN

Part of an English, probably Coalport, porcelain botanical part dessert service, comprising one oval and four octagonal dishes on gold scroll feet, and ten plates, each painted with a bloom, named on the back, damage. c1810

£700-1,000 SET   BE

An early 19thC Coalport plate, painted in the manner of William Billingsley with panels of flowers on a blue scale ground.

8.5in (21.5cm) diam

£50-150   WW

An early 19thC, possibly Coalport, tea and coffee service, decorated with wild roses, gilt foliage and borders, comprising 18 tea cups, 21 saucers, 19 coffee cups, 30 saucers, 23 small plates, five larger plates, two saucers, a slop bowl, two tall coffee cups, an oblong two-handled dish on claw and ball feet, various cracks, chips and crazing.

£900-1,200   A&G

Part of a Coalport dessert service, each piece with sprays of flowers and powder blue borders gilt with sprigs, gadrooned rims, impressed '2' and gilt '976', comprising 21 plates, four square dishes, three oval dishes, four circular dishes, two small oval dishes, two lidded tureens and a large oval comport, considerable staining wear and restoration.
c1820-25

£1,500-2,000 SET   SWO

A Coalport dessert plate, with moulded floral rim, painted with the fruit and flowers of late summer within a border, some enamel wear and staining.
c1820-25   *9.25in (23.5cm) diam*

£50-150   WW

A late 19thC Coalport fish service, with gilt scalloped edges, and decorated with gilt and polychrome fishing motifs, comprising a fish platter, a sauce tureen and saucer, and twelve plates.

Platter 23.75in (60cm) wide

£700-1,000 SET   L&T

A Coalport porcelain ten piece British topographical named view dessert service, decorated by Edward Oakes Ball, subjects include 'Tintern Abbey', 'Dover Castle and 'Buildwas Abbey', all signed 'E Ball', blue printed crown mark, each named and numbered 'X2289'.

Edward Oakes Ball (born c1873 in Jackfield, Shropshire) trained at the Coalport Pottery and became one of their principal landscape painters.
c1900-10

£1,000-1,500   TEN

A Coalport circular tapered vase, painted panel of Loch-Stack, within gilt foliated cartouche, on blue ground, with yellow neck and feet, green mark 'V7586/D', signed 'E.O. Ball', gilding to rim worn.

10.5in (26.5cm) high

£300-400   A&G

A Coalport casket and cover, with 'Moorish'-style decoration, with a turquoise ground and gilt 'jewelled' panels, painted with a cartouche, the cover with cabochon finial, printed mark, pattern no. V4229.

5.5in (14cm) high

£700-1,000   DUK

A Copeland parian bust of 'Clytie', on a bed of leaves, concave sided circular plinth, impressed 'COPELAND J94'.

Parian was a type of porcelain developed in the 1840s by Copeland & Garrett, who bought the Spode works in 1833. It has a creamy tint with a very slight sheen. Parian was used to reproduce famous sculptures in miniature and many factories produced it, including Copeland, Minton and Wedgwood. It was usually left uncoloured.

21.5in (55cm) high

£700–1,000   TEN

A large Copeland parian figure of Ruth, by W. Brodie, the standing figure modelled holding a sheaf of wheat, impressed title, sculptor, date and factory mark.

William Brodie (1815-1881) was a Scottish sculptor, elected to the Royal Scottish Academy in 1857.

c1870   *28.5in (72.5cm) high*

£400-500   SK

A Copeland parianware figure of a lady playing croquet, on a circular plinth, impressed mark 'Copyright reserved Copeland M80' and 'EA Morris SC', restorations.

17.75in (45cm) high

£350-450   L&T

A Copeland parian ware bust of Sir Titus Salt, raised on separate turned and fluted pedestal with moulded base, impressed 'John Adam Acton Fecit' and 'published by J Rhones 1877'.

Sir Titus Salt (1803-76) was a businessman, politician and philanthropist responsible for building the village of Saltaire. He made his fortune in the wool trade, and in 1853 built a wool factory of unprecedented scale, incorporating all modern engineering. His project included the construction of Saltaire, a community of housing and public buildings for the benefit of his employees.

22.5in (57cm) high

£600-800   HT

A pair of Copeland Neo-classical porcelain ewers, the S-scroll knopped handles with double snake terminals and bearded man mask, the necks with beaded edge, the rose-painted bodies over moulded leaves to a short knopped stem and foot with gilt chevron edge band, blue printed interlaced 'C' mark and 'Copeland 18'.

c1875   *14.5in (37cm) high*

£3,000-4,000   TEN

A pair of large 19thC Copeland vases, each of baluster form, with everted gilt rim, painted with summer flowers, butterflies and insects on a celadon ground, green printed mark.

1851-1885   *20in (51cm) high*

£1,000-1,500   L&T

A pair of Copeland porcelain pedestal jars, with scroll and mask-head handles, the covers with cherub knops, each foot rim painted with a band of roses, one cherub foot broken and repaired.

18.5in (47cm) high

£1,200-1,800   BE

A set of twelve early 20thC Copeland ceramic dessert plates and soup plates, pattern no. 7597, retailed by Daniell, 129 New Bond St, London, printed 'Copeland's China England', inscribed in orange.

Largest 9.75in (24.5cm) diam

£2,500-3,000   TEN

A large Copeland porcelain footbath, with trailing roses on white with turquoise band.

19in (48cm) wide

£350-450   MEA

PORCELAIN

A rare early Derby white-glazed model of St Philip, with a basket of loaves and fishes spilling over at his feet, raised on a scrolling Rococo base, some damage and restoration.

c1753 · *9.75in (24.5cm) high*

£2,500-3,000 · **WW**

ESSENTIAL REFERENCE – DERBY

- The first Derby Porcelain Factory was established in 1756 by William Duesbury, John Heath and André Planché.
- Many of the early wares were produced in white and often known as dry-edged wares
- Early wares, including tea sets, tureens and baskets, were influenced by Meissen.
- In 1770, Duesbury bought the Chelsea factory and ran it until 1784 in conjunction with Derby. Products of both factories were influenced by Sèvres and Louis XVI-style vases. The production of biscuit figures also began. Pieces were marked with an anchor and the letter 'D'.
- The Crown Derby period began in 1784 when the factory adopted a crowned D as its mark. The wares included simply decorated table-wares, Neo-classical in shape and sometimes painted with fresh naturalistic flowers, by W. Billingsley and others.
- The Bloor Derby period, a steady decline in which the factory lost all individuality, lasted from 1811-45 and the factory closed in 1848.
- Several other porcelain factories were established in Derby in 19thC, notably Royal Crown Derby Porcelain Company established in 1890 and still operating today.

A Derby dry-edge white-glazed figure of Winter, modelled by Planché, personified as a woman wearing a hooded cloak, warming her hands over a brazier, damage and restoration.

6in (15.5cm) high

£4,000-5,000 · **WW**

A Derby figure of two lovers, the girl gathering flowers in her apron with her beloved's arm around her shoulder, restored.

c1755-60 · *6in (15.5cm) high*

£600-800 · **WW**

A Derby encrusted porcelain figure of a gentleman reading a letter, standing holding a letter in his left hand, a dog at his right side in typical colours and gilt, restored.

c1770 · *7in (18cm) high*

£150-250 · **TEN**

A pair of a Derby encrusted porcelain figures of a shepherd and shepherdess, he with a dog and she with a lamb, in typical soft coloured enamels throughout, enriched with gilt, restored.

c1770-1780 · *Tallest 5.5in (14cm) high*

£250-350 · **TEN**

An 18thC Derby figure of Mars, modelled wearing armour and helmet, with emblems of war to the base, painted in polychrome, with gilding on a square gilt-lined base, incised mark 'N174'.

c1770-1780 · *6.5in (16.5cm) high*

£100-200 · **DUK**

A Derby biscuit model of two bacchantes, adorning a bust of Pan with floral garlands before an oak tree, from an engraving by Francesco Bartolozzi (1725-1815), incised 'N196', damages.
c1778   12.25in (31cm) high
£900-1,200   WW

A Derby porcelain figure of a gallant, modelled standing holding a basket of fruit before bocage, a dog at his feet on a pierced scroll moulded base, some restoration.
c1780   8.5in (21.5cm) high
£400-500   TOV

A Derby figure of John Milton, modelled standing leaning on a pile of books, supported by a gilt plinth moulded in relief with a scene.
c1790   11.5in (29cm) high
£450-550   DN

A pair of early 19thC Derby style porcelain figures, modelled as a shepherd with lamb holding a staff and a shepherdess with a sheep.
5in (13cm) high
£300-400   MEA

A pair of 18thC Derby bocage groups, one of a standing ram and a seated lamb, the other of a ewe with suckling lamb, painted, each on a shaped plinth with bocage behind.
c1770   5.75in (14.5cm) high
£1,000–1,500   L&T

Two Derby candlesticks, modelled as tree trunks, a cat winding itself around the lower branches of each, mocking the dog at the base, applied flowers, damage and restoration.
c1760-65   9.75in (24.5cm) high
£700-1,000   WW

A pair of Derby candlestick groups, each with a fox enjoying its kill, beneath a minutely flowered bocage, below a single sconce, on a gilt and scrolled base, one sconce repaired.
c1764   10.5in (26.5cm) h
£500-700   SWO

A pair of Derby Arita-style scallop-edged dishes, painted and gilded with two cranes amidst prunus, bamboo and peony, some wear to gilt and enamels.
c1770   8.25in (21cm) diam
£400-500   WW

A Derby 'Smith's blue' bordered floral plate, painted in the manner of William Billingsley with a central bouquet of flowers, with puce marks.
c1790   8.5in (21.5cm) diam
£200-300   DN

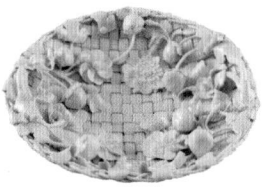

A 19thC Stevenson and Hancock Derby basket, applied with flowering and fruiting strawberries, painted marks.
8.5in (21.5cm) diam
£100-150   GORL

A set of twelve Royal Crown Derby porcelain plates, each printed with different game birds, named on reverse, signed 'D Birbeck', impressed crown and 'Derby', 'A248', printed crown and interlaced 'D' mark in red and retailer name 'T Goode & Co, South Audley St, London W', each with year cipher.
1937   9.25in (23.5cm) diam
£900-1,200   TEN

PORCELAIN

A Derby garniture, comprising a demi-lune bough pot with gilt ram-mask handles and pierced cover and two potpourri vases and covers, with puce script mark, some damage.

c1800   *Bough pot 4.25in (13.5cm) high*

£2,000-2,500   **DN**

A Derby Rococo moulded flower vase, each side painted with a colourful exotic bird, damages and restoration.

c1765   *8.5in (21.5cm) high*

£250-350   **WW**

A Derby Rococo vase, painted with birds and flowers, with applied flowerheads, small chips.

c1765   *9in (23cm) high*

£350-450   **WW**

A Bloor Derby porcelain Earl Spencer's House topographical vase, of Neo-classical two-handled pedestal baluster form, enriched in gilt and painted with a view, named on base, red printed crown and circle mark and 'Bloor Derby'.

A garniture of three Derby porcelain campana vases, each frontally painted with flowers, against a midnight blue ground enriched with anthemion trailing motifs in gilt, gold painted crown and 'D' mark.

c1810   *Tallest 7.75in (20cm) high*

£1,200-1,800   **TEN**

c1820   *11.5in (29cm) high*

£1,200-1,800   **TEN**

A pair of Royal Crown Derby ceramic vases, by Albert Gregory, with elaborate handles, on fluted socles and concave canted square bases, painted and gilt, signed, printed in iron-red, date cipher.

A garniture of three 19thC Derby vases, each of twin-handled baluster form, decorated with bold flowerheads and scrolls in the Imari palette, red painted mark.

Tallest 11.75in (30cm) high

£450-550   **L&T**

1910   *10.25in (26cm) high*

£1,000-1,500   **TEN**

A Royal Crown Derby porcelain vase and cover, enamelled by Desire Leroy, with raised and tooled gilt and painted decoration, puce backstamp 'By appointment to His Majesty the King' with date code and pattern no. '349/1409', restoration.

1903   *9.5in (24cm) high*

£2,500-3,000   **BE**

A Royal Crown Derby vase, by A.F. Wood, raised on scroll legs, the ovoid body decorated with floral swags and flowers within panelled green ground, signed 'A F Wood', with date code.

1911   *5.5in (14cm) high*

£300-350   **A&G**

A Royal Crown Derby vase and cover, decorated with gilt cartouches on a gilt decorated blue ground, below moulded gilt ring handles, printed marks including date code.

1920   *7.75in (20cm) high*

£400-500   **SWO**

A rare Derby square-lobed coffee cup, painted with flower sprays in polychrome enamels with a brown line rim.

c1755-60   *3.25in (8cm) high*

£450-550   **WW**

PORCELAIN

DRESDEN AND DRESDEN DECORATORS

- In the late 19th–early 20thC there were at least 40 porcelain workshops or decorators in and around the Saxon capital of Dresden, most of them copying the Meissen style. Many factories marked their wares with Meissen crossed swords.
- Typically, they produced hard paste porcelain, which was neither as white nor as refined as Meissen.
- Production included single figures and groups, clockcases, centrepieces, vases, baskets, candelabra and candlesticks.
- Most 19thC pieces were made in the Rococo Revival style: overly ornate, combining flowers, shells, scrollwork and figures, painted in garish tones.
- Key factories include Carl Thieme in Potschappel, the Dresden Porcelain Factory, Donath & Co. and the Voigt factory in Sitzendorf.
- Notable workshops included Richard Klemm, Oswald Lorenz and Adolph Hammann and Helena Wolfsohn. Floral sprays with gilt scroll borders and green, blue and pink scale or 'mosaic' borders were popular with these craftsmen. Porcelain is still made in Dresden.
- So-called 'Dresden' porcelain has also been made in England since the 19thC.

An early 20thC Dresden porcelain portrait vase, gold ground with stylised raised foliate border surrounding hand-painted polychrome portrait of Orientalin, artist signed 'Kiesel', printed manufacturer's mark for Richard Klemm.

13.25in (33.5cm) high

£1,200-1,800   **SK**

One of a pair of Helena Wolfsohn hexagonal vases and covers, painted with chinoiserie panels, on a yellow ground, with Augustus Rex mark.

12in (30.5cm) high

£550-750 PAIR   **GORL**

One of a pair of Dresden baluster vases and covers, painted with birds and insects, with 'AR' marks.

c1900   *17.25in (44cm) high*

£700-1,000 PAIR   **DN**

A pair of 20thC Dresden vases and covers, each with pierced flower-encrusted covers, above twin-handled flower-encrusted and painted body on a base with scroll feet and pairs of putti.

19in (48cm) high

£700-1,000   **L&T**

A late 19thC Dresden porcelain box and hinged cover, painted with panels of battle scenes reversed on a pink scale ground, restored.

9.75in (24.5cm) wide

£350-450   **DN**

A pair of late 19thC Dresden three-light girandoles, the frames encrusted with flowers and foliage and each with two cherub surmounts, marks in blue.

15.75in (40cm) high

£250-350   DN

A late 19thC Dresden porcelain plaque, painted with a Dutch-style 16thC town scene with a wealthy mother and child dispensing charity to a poor mother and infant, with impressed numerals.

8.75in (22.5cm) high

£500-700   DN

A Dresden porcelain group of musicians, wearing 17thC dress, with minute areas of restoration.

c1900   10.5in (27cm) high

£300-400   DN

A 19thC Dresden porcelain figure, of a Classical maiden wearing a leopard skin with a putto attendant.

17.75in (45cm) high

£400-500   GORL

FRANKENTHAL

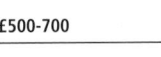

A Frankenthal 'Harmony in Marriage' group, modelled by Karl Gottlieb Lück, crowned 'CT' mark and various monograms including 'AB' for Adam Bergoll, minor chips, his sword or dagger lacking.

Frankenthal was established in 1755 in Germany by Paul-Antoine Hannong and J.J. Ringler. Main production focused on biscuit porcelain figures. Modellers included court sculptor Konrad Linck, J.W. Lanz, J.F. Luck and K.G. Luck. The factory was occupied by the French in 1795, and closed in c1800. Some figure moulds went to Nymphenburg.

c1765   6.5in (16.5cm) high

£3,500-4,500   WW

A Frankenthal figure of a young man, in a powdered wig, leaning over a forked stick, crowned 'CT' mark above date code, minor losses.

1775   4.25in (10.5cm) high

£1,200-1,800   WW

A mid-18thC Frankenthal plate, with ozier-moulded rim, painted fruit and nuts amidst scattered flowerheads, various marks including crowned 'CT' monogram, minor enamel wear.

9.5in (24cm) diam

£550-750   WW

A Frankenthal plate, painted with panels of birds, the centre with flowers within gilt borders, with script 'F'.

c1770   8.75in (22.5cm) diam

£100-200   SWO

PORCELAIN

An 18thC Liverpool blue painted plate, decorated to the well with a Chinese-style landscape scene with bold peonies, a rock and a bird in flight, the border with trailing flower and foliage.

1765–70   *6.75in (17cm) diam*

£1,000-1,500   **L&T**

A small Liverpool dish, the fluted rim in underglaze blue and gilt caiute, the centre with flowers, some wear.

c1770   *6.75in (17cm) diam*

£100-150   **SWO**

A small Liverpool dish, with fluted rim and painted with flowers.

c1770   *6.75in (17cm) diam*

£200-300   **SWO**

A small Chaffers Liverpool coffee can, the slightly tapered form painted in polychrome enamels with a trailing floral spray, some good restoration.

3.25in (8cm) high

£650-850   **WW**

A Liverpool mug, slightly waisted cylindrical body, painted in underglaze blue with a chinoiserie waterscape, enhanced in iron-red and gilding, with top strap handle terminal firing crack.

c1755   *4.25in (11cm) high*

£300-400   **SWO**

A Chaffers Liverpool coffee cup, printed in iron-red and gilt with a plumed bird, standing on one leg amidst flowering peony and foliage.

c1758   *3in (7.5cm) high*

£700-1,000   **WW**

A large Liverpool cylindrical mug, painted in underglaze blue with a willow and flowers above a Chinese fisherman.

c1765   *6in (15.5cm) high*

£600-800   **SWO**

Two Liverpool teabowls and saucers, painted with summer flowers, minute rim frits.

c1770

£100-150

SWO

A Liverpool coffee cup and saucer, brightly painted with summer flowers, cup foot rim chip.

c1770

£100-200   **SWO**

A Longton Hall blue and white coffee cup, the lower section with ribbed moulding, the plain rim painted with a blurred foliate border, indistinct mark to the base.

c1756   3.25in (8cm) high

£650-850   **WW**

A Longton Hall blue and white teabowl and saucer, painted with the 'Crossed Fence' pattern, saucer cracked.

c1756

£400-500   **DN**

A pair of 18thC Longton Hall 'Strawberry' dessert plates, the border relief moulded and coloured with a band of wild strawberries, leaves and tendrils, the well painted with flower springs.

1755–57   8.75in (22cm) diam

£1,500–2,000   **L&T**

An 18thC Longton Hall basket, scalloped border and pierced decoration to the sides, with moulded fruit and acorn decoration to the exterior above a ropetwist border to the footrim.

Longton Hall was founded in Staffordshire in 1750, by William Jenkinson, with William Littler as manager. A wide variety of wares were produced there, notably finely painted strawberry leaf dishes. Early designs were influenced by Meissen, with later pieces taking inspiration from Bow. The factory went bankrupt in 1760.

c1749–60   9in (23cm) wide

£4,000-5,000   **L&T**

LOWESTOFT

ESSENTIAL REFERENCE – LOWESTOFT

- Lowestoft was founded by Robert Brown, in Suffolk, in 1757.
- Early wares were decorated in underglaze blue. Foot-rims were often marked with a numeral. Worcester was a major influence in shape and design, but the Lowestoft porcelain was coarser than Worcester's and prone to staining.
- Overglaze colours were used from 1765.
- Porcelain quality declined after 1770. Shapes and patterns were simplified, and marks were seldom used.
- Rare birth tablets (unique to Lowestoft) and pieces inscribed for the local market are popular with today's collectors.
- Lowestoft closed in 1802.

A rare Lowestoft polychrome sparrowbeak jug, painted with a floral spray in the style of the Tulip Painter, with unusual interior blue border.

£1,000-1,500   **LOW**

An unusual Lowestoft Mandarin pattern sparrowbeak jug, with two river garden scenes, with scale decoration with vignettes.

£550-750   **LOW**

An English, perhaps Lowestoft, blue and white sauceboat, printed on one side with a kneeling European figure near a pagoda, on the opposite side a Chinese figure at an altar, with moulded leafage, painted inside rim.

c1765   2.5in (6.5cm) high

£900-1,200   **TEN**

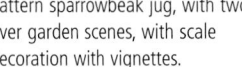

A late 18thC English, probably Lowestoft or Worcester, pear-shaped sparrow beak jug, painted with chinoiserie figures in colourful enamels.

3.75in (9.5cm) high

£200-300   **L&T**

PORCELAIN

A slightly waisted Lowestoft cylindrical blue and white mug, printed with large pagodas and man with parasol crossing a bridge and distant island scene, painted border and scroll handle.

5.5in (14cm) high

£700-1,000 **LOW**

A cylindrical Lowestoft blue and white mug, with scroll handle painted with flower sprays and inscribed 'Robt Howes 1776', within a quartrefoil cartouche.

4.5in (11.5cm) high

£3,000-3,500 **LOW**

CLOSER LOOK – A LOWESTOFT JUG

During the 1770s, the Tulip Painter produced a large number of vessels decorated with flowers, particularly a large tulip (hence the name). His identity is unknown: Thomas Rose has been suggested.

The distinctive naturalistic tulip is only found on Lowestoft porcelain.

This form of commemorative porcelain is desirable because it can be precisely dated. The original owner's name also adds a more personal interest for collectors.

A rare Lowestoft jug, with lip spout and scroll handle, painted with tulip, rose and flower sprays and inscribed within a puce, heart-shaped cartouche 'C.E. Heaman 1776'.

5.25in (13.5cm) high

£13,000-15,000 **LOW**

A Lowestoft bell-shaped blue and white mug, by Robert Allen, painted with flower sprays and inscribed 'James Crick Shottisham 1773' within a cartouche, with decorator's mark no. 5.

6in (15cm) high

£7,000-8,000 **LOW**

A cylindrical Lowestoft polychrome mug, with silver-shaped handle, painted with cornflower sprig decoration and a purple leaf cartouche and inscribed 'A Trifle from LOWESTOFT'.

3.25in (8cm) diam

£4,000-5,000 **LOW**

A cylindrical Lowestoft polychrome mug, painted with cornflower sprig decoration with a monogram and date within the pink arrowhead cartouche 'ER 1793'.

2.75in (7cm) diam

£3,500-4,500 **LOW**

A rare Lowestoft blue and white pounce pot, painted with trailing flowers and a moth and pierced with 71 holes.
c1765-68

£4,000-5,000 **LOW**

A Lowestoft octagonal polychrome spoon tray, painted with the green Redgrave pattern.

£3,000-4,000 **LOW**

A rare Lowestoft blue and white veilleuse, by Robert Allen, with two mask heads and scallop shell handles, painted with flower sprays and two butterflies, decorator's mark no. 5.

6in (15cm) high

£6,000-8,000 **LOW**

A Lowestoft blue and white coffee pot and high-domed cover, painted with an Oriental figure crossing a bridge, cottages and boats on the reverse.
c1772

£3,000-4,000 **LOW**

A rare Lowestoft blue and white moulded oval buttertub and cover, with original upstands, decorated with Oriental island cartouches and interior trailing flowers, with decorator's mark no. 6 painted in two places.

£2,000-2,500 **LOW**

A rare Lowestoft blue and white spittoon, with silver-shaped handle, printed with flower sprays and a butterfly, with crescent mark underneath.

£3,000-3,500 **LOW**

A rare Lowestoft blue and white small teapot and cover, printed with Good Cross Chapel pattern.
c1785 *4in (10cm) high*

£2,000-2,500 **LOW**

A rare Lowestoft chamberstick, with fine honeysuckle moulding and upstanding ring handle, with decorator's mark 'X'.

A chamberstick is a candleholder set in a saucer-like dish, with a handle, and a detachable conical snuffer or a slot to store scissor snuffers. Though few examples survive, chambersticks are known to pre-date the Reformation. They were typically made from non-combustible materials, particularly silver and plate.

£9,000-12,000 **LOW**

PORCELAIN

A rare Lowestoft blue and white moulded eyebath, painted with flower sprigs and interior loop border.

£3,500-4,500   LOW

A rare Lowestoft blue and white eggcup, decorated with island scene with three-tier pagoda and boy holding a shrimping net, with decorator's mark '14'.

£3,000-4,000   LOW

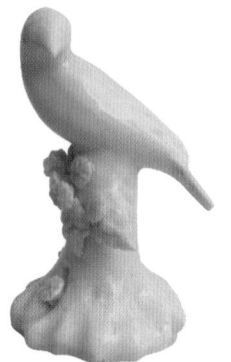

A rare Lowestoft undecorated model of a bird perched on a tree stump, applied with flowers and leaves.

c1780   2.75in (7cm) high

£4,000-5,000   LOW

A Lowestoft brown and white pug dog, seated on a green rectangular base, wearing a green collar with iron-red rosette.

£4,500-5,500   LOW

MEISSEN

ESSENTIAL REFERENCE – MEISSEN

- Founded in Germany in 1710, Meissen became the first porcelain factory in Europe, after discovering hard paste. From c1720, it made creamy white 'Böttger' porcelain.
- The factory's great period began in 1720, when J.C. Herold was appointed chief painter. He perfected the enamelling process, introducing a wider colour range with fine painting.
- The crossed swords factory mark was used from 1723. It has been much imitated by lesser factories and forgers.
- During the 1730s, Meissen became Europe's foremost porcelain factory, and its pieces were widely copied.
- Modelling became key after J.J. Kändler was appointed chief modeller in 1733, designing figures based on the Italian Commedia dell'Arte theatre tradition and street vendors. P. Reinicke and J.F. Eberlein were also notable modellers.
- Services and other domestic and decorative wares were produced. The factory's most famous service, the 'Swan' service, was designed by Kändler in 1737-41.
- The 19th century saw mass-production of pieces in the Empire, Biedermeier, Gothic Revival and Rococo styles.
- The Art Nouveau and Art Deco periods provided new inspiration with designs by Paul Scheurich and Max Esser.
- Meissen is still producing wares today.

A Meissen model of Venus and Cupid, the goddess sitting beside a flowering rose bush, attended by two doves, the base applied with flowers and leaves, a few chips to leaves.

c1750   7.25in (18.5cm) high

£1,500-2,000   WW

A mid-18thC Meissen figure of a girl, a basket of flowers hanging from a stick which rests on one shoulder, incised '19' to the reverse, minor good restoration.

5.25in (13cm) high

£450-500 WW

A mid-18thC Meissen model of a young gardener, carrying a two-handled basket, his foot resting on a hoe, blurred mark to the reverse, some restoration.

4.5in (11.5cm) high

£250-350 WW

A Meissen model of a young vintner, seated on a rocky stump with a grapevine trailing across her lap, incised '16' and blue crossed swords mark to the reverse, minor damage and restoration.

c1770 *5.25in (13cm) high*

£300-400 WW

A Meissen figure of a shepherdess, after a model by J. J. Kändler and P. Reinicke, her apron filled with flowers and a sheep at her feet, incised '27' to the base, some restoration.

6in (15.5cm) high

£2,000-2,500 WW

A Meissen group, emblematic of music, with three cherubs playing a flute and lyre on a rock work base, cancelled crossed swords mark, restored.

c1830-50 *8.75in (22cm) high*

£600-800 SWO

A pair of 19thC Meissen porcelain figures of Silenus and Flora, Silenus modelled eating a bunch of grapes with faun attendant, Flora smelling a floral posy with putti attendant, crossed swords mark and gilded '53'.

11.75in (30cm) high

£1,000-1,500 GORL

A pair of 19thC Meissen figures of a young shepherdess and a young swain, both on key moulded bases, cross swords mark in blue, incised 'F62', incised '15' in red and impressed' 122'.

Taller 7.25in (18.5cm) high

£700-1,000 HT

A large 19thC Meissen figure of Cupid, holding a basket and stood on a rocky circular base, cross swords mark, incised 'MII3' to base.

11.5in (29cm) high

£1,500-2,000 GORL

A pair of 19thC Meissen Malabar musicians, the man dressed in pink coat and floral robe playing a guitar, the woman similarly attired and playing the hurdy-gurdy, each on a Rococo scroll base, blue painted crossed sword mark.

£1,500-2,000 L&T

A 19thC Meissen figure of a boy, carrying a basket of flowers, a maul resting on his shoulder, crossed swords mark to the base, restoration.

5.25in (13.5cm) high

£500-700 WW

PORCELAIN

A near pair of 19thC Meissen sweetmeat figures, modelled as a young couple, reclining on Rococo moulded bases and holding flower-encrusted bowls, various marks including crossed swords, minor damage and restoration.

£450-550   WW

A pair of 19thC Meissen porcelain bolognaise terriers, with alert expressions, with well detailed shaggy coats, underglaze blue painted swords mark, also incised '13 891' and '13 880', restored.

Tallest 9in (23cm) high

£1,500-2,000   TEN

A 19thC Meissen model of a dog, with glass eyes, cross sword mark, impressed '880', very minor damage.

8.75in (22.5cm) high

£700-1,000   L&T

A late 19thC Meissen porcelain centrepiece, of four children playing musical instruments on graduated pedestals, with Classically draped and acanthus leaf garland base.

10in (25.5cm) high

£1,500-2,000   GORL

A pair of 19thC Meissen pagoda figures, moving heads, hands and tongues, painted with 'Indianische Blumen', crossed swords marks, he incised '156', impressed '97', she incised '157'.

7.25in (18.5cm) high

£9,000-12,000   WW

A pair of 19thC Meissen porcelain figures of a gardener and companion, he leaning on a spade with a watering can, she with basket of flowers and sickle, on circular bases.

8in (20.5cm) high

£900-1,200   HT

A 19thC Meissen model of two finches on a tree stump, no. 174, painted in naturalistic colours, crossed swords mark.

12in (30.5cm) high

£900-1,200   GORL

A 19thC Meissen figural group of four child gardeners, on spiralling pedestals, each holding a basket of flowers on drapes and acanthus garlanded bases.

10in (25.5cm) high

£1,200-1,800   GORL

A late 19thC Meissen group of Europa and the Bull, typically modelled after F. E. Meyer, with blue crossed swords mark, incised '2697', damage.

£900-1,200 DN

A pair of late 19thC Meissen models of Bacchic fauns, modelled riding goats and garlanded with fruiting vine, with blue crossed swords marks, incised '144' and '145', minor chips and losses.

Tallest 7in (18cm) high

£1,000-1,500 DN

A 20thC Meissen figure of a girl, after a model by Konrad Hentschel, wearing a floral pattern red bonnet and white dress, cuddling a black and white cat, blue painted crossed sword mark, incised 'W121' and impressed '95'.

4.75in (12cm) high

£1,500-2,000 L&T

A 20thC Meissen figure of a boy, after a model by Konrad Hentschel, drinking from a blue painted cup, with a toy horse behind his feet, underglaze blue crossed sword mark, incised 'W118'.

6.75in (17cm) high

£1,200-1,800 L&T

A 20thC Meissen figure of a girl, after a model by Konrad Hentschel, wearing a green trimmed white nightgown and trailing a doll from her left hand, blue painted crossed sword mark, impressed 'x 164' and '34'.

6.75in (17.5cm) high

£600-800 L&T

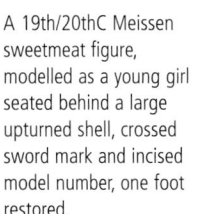

A Meissen hand-painted figurine of a boy reading a book, by Konrad Hentschel, the base inscribed '149' and painted '25'.

Konrad Hentschell worked at Meissen from 1872-1907.

1904 *4.5in (11cm) high*

£2,000-3,000 BB

A 19th/20thC Meissen sweetmeat figure, modelled as a young girl seated behind a large upturned shell, crossed sword mark and incised model number, one foot restored.

5in (12cm) high

£150-250 WW

A Meissen porcelain figure group of Europa and the Bull, on a Rococo scroll base, cancelled blue crossed swords, incised 'K/70' with press number '46', minor losses and factory filled firing cracks to base.

9in (23cm) high

£900-1,200   **BE**

A pair of early 20thC Meissen porcelain parrots, painted in reds and purples, modelled perched on branches with applied foliage, crossed swords mark.

13in (33cm) high

£1,200-1,800   **HT**

An early 20thC Meissen model of a rearing horse, with a blackamoor by its side, after the model by J. J. Kändler, crossed swords and impressed marks, old restorations.

9.25in (23.5cm) high

£550-850   **WW**

A Meissen porcelain figure, emblematic of the 'Sense of Smell', modelled after the original by Johann Carl Schonheit as a seated lady sniffing a bouquet, underglaze blue crossed swords, incised 'E.5' with press number '36'.

5.75in (14.5cm) high

£250-350   **BE**

A Meissen porcelain figure of a gallant, modelled after the original by Friedrich Elias Meyer, playing a lute, painted crossed swords mark, press number '103', slight damage to coat.

5.5in (14cm) high

£350-450   **BE**

An early 20thC Meissen mythological figural group, modelled as a maiden tended by an angel and cherubs with peacocks, on garlanded and swagged base, struck through crossed swords marks.

10.5in (26.5cm) high

£1,200-1,800   **GORL**

An early 20thC Meissen porcelain figural group, of a gardener and his lover, with child attendant.

6.75in (17cm) high

£1,200-1,800   **GORL**

An early 20thC Meissen figural group of Europa and the bull, on Rococo scroll base, crossed swords mark struck through.

This piece was a second.

9.75in (25cm) high

£900-1,200   **GORL**

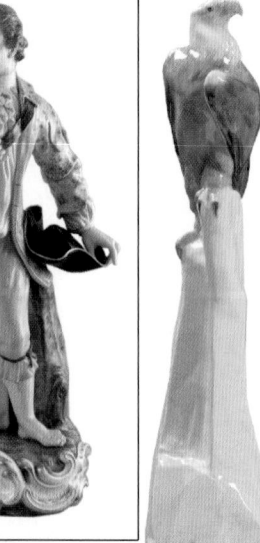

A pair of early 20thC Meissen porcelain figures, modelled as a lovers, model no. G112 and G113, on Rococo scroll base, crossed swords marks.

13.75in (35cm) high

£3,000-4,000   **GORL**

A 20thC Meissen porcelain figure of a perched eagle atop a craggy pinnacle, with incised designer's initials 'OW'.

16in (40.5cm) high

£900-1,200   **SK**

A Meissen two-handled stand or dish, painted in the Kakiemon palette with the 'Koreanische Löwe' pattern of a fabulous beast and a large insect beneath a bird in flight, crossed swords mark.

c1740   *15.5in (39.5cm) wide*

£2,500-3,000   **WW**

Two early Meissen saucers, each decorated with differing versions of 'Tischchenmuster' pattern, crossed swords mark.

c1735   4.5in (11.5cm) diam

£150-250   **WW**

A Meissen two-handled sauceboat, painted with polychrome flower sprays and raised on four stalk feet, brown line rim, faint crossed swords mark to the base, some restoration to the feet.

9in (23cm) wide

c1740-50

£250-350   **WW**

A Meissen commemorative plate, painted in blue with Augustus the Strong standing between coats of arms above dates '1708' and '1908', crossed swords mark.

This plate was probably produced to commemorate the bicentenary of the discovery of the hardpaste porcelain arcanum under the sponsorship of Augustus II.

9.75in (25cm) diam

£100-200   **WW**

An 18thC Meissen globular teapot, with puce highlighted dolphin spout and scrolling handle, with floral knop, crossed swords mark.

4.5in (11.5cm) high

£200-300   **GORL**

A small 18thC Meissen teapot, of bullet form, with gilded dolphin spout and scrolling handle, the finial moulded as a bud, painted with a landscape with figures, with crossed swords mark, restored.

3in (7.5cm) high

£400-500   **GORL**

A Meissen Böttger porcelain teabowl, applied with three sprigs of crisply detailed rose leaves and buds, and an associated Meissen saucer applied with floral branches, unmarked, minor damages.

c1715   4.5in (11.5cm) diam

£900-1,000   **WW**

A pair of Meissen cups and saucers, painted with brightly coloured exotic birds and scattered insects on a white ground, gilt rims, crossed swords mark with dots between the hilts.

c1765-70

£900-1,200   **WW**

A late 18thC Meissen tea canister, painted in blue with a bird in flight beside a flowering bush, crossed swords and star mark to the shoulders.

4in (10cm) high

£200-300   **WW**

PORCELAIN

A large late 19thC Meissen porcelain maritime ewer, with shell-form spout, seaweed S-handle topped by a cherub, neck enamel-decorated with insects, the body moulded with ocean waves, and enamelled verso with galleons and mounted with figures of Neptune, a mermaid, seahorses, turtles and fish, the foot with dolphins.

26in (66cm) high

£4,500-5,000　　　　**SK**

A 19thC Meissen vase and cover, the cover pierced with scrolls, encrusted with flowers overall, and a winged cherub to the body, raised on a socle supporting a female figure, blue painted crossed swords mark.

25.5in (65cm) high

£3,500-4,500　　　　**L&T**

A late 19thC Meissen porcelain plaque, of arched form enamelled with the 'Ascension', underglaze blue crossed swords, incised '1130' with press number '53', together with frame.

13.75in (35cm) high

£3,500-4,500　　　　**BE**

A pair of 19th/20thC Meissen armorial candlesticks, moulded with facets and decorated with sprays of 'Indianische Blumen', crossed swords and impressed marks, some small chips.

10.25in (26cm) high

£450-550　　　　**WW**

MINTON

A Minton porcelain part dessert service, comprising four circular low comports, two oval low comports, two rectangular comports and 18 plates, each enamelled with a botanical specimen, interlaced gold dot and turquoise 'jewelled' bands, impressed registration lozenge, painted pattern no. 'A. 646'.

Thomas Minton (1765–1836), the creator of the famous Willow pattern, founded his ceramics factory in Stoke-on-Trent in 1796. Minton produced soft-paste porcelain from 1798, and hard paste from 1821. Pieces were of high quality, usually copies of Sèvres or Meissen wares. The factory became famous for its majolica. Minton remains active today.

c1850

£1,500-2,000 SET　　　　**BE**

An early Victorian Minton's china supper set with fitted mahogany tray, the pieces impressed 'BB NEW STONE' to the undersides.

c1840　　　　*21.25in (54cm) wide overall*

£200-300　　　　**DN**

A large Minton oval tray, painted by Edouard Rischgitz, depicting a stag hunt in a river landscape, signed, the reverse with a painted mark, restoration to handles and some retouching.

c1870　　　　*26.75in (68cm) wide*

£150-250　　　　**WW**

A mid-19thC Minton botanical dessert service, each decorated with scalloped edge, turquoise and gilt ribbon painted and 'jewelled' border, centrally painted with flowers, comprising a high comport, a medium comport and eighteen plates, impressed diamond registration mark and impressed horseshoe mark.

1853

£1,000-1,500 SET　　　　**L&T**

A Minton porcelain 'Globe' potpourri vase and cover, painted with a landscape with a cathedral, encrusted with flowers, naturalistically moulded twig handles, crossed swords mark in underglaze blue to cover and vase.

c1820　　　　*6.75in (17cm) high*

£450-550　　　　**TEN**

A large Minton bowl, painted with large pink roses, signed 'M. Dudley', a gilt border to the interior rim, printed mark and impressed date code, minor gilt wear.

1920   9.75in (25cm) diam

£300-400   **WW**

A Minton bone china flatback model of a German peasant couple, standing on a green base inscribed 'Berne'.

c1825   5.75in (14.5cm) high

£100-200   **WW**

A pair of Minton 'The Grand Turk' and 'Turkish Lady' porcelain figures, modelled standing on Rococo bases, both elaborately enamelled, both with losses and repairs.

c1825-35   5in (13cm) high

£300-400   **BE**

A Minton cobalt blue ground vase, decorated with painted panels within elaborate gilded oak leaf garlands and rope handles, on acanthus leaf base and square foot, with pineapple knop, with puce printed Minton mark.

20in (51cm) high

£1,200-1,800   **GORL**

NEW HALL

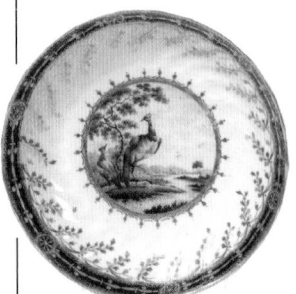

A New Hall porcelain birds in landscape saucer dish, painted in the manner of Fidelle Duvivier, of wrythen fluted shaped circular shallow form, with painted and gilt decoration.

Fidelle Duvivier was born in Tournai in 1740, but spent most of his life decorating English porcelain. He worked in London and at Worcester, and was employed by the Derby porcelain factory for four years from 1769. A letter to William Duesbury written by Duvivier in 1790 proves that Duvivier worked at New Hall and was about to leave there in 1790.

c1790   7.75in (20cm) diam

£500-700   **TEN**

An early 19thC New Hall spiral fluted jug, painted with pink roses below a floral ribboned border.

5in (12.5cm) high

£100-150   **WW**

A New Hall part tea/coffee service, pattern no. 216, painted with puce floral swags and gilt banding comprising teapot, covered sucrier, five tea bowls, four coffee cups, three saucers and a spoon rest.

£2,500-3,500 SET   **DA&H**

An unusual pair of New Hall plates, painted in pattern 2679 with scenes of the inimitable Dr Syntax after Thomas Rowlandson's prints, titled to the reverse in iron-red.

c1823-27   8.25in (21cm) diam

£1,200-1,800   **WW**

PORCELAIN

A mid-19thC Paris porcelain scent bottle and stopper, by Jacob Petit, modelled as a Levantine man, wearing elaborate costume, with blue 'JP' mark, chips to stopper.

11.75in (30cm) high

£700-1,000   DN

A pair of mid-19thC Paris porcelain figural scent bottles, by Jacob Petit, modelled as a standing Sultan and Sultana, in brightly-coloured traditional costume, underglaze blue mark.

11.75in (30cm) high

£2,000-3,000   L&T

A large late 19th/early 20thC Paris porcelain enamel-decorated cobalt blue vase, with gilt scroll and leaf handles, painted to front with figural scene, gilt borders.

21.75in (55cm) high

£650-850   SK

A pair of early 20thC Continental gilt-metal mounted Paris porcelain potpourri, damage.

9.75in (25cm) high

£650-850   DN

A mid-19thC Jacob Petit pen tray, painted with a continuous arrangement of flowers on a green ground with rich raised gilding, on four claw feet.

11.75in (30cm) wide

£200-300   WW

An early 19thC Paris porcelain cabinet cup and saucer, with a winged handle, decorated with a horse-drawn chariot on a faux marble ground within palmette borders, gilded interior, the saucer raised on three claw feet, gilt mark to the saucer.

Saucer 5.5in (14cm) diam

£700-1,000   WW

ROCKINGHAM

A small Rockingham encrusted porcelain potpourri basket and cover, with rustic arched handle, the cover with prunus blossom finial, puce griffin mark and 'Rockingham Works Brameld Manufacturer to the King', 'CL.3' in red script.

A Rockingham encrusted porcelain 'Flowers of the Union' chamberstick, fashioned as a leaf, the handle and nozzle a thistle, puce printed griffin mark and 'Rockingham works Brameld Manufacturer to the King', 'CL.2' in red script.

c1830-42

4.25in (11cm) wide

£900-1,200   TEN

c1830-42

3.25in (8cm) diam

£300-400   TEN

ESSENTIAL REFERENCE – ROCKINGHAM

● The Rockingham Pottery and Porcelain factory was probably founded on the Rockingham estate, Swinton, Yorkshire, c1745.

● Early wares were earthenware, similar to Leeds, covered in a treacly glaze, including the lidless Cadogan teapot.

● Between 1826 and its closing date 1842, it made high-quality Rococo Revival style bone china. Tea and dessert services with elaborate floral decoration were popular, as were well-modelled animal figures.

● Rockingham made a pair of metre-high vases with rhinoceros finials, c1826. At the time, they were the biggest pieces of porcelain to have been fired in one piece in England.

● The Rockingham mark (the griffin of the Rockingham family) was widely copied.

● Pieces can be difficult to identify, except through shape and pattern number.

A 19thC Rockingham porcelain Continental peasant figure, Paysanne de Sagran en Tirol, on a circular flower-encrusted base, inscribed in gilt.

1826-42	7.5in (19cm) high
£1,200–1,800	**L&T**

A Rockingham porcelain model of a crouching hare, wearing a gold collar, impressed 'Rockingham Works Brameld' and incised '110' and 'CL2' in red, cracked and restored.

c1826-42	2.5in (6.5cm) wide
£350-450	**TEN**

A Rockingham porcelain figure of a milkmaid, decorated in colour and gilt, red printed griffin mark and 'Rockingham Works Brameld', incised 'No. 2'.

c1826-1830	7in (18cm) high
£3,000-4,000	**TEN**

A pair of Rockingham porcelain pot pourri vases, each with a pierced cover, lion-head handles, on four paw feet, above plinth base, with painted floral reserves, in the style of John Creswell.

c1825	6.25in (16cm) high
£1,200-1,800	**L&T**

A Rockingham porcelain primrose-leaf moulded jug, moulded to the upper half with florets and scrolls beneath the spout, within a cup of moulded primroses leaves, puce printed griffin mark and 'Rockingham Works Brameld Manufacturer to the King', 'CL.2'.

c1830-42	7.75in (20cm) high
£300-400	**TEN**

A Rockingham porcelain topographical coffee cup and saucer, pattern no. 714 marked on cup, puce printed griffin mark and 'Rockingham Works Brameld Manufacturer to the King' and 'CL.4' in red script on the saucer.

c1830-42	Cup 2.75in (7cm) high
£250-350	**TEN**

A Rockingham porcelain Duke of Wellington trumpet vase, with solid gilt bands to the rim and foot rim, frontally with a bust portrait, puce printed griffin mark and 'Rockm Works Brameld', restored.

c1830-42	4.25in (11cm) high
£650-850	**TEN**

PORCELAIN

A late 19thC Samson model of an elephant, lifting its left forefoot, raised on an ormolu base, crossed swords mark in underglaze blue, both tusks broken off.

5.5in (14cm) high

£100-150   WW

A pair of Samson porcelain figural candlesticks, after the Chelsea originals of Mars and Minerva, standing before encrusted bocage beside scroll arms, on scroll base, with Pseudo gold anchor mark and impressed 'S'.

11.5in (29cm) high

£500-700   HT

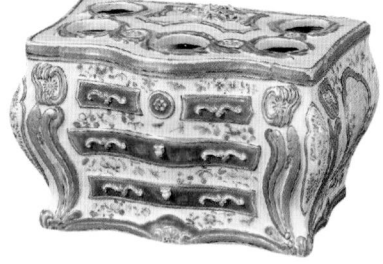

One of a pair of late 19thC Samson-style bombé commode-form porcelain tulipiers, with five openings to top, moulded with drawers, polychrome enamelling throughout, the sides with sepia landscape cartouches.

8.5in (21.5cm) wide

£350-450 PAIR   SK

A late 19thC Samson Worcester-style blue ground baluster vase and cover, decorated with exotic birds in gilt cartouche, and a pair of star shaped dishes, similarly decorated.

Vase 9in (23cm) high

£150-250   L&T

A pair of Samson famille rose porcelain covered vases, after Chinese armorial originals, painted in the typical palette with swags and flower sprays, centred by an armorial crest.

10.5in (27cm) high

£400-500   L&T

SÈVRES

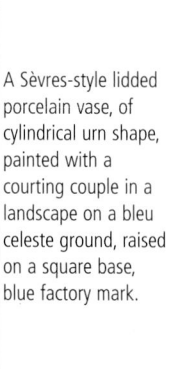

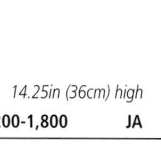

A Sèvres-style lidded porcelain vase, of cylindrical urn shape, painted with a courting couple in a landscape on a bleu celeste ground, raised on a square base, blue factory mark.

14.25in (36cm) high

£1,200-1,800   JA

A Sèvres-style Art Nouveau pedestal urn, painted with a portrait bust within gilt borders on a cobalt ground, cast gilt-metal mounts and handles, associated cover, spurious interlaced 'L's and letter 'S' mark.

9.75in (25cm) high

£150-200   FLD

A pair of late 19thC gilt-metal mounted Sèvres-style porcelain potpourri and covers.

11.5in (29.5cm) high

£700-1,000   DN

ESSENTIAL REFERENCE – SÈVRES

- The company was founded in c1738 in Vincennes, before moving to Sèvres in 1756.
- Louis XV prohibited all foreign porcelain imports (except for Chinese goods) in 1745 to protect the factory. He forbade other French porcelain factories from using more than one colour or gilding. He renamed it Manufacture Royale de Porcelaine in 1753. It had the patronage of his mistress, Madame de Pompadour, and the best painters and modellers.
- Sèvres made soft-paste until 1768 when hard-paste was introduced. Soft paste was discontinued in the early 19thC.
- After goldsmith Jean Claude Chambellan Duplessis was appointed in 1748, French Rococo style products were made, including delicate cabarets, vases in vivid colours and jardinières. Biscuit figures and porcelain plaques for mounting in furniture were also produced.
- The state monopoly was discontinued in 1780 and Royal patronage ended due to the French Revolution (1789-99). By 1800, a new period of prosperity began and it became the Imperial Factory in 1804. A rich Empire style was developed.
- Art Nouveau pieces were introduced in the late 1890s, and Art Deco in the 1920s. The factory currently produces simplified version of its 18thC pieces.

A pair of 19thC Sèvres-style vases and covers, with gilt metal mounts and diamond-form 'jewelled' decoration, scroll handles with draped swags above painted panels, on a giltmetal plinth, blue painted mark to underside of cover.

11.5in (29cm) high

£2,000-2,500   L&T

A pair of 19thC French porcelain Sèvres-style vases and covers, with shield-shaped reserves painted with women and putti representing Arts, within gilded and 'jewelled' borders, on scrolling base.

10in (25.5cm) high

£1,200-1,800   GORL

A garniture of three 19thC Sèvres-style giltmetal-mounted vases and covers, each of ovoid form, with giltmetal figural finial, foliate Rococo scroll handles and feet, the cover and body with painted panels and gilt scroll ground.

Tallest 7.75in (20cm) high

£1,200-1,800   L&T

A pair of 19thC Sèvres-style vases and covers, with giltmetal mounts and diamond-form 'jewelled' decoration, scroll handles with draped swags above painted panels, on a gilt metal plinth, blue painted mark to underside of cover.

11.5in (29cm) high

£2,000-2,500   L&T

A pair of late 19thC Sèvres-style gilt-brass mounted spirally moulded vases and cover, decorated with floral bands between pink and gilt bands.

19.25in (49cm) high

£1,500-2,000   L&T

PORCELAIN

A pair of 20thC Sèvres-style claret ground two-handled pedestal urns, each painted with a bust portrait panel with Marshals of France, M.al Lannes and M.al Soult, within a gilt border, one with repaired foot.

Marshal Soult (1769-1851), Duc de Dalmatie, joined the army in 1785 rising to Marshal in 1804. Although principally remembered as the French commander in the Peninsular War, he was also Prime Minister of France three times.

11.5in (29cm) high

£650-850   DN

A pair of Sèvres-style porcelain slender pedestal vases, each decorated in gilt with Rococo scrolls, with vignettes painted after Watteau, indistinctly signed 'F Amtrel', against a bleu de roi ground, with gilt-metal handles and bases, each bearing crossed 'L' mark, enclosing 'B' with 'A' below in blue.

c1880   *19in (48cm) high*

£1,000-1,500   TEN

A pair of late 19thC Sèvres-style dark blue ground twin-handled urns, decorated with musical scenes in reserves and 'jewelled', one restored.

17.25in (44cm) high

£2,000-2,500   DN

An 18th/19thC Sèvres-style plate, the well painted with a colourful flower spray, the blue border decorated with gilt oeil-de-perdrix, interlaced 'L's above 'BBV'.

9.25in (23.5cm) diam

£150-250   WW

A pair of 19thC Sèvres 'jewelled' porcelain cabinet portrait plates, with matching floral, gilt and 'jewelled' rims, each painted to centre with a portrait roundel in red 'jewel' surround, one depicting Mademoiselle Paulet, and the other Joseph Vernet.

9.75in (25cm) diam

£1,500-2,000   SK

A Sèvres white biscuit porcelain group, depicting two putti in a chariot pulled by a pair of goats, on rustic base, on gilded plaster and grey-veined marble rounded oblong base, with impressed mark.

17.25in (44cm) wide

£800-1,000   HT

One of a pair of late 19thC Sèvres-style blue ground and 'jewelled' cylindrical vases, decorated with scenes in reserves in the style of Antoine Watteau.

7in (18cm) high

£700-1,000 PAIR   DN

An early 20thC French Sèvres bisque bust of Madame de Pompadour, modelled by Raymond Sudre after the original by Jean-Alexandre-Joseph Falguiere, impressed marks to reverse.

31.5in (80cm) high

£1,800-2,200   SK

A large Vienna charger, with a painted Classical scene, within a gilt and enamelled border, inscribed verso 'Telemachus redux a Penelope enchiten'.

c1870   18in (46cm) diam

£1,500-2,000   SWO

A pair of Vienna porcelain cabinet plates, one decorated with 'Lohengrins Ankunft', the other 'Lohengrins Abschied', in Gothic arched gilt tooled 'frames', the rims with gilt foliage and guilloché, beehive mark in underglaze blue and 'R&M2', titled in black script.

Lohengrin is the German version of the European folk tale of the Knight of the Swan from the Middle Ages. Wagner used the story for his opera Lohengrin', first performed in 1850.

c1880   13in (32.5cm) diam

£1,200-1,800   TEN

A circular Vienna plaque, by Wagner, decorated with a circle of winged cupids and swags of flowers, fruit and leafage, red border with orange gilt scrolling leafage, gilt framed, signed 'Wagner, Vienna'.

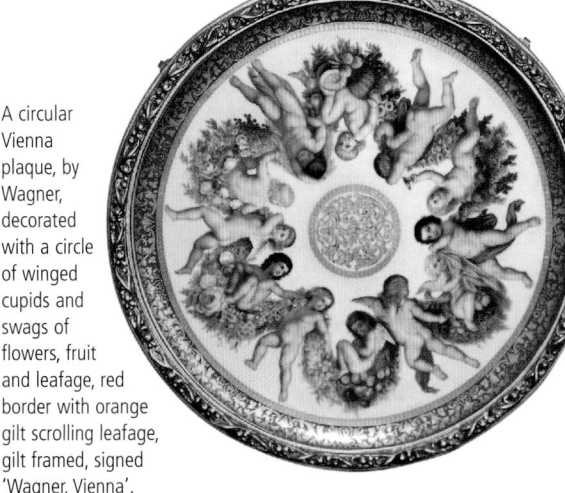

23.5in (60cm) diam

£3,000-4,000   LT

A 19thC Vienna saucer, by Komi, decorated to the well with a portrait of a lady with cobalt blue and gilt border, blue beehive mark and Rosenthal, Bavaria mark.

6in (15cm) diam

£300-400   L&T

A 'Vienna' porcelain dish, painted with three Classical maidens sharing out jewellery in a Classical interior, within typical panelled borders enriched in gilt, bearing underglaze blue painted beehive mark.

c1900   10in (25.5cm) diam

£700–1,000   TEN

A 'Vienna' porcelain 'The Flower Seller' cabinet plate, the border gilded in high relief, and centrally painted, signed 'H Muller', underglazed blue printed pseudo Vienna beehive mark, titled in gilt 'Blumenverkauferin' and '42'.

c1900   9.75in (24.5cm) diam

£900-1,200   TEN

A Vienna cabinet plate, painted with Rinaldo und Almida, script title on reverse, signed 'J Holler' in gilt, in a border of Classical maiden divided by puce panels with tiny gilded landscapes, bearing blue printed beehive mark.

c1900   13.5in (34.5cm) wide

£700-1,000   TEN

A late 19th/early 20thC Vienna porcelain plaque, painted with a scene of Classical women watching Cupid in a landscape, entitled 'Abgebitat', beehive mark, in Florentine gilt frame.

Plaque 8.5in (21.5cm) high

£1,200-1,800   GORL

A late 19thC Viennese porcelain vase, with a scene of Constantin and other figures, identified in German to underside of foot, on raised gilt ground with green accents and white 'jewels'.

21.5in (54.5cm) high

£2,000-2,500   SK

PORCELAIN

A pair of Turn Vienna porcelain two-handled vases and covers, decorated with poppies outlined in raised gilt, with red transfer printed crown and shield mark 'EW Turn Vienna', impressed '5467' and '2412'.

c1890   16in (40.5cm) high

£1,200-1,800   TEN

A late 19thC Royal Vienna porcelain portrait vase and cover, artist signed 'Meisel', below the base titled 'Bien etre', gilt blossom mark for Helena Wolfsohn factory and overglaze beehive mark.

A number of factories produced porcelain in Vienna, many of which used the Bindeschild mark. The first, founded in 1718 by Claudius du Paquier, produced porcelain similar to Böttger of Meissen. The factory was sold to the state in 1744. It produced porcelain influenced by Sèvres and later some successful Neo-Classical pieces, but was ultimately unprofitable and closed in 1864. Other notable Viennese factories include Bock (founded 1828), Goldscheider (1885) and Augarten (founded 1922), which continued the traditions of the state owned factory.

14in (35.5cm) high

£4,000-5,000   SK

A late 19thC Vienna model of a woman, probably a street trader, her wares under an arm, partially coloured, with blue shield mark, restored.

7.5in (19cm) high

£350-450   DN

WORCESTER – FIRST PERIOD BLUE AND WHITE

ESSENTIAL REFERENCE – EARLY WORCESTER

- The Worcester porcelain factory was established by Dr John Wall and apothecary William Davis in 1751, in Worcester.
- After initial failures, Wall and Davies bought Lund's Bristol porcelain factory, which gave them a source of soapstone and kilns. By 1752, they were producing porcelain that was more durable and resistant to hot liquids than that of other English factories due to the soapstone used in its batch.
- Early products were largely useful wares in shapes derived from silver, such as teapots, jugs and sauceboats. These were mainly decorated with chinoiserie designs in underglaze blue.
- Pieces made from c1752 were marked with an incised cross or line mark.
- Worcester discovered the transfer-printing technique between 1756-1758, revolutionising the ceramics market. Initially, the new technique was used to create overglaze black enamel designs from prints by R. Hancock but soon underglaze blue patterns were made. Most blue and white pieces from this period were marked with a crescent.
- In order to compete with imported Meissen wares, Worcester began to produce polychrome designs in Chinese famille-rose style in the 1760s. Coloured grounds were also introduced in shades including yellow, green and sky blue.
- In the early 1760s, Worcester adopted scale-pattern blue and crimson grounds, in imitation of Sèvres, a style which was reinforced after several former employees of Chelsea joined Worcester in 1768.
- In 1783 the factory was bought by Thomas Flight for his sons. John Flight managed the company and during his short time in charge of the factory (1783-1792) he reduced the production of blue and white lines, which had become less profitable, and replaced them with the new Neo-Classical style that he had seen in Paris.

A Worcester blue and white teapot and cover, painted with the 'Rock Strata Island' pattern beneath a hatched border, open crescent mark, minor nibbling to the finial and spout.

c1765-70   7.25in (18.5cm) high

£250-350   WW

A Worcester leaf moulded cider jug, with a mask spout, painted in blue with a sprawling floral design, workman's mark, cracked.

c1755-60   7.75in (20cm) high

£250-350   WW

A Worcester blue and white sauceboat, painted with the 'Two-Porter Landscape' pattern within moulded scrolling borders, workman's mark.

c1760   5in (12.5cm) wide

£1,000-1,500   WW

A First Period Worcester porcelain sauceboat, the exterior painted in blue in the 'Strap Flute Sauceboat Floral' pattern and the interior with a tulip, open crescent mark and incised cross.

c1770-80   6.5in (16.5cm) long

£200-300   BE

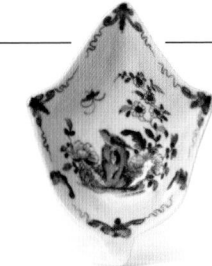

A First Period Worcester blue and white porcelain 'Rock Warbler' leaf pickle dish, centrally painted pattern within scroll and tendril rim, veining moulded to the underside, arrow painter's mark in underglaze blue.

c1760   4.25in (10.5cm) high

£650-850   TEN

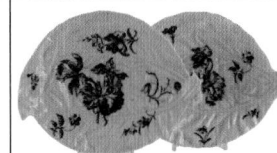

Two Worcester blue and white leaf dishes, naturalistically painted with blown flower patterns, workman's marks, one broken in half and reglued.

10in (25.5cm) wide

£150-250   WW

A pair of First Period Worcester 'Pine Cone' pattern baskets, each of pierced lobed circular form, printed in underglaze-blue, the exteriors applied with florets, crescent marks in underglaze blue.

c1765   7in (18cm) diam

£900-1,200   TEN

An 18thC Worcester blue and white porcelain plate, of scalloped circular outline, painted with the 'Hundred Antiques' pattern, underglaze blue mark.

7.5in (19cm) diam

£450-550   JA

A set of six First Period Worcester 'Pine Cone' pattern plates, each transfer printed in underglaze-blue within floral spray borders, shaped rims, open crescent marks in blue.

c1765   9.5in (24.5cm) diam

£1,000-1,500   TEN

A pair of Worcester Kangxi 'Lotus' pattern blue and white porcelain dishes, decorated with flowers against a cracked ice ground, with pseudo Chinese marks, one dish completely broken and re-stuck.

c1770-75   6.25in (16cm) diam

£200-300   HALL

A Worcester blue and white mug, painted with the 'Walk in the Garden' pattern, workman's mark, cracked.

c1758   3.75in (9.5cm) high

£150-250   WW

A Worcester blue and white mug, painted with a dragon chasing a flaming pearl, his tail flowing over the rim to continue on the interior, painted open crescent mark.

c1760-65   6in (15cm) high

£1,500-2,000   WW

A pair of Worcester porcelain teabowls and saucers, each painted in underglaze blue with the 'Feather Mould Birds' pattern, workman's marks in underglaze blue to bases.

c1765-70   4.5in (11.5cm) diam (saucers)

£350-450   TOV

A First Period Worcester blue and white oval butter dish and cover, with leaf and floral sprigged rustic handles, the frieze and cover painted with floral sprays and insects, crescent 'C' mark to base.

£300-400   DUK

PORCELAIN

ESSENTIAL REFERENCE – TRANSFER-PRINTING

- Transfer-printing is a method of decorating ceramics that was found to be both cheaper and quicker than hand painting in the mid-18thC, and is still in use today.
- An engraved copper plate is covered with ink, which has been prepared with metallic oxides. The engraved design is then transferred to paper and pressed onto the surface of the object whilst still wet with pigment. The design can then be fixed by firing.
- Transfer-printing was probably invented by John Brooks or J. Sadler.
- It was much used at the Battersea Enamel Factory (from c.1753), Bow (from c.1756), by Robert Hancock at Worcester (around 1757) and on earthenware at the Liverpool factory by John Sadler from 1756. By the late 18thC/early 19thC, most English factories used the process.
- Blue and white chinoserie designs, such as the 'Willow' pattern, were extremely popular and were often used on table ware.
- Early transfer-prints are often vastly different in shade from each other. Some designs were filled in by hand, though these are now very rare.
- By c1815 production had vastly increased, and by c1835 smoother prints could be made in a variety of colours.
- Transfer-printed ware can be distinguished from more valuable hand-painted pieces by looking for the cross-hatching left by engraving the copper plate. Sometimes the edges of a printed design do not match.

A First Period Worcester porcelain cylindrical mug, printed in black with 'The Milk Maids' and 'May Day' pattern, the reeded loop handle printed in black with strapwork.

c1760-65   *6in (15cm) high*

£900-1,200   TEN

A rare transfer-printed First Period Worcester cylindrical mug, decorated with William Pitt the Elder, shown in half-length portrait between Fame and Mars.

c1760   *3.25in (8.5cm) high*

£2,500-3,000   TEN

A transfer-printed small bell-form mug, First Period Worcester, decorated with 'King of Prussia', trophies and fame, ridged and grooved handle.

The print of battle trophies incorporates the Richard Holdship rebus and anchor and the battle honours of Reisberg, Prague, Collin, Welham, Rosbach, Breslan, Neumark, Lissa and Breslan (bis).'

c1760   *3.25in (8.5cm) high*

£900-1,200   TEN

A rare transfer-printed First Period Worcester cylindrical pint mug, decorated with 'Shakespeare between Tragedy and Comedy', depicting the Scheemakers monument to the Bard flanked by the tragic and comic muses, grooved strap handle.

c1760   *6in (15.5cm) high*

£1,200–1,800   TEN

A transfer-printed bell-form mug, First Period Worcester, decorated with 'Milking Scene' and the 'Rural Lovers', ridged and grooved handle.

c1765   *4.75in (12cm) high*

£700–1,000   TEN

A rare transfer-printed Worcester cabbage leaf jug, finely decorated with three scenes of pastoral couples, with roses above.

c1760   *7.25in (18.5cm) high*

£1,200–1,800   TEN

Two First Period Worcester transfer-printed saucer, one decorated with water birds, the other decorated with poultry and birds in flight.

A small transfer-printed First Period Worcester plate, with fluted petal rim with gilt line border framing a solitary fisherman before an arched building and ball-capped obelisk.

c1760   *7in (18cm) diam*

£350-450   **TEN**

c1760   *5in (13cm) d*

£900-1,200   **TEN**

A First Period Worcester transfer-printed bowl, externally printed with three vignettes comprising milkmaid and gallant, 'The Milkmaids', and an amorous couple, inside centre two swans and a cygnet.

c1760   *6in (15cm) diam*

£250-350   **TEN**

A First Period Worcester transfer-printed bowl, externally with three vignettes comprising 'L'Amour', a garden veranda, and an amorous couple in a Classical garden, internally to the centre with birds.

c1760   *6in (15cm) diam*

£250-350   **TEN**

A transfer-printed First Period Worcester teapot and cover, barrel-form, one side printed with figures strolling over a two-arched bridge, the other with a lady and gentlemen Grand Tourists.

4.75in (12cm) high

£700–1,000   **TEN**

A transfer-printed First Period Worcester baluster coffee pot and cover, each side with a differing view of travellers amongst statues and ruins.

c1760   *9.25in (23.5cm) high*

£700–1,000   **TEN**

A First Period Worcester transfer-printed two-spouted sauceboat, decorated with 'River Scene', crisply moulded with shell spouts between applied scroll handles, the interior printed with swans, the exterior with four cartouches.

c1760   *7.5in (19cm) high*

£1,500–2,000   **TEN**

PORCELAIN

An early Worcester coffee pot, painted with a peacock seated on rockwork amidst flowering plants, damages, cover lacking.

c1752   6.75in (17cm) high

£400-500   **WW**

An early Worcester polychrome teapot and cover, the cover with flowering prunus arched twig finial, enamelled in Chinese famille verte style, with C-shape handle and short slightly curved spout.

c1752-55

£2,000-2,500

4.5in (11.5cm) high

TEN

A Worcester teapot and cover, painted with gilt-bordered fan-shaped and circular panels of polychrome flowers on a powder blue ground.

c1770   7.5in (19cm) high

£500-700   **WW**

A Worcester blue scale ground milk jug and cover, painted with gilt-bordered C-scroll panels of insects and exotic birds, with blue 'fretted' square mark.

c1770   5.5in (14cm) high

£700-1,000   **DN**

A Worcester teapot and cover, each side painted with three Oriental figures beneath a gilt spearhead border, restoration to tip of spout.

c1778-80   6.75in (17cm) high

£300-400   **WW**

A pair of 18thC Worcester 'Blind Earl' pattern green painted sweetmeat dishes, each of circular scalloped form with a branch-form handle terminating in moulded flower buds, the well with moulded leaf decoration and painted in green with pears, plums, flowers and leaves.

The design of the Blind Earl'pattern originated at the Chelsea porcelain factory and was produced by Worcester from the 1750s. In the 19th century the pattern was named after the Earl of Coventry who lost his sight in a riding accident. He ordered a service in this pattern so that he could feel the raised decoration.

1765–70   6.25in (16cm) w

£5,000-6,000   **L&T**

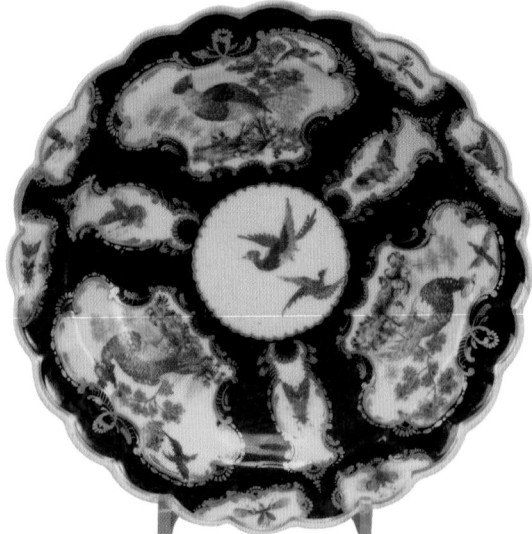

A Worcester blue scale ground plate, painted with panels of exotic birds within a scalloped rim, with blue fretted square mark.

c1770   7.75in (19.5cm) diam

£400-500   **DN**

A Worcester fluted cup, painted in the Kakiemon palette with a dragon and two crabs, the interior with a border of gilt and iron-red flowers, minor damages.

c1755-60   3.25in (8cm) high
£350-450   WW

A rare Worcester teabowl, printed and painted with two geese amongst large peony blooms in the famille rose palette, rim crack.

c1765   2.75in (7cm) diam
£400-500   WW

An unusual Worcester mug, outside decorated, with the heraldic badge of the Prince of Wales between two floral sprays on the gilt-hatched ground, a faint glaze crack.

c1770   3.5in (9cm) high
£1,000-1,500   WW

A Worcester chocolate cup, cover and saucer, painted with the 'Fan' pattern, the cover with a floral knop, seal marks, restoration to the cover.

c1765-75   5.75in (14.5cm) high
£350-450   WW

A Worcester cup, painted with four alternate sprays of colourful flowers, foliage and exotic birds, issuing from gilded cobalt blue scrolls.

c1770   3.25in (8.5cm) high
£350-450   WW

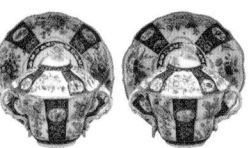

A pair of Worcester two-handled chocolate cups, covers and saucers, decorated with panels of flowers within solid blue borders with a gilt-scroll cartouche of flowers, with 'fretted' square marks, minute chips to floriform finials.

c1775
£1,500-2,000   DN

CLOSER LOOK – EARLY WORCESTER BOWL

The Chinese influence can be seen in the decoration of Oriental flowers and foliage amongst rockwork. With this level of accuracy, it is likely that Worcester decorators copied real Chinese pieces, or engravings.

This bowl comes from the First Period 1751-75, making it an early and desirable piece.

Pieces from this period have a grey-blue appearance and are fully glazed, including the foot-rims.

The eight-panelled form, which would have been relatively difficult to pot, is unusual.

A rare early Worcester bowl, moulded with eight wide panels, painted in famille verte palette with Oriental flowers and foliage amongst rockwork, minor chips to the rim, some wear.

8.5in (21.5cm) diam

£7,000-8,000   WW

An 18thC Worcester sauce tureen, cover and stand, of quatrelobed form, with twig handles and applied flowers to the terminals, decorated in the 'Dragons in Compartments' (Bishop Sumner) pattern, the cover and stand with scalloped gilt rims.

c1770   Tureen 7in (18cm) wide
£2,000-3,000   L&T

PORCELAIN

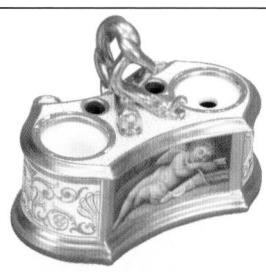

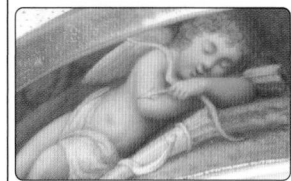

A pair of Worcester Flight, Barr & Barr Warwick urns, probably painted by Thomas Baxter with Raphaelesque panels of putti emblematic of War and Peace, damage.

c1815

£1,000-2,000

9.75in (25cm) high

DN

A Worcester Flight, Barr & Barr inkwell, with entwined snake handle and painted with a panel of a sleeping Cupid, possibly painted by Pennington, script marks, lacks covers.

c1815   6in (15cm) long

£500-700   DN

ESSENTIAL REFERENCE – 19THC WORCESTER

- The Worcester porcelain factory was bought by Joseph and John Flight in 1783. In 1793, Martin Barr also became a partner and until 1807, the factory was called Flight & Barr.
- From 1807 to 1813 it was named Barr, Flight & Barr. At this time, output included superb coloured grounds and fine hand painting by skilled artists such as William Billingsley.
- After the collapse of Oriental import, Barr, Flight & Barr made armorial ware and gilded Japanese Imari-style ware.
- From 1813-1840, the factory was named Flight, Barr & Barr. Thomas Baxter was employed from 1814-1816 and painted various subjects, including Classical style portraits.
- In 1840 the firm merged with local rival, R. Chamberlain, and the Worcester concern moved to the Chamberlain workshops. Production from this period features beautiful decoration.
- In 1852, two irishmen Richard W. Binns and William H. Kerr took over management of the factory, which became known as Kerr & Binns. Production included Parian ware and Ivory Porcelain (glazed Parian) and figures
- The factory was renamed Worcester Royal Porcelain Company (known as Royal Worcester) in 1862. By 1900, over 2500 new, elaborately decorative items were introduced in a variety of styles, including Japanese, Empire, and Greek.
- The nearby Grainger factory was sold to Royal Worcester in 1889. By 1902 many former Grainger employees, including the famous Stinton family of painters, had transferred to Royal Worcester.

An English probably Flight Barr & Barr Worcester porcelain Windsor topographical inkwell, with inserting receptacle with shallow cover with leaf finial, two tubular pen nozzles either side, on lion paw feet and integral plinth.

c1820   3.5in (9cm) high

£700-1,000   TEN

A rare Flight, Barr and Barr cylindrical mug, printed with a view of Worcester Cathedral, dated '1816' and a Barr, Flight and Barr mug painted with a view of Worcester Bridge, minor wear.

4.25in (11cm) high

£900-1,200   WW

A pair of Barr, Flight & Barr Worcester Imari dessert tureens and covers and a pair of plates en suite, each with impressed crown and 'BFB' mark, tureens also with brown printed Royal armorial and Prince of Wales feathers factory mark.

c1825   Tureens 6.25in (16cm) high

£1,500-2,000   TEN

A Barr, Flight & Barr Worcester porcelain pen and ink stand, with an entwined serpent handle, and two covers, painted with a 'Scene on the Wye, near Goodrich Castle', with painted marks and inscription, some damage.

c1800   5.5in (14cm) wide

£400-500   BE

A pair of Chamberlain's Worcester vases and covers, painted with armorial crests for the Sharp family, the reverse with panels of flowers, raised on clawed feet on circular bases, the interiors simulating marble, the covers with printed marks and the gilt inscription 'ACS August 6th 1817', damages.

1817   6.75in (17.5cm) high

£900-1,200   WW

A 19thC Chamberlains Worcester ice pail, liner and cover, the cover with gilt dolphin finial and pierced sides, the body with twin mermaid handles, raised on three gilt dolphins and a triform base, painted mark 'Chamberlains Worcester 75' to cover.

14.5in (36.5cm) high

£3,000-4,000   L&T

Two Chamberlain's Worcester plaques, one painted with a view of Lake Windermere, the other with a view of Worcester Bridge, within moulded and gilded borders, one marked, both titled, minor faults.

c1840   8in (20cm) wide

£1,500-2,000   WW

WORCESTER – GRAINGERS

A Grainger, Lee & Co. Worcester porcelain model of a red squirrel, on a rounded rectangular base moulded with scrolls picked out in gilt, impressed 'Grainger, Lee & Co Worcester', restored.

c1830-40

£250-350   TEN

A Grainger's Worcester reticulated vase, of compressed globular form with turquoise and gilt 'jewelled' ornament beneath a pierced and tapered cylindrical neck, with date letter.

1892   7.25in (18.5cm) high

£150-250   DN

A Grainger's Worcester reticulated porcelain vase and cover, the ornate reticulated body with a conforming lid, raised on a knopped and fluted stem, square foot, brown factory mark.

c1897 19.25in (49cm) high

£3,000-4,000   JA

A late 19th/early 20thC Grainger's Worcester garniture of three vases and covers, painted with exotic birds and colourful insects within gilt cartouches on a blue scale ground, printed factory marks.

8.25in (21cm) high

£400-500   WW

A Grainger's Worcester reticulated vase and cover, oviform and supported on three legs and a cushion base, enriched with gilt borders, with printed factory mark.

1901   7in (18cm) high

£150-250   DN

PORCELAIN

A small Royal Worcester porcelain reticulated pedestal vase, with stylised strapwork handles, the body decorated with a honeycomb band, gilt strapwork and painted roses, printed mark in puce, date cipher.

1898   *5.75in (14.5cm) high*

£5,000-7,000   **TEN**

A small Royal Worcester porcelain reticulated bottle vase, shape 1552, printed mark in puce, dated cipher, initialled 'PE' in burnt orange on foot.

1899   *6.25in (16cm) high*

£5,000-7,000   **TEN**

A Royal Worcester porcelain golden pheasant painted potpourri vase, lid and cover, by James Stinton, shape '293', signed, green printed crown and wheel mark, year mark.

1903   *7.25in (18.5cm) high*

£1,200-1,800   **TEN**

A Royal Worcester twin-handled vase, painted by Charles Baldwyn, with four white fan-tailed doves amidst gilded foliage, signed, printed mark and date code, restored.

1906   *9in (23 cm)high*

£1,200-1,800   **WW**

A Royal Worcester porcelain reticulated vase, by George Owen, raised on four inscroll feet moulded in high relief with baroque maiden masks, gilt printed crown and wheel mark, year mark and incised 'G Owen'.

Pierced decoration, also known as reticulation, is carried out while the clay is still soft enough to be cut with a sharp tool. George Owen (1845-1917), a craftsman at Royal Worcester, was a master in the art of piercing and each of his reticulated vases is unique.

1909   *4.25in (11cm) high*

£7,000-10,000   **TEN**

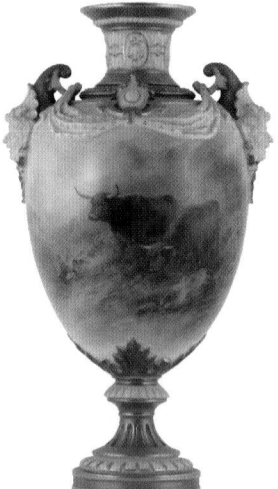

A Royal Worcester vase, with satyr head handles, painted with Highland cattle beside a mountain path, signed 'J. Stinton' for John Stinton (junior), printed mark and date code, cover lacking.

1906   *12in (30.5cm) high*

£3,000-4,000   **WW**

A pair of Royal Worcester vases and covers, each decorated with a peacock and a peahen, raised on gilded bases, signed 'Sedgley', printed marks and date codes, one knop re-glued.

1908   *15.75in (40cm) high*

£3,000-4,000   **WW**

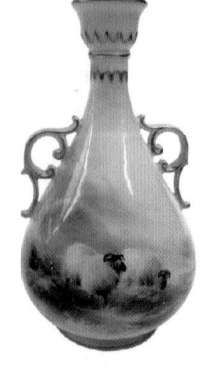

A Royal Worcester vase, Grainger's shape G995, painted with sheep in a moorland setting, signed 'H Davies' below cup-shaped blush and gilt highlighted neck, applied scroll handles, dated.

1910   *5.5in (14cm) high*

£1,200-1,800   **FLD**

A Royal Worcester porcelain potpourri vase and cover, shape G431, with four scroll-pierced vertical blush ivory panels, painted by William Powell, signed, printed mark in green, date cipher.
1912
£1,500-2,000   **TEN**

CLOSER LOOK – A ROYAL WORCESTER VASE

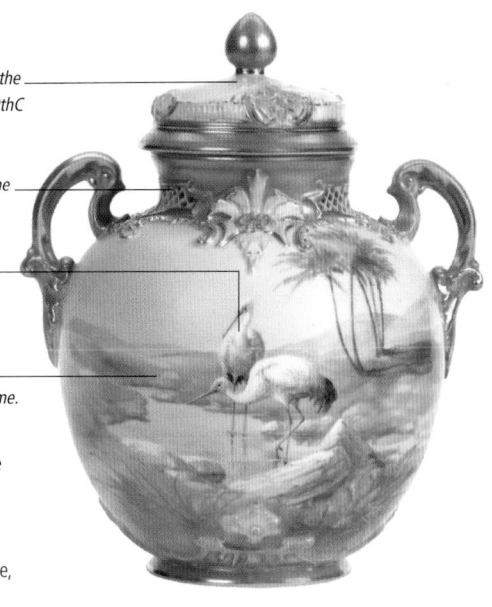

Shape 1515 is oriental and elegant. This form and the desert oasis are all typical of the late 19th/early 20thC craze for exotic wares.

This piece is in perfect condition. Any rubbing of the gilding would reduce the value considerably.

William Powell worked for Royal Worcester from 1900-1950, and was well known for his paintings of birds.

The high-quality, almost photographic image is characteristic of Royal Worcester designs of this time.

A Royal Worcester porcelain scroll-handled vase and cover, by William Powell, shape 1515, with storks in a desert oasis, within strapwork moulded and pierced borders decorated with green shot-enamel, signed, printed mark in puce, year mark, numbered '145.74' in green.
1909   *8.25in (21cm) high*
£5,000-7,000   **TEN**

A Royal Worcester twin-handled vase and cover, painted by Louis Flexman with a still life, signed, on a mottled green ground within an elaborate gilt cartouche, printed mark and date code.
1916   *12.75in (32.5cm) high*
£1,200-1,800   **WW**

A pair of Royal Worcester porcelain Highland cattle trumpet vases, by Harry Stinton, shape G923, with gold misted borders, green and puce printed crown and wheel marks, one with year mark, each signed.
1918   *8.75in (22.5cm) high*
£1,800–2,200   **TEN**

A pair of Royal Worcester porcelain painted pedestal vases, by George Moseley, shape 2160, puce printed crown and well marks, year marks, shape number and retailer's 'Maple', signed.
1929   *8in (20.5cm) high*
£1,200-1,800   **TEN**

A pair of Royal Worcester porcelain trumpet vases, shape G923, each painted with a study of a pheasant signed 'Jas Stinton' within gilt tinted and green shot enamel borders, dated.
1938   *9in (23cm) high*
£2,000-3,000   **FLD**

A Royal Worcester porcelain fruit painted campana shaped vase, by John Smith, painted with fruit, signed, crown and wheel mark.
c1960   *8.75in (22cm) high*
£1,500-2,000   **TEN**

Part of an early 20thC Royal Worcester fruit service, painted by James Stinton, signed, comprising two square dishes, two circular dishes and twelve plates, puce printed mark and date code.
1915
£3,500-4,500 SET   **L&T**

A Royal Worcester porcelain fruit painted part dessert service, by Horace Bright, comprising footed oval comport and four plates, signed, puce printed crown and wheel marks, year marks.
1919-1923
£2,500-3,500   **TEN**

PORCELAIN

A pair of Royal Worcester oval fruit painted dessert dishes and a matching dessert plate, by Richard Sebright, puce printed crown and wheel marks, year mark and 'C486' in iron-red.

1921   *10.5in (27cm) wide*
£1,800-2,200   **TEN**

A Royal Worcester jardinière, painted with orchids, the shoulders applied with a symmetric foliate design in mint green and gilt, printed marks and date code, signed 'Roberts' for Frank Roberts.

1899   *13.25in (34cm) high*
£4,500-5,500   **WW**

A Royal Worcester pedestal urn and cover, shape 2298, painted with Highland cattle signed 'John Stinton', the leaf cast handles with griffin terminals, decorated in gilt shot enamels, dated.

1917   *10.5in (27cm) high*
£3,500-4,500   **FLD**

A Royal Worcester pedestal sweetmeat dish, shape H280, signed 'Johnson', applied leaf scroll handles and raised on a moulded and fluted shot enamel spreading circular base, dated.

1918   *7.5in (19cm) high*
£2,500-3,000   **FLD**

A Royal Worcester porcelain Highland cattle painted ewer, by Harry Stinton, shape G.965, with pierced spout and shoulders, signed, green painted crown and wheel mark and date code.

1904   *6.5in (16.5cm) high*
£1,200-1,800   **TEN**

A Royal Worcester pheasant painted bowl, by James Stinton, internally and externally painted with pheasants, signed, with a misted gilt rim and solid gilded canted foot, puce printed crown and wheel mark and year mark.

1937   *8in (20.5cm) diam*
£1,500-2,000   **TEN**

A Royal Worcester porcelain fruit painted centre bowl, by John Freeman, shape 254/H, with double gilt griffin handles on scroll moulded foot, signed, crown and wheel mark in black.

1959   *15in (38cm) wide*
£3,000-4,000   **TEN**

A Royal Worcester 'Take Cover' figure group, by Eileen Soper, model RW3352, dated.

This sentimental group was part of the 'Wartime' series, which also included figures called 'The Evacuees', 'Spitfire' and 'Salvage'. The series did not sell well in wartime Britain, so very few were made.

1941   *4.25in (11cm) high*
£1,000-1,500   **FLD**

A pair of large Tournai porcelain allegorical figures, of infants, one hunting the other fishing, on circular gilded and marbled stepped bases, with painted crossed swords mark.

18in (45.5cm) high

£650-850   **GORL**

A 19thC Tournai-style sauce tureen, cover and stand, painted with scenes of rural figures, within gilt borders on a green and gilt scale ground, various marks, some wear.

Stand 9.5in (24cm) wide

£350-450   **WW**

A pair of 19thC English porcelain vases, of twin-handled urn form, painted with summer flowers and gilt borders, the handles with mask terminals raised on a square plinth.

10in (25.5cm) high

£650-750   **L&T**

A Champion's Bristol mug, painted with scattered flowers beneath a green ribbon and floral border, unmarked, a large star crack.

c1775   6in (15.5cm) high

£650-850   **WW**

A pair of dark green pâte-sur-pâte vases, probably by Brown-Westhead, Moore & Co., each decorated by Frederick Schenk with a nymph, gilt ring handles, signed, restoration to one.

c1880   8in (20.5cm) high

£600-800   **WW**

A pair of Victorian Gillet and Barndton lustre sheen porcelain centre pieces, modelled as Classically dressed women holding shells on circular shell and scroll foot bases.

17in (43cm) high

£800-1,000   **GORL**

A Pinxton coffee can and saucer, painted with a wide leafy border in gilt and purple, some wear to the gilding.

c1820   5.5in (14cm) high

£100-150   **WW**

A rare Bristol porcelain vase, of hexagonal form, painted in polychrome with butterflies, exotic birds, dragons and chrysanthemums, with shagreen and gilt borders, restored.

c1774   12.5in (31.5cm) high

£2,000-3,000   **L&T**

An English, probably Pinxton, porcelain topographical coffee cup, depicting a river valley view, perhaps Dovedale, with indented C-shape handle.

c1800   2.75in (7cm) high

£300-500   **TEN**

PORCELAIN

A Pinxton porcelain porter mug, probably by John Coke, with angled and loop handle, boldly painted with English garden flowers, with an arrow-like mark in puce enamel.

The Pinxton factory, in Derbyshire, was founded in 1796 by John Coke, with the help of William Billingsley, a talented painter who had worked for Derby. The factory produced domestic wares and tableware in a granular, yet transparent porcelain, with a brilliant glaze. In 1804 the factory was taken over by John Cutts, a Derby-trained landscape painter, and closed in 1813.

c1800   5in (12.5cm) high

£350-450   BE

An 18thC Plymouth beer mug, of inverted bell shaped form painted in underglaze blue with a pagoda landscape, painted tin mark.

The Plymouth porcelain works were set up by a Quaker chemist, William Cookworthy in 1768, who invented the first hard-paste type porcelain to be produced commercially in England. Technical difficulties meant that Plymouth porcelain was only in production for a short period, from c1768-70, after which Cookworthy relocated to Bristol.

6.25in (16cm) high

£1,500-2,000   LOC

A large Plymouth baluster footed mug, by William Cookworthy, applied with a grooved loop handle and painted with flowers in the Meissen style, with iron-red 'tin' mark, cracked.

c1768-70   6.25in (16cm) high

£400-500   DN

A Spode porcelain letter rack, enamelled with two gilt edged panels depicting English landscapes, painted to the reverse in black 'Spode' and 'Valle Crucis Abbey, Denbighshire' and to the underside 'Derwent Water, Cumberland', cracked.

c1820-30   6.5in (16.5cm) high

£600-800   BE

A Plymouth porcelain figure of a young boy, representing 'Winter', wearing a fur trimmed cloak, sanding by a brazier on a high scroll moulded base, minor chips.

c1770   5.5in (14cm) high

£450-550   BE

A Vauxhall blue and white coffee cup, painted with an Oriental river landscape with birds flying above.

c1758-60   3.25in (8cm) high

£700-900   WW

A small Vauxhall porcelain vase, of inverted baluster form, printed and overpainted in polychrome enamels with loose bouquets of summer flowers, scattered sprigs and a moth.

c1758-65   4.25in (11cm) high

£1,000-1,500   TEN

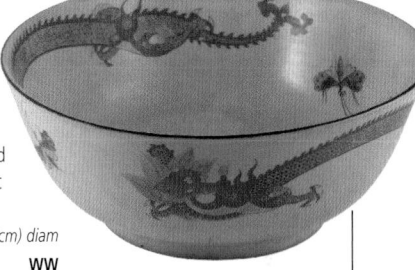

A rare early 19thC set of five Wedgwood stone china plates, painted in pink camaieu with scenes of country estates, gilded rims, impressed '1' mark, some wear.

8.5in (21.5cm) diam

£500-700 SET   **WW**

An English porcelain commemorative jug, of Queen Caroline association, with moulded satyr mask, each side with raised profile bust portrait of a gentleman, the rim inscribed 'Mr T Denman Mr Brougham'.

Thomas Denman, 1st Baron Denman (1779–1854) and Henry Brougham, 1st Baron Brougham and Vaux were both involved advising Queen Caroline, wife of George IV, on her legal position regarding the annulment of her marriage to the king.

c1820   *4.75in (12cm) high*

£350-450   **TEN**

A small English blue and white porcelain basket, of flared circular form, trellis pierced, internally and externally painted with flowers.

c1760–70   *6in (15cm) diam*

£350-450   **TEN**

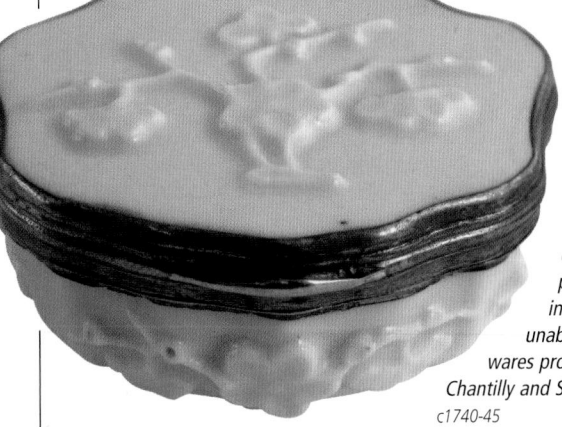

A large mid-18thC Chantilly bowl, painted in the Kakiemon palette with dragons, lion dogs and butterflies, to the interior and exterior, brown line rim, faint horn mark, restored.

10.5in (27cm) diam

£400-500   **WW**

A pair of English porcelain portrait painted plaques, by William Corden, one depicting John Osmond Deakin, Downing College, Cambridge, the other Frances Margaret Deakin, in period frames with plaques inscribed 'W M Corden 1823'.

1823   *5.75in (14.5cm) high*

£2,000-2,500   **TEN**

An 18thC Saint-Cloud circular tapered cup with matching saucer, three-quarter fluted with blue painted foliated border and scroll handle.

£400-600   **A&G**

A Saint-Cloud white-glazed box, with hinged lid, all-over moulded with branches of flowering prunus.

Saint-Cloud was the first major porcelain factory in France, beginning production of soft-paste porcelain in the early 1690s and receiving an official patent for the manufacture of porcelain in 1702. Early production imitated the forms of metalware and decoration of Oriental porcelain. Later, European designs were introduced. The factory closed in 1766, unable to compete with the sophisticated wares produced by rival French factories such as Chantilly and Sèvres.

c1740-45   *2.25in (5.5cm) wide*

£1,000-1,500   **WW**

A pair of large mid-19thC French vases and covers, each of globular form with pierced gilt scroll handles, raised on a gilt decorated socle and circular flower-painted scroll base, on later ebonised stand.

33.5in (85cm) high

£900-1,200   **L&T**

PORCELAIN

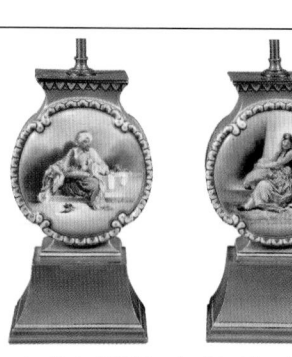

A pair of late 19thC hand-painted French porcelain Moorish vase lamp bases, each of moon flask form, on flaring painted wood bases, mounted as lamps, signed 'L. Fournier'.

Overall 13in (33cm) high

£4,000-5,000 SK

A late 19thC French porcelain figural group, of a mother and her two daughters, raised on a Rococo moulded base, damages and minor restoration.

6.25in (16cm) high

£150-250 WW

Two Karl Ens porcelain figures of parrots, each perched on a naturalistic base, printed factory marks and impressed '71401' and '71411' to bases.

Tallest 14.25in (36cm) high

£300-400 TOV

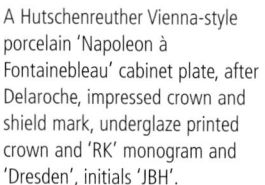

An 18thC Fulda porcelain cup and saucer, both with gilt rims, decorated with figures, underglaze blue cross mark.

Saucer 5.25in (13.5cm) diam

£2,000-3,000 L&T

A pair of early 19thC Furstenberg porcelain pedestals, with raised panels enamelled with figure subjects and bouquets within gilt borders, with blue script mark and incised 'Z', minor restoration.

3.5in (9cm) high

£300-400 BE

A Hutschenreuther Vienna-style porcelain 'Napoleon à Fontainebleau' cabinet plate, after Delaroche, impressed crown and shield mark, underglaze printed crown and 'RK' monogram and 'Dresden', initials 'JBH'.

c1900 *9.75in (24.5cm) diam*

£1,200-1,500 TEN

Three late 19thC Hutschenreuther painted porcelain portrait cabinet plates, from the Franz Xavier Thallmaier studio, each depicting a great European beauty, identified to reverse as 'Auguste Strobl', 'Anna R. Kaula' and 'Marie, Konigin von Bayern'.

The Hutschenreuther porcelain factory was established in 1814 in Bavaria, Germany, and produced mainly dinnerware and figurines. In 2000, Hutschenreuther became part of the Waterford Wedgwood Group.

9.5in (24cm) diam

£1,800-2,200 SK

A pair of Kloster-Veilsdorf porcelain figures, of a Turkish musician and female companion, modelled by Pfanger senior, losses to both figures.

The factory of Kloster-Veilsdorf (est. 1760) produced high-quality wares often imitating Meissen. The male figure seems to be based on an earlier Meissen original, which in turn was sourced from an original print by G.F. Scmidt entitled The Amorous Turk'.

c1770 *Tallest 7.75in (19.5cm) high*

£4,000-5,000 BE

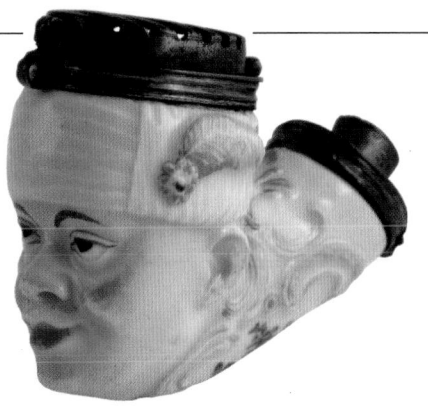

A Ludwigsburg porcelain pipe bowl, moulded as the face of a Turk, the stem with Rococo moulded scrolls and painted with flowers, fitted with metal mounts and a hinged grill lid, minor faults.

c1760   *2.75in (7cm) high*

£1,200-1,800   **WW**

A 19thC Sitzendorf porcelain bowl, of oval form encrusted with fruiting strawberries, scroll handles.

3in (7.5cm) diam

£100-200   **GORL**

A chocolate cup, the upper register with 'Indianische Blumen' above moulded flutes in Böttger lustre and green, ear-handles.

c1735

£500-700   **SWO**

A pair of late 19thC Potschappel porcelain covered vases, Carl Thieme, blue T crossed swords marks.

16.75in (42.5cm) high

£1,200-1,800   **FRE**

A large 19thC German gilt-metal mounted tureen and cover, with gilt-metal finial, pierced leaf-cast rim and stand, with lion-head and sash ring handles, the porcelain cover and bowl with basket weave borders and painted, blue painted mark.

13in (33cm) diam

£2,000-3,000   **L&T**

A late 19thC German gilt-metal mounted vase, of elongated baluster form, the body decorated with a continuous Classical scene, the neck and socle decorated with gilt trophies and scrolls.

26.75in (68cm) high

£1,200-1,800   **L&T**

A German porcelain skull stein, of half-litre capacity, the lid of pewter, engraved to the border 'Ihrem Ib. Josef z. Bleib. Erg. a.d. W.S. 1916/17 Gewidm. M.H', the skull upon a book titled 'Commersbuch' on the spine, and to the sides 'Gaudeamus Igitur', on the other 'Juvenes Dum Sumus'.

'Gaudeamus Igitur'is considered the oldest student song, and is based on a Latin manuscript of 1287. However, the modern version of the words seems to date from 1781 and the music from 1794. It is used in countless graduation ceremonies throughout the world and particularly in Europe. The first verse is as follows: While we are young (juvenes dum sumes)/ Sung out in gleeful tones/ Youth's delightful frolic/ And old age so melancholic/ Earth will cover our bones.'

1916/17   *7in (18cm) high*

£350-450   **TEN**

POTTERY

Pottery sellers began this last year somewhat tentatively, anxious about the state of the economy and the implications of a downturn on the antiques trade. Thankfully, the greatest fears have been allayed for the time being, and there continues to be a core number of keen buyers for pottery. Having said this, there has been a noticeable shift in buying patterns – in particular, there is growing interest in high-end pieces, but a cooling of interest in mid-priced and lower-end examples.

Sales of British pottery have been mixed. At the top end, items of quality and/or rarity continue to achieve good prices, as they have done for several years. Collectors of early English wares dominate the field, showing most interest in early Delftware and unusual pieces. Blue and white transfer printed topographical scenes have always been popular with buyers, and exceptional pieces are seen less often, which could push prices up. Areas that have enjoyed less interest during the last twelve months, are painted Chinoiserie creamware items, which has demonstrated poorer sales than in previous years.

Continental pottery is selling reasonably well, particularly the more exceptional examples. Serious collectors are prepared to pay strong prices for early, rare and beautiful maiolica and Hispano-Moresque items of quality; for example, Christie's sold an early armorial Valencian dish for £34,850 in the early part of this year. In general, buyers are looking for pieces that are in excellent condition, feature strong colour and are of rare design. Marked and dated pieces command the highest prices, and several items are

known to have sold at auction for around £16,000 earlier this year. Edinburgh auction house Lyon & Turnbull sold a second half 16th century Hispano Moresque Valencia (Narbonne) maiolica albarello for £20,000 early in 2009.

For the more modest collector, good pieces of English slipware and delftware are still to be had for the low end of four figures. Woolley & Wallis of Salisbury offered an unusually large private collection of delftware drug jars in its October 2009 sale, which attracted strong bidding from international dealers and private collectors. Again, it was the most rare pieces that attracted the highest interest, but demand was consistent for the less exotic items.

More recent trends in this market include a growth of interest in modern ceramics (post First World War) and, in particular, those that define a period style or commemorate an event. Earlier this year a 'marina green' George VI Coronation tankard by Eric Ravilious realised a world record of £1,650. While versions of the mug are usually estimated to realise in the region of £300 at auction, they were made using different colourways, of which marina green is the rarest.

Another market worth looking at is that of Eastern European pottery, with prices on the increase and looking set to stay that war. Earlier this year, a bowl by Zsolnay made £680 against an estimate of £180–220. Postwar pieces made in Poland, Czechoslovakia and Hungary are generally overlooked, and this could conceivably become a new growth area over the next few years.

Clockwise from top: Bristol blue delftware charger c1700 £14,100 at Anderson & Garland; George VI Coronation tankards £1,650 and £1,150 at Anderson & Garland; delftware drug jar c1740 £881 at Woolley & Wallis.

A Bristol delft plate, naively painted with initials 'AB' and date above and below cottages, the border with lanterns, minor chips.

1733   8.25in (21cm) diam

£3,000-4,000   SWO

A delftware charger, probably Wincanton or Bristol, painted with a castle surrounded by boats within an octagonal panel, stylised flowers in panels around the border, on a powdered manganese ground.

c1740-50   11.5in (29.5cm) diam

£350-450   WW

A delftware blue and white plate, probably Bristol, with a central circle and the monogram 'WEL 1738' surrounded by radiating fronds.

This plate is one of a small number of services made for a group of Chester County Quakers in Pennsylvania. It was most likely to have been made for William (1688-1747) and Elizabeth (1720-1773) Levis.

1738   9in (23cm) diam

£20,000-30,000   POOK

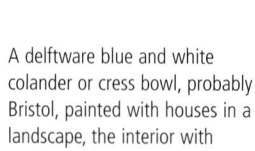

A Bristol polychrome delft dish, painted in sage green, manganese and yellow ochre with stylised tulips, crack.

c1750   13.5in (34cm) d

£250-350   SWO

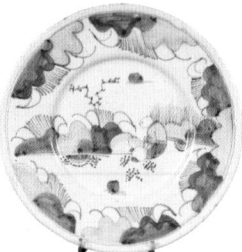

An English delft blue and white plate, Bristol, Brislington or London, painted in the Transitional style with a seated figure in a rocky landscape, cracked.

8.25in (21cm) diam

£250-350   DN

A mid-18thC Bristol delft panel of four titles, each painted in polychrome with a basket and a vase of flowers with bianco-sopra-bianco borders.

Bianco-sopra-bianco, literally white-on-white, is a decorative technique first used in 16thC Italy, where designs in an opaque white were laid over a milk-white tin glaze, particularly around rims and borders. It was used at Lambeth, and extensively at Bristol.

£600-800   SWO

A late 17thC oval delftware three-footed bowl, probably Brislington, with rope-twist handles, the interior painted with a figure, the sides with rockwork and foliage, small glaze chips.

8.25in (21cm) wide

£1,000-1,500   WW

A delftware blue and white colander or cress bowl, probably Bristol, painted with houses in a landscape, the interior with concentric bands, restored.

c1760-70   9.25in (23.5cm) wide

£300-400   WW

A delftware plate, probably Lambeth, painted in polychrome enamels with stylised tulips on a pale blue ground, some crazing to the glaze.

c1720-30   9in (23cm) diam

£200-300   WW

A delftware flowerbrick, perhaps Liverpool, the recessed top set with a central rectangular hole and twelve smaller round holes, minor chips.

c1740-60   6in (15.5cm) wide

£900-1,200   WW

ESSENTIAL REFERENCE – DELFTWARE

- The Netherlands began producing tin-glazed earthenware in the late 15thC. Potteries grew up in Amsterdam, Haarlem, Rotterdam and Delft, which became the most important centre by the late 17thC.
- Dutch Delft ware has a gritty texture, thick glaze and often some 'peppering' to the surface, due to air bubbles bursting during firing. Chipping is common, especially around the rim.
  - Decoration was initially based on Chinese blue and white. By the late 17thC a range of colours was produced, typically purple, red, green and black. Common designs include Biblical scenes and copies of Oriental polychrome decoration.
  - Britain began producing tin-glazed 'delftware' from the mid-16thC. British pieces were typically less finely potted than Dutch Delft and the glaze is often tinged blue or pink. Key production areas were Lambeth, Liverpool and Bristol.
    - By the early 18thC, British delftware was more refined, with a smoother glaze than Dutch wares. Patterns included bold floral designs and British landscapes in blue and white.
      - Polychrome is less common and colours are muted due to the absorbency of the tin-glaze. Inscribed or dated pieces are rare and desirable.

A delftware guglet or water bottle, probably Liverpool, the globular body painted in blue with floral sprays beneath scrolling bands and fern fronds, some restoration.

c1750-60   7.75in (20cm) high
£550-750   WW

An English, probably Liverpool, blue and white delft shallow circular dish, brown rim, the underside with blue encircling line and double concentric ring to the centre.

c1745   14.5in (36.5cm) diam
£650-850   TEN

A rare, possibly Liverpool, delft plate, painted in blue with an unusual scene of a tower billowing smoke, approached by a bridge, rubbing to the rim.

c1750   8in (21.5cm) diam
£200-300   SWO

A delftware mug, possibly Liverpool, the slightly waisted body painted in blue with a symmetrical floral design, the wide strap handle with horizontal dashes, some restoration to the rim.

c1760-70   6.5in (16.5cm) high
£1,000-1,500   WW

A delftware blue and white teapot stand, probably London, painted with Oriental foliage before small buildings within a plumed border raised on three flat scrollwork legs, glaze chipping, crack and wear.

c1720   5.25in (13.5cm) wide
£1,500-2,000   WW

An early 18thC delftware blue and white dish, probably London, painted with a rabbit before a large tree, the rim with concentric bands of blue, chips to the rim.

9in (23cm) diam
£900-1,200   WW

A mid-18thC London blue and white delft plate, painted with a willow, maple, bamboo and lotus.

13.25in (33.5cm) diam
£200-300   SWO

A delftware puzzle jug, London or Liverpool, painted in blue with flowers either side of a verse challenging the drinker to 'try y'Skill', the handle with a series of swirls and dashes, minor faults.

c1750-70   6.75in (17cm) high
£1,200-1,800   WW

A mid-18thC English delft blue and white flower-brick, possibly London, painted with stylised mimosa, cracked.

6in (15cm) long
£300-400   DN

A delftware blue and white shallow teabowl, painted with a house within stylised shrubs and trees, minor glaze chips and cracks to the rim.

c1760-70   3in (7.5cm) diam

£600-800   WW

A rare delftware bowl, the interior painted with a double-masted ship flying the British White Ensign, titled 'Success to the Active 1769', the exterior painted with an Oriental landscape, cracked.

The Active was a warship during the Seven Years' War, and under Captain Sawyer was responsible for the capture of the Spanish treasure ship, the Hermione, still thought to be the richest prize ever taken.

9in (23cm) diam

£5,000-6,000   WW

An 18thC delftware wet-drug jar, painted in blue with a cartouche of shells and putti around the black inscription 'S. Croci', minor glaze wear.

Syrup of saffron was used in the 18thC as colouring and flavouring in medicinal preparations but sparingly, as it was an abortifacient and a fatal poison in larger quantities. It was also used to treat nervous disorders.

6.5in (16.5cm) high

£1,200-1,800   WW

A small delftware wet-drug jar, with the inscription 'S: E: Spin: Cerv' within a scrolling cartouche of cherubs, shells and floral motifs, with strapwork handle and raised on a flared foot, minor chipping.

c1730-50   6.75in (17.5cm) high

£1,500-2,000   WW

A delftware dry-drug jar, painted in blue with the inscription 'C.Ros.Rub' within a cartouche of cherubs and stylised flowers, blue line mark to the base, small restored foot-rim chips.

The inscription relates to the preparation 'Conserve of Red Roses', used as a treatment for consumption because of its soothing properties on the digestive and respiratory systems.

c1740-60   7.75in (20cm) high

£900-1,200   WW

A late 17th/early 18thC lobed delft dish, the well painted with a portrait of King William within a border of yellow flowers and foliage, a short crack, minor rim chips.

13.5in (34.5cm) diam

£1,200-1,800   WW

A delftware Adam and Eve charger, painted and sponged in blue, green and manganese with the couple either side of a tree in which sits the serpent, proffering the forbidden fruit to Eve.

Tin-glazed earthenware 'blue-dash' chargers were made in London and Bristol c1630-1740. Popular motifs include abstract, floral, patriotic and religious images in blue, green, tawny-yellow and brown. Images of Adam and Eve were particularly common and as the fruit Eve hands Adam is typically orange, it is possible that they were intended as a satire on the ascension of William and Mary of Orange.

c1740   13in (33.5cm) diam

£5,000-7,000   WW

A delftware pill slab, painted in blue with the arms of the Worshipful Society of Apothecaries and their motto 'Opiferque Per Orbem Dicor', surface wear and restoration.

c1775-1800   11.75in (30cm) long

£3,000-4,000   WW

A rare manganese delft tile, moulded in the form of a sun dial, dated. This is an extremely rare subject.

1771   *7.25in (18.5cm) wide*

£700-1,000   **SWO**

A delftware posset pot and cover, painted in blue with trellised bridges within stylised bamboo, the mushroom knop to the cover painted with concentric circles, some restoration.

c1720-30   *7.75in (20cm) high*

£2,000-3,000   **WW**

An English delft double inkwell, the sides painted with Fazackerly scrolls and flowers, the top blue and white, chips.

c1760   *5in (13cm) wide*

£600-800   **SWO**

Two similar mid-18thC Dutch Delft blue and white flower-bowls and pierced covers, painted with stylised foliage, chipped.

7.5in (19cm) diam

£550-750   **DN**

A 17thC Dutch Delft petal rim dish, decorated with a central portrait of William of Orange crowned within stylised tulip borders.

13.75in (35cm) diam

£350-450   **GORL**

An 18thC Dutch Delft model of a dog, seated on a rectangular base, painted in blue with leaf fronds and geometric dots, extensively damaged and repaired.

7.5in (19cm) high

£550-750   **WW**

A pair of Dutch Delft polychrome figures of horned cows, each painted with flowers and raised on canted rectangular bases, marked with monogram 'AG'.

7.75in (20cm) wide

£150-250   **FLD**

An early 18thC Dutch Delft jug, painted in blue with an Oriental figure seated amidst rockwork before bamboo and plantain, minor glaze chips to the rim and handle.

5.5in (14cm) high

£700-1,000   **WW**

A 19thC Dutch Delft blue and white ewer, painted with figures in an Oriental landscape, the handle applied with the remains of a metal hinged cover, '6' mark to the base, glaze chips and cracks.

9.75in (25cm) high

£100-150   **WW**

Two 19thC Dutch Delft ewers with winged spouts, painted in blue with figures in landscapes between stylised foliate and floral borders, one with an armorial crest, painted marks, restoration.

9.75in (25cm) high

£100-200   **WW**

ESSENTIAL REFERENCE – DUTCH DELFT FACTORIES

- Dutch Delft ceramists had been imitating tinglazed maiolica (originally from Spain and Italy) from the early 16thC.
- The industry expanded from c1650, after the cessation of imports of Chinese porcelain into Holland. Potters in the town of Delft began to emulate Chinese designs, filling the gap in the market. For this reason, the designs of much early blue and white Delft is similar to Chinese wares, including motifs such as Dog of Fo finials.
- Soon factories in other Dutch towns, such as Amsterdam, Delfshaven, Gouda and Haarlem, also began to produce tinglazed earthenware.
- Imports from China resumed after 1680. By this time there were more than 30 potteries in Delft and their products had developed a style of their own. Other colours were used, and new themes included local landscapes and flowers.
- Important Delft factories include The Greek A factory, The Metal Pot, The Porcelain Claw factory and the Golden Flowerpot.
- By the mid-18thC, many Delft ware factories had gone out of business.

Six similar mid-18thC Delft De Porceleyne Caleuw blue and white chargers, similarly decorated with the 'Peacock' pattern, blue claw marks, some old damage.

Largest 13.75in (35cm) diam

£900-1,200   DN

An 18thC Dutch Delft circular plate, decorated with a figure holding a flag, inscribed 'Vivat Orange'.

9in (23cm) diam

£300-400   L&T

A late 18thC Delft blue and white tile, painted with two figures holding clubs or kolve.

The Dutch game of kolf of kolven, where the aim is to be first to hit a post at the opposite end of the court or ice-rink, is believed to have given its name to the popular game of golf.

5in (13cm) high

£100-200   WW

An 18thC Dutch Delft five-piece mantel garniture, each piece an octagonal shape, consisting of three covered vases with foo dog finials, and two vases, each decorated with a male figure battling a seven-headed dragon, the subject possibly from 'The Two Brothers' by the Brothers Grimm, with hatchet marks.

Vases 13in (33cm) high

£3,500-4,500   SK

A 19thC Dutch Delft octagonal vase, with moulded Rococo scroll, painted in blue and later enamelled with a basket containing a flowering shrub, the reverse with flower and butterflies, restored.

11.75in (30cm) high

£80-120   WW

A 19thC Dutch Delft vase and cover, of lightly ribbed form, the cover surmounted with a bird, painted 'AK' monogram, damages and restoration.

18.5in (47cm) high

£200-300   WW

A 19thC French faience cistern and cover, painted with floral swags and delicate stylised foliage, extensively damaged and repaired.

23in (58.5cm) high

£150-250   **WW**

A pair of 19thC Lille faience dishes, of elaborate crest form, painted with scenes of lovers in a landscape, within elaborate scrolling borders, with mock armorial.

9.75in (25cm) wide

£100-150   **GORL**

A Strasbourg faience dish, painted with an Oriental figure standing on a riverbank beside bulrushes and rockwork, painted mark for Joseph Hannong, damage and restoration.

c1770   *14.25in (36.5cm) wide*

£250-350   **WW**

A 19thC Nove faience monteith, painted with large flowers above a scrolling foliate border, the interior with stylised leafy swags, painted 'Nove' mark, damage and restoration.

13.75in (35cm) diam

£300-400   **WW**

A late 18thC German faience pewter-mounted tankard, enamelled in blue, yellow, green, manganese and red, touch marks under cover, devoid of pewter foot rim.

9.75in (25cm) high

£350-450   **BE**

A pair of 19thC faience albarelli, painted in polychrome with a cartouche, one titled 'R. Zinziber', the other 'R. Turbith', glaze wear and minor chipping.

R. Zinziber (root ginger) was used to settle the stomach and sometimes to disguise the taste of other medicines. R. Turbith (turpeth) was given as a cathartic and purgative.

10.25in (26cm) high

£400-500   **WW**

MAIOLICA

An Italian 16thC-style maiolica Urbino-style round dish, decorated with a biblical scene, possibly representing Hagar and the Angel, Genesis 16 v. 7, within a yellow-line bordered rim.

12.5in (32cm) diam

£400-500   **DN**

Two 19thC Italian maiolica plates, decorated with zoophiliac scenes of women or dryads with goats and Pan in a woodland setting, the reverse with scrolling foliate designs, both restored.

8.75in (22.5cm) diam

£250-350   **WW**

A 19thC Italian maiolica charger, bearing the inscription 'MANTUAE MARG.s ALOISIU.s GONZAGA', the underside inscribed 'ANDES.ME.FECIT', with paper label for the Winifred Dibben Collection, with repaired rim chips.

16.75in (42.5cm) diam

£400-500   **DN**

A 19th/20thC Italian maiolica istoriato dish, painted with the Rape of the Sabine Women within a border of Renaissance-style figures and putti, titled to reverse, a section broken and repaired.

Istoriato, Italian for 'with a story on it', is a type of decoration used on maiolica.

11.75in (30cm) high

£700-1,000   **WW**

A set of three Deruta maiolica drug jars, decorated with fruit and foliage framing a yellow circle with the letters 'S' and 'M' and a blue painted band labelled with the contents, the handle painted with an angel, 'SV LVPOLORV', 'OL ROSAT COMP' and 'MIV CITONI', damages.

Deruta, in Umbria, was an important centre of Italian maiolica production from the 16thC.
c1600

£8,000-10,000   **L&T**

A 17th/18thC Italian Deruta-type maiolica portrait vase, decorated with musical instruments and scrolls framing three portraits surrounding the body.

11.75in (30cm) high

£350-450   **SK**

A 19thC Cantigalli maiolica globular vase, painted with a profile portrait of a young man with tousled hair, on a ground of swirling flowers in yellow, green and ochre, cockerel mark to the base.

11.75in (30cm) diam

£600-800   **WW**

A 16thC Italian maiolica albarello, the waisted form painted with a foliate design in shades of green, yellow and blue, with a few small chips.

10in (25.5cm) high

£2,500-3,500 WW

A 17thC Italian Tuscan tin glazed earthenware albarello, polychrome decorated crest to a waisted vase with blue foliate design, titled 'EIL IND MA'.

7.75in (19.5cm) high

£800-1,200 SK

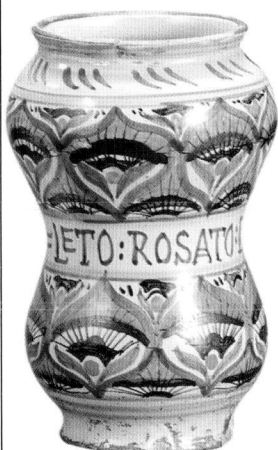

A 17thC Italian Faenza maiolica tin glazed albarello, polychrome decorated with foliage to the waisted vase with central inscription 'LETO:ROSATO:D:MELE'.

9in (23cm) high

£800-1,200 SK

A 17thC Italian maiolica albarello, named for Triafar, within scrolling floral borders, decorated with a winged cherub mask and a fleur-de-lys, impressed marks indistinct.

7.75in (19.5cm) high

£1,000-1,500 GORL

A 17thC Italian maiolica albarello, named for Diaprunislvn, within scrolling blue foliate borders, highlighted with a yellow cartouche, dated.

1687 *7.25in (18.5cm) high*

£1,000-1,500 GORL

An early 18thC Italian Capellotti maiolica tin glazed albarello, blue decorated 'alla Rouen' ware with cartouches of a bird in a landscape and a floral vine to a scrolled foliate ground.

9.75in (25cm) high

£1,500-2,000 SK

A 17thC Italian maiolica plaque, depicting a bishop saint in low relief wearing ecclesiastical robes with 'CG' monogram, inscribed 'Semi Dio'.

Plaque 13in (33cm) high

£400-500 GORL

A pair of late 19thC Italian maiolica roundels, one painted with Minerva, the other with Galatea, both accompanied by putti and depicted with articles signifying their attributes.

10.25in (26cm) diam

£1,500-2,000 FRE

POTTERY

A 19th/20thC Italian Della Robbia-style earthenware tile, polychrome enamel decorated with relief depiction of the Virgin Mary and Christ Child with cherubs, wide border of fruits and foliage.

33in (84cm) high

£550-750   **SK**

A 19th/20thC Italian maiolica semi-circular plaque, in the Della Robbia style, moulded with The Annunciation, unmarked, damages.

17.75in (45cm) wide

£450-550   **WW**

A 17thC Sicilian Caltagirone maiolica wet-drug jar, polychrome decorated with foliage, a portrait below the handle.

7.5in (19cm) high

£1,200-1,800   **SK**

A 17th/18thC Caltagirone maiolica small globular jar, painted with scrolling flowers and leaves in a palette of green, yellow and ochre against a blue ground, some glaze wear.

3.75in (9.5cm) high

£100-200   **WW**

An 18thC Sicilian maiolica vase, polychrome decorated with a scroll framed portrait to one side, dated.

1787   7.75in (19.5cm) high

£300-400   **SK**

A 17th/18thC maiolica wall font, probably Caltagirone, painted with St Catherine and inscribed 'S. Chatarina', chips.

£1,300-1,800   **WW**

A pair of 18thC Iberian maiolica waisted albarelli, one named for 'U ~ AVREO' and the other 'R ~ RVYBARB', one repaired.

9.75in (25cm) high

£750-1,000   **DN**

Two similar 18thC Iberian maiolica waisted albarelli, painted in blue with foliate cartouches of a cross with tassel-surmounted with a crown, one inscribed '60', one chipped and repaired.

Tallest 10.75in (27.5cm) high

£1,200-1,800   **DN**

An 18thC Spanish Talavera maiolica bowl, centrally painted with the head of a mule, within a broad band of stylised trees, yellow and green lines to the rim, on a flared circular foot.

12.5in (31.5cm) wide

£550-750   **TEN**

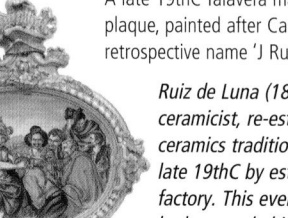

A late 19thC Talavera maiolica oval wall plaque, painted after Caravaggio, bearing retrospective name 'J Ruiz de Luna Talavera'.

Ruiz de Luna (1863-1905), a Spanish ceramicist, re-established the ceramics tradition in Talavera in the late 19thC by establishing his own factory. This eventually closed but he had succeeded in reviving Talavera as a centre for traditional wares.

19.5in (50cm) high

£500-700   **TEN**

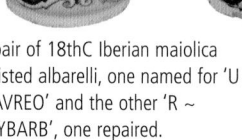

Two maiolica dishes, decorated in a palette of blue, yellow and green, with allegorical figures within a scrolling foliate border, painted marks, extensively damaged.

12.75in (32.5cm) diam

£350-450   **WW**

A late 18th/early 19thC Liverpool creamware bowl, black printed to the interior with a sail ship, to the exterior with four figural vignettes within floral sprigs.

Liverpool was well known for transfer decoration on ceramics and remained the centre of this niche for many years.

11.5in (28.25cm) wide

£350-450   **HT**

A large Documentary Liverpool creamware jug, printed in black and overpainted with 'Tom Truelove Going To Sea' and 'Jack Spritsail Coming On Shore' after Mollart, 'The Waterman' vignette beneath the handle, and with Masonic symbols after F. Morris Shelton.

c1790   *13.5in (34.5cm) high*

£1,800-2,000   **TEN**

A Liverpool creamware jug, decorated with 'An East View of Liverpool Light House & Signals on Bidston Hill', the reverse with a printed explanation of the signals, 2.75in (5cm) crack.

Flag no. 40, 'Enemies', perhaps indicates that this jug was made after the declaration of war between Britain and France in 1803.

7in (18cm) high

£1,200-1,800   **WW**

An early 19thC Liverpool pitcher of nautical interest, one side depicting the 'Apotheosis' of George Washington, the reverse inscribed 'Peace Plenty and Independence' beneath an eagle with outstretched wings, bearing the monogram of Captain George A. Robinson.

10in (25.5cm) high

£3,500-4,500   **POOK**

A Staffordshire, possibly Wedgwood, creamware commemorative jug, printed to one side with an American brig, the other with George Washington and a figure with liberty bonnet gesturing towards His Majesty's loyal Canadian provinces, opposite a seated figure of Benjamin Franklin resting a copy of the Declaration of Independence upon his knee, small chips and scratches.

The jug may commemorate the death of George Washington, first President of the United States (1732-99). This may not only have been produced for export but also for British supporters of the rebellious colonists of the American War of Independence, particularly the Whigs.

c1800   *10.25in (26cm) high*

£2,000-3,000   **DN**

A creamware mug, printed in black with four riders on horseback watching the hounds chasing the fox, beneath a tree.

c1770-80   *6in (15.5cm) high*

£300-400   **WW**

A Wedgwood & Co. creamware mug, ribbed strap handle, transfer-printed and enamelled with 'An East View of Liverpool Light House... Bidston Hill', impressed marks, chip.

c1800   *5in (13cm) high*

£600-800   **BE**

POTTERY

A 19thC Staffordshire campana-shaped two-handled frog and lizard mug, painted with flowers, dedicated to Charlotte Fairburn, on circular foot, crazed, on handle thumbpiece chip, dated.

1845 *8in (20.5cm) high*

£200-300 **A&G**

A 19thC 'Semi China' mug, with an internal partition, printed with figures in an Oriental landscape and a cartouche containing the inscription 'G Tyrer's Improved Soda Font, Liverpool', printed mark.

5.5in (14cm) high

£300-400 **WW**

An 18thC Dutch decorated creamware plate, with feathered rim, painted with Prince William of Orange and his intended, facing each other either side of an orange tree, incised 'X' to the base, restored.

8.75in (25cm) diam

£150-200 **WW**

A Leeds creamware teapot, the cover with convolvulus flower finial, painted on one side with a plough and inscription 'God Speed The Plough', on the other with a chinoiserie bridge over a lake, restoration.

c1770 *5in (12.5cm) high*

£1,800-2,200 **TEN**

A cylindrical Leeds creamware teapot, with flowerhead finial, with ogee strapwork handle and acanthus decorated spout, decorated on both sides with a ho ho bird standing near flowers in colours.

c1770 *6in (15cm) high*

£1,000–1,500 **TEN**

A Staffordshire creamware cauliflower-moulded tea canister, of William Greatbatch type, with associated metal cover, partially green glazed.

c1765 *4in (10cm) high*

£300-400 **DN**

ESSENTIAL REFERENCE – CREAMWARE

A Leeds creamware teapot, the ogee domed cover with acorn finial and painted with flower sprays within pierced gallery, painted on each side with Chinese maiden holding a parasol, on swept foot.

c1770 *6in (15cm) high*

£2,000-3,000 **TEN**

- Creamware was developed in the mid-18thC by the potteries of Staffordshire, led by Josiah Wedgwood.
- The clay was mixed with flint to produce a lightweight, close-grained surface that was then covered in a thin layer of ivory-tinted lead glaze. The material was durable, relatively cheap, and as thin as porcelain. Creamware could be finely moulded before being painted or printed over the glaze.
- Josiah Wedgwood developed an improved type of creamware in 1765, which he named 'Queensware' after Queen Charlotte granted him a royal warrant for his invention.
- By the late 18thC creamware was the standard household pottery throughout Europe, driving many tin-glazed earthenware factories out of business.

A cylindrical Leeds creamware teapot, painted on one side with stylised heart with inscription 'When Lovers Act There (sic) Part They Make a Double Heart', the opposite side with a single heart and crossed arrows, restored.

c1770 *5in (12.5cm) high*

£2,000-3,000 **TEN**

A probably Derby creamware teapot, Cockpit Hill, crabstock handle and spout, painted on one side with a woman seated by an altar inscribed 'Solitude Is My Choice', the other with a church, the cover with a house and a bird.

c1780 *4.5in (11.5cm) high*

£1,500-2,000 **TEN**

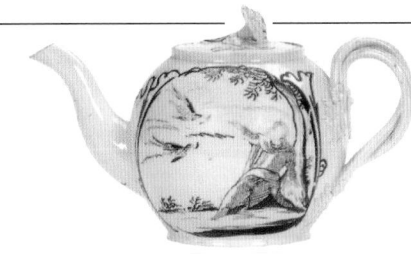

A Leeds creamware teapot, the flat lid with flowerhead finial, the reeded cross-over handle with flowerhead and leaf terminals, painted on each side with a Biblical figure gesturing towards birds.

c1780   4in (10cm) high

£700-1,000   **TEN**

CLOSER LOOK – A LEEDS CREAMWARE TEAPOT

The Leeds pottery was founded at Hunslet, near Leeds in c1760 and run by Humble, Greens & Co. from 1770 to 1775. It began to make creamware similar to that of Wedgwood soon after 1770, though Leeds' creamware had a less even and more yellow-tinged glaze.

This teapot features an unrecorded print, which may account for its high value, as it would be rare.

A Leeds creamware teapot, with ogee strap handle and acanthus decorated spout, decorated with vertical bands of textile inspired design, slight restoration to tip of spout, hairline crack to rim.

c1780   5.25in (13.5cm) high

£5,500-7,500   **TEN**

The figures examining the book, chart and the ships mast seem to be part of a celebration of trade. The sun and moon and the figure of Justice represent mercy and fairness in commercial endeavours.

A Leeds creamware teapot, printed and coloured on one side with figures examining a book, near a sailing vessel, on the other a stylised map of world, the sun, moon and a figure of Justice amongst clouds and Hebrew inscription, damage.

c1780   5.25in (13.5cm) high

£11,000-13,000   **TEN**

A creamware teapot and cover, commemorating 'The Revd John Wesley A.M.', the portrait of Wesley surrounded by the names and miniature portraits of 15 contemporaries, marked 'T. M. B.', dated.

1790   5.25in (13.5cm) high

£250-350   **LT**

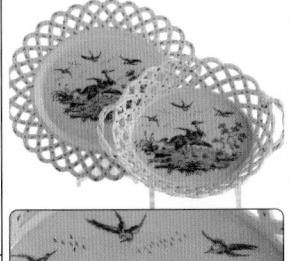

A creamware basket and stand, with reticulated sides and rim, printed in black with exotic birds besides a river in the manner of Sadler's Liverpool Birds, crack to the stand.

c1775-85   10.5in (26.5cm) wide

£350-450   **WW**

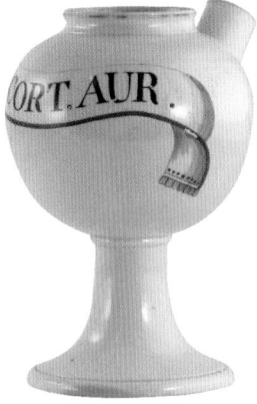

A late 18thC creamware wet-drug jar, painted with a purple banner containing the rare title 'S. Cort. Aur.'

Syrup of orange peel (cortex aurantiorum) was more commonly used in confectionary.

8.25in (21cm) high

£600-800   **WW**

A Yorkshire or Tyne & Wear creamware baluster coffee pot and cover, painted with flowers and 'John & Pheby Watson' with the verse 'Long may you live etc'.

c1790-1800   10in (25.5cm) high

£250-350   **A&G**

POTTERY

A Yorkshire pearlware cow creamer, with looped tail handle, sponged in ochre and brown, with milkmaid seated at the side, on a pale green washed cut serpentine base with brown line border.

c1790   *5.25in (13.5cm) high*

£900-1,200   **TEN**

An early 19thC Yorkshire pearlware cow creamer and cover, the standing cow sponge-decorated in pink and black, with a milkmaid wearing a similar decorated dress, on a green sponged canted rectangular base.

5.75in (14.5cm) high

£350-450   **TEN**

An early 19thC Yorkshire pearlware cow creamer and cover, ochre and black sponge-decorated, beside a milkmaid wearing an ochre top and blue striped skirt, on a blue sponged canted rectangular base.

5.5in (14cm) high

£350-450   **TEN**

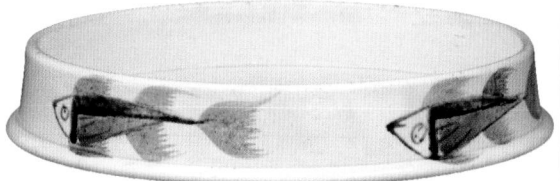

An early 19thC pearlware char dish, painted with a collar of green and brown fish with yellow fins.

7in (17.5cm) diam

£250-350   **FLD**

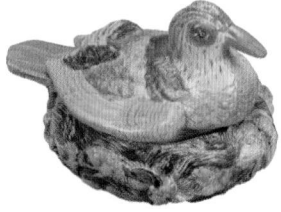

A Staffordshire pearlware sauce tureen and cover, modelled as a duck sitting on a nest, painted with coloured enamels, restored.

6.75in (17cm) long

£300-400   **DN**

A pearlware oval section jug, moulded in relief with two untitled heart-shaped panels of children, 'Mischievous Sport' and 'Sporting Innocence', painted with Pratt-type colours, small rim chip.

c1795   *4.75in (12cm) high*

£200-300   **DN**

An enamel decorated pearlware jug, with 'Success to the plough' verse, a wheat sheaf and farm tools below a floral border.

c1800   *9.5in (24cm) high*

£150-250   **FLD**

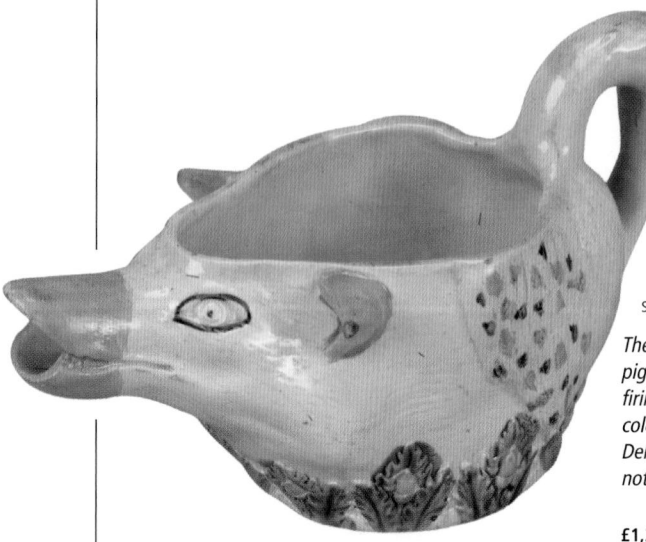

An early 19thC pearlware fox-mask and swan sauce tureen, with fox-mask spout and swan-neck handle, painted with Pratt-type colours, small chips to ear tips.

The blue, yellow, brown and green pigments, which could withstand high firing temperatures, were known as 'Pratt colours' after the Pratt family from Lane Delph, Staffordshire, although theirs was not the only factory to make Prattware.

7.75in (19.5cm) long

£1,200-1,800   **DN**

A Hartley, Greens & Co Leeds transfer-printed pearlware pottery coffee pot and cover, transfer-printed with bands of tong and dart, and a view of an Indian temple, impressed with maker's name.

c1800   *11in (28cm) high*

£350-450   **TEN**

An early 19thC Wedgwood pearlware ice pail, with deep dished lid with entwined scroll handle, and on three bun feet, printed and painted in Imari colours with japonaiserie flowers, impressed 'Wedgwood', restored.

Josiah Wedgwood is generally credited with the invention of pearlware c1780, which was intended as an improvement on creamware. However, although the name came from Wedgwood's 'Pearl White', a number of other factories developed a similar product at the same time.

7.75in (19.5cm) high

£250-350   **TEN**

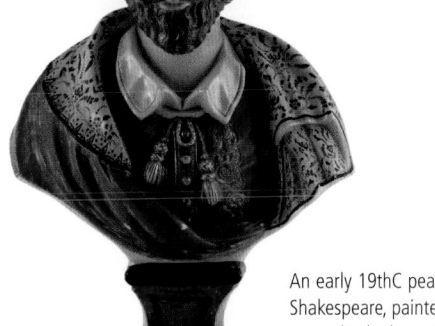

An early 19thC pearlware bust of Shakespeare, painted in polychrome enamels, the base decorated in pink lustre and titled 'W: Shakespear', minor damages.

17.25in (44cm) high

£2,000-3,000   **WW**

A Staffordshire pearlware pottery bust of Tsar Alexander I, with impressed inscription 'Alexander Aet. 35 Moscow Burnt Europe Preserved 1812', in typical bright colours, upon a later painted wood plinth.

Tsar Alexander I witnessed Napoleon's troops enter Moscow in 1812 and the Fire of Moscow that followed, which destroyed around three-quarters of the city.

c1815   11.5in (29.5cm) high overall

£550-750   **TEN**

An early 19thC English pearlware pottery figure of an actor, the square base with frontal inscription in blue 'Not Am I A Gentleman? Upon Your Soul The Mother', impressed '20'.

6.25in (16cm) high

£300-400   **TEN**

A Staffordshire pearlware bear and dog cistern.

Bearbaiting was a popular pastime in Georgian England and the subject was often depicted in pottery. The bear's body is covered in tiny clay parings to simulate fur.

c1800   12.5in (32cm) high

£4,000-5,000   **POOK**

A late 18th/early 19thC pearlware model of Buddhai Ho Shang, wearing a black robe, holding a flask in one hand, the other hand resting on one knee, holding a goblet, some damage.

4.75in (12cm) high

£150-200   **WW**

A pair of early 19thC pearlware chickens, a hen and a cockerel, each naturalistically coloured, one impressed '13', chips to both beaks and bases.

7.75in (20cm) high

£2,000-2,500   **SWO**

A rare Sunderland pearlware pottery remembrance obelisk, Southwick, two registers painted with continuous memorial inscription in black, painted with bouquets of flowers, edged with pricked and dentil incised detail, the base inscribed 'Nov 12 1897'.

1897   10in (25.5cm) high

£200-300   **TEN**

A large Sunderland armorial lustre bowl, Dixon Austin & Co., the exterior with a view of Sunderland Bridge, shipping scenes and farming implements, the interior with an armorial probably for the Delmy family, damaged and restored.

The iridescent surface of lustreware is produced by using metallic pigments, usually silver or copper, applied to a fired glazed piece and then fired again at a lower temperature.

c1810-20   15.25in (39cm) high

£350-450   **WW**

A 17thC-style Burgess & Leigh lustre charger, by L. T. Swettenham, with an English Civil War soldier, initialled 'L. T. S.' and dated.

1820

£450-550   **LT**

A rare North Shields pottery tankard, for the 1826 Northumberland Election depicting 'A Heat between the four candidates at Alnwick BELL, LIDDELL, BEAUMONT & HOWICK', transfer-printed, with lustre bands.

Pieces related to the 1826 General Election and including Lord Howick are rare, as Howick pulled out of the contest after only a few weeks of campaigning.

1826   4.5in (11cm) high

£1,000-1,500   **A&G**

A large Sunderland 'King William IV' and 'Cast Iron Bridge' pottery jug, printed in underglaze black and naively overpainted in colours with an equestrian portrait of the King, opposing a view of the Iron Bridge, and flanking a Masonic verse.

c1825   9.25in (23.5cm) high

£900-1,200   **TEN**

A large Sunderland 'Cast Iron Bridge' pottery jug, printed and naively overpainted with 'A West View of The Iron Bridge', and a Masonic verse, with pink lustre borders and wrigglework ground.

c1830   9in (23cm) high

£400-500   **TEN**

A large Sunderland 'Cast Iron Bridge' pottery jug, printed and painted with 'A West View of the Iron Bridge', flanked by 'The Mariner's Compass' and verse 'When first I was aforemast man…'.

c1830   9.25in (23.5cm) high

£450-550   **TEN**

A Sunderland pink lustre Grace Darling jug, for Isaac & Sarah Brown, painted and printed with the famous Victorian sea rescue and inscribed, 'William Darling & his daughter Grace Horsley Darling / The Forfarshire streamer lost on Sept 7th 1838'.

1839   9.5in (24cm) high

£2,200-2,800   **TEN**

A Sunderland-style pottery jug, probably Tyneside, printed and over enamelled with a portrait of 'Susan & William', verso with the Iron Bridge and beneath the spout a verse 'Here's to the wind that blows', crack under base.

c1840-60   7.25in (18.5cm) high

£800-1,000   **BE**

A large Sunderland lustreware baluster jug, transfer-printed with a ship 'Northumberland 74'.

9.5in (24cm) high

£400-500   **L&T**

A large early 19thC blue and white Brameld platter, printed with the 'Returning Woodman' pattern within a trompe d'oeil gadrooned border, impressed 'Brameld +1'.

21.25in (54cm) wide

£700-1,000 **WW**

A 19thC Davenport blue printed venison dish, decorated with cows by a bridge, with a house in the background, impressed anchor mark.

20in (51cm) wide

£250-350 **L&T**

A 19thC Davenport blue printed ashet, depicting two figures in a landscape with trees and rockwork, with a building behind, impressed anchor mark.

20.75in (53cm) wide

£180-250 **L&T**

A 19thC Davenport blue printed venison dish, centred by a roundel with the head of a Roman Emperor surrounded by gardening motifs and large scroll decoration.

18in (46cm) wide

£900-1,200 **L&T**

A Staffordshire blue and white earthenware meat plate, printed with 'The Durham Ox', after John Boultbee (1753-1812), restored crack.

The Durham Ox was a product of intensive breeding and was prized for its Great size and perfect shape and configuration.' Its owner, John Day, toured Britain exhibiting the ox, who became a popular attraction at agricultural fairs and other events. In one day, London tourists paid a total of £97 in admission fees to see him. 'The Durham Ox' also became a popular pub name.

c1820 *20.75in (53cm) wide*

£700-1,000 **SWO**

A 19thC Spode 'Shooting a Leopard in a Tree' pattern blue printed venison dish, from the 'Indian Sporting' series, impressed and printed mark.

The Indian Sporting series was introduced by Spode c1815 and included illustrations after Samuel Howitt from the publication 'Oriental Field Sports' by Captain Thomas Williamson.

20.25in (51.5cm) wide

£1,200-1,800 **L&T**

A 19thC Heathcote & Co 'Castle and River' pattern blue printed venison dish.

20.25in (51.5cm) wide

£350-450 **L&T**

An early 19thC Boston State House blue transfer decorated Staffordshire pottery platter, by Rogers & Son, Longport, England, depicting the Boston State House with cows grazing, impressed maker's mark on reverse.

18.5in (47cm) wide

£1,200-1,800 **SK**

POTTERY

A pair of early 19thC blue and white meat plates, with a scene of Pashkov Palace, Moscow, within floral borders.

19in (48cm) wide

£600-800   **GORL**

A rare pearlware sample meat dish, printed in underglaze blue with numerous samples of border patterns, variously inscribed 'Breakcup, Salad', 'Sup M', 'Sup C', 'C Dish' and 'Tea C', indistinctly inscribed.

c1810   19in (48.5cm) wide

£700-1,000   **TEN**

One of two 19thC 'Guy's Cliff, Warwickshire' blue printed ashets, with impressed mark '11/20'.

15in (38cm) wide

£150-250 PAIR   **L&T**

A 19thC Clews blue and white torus-shaped flask, printed with four roundels of a figure leaning on rocks before flowers, on a dense floral ground.

7.75in (20cm) high

£400-500   **WW**

A Spode pearlware blue and white printed 'Caramanian' series drainer, printed with the 'Castle of Boudron in the Gulf of Stancio' pattern, with impressed mark.

c1815   14.5in (37cm) wide

£600-800   **DN**

A Staffordshire blue and white transfer-printed pottery English topographical miniature dinner service, the patterns including Kenilworth Priory, Embdon Castle, Lechlade Bridge, Donnington Park, and De Gaunt Castle, most pieces with blue printed titled curtain drape and floral mark.

c1820-30

£1,200-1,800   **TEN**

A large early 19thC Wedgwood blue and white pearlware footbath, printed with Chinese pagodas in a river landscape beneath a wide floral border, impressed 'WEDGWOOD', star cracks to the base.

19.75in (50cm) diam

£800-1,000   **WW**

An early 19thC large pearlware punch pot and cover, printed in blue with figures in a Chinese riverscape, the damaged spout with metal replacement.

15.75in (40cm) high

£100-150   **WW**

A late 18thC English pearlware bowl, the interior printed in blue with a black man blowing a horn before buildings and mountains, minor faults.

11.25in (28.5cm) diam

£100-150   **WW**

A Prattware figure of a standing naval officer, wearing naval hat and a blue jacket with mustard collar, holding a sword in his left hand on a pricked and spotted square base.
c1790   4.75in (12cm) high
£250-350   TEN

A pair of early 19thC Staffordshire 'Departure and Returned' figural groups, modelled as a sailor and his wife.

The Victorian era saw a series of international conflicts involving the British navy, and sentimental groups of sailors leaving their loved ones found a ready market with patriotic members of the British public.
9in (23cm) high
£200-300   GORL

A rare early 19thC Prattware portrait bust of Queen Caroline, brightly coloured with waisted socle.

During the 19thC there was an increase in demand for figures of famous people. The resemblance to the individual was often poor, as the same mould was often used for different subjects.
8.25in (21cm) high
£1,200-1,800   GORL

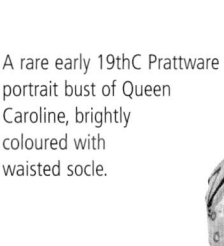

ESSENTIAL REFERENCE – STAFFORDSHIRE POTTERIES

The Staffordshire ceramics trade grew up in the mid-17thC around the five towns of Stoke, Burslem, Hanley, Longton and Tunstall, after local farmers found a market selling butter pots.

- Rich natural resources of clay and coal, which could be dug from the road as 'potholes', helped to develop the local trade into a thriving industry.
- The first Staffordshire figures were manufactured c1740 as an affordable alternative to the fine porcelain models by European companies such as Sèvres and Meissen.
- By the 19thC Staffordshire was home to more than 1,000 pottery and porcelain factories, including the highly successful firms Spode, Ridgway and Wedgwood.
- Designers and potters moved between factories and pieces were left unmarked, so it is hard to ascribe figures to individual firms.
- The development of canals, and by 1848, the railway to Stoke, allowed wares to be transported across England, or to the port at Liverpool for shipping overseas to America and India.

A Staffordshire earthenware figural New Marriage Act group, depicting a clergyman residing over a wedding within an arch titled and with verse.
c1825   6.5in (16.5cm) wide
£300-400   GORL

A Prattware watch-stand, modelled as a longcase clock between two figures leaning on plinths, some restoration, together with a pocket watch movement.
c1820-26   11in (28cm) high
£650-850   WW

A pair of 19thC Staffordshire models of cows, with a milkmaid and cowherd, minor damages.
6.75in (17.5cm) high
£100-200   WW

A pair of early 19thC Staffordshire figures of a lady archer and huntsman.
7in (18cm) high
£350-450   DUK

Two Staffordshire pottery figures of jockeys, each holding crops in their upraised right hands, with light green jackets and floral waistcoats, and yellow topped black boots, on circular bases.
c1830   6.75in (17cm) high
£550-750   TEN

POTTERY

A Staffordshire cricketing group, depicting a batsman and a wicket keeper.

c1845   *7in (17.5cm) high*

£350-450   **SWO**

A Staffordshire cricketing group, depicting a bowler and a waiting batsman.

c1845   *6.5in (16.5cm) high*

£250-350   **SWO**

A pair of 19thC Staffordshire flatback figures, of jockeys mounted on chestnut horses.

9in (23cm) high

£250-350   **DUK**

A group of four Staffordshire pottery groups of cricketers, each with a batsman and bowler in traditional sporting attire and on lobed-shaped oval bases with gilt line, variously restored.

c1850–70   Tallest 6.75in (17cm) high

£1,000-1,500   **TEN**

A rare Staffordshire boxing 'Heenan and Sayers' group.

This group records the match between John Carmel Heenan, a heavyweight bare-knuckle fighter from New York State, and Tom Sayers, an English middleweight champion, at Farnborough, in April 1865. The result was a draw.

c1865   9.25in (23.5cm) high

£500-700   **SWO**

A large Staffordshire figure of a batsman, standing before the wicket, wearing an orange cap and sash, a small chip to the front of the stumps.

c1865   13.25in (33.5cm) high

£550-750   **WW**

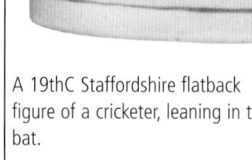

A 19thC Staffordshire flatback figure of a cricketer, leaning in to bat.

13in (33cm) high

£700-1,000   **DUK**

A late 18thC Ralph Wood style Toby jug, decorated with translucent green, yellow and brown splashed glazes, octagonal base, some hairlines and chips.

10in (25.5cm) high

£900-1,200   **LT**

A late 18thC Ralph Wood Toby jug, decorated with translucent glazes in shades of green, cobalt, blue and brown, octagonal base.

9.75in (25cm) high

£1,500-2,000   **LT**

A Yorkshire pearlware Toby jug, typically modelled and decorated with Pratt-type glazes, small rim chips.

10.25in (26cm) high

£900-1,200 DN

A Prattware George III and Queen Charlotte Bacchus and Satyr Toby jug, modelled with Bacchus sat on a barrel, a tiny figure wrapped in a cloak at his feet, the satyr leaning on his back, the barrel ends moulded with bust portrait of King and Queen, chained monkey handled, restored spout.

c1800 *12in (30.5cm) high*

£500-700 LT

A Staffordshire pearlware Toby jug, typically modelled and decorated with Pratt-type glazes, restored hat.

c1800 *9.75in (25cm) high*

£1,200-1,800 DN

A Staffordshire Pearlware Toby jug, blue and white decorated, with brown jug, pipe missing, some restoration.

11in (28cm) high

£300-400 LT

ESSENTIAL REFERENCE – TOBY JUGS

- **Toby jugs were produced from the mid-18thC mainly by the Staffordshire potteries. The most common form is the 'Toper' or ale drinker, a comical seated man wearing a tricorn hat with a drink in his hand, many variations of the Toby jug were made, including the 'Thin Man', the 'Collier', the 'Sharp Face', 'Rodney's Sailor' and the 'Admiral Howe'.**
- **The name 'Toby jug' may have been based on the well-known character Harry Elwes, who was nicknamed Toby Philpot ('fill pot') because of his legendary capacity for drink.**
- **The tricorn hat forms the spout of the jug and originally had a cover, which is usually missing. If the original cover is present it can considerably increase the value of the piece.**
- **Some of the best examples of Toby jugs were made by the Wood family, from Burslem in Staffordshire, who produced well modelled earthenwares with carefully applied colours from c1765. Pieces by Ralph Wood II (1748-1795) are amongst the most desirable.**
- **Impressed marks or labels enhance the value.**

A rare late 18thC Ralph Wood style 'Admiral Lord Howe' Toby jug, modelled wearing a tricorn hat and holding a jug of ale, seated on a barrel with a dog at his feet, with a green rustic handle.

10in (25.5cm) high

£1,500-2,000 GORL

A T. & J. Hollins pottery Toby jug, dressed in blue coat, green breeches, black shoes and hat, clutching a foaming tankard, octagonal base with impressed mark, restored hat.

c1800-1820 *9.75in (25cm) high*

£700-1,000 LT

A 19thC Staffordshire standing snuff-taking Toby, his tricorn hat forming a cover, his left hand returning his snuffbox to his pocket while the other powders his right nostril, minor wear and a faint base crack.

13in (33cm) high

£80-120 WW

POTTERY

An early 19thC Prattware model of a sheep, recumbent upon a base splashed with green, blue and ochre, minor chipping to the base.

3.25in (8.5cm) high

£300-400   WW

An early 19thC pair of Prattware lions, on sponge-decorated bases, restored.

Staffordshire potters made a range of wild animals, mostly in pairs. The figures are often surprisingly accurate, even though the potters rarely studied the animals from life, usually working from engravings.

4.25in (11cm) high

£1,200-1,800   WW

An early 19thC Staffordshire model of a recumbent horned sheep, painted with brown and green splashes.

6in (15.5cm) long

£900-1,200   DN

A Staffordshire pottery figure group of a lion seated above a tiger, on green foliage base, possibly originally part of a spill vase or centrepiece, polychrome decorated.

6.5in (16.5cm) high

£250-350   LT

A 19thC Staffordshire flatback model of a cat, with black sponge decoration.

Flatback pieces were designed to stand on a mantelpiece and so have little or no modelling on the back, which made them easier to mass produce.

3.5in (9cm) high

£150-200   DUK

A pair of rare mid-19thC Staffordshire spill vases, modelled as leopards with heads turned and one foreleg raised, on a mossy ground, minor restoration to both.

Spill vases were small containers designed to hold the rolled-paper spills that were used for lighting the fire.

7.75in (19.5cm) high

£550-750   WW

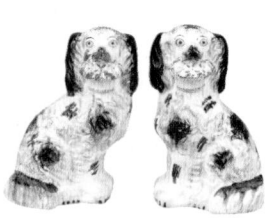

A pair of mid-19thC Staffordshire models of spaniels, with baskets of flowers in their mouths, modelled facing left and right and seated on their haunches, black patches.

7.75in (20cm) high

£500-700   DN

A pair of mid-19thC Staffordshire spaniels, each modelled seated and carrying baskets of flowers in their muzzles, enamelled with liver patches.

8.25in (21cm) high

£250-350

A pair of 19thC Staffordshire Dalmatians, sitting on blue oval bases.

5in (13cm) high

£450-550   L&T

A Staffordshire pottery figure of an ape, seated on a mossy knoll amongst bananas and skins, with black coat, and green, brown and yellow detail to the rustic oval knoll, gilt line to the base.

c1860   *10.25in (26.5cm) high*

£1,200-1,800   TEN

A pair of 19thC Staffordshire treacle glazed lions, each with one paw on a ball, with tails swished and unusually large teeth, on square stepped bases.

9in (23cm) wide

£1,500-2,000   GORL

A pair of Victorian Staffordshire greyhounds, each modelled with a rabbit at its feet, wearing gilded collars, restored.

7.25in (18.5cm) high

£150-200   GORL

A pair of Victorian Staffordshire models of zebras, on oval rockwork bases.

Zebra models were made from c1845, but it was not until c1850 that correctly modelled zebras appeared. Earlier figures of zebras were made from horse moulds and painted with stripes.

5in (12.5cm) high

£250-350   GORL

A mid-19thC Staffordshire water/gin figure, modelled as a double-sided man.

8.25in (21cm) high

£250-350   L&T

A pair of 19thC Staffordshire figures of girls with deer, on shaped naturalistic bases.

7in (18cm) high

£100-200   L&T

IRONSTONE

A miniature Mason's side-handled jug, painted with flowers and fences in a typical Japanese-style pattern, some wear to the gilding.

c1815-25   *1.75in (4.5cm) high*

£150-200   WW

Part of a Turner's patent Ironstone part dinner service, decorated in the Imari palette, comprising one large and one small oval tureen and cover, four rectangular serving dishes, a venison dish, a dish and drainer, two sauce tureens and three stands, 12 graduated ashets, 10 soup bowls, five dessert bowls, eight side plates, and a gravy boat, some pieces lacking covers.

Tureen 13.75in (35cm) wide

£1,500-2,500 SET   L&T

A large pair of Mason's Ironstone vases and covers, painted pattern no. '6418', with scrolling dragon handles and domed covers with entwined dolphin finials, one cover restored, one cracked.

A large 19thC potpourri vase and cover, of baluster form, the pierced cover with gilt lion finial, boldly decorated with flowers in the Imari palette.

17in (43cm) high

£600-800   L&T

Ironstone was patented by Charles James Mason in 1813 as an alternative to porcelain. It contained ironstone slag and cobalt oxide, and was an extremely strong material, even being used to make fireplaces and furniture. Mason's Ironstone was very successful and was exported to markets in Europe and America. When Mason's patent expired in 1827, rival firms, such as Spode and Davenport, began manufacturing similar wares. Pieces were frequently decorated with colours and patterns inspired by Oriental ceramics, particularly Imari designs.

c1845

£3,500-4,500   BE

Part of a mid-19thC Ironstone part dinner service, with Chinese-style decoration, a lobed oval tureen and cover with flowerhead finial and scroll handles, six graduated ashets, four oval vegetable dishes, a footed square serving dish, 18 meat plates, 14 fish plates, 11 soup bowls, seven side plates and three stands.

£2,500-3,500 SET   L&T

A Wedgwood jasperware bowl and cover, decorated with two putti at play with a butterfly and a dog, the reverse with a young maiden and child, impressed 'Wedgwood', minor faults.

c1765   5.5in (14cm) high

£300-400   **WW**

A 19thC Wedgwood solid light blue jasper plaque, the roundel with applied white Classical depiction of 'The Apotheosis of Homer', with impressed mark.

16in (40.5cm) diam

£2,500-3,500   **SK**

An early 19thC Wedgwood dark blue jasper dip crocus basket, cover and stand, with pierced convex cover, engine-turned dicing and pierced sides, impressed mark.

9in (23cm) high

£2,500-3,500   **SK**

A 19thC Wedgwood three-coloured jasperware two-handled jardinière, each side applied with a ribboned mauve cameo of a lady above laurel, raised on three ball feet, impressed 'WEDGWOOD' to the base, small chips to base.

10in (25.5cm) high

£450-550   **WW**

CLOSER LOOK – A WEDGWOOD JASPERWARE VASE

This piece is based on a vase dating from the 1stC BC that was discovered in a Roman garden in 1566 and acquired by the Borghese family. The piece is typical of the Neo-classical period, when many considered the accurate imitation of a Classical masterpiece a higher achievement than artistic originality.

A 19thC Wedgwood solid light blue jasperware Borghese vase and cover on pedestal base, the vase with applied white Classical figures in relief, foliate, gadroon and fruiting grapevine borders, the pedestal base with trophies and ornaments between fruiting grapevine festoons terminating at leopard masks with ribbons, bands of lotus and laurel and berry borders, impressed marks.

Vase 19in (48cm) high

£12,000-15,000   **SK**

The Borghese vase was one of the largest of the pieces produced by Wedgwood in Jasperware. It was extremely difficult to make so few copies were produced.

The applied white relief typical of Jasperware was inspired by the cameo technique used in Antique Roman glass. The relief is crisp and very refined. Wedgwood sometimes touched the shallowest parts of the relief with a slightly darker colour to give the impression of translucence and enhance the delicacy of the moulding.

Josiah Wedgwood arranged for copies of the Borghese vase and other important Roman Classical pieces to be made by John Flaxman and other artists between 1787-90.

A 20thC Wedgwood dark blue jasper dip vase and cover, with upturned loop handles, applied white Classical figures bordered with a variety of foliate designs, with impressed mark.

11.75in (30cm) high

£650-850   **SK**

A 19thC Wedgwood dark blue jasper dip Portland vase, with applied white Classical figures, the base with a man wearing a Phrygian cap, with impressed mark.

10in (25.5cm) high

£1,500-2,000   **SK**

A pair of Wedgwood sage green jasperware Classical wine and water ewers, limited edition 12/25, the wine ewer featuring a satyr, the water ewer featuring Triton, in their original boxes with certificate of authenticity.

16.5in (42cm) high

£1,500-2,500   **GHOU**

A 19thC Wedgwood green jasper dip wall clock, decorated with Dancing Hours, with impressed mark, mounted in a contemporary giltwood frame and with a modern movement.

17in (43cm) high

£2,000-3,000   **SK**

A Wedgwood yellow jasper dip vase, with applied black jasper acanthus leaf border above a running grapevine and scrolled ribbon band, acanthus leaves and bell flowers to foot and base, with impressed mark.

c1930   12in (30.5cm) high

£1,200-1,800   **SK**

A Wedgwood yellow jasper dip vase and cover, with upturned white jasper handles, applied black Classical figures in relief with foliate borders, with impressed mark.

c1930   15in (38cm) high

£1,500-2,000   **SK**

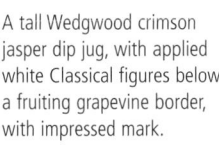

A tall Wedgwood crimson jasper dip jug, with applied white Classical figures below a fruiting grapevine border, with impressed mark.

c1920   7.75in (19.5cm) high

£200-300   **SK**

A 19thC Wedgwood black jasperware dip plaque, of rectangular shape with applied white relief depictions of putti at play, impressed mark, mounted in an ebonised wood frame.

Plaque 15in (38cm) wide

£1,500-2,000   **SK**

A Wedgwood black jasper dip 'Blind Man's Bluff' plaque, with applied white figural relief, impressed mark, mounted in a mahogany frame.

c1860   Plaque 11.25in (28.5cm) wide

£1,500-2,000   **SK**

A Wedgwood & Bentley black basalt vase and cover, with 'the Dancing Hours' modelled by William Hackwood encircling the body, impressed factory mark, chip to cover, restoration to handle.

c1775   14.25in (36cm) high

£1,500-2,000   **WW**

A pair of Wedgwood black basalt statuettes of seated Greek sphinxes, both impressed 'WEDGWOOD', one impressed 'W', the other 'E'.

Sphinxes of this form were in production from about 1770, with and without 'lotus' nozzles or candle holders. By 1773, when they were listed in the first Wedgwood & Bentley catalogue, at least eight models of Grecian and Egyptian sphinxes were in production. Some were copied from engravings such as those that appeared in Montfaucon's 'L'Antiquité Expliquée' published 1719-24.

c1800   8.75in (22.5cm) high

£2,500-3,500   **TEN**

A pair of early 19thC Wedgwood black basalt twin-handled amphora vases, decorated with a continuous scene emblematic of the Arts, within acanthus leaf and laurel borders, impressed mark.

10in (25.5cm) high

£800-1,000   GORL

POTTERY

ESSENTIAL REFERENCE – WEDGWOOD FACTORY

- Josiah Wedgwood set up his own business in Staffordshire in 1759, becoming the most successful manufacturer of creamware, called 'Queensware'. He then produced a more refined version of creamware, called pearlware.
- Jasperware, a form of unglazed stoneware introduced in c1767, became one of the company's most popular products.
- Wedgwood was one of the first potters to commission leading artists, such as John Flaxman, to create his designs.
- Wedgwood was one of the first potteries to mark wares systematically. The pre-Etruria wares are rarely marked, but other pieces are impressed with either Wedgwood and Bentley, 'WB', or Wedgwood alone. From 1860 a date coding system using three letters was adopted.
- A master self-publicist, Wedgwood built a reputation for high-quality wares that has endured through the centuries.
- Etruria was the main Wedgwood factory from 1769-1950.

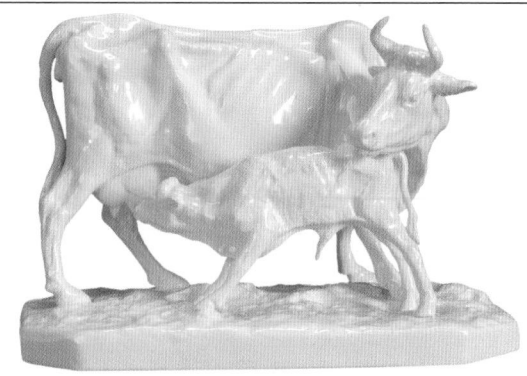

A Wedgwood Queensware cow group, the cream-coloured body modelled as a cow with calf and set on a rectangular base, with impressed mark.
c1873   *13in (33cm) wide*
£3,500-4,500   SK

A pair of early 19thC Wedgwood encaustic decorated black basalt vases, with upturned loop handles, each with iron red, black and white decorated Classical figures, with impressed marks.

Basalt was one of Wedgwood's most popular wares, and was produced in the Etruria factory which specialized in ornamenal pieces.
11.5in (29cm) high
£6,500-8,500   SK

A 19thC Wedgwood creamware dessert service, for James Powell & Sons, London, comprising 12 shaped vine border plates and four shaped and stemmed serving dishes, each with two interlaced rustic handles.
£1,200-1,800   MEA

A Wedgwood Queensware 'Persian' pattern charger, by Millicent Taplin, blue and green enamelled in a lustrous glaze, impressed mark.
c1920   *21.75in (55cm) diam*
£2,500-3,000   SK

A Wedgwood Queensware boat race day bowl, designed by Eric Ravilious, polychrome enamel decorated to black transfer prints, impressed and printed marks.
c1938   *10.25in (26cm) high*
£3,500-4,500   SK

A Wedgwood 'Mistress Ford' circular wall plaque, painted by J. P. Hewitt in enamels against a raised gold foliate ground, with impressed mark.

15.25in (39cm) diam
£400-500   SK

A Wedgwood 'Sir John Falstaff' circular wall plaque, painted by Thomas Allen in enamel against a raised gold foliate ground, with impressed mark.

c1886   6in (15cm) diam

£400-500   **SK**

A Wedgwood earthenware charger, painted with a lady in a feathered hat in medieval style by G. Siever, signed and dated, impressed Wedgwood and date code, printed mark 'G L Siever & Co, Worcester'.

G.L. Siever is recorded as decorating both Wedgwood and Worcester blanks in Worcester.

1888   18.75in (47.5cm) diam

£150-250   **SWO**

A Wedgwood & Bentley variegated Porphyry vase and cover, the surface decorated to imitate the hardstone phorphyry, mounted on a white jasper plinth, with impressed mark.

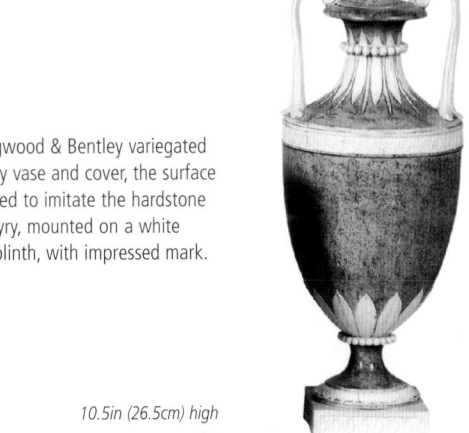

c1775   10.5in (26.5cm) high

£3,500-4,500   **SK**

A late 18thC Wedgwood crocus pot and cover with surface agate, with pierced cover with four bulb reservoirs, the all-over agate in browns, tans and iron red to a pearl glazed ground, traces of gilding, impressed upper-lower case mark.

Surface agate is achieved by blending different coloured slips on the surface of the stoneware.

7in (18cm) diam

£3,500-4,500   **SK**

A late 18thC Wedgwood glazed white terracotta flowerpot, barrel-shaped in the 'Devonshire hoop' manner, with brown staves, green hoops and ring handles, with scalloped rim, and impressed mark.

5.5in (14cm) diam high

£500-700   **SK**

A Wedgwood white terracotta bouquetière and cover, with pierced basketweave cover, the bowl with twig handles and basketweave body coloured with buff slip, with impressed mark.

c1785   10in (25.5cm) long

£1,500-2,000   **SK**

A Wedgwood caneware milk jug, with moulded bamboo handle and neck, bacchanalian boys in relief and trimmed in a brown enamel, with Prince of Wales feather below the spout, engine-turned band at foot, with impressed upper-lower case mark.

c1785   5.5in (14cm) high

£1,500-2,000   **SK**

An early 19thC Wedgwood caneware bamboo flower vase, modelled as four spills simulating bamboo, of differing heights, all atop a naturalistic freeform base, with impressed marks.

4.5in (11.5cm) high

£700-1,000   **SK**

POTTERY

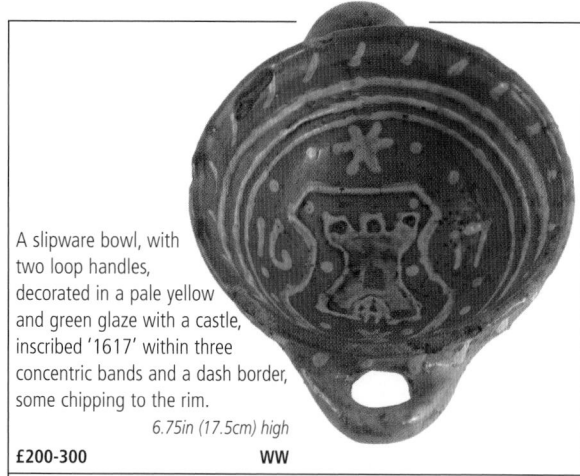

A slipware bowl, with two loop handles, decorated in a pale yellow and green glaze with a castle, inscribed '1617' within three concentric bands and a dash border, some chipping to the rim.

6.75in (17.5cm) high

£200-300   WW

A set of six early 19thC Giustiniani, Naples Ancient Greek style 'skyphos' terraglia bowls and stands, imitating Attic wares, impressed 'Giustiniani'.

The Giustiniani was an important family of potters in Naples, active from the early 18thC to late 19thC.

Stands 7.25in (18.5cm) wide

£2,500-3,500   TEN

A French footed pottery oval dish, by the School of Bernard Palissy, modelled in low relief with a figure of Plenty in a garden, within a lambrequin border, section of foot missing and some surface wear.

Bernard Palissy (c1510-c1590) was a celebrated French potter probably best known for his 'rustic' wares with applied decoration. At his death he was followed by a school of imitators who sought to copy his style and technique. His style was immensely popular in France and Britain in the 18th and 19thC, achieving an almost mythical status. Few pieces survive today that can be surely attributed to Palissy or his workshop.

c1630

£5,000-7,000   DN

A large 19th/20thC oval slipware dish, with a pinched rim, the combed decoration in brown and cream.

15.5in (39.5cm) diam

£250-350   WW

A Yorkshire pearlware pottery puzzle jug, with three trumpet spouts and a C-shape handle, with pierced decoration and painted in underglaze blue with two gentlemen seated at a table, bearing the number '666'.

c1790   *7.5in (19cm) high*

£1,500-2,000   TEN

An early 20thC tin-glazed earthenware Passover dish, the white ground with aubergine and green Hebrew text, grape clusters and a central figure of a shepherd with a city in the distance, imperfections, wear.

12in (30.5cm) diam

£1,000-1,500   SK

An early 20thC Henriot Quimper dish, after Alfred Beau, painted with a scene of Breton villagers, within a green foliate border broken by the arms of Brittany.

12in (30.5cm) diam

£450-550   WW

A Brameld caneware Neo-classical-style jug, the border moulded in relief with musical putti and anthemion with 'horses hoof and tail' handle, raised cartouche Brameld mark.

9.5in (24cm) high

£450-550 **DUK**

An early 19thC Castleford moulded jug, painted with panels of rural scenes within blue line borders, impressed '30' to the base.

4.75in (12cm) high

£150-250 **WW**

CLOSER LOOK – MEASHAM SMOKER'S COMPENDIUM

The piece is complete, and in excellent condition, which is rare for an item with several parts.

Although there are some small chips, there is no major damage or restoration. It would be unusual to find an item like this without minor chipping so this does not detract from its value.

Wares from Measham Pottery are often roughly made, but this item is well potted and nicely glazed, with attractive applied flowers and leaves.

Highly unusual pieces, such as this, are desirable to collectors.

Four late 18thC Whieldon octagonal plates, with serrated edges, decorated in a mottled brown glaze, minor faults.

9.75in (25cm) diam

£350-450 SET **WW**

A Davenport, Longport terracotta and encaustic painted wine cooler, the side handles as grotesque masks, with bold key pattern band to the rim and fluting to the base.

c1820 *9.5in (24cm) high*

£500-700 **TEN**

A Measham pottery smoker and drinker's compendium, of 'tower' form, surmounted by a cylindrical candlestick applied with florets and leaves, over a goblet, a cylindrical tobacco jar, with inner lid/weight, the whole raised upon a spittoon base, in typical mottled brown glaze.

c1880 *16in (40.5cm) high*

£6,000-8,000 **TEN**

A tin-glazed terracotta figure of Judith with the head of Holofernes, in the manner of Giovanni della Robbia, on moulded plinth base.

25in (63.5cm) high

£2,500-3,500 **GORL**

A pair of 19thC Alloa brown glazed spaniels, by John Petrie, impressed marks.

11.75in (30cm) high

£500-700 **L&T**

An 18thC black basalt bust of George II, after John Michael Rysbrack, after the reduced replica in ivory by Gaspar Van der Haagen, upon a square pedestal.

9.75in (25cm) high

£900-1,200 **TEN**

A mid-18thC Staffordshire white salt-glazed stoneware pink ground teapot and cover, the globular shape with crabstock handle and spout, the deep pink ground decorated with flowers.

5in (12.5cm) high

£1,500-2,000   SK

A mid-18thC Staffordshire white salt-glazed stoneware teapot and cover, the globular shape with crabstock handle and spout, twig finial, polychrome enamel decorated with Chinese figures in a garden landscape.

4.75in (12cm) high

£2,500-3,000   SK

A Staffordshire pink ground salt-glazed stoneware teapot and cover, the globular shape with moulded crabstock handle and spout, pink enamel ground with polychrome floral designs in reserves, acorn finials.

c1760   *5in (12.5cm) high*

£1,500-2,500   SK

ESSENTIAL REFERENCE – STONEWARE

- Salt-glazed stoneware is made by firing pottery in the kiln at a high temperature and then throwing in salt, which combines with the clay to form a thin, glassy glaze with a distinctive granular 'orange peel' surface.
- Developed in Germany, the technique spread to England in the mid-17thC, where it was patented by London-based potter John Dwight. Early English production imitated typical German wares, including mugs, jugs and tankards, decorated with moulded relief and a two-tone brown wash.
- Salt-glazed wares were probably first produced at the end of the 17thC in Staffordshire by John and David Elers. By the 1720s the Staffordshire potters had refined the material in order to compete with imports of Chinese porcelain, sometimes decorating pieces with Oriental-style designs.
- Teawares and tablewares were the commonest products, but decorative items such as seated cats and other animals were also made. Early sculptural pieces attract high prices.
- Salt-glazed ware was often finished with moulded decoration and typically glazed in a cream colour, although other coloured grounds, such as blue or aubergine, were also used. From c1750, pieces were also decorated in coloured enamel, and sometimes transfer-printed.
- By the 18thC the main centres of production were Staffordshire, Nottinghamshire, London and Bristol.
- Brown wares continued to be made throughout the 18th and 19thC in London at Mortlake, Fulham and Lambeth.

A 17thC English salt-glazed stoneware white-metal mounted ewer, of globular form with loop handle and mottled brown glaze, some damage.

7in (18cm) high

£250-350   DN

An early 18thC salt-glazed stoneware metal-mounted tankard, of Dwight of Fulham type, the metal rim with foliate lappets, cracked.

6.5in (16.5cm) high

£500-700   DN

A Documentary London cylindrical stoneware quart mug, perhaps Vauxhall, inscribed 'Tho. Gilbert' above a coat-of-arms and with hunting scenes, grooved strapwork handle, with silver mounted rim and foot.

1722   *8.5in (21.5cm) high*

£2,500-3,500   TEN

A mid-18thC Staffordshire white salt-glazed stoneware globular teapot and cover, with moulded crabstock handle and spout, twig finial, polychrome enamel decorated with castles and figures in a landscape.

4.25in (11cm) high

£3,500-4,500   SK

A Vauxhall large stoneware hunting mug, with a bust of Queen Anne flanked by two beefeaters and Boscobel oak trees above running hounds, the handle riveted, the rim inscribed 'Thomas Sprito Mrs Jane Sprito 1730'.

8.5in (21.5cm) high

£2,000-2,500   WW

An English stoneware silver-mounted jug, of Mortlake type, typically decorated with a tavern scene, hunting and other subjects, with later silver mounts, handle cracked and glued, hallmarked for 1825 and 1841.

c1800　　*10.5in (27cm) high*

£550-750　　**DN**

A black glazed stoneware bust of Nelson, wearing the Order of the Garter and sash on a waisted square socle moulded with trophies of war and titled 'Nelson'.

Vice Admiral Horatio Nelson (1758–1805) was a British naval officer who famously served during the Napoleonic Wars. He won many victories, including the Battle of Trafalgar (1805), during which he was killed. Nelson is commemorated on objects and monuments.

c1800　　*7.75in (20cm) high*

£900-1,000　　**TEN**

A small probably 17thC German salt-glazed stoneware Bartmann jug or Bellaramine, of typical swollen form, the neck embossed with a bearded mask above an oval medallion, minor losses and wear.

9in (23cm) high

£350-450　　**BE**

Two similar 17thC German salt-glazed stoneware Bellarmine jugs, each typically moulded with a bearded mask above an oval boss, small foot rim chips.

Bellarmines are bulbous jugs that were initially produced in Cologne and Frechen during the 17thC. They are named after Cardinal Roberto Bellarmino (1542-1621), an opponent of Protestantism. They typically have a mottled brown glaze and genuine examples should have an oval mark like a thumbprint to the base, made when the piece was removed from the wheel.

Tallest 9in (23cm) high

£800-1,000　　**DN**

An early 18thC German Kreussen pewter mounted Apostle tankard, the moulded body with sheep surrounded by titled Apostle figures bordered with bands of foliage.

6in (15cm) high to rim

£650-850　　**SK**

An early 19thC Scottish brown salt-glazed stoneware flask, Alloa Pottery, applied with a repeated figure of a fisherman between sunflower sprigs and a grapevine border, pewter mounts, inner stopper and cover, impressed 'M' to the base.

9.5in (24cm) high

£150-250　　**WW**

POTTERY

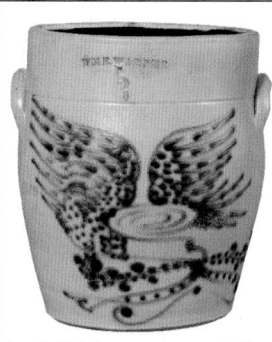

A mid-19thC stoneware crock, New York, three gallon capacity, the front decorated with a freehand spreadwing eagle, marked 'WM E. Warner West Troy', with minor base chips.

11in (28cm) high

£6,500-8,500 **SK**

CLOSER LOOK - A REMMEY STONEWARE PITCHER

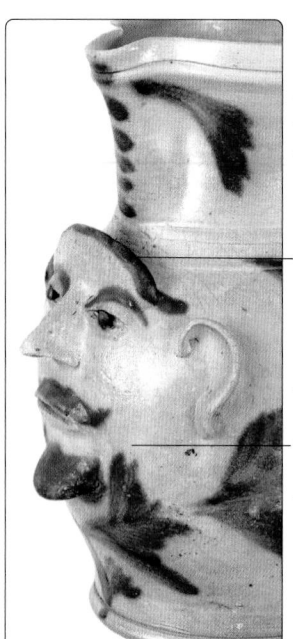

This piece is attributed to Richard Remmey, who came from an important American family of potters. He worked in Philadelphia in the late 19thC.

The cobalt blue floral decoration and facial highlights are delicately painted.

The relief face may be a likeness of a real person.

It is technically difficult to mould a face on a jug, and examples are rare, increasing their desirability.

A rare Philadelphia stoneware pitcher, attributed to Richard Remmey, with relief face of a man with cobalt highlight moustache, eyes, brow and goatee.

10.25in (26cm) high

£50,000-100,000 **POOK**

A 19thC Pennsylvania stoneware pitcher, with vibrant cobalt tulip decoration.

9in (23cm) high

£2,500-3,500 **POOK**

A 19thC stoneware pitcher, with cobalt floral decoration, impressed 'Wells & Richards Reading Berks Co. Pa'.

13in (33cm) high

£6,000-8,000 **POOK**

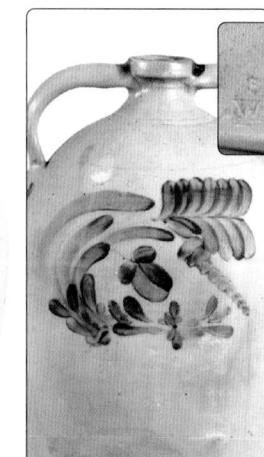

A 19thC stoneware lidded crock, with cobalt flower, impressed 'TH Willson & Co. Harrisburg PA'.

10in (25.5cm) high

£2,500-3,500 **POOK**

A large 19thC two-handled stoneware jug, with cobalt blue grape decoration, the reverse with a large floral spray, impressed 'Sipe & Sons Winsport Pa'.

20.5in (52cm) high

£5,000-7,000 **POOK**

A Edward VII Coronation oval plaque, by Hammersley, moulded with head in profile on a gilt reserve within a turquoise border decorated in colours and gilt.

c1902   10in (25cm) high

£80-120   **SAS**

An earthenware Toby jug, made to commemorate the proposed coronation of Edward VIII, the handle in the shape of an initial 'E', by Bretby pottery.

c1936   4in (10cm) high

£60-70   **H&G**

A Paragon King George VI and Queen Elizabeth Coronation preserve pot.

c1937   4in (10cm) high

£50-60   **RCC**

An Elizabeth II souvenir coronation compact, by Le Rage.

1953

£40-60   **MGT**

A Minton bone china loving cup and cover in the shape of an orb, made to commemorate the coronation of Queen Elizabeth II, in a limited edition of 600.

A limited edition of 60 coloured versions were also produced, which are worth £1,800-2,200.

c1953   6in (15cm) high

£450-550   **H&G**

CERAMICS

A Staffordshire Queen Victoria Coronation six-sided plate, in excellent condition and bright colours.

1837   *7.5in (19cm) wide*

£500-600   **RCC**

A cylindrical earthenware mug, decorated in pink lustre and printed in black with half-length seated portraits of Queen Victoria, centred by a crown named Victoria and a starburst and inscribed 'A Present for Eliza', minor chip to foot.

1837

£800-1,000   **SAS**

A Queen Victoria and Prince Albert Royal Wedding plate, unmarked.

1840   *6.25in (16cm) diam*

£350-450   **RCC**

A twin-handled plate decorated in pink lustre and printed in pink and enamelled in colours with portraits entitled 'Victoria and Albert'.

c1851   *8.75in (22cm) diam*

£50-80   **SAS**

A Staffordshire 'Queen Victoria with Prince Consort (152) potlid.

5in (13cm) diam

£200-300   **SAS**

An octagonal plate, made to commemorate the golden jubilee of Queen Victoria.

c1887   *10in (22.5cm) diam*

£240-290   **H&G**

A Doulton Burslem Queen Victoria Diamond Jubilee beaker.

c1897   *3.75in (9.5cm) high*

£120-135   **RCC**

A Queen Victoria commemorative plate, featuring an unusual three-quarter-length portrait, possibly German.

10.5in (26.5cm) diam

£80-100   **RCC**

A Doulton Lambeth jug in memoriam to Queen Victoria.

c1901   *8in high*

£550-625   **H&G**

A Copeland tazza in memoriam to Prince Albert, produced for the Art Union of London.

c1861   *16in diam*

£950-1,250   **H&G**

A probably Bucks or Montgomery County, Pennsylvania redware two-handled bowl, with yellow and green ellipses, flanked by black dots.

c1800   *4.25in (11cm) high*

£4,000-6,000   **POOK**

A Nockamixon Township, Bucks County, Pennsylvania pierced redware covered bowl, attributed to Jared or David Haring, with lamb finial, with dark brown manganese glaze with rope twist handles.

From the Shelley Collection.

6.5in (16.5cm) high

£1,200-1,800   **POOK**

An Pennsylvania glazed redware pierced stainer basket, dated 1815 inside the bowl, with overall yellow glaze with sgraffito trailing vines and outlines.

From the Shelley Collection.

10.5in (26.5cm) diam

£2,500-3,500   **POOK**

A Montgomery County moulded and wheel-thrown redware sugar bowl, attributed to John Nice, Upper Salford Township, with elaborate knop, bead-and-scroll decoration on lid, the base with two applied twisted handles with overall brown glaze, white dot slip decoration and footed base.

From the Shelley Collection

c1830-40   *7.25in (18.5cm) high*

£8,000-12,000   **POOK**

A 18thC Moravian glazed redware covered sugar bowl, North Carolina, with applied handles and yellow and black manganese slip leaf and line decoration.

From the Shelley Collection.

5.25in (13.5cm) high

£5,000-7,000   **POOK**

A late 18thC North Carolina Moravian redware sugar bowl, with yellow honeycomb slip decoration with green leaves on an orange ground, 3.75 ins high

From the Shelley Collection.

£400-600   **POOK**

A Moravian slip decorated redware deep bowl, Hagerstown area, inscribed "Anno 1857", with profuse yellow, green and brown star and scalloped decoration on an orange glazed ground.

From the Shelley Collection.

13in (33cm) diam

£4,000-6,000   **POOK**

An 18thC American redware shallow bowl, Pennsylvania, with swirl and coggled sgraffito decoration on a green and yellow glazed ground.

From the Shelley Collection.

11.75in (3cm) diam

£600-800   **POOK**

A 19thC Bucks county, Pennsylvania redware bowl, with scalloped rim, the interior sides decorated with yellow, black, and green tulips centering on a group of daisies.

6.5in (17cm) diam

£20,000-30,000   **POOK**

A late 19thC Virginia redware covered sugar bowl, by Anthony W Baecher, stamped on lid, body, and underside of base "Baecher Winchester VA", the lid with bird finial, the body with overall decoration of trailing floral vines and unusual green and brown mottled glaze.

6.25in (16cm) high

£25,000-35,000   **POOK**

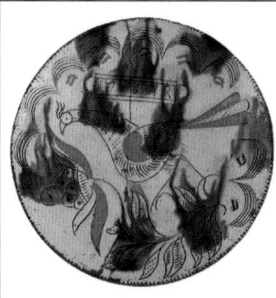

A rare Philadelphia stoneware pitcher, attributed to Richard Remmey, with relief face of a man with cobalt highlight moustache, eyes, brow and goatee.

10.25in (26cm) high

£50,000-70,000   **POOK**

A Montgomery County, Limerick Township, Pennsylvania sgraffito redware dish, attributed to George Hubener, with an inscribed border surrounding a three flower tulip vine.

1785   *12.25in (31cm) diam*

£220,000-280,000   **POOK**

A redware plate, with central decoration of a bird and branch within a border with script, the reverse inscribed 'F. Goff Lancaster Penna 1807'.

1805

£350-450   **POOK**

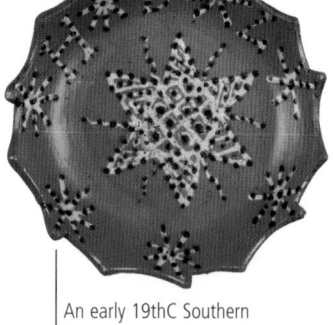

An early 19thC Southern Pennsylvania redware plate, with central star surrounded by seven asterisks and the initials 'HBL', with scalloped border.

7in (18cm) diam

£1,200-1,800   **POOK**

An early 19thC Montgomery County, Upper Salford Township, Pennsylvania sgraffito-decorated redware plate, attributed to John Neis, the central tulip flower with perched bird within an inscribed border.

11.25in (28.5cm) diam

£7,000-10,000   **POOK**

A south-eastern Pennsylvania sgraffito-decorated redware plate, initialled 'NM', decorated with a green eagle with outstretched wings.

1811   *12in (30.5cm) diam*

£8,000-10,000   **POOK**

A Bucks County, Haycock Township, Pennsylvania sgraffito-decorated redware plate, attributed to Conrad Mumbouer, with tulip vine and stylised floral pinwheel decoration.

c1815   *11.75in (30cm) diam*

£50,000-70,000   **POOK**

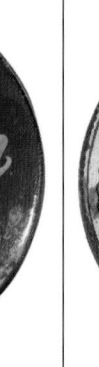

A 'William & Mary' slip-decorated redware plate, attributed to the Smith Pottery, Norwalk, Connecticut, the plate with coggled rim, with yellow slip-trailed inscription.

1825-50   *11in (28cm) diam*

£10,000-15,000   **SK**

A south-eastern Pennsylvania sgraffito-decorated redware plate, with central tulip vine surmounted by birds and pinwheels within a squiggle line border, inscribed indistinctly verso, dated 'May 25, 1828'.

1828   *12.25in (31cm) diam*

£7,500-9,500   **POOK**

A Montgomery County, Pennsylvania sgraffito redware dish, by Samuel Troxel, with central eagle with outstretched wings beneath a banner inscribed 'Liberty' and above a potted tulip vine, inscribed verso 'Samuel Troxel Potter 1825'.

1828   *11.5in (29cm) diam*

£40,000-60,000   **POOK**

A 19thC Pennsylvania redware loaf dish, with a yellow slip decoration.

16.5in (42cm) high

£3,000-4,000   **POOK**

A Medinger sgraffito redware charger, the decoration attributed to McAllister, after a design by Troxel, with spread-winged eagle below potted flowers.

c1900   *12.25in (31cm) diam*

£3,000-4,000   **POOK**

A pair of 19thC Bennington glazed spaniels, with coleslaw hair.

8.25in (21cm) high

£1,800-2,200   **POOK**

A 19thC Strasburg, Virginia redware wall pocket, attributed to S. Bell & Son, with bird and floral decoration on a mottled green and brown glaze.

5.5in (14cm) high

£5,500-6,500   **POOK**

A 19thC Shenandoah Valley redware inkwell, attributed to Anthony Baecher, Winchester, Virginia, in the form of a bear with coleslaw mane.

7.25in (18.5cm) high

£5,000-10,000   **POOK**

LEFT: A 19thC redware figure of a seated dog, attributed to the Bell Potters, holding a basket.

4.75in (12cm) high

£5,000-7,000   **POOK**

CENTRE: A 19thC redware figure of a dog, attributed to the Bell Potters, holding a basket with a bottle.

5.5in (14cm) high

£4,000-6,000   **POOK**

RIGHT: A 19thC redware figure of a standing dog, attributed to the Bell Potters.

3.75in (9.5cm) high

£2,000-3,000   **POOK**

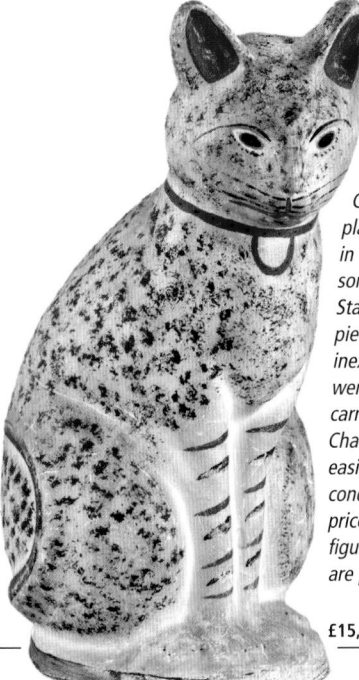

A large 19thC chalkware cat, with black sponge decorated body and red collar.

Chalkware is made of plaster of paris decorated in watercolors, and was sometimes cast using old Staffordshire moulds. The pieces were intended as inexpensive ornaments and were frequently used at carnivals as prizes. Chalkware damages very easily, so pieces in good condition fetch the highest prices. Rarer chalkware figures, such as Santa Claus, are particularly valuable.

15.25in (38.5cm) high

£15,000-25,000   **POOK**

A late 19thC American redware fox-form canister, with coleslaw mane and exaggerated facial features.

10.5in (26.5cm) high

£1,500-2,500   **POOK**

ORIENTAL

Despite headlines of a global financial slump, falling house prices and job losses, the Asian antique and decorative arts market can genuinely boast that it has never been stronger. The market thrived throughout 2009, thanks largely to the unremitting domestic demand for traditional art, coupled with the buying power of China's ardent and prosperous collectors. Auctioneers, domestic and foreign dealers and sellers at every level – from casual pickers to international brokers – have had the opportunity to do well in the Chinese arts trade.

Initially, interest in Chinese antiques was very broad, with almost anything finding a buyer. More recently, however, collectors have begun to seek the more decorative wares, rather than simply archaic and/or esoteric pieces, and this has been reflected in auction house salerooms. Rare and fine decorative objects from the Song dynasty (960–1279) through to the 18th century, sell at a premium and rarely fail to find buyers willing to pay for them. Today's collectors are also buying the better quality 19th- and even 20th-century decorative wares, and prices of these have seen an increase in value over the past year as a result. Attractive jades, ivories and porcelains from the late Qing dynasty (1683–1895) are of particular interest and collectors will bid competitively to acquire them. This has been a boon for the owners and inheritors of domestic estate collections, which often contain pieces of lesser rarity and little cultural significance but considerable attractiveness and that are very early.

Among the more publicised pieces in the last twelve months was an 18th-century imperial jade water buffalo (see page 3), which Woolley & Wallis in Salisbury sold in May for a £3.4 million hammer price, breaking its own record for any object in a UK regional saleroom and sending shockwaves through London and Hong Kong.

However China has also been flexing its muscles politically. This was demonstrated at Christie's Yves Saint Laurent-Pierre Bergé sale, where two Qing dynasty bronze fountain heads – once part of a zodiac water clock from Beijing's looted Summer Palace – were bid to a world record price of €28m (£25.4m) before the buyer announced that he would not pay, and had only bid as a patriotic act of protest.

The Japanese art market, as well as that for Korean, Indian, Middle Eastern and Southeast Asian wares, has seen interest in only the finest of items, while the mid-price market (£1,500–5,000) has remained flat. Nevertheless, shrewd buyers could bolster that middle market in the forthcoming years by taking advantage of the currently low prices.

The close of 2009 was a healthy one for Asian art, with auction houses witnessing busy evening receptions and the frenzied bidding in the salerooms. At Sotheby's in London an 18th century jade Imperial seal fetched £3.15m and again created a small political storm about looted art treasures. The market remains an unpredictable one, with many pre-sale estimates being wildly inaccurate, and this trend may continue for the next year at least.

From top: Yongzheng bowl £280,000 at Martel Maides; one of a pair of Yongzheng famille rose bowls, £1,020,000 at Martel Maides; one of a pair of 18th century Chinese pottery parrots £170,000 at Plymouth Auction Rooms.

ORIENTAL

CHINESE REIGN PERIODS AND MARKS

Imperial reign marks were adopted during the Ming dynasty, and some of the most common are illustrated here. Certain emperors forbade the use of their own reign mark, lest they should suffer the disrespect of a broken vessel bearing their name being thrown away. This is where the convention of using earlier reign marks comes from – a custom that was enthusiastically adopted by potters as a way of showing their respect for their predecessors.

It is worth remembering that a great deal of Imperial porcelain is marked misleadingly and pieces bearing the reign mark for the period in which they were made are therefore especially sought after.

Early Periods and Dates

Xia Dynasty	*c2000 - 1500BC*	Three Kingdoms	*221 - 280*	The Five Dynasties	*907 - 960*
Shang Dynasty	*1500 - 1028BC*	Jin Dynasty	*265 - 420*	Song Dynasty	*960 - 1279*
Zhou Dynasty	*1028 - 221BC*	Northern & Southern Dynasties	*420 - 581*	Jin Dynasty	*1115 - 1234*
Qin Dynasty	*221 - 206BC*	Sui Dynasty	*581 - 618*	Yuan Dynasty	*1260 - 1368*
Han Dynasty	*206BC - AD220*	Tang Dynasty	*618 - 906*		

Ming Dynasty Reigns

Hongwu	*1368 - 1398*	Jingtai	*1450 - 1457*
Jianwen	*1399 - 1402*	Tianshun	*1457 - 1464*
Yongle	*1403 - 1424*	Chenghua	*1465 - 1487*
Hongxi	*1425 - 1425*	Hongzhi	*1488 - 1505*
Xuande	*1426 - 1435*	Zhengde	*1506 - 1521*
Zhengtong	*1436 - 1449*		

Ming Dynasty Marks

大明靖年製嘉 | 大明慶年製隆 | 大明曆年製萬 | 大明啟年製天 | 崇禎年製

Jiajing *1522 – 1566* | Longquing *1567 – 1572* | Wanli *1573 – 1619* | Tianqi *1621 – 1627* | Chongzhen *1628 – 1644*

Qing Dynasty Marks

大清治年製順 | 大清熙年製康 | 大清正年製雍 | 大清隆年製乾 | 嘉慶年製 | 大清光年製道

Shunzhi *1644 – 1661* | Kangxi *1662 – 1722* | Yongzheng *1723 – 1735* | Qianlong *1736 – 1795* | Jiaqing *1796 – 1820* | Daoguang *1821 – 1850*

大清豐年製咸 | 大清治年製同 | 大清緒年製光 | 大清統年製宣 | 年製崇禎

Republic Period

Xianfeng *1851 – 1861* | Tongzhi *1862 – 1874* | Guangxu *1875 – 1908* | Xuantong *1909 – 1911* | Hongxian (Yuan Shikai) *1915 – 1916*

ESSENTIAL REFERENCE – THE TANG DYNASTY

The Chinese Tang dynasty (618-906AD) was a time of great cultural and economic prosperity, when ceramic art achieved high status. The dynasty was founded by the Li family, who seized power during the decline of the Sui dynasty. The Tang dynasty was interrupted from 690 to 705BC by the Second Zhou dynasty after Empress Wu Zetian seized power, becoming the first and only Chinese empress regnant.

- The Tang dynasty is particularly famed for the pottery burial wares made of a soft, absorbent pottery (modern copies are usually harder) that revived traditions of the Han dynasty (206BC-220AD). These fine white-bodied pieces – Xing and Yueh wares – eventually led to the production of true porcelain.
- The glaze on Tang wares is particularly distinctive as it has a bright, glassy appearance.
- In the low-fired range the most characteristic wares of the period are the sancai ("three colour") wares, which became widespread in the Tang dynasty. These wares included earthenware vessels, and models made as tomb

guardians. The faces of figures were often left unglazed and painted with coloured pigments after firing.

- The best examples of tomb figures are arguably the powerfully modelled horses and camels, with superbly modelled tack. They were decorated with sancai glazes in lead-fluxed green, amber, brown, cream and blue. These glazes were splashed or poured over the piece's upper section and allowed to drip and run.
- Tomb figures first came on the European market in 1909. Because these wares have been buried for such long periods they are usually relatively undamaged; nevertheless they can be very reasonably priced. However, collectors should be aware that there are fakes on the market – the success of Tang burial figures was so immediate and so great that by 1912 there was already a factory producing fakes in Peking, and these can be extremely difficult to recognise.
- Yingqing, one of the earliest Chinese porcelains, was developed in this era.

A Chinese Tang Dynasty pottery model of a horse, standing four-square, wearing a saddle and with traces of painted bridle and harness.

13.5in (34cm) high

£1,500-2,000   L&T

A Chinese terracotta standing horse, with arched neck and downward looking head, wearing a saddle, standing on all fours on a rectangular plinth, with vestiges of original polychromy.

14in (35.5cm) long

£1,800-2,200   TEN

A Chinese Tang Dynasty stoneware globular ewer, with a clear glaze and an iron splash to one side.

7in (17cm) high

£500-600   WW

A Chinese, probably Tang period, San Tsai cup, made in the form of a head of a mythical animal.

3in (7.5cm) high

£300-400   SK

An early 10thC Chinese butterfly-shaped vase, the decoration of underglaze blue and red, with edge fritting.

15.25in (39cm) high

£1,200-1,800   SK

A Chinese Song Dynasty light blue Yingqing hexafoil bowl, of deep moulded form, white petal-shaped rim with a well-moulded foot, with a timber stand.

5in (12.5cm) diam

£300-400   FRE

ORIENTAL

A Chinese Song/Jin Dynasty Cizhou painted meiping, of small attenuated form, inverted mouth, well-painted iron-brown peony and issuing leaves over a white slip.

9.5in (24cm) high

£700-1,000   FRE

A Chinese Yuan Dynasty tea-dust type and mottled glaze stoneware wine jar, the short neck glazed brown with ivory issues from a tapering green glazed ovoid body, terminating in a circular foot.

26in (66cm) high

£500-600   FRE

A rare Five Dynasties, Northern Song Dynasty early 'Yaozhou' relief-carved globular ewer, the body finely carved, with flat strap diaper-moulded ear handle and a curved spout, on a high flaring foot, the light grey stoneware covered overall with a pale-green glaze with even craquelure save for the foot rim.

Ewers of this elegant form and deeply carved flower decoration seem to be among the earliest green-glazed wares made at the 'Yaozhou' type site at Huangpu in Tongchuan county, Shaanxi province. This ewer is a particularly well-preserved example and features a beautiful even glaze and exceptionally bold carving.

7.75in (19.5cm) high

£120,000-150,000   SOT

A large Chinese probably Yuan Dynasty Junyao bowl, decorated with a lavender glaze, pooling around the foot.

8.75in (22cm) diam

£550-650   WW

An unusual Chinese Yuan Dynasty stoneware jar, with a ribbed barrel-shaped body, painted in iron-red with a figure riding a donkey with an attendant, the reverse with a brown flower and cloud motif, minor faults.

5in (12.5cm) high

£400-500   WW

A Chinese Tang Dynasty marble-glazed double gourd earthenware vase, simulated marble yellow and brown glaze.

8in (20.5cm) high

£3,000-4,000   FRE

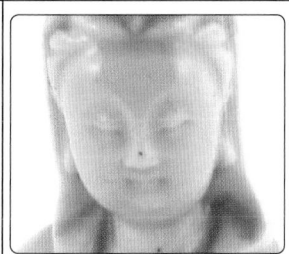

A small 18thC Chinese blanc-de-Chine figure of Guanyin, the goddess, sitting with one knee raised on a cloud scroll, on a wood stand in a fitted box.

4.25in (11cm) high

£550-650   **WW**

A Chinese early Qing dynasty blanc-de-Chine Dehua elephant censer, of two section form, the cover carved and moulded to show three musicians, on a howdah, over an elephant, delicately incised.

12in (30.5cm) high

£2,000-3,000   **FRE**

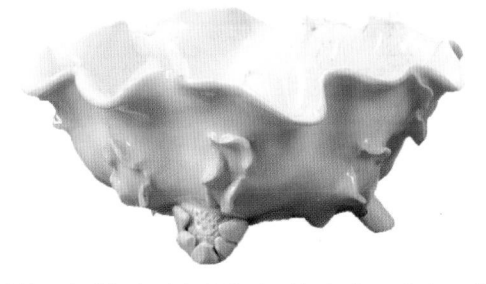

A 19thC blanc-de-Chine bowl, the Te Hua bowl in the shape of a lotus plant.

7.25in (18.5cm) diam

£200-300   **SK**

A large 18thC Chinese blanc-de-Chine figure of Guanyin, with detailed head crown, bead jewellery and robe, seated over a rocky outcrop, slight blue hue to white glaze, on solid unglazed base.

22in (56cm) high

£12,000-18,000   **FRE**

An 18thC Chinese blanc-de-Chine figure of an Immortal holding a dragon, on cloud base, with traces of the original hair insets.

13in (33cm) high

£500-600   **SK**

A Chinese blanc-de-Chine figure of the Goddess of Mercy, with the mark of Hsu Yu Yi.

c1910   *13in (33cm) high*

£150-250   **SK**

ORIENTAL

A probably early 16thC Chinese Ming Dynasty celadon glazed and incised jar, the unglazed rim possibly ground down or lacking cover, the body incised with a peony and leaves, unglazed base, raised on a circular foot.

7in (18cm) high

£1,200-1,800   FRE

A rare Chinese Ming Dynasty celadon one hundred rib jar and cover, the body of bulbous form beneath a lotus leaf formed lid, with stem knop.

8.5in (21.5cm) high

£2,000-2,500   GORL

An 18thC Chinese celadon vase, of waisted tapering cylindrical form with concentric blue circles to base.

5.5in (14cm) high

£350-450   L&T

A Chinese Tongzhi celadon vase, Fang Hu of Kuan type, with Tongzhi mark, with fitted hardwood stand.

12in (30.5cm) high

£7,000-8,000   SK

A large Chinese celadon vase, probably Qianlong period, with allover moulded scroll and stylised foliate and geometric bands, blue painted character mark.

This style of decoration takes inspiration from archaic bronzes.

15in (38cm) high

£8,000-10,000   L&T

A large 15thC Ming Dynasty Longquan celadon barbed-rim dish, carved to the interior with a medallion enclosing a peony spray, covered overall in a thick bluish-green glaze.

Celadon is a European term for wares with the iron-derived, semi-translucent, usually greenish glaze developed in the Song Dynasty (960-1279). The glaze is usually laid over a relief or incised pattern. Pieces dating from the Song period are extremely rare.

18.5in (47cm) high

£100,000-150,000   SOTH

A Chinese Ming Dynasty carved celadon glazed bulb bowl, the rim worked to show two stud bands enclosing a trellis-diaper over three carved mask feet, the orange-fired interior worked in low relief, orange-fired foot, over an 18thC hardwood stand.

12.5in (32cm) diam

£3,000-4,000   FRE

A pair of Chinese Liao Dynasty ovoid pottery vases, with flared slender necks, with a green glaze falling short of the foot.

The Liao Dynasty was a regime founded in 916 by an ethnic minority called the Qidan (Khitan) who lived in the northeast areas of China. The title of the Qidan kingdom was officially changed to Liao in 947, with Balin Left Banner (in current Inner Mongolia) as its capital city.

14in (35.5cm) high

£1,500-2,000   **WW**

An 18thC Chinese export baluster vase, decorated with prunus on a cracked-ice ground within formalised borders, substantial damage to rim.

20in (51cm) high

£1,000-1,500   **DUK**

A Chinese Qing Dynasty langyao glazed jar and bronze cover, tall circular foot, orange buff recessed base, bronze ruyi band cover.

12in (30.5cm) high

£300-400   **FRE**

A large 18thC Chinese langyao vase, of pear form, well potted straight neck issuing from pear compressed body over a raised foot, strawberry to dark purple glaze to body, repainted recessed foot.

Sang-de-boeuf is a brilliant red glaze developed in Ming dynasty, during the reign of Wanli 1573-1619.

18in (45.5cm) high

£650-850   **FRE**

A pair of 19thC Chinese flambé double gourd vases, the bodies with an allover speckled red glaze, the rim with a cream glaze outline, general peppering effect to the glaze.

9.5in (24cm) high

£1,000-1,200   **WW**

A 19thC Chinese sang-de-boeuf and parcel gilt porcelain vase, the neck painted with scroll edged panels depicting prunus, peonies, butterflies, fruiting blossoms with birds.

16.25in (41cm) high

£1,500-2,000   **TEN**

A small Chinese vase, decorated with a robin-egg glaze, the neck encircled by a bifid dragon, the base moulded with a six character Qianlong mark.

6.75in (17.5cm) high

£200-300   **WW**

A 19thC Chinese robin-egg glaze bottle, with a short, slender neck, broad-shouldered body tapering to a circular base, glazed a mottled dark blue, black underglazed base.

7.5in (19cm) high

£200-300   **FRE**

A 19thC Chinese monochrome blue vase, in deep cobalt blue.

19in (48cm) high

£600-800   **SK**

A Chinese bottle vase, of compressed form, with a flambé purple glaze and a ribbed neck, a four character Yongzheng mark but later, flakes to foot and faint cracks.

10.25in (26cm) high

£1,200-1,500   **WW**

ORIENTAL

A Chinese vase with an inverted pear-shaped body, and everted rim, decorated with a pale blue monochrome glaze, a later four character Yongzheng mark.

12.5in (32cm) high

£300-400   **WW**

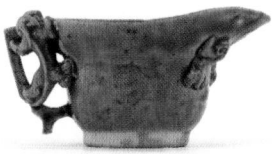

A Chinese Kangxi period turquoise glazed libation cup, the handle and spout each applied with a small kylin.

4in (10cm) wide

£200-300   **WW**

A pair of 19thC porcelain covered bowls, in robin-egg blue glaze, with Qianlong six-character mark in red, one with a small chip.

7.25in (18.5cm) diam

£200-300   **SK**

CLOSER LOOK – A JUN WARE FLOWERPOT

Dating these receptacles has long been debated. The discovery of a mould fragment for coins inscribed with the Xuanhe reign name together with fragments of numbered 'Jun' vessels suggested a date from the Northern Song (12thC). Recently however, the coin mould dating has been dismissed and a dating of the early Ming dynasty (15thC) is now largely accepted for 'Jun' ware, following stylistic comparison with flower receptacles in celadon and blue-and-white from the Longquan and Jingdezhen kilns, which are more precisely datable.

These bright blue or purple 'Jun' ware flower receptacles in mould-made shapes, are inscribed on the base with numbers from one to ten.

The temperature and atmosphere in the kiln were critical to successful firing. The purple shade was a difficult colour to control in the kiln and is not common.

A rare early Ming Dynasty 'Jun' mallow-shaped lavender-glazed flowerpot, highlighted with cascades of sky-blue and deep pinkish-purple, with bracket-lobed flaring sides, the base with five drainage holes and incised with the number san (three).

10.75in (27.5cm) diam

£300,000-350,000   **SOT**

A pair of unusual Chinese tea-dust glaze vases, of fluted double gourd shape, each with triple neck.

9.5in (24cm) high

£1,000-2,000   **A&G**

An 18thC Chinese mirror-black glaze vase, white ground rim, unglazed foot, with blue rings.

6in (15cm) high

£350-450   **FRE**

A large 19thC Chinese porcelain model of a water buffalo, on a wooden stand.

20.5in (52cm) wide

£3,000-3,500   **WW**

A pair of late 19thC Chinese Guan style vases, flared, iron oxoid washed rims, overall crackle design.

15.5in (39.5cm) high

£2,000-3,000   **TEN**

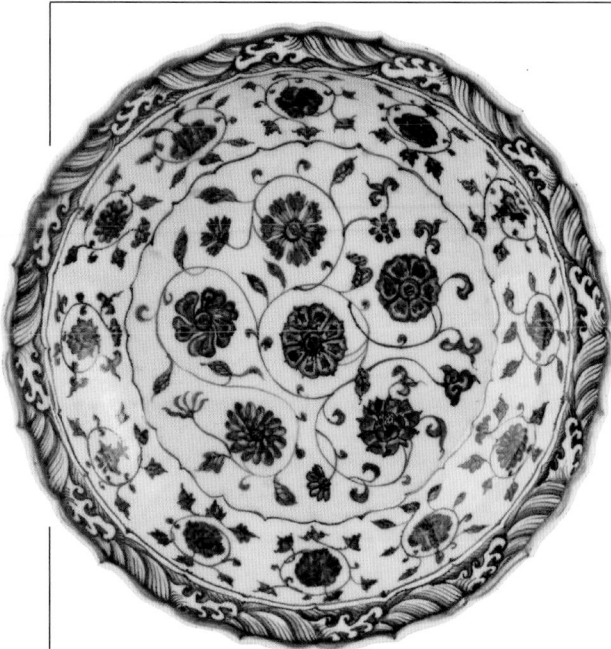

A Chinese Yongle period barbed rim charger, the underglaze-blue of inky blue and black tone, with 'heaped and piled' effect, painted with flowers and floral sprays, the white base unglazed.

The high value of this dish can be attributed to its fine painting and its age. It comes from the Yongle period (1403-24) in the Ming Dynasty, evidence for which can be seen in the 'orange peel' glaze (a dimpled surface) and the 'heaped and piled' effect, caused by unevenly applied cobalt oxide. Pieces sold by major auction houses with documented provenance from British collections going back to the 1920s and 1930s, such as this charger, sell well to the major Chinese collectors.

13.5in (34cm) diam

£450,000-600,000   **SOTP**

A Chinese Wanli period blue underglazed charger, with a curvilinear rim, decorated with freely painted diaper band, lotus flowers and reeds enclosing a medallion of swimming fish, the outer wall painted with Buddhistic symbols.

13in (33cm) diam

£3,000-4,000   **FRE**

A late 16thC/early 17thC 'Kraak Porselein' blue and white dish, painted with scholars on a veranda, the border with peasant figures and flowers, the underside with five lobed and floral reserves.

18in (46cm) diam

£900-1,200   **TEN**

A large Chinese Ming Dynasty 'European subject' blue and white charger, Swatow, Guangdong Province, geometric and foliate sprigs to rim, central medallion of tall mast ships and European landscape, with repaired rim.

Named after the port of Shantou (Swatow), Swatow wares are roughly decorated porcelains that were produced around the city of Chaozhou in Guangdong Province from the mid-16thC for export.

18.5in (47cm) diam

£4,000-5,000   **FRE**

A large Chinese Kangxi period blue and white charger, of slightly rounded form, painted Indian lotus pods issuing scrolling leaves worked to inner and outer walls, raised circular recessed foot, with Kangxi mark.

15in (38cm) diam

£900-1,200   **FRE**

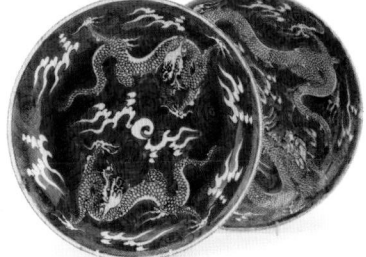

A near pair of Chinese Kangxi period blue painted chargers, each decorated with two dragons chasing pearls of wisdom amongst clouds, blue painted lozenge mark.

Larger 13.75in (35cm) diam

£1,000-1,500   **L&T**

A large Chinese Kangxi period moulded blue underglazed charger, of foliate lotus petal form, painted in cobalt blue to show a profusion of floral sprigs, flowers and peacocks, with blue Artemisa mark.

14.5in (37cm) high

£2,500-3,500   **FRE**

ORIENTAL

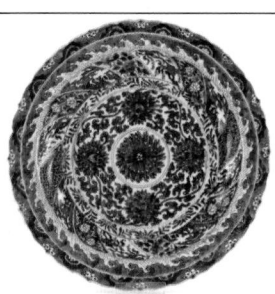

A Chinese Kangxi period blue and white moulded charger, painted with a central flower surrounded by bands of flowers, foliage and waves, the base with a Mandarin mark of honour, restoration to rim.

14.5in (36.5cm) diam

£400-500   WW

A Chinese Kangxi period blue and white porcelain shallow circular dish, decorated with peony blossoms amongst tendrils and leaf scrolls, two sprigs painted to the underside, with a similar dish.

15.25in (38.5cm) diam

£550-750   TEN

A shallow Chinese Kangxi period export blue and white porcelain dish, painted with moulded, petal-shape panels with Buddhistic emblems, similarly decorated to outside, six-character Kangxi mark.

10in (25.5cm) diam

£450-550   TEN

ESSENTIAL REFERENCE – SHIPWRECK CARGOES

With so many ships carrying tea, porcelain, spices and silk from China to India and Europe from the 17thC onwards, it was inevitable that a significant number should sink before completing their journeys.

- From the mid-1980s, wrecks of Chinese trading vessels have been discovered and salvaged by teams of deep-sea divers. Each wreck is an important archaeological find, revealing previously unseen Oriental ceramics that might not have survived had it not been for the disaster that sent them to the bottom of the sea. It is interesting to imagine how fashions and ceramics history would have changed if these pieces had reached their intended destination. Collectors are often also interested in these pieces as they are bound up with their own intriguing story: where was the ship headed; what caused it to sink?
- In general, the longer a cargo has been on the market, the rarer pieces have become as more and more is sold on. The Hatcher Cargo (the first on the market in 1984) is therefore desirable, though the Vung Tau Cargo (discovered in 1990) and the Diana Cargo (discovered in 1994) are

becoming increasingly sought after. Eventually, however, all shipwreck cargos will be rare.

- As inventories are rare, shipwreck cargoes can be difficult to date. The Nanking Cargo (lost in 1752 and discovered in 1986) is a notable exception, as it was being shipped aboard the 'Geldermalsen', a ship registered to the Dutch East India Company. The Nanking cargo included 171 dinner services, as well as many tea and coffee services, predominantly decorated with blue and white landscapes. As it came from a time when shapes had become more standardised and less decorative designs were being used, this cargo revealed little about historical porcelain, but pieces from the Nanking cargo are highly collectable. This is due to the detailed ship's records and the highly publicised auction of its contents at Christie's in Amsterdam in 1986.
- Prices can range from £50 to thousands of pounds. Blue and white wares are consistently popular, as are items encrusted with coral and limpets, which are valued for their aesthetic appeal.

A Chinese blue and white stem dish, decorated with Buddhist emblems, gourds and foliage, on a spreading circular foot, the inside of the base with a six-character mark of Yongzheng.

7in (18cm) diam

£3,500-4,500   DUK

A rare large Yongzheng period blue and white 'Dragon' dish, the wide vessel with curved sides rising to a flat everted rim, painted in deep underglaze-blue with a five-clawed dragon clasping a shou medallion, all atop a short foot, the base with a six-character Yongzheng mark.

This dish is rare for its unusual depiction of the shou medallion. In comparable works, the shou character floats freely between the five-clawed feet of the dragon, but here the dragon is tightly clutching it in three-clawed feet.

17.75in (35cm) diam

£90,000-120,000   SOT

A set of four 18thC Nanking porcelain deep dishes, blue painted with a river scene and dwellings on the shore line.

9.5in (24cm) diam

£150-250   DA&H

An 18thC Chinese blue underglaze charger, of slightly rounded form, painted interior of Immortals among a mountainous landscape, marked.

13.5in (34cm) high

£2,500-3,500   FRE

Two 18thC Chinese blue and white rectangular dishes, painted with a pagoda and three other houses, one with an incised character.

9.75in (24.5cm) wide

£150-250   WW

An unusual early 17thC Chinese blue and white bowl, the interior painted with the god Shoulao and a band of Arabic-style script, the exterior depicting Daoist Immortals and shou characters, gilt-metal rim, with six-character Chenghua mark, hairlines.

8.75in (22cm) diam

£3,000-4,000   WW

A Chinese Qing Dynasty large Ming-style copper-red underglazed bowl, painted with peonies, chrysanthemums and foliage, Roman key to foot circular foot, orange buff unglazed base.

15.5in (39.5cm) diam

£2,500-3,500   FRE

A Chinese Kangxi period blue and white square-section bowl, painted with figures in various outdoor pursuits, with Chih seal mark.

6in (15cm) diam

£700-900   WW

A large 18thC underglaze gilt-bronze mounted jardinière, with cast acanthus leaf band rim, bowl depicting sea creatures, raised on a shell and C-scroll three-legged base.

15in (38cm) diam

£3,000-4,000   FRE

A pair of Chinese Tongzhi period blue-painted bowls, each decorated with an Immortal to the well and further Immortals to the exterior, blue painted Tongzhi mark.

8.5in (22cm) diam

£4,500-5,500   L&T

A Chinese porcelain large, shallow bowl, painted with dragons chasing pearls, amongst waves and fish, with red enamel, a later possibly Guangxu six-character mark.

41.25in (104.5cm) diam

£900-1,200   TEN

ORIENTAL

A large Chinese Ming Wanli period blue and white 'lotus' jar, with scroll-decorated neck and painted lotus flower and leaf body, unglazed base raised on a short foot.

14.5in (37cm) high

£5,500-6,500   **FRE**

A Chinese blue and white globular jar, painted with lotus flowers and leaves between two bands of symbols from the 'Eight Precious Things', the base with a hare mark as a symbol of intelligence and longevity.

c1600   *3.75in (9.5cm) high*

£300-400   **WW**

An early 17thC Chinese kraak square-section flask, painted in blue with panels of peony, chrysanthemum and auspicious objects, the shoulders with stylised ruyi fungus, with a few chips to neck.

7.25in (18.5cm) high

£700-800   **WW**

A rare Chinese Ming Dynasty underglazed 'double bird' wine jar, moulded as joined ducks, one decorated with a blue head, the other primarily unglazed, the domed cover revealing a single hollow chamber, unglazed flat base.

5in (13cm) long

£3,500-4,500   **FRE**

A Chinese Ming period Swatow ware porcelain jar, the underglaze blue decoration of flowers with a border of Fu dogs and cash coins.

9.5in (24cm) high

£350-450   **SK**

A pair of Chinese Kangxi period oviform jars, with underglaze blue and red with carved celadon accents, with designs of scholars in landscapes.

8.25in (21cm) high

£6,000-7,000   **SK**

A large Chinese Kangxi period blue and white moulded covered jar, moulded with eight petal bands to collar and base, painted to show Buddhistic symbols, the body painted to show court beauties.

9.5in (24cm) high

£1,200-1,800   **FRE**

A late 19thC Chinese blue and white covered jar, cover painted to show boys at play, the wide-shoulder base painted to show ladies amongst bands of phoenix, with four-character Kangxi mark.

11in (28cm) high

£3,500-4,500   **FRE**

A large Chinese blue underglazed jardinière, of octagonal form, the everted rim issuing from a diaper of ruyi heads and leaf band enclosing a figural landscape of various Immortals.

23in (58.5cm) high

£1,500-2,000   **FRE**

ESSENTIAL REFERENCE – CHINESE BLUE & WHITE

China's first underglaze blue pieces were produced in the mid-14thC using cobalt imported from Persia. The method of painting cobalt oxide onto white porcelain before the final firing is still used today.

- A very fine painting style had developed by the late Ming period (1368-1644), though occasionally the blue filtered through glaze, creating a pooled effect known as 'heaped and piled'. This was later imitated in the Qing period (1644-1911) as a sign of quality.
- Blue and white pieces produced during the reign of Chenghua (1465-87) are widely regarded as examples of the finest porcelain ever produced. They have light, thin bodies and a glassy glaze. Designs of dragons, phoenixes, landscapes and flower scrolls were applied evenly, in dark blue in the early Chenghua pieces and lighter blue on later pieces. Standards were maintained during Hongzhi's reign (1488-1505), but after this they began to decline, with poorer clay being used and more casual brushwork.

- By the end of the Ming dynasty, large quantities of blue and white wares (known as kraak porcelain after the Portuguese carrack ships that carried them) were being shipped to Europe. Panels were used increasingly on bowls and dishes, with decoration radiating outwards from the centre. Transitional ware, dating from the same period, is heavier, better potted and more refined.
- Production in the late 17thC was dominated by blue and white garnitures, and dinner and tea services for export to Europe. Some polychrome pieces were also produced, but these were more expensive.
- Pieces with a genuine date mark can be worth ten times as much as unmarked pieces from the same period. Unmarked pieces can be dated by style, date, and colour, as well as by the nature of porcelain and potting. Ming porcelain has blue tinge to the body. Late Qing porcelain is pearly white. 17thC Chinese porcelain had orange tint, which has never been seen on European porcelain.

A rare Ming Dynasty Jiaqing period blue and white Portuguese market bottle vase, painted in cobalt blue tones with the monogram 'HIS', with trellis-diaper and running horse and bands to top and bottom.

c1540-1550   7.25in (18.5cm) diam

£100,000-120,000   SOTH

A rare Ming Dynasty Wanli period blue and white Portuguese market bottle vase, painted in cobalt blue with the arms of the Portugese 'Vilas Boas e Faria' with an eagle crest, all above flowers issuing from rockwork.

This bottle is modelled following a European glass shape, known also from European stoneware and faience. Such bottles would have been fitted with a pewter screw top. These bottles were used mainly for spirits and were designed to be stored in wooden boxes for easy transportation on ships.

c1590-1610   12in (30.5cm) high

£120,000-180,000   SOTH

A Chinese Ming style blue and white bottle vase, the body painted to simulate 'heaping and piling' with bands of lotus and leafy tendrils, the base with a Qianlong seal-mark, drilled.

14.75in (37.5cm) high

£20,000-25,000   DUK

A small Chinese Transitional period blue and white gourd-shaped vase, painted with two figures, the upper bulb with stylised flowers, with gold leaf repair to the rim.

c1640   7.75in (19.5cm) high

£600-800   WW

CLOSER LOOK – AN ARMORIAL BLUE & WHITE FLASK

A large Chinese Kangxi period blue and white vase, drilled for a lamp, of unusual pear form, painted in cobalt blue with court scene and landscape, on unglazed foot, six-character Kangxi mark.

18in (46cm) high

£2,000-3,000   **FRE**

A large Chinese Kangxi period blue and white beaker vase, painted with a continuous landscape of fisherman at top and mountain range to base, unglazed foot, double blue rings and old collection label.

17.25in (44cm) high

£18,000-22,000   **FRE**

This piece may have been a royal commission from Philip II (1527-98) dating from 1580-95. Philip II had a vast collection of Chinese pieces, allegedly three-thousand items. However, these flasks may have been ordered by a knight of the Order of Aviz or of the Order of Christ during the Spanish occupation of Portugal, between 1610-20. Such an interesting history can only increase the value of an object like this.

The shape is a copy of an Islamic metal flask and would have been made specifically for the export market. Very few pieces were made in this form.

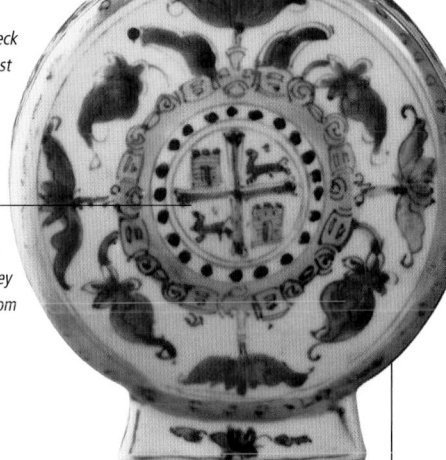

Certain design elements found on these flasks, such as the flowers painted on the neck and body, strongly suggest a 17thC date.

The arms of Spain painted on one side show that this piece was a special commission. They may have been copied from a coin.

One of a pair of Chinese Kangxi period blue underglaze baluster vases, converted to lamps, painted with mountain landscape, one heavily restored.

10in (25.5cm) high

£600-800 PAIR   **FRE**

A Chinese Kangxi period blue and white vase, painted with figures, plantain and rockwork, with small chips around the foot rim and the neck replaced.

8.5in (21.5cm) high

£550-750   **WW**

A rare Ming Dynasty Iberian market armorial blue and white pilgrim flask, the slightly convex circular body rising from a short spreading foot and painted to the front face with the arms of Spain.

c1610-20   *11.75in (30cm) high*

£120,000-180,000   **SOTH**

A Chinese Qianlong blue and white double gourd vase, painted with bats carrying Buddhist emblems and pa-chi-hsiang, lotus scroll, foot and neck with key fret bands, hairline.

17.75in (45cm) high

£7,000-9,000   **WW**

A large Chinese, probably Qianlong period, blue and white hexagonal vase, with branches, key fret and lappet bands, base with 6-character Qianlong mark, neck reduced.

24.75in (63cm) high

£1,500-2,000   **WW**

A large Chinese blue and white meiping vase, painted in the Yuan style, with a band of peony between borders of lappets and clouds collars, wear, mounted as a lamp.

16.25in (41cm) high

£6,000-8,000   **WW**

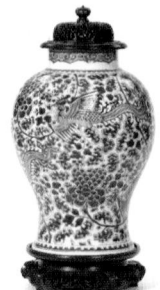

A late 18thC/early 19thC Chinese export blue and white porcelain baluster vase, body with phoenix in flight and peonies, later associated carved wood cover and stand.

13.75in (35cm) high

£1,500-2,000   **TEN**

A large early 19thC Chinese square-section vase/tea jar, painted with a continuous scene with small figures, boats and pagodas in a watery landscape, with small cracks to the neck.

13.25in (33.5cm) high

£350-450   **WW**

A pair of mid 19thC Chinese square ogee decorated vases, decorated with scholars and flowers in underglaze blue.

15in (38cm) high

£4,000-5,000   **SK**

CLOSER LOOK – MING-STYLE VASE

This vase represents one of the finest porcelain designs, influenced by earlier Ming ceramic patterns but adapted to suit contemporary Qianlong period taste. The vase is impressive for its large size, with meticulously detailed painting and fine potting. The vivid blue glaze is a reflection of the technical ability of the potters working in the Imperial kilns at Jingdezhen under the guidance of China's most famous Superintendent Tang Ying.

The Qianlong emperor is known to have commissioned artists to make pieces that were challenging and impressive. The making of such large vessels, together with the complex decorative techniques indicates that artists were encouraged to be ambitious in their repertoire.

This hu required considerable expertise from the potter, who drew on archaic styles and forms while creating a piece that was contemporary. Reference to archaic bronze hu would have been appreciated by the emperor who was a collector of archaic pieces. He was also a follower of Tibetan Buddhism and the religious reference, such as the symbols of the Eight Buddhist Emblems, would have been preferred motifs.

A large Qianlong period Ming-style blue and white vase, the high rounded shoulders set with two archaistic taotie masks supporting mock ring handles, with contrived 'heaping and piling' effect, with 'Hu' sealmark.

£300,000-400,000   **SOTH**

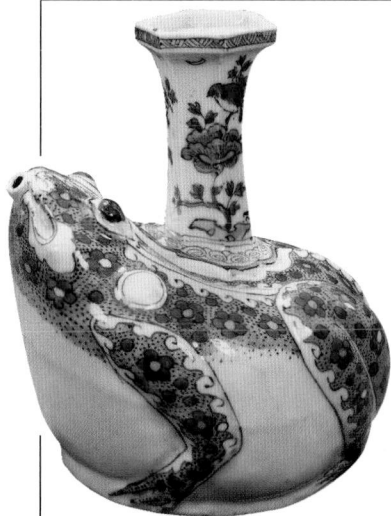

A rare Ming Dynasty Wanli period blue and white 'Frog' kendi, naturalistically modelled as a crouching frog, a short spout issuing from its mouth and tall hexagonal trumpet-shaped handle supported on its back.

This piece is extremely rare for its hexagonal handle and moulded features, such as the bulging eyes and ridge running down its body.

7.25in (18.5cm) high

£45,000-55,000   SOTH

A Chinese Kangxi period porcelain cup, of flared cylindrical form, painted in underglaze blue with three figures in a boat beneath script, six-character mark in underglaze blue.

10in (25.5cm) high

£1,000-1,500   TEN

A Chinese Kangxi period blue and white cup and underplate, cup of deep U-shape raised on a small foot, together with an underplate both decorated with lotus flowers and foliate scrolls.

Underdish 5.5in (14cm) diam

£350-450   FRE

A rare 17th/18thC Chinese blue and white drum-form brush stand, the top recessed with three circular brush pots, rectangular inkpot and a central water pot, all with moulded covers and painted, with two-character mark.

It is extremely rare to find drum form brush stands with period insert covers.

5.5in (14cm) wide

£3,500-4,500   FRE

Twenty Ca Mau 'Peacock' pattern tea bowls and saucers, each painted with a peacock within crimped segmented floral borders, the undersides with a simple underglaze blue meander.

c1725   *Saucer 5in (12.5cm) diam*

£500-600 SET   HALL

ESSENTIAL REFERENCE – CA MAU PORCELAIN

In 1998, a Vietnamese newspaper reported that a shipwreck filled with 18thC Chinese porcelain had been discovered by fishermen working off the coast of the Ca Mau peninsula, Vietnam and was in the process of being dredged. The government soon intervened and a team of conservators and divers began to excavate the site. More than 130,000 pieces of porcelain were retrieved from the site, of which 76,000 were selected for sale in 2006.

- **The wreck was probably a Chinese junk heading for the Dutch trading port of Batavia (present-day Jakarta), which had sunk after a fire on board.**
- **All Ca Mau porcelain was made at Jingdezhen for the European market. It can be dated to the Yongzheng period (1723-35), and can be narrowed down to c1725 by the presence of pieces of porcelain in the same style as pieces made in the reign of the emperor Kangxi, who died in 1722.**
- **Ca Mau patterns include 'Fisherman', 'Lotus and flowerhead', 'Fallow dear', 'Peacock' and 'Butterfly'.**

A 19thC Chinese blue and white brush pot, of a gathering of scholars, with a Wen Chang Shan Tou hallmark on the base.

7.25in (18.5cm) high

£350-450   SK

A 19thC Chinese blue and white octagonal garden seat, painted with scrolling flowers and foliage.

19in (48cm) diam

£500-600   WW

One of a pair of 19thC Chinese blue and white garden seats, moulded with studs, painted with dragons, pierced with cash symbols, damage.

18.25in (46.5cm) high

£2,000-3,000 PAIR   WW

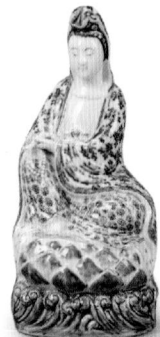

A 19thC Chinese porcelain seated figure of the Goddess of Mercy, her robes and throne decorated in underglaze blue.

10.75in (27.5cm) high

£450-550   SK

ORIENTAL

An 18thC Kangxi period famille verte plate, with a design of a woman and children in a garden, with diapered borders with floral reserves, artemesia mark on the base, small hairline.

8.5in (21.5cm) diam

£450-550   SK

A Chinese Qianlong period porcelain famille verte charger, painted in typical palette with a bird, tree, chrysanthemums, within a panelled border with fish, the reverse with matching decoration.

15in (38cm) diam

£800-1,000   TEN

A large Chinese Kangxi period famille verte dish, painted with five panels containing animals, the border with six small panels on a floral diaper ground, with artemesia mark, restored.

Famille Verte, literally meaning 'green family' is a style of polychrome porcelain that features a bright copper green. It was adopted during the Kangxi period (1662-1722), having evolved from the five colour Wucai style developed in the 16thC.

15.25in (38.5cm) diam

£2,500-3,500   WW

A large Chinese Kangxi period famille verte bowl, painted with flowers.

12.25in (31cm) diam

£2,000-3,000   WW

A Chinese Kangxi period famille verte bowl, the exterior painted with four peony flowerheads on a green leaf scroll ground, with a hairline crack.

7.75in (20cm) diam

£350-450   WW

A Chinese Kangxi period famille verte bowl, moulded with ribs and painted with panels containing crickets and other bugs on a scrolling ground, cracked and restored.

7in (18cm) high

£900-1,200   WW

A Chinese Kangxi period famille verte moulded bowl, painted with panels depicting flowers issuing from rockwork and insects, with a shop mark, rim crack.

8.25in (21cm) diam

£800-1,000   WW

A 19thC Chinese famille verte jardinière, painted with four panels containing censers on a green ground with mythical beasts amidst flowers, with a turned and carved wood stand.

£250-350   WW

A pair of small late 19thC Chinese famille verte jardinières, each of semi-ovoid form, the frontal panels decorated with a pheasant amongst flowering peonies, on the reverse with chrysanthemum panels.

8.5in (22.5cm) high

£500-700   TEN

A large Chinese Kangxi period famille verte covered jar, of octagonal form, the decorated iron-red and enamel painted body depicting a figural landscape, the unglazed base with recess and double rings.

20.5in (52cm) high

£2,500-3,500   **FRE**

An 18thC Chinese famille verte vase and cover, with underglaze blue decoration and overglaze scrolling floral decoration with infants picking flowers, mainly in shades of green.

16.5in (42cm) high

£550-750   **GORL**

A pair of 18thC Chinese famille verte porcelain vases, converted to lamps, underglazed in blue and enamelled to show red and yellow chrysanthemums and other floral sprigs, and a scholar's studio.

Porcelain 11in (28cm) high

£5,500-7,500   **FRE**

An 18thC/19thC Chinese baluster vase, with famille verte decoration of women boating in a lotus pond.

17.5in (44.5cm) high

£2,000-3,000   **SK**

A 19thC Chinese famille verte vase, decorated with rose decoration of a dragon chasing the pearl of wisdom, with elaborate Qianlong mark, on hardwood stand.

16in (40.5cm) high

£900-1,200   **GORL**

A 19thC Chinese famille verte vase and cover, painted with ladies in boats picking lotus and with other figures, the cover damaged, the base drilled.

17.75in (45cm) high

£250-350   **WW**

A Chinese porcelain vase, painted in famille verte palette with peacocks, within a geometric border, four-character Jiaqing marks in underglaze blue.

18in (45.5cm) high

£900-1,200   **HT**

A 19thC Chinese Canton box and cover, painted in the famille verte palette the box with a dividing section, losses to the paint and gilding.

7.5in (19cm) wide

£200-300   **WW**

An 18thC Chinese rose verte circular box and cover, painted with a boy sheltering beneath a large lotus leaf.

3.75in (9.5cm) high

£150-200   **WW**

ORIENTAL

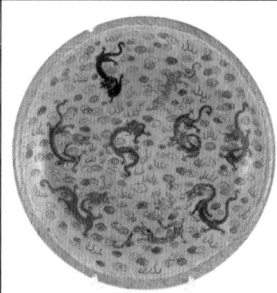

A Chinese Kangxi period porcelain charger, the lime green floral centre surrounded by famille rose enamels of the 'Eight Precious Things', with Kangxi mark.

15in (38cm) diam

£2,500-3,500   SK

A large 19thC Chinese famille rose yellow ground dish, painted with nine dragons chasing three pearls, the reverse with a six-character Yongzheng mark, damage to the rim.

20.5in (52cm) diam

£600-800   WW

ESSENTIAL REFERENCE – FAMILLE ROSE

Famille rose was popular during the Yongzheng period (1723-1735). It virtually replaced the famille verte palette, which had been developed during the Kangxi period (1662-1722).

- Famille rose uses predominately rose pink and purple shades, combined with green and yellow.
- As well 'fencai' or 'ruan cai' (meaning 'soft colours) the Chinese referred to this palette as 'yang cai': 'foreign colours'. This is because it was developed from combination of Eastern and Western enamels. The pink-hue was derived from gold chloride, which was introduced into China from Europe by Jesuit missionaries. This is notable as the only advancement in Chinese ceramics made by Europeans, rather than by the Chinese.
- Famille rose enamels were of higher quality than those of famille verte. Their brighter colours and improved opacity allowed the depiction of more complex images.
- Typical decoration includes panels of figures, landscapes or interior scenes and motifs, such as rockwork, branches, flowers and birds.
- During the 18thC and 19thC, vast quantities of famille rose ceramics were exported to Europe, and fashionable wealthy families had famille rose dinner services decorated with armorial designs.

A pair of 19thC Chinese Islamic market Canton famille rose plates, painted with panels of birds and flowers around gilt calligraphy roundels.

9.75in (25cm) diam

£400-500   WW

A Kangxi period porcelain cup, decorated with figures on a palace terrace in famille rose enamels, with Kangxi mark.

3.5in (9cm) diam

£1,200-1,800   SK

An 18thC Chinese famille rose fluted sugar bowl, applied with lotus flowers and leaves and painted with a cockerel, a hen and chicks.

4.5in (11.5cm) wide

£600-800   WW

A Chinese Qianlong period famille rose tureen and cover, moulded with ribs and painted with colourful insects amidst flowers, the knop as a flower head.

This tureen would have been part of a large dinner service which were popular with wealthy European and American clients. Famille rose wares were widely copied in Europe.

11.5in (29cm) high

£2,000-3,000   WW

One of two Chinese Qianlong period famille rose bowls, with floral decoration.

9in (23cm) diam

£450-550 PAIR   L&T

One of two late 18thC Chinese famille rose Rockefeller pattern circular bowls, with everted rims, painted with figures on a terrace.

8.25in (21cm) diam

£550-750 PAIR   WW

A pair of small 19thC Chinese famille rose bowls, each painted with two scaly dragons in pursuit of flaming pearls, four-character mark.

3.25in (8.5cm) diam

£500-700　　　　　　　　　　WW

A Chinese Tongzhi period famille rose bowl, decorated with nine Buddhist lion dogs on a colourful scrolling ground, with Tongzhi character seal mark.

6.5in (16.5cm) diam

£250-350　　　　　　　　　　WW

A pair of 19thC Chinese pottery lotus-form jardinières, with associated zinc liners, on wave-form bases applied with grimacing toads, slight damage.

6in (15.5cm) high

£400–500　　　　　　　　　　TEN

A large 20thC Chinese Canton famille rose bowl, decorated with a watery landscape, Qianlong six-character seal mark.

15.25in (39cm) high

£700-900　　　　　　　　　　WW

A Chinese Yongzheng period famille rose pear-shaped vase, with a flared foot, painted with insects amidst peonies and with a lily to the reverse, chips.

14.5in (36.5cm) high

£800-1,000　　　　　　　　　WW

A pair of large Qianlong period European market famille rose vases and covers, surmounted by tall lotus bud finials, the bodies decorated in underglaze blue and colourful enamels with gilt highlights, on later gilt stands.

Vases of this type would have been reserved for the wealthiest clients. The phoenix among flowers and rockwork was a popular motif for these types of vases. Examples like this decorated in underglaze blue and colourful enamels are rarer than those decorated purely with enamels.

53in (134.5cm) high

£100,000-120,000　　　　　SOT

A Chinese Qianlong period green ground famille rose wall vase, inscribed with an Imperial poem.

£160,000-180,000　　　　　SOTP

A pair of Chinese Qianlong period export porcelain famille rose vases and covers, one cover restored, the other cover an English replacement.
c1750   *18in (45.5cm) high*
£3,000-5,000   **TEN**

£550-750   **FRE**

A large Qianlong period famille rose covered vase, converted into a lamp, the body decorated in enamel, showing detailed figural landscape, with later gilt-metal mounts.

Jar 16in (40.5cm) high

An 18thC Chinese famille rose baluster vase, with spiral moulded neck and foot, decorated with pink scales, the body with European flower sprays, with small foot chips.
8.75in (22cm) high
£350-450   **WW**

A pair of 18thC Chinese hexagonal vases and covers, delicately painted in the famille rose palette, the knops modelled as lion dogs, the gilding mostly lacking on one vase, extensive damage.
18in (45.5cm) high
£2,000-3,000   **WW**

A large pair of 19thC Chinese Canton famille rose baluster vases, decorated with painted panels, with carved wood stands with inset soapstone tops, restoration.
56in (142cm) high
£5,000-6,000   **WW**

A large 19thC rose medallion baluster form vase, the foliate moulded neck applied with gilt Fu dogs in reverse, with butterflies, figural groups and millefleurs.
36in (91.5cm) high
£1,500-2,000   **FRE**

One of a pair of 19th/20thC Chinese famille rose covered jars of baluster form, in the export style.

18.75in (47.5cm) high
£2,500-3,500 PAIR   **FRE**

A 19thC Chinese Canton famille rose vase, decorated with exotic birds, butterflies and flowering shrubs, flaked.
14in (35.5cm) high
£250-350   **WW**

A pair of late 19thC Chinese famille rose porcelain bottle vases, painted with a pair of sky dragons chasing the cosmic pearl over waves
8.75in (22.5cm) high
£500-600   **TEN**

A small Chinese, Hongxian period, famille rose vase, with pomegranate branch and chrysanthemum, with four-character Hongxian mark.
3.25in (8.5cm) high
£120-180   **WW**

A pair of Chinese Republic period famille rose lanterns and stands, in two parts.

13in (33cm) high
£1,000-1,500   **FRE**

A large 19thC Chinese rose medallion porcelain palace vase, of baluster form, with dragon-form handles and decorative accents, painted with elaborate scene of courtly figures.

51in (129.5cm) high

£14,000-16,000   **SK**

A pair of early 19thC Chinese famille rose export tureens and covers, painted with the American eagle with outspread wings, one tureen with frits around the edge, both with rubbed gildings.

9.25in (23.5cm) wide

£250-350   **WW**

A 19thC Chinese square-section brushpot, or container, painted in the famille rose palette with elegant ladies, gilding to the rims missing.

4.5in (11.5cm) high

£250-350   **WW**

An early 20thC Chinese rose medallion porcelain garden seat.

18.5in (47cm) high

£1,500-2,000   **SK**

A 20thC Chinese famille rose model of a writhing coral-coloured dragon, standing on colourful clouds, restoration to extremities.

10.25in (26cm) high

£350-450   **WW**

CLOSER LOOK – A QING EXPORT FIGURE

This figure is one of the finest examples of famille rose figures made for the export market in China during the 18thC.

It is often referred to as 'Lady Duf', 'Duf' being the Chinese phonetic shortening of the name Durven. Diederick Durven was a lawyer in Delft, Holland, when in 1705 he was appointed to be the Council of Justice in Batavia. Sailing to the Dutch East Indies in 1706 with his wife, Anna Catharina de Roo, he remained with the Dutch East India Company in Batavia until the end of his appointment as Governor from 1729 to 1732.

Howard and Ayers, ibid., p. 613, suggest that the subject of this figure is 'presumably drawn from European prints'.

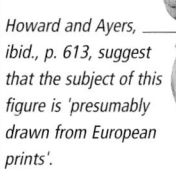

A rare Qing Dynasty export figure of a Dutch lady, modelled standing with her hands at her sides, her face with rosy cheeks and a gentle smile framed by a winged lace cap.

c1735-45   *16.5in (42cm) high*

£80,000-100,000   **SOTH**

ORIENTAL

A 19thC Chinese famille noire frog-form bowl and cover, with fruit-form finial and pink ribbon borders, painted all over with butterflies.

12.25in (31cm) wide

£500-700   L&T

A Chinese Kangxi period famille noire box, enamelled to show cartouches of figures among a landscape on a geometric enamel ground, unglazed interior, on bracket feet.

5in (13cm) long

£1,500-2,000   FRE

One of a pair of 18thC Chinese export armorial plates, with polychrome and gilt-painted arms and motto 'S P F S, TUTISSIMA CELS' and with spearhead border.
The motto should read 'SPES TUTISSIMA COELIS', but the 'o' has been omitted.

c1748   *9in (23cm) diam*

£900–1,200 PAIR   L&T

ESSENTIAL REFERENCE – CHINESE ARMORIAL

In the 17th and 18thC, Chinese porcelain was a status symbol in the West. From the early 18thC, especially wealthy Europeans and North Americans began to commission armorial dinner services, decorated with their crests and coats of arms. These could cost up to ten times as much as a comparable export service.

- In England, only companies and families with Letters Patent from the College of Arms were entitled to own armorial ceramics.
- The pieces were lavishly decorated in underglaze blue, famillie verte, or the later famille rose palette, and are often embellished with gilding.
- At this time, most commerce with the Orient was controlled through organisations such as the East India Company, which, but armorial porcelain was commissioned and traded on a small scale.
- Armorial services were often given as wedding gifts. They often depicted the coat of arms of one spouse impaling or standing beside the arms of the other
- By the late 18thC European makers had also begun to produce high quality porcelain, and so the prestige of armorial ceramics declined.
- These examples for the American market are extremely rare, particularly with the naval connection.

An 18thC Chinese Qianlong export porcelain armorial dinner service, possibly decorated with the arms of the Collier family, comprising tureen and cover, three meat plates, a sauceboat and 15 bowls.
1755

£5,000-7,000   GORL

An 18thC Chinese famille rose armorial bottle, with a scroll-decorated white metal collar and stopper.

9.75in (24.5cm) high

£2,500-3,500   L&T

A pair of early 19thC Chinese export porcelain bough pots, each with large depiction of an American ship and bearing the monogram of Captain George A. Robinson.

8.75in (22cm) high

£10,000-12,000   POOK

A Chinese armorial trencher salt, decorated with the arms of Warne within Fitzhugh borders.

c1780   *3.5in (9cm) diam*

£800-1,000   WW

A large pair of 'Chinese Imari' Kangxi period soldier vases and covers, each body of slender baluster from, painted with a hunting landscape scene within floral panels, the domed covers similarly decorated and surmounted by later biscuit lion finials.

Chinese Imari vases of this size, decoration and quality are extremely rare. Wares painted in underglaze blue, overglaze iron-red and lavish gold are after Japanese Imari porcelain made in Arita, Kyushu, for export to the Netherlands from the late 17thC. Japanese Imari wares also reached Europe via China, and success in this trade led Chinese potters to make Imari imitations at the kilns in Jingdezhen, Jiangxi province, which proved to be a cheaper and a much more profitable business for all parties involved. Chinese Imari wares primarily imitate the colours but are not close copies of the Japanese originals. In shape and decoration, Chinese Imari wares are often similar to contemporary blue and white garnitures made for the export market. Production of Chinese Imari wares reached its peak in the 1720s and 1730s when it became one of the main group of orders by the Dutch East India Company operating in China.

50.75in (129cm) high

£180,000-220,000   SOTH

An 18thC Chinese Imari white-metal mounted kendi, with white metal mounted domed rim, cover and spout with pressed lotus scrolls, the slender neck issuing from a ribbed bulbous body, raised on a short foot.

9.5in (24cm) high

£400-500   FRE

An early 18thC Chinese Imari dish, painted with flowers.

8.75in (22cm) diam

£80-120   SWO

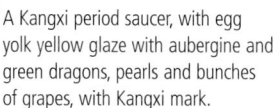

A pair of large Chinese Jiajing period saucer dishes, decorated with dragons within scrolling lotus borders, in shades of red oxide and green, the outside decorated with phoenix within scrolling foliage, with six-character Jiajing mark.

30in (76cm) diam

£1,500-2,500   GORL

A Kangxi period saucer, with egg yolk yellow glaze with aubergine and green dragons, pearls and bunches of grapes, with Kangxi mark.

5.25in (13.5cm) high

£600-800   SK

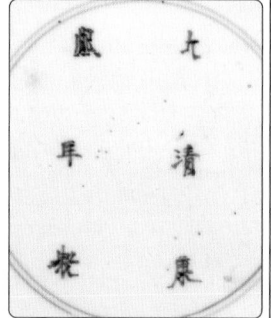

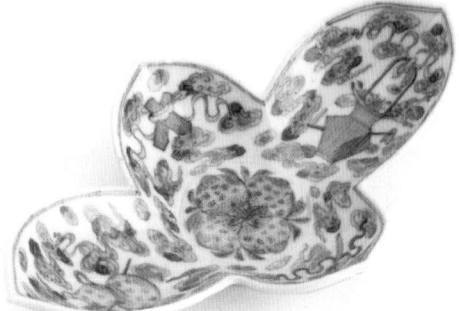

A rare Chinese Kangxi period blue underglazed and Wucai decorated charger, blue underglazed lotus band to rim, central medallion of enamelled fruit, lotus and foliate sprigs, recessed foot, with six-character Kangxi mark.

13in (33cm) diam

£2,000-3,000   FRE

A Chinese Yongzheng period quatrefoil leaf-form doucai dish, decorated with a stylised flowerhead to the well, with good luck symbols and polychrome clouds to the interior sides and exterior.

7.5in (19cm) wide

£2,000-3,000   L&T

ORIENTAL

An 18thC Chinese square moulded dish, painted in the doucai palette with auspicious objects, the border with flowers and scrolling tendrils.

7.25in (18.5cm) wide

£600-800   **WW**

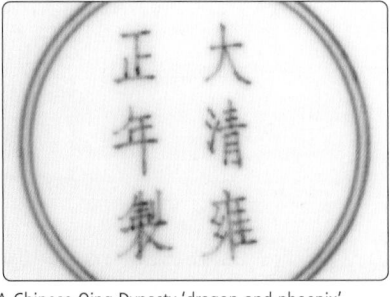

A Chinese Qing Dynasty 'dragon and phoenix' doucai saucer dish, decorated with red enamel and blue underglaze, raised on a short circular foot, with Yongzheng mark inside double rings.

8in (20.5cm) diam

£2,500-3,500   **FRE**

A Chinese Guangxu period plate, painted with two standing cranes, a pine tree, peony and a pair of bats, the reverse with three flower sprays, with a six-character Guangxu mark, rubbing to the gilt rims.

10.5in (26.5cm) diam

£200-300   **WW**

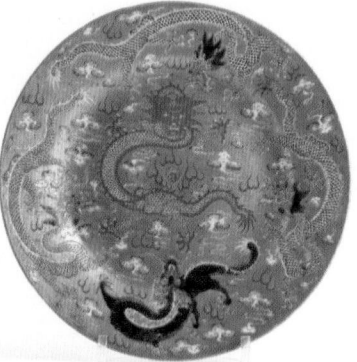

An early 20thC Chinese gold ground dish, decorated with five fierce and colourful dragons chasing a central flaming pearl, the reverse with a six-character Qianlong seal mark.

7.5in (19cm) diam

£300-400   **WW**

A Chinese dragon dish, painted with five scaly yellow dragons pursuing flaming pearls on a blue ground, with a six-character Guangxu mark but later.

7.75in (20cm) diam

£150-250   **WW**

A rare Ming Dynasty Jiajing period green and yellow bowl, with Jiajing mark.

£80,000-100,000   **SOTP**

A Chinese Jiaqing blue and white and polychrome enamelled bowl, of ogee-sided circular shape, internally decorated in underglaze blue with flowers and a kite motif, externally with floral and fruit sprays against a pink enamel and incised ground, with seal mark of Emperor Jiaqing.

6in (15cm) diam

£19,000-21,000   **TEN**

A rare small Qianlong period bowl and cover, the exterior painted in enamel on a pink ground incised with feathery scrollwork, the interior glazed white, the cover centred by a flaring stem knop, with gilt rims and foot, seal marks.

These items belong to a special group of wares, of which there are few examples, where the design is reserved on a monochrome enamel ground, incised with fine needle-point etching of endless scrolling fronds. This complicated and laborious decorative technique was developed in the Imperial kilns at Jingdezhen under the direction of Superintendent Tang Ying, during the Qianlong period. Tang Ying's talent for design, combined with the high level of technical ability at the kilns made the manufacturing of such pieces possible.

Bowl 4in (10cm) diam

£60,000-80,000   SOT

A Wanli period wucai bowl, the delicately potted rounded sides rising from a short tapering foot to a flaring rim, decorated to the interior with a dragon medallion, the exterior depicting an Immortal and mythical beasts, with Wanli mark.

3.5in (8.5cm) diam

£4,000-5,000   SOTH

A Chinese Qianlong period wucai dragon and phoenix bowl, typically decorated with the mythical beasts amidst leaves and flowers, with six-character Qianlong mark, minor restoration to the rim.

6in (15.5cm) diam

£3,000-4,000   WW

A Chinese Qianlong period bowl, the exterior decorated with twelve cranes amidst rockwork and fungus beneath pine trees, with a six-character Qianlong mark.

5.5in (14cm) diam

£600-800   WW

A pair of 19thC Chinese blue and white and yellow ground bowls, each semi-ovoid bowl decorated with stylised flowerheads on leafy tendrils against a solid yellow ground, with gilded rims.

10.5in (27cm) diam

£1,000-1,500   TEN

One of a pair of 19thC Chinese trefoil section cups, decorated in coloured enamels with flowers over a pale green graviatta ground.

3.75in (9.5cm) high

£250-350 PAIR   DN

A pair of small 20thC Chinese doucai bowls, painted with medallions, the base with six-character Qianlong marks, one with two faint glaze cracks.
Doucai, or 'contrasting colours', was developed 1465-87.

4.5in (11.5cm) diam

£1,500-2,000   WW

A Ming Dynasty Jiajing period polychrome jar, with Jiajing mark.

5in (12.5cm) high

£80,000-120,000 SOTP

ORIENTAL

ESSENTIAL REFERENCE – WUCAI

The Wucai style of decoration was introduced during the Jiajing reign (1522-66). Wucai means 'five colours' but the number of colours used can vary. It features bright, eye-catching shades of red, yellow, green, blue and purple painted in densely arranged brushstrokes. Golden and black paints were also used.

- Wucai is also called yingchai ('hard colours') as it has clear lines and the firing temperature is slightly higher than that of famille rose.
- While underglaze-blue outlines were still used, they were often replaced with overglaze black or red on Wucai pieces.
- Wucai decoration was used on large and small pieces.
- Decoration on Wucai pieces was different and generally less refined than that used on the earlier Doucai style, with which it shared a palette. Doucai pieces were often decorated with figures, plants, animals and landscapes; Wucai pieces were more likely to feature fish, water-weed, ducks and figure scenes, as well as winged dragons with flowers or jewels in their mouths, arranged around bowls or jars, or used as circular medallions.
- The finest pieces date from the Wanli period (1573-1619).

A 17thC Chinese Transitional period Wucai vase, decorated with blue underglaze and red, green and yellow enamel to show a figural landscape, with Japanese silk cover and tomobako.

10in (25.5cm) high

£5,000-6,000   **FRE**

A 17thC Chinese Transitional period Wucai porcelain jar, blossoms enamelled to neck, body enamelled to show boys during a dragon show amongst foliate landscape, with unglazed base.

10in (25.5cm) high

£6,500-7,500   **FRE**

A pair of Chinese Kangxi period spiral-moulded Wucai vases, the covers moulded as lotus, the bodies brightly decorated with an abundance of flowers amidst foliage, on vase with a crack.

12in (30.5cm) high

£2,500-3,500   **WW**

A pair of Chinese Kangxi period rosewater sprinklers, of Islamic form, painted in iron-red and gilt, with flowers and foliage.

7.25in (18.5cm) high

£650-850   **WW**

A Chinese double gourd vase, decorated with flowers and scrolls and tied around the middle with a pink sash, the base with a Qianlong seal-mark incised and in gilt.

15.25in (38.5cm) high

£6,500-7,500   **DUK**

An unusual Chinese square-section vase, decorated with a pale celadon glaze upon which five small boys climb, a Qianlong seal mark, with a wood stand, damages.

8.5in (21.5cm) high

£7,000-8,000   **WW**

A pair of large 18th/19thC Chinese export-style jardinières, gilt and enamel painted, the sides applied with two orange glazed faces supporting brass free-hanging handles, over gilt-metal stands.

10in (25.5cm) diam

£7,000-8,000   **FRE**

A pair of 19thC Cantonese porcelain baluster vases, each with Fu dogs in gilt to the neck and dragons to each shoulder, typically decorated with panels of Manchu court figures.

17.25in (44cm) high

£2,000-3,000　　　　　TEN

A Chinese Republic period blue underglaze and enamelled vase, the body painted with a court scene among a continuous landscape, over a circular foot, with Qianlong mark.

13in (33cm) high

£2,500-3,500　　　　　FRE

A large pair of 19thC Chinese pottery lion dogs, one with its paw raised on a cub, the other with its paw raised on a globe, each on a swagged rectangular plinth.

23.75in (60cm) high

£700-1,000　　　　　L&T

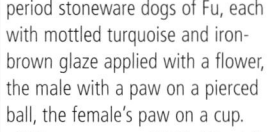

One of a pair of Chinese Xuandong period stoneware dogs of Fu, each with mottled turquoise and iron-brown glaze applied with a flower, the male with a paw on a pierced ball, the female's paw on a cup.

c1900　　　　*15.75in (40cm) high*

£700-1,000 PAIR　　　　TEN

A Chinese yellow ground censer, the three sections of flattened rectangular shape, the pierced cover with qilin finial, on pierced hardwood stand.

14.25in (36cm) high

£800-1,000　　　　　GORL

A small 19thC Chinese canton oval tureen and cover, painted with figures on verandas above floral borders, inscribed 'JH'.

8.5in (21.5cm) high

£200-300　　　　　WW

CLOSER LOOK – A POLYCHROME HOUND

The quality of the modelling shows that this is an exceptional example – note the detailing of the ears, nostrils and the open mouth with teeth, and the exquisite detailing of the floral collar.

While many smaller figures of hounds are known, large examples are rare and therefore sought after.

The dog is one of the six domestic animals of China and is considered a symbol of fidelity as it is in the West. A pair of dogs made of silver thought to have come from the Summer Palace, Beijing, suggests that it is highly likely that figures of hounds were not made solely for the export market.

The separate front legs and carefully detailed paws add to the lifelike qualities of this piece.

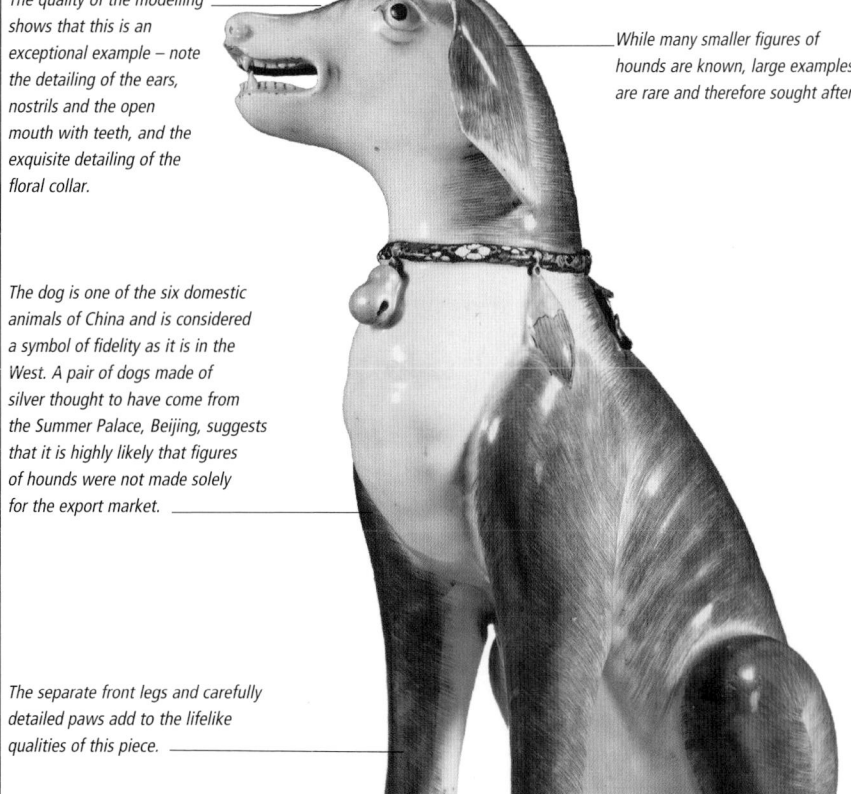

A rare early Qianlong period model of a hound, naturalistically modelled, wearing a floral collar with fixed pendent tassels and a gilt bell, the coat in shades of iron-red and black.

20.75in (52.5cm) diam

£40,000-60,000　　　　　SOTH

ORIENTAL

A Japanese Imari dish, painted with a phoenix above a pond, within a border of flowers and rockwork, with surface wear.

c1700   12.5in (32cm) diam

£200-300   **WW**

A large pair of Japanese Imari fluted dishes, decorated with birds and foliage.

c1800   18.5in (47cm) diam

£500-700   **WW**

A large 19thC Japanese Imari charger, of stepped shallow rounded form, decorated in iron-red gilt and cobalt blue with chrysanthemums, peony and a central medallion.

21.25in (54cm) diam

£1,500-2,000   **FRE**

A large 19thC Imari circular dish, all-over decorated with pagodas, flowers and birds.

22.75in (58cm) diam

£800-1,000   **LT**

A large late 19thC Japanese charger, of slightly rounded form, enamelled and underglazed in the typical Imari palette.

24in (61cm) diam

£450-550   **FRE**

A large late 19thC Imari charger, decorated with flowers against a panelled background inside a conforming border.

Imari porcelain was developed in late 17thC Japan and matured as a style c1800. It was made in and around Arita, and shipped to Europe from the port of Imari. Its distinctive palette is dark underglaze blue with iron-red, gold and sometimes purple, and designs often include a flower-basket pattern. Imari was copied in China, Holland and the UK.

18in (46cm) high

£2,000-3,000   **MEA**

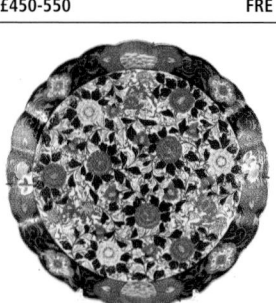

A large late 19thC Japanese Imari charger, enamelled to show four cartouches of seated gentlemen framing a central medallion.

24in (61cm) diam

£400-500   **FRE**

A 20thC Japanese Imari charger, painted with lion dogs, the border depicting cranes and mountain landscapes, wear to the gilt rim.

16in (40.5cm) diam

£200-300   **WW**

A large 19thC Imari porcelain jardinière, with reeded body decorated with colourful flowers on a dark blue and white ground.

19in (49cm) high

£1,200-1,800   **MEA**

A large late 19thC Japanese Imari bowl, of U-shape decorated to show a central medallion framed by reversed scroll enamelled panels.

16in (40.5cm) wide

£500-700   **FRE**

A large late 19thC Japanese Imari bowl, of deep U-shape form, enamelled in the Imari palette, raised on a circular foot.

£2,000-3,000   FRE

A large 19thC Japanese Imari baluster vase, decorated with flowers and geometric forms to the borders, and with opposed figural panels.

£900-1,200   L&T

A pair of Japanese Meiji Imari vases, necks painted on the inner rim, bodies with panels depicting shi shi dogs and sea dragons.

Tallest 36.25in (92cm) high

£3,000-4,000   TEN

A 19thC Japanese Imari floor vase, moulded shi shi in reverse, enamelled and gilded Imari palette to body, repair to foot.

43in (109cm) high

£1,200-1,800   FRE

A large 19thC Imari baluster vase and cover, decorated on a white ground with colourful flowers and alternate panels.

24in (63cm) high

£1,000-1,500   MEA

One of a pair of 19thC/20thC Japanese Imari umbrella stands, blue underglazed band to collar and base enamelled scene of bijin to body.

25in (61cm) high

£1,500-2,000 PAIR   FRE

A 19thC garniture of three Japanese Imari vases and covers, the lids with lion dogs resting their paws on brocade balls, damages.

17.75in (45cm) high

£900-1,200   WW

A large early 20thC Japanese Imari covered koro, the cover surmounted by a glazed and gilt shi shi, foliate moulded, with rim handles and raised on three mask and paw legs.

17in (43cm) high

£3,500-4,500   FRE

ESSENTIAL REFERENCE – SATSUMA

Satsuma wares take their name from a feudal province at southern tip of Japanese island of Kyushu.

- Following Japan's invasion of Korea in 1597, the potteries benefited from an influx of Korean master potters, who began to make the first Satsuma ceramics. These were simple Karatsu-style tea ceremony wares, often with a crackled yellow glaze over a cream ground.
- Pieces were relatively unsophisticated until the late 18thC, when the potters learned decorative techniques from potters in Arita and Koto.
- 'Satuma' has since become a generic term for the cream-coloured Japanese pottery exported to the West from c1850, much of which was made at Kyoto.
- This pottery had a clear, yellowish, finely crackled glaze and was often decorated with figures, flowers and butterflies in polychrome enamels and gilding. Many designs use perspective to create complex multi-layered scenes. Some pieces were artificially aged with tea, sulphuric acid or smoke.
- Quality varies, from the oldest carefully decorated pieces to more recent, gaudy items made for export.

A large Meiji Period Satsuma vase, the neck with tied bundles of stalks applied as handles, the decoration painted primarily in green and turquoise hues for the foliage, with pink and burnt orange flowers.

19in (48.5cm) high

£5,000-7,000   RGA

A large early 20thC Satsuma two handled-baluster vase, heavily enamelled, with mask handles, iron-red seal mark and gilt-inlaid clay two-character mark.

18.25in (46cm) high

£1,200-1,800   HALL

A large late 19thC Japanese Satsuma baluster vase, decorated with dragons within raised black and red enamel panels of daoist symbols and precious objects, firing crack to base enamelled in black.

15.25in (39cm) high

£1,500-2,000   HALL

A Japanese Meiji period Satsuma vase, decorated with raised enamel scene depicting a three-claw dragon, within a thousand faces pattern, signed.

13.75in (35cm) high

£650-850   JA

A late 19thC Japanese Satsuma vase, decorated with birds in a flowering prunus tree and hollyhocks against a basketry fence, signed.

18in (46cm) high

£900-1,200   SK

One of a pair of large Japanese Meiji period Satsuma vases, each painted and gilt with figural and landscape panels.

18.5in (47cm) high

£2,000-3,000 PAIR   JA

A pair of Meiji Period Satsuma decorated vases, each with gaping shi shi masks on the shoulder, painted in thick enamel colours and gilding, signed Satsuma yaki.

These vases are a good example of two styles merging into one. Overall the thick, jewel colours of the enamels, outlined in gilt, combined with the bold, imposing decorative scheme are typical of one school. However, sprays of delicate rust-red kiku are equally typical of the 'Audsley-Bowes' taste.

12in (30.5cm) high

£5,000-6,000   RGA

A large pair of Japanese Meiji period Satsuma ovoid vases, with elaborate gilt-metal mounts to the rims, the feet formed as elephant heads, the bodies decorated with Immortals.

34.25in (87cm) high

£2,500-3,500   **WW**

A pair of Japanese Meiji period Satsuma vases, of ovoid form, each decorated with opposed panels, of two ladies and a child in a landscape on one side and pheasants to the other.

10in (25.5cm) high

£700-900   **L&T**

CLOSER LOOK – A SATSUMA VASE

This vase features an intricate, highly unusual simulated basket-weave ground.

In 1868 the Meiji emperor was restored to power and Japan was once more opened to the Western world, after its isolation during the Edo period (1600-1868). Arts and crafts, such as lacquer wares, metalwares, enamels and ceramics, were encouraged as a display of Japanese skill. They were shown to great acclaim and influence at international exhibitions.

This vase demonstrates the full glory of Japanese flora in a single piece. Each flower is so perfectly drawn that it is easy to identify prunus, pomegranates, clematis, iris, peonies, gourds, carnations, lilies, maples, wisteria, hydrangea and chrysanthemums. The drawing is exquisite and the attention to detail meticulous.

A large Meiji Period Satsuma earthenware floor vase, the skittle shaped body cleverly potted to resemble a basket with a tied rope handle round the neck, painted throughout in delicate overglaze enamel colours and gilding with roundels of flowers floating like bubbles between brocade bands.

29in (73.5cm) high

£10,000-15,000   **RGA**

A large Japanese Meiji period Satsuma vase and cover, the cover with shi shi finial, the body decorated with warriors and geometric and floral borders.

26in (66cm) high

£550-750   **L&T**

One of a pair of large rare 19th/20thC earthenware Satsuma vases, four handles joined by chain link, with impressed gourd mark, minor losses.

14.5in (37cm) high

£1,800-2,200 PAIR   **FRE**

A Satsuma pottery lotus vase, enamelled and gilded with dense foliate designs, painted Satsuma mon in orange and inscribed in gilt.

c1900   *7.25in (18.5cm) high*

£350–450   **TEN**

A Japanese Meiji period Satsuma vase, by Yabu Meizan, of onion form with elongated flared neck, decorated with flowers in gilt and colours, signed.

7.5in (19cm) high

£5,500-6,500   **L&T**

A Japanese Meiji period Satsuma vase, by Yabu Meizan, decorated with figural and landscape panels, on a ground of flowers above a geometric border and irises on a cream ground, signed.

4.75in (12cm) high

£5,500-6,500   L&T

An unusual Meiji Period Satsuma vase, the neck set in a moulded collar of chrysanthemum petals, painted in muted overglaze enamels and gilding, raised on three small, lobed feet, signed.

7in (18cm) high

£7,000-9,000   RGA

A small Meiji period Satsuma reticulated tripod koro, by Toukouzan, the squat body applied with elephant mask handles, the domed cover with a double layer of pierced basket-weave, signed in gilt.

3.5in (9cm) high

£5,000-6,000   RGA

A Meiji Period Satsuma reticulated tripod koro and cover, by Yoshida, the cover intricately pierced, signed 'Satsuma Yoshida' in black ink with red kakihan, in original box.

4.25in (11cm) high

£5,000-7,000   RGA

A Japanese Meiji or Taisho period Satsuma box and cover, the cover surmounted by a gilt dog finial, signed, on a pierced hardwood stand.

11.75in (30cm) high

£900-1,200   L&T

 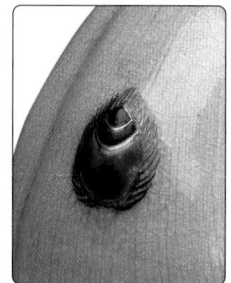

An unusual Meiji period Satsuma vessel in the form of a minogame, by Isoniwa, its tail curved over its back to form a handle, the cover made by one of the hexagons in its shell, sparsely decorated overall with gilt detailing and a tama in coloured enamels, signed 'Isoniwa' in gilt.

8in (20.5cm) high

£5,000-7,000   RGA

JAPANESE ARITA

An 18thC Japanese Kakiemon-style decagonal bowl, with kiln mark, minor frits to the rim.

8.25in (21cm) diam

£400-500   WW

An 18thC Japanese Arita bowl, decorated in gilt and enamel colours, with birds amidst fruiting branches and flowers.

6in (15cm) diam

£100-200   WW

An 18thC Japanese Arita blue and white charger, painted with peonies, chrysanthemum and auspicious symbols.

18.25in (46.5cm) diam

£700-1,000   WW

A large late 19thC Japanese Arita blue and white incense vase on stand, painted with archaic masks, geometric scrolls and foliate blossoms, gilt-metal mounts.

24in (61cm) high

£1,500-2,000   FRE

A 19thC Japanese Arita floor vase, enamelled and gilded bands of floral sprigs, with blue underglazed rim, interior and base.

36in (91.5cm) high

£1,200-1,800   FRE

A large 19th/20thC Japanese enamelled porcelain jardinière, blue underglazed and red leaf band to rim, four medallions enamelled to body on a ground of gilt sprigs.

15in (38cm) wide

£150-250 FRE

A Japanese late Meiji period earthenware bowl, painted with fan and leaf outlined reserves against a diapered ground.

6in (15.5cm) diam

£350-450 TEN

A Japanese Meiji earthenware bowl, of chrysanthemum outline, painted with a family group, with six-character mark, possibly Kinkozan Sobei VII.

6.5in (16.5cm) diam

£500-600 TEN

A large Japanese Meiji period porcelain bowl, painted with shi shi dogs, with old Japanese label with inscription and later associated ebonised wood stand.

13.5in (34.5cm) diam

£500-600 TEN

A late 17th/early 18thC Kakiemon-style enamelled hexagonal 'Hampton Court' vase, painted with paired red and yellow flag irises on turquoise-leafed stems with lapis blue details.

Vases known as 'Hampton Court' vases are so-called after a pair of hexagonal covered Kakiemon vases recorded at Hampton Court Palace, London, in an inventory of 1696.

15in (38cm) high

£11,000-14,000 TEN

A 19thC Japanese Kyoto Yaki vase, of double gourd form, with thick crystalline glaze with enamelled flowers and butterflies.

14in (35.5cm) high

£550-750 SK

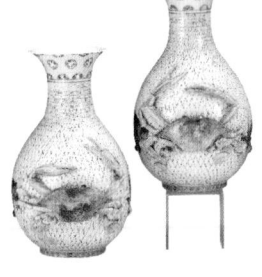

A pair of large Japanese applied porcelain vases, attributed to Makuzu Kozan, the flared mouths painted with gilded roundels, the bodies with black lace enamel and aquatic animals.

14in (35.5cm) high

£3,000-4,000 FRE

ESSENTIAL REFERENCE – MAKUZU KOZAN

Miyagawa (Makuzu) Kozan (1842-1916) was one of the greatest potters of the Meiji era. He was appointed artist to the Japanese Imperial household in 1892.

● **Born in Kyoto, he took over the family ceramics business in 1860, at the age of nineteen. In 1870, he opened a workshop in Yokohama and reached his artistic height during the 1880s.**

● **His style is typically detailed and delicate, the designs asymmetric.**

● **Most of Kozan's pieces bear his stylized signature in underglaze blue. However, care should be taken when identifying his works, as pieces made by other hands and signed 'Makuzu Kozan' have been made through the 20thC.**

A large vase, by Makuzu Kozan, painted with bold bamboo branches, with a six-character seal mark to the base.

c1910 *22in (56cm) high*

£5,000-6,000 WW

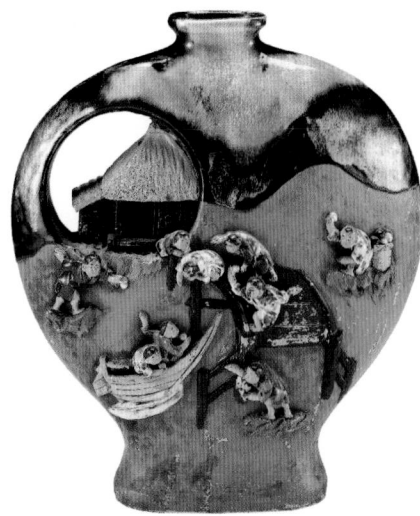

A large early 20thC Japanese Sumida Gawa vase, potted to show an openwork hut forming an arched handle, glazed high relief figures to the body, flambé glaze to the mouth and shoulder.

15in (38cm) high

£1,200-1,800 FRE

A large early 20thC Japanese Sumida Gawa vase, the flambé glaze to neck and shoulder, five high relief figures walking a ledge over a ribbed red vase body, with four-character seal.

Taking its name from the Sumida river (gawa meaning river), Toyko, Samida Gawa ware was made for export to the West from the late 19thC. Most pieces are everyday objects such as teapots, vases and mugs, partly glazed in orange-red, blue, brown, black, green, purple, or off-white, and decorated with figures in relief. The factory moved to Yokohama in 1924 and closed c1940.

18in (45.5cm) high

£1,200-1,800   FRE

A large early 20thC Japanese Seto studio blue underglaze vase, of Chinese hu form, two elephant and ring stylised handles, with scrolling leaf motif underglazed to body, with script to base.

18.5in (47cm) high

£2,500-3,500   FRE

A Japanese famille rose ovoid vase, with a turned wood cover, the body painted with butterflies amidst a multitude of flowers.

c1900   11.75in (30cm) high

£150-250   WW

A pair of early 20thC Noritake porcelain vases, gilded rims, painted en grisaille and sparse colours, both indistinctly signed, possibly 'S Takawayti' both with green printed 'Noritake' and circular rebus.

9.75in (24.5cm) high

£500-700   TEN

A 19thC Japanese blue and white bottle, decorated with three roundels of the Three Friends, on a ground of stylised aquatic plants, the base with an incised crane mon.

15.5in (39.5cm) high

£150-250   WW

An 18thC Japanese blue painted ewer, with white metal domed cover and mounts, decorated with impressionistic figures in a landscape and stylised flower and foliage.

9in (23cm) high

£2,500-3,500   L&T

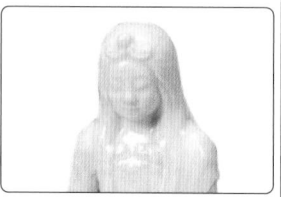

A 19thC Japanese Hirado ware porcelain figure of Manjushri, seated on the back of a lion.

5.5in (14cm) long

£150-200   SK

A rare 14th-16thC Japanese Majapahit Kingdom pottery piggy bank, with a small coin slot to his back, the surface burnt to a reddish black, with old firing faults.

11.5in (29cm) wide

£2,500-3,500   WW

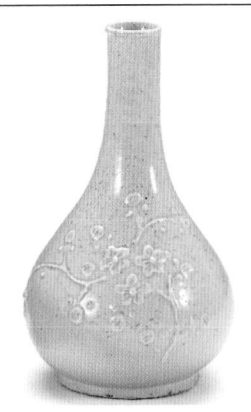

A Korean Choson period white/light green glazed and applied vase, incised swirl to base, sand deposit to base, applied to body with incised floral sprays in reverse.

10.5in (26.5cm) high

£1,200-1,800   FRE

A 19thC Korean pottery water dropper, in the form of a peach, potted with applied leaves and branch as base.

6in (15cm) high

£1,500-2,000   FRE

A large 18th/19thC Korean porcelain globular vase, freely painted in underglaze blue with flowering branches and a bat beneath a stylised scroll border to the shoulders.

6.25in (16cm) high

£4,500-5,500   TEN

THAI CERAMICS

A 13th/14thC Thai incised celadon bowl, the U-shaped thinly potted bowl with incised rings to rim and four petal lotus to interior, raised on a short circular foot.

10in (25.5cm) diam

£1,000-1,500   FRE

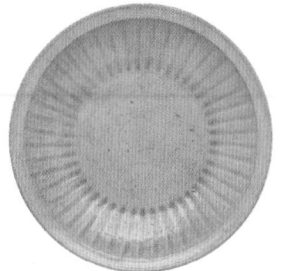

A 14th/15thC Thai or Khmer celadon glazed dish, fluted rim, raised on a small unglazed foot.

14in (35.5cm) wide

£2,000-3,000   FRE

A 15thC Thai Sawankaloke celadon stem bowl, decorated with a wide band of crosshatch motif.

7in (18cm) high

£250-350   FRE

A 14th/15thC Sawankaloke celadon covered jar, the slightly domed cover is surmounted by a triangular finial, the body decorated with cross-hatching and circular bands.

8.5in (21.5cm) high

£350-450   FRE

A 15thC Thai Sawankaloke blue and white kendi, an open lip over a slender neck leading to a globular body with a wide spout, decorated in scrolls and reverse panels of flowerheads and animals.

7in (18cm) high

£200-300   FRE

A 15thC Thai partially brown glazed stoneware jar, domed shoulders applied to with S-shaped stylized handles in reverse leading to a tapering and ring incised body, on an unglazed foot.

13in (33cm) high

£500-1,000   FRE

A 15thC Thai Sawankaloke iron-brown glazed urn, with four applied lug handles to the shoulder, finely incised with bands and wave-like patterns.

17in (43cm) high

£700-1,000   FRE

ORIENTAL

A large 19thC Middle Eastern pottery vase, painted and incised marks to base, glaze chips.

17in (43cm) high

£250-350   **WW**

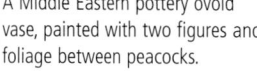

A Middle Eastern pottery ovoid vase, painted with two figures and foliage between peacocks.

c1900   *10.5in (27cm) high*

£100-200   **WW**

A 19thC Persian hexagonal tile, the green ground with a hunt scene depicting a mounted swordsman and a lion.

£250-350   **SK**

A 19thC Syrian Iznik style stoneware jar, with a floral design in blue, red and green on a white ground, repairs.

10in (25.5cm) diam

£650-850   **SK**

A Channakale seated model of a camel, decorated with a yellow and green glaze.

c1900   *5.5in (14cm) high*

£650-850   **WW**

An 18thC Kutahya (west Anatolia) pottery beaker, painted with four large leaf and flower motifs and bordered by leaves, with small rim chips.

3.25in (8.5cm) high

£350-450   **WW**

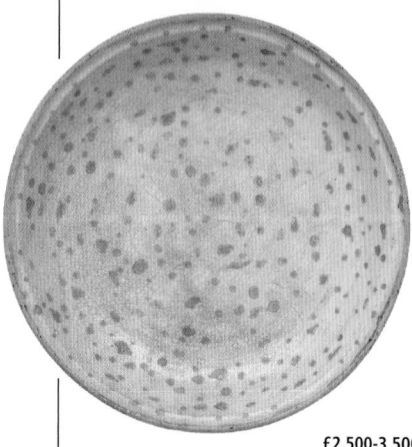

A rare 15thC Vietnamese glazed dish, of slight U-shape hollow form raised on a small circular foot, decorated with scattered green splashes and painted lotus petals to the underside and finely incised.

14in (35.5cm) diam

£2,500-3,500   **FRE**

An unusual Iznik style ewer, the two central panels decorated with a figure and a pavilion within foliate decoration, raised with bubbled gold glaze, engraved gilded European hinge mouth.

14.25in (36cm) high

£2,000-3,000   **GORL**

A probably 17thC Chinese cloisonné hookah base, decorated with flowerheads and scrolling foliage, damaged and repaired.

6.25in (16cm) high

£1,000-1,500   WW

`A Chinese Qianlong period cloisonné enamel and gilt-bronze mounted 'lotus' vase, enamelled to show Indian lotus and scrolling leaves on a green ground, mounted coiled qilong to shoulder and neck, drilled to base.

11.5in (29cm) high

£2,000-3,000   FRE

CLOSER LOOK – A QIANLONG CLOISONNÉ EWER

The cloisonné technique dates back to 1400BC. To create the design, thin strips of metal were soldered on to the surface to form individual cells. These were filled with powdered enamel and then fired in a kiln.

It is rare to find ewers made in cloisonné enamel and even rarer to find an imperial reign mark indicating that the ewer was made for the Palace.

This ewer was probably made as a wedding gift for the Emperor and Empress. The spout in the form of a phoenix head and the dragon tail decoration represent good fortune and blessings, while the two facing dragons on the swing handle symbolize a happy reunion (xi xiangfeng). The swing handle is also decorated with 'wish-granting' clouds (ruyiyun), which symbolize the granting of all wishes.

Only one other similar ewer, possibly the pair to this, is recorded, in the National Palace Museum, Taipei. The two ewers follow the design of an earlier type of Ming ewer. Qing craftsmen adapted earlier models by adding their own design elements to create vessels that were contemporary and individual.

A rare Chinese Qianlong period cloisonné enamel ewer and cover, with gilt-bronze spout and handle, decorated with a wide band of Indian lotus strapwork on a turquoise ground, below a band of gilt-bronze lappets to the shoulder, with Qianlong mark.

12.5in (31.5cm) high

£120,000-180,000   SOTH

A Qianlong period cloisonné enamel 'Squirrel and Grapevine' brushpot, decorated with squirrels climbing on leafy grape vines, all supported on four ruyi-shaped feet.

6.25in (15.5cm) high

£10,000-15,000   SOTH

An 18thC Chinese cloisonné gu-shaped vase, decorated in bright polychrome enamels with geometric motifs and lotus scrolls, the foot incised with a dot motif, some rubbing to the gilding.

6.75in (17cm) high

£2,500-3,500   WW

A large 18thC Chinese cloisonné covered vase, the gilt-metal finial with Indian lotus flowers and scrolling leaves, decorated overall with lotus flowers, Fu bats and antiques on a blue ground.

17in (43cm) high

£4,000-5,000   FRE

A large pair of 19thC Chinese cloisonné and gilt-metal wine buckets, incised band to rim, the body enamelled with flowers bisected by gilt-metal vertical struts, bound by bands of ribbon rings.

8.25in (21cm) high

£8,000-10,000   FRE

A 19thC Chinese cloisonné enamel gilt-metal mounted jardinière, enamelled to show a ruyi cloud band and foliage over a blue and gilt wire Greek-key ground, with slate and gilt-metal mounts.

12in (30.5cm) wide

£3,000-4,000   FRE

A large 19thC Chinese gilt-metal and tripod cloisonné enamel censer, the rim issuing coiled qilong, over a gilt wire enamelled body of Indian lotus and scrolling leaves, raised on three feet.

11in (28cm) wide

£1,500-2,000   FRE

A pair of late 19thC Chinese cloisonné dragon ewers, the handles formed as dragons, the bodies worked as three sky dragons pursuing a cosmic pearl, on a short circular feet.

12.25in (31cm) high

£1,000-1,500   TEN

A Chinese Qing Dynasty cloisonné enamel and gilt-metal jardinière, decorated with Indian lotus and scrolls worked in gilt wire, applied with dragon forms and raised on gilded bracket feet.

9.5in (24cm) high

£1,200-1,800   FRE

A 20thC Chinese cloisonné basket and cover, with bright enamels, the lid reticulated, the handle engraved with a scrolling flower motif.

6in (15.5cm) wide

£1,000-1,500   WW

A large 19thC Chinese cloisonné and gilt-metal enamel charger, rim enamelled with Indian lotus, gilt and Roman-key band, Lingzhi band and foliate scrolls, underside well with butterflies and floral sprigs.

15in (38cm) diam

£2,500-3,500   FRE

A large pair of 20thC Chinese cloisonné, jadeite and copper lanterns, surmounted with enamelled finial, over a pagoda-like yellow and jadeite section, covering an openwork lantern, on a twin-handled enamelled base, with wooden stand.

113in (287cm) high

£60,000-80,000   FRE

A 17thC Chinese bronze censer, made for the Islamic market, carved with three panels of Arabic calligraphy divided by stylized lotus, all raised on three feet, with four-character mark.

2.75in (11cm) wide

£2,000-3,000   WW

A Chinese Qianlong period bronze tripod censer, cast with a key fret band, the base with a four-character mark, Yu Tang He Wan.

6in (15.5cm) wide

£700-800   WW

A large probably 18thC Chinese bronze incense burner and cover, in the form of a double finger citron, seal mark to base, traces of gilding.

19.25in (49cm) wide

£900-1,200   WW

A rare Chinese Qianlong/Jiaqing period gilt-metal, white metal, enamelled and carved shell mechanical 'lotus' vases, comprising twelve gilt-metal and filigree lotus petals, each hinged and opening to reveal a recess, operated by three mechanical brackets to base, over a carved shell and gilt-metal and enamelled base.

8in (20.5cm) high

£2,500-3,500 **FRE**

A 17thC Chinese gilt-bronze circular box and cover, made for the Islamic market, the top with the Arabic inscription 'Alhamduli Allah' meaning 'Praise God', within a scrolling foliate border.

4.25in (10.5cm) diam

£1,200-1,800 **WW**

An unusual Chinese probably Kangxi period paktong and enamel gu-shaped vase, elaborately decorated with panels of figures, cranes, bats, fruit and calligraphy, the borders with key fret bands.

10.75in (27.5cm) high

£700-1,000 **WW**

A Chinese gold shoe, 'The Nanking Cargo', with five stamped marks.

Originally owned by a diver from the crew who found the Nanking Cargo on the Admiral Stellingwerf reef, one hundred miles from Singapore, in 1985. The vendor was part of the team that discovered and salvaged both the cargoes of porcelain from the Chinese junk known as the 'Hatcher Collection' (Ming) and the 'Nanking Cargo', which included 167 gold bars and Nanking Shoes. The cargo came from the wreck of the 'Geldermalsen', which sank in South China Seas in 1752 on its way to the Netherlands. Research into the sinking had informed the team that there was a box of gold on board in the captain's cabin but they searched this area of the wreck without success. According to a report made in old Dutch, the ship's captain ordered the box to be taken to the companion way, so after reconsideration, the gangway was checked (which was situated on the deck over the ship's kitchen and gallery and had a brick chimney) and the divers began to find bars amongst the bricks of the gallery. The vendor describes one of the most memorable moments of his life, 'for, while digging in the black silty bottom mud with my gloved hand I suddenly came across a small heavy object, which when brought into the light was completely black, but when I wiped it with my glove became gleaming gold!'

c1750 *3.25in (8cm) wide 13oz (372g)*

£10,000-15,000 **TEN**

A Chinese probably Ming-period gilt-bronze figure of a Puxian, seated on an elephant holding a book in her left hand.

8.75in (22cm) high

£4,500-5,500 **DUK**

A large 19thC Chinese bronze bell, the loop cast as a twin headed mythical beast.

23.5in (60cm) high

£300-400 **WW**

A Chinese silver-inlaid bronze figure of a Guanyin, in a seated position, with a silver dot to the forehead, the robe inlaid with geometric design, two-character mark, lacking hand and hairpin.

8.25in (21cm) high

£2,000-3,000 **L&T**

ORIENTAL

An early 20thC Chinese silver tea kettle on stand with burner, by Wang Hing, with applied and engraved foliate decoration and faux bamboo handle, the stand with faux bamboo supports.

11in (28cm) high 39oz (1,106g)

£700-1,000   **GORL**

A large 19thC Chinese silver jewellery box, hand beaten, chased and repoussé decorated, interior fitted with a velvet-lined removable insert, locking mechanism and lobed carrying handle.

13in (33cm) wide

£1,200-1,800   **JA**

An early 20thC Chinese silver coloured metal four-piece tea service, Luen Hing, Shanghai, chased and engraved with bamboo fronds, stamped marks.

11.75in (30cm) high Total 65.75oz (1,864g)

£1,000-1,500   **DN**

A Chinese export silver vase, by Wang Hing & Co., Hong Kong, the undulating rim with cherry blossoms, the body and foot decorated with dragons.

The West imported Chinese silver from the late 18thC-early 20thC, but the silver export trade was never as large as that for Chinese porcelain. One of the best-known silver export craftsmen was Wang Hing, who worked in Hong Kong between 1880 and 1910, and also had an outlet in Canton. Like many craftsman he used Western letters – 'WH' or 'Wang Hing' – to mark his pieces. The number '90' often appears alongside his mark to indicate the grade of silver – not quite sterling quality. His output included a range of items, from tea sets to trophies.

c1900   *9in (23cm) high*

£3,500-4,500   **FRE**

CHINESE ENAMEL

A pair of 18thC Chinese Canton enamel saucer dishes, each depicting a domestic courtyard scene, the exterior with a border of flowers to the base.

6.25in (16cm) diam

£2,500-3,500   **L&T**

An 18thC Chinese Canton enamel box, with gilt-metal mounts, decorated with figure and birds within a reeded waterscape on a puce ground.

3.25in (8.5cm) wide

£1,500-2,000   **L&T**

An 18thC Chinese Canton enamel box, cover with repoussé enamel, border with foliate rim on yellow ground with a figural scene, and chased figures in relief to the sides.

4.25in (11cm) wide

£2,000-3,000   **L&T**

Plique à jour, from the French 'open to light' is a technique where translucent enamels are set within cells in a metal mould, rather like a stained glass window. Once the backing material has been removed it is the metal strips that hold the enamels together, unlike the technique of cloisonné, where the enamel is applied to the supporting surface.

A Chinese plique à jour stem cup, decorated with birds above peony bamboo and prunus.

4in (10cm) high

£300-400   **WW**

A Shibayama vase, the gold lacquer body inset with mother-of-pearl, stained ivory and tortoiseshell, the mouth with bronze mounts and the whole resting on bronze dragon feet, one flower reset.

c1880 *9in (17.5cm) high*

£2,500-3,500 **SWO**

A large 19thC Japanese Qing Dynasty bronze jardinière, of baluster form, decorated with panels of birds in relief, surmounted by applied elephant heads, floral ground.

14.5in (37cm) high

£700-1,000 **JA**

A pair of Japanese Meiji period bronze Bactrian camels, dark brown patina, each raised on a naturalistic carved hardwood base, character marks to the underside of each.

Camel 7in (18cm) high

£3,000-4,000 **FRE**

A Japanese Meiji period bronze figure group of a boy and water buffalo, attributed to Genryusai Seiya, cast seal mark on the belly of buffalo.

19.5in (49.5cm) wide

£1,500-2,500 **TEN**

A pair of Japanese Meiji period bronze models of doves, their plumage finely detailed, each signed beneath the breast and raised on a root wood stand.

12.25in (31cm) wide

£2,000-3,000 **WW**

A late 19thC Japanese Shibayama pheasant, naturalistically modelled in carved ivory and mother-of-pearl, the legs of bronze, signed Tomoyuki on a reserve.

Shibayama is the technique of semiprecious shell inlay on lacquer and ivory pieces. It is named after the Japanese town of Shibayama, Sanbu District, where it originated.

8.75in (22cm) wide

£2,500-3,500 **SWO**

A Japanese white metal crane, naturalistically modelled and standing on a carved hardwood stand.

14.5in (37cm) high

£1,200-1,800 **L&T**

A Japanese bronze figure modelled as an elephant fighting two tigers, with dark brown patination and ivory tusks, signed, raised on oval wood base.

14in (35.5cm) wide

£450-550 **HT**

A 19thC Japanese Meiji period iron lantern, surmounted by an egret above a stylised lotus leaf, over a pierced barrel and double lotus leaf column, over a fret-carved base.

78in (198cm) high

£8,000-10,000 **FRE**

A Japanese Meiji period musen enamel vase, decorated with carp rising from cloudy waters, the rim and foot with silver-plated mounts.

9.5in (24cm) high

£350-450 **WW**

ORIENTAL

A probably 14th/15thC Sino-Shan bronze two-frog drum, from Laos, of typical cylindrical form, decorated with four pairs of mating frogs, with a later hardwood stand.

Most of these drums originate from the Kha people living in the hills and mountains of northern Laos, east of Ban Houie Sai and west of Luang Prabang. These drums, commonly known as Kha drums in Laos, are related to the idea of fertility and are decorated with bronze frogs, symbols of water and rain, around the top. The sound of the drum, when suspended by its handle, is likened to the roar of thunder or bellowing of a bullfrog, a harbinger of rain.

23.25in (59cm) diam

£1,800-2,200   L&T

A large 18th/19thC bronze Shan drum, with a ten-point star to the centre flanked by radiating conforming circles terminating in four applied animal groupings.

18in (45.5cm) high

£3,500-4,500   FRE

A large 18th/19thC Khmer bronze offering bowl, the cover moulded with an openwork flared circular handle, covering a U-shaped base.

10in (25.5cm) high

£500-700   FRE

A 19thC South East Asian silver coloured metal bowl, embossed with vignettes of rural figures, above the 12 signs of the Zodiac, raised on a moulded foot.

7.5in (19cm) high

£350-450   WW

A 19thC Islamic brass ewer, modelled as a cockerel, incised with floral patterns, with a hinged lid and raised on a round base.

9.5in (24cm) wide

£450-550   WW

CHINESE IVORY

A Chinese stained ivory group of a cricket, sitting on a cabbage leaf, stained in naturalistic colours, with red berries to one end.

6.25in (16cm) wide

£2,000-3,000   L&T

A set of early 20thC Chinese ivory Immortals, each carved with his or her attributes, with black highlighted areas, and raised on a stepped square base.

9in (23cm) high

£5,000-6,000   L&T

CLOSER LOOK – CHINESE IVORY FIGURES

The size of these is appealing to a variety of collectors: big enough to impress, without being showy. These single-piece models are well carved in a convex form that reflects the natural contour of the elephant tusk. The stands are also of high quality.

The good, consistent ivory patina is a testament to the piece's age. Earlier pieces tend to have a darker, more burnished patina (often cracked), whilst later pieces may be too light to show off the details and dimension of a well-carved piece.

There are eight legendary immortals in the Taoist tradition, which embody its ideals and are among the most desirable subjects in carved Chinese art. The immortals were often depicted in a whimsical manner, appealing to buyers wishing to avoid more severe religious subjects.

A pair of large 19thC Chinese Immortals, carved in high and low relief to show elongated eyebrows and openwork staff, stained, silver inlaid and enamelled stands.

15.25in (39cm) high

£12,000-18,000   FRE

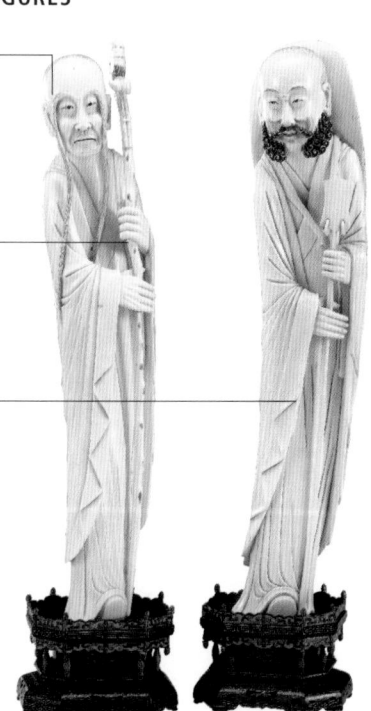

A set of eight late 19th/early 20thC Chinese ivory Immortals, each carved in a standing pose with their attribute, with stained highlights, on a pierced stained wood stand.

The eight Immortals were revered by Daoists and are believed to be figures of prosperity and longevity. They represented eight factors in Chinese daily life: men and women, old and young, rich and poor, noble and lowly. The stories of the eight Immortals were traditionally very popular; temples were dedicated to them, and they are frequently represented in Chinese art.

6in (15.5cm) high

£2,500-3,500   L&T

A Chinese carved elephant tusk figure of Guanyin, the elegant goddess with elaborate chignon supporting a diminutive figure of Buddha, a phoenix bird at her side, the base with character marks.

c1930   *22.5in (57cm) high*

£2,500-3,500   TEN

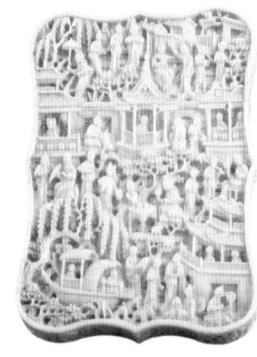

A 19thC Cantonese carved ivory serpentine card case, decorated with figures and pavilions.

£900-1,200   GORL

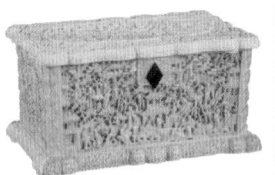

A 19thC carved Cantonese ivory casket, carved with a central view of figures in pavilions with phoenix carved spandrels, the lid now detached.

6.5in (16.5cm) wide

£2,000-3,000   GORL

A 19thC Chinese ivory veneered tea chest, decorated with reticulated panels carved with flowers and geometric designs, raised on four turned feet, damage.

9.5in (24cm) wide

£700-1,000   WW

CLOSER LOOK – CHINESE IVORY WRIST RESTS

There is a long history of ivory-carving in China, with examples found in tombs dating from the Shang Dynasty (18th-12thC BC).

It is unusual to find a pair of ivory wrist rests with complementary themes, such as the matching daytime and night-time representations of a landscape seen here.

These wrist rests represent the best of the 19thC ivory pieces and feature great depth of carving: the figures stand proud and there is delicacte pierced work: through a window, we can see that there is a man who has fallen asleep at his desk.

A pair of mid-19thC Chinese carved ivory wrist rests, each representing Day and Night, worked with scenes of scholars, on wood stands.

14.5in (36.5cm) long

£9,000-12,000   TEN

A 19thC Chinese Canton carved ivory brushpot, delicately decorated with figures, the foot reticulated with flowers and leaf scrolls.

5.25in (13.5cm) high

£1,200-1,800   WW

A Chinese export carved ivory ball on stand, pierced outer sphere in high relief, inner spheres with pierced motifs.

c1890   *13.5in (34.5cm) high*

£1,200-1,800   TEN

ORIENTAL

A Japanese Meiji period carved ivory figure group, of a mother standing wearing a decorative kimono with children, incised three-character mark.

4.25in (10.5cm) high

£2,000-3,000   TEN

A large Japanese Meiji period Tokyo school carved ivory figure, of an elderly man standing with a basket of fruit over his arm, on a naturalistic base, signed.

12.25in (31cm) high

£5,000-7,000   L&T

A Japanese Meiji period ivory of two Pekinese puppies, playing with roses, with two character signature.

6.25in (16cm) wide

£1,000-1,500   WW

A Japanese Meiji period ivory carving of a man, unsheathing a katana, three-character signature, wooden stand, small chip.

4.75in (12cm) high

£2,500-3,500   WW

A Japanese Meiji period ivory carving of a man, holding a processional banner, with a matched wood stand, minor damage and the signature lacking from the base.

12in (30.5cm) high

£1,000-1,500   WW

A Japanese carved ivory group of a fisherman and little boy, on a rustic plinth with sea rocks and shells, two-character mark incised onto inset red kakihan.

c1910   6in (15cm) high

£1,000-1,500   TEN

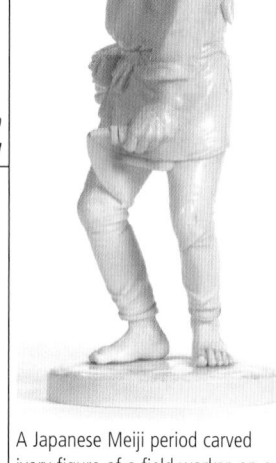

A Japanese Meiji period carved ivory figure of a field worker, on a shaped oval plinth, engraved two-character mark and stylised seal mark on the base.

9.75in (25cm) high

£700-1,200   TEN

A large Japanese one piece carved ivory figure of a maiden, dressed in foliate kimono, and holding a shamisen in her right hand, with two-character engraved mark.

c1930   19in (48.5cm) high

£700-1,000   TEN

A Japanese Meiji period turned ivory, gilt and shibayama decorated vase, with mother-of-pearl side handles as dragons, the base inset with mother-of-pearl kakihan, incised two-character mark, with palm wood stand.

Overall 6.75in (17.5cm) high

£1,200-1,800   **TEN**

CLOSER LOOK – JAPANESE IVORY

Japanese brush pots are rarer than examples from China, where the brush pot is known as one of the "four treasures of the scholar".

The height and lid are typically Japanese features. Much of the piece's appeal is in its successful combination of the Japanese and Chinese styles.

The carving depicts 16 Buddhist rakan – pious ascetics witness to the ascension of the Buddha Sakyamuni – standing under palms and dragons flying overhead. This Buddhist iconography is more reminiscent of Chinese art than typical Meiji carvings.

A large late 19thC Japanese elephant ivory covered brushpot, carved in high and low relief, raised on a scrolling reticulated base.

12in (30.5cm) high

£5,000-6,000   **FRE**

A Japanese Meiji period shibayama card case, decorated with quail beneath chrysanthemum, flowers and insects, the reverse with cranes beneath bamboo.

4.5in (11.5cm) long

£2,000-3,000   **TEN**

A large late 19thC Japanese elephant ivory bird study, carved single section, openwork to tail feathers, insert eyes, with metal legs and feathers.

7in (18cm) long

£4,500-5,500   **FRE**

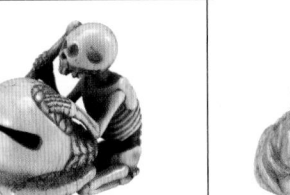

A 19thC Japanese Tomochika signed netsuke, modelled a skeleton beating a drum.

Netsuke are decorative 'toggles'.

1.5in (4cm) high

£300-400   **FRE**

An early 19thC Japanese shi shi study, modelled seated with pup, front paws resting over a ball, with period patina.

1.75in (4.5cm) long

£2,000-3,000   **FRE**

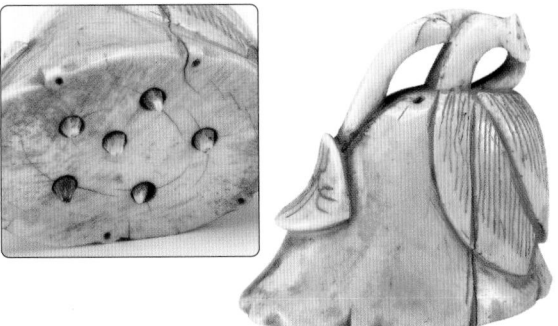

A late 19thC Japanese ivory lotus pod reticulated study, open stem to crown issuing from a stylised hanging pod carved in low relief to show eaves, the underside reveals six reticulated seeds.

2in (5cm) high

£300-400   **FRE**

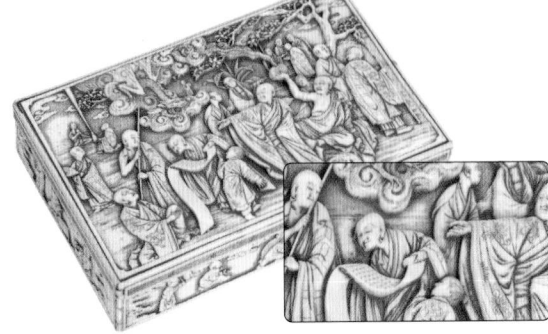

A Japanese Meiji period relief carved ivory box, the pull-off lid worked in high relief with nineteen monks, with Buddhistic entities and attendants in a wooded landscape.

72.5in (18.5cm) wide

£1,500-2,000   **TEN**

A Chinese Song Dynasty rhinoceros horn libation cup, the tip of a dark brown to black hue leading to a light and golden brown to the mouth.

3.25in (8cm) high

£20,000-25,000　　**FRE**

CLOSER LOOK – JAPANESE RHINOCEROS HORN LIBATION CUP

Rhinoceros horn is the most highly treasured and scarce of all organic Asian art materials. Libation horns of such a scale fetch extremely high prices.

Rhino horn, like ivory, grows more attractive with age. This has aged to a beautiful golden hue and is masterfully carved.

Artificially aged horn, buffalo horn passed off as rhino, and old pieces of horn newly carved have recently appeared on the market, but the strong provenance of this piece was able to prove it was genuine.

The elaborate hardwood stand adds substantial value to the horn.

A large 19thC Chinese carved rhinoceros horn libation cup, over an ebonised carved stand.

25in (60cm) high overall

£30,000-40,000　　**FRE**

A 19thC Japanese antler ruyi sceptre, carved to show two lingzhi heads, issuing from a naturally shaped antler handle, artist's seal.

12in (30.5cm) long

£1,500-2,000　　**FRE**

A set of three 19thC Japanese Kiseruzutsu, including naturalistically carved stag horn case in the form of a branch, a well-patinated wood case and a carved bone double-ended case.

A kiseruzutsu is a Japanese tobacco pipe case.

£350-450

Longest 8in (20.5cm) long

FRE

An early 20thC Chinese horn box, carved in detail with animals and birds, the hinged lid with a bat and two dragons, the reverse with a belt clasp shaped as a cicada.

3in (7.5cm) high

£200-300　　**WW**

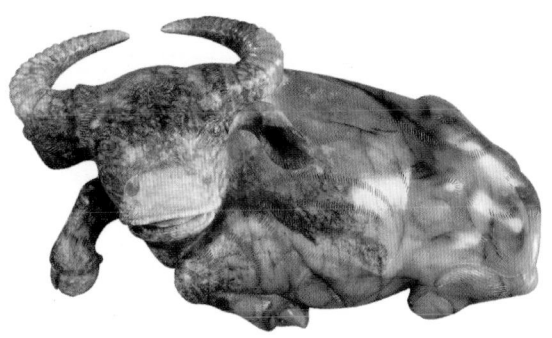

A Ming period jade water buffalo, the reclining figure in celadon green stone with black markings and tan areas.

11.5in (29cm) wide

£25,000-35,000

SK

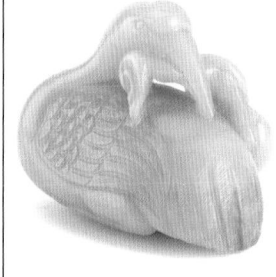

A 17thC Chinese jade bi disc, carved in relief with two mythical creatures.

3.5in (9cm) diam

£250-350

WW

An 18thC Chinese jade crane, naturalistically modelled with its head turned over its back, holding a branch of fruit in its mouth.

2.25in (5.5cm) wide

£1,500-2,000

L&T

An 18th/19thC Chinese white jade pendant, carved on each side with an archaic chilong dragon.

1.75in (4.5cm) long

£900-1,200

WW

A 19thC Chinese pale celadon jade belthook, carved with a bifid dragon.

4.75in (12cm) long

£100-200

WW

A 19th/20thC Chinese celadon jade duck, turning his head round, holding a lotus pod and leaf in its beak.

2in (5cm) wide

£250-350

WW

A Chinese spinach jade model of cicada, with protruding eyes.

2.25in (5.5cm) high

£400-500

WW

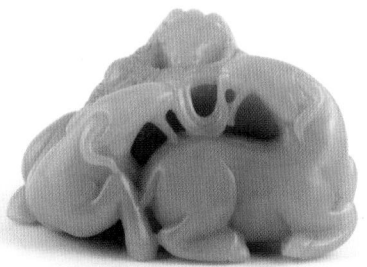

A Chinese jade carving of three goats, all holding ruyi scrolls in their mouths with a central yin yang roundel, symbolising prosperity in the New Year.

4in (10cm) wide

£250-350

WW

A small white jade dish, formed as a lotus leaf upon which a small frog crouches.

2.5in (6.5cm) wide

£250-350

WW

A Chinese celadon jade carving of two lion dogs, probably a mother and pup, with long coats on their backs.

2.5in (6.5cm) wide

£200-300

WW

An unusual Chinese Qing Dynasty tortoiseshell pewter and yingmu artemisia leaf-form box, the pewter-bound tortoiseshell cover reveals a pewter-lined interior, the outer wall of yingmu, on a pewter base.

9in (23cm) long

£650-850   FRE

A Chinese Qing Dynasty Daoist coconut and coral applied libation cup, the dark coffee-brown shell enhanced and applied with two circular coral eyes to resemble a beetle.

7in (17.5cm) long

£700-1,000   FRE

A rare Chinese Qing Dynasty whalebone brushpot, of plain cylindrical form, comprised of a single, well-hollowed bone of a light smooth porous texture.

5in (12.5cm) high

£300-400   FRE

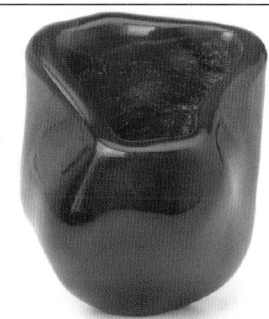

A rare 18thC Burmese hollowed amber wine cup, of waisted and bulbous cylindrical form, hollowed from a single section of rich orange-brown amber, inset circular base.

2in (5cm) high

£300-400   FRE

HARDSTONE & SOAPSTONE

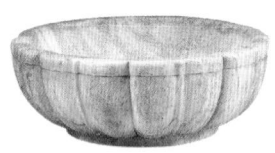

A pair of monumental Chinese Ming Dynasty marble basins, of foliate petal form, incised ribbed petals to interior and outer wall, fine grey vein throughout.

28in (71cm) diam

£18,000-22,000   FRE

An unusual Chinese Qing Dynasty malachite mottled green and blue russet brush rest, of mountainous form with several worked brush troughs, over a dark hardwood stand.

3in (7.5cm) high

£1,500-2,000   FRE

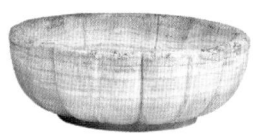

A Chinese Qing Dynasty pudding stone lotus brush wash, with scalloped edge, purple colour to ivory stone and ground pattern, with white incision to base.

13in (33cm) wide

£650-850   FRE

A 17thC Chinese rock crystal brush rest with carved zitan base, of undulating mountainous form, carved with riverlet body fitted over a finely carved openwork zitan stand.

3.5in (9cm) long

£1,000-1,500   FRE

A rare Chinese Ming Dynasty or earlier burial ruyi sceptre of Shandong limestone, the lingzhi head foliate-shaped, the central medallion inscribed with a character for longevity banded by freely carved Fu bats, a second medallion to the stem centre worked to show a blossoming lotus within a diaper band, terminating bat medallion.

£700-1,000   FRE

A Chinese Qing Dynasty rock crystal and coral rosary bracelet, with a silk cord joining a green glass medallion and two purple semi-precious stone and yellow metal filigree lustres.

£1,200-1,800   FRE

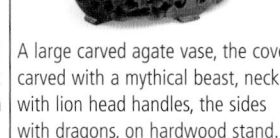

A large carved agate vase, the cover carved with a mythical beast, neck with lion head handles, the sides with dragons, on hardwood stand.

10.5in (27cm) high

£600-800   L&T

A 19thC Chinese soapstone carving of Shoulao, standing, holding the peach of immortality.

8.25in (21cm) high

£350-450   WW

A large Japanese wood carving of Gama Sennin, the god stands contemplating his toad, holding a gnarled staff, the base with three lines of calligraphy, with minor repairs.

Gama Sennin is a benign Japanese sage who is always accompanied by a toad and can assume the shape of a snake or change his skin and become young again. He possesses the secret of immortality.

23.5in (60cm) high

£700-1,000   WW

A Japanese Edo period boxwood okimono of a pup with ball, with detail to face, ball and underside, of coiled form.

1.5in (4cm) high

£300-400   FRE

An early 18thC Chinese Qing dynasty bamboo brushpot, main frieze relief-carved in high relief with peonies, bracketed foot rim.

6.5in (16.5cm) high

£550-750   TEN

A 19thC Japanese bamboo lacquered box, split bamboo to the exterior, the interior lacquered red and black over cloth.

10in (25.5cm) wide

£300-400   FRE

A Japanese hanakoga basket, of finely woven split bamboo construction, the body of open latticework, insert single section bamboo stand, base signed 'Chikuunsai Kore Wo Tsukuru'.

24in (61cm) high

£1,800-2,200   FRE

A Chinese bamboo brushpot, carved with two cranes standing beside a large pine tree, the reverse with ruyi fungus and bamboo.

5.5in (14cm) high

£200-300   WW

CLOSER LOOK – BAMBOO CARVING

Figures of the demon queller Zhong Kui are placed at the door to banish evil spirits in the Dragon Boat Festival.

According to legend, he was an 8thC scholar who achieved top marks in the Civil Service examinations but his disfigured face repulsed the emperor and his honours were stripped. The emperor later gave him the title of Demon Queller after Zhong Kui dispelled ghosts from his nightmare.

This group was carved by the skilled sculptor Zhu Zhizheng (alias San Song) of Jiading, Jiangsu province. He is believed to have been active during the reigns of Tianqi (1620-27) and Chongzhen (1627-44). The Zhu family founded the Jiading school of bamboo, which flourished until the 18thC.

A 17thC bamboo carving of Zhong Kui, carved with fine detail, a small attendant demon on his back and a seated demon below, signed 'San Song' with an inscription translated as 'The ears have good news'.

6in (15.5cm) high

£100,000-150,000   SOT

A Chinese bamboo brushwasher, carved with prunus blossom.

4in (10cm) high

£300-400   WW

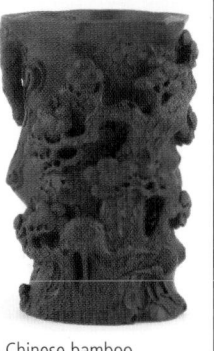

ORIENTAL

A rare Chinese Qianlong period cinnabar lacquered yixing teapot, carved in high relief lotus scrolls overall, with two medallions of boys at play to body, petal band base, all on yixing pottery base and cover.

8.5in (21.5cm) wide

£3,000-4,000　　　　　　　　　　FRE

A Chinese Qianlong period carved cinnabar lacquer-covered box, domed cover, wide foliate rimmed base, carved in medium relief to show foliate profusion, incised under rim, missing finial.

6in (15cm) high

£1,500-2,000　　　　　　　　　FRE

A 19thC Chinese red cinnabar lacquer dish, moulded and carved with four figures in a garden, the border with flowers and scrolling foliage, a few small losses.

8.75in (22.5cm) diam

£400-500　　　　　　　　　　　WW

A pair of 19thC Chinese lacquer peach-shaped boxes, both carved with a Daoist Immortal in a landscape, with fruit borders, damages, with wood stands.

5.5in (14cm) high

£600-800　　　　　　　　　　WW

CLOSER LOOK – LACQUER COVERED CENSER

Censers are important objects in Chinese culture, and hearken back to the country's earliest bronze-age civilizations, when metalworkers crafted elaborate vessels for the ritual burning of incense. In the 20thC, the censer was adopted as a symbol of integrity.

This censer was probably made during the reign of the Qianlong Emperor (1736-95), when several traditional Chinese art forms reached the pinnacle of refinement.

Like the more heralded jade and porcelain of the same period, 18thC cinnabar lacquer is still celebrated for its peerless delicacy and splendour.

The geometric ground is tightly carved and precise and the raised scroll and mask-and-claw legs curve and flow elegantly.

A 17thC Chinese mother-of-pearl and lacquer, lac burgate five tier octagonal box, of foliate form, with detailed inlay on black lacquer, raised on a foliate base.

9.5in (24cm) high

£4,500-5,500　　　　　　　　FRE

An 18thC Imperial Chinese carved cinnabar lacquer covered censer, surmounted with a coral handle, the cover and base carved in medium relief, opening to reveal original gilt-metal bowl.

5.5in (14cm) wide

£8,000-12,000　　　　　　　　　　　　　　FRE

A Chinese early Qing Dynasty bone inlaid and black lacquer document box, bone panelled cover enclosing a figural landscape, with Buddhistic symbols to side panels, sprigs to base, biaton lock-plate.

13in (33cm) long

£2,500-3,500   FRE

A Chinese export lacquer sewing box, with ogee moulded borders to the hinged lid revealing a fully fitted interior containing ivory and bone implements, the whole decorated with Manchu courtiers against a foliate and trellis ground.

c1820   14.5in (36.5cm) wide

£700-1,000   TEN

An early 19thC Chinese export lacquer tea caddy, decorated in shades of gilt with landscape panels, the interior with two engraved silver coloured metal canisters, on gilt and red-painted dragon feet.

8.75in (22cm) wide

£700-1,000   DUK

A 19thC Chinese export black lacquer and gilt gaming box, painted exterior, the interior fitted with seven covered boxes and two playing card-themed trays.

15in (38cm) wide

£550-750   FRE

A late 19thC Japanese gold and black lacquer writing box, or Suzuribako, and document box, or Ryoshibako, both boxes lacquered gold to a black ground.

Longest 16in (40.5cm) long

£1,200-1,800   FRE

A 20thC Japanese lacquer ashtray, depicting two dunlins, one preening its feathers, the borders with reeds and pink flowers, signed 'Namyki', with minor flakes.

5.25in (13.5cm) wide

£1,200-1,800   WW

An 18thC Chinese lacquered coconut bowl, carved with a landscape and figures, with seven characters and two seals, restored.

4.25in (11cm) diam

£600-800   WW

GLASS

A Chinese Qing Dynasty five colour overlay Imperial yellow covered jar, probably Palace Workshops, Beijing, ribbed blue finial surmounts a cover overlaid with blue lingzhi heads, the base overlaid with five colours, raised on a short blue ring foot.

3.5in (9cm) high

£1,500-2,000   FRE

A pair of Chinese red and white overlay glass shaft and globe vases, each cut in high relief with a pair of song birds and a flowering prunus tree, with rim bands.

c1940   13.75in (35cm) high

£700-1,000   TEN

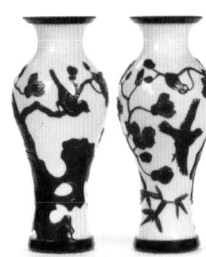

A pair of Chinese 'Pekin' blue overlay glass baluster vases, birds in relief in a blossoming magnolia tree growing from rocks, with solid blue bands to the rim and foot.

c1940   14in (35.5cm) high

£700-1,000   TEN

One of a pair of late 19thC Chinese reverse painted glass pictures of maidens, each depicted within an oval reserve surrounded by flowers and foliage, in stained wood moulded frames.

16in (41cm) wide

£400-500 PAIR   DN

ESSENTIAL REFERENCE – SNUFF BOTTLES

- Snuff-taking was introduced to China from the West probably in the late 17thC. It soon spread from the court throughout the country. The small bottles used for storing powdered medicines were suited to this new substance, with the addition of a stopper of a different material with a spoon hanging from it.
- Produced throughout the 18thC, most snuff bottles date from the Daoguang period (1821-50).
- Most were made from glass. Hardstones were also used, particularly nephrite jade, which was common towards the end of the 18thC. Bottles were also made from porcelain, lacquer, amber, coral or ivory, or adapted from natural objects, such as nuts.
- Decoration such as enamelling and cloisonné were applied. Jade, hardstone, ivory and lacquer bottles were often carved, most in shallow-relief, but deep-relief examples are also known. Carved overlay glass decoration was used from the early 18thC. By the end of the 19thC, the technique of painting inside glass had been perfected.
- Snuff bottles are still produced in China today, where they are mainly sold as tourist items.

A large Chinese chalcedony snuff bottle, of rounded square form with a galloping bannerman in relief, with metal and green jadeite stopper.
1760-1850   *3.25in (8cm) high*
£1,500-2,000   **L&T**

A Chinese jade snuff bottle, of rounded square form, carved with a kylin and pierced rocks, with metal and pink stone stopper.
1800-1850   *2.75in (7cm) high*
£1,000-1,500   **L&T**

A large early 19thC Chinese white jade faceted snuff bottle, of true white hue faceted body, worked in reverse with radiating lotus petals.
2.5in (6.5cm) high
£1,500-2,000   **FRE**

A 19thC Chinese jade snuff bottle, carved from a rounded pebble, two bifid dragons carved beneath the coral stopper.
3.25in (8cm) high
£350-450   **WW**

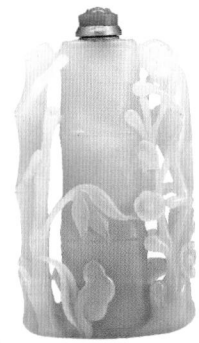

A Chinese white jade snuff bottle, with true white jade tone, low-relief carved to show a cartouche of boys, worked in reverse, jadeite stopper.
2.5in (6.5cm) high
£1,500-2,000   **FRE**

A 19thC Chinese jade snuff bottle, of tapering baluster form, carved with shou characters, between indented bands of lappets.
2.5in (6.5cm) high
£350-450   **WW**

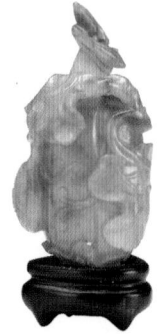

A late 19thC Chinese green and celadon jadeite snuff bottle, of tall melon form, carved in high relief to show lotus and insects, wood stand.
3in (7.5cm) high
£1,800-2,200   **FRE**

A Chinese black and white jade snuff bottle, carved with a cat looking at a flying bird, the reverse with a butterfly above an orchid.
c1900   *3in (7.5cm) high*
£350-450   **WW**

A 19thC white-grey jade snuff bottle, carved in high relief to show a bamboo stem and a monkey, with blossoms and bamboo.
3.5in (9cm) high
£900-1,200   **FRE**

A Chinese Qianlong period famille rose painted white glass snuff bottle, painted with scroll band to neck, and landscape scene in reverse, with Qianlong mark to base, with jadite stopper.

2.5in (6.5cm) high

£2,500-3,500   FRE

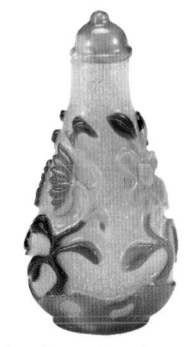

A rare Chinese Qianlong period faceted blue glass snuff bottle, of elongated form, the base with a four-character mark, a tiny flat chip to the rim.

3in (7.5cm) high

£1,500-2,000   WW

A 19thC Chinese five colour overlay snuff bottle, the snow flake bottle of overall pear form, agate stopper.

3in (7.5cm) high

£900-1,200   FRE

A Chinese snuff bottle, the yellow metal moulded and carved as an elephant, a silver coloured metal stopper.

3.25in (8.5cm) high

£550-750   WW

A Chinese chalcedony snuff bottle, of rounded square form, with hehe twins carved in relief, with pink stone stopper.

1780-1850   2.75in (7cm) high

£1,500-2,000   L&T

A Chinese chalcedony snuff bottle, of flattened squat ovoid form, carved with a horse and a monkey on a tree stump, later glass stopper.

1800-1850   2.5in (6.5cm) high

£600-800   L&T

A 19thC Chinese amber snuff bottle, tapering form, carved in high relief with double gourds and leaves, coral stopper, wood stand.

Bottle 3in (7.5cm) high

£900-1,200   FRE

A Chinese jasper ochre snuff bottle, depicting a horse and monkey carved in relief, a peach above, with coral stopper.

1800-1850   3in (7.5cm) high

£1,500-2,000   L&T

A large 19thC Chinese octagonal section famille rose snuff bottle, painted with a seated dignitary and 12 standing figures in a continuous landscape.

4.5in (11.5cm) high

£350-450   WW

A Chinese moulded porcelain snuff bottle, with coral glaze, of globular form, relief-decorated with fish, plants and good luck symbols, with modern porcelain stopper.

1780-1830   3in (7.5cm) high

£500-700   L&T

ORIENTAL

A 19thC huangyangmu boxwood erotic snuff bottle, finely carved in medium relief to show an Immortal embraced by two female attendants, carved in reverse, head removes to reveal hollowed interior.

2.5in (6.5cm) high

£150-250   FRE

A large early 19thC Chinese elephant ivory snuff bottle, the oval cover worked to show an open pagoda, over a tapering body carved in openwork and high relief to show a figural landscape, with wood stand.

4in (10cm) high

£600-800   FRE

A 19thC Chinese coral snuff bottle, blossom carved cover, over reticulated body carved to show four Fu cubs chasing balls, with wood stand.

3in (7.5cm) high

£550-750   FRE

An unusual 19thC Chinese 'dragon' snuff bottle, enamelled stopper, the body worked in gilt wire to show a five-claw yellow dragon, with an oval foot.

2.75in (7cm) high

£1,500-2,000   FRE

A Chinese enamel snuff bottle, of baluster form, enamelled to show a court scene framed by ruyi cloud band, gilt-metal stopper and base, with carved coral stopper.

2.75in (7cm) high

£400-500   FRE

A 19thC Chinese carved ivory snuff bottle, decorated with four figures in a garden amidst rockwork and leafy trees.

3.25in (8cm) high

£150-250   WW

A Tibetan semi-precious stone snuff bottle encrusted with turquoise and coloured stones.

3.25in (8cm) high

£250-350   DN

PAINTINGS

A set of four early 19thC Chinese gouache palace paintings, each depicting figures in front of palace buildings and gates, framed and glazed.

18.75in (48cm) wide

£2,500-3,500   L&T

A rare engraving from the set recording the Emperor Qianlong's military campaign, depicting the battle of Kulonggui, a great Chinese victory against the Hui Muslim tribe in 1755, after a drawing by Jean Damascene, engraved by Jacques Aliamet (1728-1788).

34.75in (88.5cm) wide

£450-550 **WW**

Two from a harlequin set of six Japanese woodblock prints, four depicting courtesans, after Utamaro (1753-1806), another depicting a courtesan, after Eisho (active until 1790), and another depicting ladies in a domestic scene, after Kiyonaga (1752-1815), each mounted in a plain ebonised frame.

15.25in (39cm) high

£1,500-2,000 SET **L&T**

Ginko Adachi (Japanese, active 1874-1897), 'Court Women Studying', colour woodblock, signed 'Adachi Ginko hitsu', oban triptych, framed.
1879

£250-350 **FRE**

Toshihide Migita (Japanese, 1863-1925), 'Fierce Battle at Pyongyang', colour woodblock, signed 'Oju Toshihide' and with artist's seal, oban triptych, framed.
1894

£300-400 **FRE**

Hiroshi Yoshida (Japanese, 1876-1950), 'Fujiyama from Okitsu', from the 'Ten Views of Fuji' series, colour woodblock, 'Yoshida' signature and 'Hiroshi' seal, 'Jizuri' seal, framed.
1928 *15.75in (40cm) wide*

£400-500 **FRE**

PAINTING ON SILK

One of a large pair of 19thC Chinese paintings on silk, depicting Immortals in landscapes, each signed, framed and glazed, one glazing panel cracked.
58in (147cm) high

£400-500 PAIR **WW**

A large 19thC Chinese watercolour on silk, painted with pheasants amidst pierced rockwork, peony and bamboo, framed and glazed.
60.25in (153cm) high

£350-450 **WW**

One of a set of four Chinese paintings on silk, of beautiful young ladies in interiors engaged in domestic pursuits.
c1900 *29.25in (74cm) high*

£900-1,200 SET **WW**

A rare early 20thC Japanese Miyata Shizan (1889-1971) painting on silk, mineral pigments, clam shell gesso and sumi ink, scroll mounted, signed and sealed by Miyata Shizan.
100in (254cm) high

£10,000-15,000 **FRE**

ORIENTAL

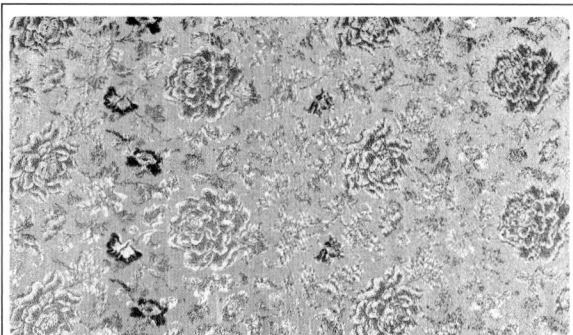

A large late 1830s Chinese bolt of brocaded yellow satin, for the European market, woven with large repeat peonies, scrolling green foliage and peach convolvulus against a brilliant yellow satin ground.

Identical brocaded silk panels cover the walls and upholstery of the Yellow Drawing Room at Chatsworth. The material was purchased by the sixth (Bachelor) Duke and hung at Chatsworth in 1839. In his 1844 handbook he describes the design as Indian, though in fact it is chinoiserie 'More Indian silk, yellow bought at the Custom House at the same time as the red'. The curtains were first of all put up in the Library but then moved to the Dining and Drawing rooms.

518.5in (1317cm) long

£4,000-5,000 KT

A 19thC kesi military front rank badge, woven with a tiger, painted and woven on a gold and black ground, mounted.

The tiger was emblematic of courage and military prowess.

1850-70 *12in (30cm) wide*

£400-500 KT

One of a pair of late 19thC Chinese embroidered hangings, the eau de nil satin ground embroidered with large coiling sea dragons, sea spray, flaming pearls, and sea creatures.

128in (324cm) long

£3,000-4,000 PAIR KT

A Chinese embroidered silk panel, decorated with exotic birds in trees above lion dogs, four lines of calligraphy, mounted in a hardwood and mother-of-pearl frame.

c1900 *53in (135cm) high*

£6,000-8,000 WW

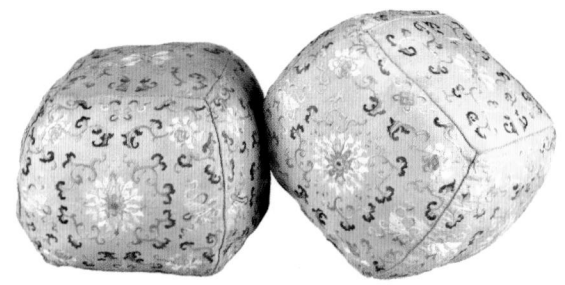

A pair of late 18thC Chinese embroidered square cushions, worked in pastel floss silks with floral medallions, blue scrolling foliage and shells.

9in (23cm) wide

£1,000-1,500 KT

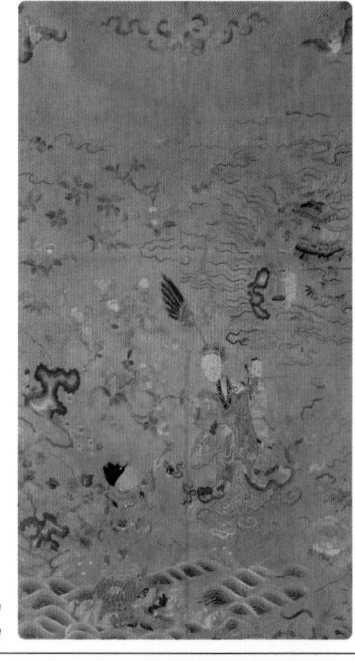

A 19thC Chinese embroidered panel, depicting three figures in a pagoda landscape, framed and glazed, some damage.

36.25in (92cm) high

£200-300 WW

A 19thC Imperial Chinese Guangxu period embroidered silk wall panel, the large central five-clawed dragon with couched stitch gold wrapped thread scaly body, with four smaller dragons encircling.

140in (356cm) long

£5,000-7,000 RTC

A large early 20thC Chinese embroidered wall panel, roundel of five couched gold thread dragons amid floss silk cloud scrolls, smaller dragon to the sides and border.

100in (267cm) wide

£800-1,000 KT

A 19thC Chinese embroidered female sleeveless tunic, with silk embroidery of blue scrolling clouds, flaming pearls and worked golden thread dragons, silk lishui band.

37in (94cm) high

£1,500-2,000   FRE

A large Chinese Qing Dynasty silk embroidered robe, embroidered with eight round symbols enclosing gold-thread dragons and various Buddhistic symbols.

58in (157.5cm) high

£4,000-5,000   FRE

A 19thC Chinese silk embroidery 'dragon' robe, of typical form, gold thread dragons over a purple ground.

88in (223.5cm) high

£5,000-7,000   FRE

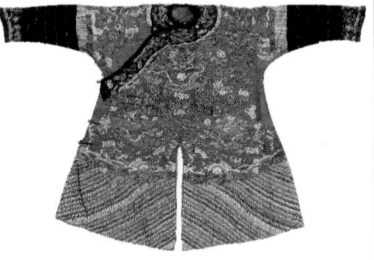

A rare Chinese Qing Dynasty kesi tunic, well worked kesi body showing Fu bats, gold thread dragons, Buddhistic symbols all over lishu and lingzhi base, losses.

This tunic was acquired by an American diplomat to China during the late 19thC.

37in (94cm) high

£2,500-3,500   FRE

A Chinese Dowager style and period woman's court robe, with tight embroidery sprigs and blossoms to yellow ground.

This tunic was acquired by an American diplomat to China during the late 19thC. This provenance is important for value.

55in (139.5cm) high

£2,000-3,000   FRE

A late 19thC Chinese silk embroidered dragon robe, decorated with five-claw gold thread imperial dragons chasing the pearl of wisdom against a blue ground.

52in (132cm) long

£1,000-1,500   GORL

A late 19thC Chinese dragon robe, embroidered with three coiling gold dragons chasing flaming pearls among clouds, bats and shou medallions, above polychrome waves.

56in (142cm) high

£4,000-5,000   TEN

A 19th/20thC embroidered silk dragon robe, five-clawed satin-stitched dragons on yellow satin ground, reworked in a central opening jacket with indigo blue satin stitch borders.

46in (117cm) long

£1,200-1,800   RTC

A rare early 20thC Chinese theatrical costume, handmade from embroidered silk, silvered metal and white glass or stone applied disks and gold thread.

Commissioned in China during the 1920s as a replica of a costume worn by opera actor Mei Lang Fang in Peking (Beijing).

£700-1,000   FRE

ORIENTAL

CLOSER LOOK – ALTAR TABLE

This table has excellent provenance: it was originally brought to the United States by an American diplomat and was later displayed at the Philadelphia Museum of Art.

Fine carving and openwork panels lend the piece a gracefulness that belies its bulky weight and size.

An 18thC Chinese hongmu altar table, the four-plank framed top over carved apron, raised on straight legs joined by a lingzhi-shaped panel carved in low relief.

124in (314cm) wide

£80,000-100,000 FRE

This table was probably a centrepiece in the grand entrance hall of an esteemed official during the long and celebrated reign of the Qianlong emperor (1735-1799).

It features dragon and lingzhi motifs, two sacred and important emblems of authority and prosperity.

A 16th/17thC Chinese huanghuali recessed leg side table, with single-plank top over straight beaded and joined legs supporting a strut latticework apron.

71in (180.5cm) long

£15,000-20,000 FRE

A Chinese early Qing Dynasty nanmu recessed leg table, the single plank top applied with two small everted flanges, supported by a beaded S-scroll apron joining four beaded straight legs.

105in (266.5cm) wide

£5,500-6,500 FRE

An unusual 17th/18thC Chinese tielimu and burlwood wine table, burl insert top framed by tielimu planks, over high strut supported stretcher, straight beaded legs terminating in hoof feet.

29in (73.5cm) wide

£400-500 FRE

A Chinese Qing Dynasty late Ming-style huanghuali recessed leg side table, the well-matched double-plank insert 'ice-plate' framed top over a plain apron and matched spandrels, raised on rounded legs.

75in (190.5cm) wide

£30,000-40,000 FRE

A Chinese Qing Dynasty huanghuali painting table, the figured double-plank insert 'ice plate' framed top, raised on four straight and beaded square legs, terminating in high hoof feet.

68in (173cm) long

£60,000-80,000 FRE

An 18thC Chinese hardwood rectangular low table or stand, above a pierced key fret frieze, on square-section legs with stylised scroll feet, minor damages.

31.5in (80cm) wide

£500-600 WW

ORIENTAL

A Chinese carved hardwood stand.
c1800

£200-300   DN

A Chinese mid-Qing Dynasty jichimu
and softwood side table, the
rectangular softwood plank framed
by figure jichimu planks, waisted
edge over a high-humpback
stretcher terminating in a carved
hoof foot.
36in (91.5cm) wide

£1,000-1,500   FRE

A mid-19thC Chinese lacquer games
table, gilt decorated, the top with a
central drop-in cover, released from
the underside to reveal a chequer
board on the reverse, the interior
with backgammon, revolving on a
birdcage, cracks, repairs.
24.5in (62cm) wide

£650-850   WW

A late 19thC Chinese hongmu
table, marble insert top, inlaid with
mother-of-pearl, and raised on outswept claw feet.

24in (61cm) wide

£1,000-1,500   FRE

A 19thC Chinese
rectangular side table,
the side with an
openwork cash frieze
on humpback crossed
stretchers.
37in (94cm) wide

£550-750   WW

A Chinese lacquer
and ebonised coffee
table, inlaid with
mother-of-pearl and
various semi precious
stones, on bracketed
supports.
37.25in (95cm) wide

£900-1,200   WW

SEATING

A pair of 19thC Chinese ash elbow
chairs, with backs of 'cardinal's hat'
design, with panelled seats and
moulded square legs with stretchers.

£500-700   TEN

A pair of 19thC Chinese hongmu and marble
'dreamstone' insert meditation chairs, the back
with circular marble insert, spandrels to seat,
over beaded apron and straight legs, joined by a
foot rest.
36in (91.5cm) high

£1,500-2,000   FRE

A 19thC Chinese hongmu, marble inset and
mother-of-pearl inlaid Qing chair, the back with
a grey and white 'dramstone' panel, the marble
seat framed by hongmu planks, on square-
section legs and stretchers.
38in (96.5cm) high

£900-1,200   FRE

ORIENTAL

A large late 19thC Chinese hardwood and marble chair, the multi-panel marble-inset back and sides above a burr wood panel seat, on square moulded legs with a conforming openwork apron.

42in (107cm) high

£1,500-2,000   L&T

A pair of lacquered Chinese Ming-style armchairs, with pierced and carved splats above shaped open arms and panelled seats, with pierced and foliate-carved aprons, on square-section legs, finished in red-brown lacquer.

£1,000-1,500   L&T

A pair of Chinese Qing Dynasty mixed wood chairs, with protruding top rail, carved vertical back rail, shaped arms supported by posts, plank seat, together with a strut back chair.

40in (101.5cm) high

£900-1,200   FRE

A pair of Chinese Ming-style lacquered bamboo armchairs, the wrap-around backs with downswept outscrolling arms and fretted splats above solid seats on bamboo framed legs.

£900-1,200   L&T

An early 19thC Chinese hongmu bench, straight back inset with panels carved to show foliate scrolls and sprigs, straight plank arm rests over straight square legs.

74in (71.5cm) wide

£3,500-4,500   FRE

A pair of 18thC Chinese jichimu stools, the square 'ice-plate' framed top over waisted openwork panels, and spandrel-applied apron, on straight legs terminating in hoof feet, joined plank base.

13.25in (33.5cm) wide

£5,000-6,000   FRE

A 19thC Chinese hongmu bench, carved straight back rest, straight arms and square straight legs.

£1,500-2,000   FRE

A 19th/20thC Chinese hardwood barrel-shaped stool, with five legs joined by a circular stretcher, the top inset with burr wood, the rim with simulated studs, minor damages.

18.5in (47cm) high

£700-1,000   WW

A Chinese Kangxi period famille rose table screen and hardwood stand, the porcelain screen decorated in enamel, with huanghuali frame and stand.

27in (68.5cm) high

£2,500-3,500 **FRE**

An 18thC Chinese dreamstone and zitan scholar's screen, with purple-golden thread zitan plank framed screen, mountainous grey and white stone, over a simple strut and bracket stand.

11in (28cm) high

£8,000-12,000 **FRE**

An 18thC Chinese carved turquoise and hardwood table screen, carved in medium and high relief, inscribed with five rows of script, over a hardwood stand.

6.5in (16.5cm) high

£3,000-4,000 **FRE**

A large pair of 19thC Chinese enamel, applied and gilt-metal table screens on stands, applied with coloured stones and jadeite on an unusual enamel ground, both over elaborate hardwood stands, raised on bracket feet.

28in (71cm) high

£7,000-8,000 **FRE**

A pair of early 19thC Chinese white jade inset hardwood table screens and stands, the carved white jade panels with gilt-decorated inscribed poetic script verso, in latticework hardwood frame, on similar carved stands.

15in (38cm) high

£15,000-20,000 **FRE**

A pair of miniature 19thC table screens, each formed as a pierced jade plaque of a standing lady holding a vase, mounted in a burr wood panel, each on a wooden stand.

5in (12.5cm) high

£400-500 **WW**

A Japanese Meiji period Shibayama screen, decorated to one side with figures on a blue ground, the reverse with a bird in flight, signed, in hardwood frame in pierced and carved trestle stand.

42in (106.5cm) high

£1,200-1,800 **L&T**

A 19thC Chinese six panel jade, quartz and ivory applied floor screen, on a black lacquer ground, with hongmu frame.

75in (191cm) high

£7,000-8,000 **L&T**

A 19thC Chinese wood framed, paper and silk lined six-fold screen, hand-painted with a river and mountain landscape on a gilt background.

68.25in (173cm) high

£3,000-4,000 **ADA**

A 19thC Chinese lacquer, mother-of-pearl and ivory-inlaid four-fold draught screen, depicting waterbirds amidst foliage, with similarly decorated verso and foliate-pierced frieze panels, within a moulded rosewood frame with brass flush hinges.

60.25in (153cm) high

£3,000-4,000 **L&T**

A 19thC Chinese lacquer, hardstone and ivory-applied four-fold dressing screen, with figural panels, depicting exotic birds on verso.

72in (183cm) high

£2,000-3,000 **L&T**

ORIENTAL

CLOSER LOOK – A KANGXI COROMANDEL SCREEN

As well as revealing the year of construction and the piece's original recipient, the inscription provides a glimpse of local 17thC bureaucracy: the honoured magistrate Wen Linlang was presented with this screen by his disciple/protégé/deputy Zhao Jinmei. The names of over 400 city council men are also included.

The Kangxi period (1661-1722) is noted for its artistic excellence.

The costumes, architecture, activities and even plantlife depicted provide invaluable reference points for researchers and admirers of Chinese culture.

The high-quality carving and the good condition make this screen extremely rare and desirable.

A Chinese Kangxi period twelve panel coromandel screen, depicting still-lifes and landscapes, the reverse carved to with calligraphic script in a border of foliate scrolls and flowers.

1682   *106in (269cm) high*

£50,000-70,000   **FRE**

STORAGE

One of a pair of rare 18thC Chinese huanghuali chest-on-stands, set with corner lingzhi-form mounts and banding to the hinged top, the lock plate flanked by doors, shaped bracket base raised on a late 18thC/early 19thC Chippendale-style stands.

39.5in (100.5cm) high

£6,000-8,000 PAIR   **FRE**

A Chinese late Qing Dynasty lacquered, painted and applied cabinet-on-stand, mineral applied twin door depicting figural landscape, over a two drawer stand, raised on straight legs.

40in (101.5cm) wide

£700-1,000   **FRE**

A pair of Japanese Meiji period ivory and shibayama miniature cabinet-on-stands, with chased metal mounts and hinges, the doors enclosing four long drawers with bird-form metal handles and decorated with flowers and insects, raised on a gilt decorated lacquer stand.

5in (12.5cm) wide

£4,500-5,500   **L&T**

A Japanese Meiji period lacquer table cabinet-on-stand, with foliate-chased metal mounts, on cabriole legs.

19.75in (50cm) wide

£700-1,000 **L&T**

CLOSER LOOK – A CHINESE TABLE CHEST

Only a wealthy scholar or official would been able to purchase this fine piece to store his seals, incense, ink, paste and other important and other costly table items.

Zitan is a dense and dark wood grown only in the Indian subcontinent that was rare and expensive in the 18thC. The almost dark purple hue of the wood is interspersed with deep 'golden threads' throughout the grain.

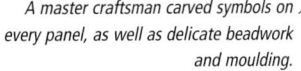

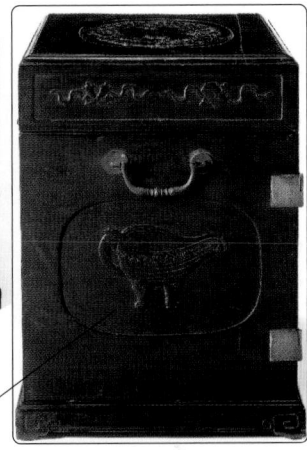

A master craftsman carved symbols on every panel, as well as delicate beadwork and moulding.

An 18thC Chinese carved full zitan table chest, hinged carved cover to the top, biaton lock-plate and mounts, two carved panel doors enclosing seven drawers, raised on a carved bracket base.

16in (40.5cm) high

£12,000-18,000 **FRE**

A pair of early 20thC Chinese brown lacquer decorated and hardstone-inlaid cabinets, the lower doors enclosing central shelves with two drawers, raised on stile feet with brass caps.

27.5in (70cm) wide

£7,000-9,000 **L&T**

An early 19thC Chinese export gilt and polychrome lacquer chest-on-stand, the cupboard doors enclosing shelves, the sides with brass carrying handles, the stand with shaped apron, on bulbous turned legs.

40.25in (102cm) wide

£5,000-6,000 **L&T**

A set of late 19th/early 20thC Japanese carved hardwood and relief-decorated hanging wall shelves, with applied mother-of-pearl and bone decoration, faults, elements missing.

28.25in (72cm) wide

£150-250 **DN**

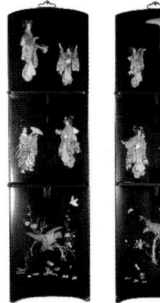

A pair of Japanese black lacquer hanging wall shelves, inset in bone, ivory and mother-of-pearl with figures and birds of prey, minor faults.

c1900 *41.75in (106cm) high*

£400-500 **WW**

A Chinese huanghuali mirror stand and table chest, with hinged open latticework mirror, bracketed over two matched hinged doors that reveal two short drawers over a single long drawer.

16in (40.5cm) wide

£6,500-7,500 **FRE**

A rare mid-18thC Chinese export amboyna and ebony table bureau, with ornate silver escutcheons and side handles, the lock plate with monogram, on squat bun feet, with two keys.

18in (46cm) wide

£3,000-5,000 **L&T**

FURNITURE

The antique furniture market is arguably one of the hardest hit by the recent economic downturn – a trend that many claim began as early as September 11 2001, when American buyers simply stopped travelling to Europe, forcing export sales to fall through the floor. A similar drop in trade from Japan occurred at the same time, possibly owing to that country's own financial woes. Prices have fallen year on year, exacerbated in the last 12 to 18 months by a growing lack of domestic interest. Dealers and auction houses have seen a dramatic slow down as buyers become increasingly cautious.

Although pieces of high-quality furniture and more unusual items continue to sell – and sell well – more ordinary pieces are proving increasingly difficult to find buyers for. Prices for most run-of-the-mill items, including much average Georgian furniture, are down by about 20–30 per cent in the wake of the Lehman Brothers collapse in September 2008. People are considerably more selective when buying. This naturally causes a problem with supply too, with sellers becoming increasingly reluctant to consign good pieces to auction while prices remain so depressed.

It is not all doom and gloom, however. The 2009 September sales seemed to suggest something of a turning point, partly as they included the sale of a couple of private collections, which do very well on the whole. One such collection, stock from the London dealer Nicholas Squire, did well as it mixed modern and antique pieces with a strong 'look' that Squire excelled at. This fact, combined with an appealing and attractive catalogue presentation, led to a different trend in the bidding and the sale was boosted.

Georgian and Regency pieces seem to sell better than their heavy Victorian cousins. In general, however, people are not buying one style over another – for example, Rococo over Regency – but are looking for high-quality pieces across the board. Brown furniture, which has been out of fashion for several years, is becoming appreciated again. Sturdy, good-quality, functional pieces still represent excellent value for money: a Victorian chest of drawers can cost as little as £100–150, with only exceptional examples going to £400–500.

Times like this are good for buyers, who can currently find fine-quality pieces at much lower prices than have been seen before. Prices will definitely rise once things pick up, and so such purchases make good long-term investments. Always consider size and quality when buying: a large Georgian dining table will fetch more than a smaller one, partly due to its rarity. Look out for Edwardian pieces, which can make an affordable entry point to the Georgian style. When buying chairs, bear in mind that the larger the set of chairs, the larger the price – for each pair over four or six, the price nearly doubles – and look out for more 'generous' chairs that are well-proportioned and balanced. Finally, always consider the quality of the wood and grain, as well as the construction, carving and date; pieces stamped with a maker's name always sell for a premium.

An important George III mahogany concave breakfront bookcase in the manner of Thomas Chippendale, possibly Irish, £27,000 at Lyon & Turnbull.

ESSENTIAL REFERENCE – WINDSOR CHAIRS

The Windsor chair is the best-known country chair in both Britain and America. Its legs, arms and spindle-back are dowelled into a saddle seat. This is shaped to prevent the sitter from sliding forward: the sides and back are scooped away from a central ridge, resembling the pommel of a saddle. Most examples are arm-chairs.

- This form is said to have originated around Windsor and the Thames Valley, which is probably where the name originates. Another explanation is that George III sat in one while sheltering in a forester's cottage in the middle of a hunt in Windsor Great Park.
- The main centre of the Windsor chair-making industry in the 18thC was High Wycombe, Buckinghamshire, and the cheapness and lightness of the Windsor chair meant that it could be easily transported from there around the country.
- There are two basic types of Windsor chair. The earliest form, the comb-back, which has a horizontal toprail, was introduced in the late 17thC or early 18thC, and is popular in North America. The hoop-back, or bow-back, which became fashionable in the mid-18thC, has a rounded toprail, formed by steaming and bending the horizontal bar into a semi-circle, which then forms the arms and the mid-support for the spindles. Some British hoop-backs feature a splat, which may be pierced or decorated. The now common 'wheel' splat chair began to appear at the end of the 18thC.
- Traditional Windsor chairs were made in ash, yew, beech and birch, by wood-turners. British examples usually have an elm seat, which has a good cross-grain strength that resists splitting when holes are placed close to the edge of a seat. For this reason English Windsor chair seats are generally not as thick as the seats of North American Windsors, which are typically made from pine or popular wood.

- Much of the the appeal of Windsor chairs lies in their restrained ornamentation, which is often limited to the natural grain and colour of the wood. Over time, ash develops a rich honey-brown patina, and cherry a rich red hue, and these are sought after. Early pine Windsor chairs were sometimes painted for use outdoors, but most were left plain.
- The most elaborate form of Windsor chair is referred to as the 'Strawberry Hill' design, after a house at Twickenham, which featured windows with a distinctive Gothic shape, much like the toprail of the chair. These 18thC Gothic-style chairs were almost always made from yew, and are sought after.
- Windsor chairs (and their variant styles) were mass-produced from the late 19thC. In the early 20thC it became popular with civil and military institutions, who mainly ordered side chairs.
- It is unusual to find sets larger than six, and there may be marginal differences in turning and carving within the set.
- British chairs may be marked with a maker's label or stamped with initials or a name on the outside edge of their seats. American chairs are sometimes branded underneath the seat.

A George III yew, elm and beech Windsor chair, the hoop-back with a pierced and shaped central splat, with a shaped and out-turned armrail on turned uprights, the saddle seat on cabriole front legs with a curved stretcher and turned rear legs.

40in (101.5cm) high

£2,000-2,500   DUK

An ash and yew high-back Windsor armchair, faults.
c1800

£350-450   DN

A first-half 19thC elm and yew wood child's Windsor elbow chair.
27.25in (69cm) highest

£250-350   DN

A second-quarter 19thC ash, oak and fruitwood child's high-back Windsor armchair, the arched spindle back and crescent arm rail above the solid seat, on turned tapering legs.

£600-800   DN

A mid-19thC elm and yew wheel-back Windsor armchair.

£400-600   **DN**

A 19thC yew and elm Windsor chair, the high double-bow back with shaped and pierced splats and turned arm supports, the seat on turned legs joined by a crinoline stretcher.

£1,000–1,200   **TEN**

A mid-19thC child's yew wood Windsor chair, the pierced splat back with spindle supports and solid elm seat raised on turned legs and crinoline understretcher.

£400-500   **A&G**

A 19thC Nottinghamshire ash and elm Windsor chair, the rounded back with pierced splat and turned supports, the seat on turned legs with crinoline stretcher, stamped 'F WALKER ROCKLEY'.

£600-800   **TEN**

A matched set of six 19thC Nottingham yew wood Windsor chairs, the low double-bow backs with pierced splats and turned arm supports, the seats on turned legs with crinoline stretchers.

£2,500-3,500   **TEN**

An 18th/19thC ash stickback chair, the high comb back between straight arms, the seat raised on staked legs.

£600-800   **TEN**

Two of a set of eight ash Lancashire ladder-back chairs, with rush seats, on turned legs and stretchers, including two elbow chairs.

£1,200-1,500 SET   **TEN**

Three of a set of seven late 19thC elm spindleback chairs, including a carver.

£1,100-1,300 SET   **DN**

A late 18thC New England green-painted bow-back high chair, old surface, imperfections.

36in (91.5cm) high

£4,000-5,000   SK

A late 18thC New England sack-back Windsor chair, the surface of brown over green paint.

37.75in (96cm) high

£2,500-3,000   SK

A pair of coastal New Hampshire or North Shore, Massachusetts carved and turned black-painted maple side chairs, the arched and moulded crests with flanking carved ears above conforming stiles and splats over block, vase and ring-turned legs topped by concentric circles and joined by a bulbous medial stretcher and tripartite side stretchers, early surface of black paint over red.

c1730   *49in (124.5cm) high*

£80,000-100,000   SK

A late 18thC New England sack-back Windsor chair, the surface of brown over green paint.

37.75in (96cm) high

£2,500-3,000   SK

A set of five American Philadelphia birdcage Windsor chairs, comprising four side chairs and one armchair, the side chairs retaining their original off-white surface, initialled by the maker Thomas Rain.

c1805

£2,500-3,000   POOK

A New England continuous-arm Windsor high chair, green-painted with yellow striping, paint wear.

c1810   *36.5in (93cm) high*

£1,500-2,000   SK

A mid-19thC Shaker maple side chair with tillers, probably Enfield, New Hampshire, minor imperfections.

41in (104cm) high

£1,800-2,000   SK

A New England painted rocking chair, the crest rail with a grisaille stencil-decorated scene of a steam locomotive and town, the seat with vibrant ochre and orange graining.

c1850

£900-1200   POOK

A set of six 19thC Pennsylvania painted plank-seat chairs, retaining their original decorated surface.

£900-1200   POOK

FURNITURE

A late 17thC joined oak settle, the back with three fielded rectangular panels between downcurved arms, the squab seat on moulded rails and baluster legs joined by stretchers.

70.75in (180cm) wide

£1,000-1,200   **TEN**

An 18thC joined oak settle, the back with three fielded panels below a carved frieze of leaves and flowers with initials 'KWI' (?) and dated, with baluster and block supports joined by a carved stretcher.

1718   174.75in (190cm) wide

£500-700   **TEN**

A George II carved oak box seat settle, the top rail carved 'R 1734 M', above five double heart and foliate-carved panels, alterations.

70.75in (180cm) wide

£600-900   **L&T**

A George II Yorkshire oak settle, the quintuple ogee arch-fielded panel back above a downswept arm and outcurved padded arm, seat formerly string, on tapered short circular legs.

80.25in (204cm) wide

£400-600   **L&T**

A George II oak settle, with five-panelled back and welled cushion seat on cabriole legs and pad feet, damage.

53in (134.5cm) wide

£500-800   **GORL**

An early 19thC mahogany and elm hall bench, the back with reeded spar splats above downswept arms on baluster supports, legs united by a double H-stretcher, one arm replaced.

80.25in (204cm) wide

£1,000-1,200   **L&T**

A Victorian Gothic carved oak pew, the moulded top rail over pierced arcaded back with two carved traceried panels below, plank seat, raised on square legs joined by an H-stretcher.

58.25in (148cm) wide

£500-800   **HT**

A late 19th/early 20thC caned and beech child's settee.

25in (64cm) wide

£120-180   **DN**

DINING CHAIRS

A pair of George II walnut side chairs, with solid splats, repair.
c1735

£1,200-1,800   **DN**

A pair of mid-18thC French walnut chairs, the seats covered by verdure tapestry fragments, faults.

£300-500   **DN**

A pair of 18thC American Queen Anne provincial walnut side chairs, each with solid vasiform splat and scrolled uprights, slip-seat, and cabriole legs ending in pointed pad feet.

18in (45.5cm) high

£900-1,200   **SK**

A set of four American Queen Anne mahogany dining chairs, each with a yoke crest and vasiform splat, above a slip seat supported by cabriole legs terminating in pad feet.
c1760

£4,500-5,000   **POOK**

A set of three George III mahogany bell-carved dining chairs, in the manner of Alexander Peter, the reeded yolk-shaped top rails decorated with husks and a rocaille cartouche enclosing a bell motif, the entrelac splats above floral gros point needlework drop-in seats with caddy-moulded and blind 'guilloche fret' carved rails, on chamfered square section legs joined by pierced H-stretchers.

£3,500–4,500   L&T

An American Philadelphia Chippendale mahogany dining chair, attributed to the workshop of Thomas Tuft, the serpentine crest with voluted ears, above a gothic splat flanked by fluted stiles, above a trapezoidal slip seat supported by acanthus-carved legs, terminating in claw-and-ball feet.

c1780

£10,000-12,000   POOK

A pair of George III mahogany and hide upholstered dining chairs, on four scroll-carved cabriole legs with pad feet.

£1,000-1,200   L&T

Two of a set of seven George III mahogany dining chairs, including a pair of armchairs with scroll-moulded arms, the pierced waved ladderbacks above overstuffed seats, on square chamfered legs joined by H-stretchers.

£2,000-2,500 SET   L&T

Two of a set of seven George III mahogany dining chairs, the moulded backs with shaped top rails and S-scroll and oval pierced backs, the drop-in seats on square tapering legs joined by H-stretchers.

£2,000-2,500 SET   L&T

One of a set of nine George III mahogany hoop-back dining chairs.

c1790

£1,700-2,000 SET   DN

A set of six 18thC Dutch William & Mary carved walnut side chairs, each with a curved backrest and shell-carved cresting, overupholstered seat and cabriole legs ending in pad feet.

£1,200-1,500   SK

Two of a set of six George III mahogany dining chairs, the square vertically-railed backs over overstuffed seats, on square moulded and tapered legs with stretchers.

c1790

£1,200-1,800 SET   TEN

Four of a set of eight George III mahogany dining chairs, including two carvers.

£4,500-5,500 SET   DN

FURNITURE

Two of a set of six single and two arm George IV mahogany dining chairs, with reeded cresting rails above seats covered in floral trellis pattern tapestry, raised on turned tapering legs.

£700–1,000 SET   **A&G**

A set of five George IV mahogany dining chairs, in the manner of Gillows, including an armchair.

c1825

£300-500   **DN**

A set of six Regency mahogany and brass-inlaid dining chairs, the scrolled backs with turned top rails and tabletted mid-rails, the caned seats with loose squabs between moulded rails, on sabre legs.

£900-1,200   **TEN**

One of a set of six George IV mahogany dining chairs, the shaped-bar top rails with volute-scrolled ends over paired horizontal mid-rails, the drop-in seats between moulded rails, on sabre legs.

£700–900 SET   **TEN**

A pair of William IV mahogany armchairs, and three other dining chairs of similar design and date, damage.

c1835

£700-900   **DN**

One of a set of eight William IV rosewood dining chairs, with curved-bar backs and scrolling mid-rails over drop-in seats, originally caned, on lotus-carved and turned legs, stamped to the seat rails 'TJ'.

£2,200-2,700 SET   **TEN**

Two of a set of four 19thC Hepplewhite-style mahogany dining chairs, the arched crest rail carved with bell flowers above a pierced anthemion and vase-shaped splat, the seats upholstered in green velvet and raised on squared tapering reeded supports and blocked feet, joined by H-stretchers.

£500-700 SET   **ADA**

Two of a set of nine mid-19thC mahogany dining chairs, one with arms, with plain crest rails above carved mid-rails and uprights, the drop-in seats covered in brown hide, raised on octagonal and turned tapering legs, some repaired.

£2,000-2,500 SET   **A&G**

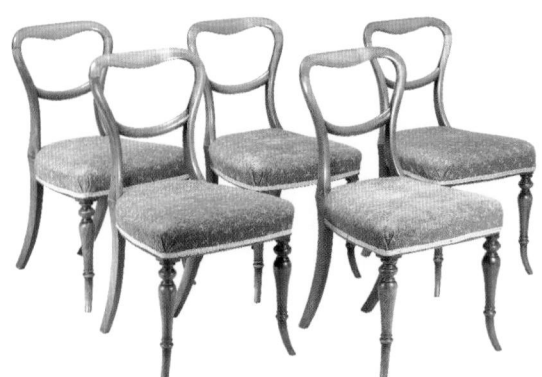

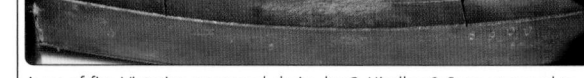

A set of five Victorian rosewood chairs, by C. Hindley & Sons, stamped to the seat rail 'C HINDLEY & SONS LATE MILES & EDWARDS 134 OXFORD ST LONDON 8906'.

c1860

£300-400   **DN**

Two of a set of eleven Victorian oak-framed dining chairs, the rectangular padded scrollover backs above stuffover seats, on turned tapering legs, upholstered in Jacobean-style tapestry, including one open armchair.

£1,100-1,600 SET   L&T

One of a set of six Victorian mahogany dining chairs, the backs with pierced splats and plain uprights, the upholstered seats raised on turned and fluted tapering legs with casters.

£450-650 SET   A&G

A set of five late 19thC Dutch mahogany and marquetry chairs, including one armchair.

£550-750 SET   DN

One of a set of six Chippendale Revival mahogany dining chairs, the undulating backs and pierced interlaced splats carved all over with scrolls and acanthus, including two elbow chairs.

£2,000-3,000 SET   TEN

Two of a set of twelve late 19thC Hepplewhite-style mahogany dining chairs, the arched backs with pierced splats and carved classical motifs, the overstuff seats upholstered in blue-and-beige patterned fabric, raised on square tapered forelegs and joined by an understretcher.

£3,000-3,500 SET   TEN

A set of eight late 19thC George III style ladder-back mahogany dining chairs, including a pair of armchairs, repairs.

£1,800-2,200 SET   DN

A matched set of ten late 19thC Victorian mahogany and satin birch dining chairs, including a pair of armchairs.

£800-1,200 SET   DN

A set of ten late 19thC George III style mahogany dining chairs.

£2,000-2,500 SET   DN

Two of a set of ten George III style mahogany dining chairs, the serpentine top rails with pierced Gothic-style vase-shaped splats, over drop-in seats, raised on fluted square tapering legs joined by H-stretchers, including two armchairs.
c1900

£5,000-6,000 SET   L&T

A set of eight North Italian carved, painted and parcel-gilt wood dining chairs, including two armchairs.
c1900

£2,200-3,000 SET   DN

FURNITURE

A pair of 17thC carved walnut armchairs with a pair of later carved walnut side chairs, each with a padded back and seat with spiral turned supports.

36in (91.5cm) high

£500-800   FRE

A pair of late 17thC and later carved beech chairs, with caned backs.

£400-600   DN

Two of a set of six late 17thC-style Continental baroque fruitwood-inlaid walnut side chairs, each with trapezoidal backrest inlaid with an armorial panel with penwork designs, shaped seat inlaid with a star, on square legs joined by a shaped stretcher.

21in

£2,000-2,500 SET   SK

A George I Irish carved walnut side chair, the waisted cartouche-shaped back with scallop shell cresting above an acanthus and paper scroll carved vase-shaped splat and balloon-shaped seat rail with drop-in needlepoint pad with early restored floral woolwork cover, on bold eagle mask carved cabriole legs with trailing acanthus, ending in upswept scroll feet, the plain tapering rear legs on pad feet.

£3,500–4,500   L&T

One of a pair of George II walnut chairs.

c1735

£3,500-4,500 SET   DN

An American Philadelphia Chippendale walnut shell-carved side chair.

c1755-95   *40in (101.5cm) high*

£8,000-10,000   SK

A mahogany child's chair, the rectangular back with arched crest rail, above a pierced vase splat, and a drop-in seat and square section legs.

c1780 and later

£350-450   DN

A set of six American New York Federal mahogany inlaid side chairs, the square crests inlaid with festoons of bellflowers and pendant flowers over serpentine seats, on bellflower and cuff-inlaid front legs, original surface, very minor imperfections.

1790-1805   *36.5in (93cm) high*

£55,000-60,000   SK

A Regency ebonised side chair, with gilt-brass mounts and a cane seat.

£120-180   WW

A set of six mid-19thC Pennsylvania painted plank-seat chairs, each retaining vibrant red and yellow floral decoration on a black and red ground with yellow pinstriping.

£10,000-12,000   **POOK**

Three of a set of fourteen mid-19thC Pennsylvania painted plank-seat lodge chairs, each with a half-spindle back with fruit decoration, inscribed 'No 122 I.O.F.', including two armchairs.

£18,000-22,000   **POOK**

ESSENTIAL REFERENCE – BLACK FOREST

Black Forest carvings originated in the early 1800s in Brienz, Switzerland, where there was a small-scale local industry of wood carvers. However, people often think they are German. By the mid-19thC, the popularity of the carvings spread, due to wealthy Victorian tourists visiting Brienz and other picturesque Swiss resorts such as nearby Interlaken and Luzern.

- A huge range of items was produced, from carved wooden bears, stags, dogs, birds and other animals to religious scenes, furniture and works of art.
- In Europe, ownership of Black Forest carvings became a symbol of wealth and prestige. In the US there was great demand for pieces featuring native animals such as eagles.
- From the mid to late 19thC, Black Forest carvings were exhibited at International Exhibitions in London, Chicago and Paris, confirming their status as works of art.
- Due to a current revival of interest, the best pieces of Black Forest carving are once more highly sought after.
- Signed pieces and those by important names, such as the Huggler family, command a premium.

One of a pair of Reformed Gothic walnut side chairs, by Lamb of Manchester, old repairs, lacking casters.

James Lamb (1816-1903) was the leading Manchester cabinetmaker of his day.

                              33in (84cm) high

£350-550   **DN**

A late 19thC Syrian mother-of-pearl inlaid folding side chair, with a foliate and script-decorated shaped crest above a five-slat backrest, small losses including two finials to the back.

                          22.75in (58cm) high

£100-200   **WEB**

A pair of German antler salon chairs, the rounded backs formed from two fallow antlers supporting a central green hide-effect oval cushion, with padded sprung seats and on red and fallow deer antler supports.
c1890

£1,500-2,000   **TEN**

A Swiss Black Forest carved chair, in the form of a standing bear, the seat with incised scrolling and on cabriole legs.
c1900   *43.25in (110cm) high*

£6,000-8,000   **SOTH**

A set of six late George III mahogany medallion-back hall chairs, in the style of Mayhew and Ince, the seat rails with maker's stamp 'W.E.'

£6,500-7,500　　　L&T

A pair of Regency mahogany hall chairs, each boldly-carved cartouche-shaped back above a solid channel-moulded seat, on turned and reeded tapering legs.

£1,200-1,700　　　L&T

A pair of George IV mahogany hall chairs, in the manner of Gillows, the deep scallop shell, tablet and C-scroll backs above oval dished seats, one initialled 'SG' to seat rail.

£2,000-2,500　　　L&T

A pair of George IV mahogany hall chairs, each with reeded cartouche-shaped back, the solid seats with reeded rails, on reeded-front sabre legs headed by carved roundels.

£1,000-1,500　　　L&T

One of a set of four George IV armorial mahogany hall chairs, each shield-shaped back with a decorated centre panel, on turned baluster legs.

£2,300-2,800 SET　　　MEA

One of a pair of William IV carved mahogany hall chairs by Gillows, each with scallop-shell back and painted shield monogram.
c1830

£4,500-5,000 SET　　　DN

A pair of Victorian mahogany hall chairs, with scroll and leaf-carved armorial backs above a serpentine-front panel seat raised on cabriole legs.

£1,200-1,500　　　ADA

A pair of Victorian Gothic Revival oak hall chairs, the twin pierced lancet-arch backs with carved scrolling foliage, the moulded seats on canted square arch-carved legs.

£900-1,200　　　L&T

ESSENTIAL REFERENCE – HALL CHAIRS

From the 18th century onward, a formal wooden chair, with a high back and a hard seat could be found in the halls or corridors of grand houses. They may have been inspired by similar *sgsbello* chairs used in 16thC Italian palaces.

● They were used by servants and tradesmen waiting to enter the main rooms, and consequently often lacked upholstery and arms.

● They are usually found in sets of four or more, although single chairs can be found.

● Typically these bold and simple chairs were made of oak or mahogany, which was particularly suitable for hall furniture, as it is hard-wearing and capable of taking a glossy polish.

● Chair backs were often carved with Classical motifs or the crest or coat of arms of the family who commissioned them. In some cases they were carved with motifs intended to impress guests and to emphasise the social status of the home-owner.

● Numerous designs for hall chairs are featured in Thomas Chippendale's 'The Gentleman and Cabinet-Maker's Director', George Hepplewhite's 'The Cabinet-Maker and Upholsterer's Guide', and Thomas Sheraton's 'The Cabinet Dictionary'. From this it can be deduced that hall chairs were highly regarded.

A pair of Swiss Black Forest carved hall chairs, each back with a bear among oak boughs and leaves, with a solid seat, the legs carved to simulate trees and bears.
c1900

£10,000-12,000　　　SOTH

ESSENTIAL REFERENCE – REGENCY STYLE

The Regency style, named after the regency (1811-20) of George, Prince of Wales (later George IV), was prevalent in Britain from 1790-1830.

● The period saw a continuation of interest in Neo-classical tastes that began earlier in the 18thC.

● Forms were rectilinear, light and well proportioned, although heavier than Georgian pieces. Master silversmiths such as Paul Storr and Benjamin Smith created copies of the Warwick vase and other historical pieces, in silver or silver-gilt.

● Luxurious materials were used, including brass inlay and figured woods on furniture and ivory and ebony handles and finials on silver. Figurative marquetry and painted furniture went out of fashion. Instead much was made of the wood as a feature, emphasising the attractive grain. Mahogany remained the most popular wood, but rosewood, satinwood, zebrawood and amboyna were also much used, particularly for small pieces of furniture, such as occasional tables.

● Notable cabinet-makers include Thomas Chippendale the younger, George Bullock, and Gillows.

● The lyre was among the most commonly used decorative forms in classically inspired pieces. Originating in both Ancient Greek and Roman art, it became an enduring motif in Regency furniture. It is frequently seen on chair backs.

● The French Empire style, which drew heavily on Classical Roman imagery, was influential in Regency designs. Regency pieces can be distinguished from their French Empire counterparts by the lack of heavy gilt-bronze mounts and Napoleonic emblems, such as bees and 'N's.

A Regency carved rosewood and upholstered long stool, the end supports modelled as lyres.

c1820   37in (94cm) wide
£2,500-3,000   DN

An early 20thC Regency-style carved, ebonised and parcel-gilt wood X-frame stool, with ram's head finials.
£700-900   DN

A large George IV simulated rosewood and button-upholstered stool, of rectangular form and covered in patterned gold fabric, on parcel-gilt baluster-turned legs ending in brass caps and casters.
54in (137cm) long
£1,800-2,500   L&T

A William IV mahogany and rosewood music stool, with floral needlework cover and acanthus-carved stem.
c1830   19.25in (49cm) high
£300-400   DN

An early 19thC faux-rosewood and tapestrywork covered stool, later recovered.
£250-350   DN

A mid-19thC probably Anglo-Indian carved rosewood and upholstered stool, later seat section.
30.25in (77cm) wide
£400-600   DN

FURNITURE

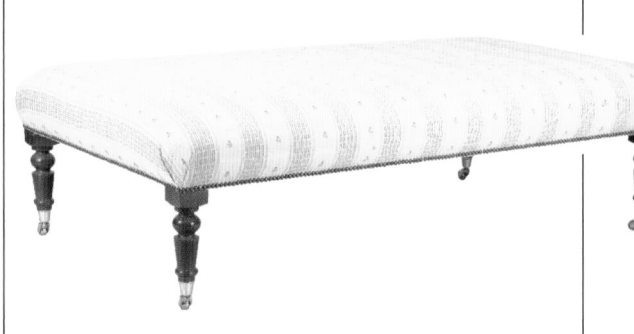

A Dutch marquetry stool, inlaid urns with flowers and foliage, the drop-in leather seat to cabriole legs and claw-and-ball feet, cracks, losses to marquetry.

29in (73.5cm) wide

£600-800   WW

A mid-20thC mahogany and upholstered centre stool.

57in (145cm) long

£600-800   DN

WINDOW SEATS

An early 19thC Regency mahogany window bench, with scrolled ends carved with leaftips, blue loose cushion seat, ogee frieze and circular, reeded legs.

51.75in (131.5cm) wide

£2,000-2,500   SK

A 20thC Regency-style ebonised and parcel-gilt window seat.

65.25in (166cm) wide

£700-900   DN

A George IV mahogany window seat.

c1825   *39.75in (101cm) wide*

£600-800   DN

One of a pair of Continental carved mahogany upholstered window seats.

c1900   *25.5in (65cm) wide*

£500-700 SET   DN

A 17thC and later Charles II carved oak panel-back armchair.

£3,000-3,500   DN

A mid-19thC north Italian 17thC-style carved walnut hall armchair, repair.

£350-550   DN

A near pair of late 19thC 17thC-style carved oak panel-back armchairs.

£500-700   DN

A 19thC oak high panel-back armchair in late 17th/early 18thC style.

£200-300   DN

A Chinese Chippendale mahogany armchair, the trellis back with gadrooned pagoda-shaped top rail above outsplayed trellis-filled arms and drop-in seat with caddy-moulded rail, on similarly moulded and chamfered square-section legs headed by angle frets.

£3,000-4,000   L&T

A George III oak corner armchair, faults, repair.

c1770

£500-700   DN

A George III mahogany armchair, the rectangular back with pierced vase splat above a pair of serpentine arms with scroll terminals, the hinged seat above a shaped frieze and moulded square-section legs.

c1780

£150-200   DN

THE 'BLETHERIN' BITCH' CHAIR

A late 18thC Scottish provincial stained-elm open armchair, the Burns 'Bletherin' Bitch' chair, with shaped top rail above silver presentation plaque in the form of a thistle, over vase splat, later upholstered seat, scroll arms and square section chamfered legs united by stretchers.

The strong provenance of the 'Bletherin' Bitch Chair' increases its interest. It took its name from its original owner Mr James Humphrey, who featured in a poem by Robert Burns about a man described as a 'bletherin' bitch' because he readily engages in arguments, but with little knowledge on the subject. Despite this unflattering portrayal, Humphrey enjoyed introducing himself to visitors with 'Please Sir, I'm the bletherin' bitch'. The chair was presented in 1921 to the Glasgow Philological and Literary Club, popularly known as the OURS Club, by Glasgow's best-known antiques dealer, Muirhead Moffat, on the occasion of its 50th anniversary. Moffat obtained it from the fine art dealer Craibe Angus, an authority on Burns. Its previous owner was Alexander Marshall, who loaned it for display in the 1896 Burns Exhibition at the Royal Glasgow Institute of Fine Arts.

£4,000-6,000   L&T

FURNITURE

One of a set of six George III mahogany elbow chairs.
c1790 and later
£750-1,000 SET   DN

A Regency mahogany-framed library bergère, the moulded rectangular framed back above enclosed arms on baluster supports and moulded seat rail with squab cushion, on turned tapering legs ending in brass socket casters, the whole with split cane upholstery.
£1,800-2,200   L&T

An American Federal New Hampshire mahogany easy chair frame, with serpentine crest and sides continuing to outward scrolling arms, on casters.
c1820   *45in (114.5cm) high*
£1,500-2,500   SK

A Regency rosewood bergère chair, the caned horseshoe back and side with scrolled arm terminals, over a squab seat on plain rails, turned and reeded legs with casters.
£2,000-2,500   TEN

A George IV mahogany and caned swivel armchair, later canework.
c1825
£200-300   DN

A William IV mahogany and caned library bergère armchair, the cartouche-shaped back and downswept arms with lappet-carved scroll terminals, the seat on octagonal baluster-shaped tapering legs, brass caps and casters, damage.
c1835   *20in (51cm) wide*
£200-300   DN

CLOSER LOOK – SIR WALTER SCOTT'S CHAIR

There is a strong market for well-proportioned, pleasing Regency pieces that are good examples of their kind. The provenance of this piece increases the value: the novelist Sir Walter Scott (1771–1832) owned the chair until 1826.

Well-executed pieces after the design of important designers such as Thomas Hope (1769-1831) command high prices. An influential figure, Hope was an advocate of the Neo-classical style.

In 1807, Thomas Hope published his designs in his book 'Household Furniture and Interior Decoration', including measurements and instructions for craftsmen.

A Regency simulated-mahogany open armchair, the Sir Walter Scott Parlour Writing Chair, after a design by Thomas Hope, the turned back rail above two narrow slotted cross rails and a split-cane upholstered seat flanked by downscrolling open arms on claw-carved terminals, the seat rail with a silver plaque inscribed 'Sir Walter Scott's Parlour Writing Chair, 39 Castle Street, Edinburgh', on turned and splayed tapering legs.

Sir Walter Scott (1771–1832) one of Britain's most famous novelists, moved to 39 Castle Street in 1801 and it remained his Edinburgh home until financial disaster forced him to sell the house and its contents in 1826.

£5,000-7,000   L&T

A second-quarter 19thC oak and caned armchair.

£450-550   DN

A Victorian mahogany carved child's high chair.

c1860   *35.5in (90cm) high*

£350-450   DN

A Gothic Revival 'Glastonbury' chair, Howard & Sons, with a parquetry veneered back, applied metal label 'Howard's Patent Parquetrie No. 1548 Berners St. London'.

33.5in (85cm) high

£350-550   DN

A late Victorian satinwood and painted Sheraton Revival open armchair, the pierced splat back decorated with flowers and plumes of feathers, the overstuffed seat on square tapering legs.

£1,200-1,500   WW

A Victorian papier mâché child's chair, with gilt foliage decoration and a bee to the top rail and a re-caned seat, old restoration and metal braces.

25.5in (65cm) high

£40-60   WW

A late 19thC mahogany elbow chair, with high trellis-pattern back, the drop-in seat raised on chamfered square legs with pierced bracket decoration and understretchers.

£600–800   A&G

A German antler-mounted armchair, the arched back formed from fallow deer antlers, the arms and legs of red deer antlers with Fallow stretchers.

c1880

£900-1,200   TEN

A late 19thC probably Russian carved mahogany and marquetry armchair, with stylised lion mask terminals and paw feet.

£700-900   DN

A late 19th/early 20thC oak and leather upholstered desk chair.

£300-400   DN

A Swiss possibly Brienz carved wood and marquetry-inlaid armchair, the scroll-form shield-back centred by an ogival-arched panel inlaid with two chamois on a grassy knoll, framed with edelweiss and alpine rose, with overlapped scale decorated downscrolled arms with lion mask terminals, seat inlaid with a stag among edelweiss, the seat hinged, originally for a musical box movement, now lacking, upon scroll legs.

c1900   *47in (119.5cm) high*

£500-700   TEN

FURNITURE

A late 17thC-style Spanish stained walnut and upholstered armchair.

£1,000-1,200

L&T

A pair of 17thC-style upholstered elbow chairs, covered in faded floral mock tapestry, the shaped arched backs between padded arms with scrolled terminals, the sprung seats on scrolled forelegs with scroll-carved fore-rails and stretchers.

£700-900

TEN

A pair of mid-18thC Louis XV open armchairs.

£1,300-1,800

DN

A pair of Louis XV style carved hardwood open armchairs.

£1,000-1,200

DN

A pair of late 19thC Lois XVI style carved, painted and parcel-gilt wood fauteuils, with light blue upholstered seats and backs.

£1,000-1,500

DN

A pair of George II 'Gainsborough' armchairs, with rectangular upholstered backs, seats and arms on leaf - and flower-carved uprights, on heavy-carved cabriole legs with scrolling feet.

38in (96.5cm) high

£7,000-9,000

DUK

One of a pair of late 19thC American Louis XVI-style giltwood fauteuils à la Reine, of typical form with foliate-carved frame, leaf-carved and fluted, circular and tapered legs.

37in (94cm) high

£2,000-2,500 SET

SK

One of a set of four late 19thC Empire-style mahogany and upholstered fauteuils, each with gilt-brass flowerhead roundels, the moulded frames and arms enclosing needlework fabric, the seats and backs on ring-turned tapered legs.

£1,800-2,200 SET L&T

One of a pair of Georgian-style mahogany framed elbow chairs, upholstered in red-gold damask, the slightly arched backs between outcurved arms with eagle's head terminals, the square seats on carved cabriole legs with claw feet.

£1,600-2,000 PAIR TEN

A pair of Empire giltwood fauteuils, in the style of Jacob Frères, the rectangular backs above padded scroll arms with lappet-carved terminals and quatrefoil rosette decoration above bowed seats, on lappet-carved sabre legs, upholstered in plush velvet and gilt brocade.

39.25in (100cm) high

£4,000-5,000 L&T

CLOSER LOOK – HEPPLEWHITE CHAIRS

George Hepplewhite is best known for his The Cabinet-Maker and Upholsterer's Guide, published in 1788. This pattern book, along with similar publications by Thomas Chippendale and Thomas Shearer was hugely influential on the furniture designs of the late 18thC and early 19thC.

This chair is based on the French 'fauteuil', or armchair, style that was first seen in the early 18thC. In a bid for greater comfort, such chairs had padded backs and armrests and – for the first time – stuffover seats.

The mahogany frame of the seat is very much in the Rococo style that dominated the early 18thC, which can be misleading when dating the piece. Of all the furniture forms, the armchair was among the last to adapt to the influences of the Neoclassical style that emerged from 1760 onwards.

It is unusual to find chairs from this period with their upholstery intact. Make sure that any wear is consistent with the chair's age.

A George III 'French Hepplewhite' mahogany-framed elbow chair, the cartouche-shaped back above outswept padded arms with scrolled terminals and fluently executed 'swept' acanthus to their lower portions, the serpentine stuffover seat with a foliate-carved apron rail, on rocaille-carved cabriole legs ending in brass socket casters, the whole in close-nailed blue woven-silk upholstery.

36in (91cm) high

£3,000-5,000 L&T

FURNITURE

A 19thC Continental Empire-style mahogany and brass-mounted elbow chair, the back applied with brass rinceaux and anthemia between reeded downscrolled arms.

£300–500   TEN

A pair of early 19thC French giltwood-framed fauteuils, with scroll-carved cartouche-shaped backs.

£3,000-3,500   L&T

Two of a set of four 19thC Empire-style padouk and gilt-metal-mounted open armchairs.

£3,500-5,500 SET   DN

Two similar French Charles X mahogany elbow chairs, with broad horseshoe-shaped backs, close-nailed leather overstuffed seats and sabre legs.

£800-1,000   TEN

One of a set of four Regency mahogany elbow chairs, the reeded frame with six-bar top rail and similar horizontal splat. each centred by a satinwood tablet with boxwood and ebony stringing, downswept arms on baluster supports, overstuffed seat, on turned tapering legs and peg feet.

£800-1,000 SET   HT

CLOSER LOOK – A LIBRARY CHAIR

The piece is a typical example of its period and is in excellent condition. Two features increase the interest of the piece: an adjustable brass and mahogany bookrest is attached to one arm and a candle dish to the other.

Well-proportioned Regency pieces that are pleasing to the eye sell well.

Finely reeded tapered legs add to the appeal.

The mahogany frame and leather upholstery are a good colour.

A Regency mahogany and caned library chair, the rectangular back with a reeded frame between padded arms and caned sides, with an adjustable brass and mahogany bookrest on one arm and a candle dish on the other, the caned seat with a loose leather squab, on plain rails and turned reeded and tapered legs with casters.

£3,500–5,000   TEN

A late Regency 'goncalo alves' open armchair, the ring-turned faux bamboo back to padded arms and loose seats and back upholstered with damask fabric, with scroll arms on turned and tapering supports to brass casters, back legs spliced.

Goncalo alves is a hardwood that grows in tropical forests. It is sometimes known as zebrawood or tigerwood for its dramatic markings in colours ranging from light to reddish brown, and deep mahogany to almost black. It is highly prized for its beauty.
c1820

£1,500-2,000   **WW**

One of a pair of Anglo-French mahogany library armchairs, the shaped back with leaf cresting.

c1830

£1,800-2,600 PAIR   **MEA**

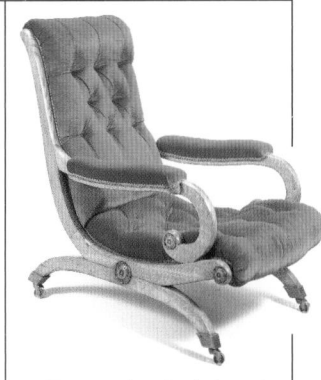

A William IV oak and upholstered library chair.

c1835

£400-600   **DN**

A 19thC upholstered elbow chair, the scrolled back with padded panel in a reeded frame, on turned and reeded legs with casters.

£1,000-1,200   **TEN**

A Victorian Rococo-style carved walnut armchair with companion nursing chair.

c1865

£800-1,000 SET   **DN**

One of a pair of Victorian carved walnut armchairs, upholstered in red leather.

c1870

£400-600 PAIR   **DN**

A 19thC French walnut fauteuil, damage, repair.

25.5in (65cm) wide

£300-400   **DN**

A Victorian walnut Rococo Revival revolving conversation seat, in the form of two chairs with integral table.

66.25in (168cm) wide

£2,300-2,600   **DN**

One of a pair of unusual ship's mahogany open armchairs, with ornate carved cresting rails above the padded backs, arms and upholstered seats, the arm terminals carved with acanthus leaves, raised on turned and fluted tapering legs with curved understretchers.

£1,000-1,200 PAIR   **A&G**

An American William & Mary beech easy chair, with an arched back, scrolled arms, and turned legs joined by stretchers, terminating in Spanish feet.
c1710

£4,000-5,000   **POOK**

A French Baroque-style giltwood and velvet upholstered armchair, with tasselled red velvet upholstery, scrolled arms and foliate-carved hand-holds, short cabriole legs ending in gadrooned feet, with X-form stretchers.

£700-1,000   **SK**

A late 19thC George II style walnut-framed wing armchair.

£1,200-1,400   **DN**

An early George III mahogany wing armchair, upholstered in green dralon, cabriole front legs with scallop knees, claw-and-bal feet.

£3,500–4,500   **L&T**

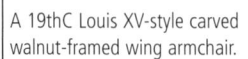

A 19thC Louis XV-style carved walnut-framed wing armchair.

£1,200-1,500   **DN**

One of a pair of 19thC American Louis XV-style walnut and needlepoint upholstered bergères à la Reine, of typical form, foliate-carved frame, needlework depicting animals, figures, and foliage.
24in (61cm) wide

£2,500-4,000 PAIR   **SK**

A pair of late 19th/early 20thC Louis XV-style carved walnut and upholstered fauteuils and a stool.

£500-700   **DN**

A Louis XV-style carved walnut sofa and chair en suite.
c1930   *76in (193cm) wide*

£700-1,200   **DN**

ESSENTIAL REFERENCE – WING ARMCHAIRS

Wing chairs are fully upholstered armchairs, with "wings" at the sides of the chair-back in an attempt to keep out draughts. They were originally designed for the elderly and infirm.

- The first recorded examples were made from the 1670s in France, where they were known as bergere en confessional, because the sitter's identity was concealed.
- Wing Chairs were first made in England in the late 17thC, when they were described in contemporary inventories as "easie" chairs. They remained fashionable until the mid-18thC, and are still produced today. In the 20thC Arne Jacobsen notably revived and moderised the design.
- They were typically made of walnut, or beech stained to look like walnut. From the 18thC, mahogany was also used in Britain, with maple being used in North America.
- The more refined examples from the early to mid-18thC were upholstered in gros and petit point needlework, often with figures in a floral border on the back.

A George III mahogany wing armchair, damages.

c1780

£600-800   DN

A 20thC George III-style mahogany wing armchair.

£500-700   DN

A 19thC George III style mahogany and blue upholstered wing armchair.

£400-600   DN

A 20thC George III style oak framed wing armchair.

£400-600   DN

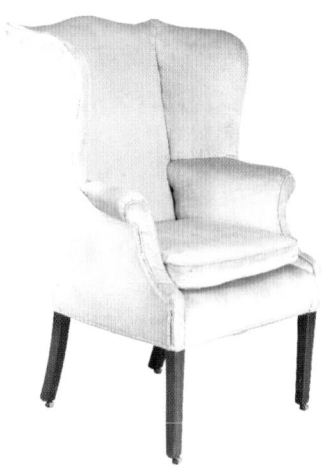

A George III mahogany wing armchair.

c1790

£1,200-1,600   DN

A 19thC Louis XVI style duchesse brisée, the carved and painted frame upholstered with striped silk, on turned stop-fluted supports, comprising an armchair and a stool.

£1,000-1,200   WW

An early 20thC George III-style button-back tub armchair, covered in raw silk.

38.25in (97cm) high

£250-350   DN

A French giltwood and upholstered fauteuil, the curved back, arms and cushioned seat covered in dark blue acanthus-and-shell striped fabric, moulded frame, the arms with ram's head terminals, on fluted turned tapering legs.

£600-900   L&T

ESSENTIAL REFERENCE – BIEDERMEIER

Biedermeier was a decorative style that was produced mainly between c1805 and 1850 in Germany, Austria and Scandinavia. Its development was associated with the revival of the German furniture trade after the defeat of Napoleon and the increasing prosperity of the middle classes.

- It was influenced by the French Empire style, with simple, clean lines and geometric shapes, and an absence of elaborate ornamentation.
- The emphasis on practicality and comfort earned the style its popularity with the middle classes, although it was also used in the private areas of noble houses.
- Light-coloured indigenous woods, especially maple, cherry and birch, were favoured, and pieces often incorporated large areas of flat veneer to show off the grain of the wood. Upholstery was generally flat and square, made of silk or horsehair, and occasionally coil-sprung.
- By the mid-19thC, the style had begun to seem dated and the name 'Biedermeier' was coined, being derived from bieder (plain) and Meier, a very common German surname.
- In the late 19thC and early 20thC there was a revival of interest in the style, when it became highly sought after and widely copied.

A pair of 19thC Neo-classical parcel-gilt bergères, the backs carved with anthemia, the arms in the form of cornucopia ending in ram's mask terminals, the seats centred with foliate motifs, on sabre legs with rosette capitals ending in hairy paw carved feet.

36.5in (93cm) high

£3,000–4,000   L&T

A William IV mahogany-framed armchair, the rounded rectangular back above out-scrolling arms, on short faceted legs headed by rosettes and ending in brass socket casters.

£700-900   L&T

A pair of Biedermeier maple bergères, each with gently sloped backrest, outscrolled arms and square tapered legs.

c1825   *21in (535.5cm)*

£2,500-3,000   SK

A 19thC upholstered throne armchair, originally made for Prince Ernst of Hanover, the rectangular back panel with raised uprights above broad outset open arms with raised terminals and upholstered seat, on turned legs, the whole covered in gold velvet with decorative tassels, distressed.

38.25in (97cm) high

£500-800   L&T

A William IV mahogany library chair, carved with acorns and trailing foliage, the seat rail stamped 'B'.

c1835

£2,000-2,500   DN

A 20thC Louis XV style green painted sofa.

68.5in (174cm) wide

£700-900 DN

An Edwardian Chippendale-style mahogany two-seater settee, with padded back and overscrolling arms and serpentine seat raised on blind fretwork square supports and fretwork stretcher, distressed upholstery.

£1,500-2,000 ADA

A 19thC French Louis XVI-style carved giltwood and upholstered canapé and one of a pair of chairs, the padded open arms, seats and backs covered in floral-patterned pink fabric, the gilt foliate-tied reeded moulded frames with floral basket cresting, paterae and acanthus leaf carving, on lotus leaf-carved spiral fluted tapered legs.

Sofa 58.25in (148cm) wide

£1,000-1,500 SET L&T

A George III mahogany sofa, faults, repairs.

c1790 *76.25in (194cm) wide*

£1,500-2,000 DN

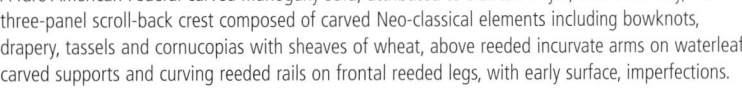

A rare American Federal carved mahogany sofa, attributed to Duncan Phyfe, New York City, the three-panel scroll-back crest composed of carved Neo-classical elements including bowknots, drapery, tassels and cornucopias with sheaves of wheat, above reeded incurvate arms on waterleaf-carved supports and curving reeded rails on frontal reeded legs, with early surface, imperfections.

Duncan Phyfe (1768-1854) was known as the 'United States Rage' during the more than 50 years he made furniture for the social and mercantile elite of New York, Philadelphia and the American South. Phyfe's pre-eminence in furniture lasted from the 1790s until his retirement in 1847. He remains America's best-known cabinetmaker.

1792-1815 *77.5in (197cm) wide*

£20,000-30,000 SK

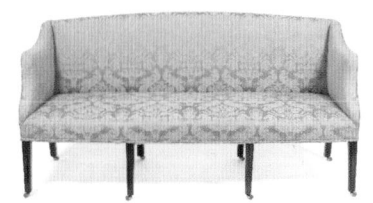

A George III mahogany-framed settee, upholstered in green print damask, the slightly arched back between downswept rounded arms and overstuffed sprung base, raised on eight square tapered legs and brass casters.

73.25in (186cm) wide

£2,500-3,000 TEN

A mahogany sofa, some faults.

c1800 and later *70.75in (180cm) wide*

£2,000-2,500 DN

An American Portsmouth, New Hampshire Federal mahogany sofa, with arched back and scrolled arms, supported by turned and reeded legs.

c1810

£1,500-1,800 POOK

An early 19thC American Federal carved mahogany and bird's-eye maple inlaid sofa, from north New England, old refinish, very minor imperfections.

75.5in (192cm) wide

£2,000-3,000 SK

An early 19thC Empire parcel-gilt mahogany and upholstered sofa.

92.5in (235cm) wide

£500-700 DN

A Regency mahogany-framed settee, the rectangular back with enclosed downswept arms on baluster terminals, the plain veneered seat rail on three slender turned and reeded front legs ending in brass socket casters, the whole covered in gold and pale yellow damask with bolster cushions.

76in (193cm) wide

£2,000-2,500   L&T

A Regency mahogany sofa, faults.

c1815   *67in (170cm) wide*

£1,500-2,000   DN

A Regency rosewood and brass-inlaid chaise longue, covered in gold cotton velvet, with two bolsters, the shaped back and scrolled ends over a loose squab on straight rails and sabre feet with brass paw caps and casters.

84.25in (214cm) wide

£6,000-7,000   TEN

An American New York Classical mahogany sofa, with dolphin-form arms and carved legs.

c1825   *92in (233.5cm) wide*

£1,500-2,000   POOK

A George IV mahogany chaise longue, upholstered in primrose damask, with scrolled ends and padded scrolled back, the loose squab cushion on a moulded rail and gadrooned sabre feet with casters.

73.5in (187cm) wide

£1,500-2,000   TEN

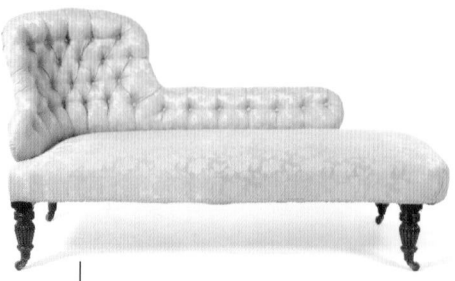

A William IV chaise longue, the shaped back and armrest upholstered in buttoned silk damask, the sprung base with shallow serpentine front, raised on stout turned and fluted legs with brass casters.

68.75in (175cm) wide

£700–900   TEN

An early Victorian mahogany and upholstered sofa, with graduated scrolling ends and reeded legs.

c1840

£300-500   DN

A mid-19thC mahogany and caned adjustable daybed.

75.5in (192cm) long

£600-800   DN

A late 19thC Victorian walnut-framed Chesterfield sofa.

£2,000-2,500   **DN**

An early 20thC tan leather Chesterfield two-seat sofa.

£800-1,000   **DN**

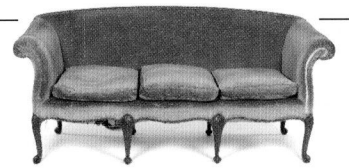

A mahogany-framed sofa, upholstered in grey-green velvet, the slightly arched back with a gadrooned toprail between rolled sides, the sprung serpentine seat with three loose cushions to the back, on carved cabriole legs with scrolled toes.

82.75in (210cm) wide

£1,000-1,500   **TEN**

A 19thC French giltwood two-seat canapé, with upholstered back and open arms, the seat covered in cream tapestry, with carved floral and moulded decoration, raised on fluted tapering legs.

42in (106.5cm) wide

£600-800   **A&G**

A Victorian rosewood button-back chaise longue, the arched back flowing from right to left, with moulded acanthus-carved scroll arms, raised on cabriole legs terminating in C-scrolls with brass casters.

69.75in (177cm) wide

£400-600   **L&T**

A late Victorian nine-piece walnut salon suite, comprising an open-arm settee with rectangular buttoned back decorated with blind fret carved foliate scrolls to the central panel, flanked by pierced and carved foliate motifs, with padded arms and seats covered in salmon pink tapestry, raised on square tapering legs with casters, a lady's and a gentleman's easy chair, and six standard chairs.

63in (160cm) wide

£900-1,200 SET   **A&G**

An American Edwardian painted satinwood double chair-back settee, painted with floral bouquets and trailing flowers, the double shield-shaped back with outswept arms, over a padded seat and raised on slender square tapered legs.

39.5in (100.5cm) wide

£700-1,000   **FRE**

A French-style fruitwood-framed and upholstered low seat, on cabriole legs, the frame carved with rosebuds and scrolls.

£1,000-1,200   **ADA**

An Edwardian three-piece mahogany-framed bergère suite, each with rope-twist top rail terminating in acanthus-carved C-scroll arms over caned back, the loose-cushioned seat with foliate-carved frieze panel, raised on squat carved cabriole legs terminating in C-scroll feet.

78.75in (190cm) wide

£900-1,200 SET   **L&T**

A 20thC Continental coromandel quarter-veneered sofa, reupholstered.

78.75in (200cm) wide

£600-800   **DN**

A Charles II oak refectory table, the top of triple-plank form, the six columnar turned legs on square feet with peripheral stretchers, the top planks with dividing cuts.

116in (295cm) wide

£10,000-12,000   **SOTH**

A large 17thC-style oak and elm refectory dining table, the rectangular top of four-plank design with cleated ends above guilloche frieze and four gadrooned and leaf-carved melon-bulb legs on block feet united by an H-stretcher.

120in (305cm) long

£3,000-3,500   **L&T**

A 17thC and later oak refectory table, on a baluster and blocked frame.

31.5in (80cm) wide

£1,200-1,600   **DN**

A late 19thC 17thC-style oak refectory table.

60.25in (153cm) wide

£500-700   **DN**

An 18thC oak refectory table, with frieze drawer.

59.5in (151cm) long

£700-1,000   **DN**

An 18thC oak refectory-style table, the three plank top and plain frieze raised on square tapered legs, joined by a central square moulded understretcher, drawer opening to one end.

32in (81cm) wide

£4,500-5,500   **HT**

An early 19thC cherry wood refectory table.

81in (206cm) wide

£3,000-4,000   **DN**

A large 19thC yew fold-over harvest table, the hinged top with cleated ends above a frieze fitted with a drawer to each end and raised on tapering block legs united by an H-stretcher.

78in (198cm) long

£2,000-4,000   **TOV**

ESSENTIAL REFERENCE – GATELEG TABLES

Gateleg tables have hinged tops consisting of one or two leaves that open out, and are supported on pivoting legs joined by stretchers.

- Introduced in the 16thC, the design became most popular in the late 17thC.
- Most have circular or oval tops, but square and octagonal tops are known.
- Most examples were made in oak or elm.

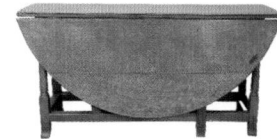

A William & Mary oak gateleg dining table, the oval top on eight turned and tapering supports, united by plain side stretchers on four short splay feet, lacking frieze drawer.

61in (155cm) wide

£1,500-2,000   HALL

An early 18thC oak gateleg table.

c1720   *63in (160cm) wide*

£1,300-1,500   DN

An early 18thC oak gateleg table, the oval top over a drawer to each end, on ball, ring and baluster supports joined by a plain stretcher, on turned feet, restorations.

69.75in (177cm) wide

£1,300-1,500   TEN

An 18thC joined oak gateleg dining table, the oval top raised on baluster supports and plain stretchers, on turned feet.

63.5in (161cm) wide

£1,600-2,000   TEN

A Victorian mahogany double drop-leaf Sutherland table, the moulded top decorated with ebony stringing and raised on turned gateleg mechanism and twin-pillar end supports with splayed feet, brass toecaps and casters.

£1,500-1,800   ADA

BREAKFAST TABLES

A George III mahogany breakfast table, the crossbanded round-cornered top on tapered, lotus-carved pillar with four reeded sabre legs, brass caps and casters.

66.25in (168cm) wide

£2,000-3,000   TEN

CLOSER LOOK – A GEORGE III MAHOGANY BREAKFAST TABLE

Designed for serving a master or mistress in the bedroom, this style of breakfast table appeared in Thomas Chippendale's The Gentleman and Cabinet-Maker's Director of 1762.

The design is compact, with drop leaves that can be folded down for storage against a wall when not in use. The inward-curving doors at one end open outwards – an innovative feature that allows the diner to sit comfortably at the table without banging their knees.

Pieces that follow a Chippendale pattern are likely to be more valuable, particularly if they are faithful to the original.

A George III mahogany breakfast table, after a design by Thomas Chippendale.

c1790   *28in (71cm) high*

£8,000-12,000   DN

A George III mahogany dining table, the circular crossbanded top on a gunbarrel pillar and four swept sabre legs, brass caps and casters.

53.5in (136cm) diam

£1,500-2,000   TEN

A George III mahogany breakfast table, the oval top raised on a ring-turned gunbarrel pillar with four reeded sabre legs, brass caps and casters.

53.5in (136cm) wide

£500-700   TEN

A Victorian amboyna and carved giltwood breakfast table, by T. & G. Seddon, London, the faded circular tilt-top with an entwined scroll gilt-brass mount to its edge, the pedestal column with gadrooned and lotus leaf collars on a triform base with scroll mouldings and fluted scroll feet with concealed casters, top of pedestal stamped twice 'T&G SEDDON' and also 'I. WILSON 68 GREAT QUEEN STREET LONDON'.

52.25in (133cm) diam

£15,000-20,000   **L&T**

A Victorian walnut and marquetry breakfast table, the circular radial veneered tilt-top inlaid with a central bouquet and an ornate entwined foliate and flowerhead scrolling border, on a bulbous gadrooned column with triple moulded downswept legs with leaf scroll feet and casters.

53.5in (136cm) diam

£3,000-4,000   **L&T**

PEDESTAL DINING TABLES

A George II and later mahogany three-pillar dining table, the round cornered top with a moulded edge, on ring-turned pillars and platform bases with hipped sabre legs, brass caps and casters and two additional leaves.

119in (302cm) long

£6,000-8,000   **TEN**

A 19thC George III mahogany two-pedestal dining table, with rectangular top and rounded corners and a reeded edge, each turned pedestal on four downswept legs ending in brass cap casters, with one leaf.

Extended 74in (188cm) wide

£3,000–4,000   **SK**

A 19thC mahogany three-pillar dining table, of bow-ended outline, the satinwood-crossbanded top with reeded edge above baluster-turned supports, on reeded triform downswept legs ending in brass box casters, with two leaf insertions.

131.5in (334cm) wide

£1,800-2,500   **L&T**

A 20thC Regency-style mahogany D-end extending dining table, with two additional leaf insertions, the reeded edge above twin baluster-turned columns, each issuing three reeded downswept legs, brass lion paw caps and casters.

58.5in (146cm) wide unextended

£600-800   **DN**

An American late 19thC Federal-style mahogany three-pedestal dining table, with a reeded-edge top and urn standards, supported by downward sloping legs, terminating in brass animal paw casters.

150in (381cm) wide

£6,000-7,000   POOK

A William IV rectangular mahogany extending dining table, raised on a pair of reeded pedestals, each with four splay legs, moulded brass feet and casters, with a spare leaf.

Extended 98in (249cm) wide

£6,000-8,000   A&G

A William IV mahogany twin pedestal dining table, on bulbous canted columns and carved paw feet, including an extra leaf.

75.25in (191cm) wide

£1,800-2,500   DN

DROPLEAF DINING TABLES

A George II mahogany dropleaf table, the oval top with rounded edge above four cabriole legs with boldly carved still leaf decoration, on claw-and-ball feet, with gate action.

50.5in (128cm) wide

£3,800-4,200   L&T

An American Philadelphia Chippendale mahogany dining table, the rectangular top supported by two dropleafs with notched corners, over a frame with scalloped ends supported by cabriole legs terminating in claw-and-ball feet, retaining old dry surface.

c1765   *41.75in (106cm) long*

£10,000-13,000   POOK

An early George III mahogany dropleaf table, of oval form with moulded edged top, arched frieze with drawer having turned brass handle, scroll carved cabriole legs terminating in hoof pad feet.

47.5in (120.5cm) wide

£400-600   HT

A George III mahogany bow-end dining table, the rounded rectangular top with two demi-lune ends and a dropleaf centre section above a plain frieze with beaded edge, on square tapering legs ending in spade feet.

127.5in (324cm) extended

£3,000-4,000   L&T

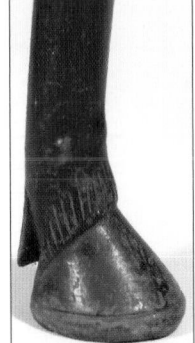

A George III mahogany dropleaf table, on cabriole legs with hoof feet.

37in (94cm) wide extended

£700-1,000   DN

A Regency mahogany extending dining table, in the manner of Gillows, the rosewood crossbanded top with D-shaped ends on a patent action extending base with six turned tapering fluted legs terminating in brass toes and casters.

£4,500-6,000 DUK

A George IV mahogany 'scissor action' extending dining table, the well-figured rounded rectangular top with reeded edge incorporating three leaf insertions, the action stamped 'WILKINSON MOORFIELDS', on turned tapering reeded legs ending in brass socket casters, the patent action allowing the table to fold down to a side table, complete with curved brass leaf clips.

In 1784 Joshua Wilkinson and his eldest son acquired premises at 7 Broker's Row, Moorfields, trading as Wilkinson & Sons. By 1790, the firm acquired further premises at 9 and 10 Broker's Row. Wilkinsons became renowned for specialising in well-made patent card and dining tables, which were, as one of their advertisements emphasised, equally remarkable for their 'ornamental effect' as the 'singularity of principles' on which they were made. In 1808 the partnership divided and William Wilkinson moved his operation to Ludgate Hill, while Thomas Wilkinson continued at 10 Broker's Row until 1828. The 'Moorfields' stamp on this table therefore reflects the firm at its peak period of production.

A large mahogany extending dining table, in the manner of Gillows, incorporating six leaves.

c1830 *217.25in (552cm) long*

£15,000-18,000 DN

50in (127cm) wide

£18,000–22,000 L&T

A William IV mahogany extending dining table, with three additional leaves, stamped 'JAMES WINTER & SONS, 101 WARDOUR ST SOHO, LONDON'.

c1835 95.25in (242cm) wide

£2,500-3,500 DN

A William IV mahogany extending dining table, with a moulded top on lotus-carved baluster legs with casters, including four additional leaves, two original and two later.

137in (348cm) long

£2,700-3,500 TEN

A William IV mahogany extending dining table, with three additional leaves, stamped 'JAMES WINTER & SONS, 101 WARDOUR ST SOHO, LONDON'.

c1835 *95.25in (242cm) wide*

£2,500-3,500 DN

An early Victorian mahogany extending dining table, the rectangular D-end top with a moulded edge on a deep frieze with heavy turned legs with carved paterae tops and brass wheel casters, with two matching central legs and five additional leaves, the table closing to form a circular table.

197in (500.5cm) long fully extended

£7,000-10,000 DUK

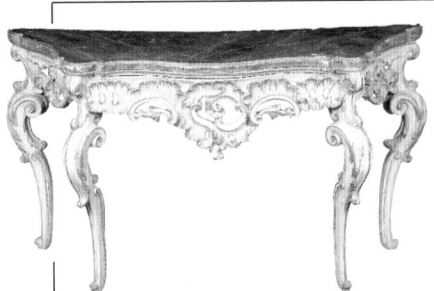

A mid-18thC and later Louis XV carved, painted and parcel-gilt wood pier table.

54in (137cm) wide

£1,700-2,200   DN

A late 18thC George III inlaid mahogany demi-lune side table, the top inlaid with crossbanding and stringing, with a central inlaid panel, above a frieze drawer and two sham drawers, on square, tapered legs ending in spade feet.

52in (132cm) wide

£2,000–2,500   SK

A George III inlaid sycamore pier table of semi-elliptical form, the top crossbanded and centred by a husk patera issuing radial veneers, the frieze centred by a shell patera and raised on square tapering banded legs with ebony stringing.

62.25in (158cm) wide

£13,000-18,000   ADA

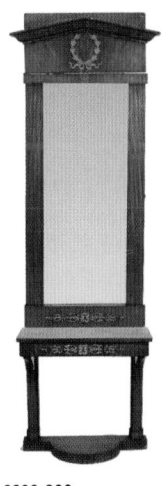

An early 19thC Empire mahogany and gilt metal mounted console table and mirror.

Table 30.75in (78cm) wide

£600-800   DN

A Regency giltwood console table, with a white marble top above a leaf and shell carved and moulded frieze, on lion monopodia and paw feet.

44in (112cm) wide

£2,500-3,500   DUK

An Empire gilt-bronze mounted onyx top pier table, the rectangular top above a conforming frieze mounted with classical motifs, on column form supports, backed by a mirror, on a plinth base.

47in (119.5cm) wide

£1,800–2,200   SK

ESSENTIAL REFERENCE – EGYPTIENNERIE

Eygptiennerie describes forms and motifs inspired by ancient Egyptian art and architecture. From the 16thC, motifs such as sphinxes and obelisks were used in the applied arts.

- In the late 18thC and early 19thC, the vogue for Egyptian ornament reached its peak, as part of the Regency, Empire and Federal styles, inspired by Napoleon's campaigns in Egypt of the 1790s and the publications of Baron Vivant Denon.
- Typical motifs include hieroglyphs, winged griffins, palmettes and lotus leaves.
- The fashion for Egyptian style continued as a strand of Historicism throughout the 19thC.
- The discovery of the tomb of Tutankhamen in 1922 led to a revival in popularity, which is especially evident in Art Deco jewellery.

A 19thC North European Empire-style mahogany, ebonised, parcel gilt and metal mounted pier table, with twin monopodial sphinx supports.

37.75in (96cm) wide

£2,300-2,800   DN

FURNITURE

A William IV carved rosewood pier table, with rectangular top, plain frieze and beaded edge raised on boldly carved and gadrooned legs, with mirrored back and plinth base.

c1835   *59in (150cm) wide*
£6,000-7,000   **SK**

A French figured walnut and marble-mounted console table.

c1860   *45.25in (115cm) wide*
£600-800   **DN**

A Victorian black japanned, parcel-gilt and painted console table, the demi-lune mould top decorated with figure and pagodas in a landscape, the floral painted frieze on a turned fluted central support and shaped triform under tier, decoration later.

35.75in (91cm) wide
£200-400   **L&T**

A 19thC Empire Revival painted pier table and mirror, each with carved Egyptian and other motifs including patera and herm figures, recessed pilasters inlaid with anthemion, table with faux marble top and frieze drawer and platform stretcher.

Table 36.5in (93cm) wide
£1,000-1,500   **SK**

A matched pair of 20thC grey painted wrought iron console tables, each with shaped marble tops, now overpainted, above a pierced frieze centred by a foliate motif, on cabriole legs capped with acanthus, joined by scrolling stretchers and scroll feet.

39.25in (100cm) wide
£1,000-1,500   **TEN**

SIDE TABLES

A late 17thC Jacobean oak side table, the rectangular top above a panelled frieze drawer, on block and ring-turned legs joined by stretchers.

28.5in (72.5cm) wide
£3,000-4,000   **SK**

A late 17thC and later William & Mary walnut side table, with geometric crossbanded top above a frieze drawer, adapted.

35in (89cm) wide
£1,300-1,800   **DN**

An early 18thC oak single-drawer side table.

30.25in (77cm) wide
£650-850   **DN**

An early 18thC joined oak side table, the moulded top over a frieze drawer, on baluster legs joined by a waved X-stretcher, on ball feet.

30in (76cm) wide
£1,700-2,000   **TEN**

A George II oak two-drawer side table.

c1750
£250-350   **DN**

A mahogany side table, top altered.

c1750   33.75in (86cm) wide
£1,500-2,000   **DN**

A 19thC Irish mahogany lobby table, the rounded rectangular top with moulded edge above a rosette-carved frieze with a pair of recessed drawers, on scroll-carved front legs ending in massive carved lion paw feet.

58.75in (149cm) wide

£3,500-4,500   L&T

A mid-19thC Irish mahogany serving table, the top of serpentine outline with broad moulded edge and a recessed frieze drawer, on four bold acanthus-carved volute scroll legs with shaped plinth bases, each attached to the top on metal slides stamped 'Cope & Collinson'.

98.5in (250cm) wide

£14,000-20,000   L&T

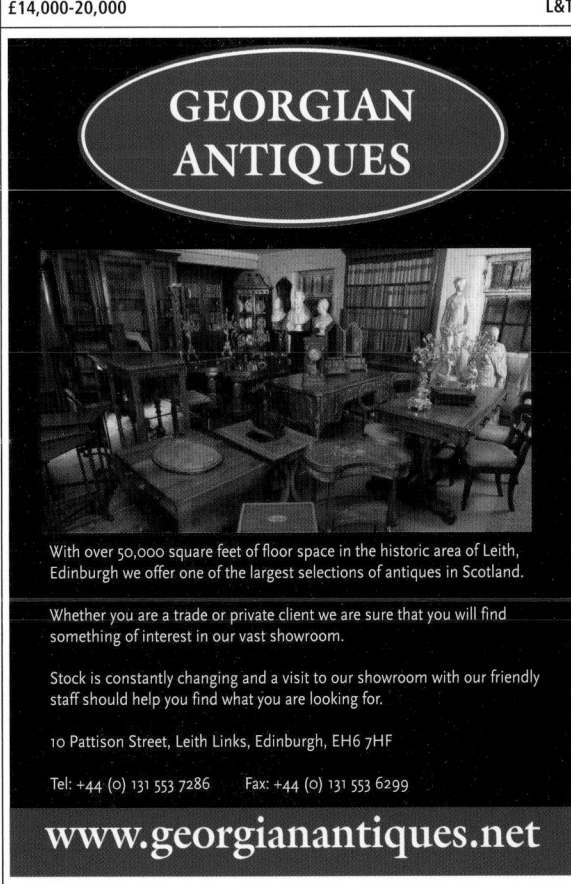

FURNITURE

An American Pennsylvania painted walnut diminutive tavern table, with an oval top and baluster-turned legs joined by an H-stretcher, retaining an old green/blue surface.

c1760   *25in (63.5cm) high*

£3,500-4,500   **POOK**

A George III walnut and oak cricket table, faults.

c1780   *26.25in (67cm) diam*

£1,200-1,400   **DN**

A late 18thC and later oak cricket table.

25.25in (64cm) diam

£600-800   **DN**

A late 18thC American probably New England, cherry, birch and pine red-painted splay leg table with drawer.

32.5in (82.5cm) wide

£5,500-7,000   **SK**

A George IV mahogany reading table, the rectangular moulded-edge top on an adjustable square stem to a stepped base and X-shape supports, on brass caps and casters.

26.75in (68cm) wide

£500-700   **WW**

One of a pair of French bird's-eye maple and marquetry occasional tables.

c1835   *24.75in (63cm) high*

£2,000-3,000 PAIR   **DN**

A William IV rosewood and marble-top occasional table, the rectangular cube parquetry top decorated with specimen marbles within a black veined marble border, the turned and lappet-carved pedestal on a quadripartite platform base with bun feet.

18.5in (47cm) wide

£1,600-2,000   **L&T**

A William IV rosewood occasional table.

c1835   *22in (56cm) wide*

£1,000-1,400   **DN**

A small 19thC occasional table, the square crossbanded flip top with rounded corners on a turned stem on tripod base.

£850-1,000   **MEA**

A 19thC satinwood and mahogany crossbanded occasional table, adapted.

18in (46cm) wide

£350-450   **DN**

FURNITURE

A Regency mahogany drum table, with four real and four sham drawers raised on a ring-turned pillar and four reeded sabre legs, brass caps and casters.

41.75in (106cm) wide

£2,500–3,000   TEN

A Regency rosewood, crossbanded and cut-brass inlaid tilt-top breakfast table, the circular top with a crossbanded border decorated with anthemia and griffins bounded by arabesque scrolls, on a stepped and beaded pedestal and inswept platform base raised on four short sabre legs ending in brass claw caps and casters, the whole inlaid with brass stringing.

51.25in (130cm) diam

£5,500-6,500   L&T

A Regency burr-elm centre table, attributed to William Trotter, the circular radial veneered burr-elm tilt-top enclosed by satinwood, partridgewood and further satinwood crossbanding above a ribbed frieze, the square tapered panelled pedestal with reeded scroll corner corbels, and acanthus-carved hipped sabre legs ending in brass caps.

William Trotter was born into a family of merchants in 1772, descended on the maternal side from the family of John Knox. He became a member of The Merchant Company in 1797 and by 1809 he was sole proprietor of the firm Young & Trotter. In 1819 he was elected master of The Merchant Company. Trotter continued to trade from 9 Princes Street, Edinburgh until his death in 1833. Trotter was regarded as perhaps the most eminent of all Scottish cabinetmakers.

53.25in (135cm) diam

£4,000-6,000   L&T

A Charles X marble top and parcel gilt centre table, the circular rouge royale marble top above a faceted baluster stem with three-sided base, with gilded corbels and paw feet, on casters.

39.5in (100.5cm) diam

£2,200–2,800   SK

A George IV mahogany drum library table, the top incorporating four drawers.

c1825   *52.25in (133cm) diam*

£3,000-4,000   DN

A William IV mahogany centre table, the radial-veneered and rosewood-crossbanded top on a hexagonal waisted baluster column, the triform concave base with scroll feet and casters.

35.5in (90cm) diam

£2,000-2,500   L&T

A William IV rosewood centre table, the circular top above a convex apron, on a concave faceted triform stem with scroll corbels, the triform platform base with lappet scroll feet and casters.

36.25in (92cm) diam

£1,800-2,200   L&T

ESSENTIAL REFERENCE – J.H. BELTER

John Henry Belter (1804-63) was a German furniture maker who emigrated to America in 1840. He eventually replaced Duncan Phyfe as New York's best-known cabinet maker.

- **Belter's name is associated with a type of New York furniture made with elaborately carved, pierced and upholstered bentwood.**
- **He favoured rosewood, a material that lacked sufficient strength for carving and was difficult to use for veneering. Belter developed a process to make laminated rosewood consisting of six to eight layers which could be used for carved and curved pieces with elaborate ornament.**
- **Between 1847 and 1860, he patented many machines and processes related to making his innovative furniture.**
- **Stylistically his furniture was Neo-Rococo, with lots of carved work, both in relief and the round.**
- **His firm went bankrupt in 1867.**

A carved Rococo rosewood marble-top centre table, attributed to J. H. Belter, the oval Carrera marble top with serpentine 'bull nose' edges fitted to the conforming frieze, ornately carved with floral sprays, raised on four floral-and-foliate carved cabriole legs joined by a carved serpentine X-stretcher centring a large carved finial in the form of a floral bouquet, the whole raised on wooden casters within brass fitting.

c1860   *35.5in (90cm) wide*

£15,000-20,000   **JDJ**

A mid-Victorian rosewood centre table, the top of serpentine outline with moulded edge and shaped apron with leaf-carved escutcheons, enclosing a pair of frieze drawers on profusely carved cabriole legs united by pierced and floral-carved X-stretchers surmounted by an urn-shaped boss, on china casters.

60.25in (153cm) wide

£900-1,200   **L&T**

A Victorian figured walnut oval centre table.

c1870   *50in (127cm) wide*

£700-1,000   **DN**

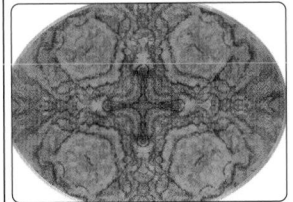

A Victorian walnut centre table, the radially quarter-veneered oval top with moulded edge and plain frieze, supported on a ring-turned pillar with four leaf-carved scroll feet and brass casters.

57.75in (147cm) wide

£2,300–2,800   **TEN**

A Victorian figured walnut oval centre table.

c1870

£400-600   **DN**

A Victorian circular specimen timber centre table, the segmented top crossbanded and inset with veneers of yew, rosewood, coromandel, fruitwood, walnut, etc., on an octagonal tapering stem with circular platform and scroll legs.

36in (91cm) diam

£1,500-2,000   **MEA**

A Victorian rosewood oval centre table, the top with a moulded edge, on double scroll supports with central shells, the downswept legs with brass casters and joined by a turned pole stretcher.

53.25in (135cm) long

£1,200-1,500   **L&T**

A late 19thC boulle and gilt-metal mounted centre table, of serpentine outline.

39in (99cm) wide

£1,300-500   **DN**

A French Regence-style gilt-brass mounted ebony bureau plat.

c1850   *49.25in (125cm) wide*

£2,000-2,500   DN

A late 19thC Louis XV style kingwood bureau plat, with gilt metal mounts, the serpentine moulded-edge top inset with gilt-tooled leather above three banded frieze drawers, with pull-out slides to each side, on cabriole legs.

47in (199.5cm) wide

£900-1,200   WW

A mid-18thC German kingwood and marquetry small writing table, the quarter-veneered serpentined top with a crossbanded edge and finely inlaid central floral basket, below a lateral drawer and a baize inset writing slide, the apron inlaid with foliate wreaths above slender cabriole legs.

26.5in (67cm) wide

£1,500-2,500   L&T

A George III mahogany and red leather inset partner's writing table.

c1800   *45.25in (115cm) wide*

£700-1,000   DN

A George IV mahogany dressing or writing table, with four drawers and reeded legs.

c1825   *48in (122cm) wide*

£700-1,000   DN

A William IV mahogany writing table, Gillows of Lancaster, the drawer stamped 'GILLOW'.

c1830   *48in (122cm) wide*

£2,500-3,000   DN

A late Victorian rosewood and marquetry writing table, retailed by Maple & Co., the raised mirrored back flanked by two drawers either side, the top inset gilt-tooled leather above three frieze drawers two stamped 'Maple & Co.', on square tapering legs and ceramic casters, losses to inlay.

Maple & Co. was a well-known furniture maker from the Victorian period: the Maple & Co. Warehouse was recognized as one of the 'Sites of London', and as such was often visited by distinguished tourists and others from all parts of the world. In 1980 Maple & Co. joined with Waring and Gillow becoming Maple, Waring and Gillow.

42in (107cm) wide

£600-800   WW

A 19thC Louis XV-style gilt bronze mounted kingwood bureau plat, with a shaped top, raised on cabriole legs.

36in (91.5cm) wide

£1,000-1,500   FRE

An Edwardian satinwood and inlaid kidney-shaped writing table, inlaid throughout with trailing husks and bell flowers, the curved superstructure incorporating three small drawers above a tooled green leather inset top, above a central drawer flanked by a pair of small drawers, on Ionic-capped square tapered legs ending in spade feet with brass casters.

42in (107cm) wide

£2,000-3,000   L&T

An Edwardian mahogany and satinwood lady's writing table, the top with a leather-lined writing surface and a raised shelf with pierced brass gallery, above a central recess and two pairs of short drawers, above two frieze drawers, on square tapering legs and casters.

35.5in (90cm) wide

£1,000-1,200   DUK

A Regency mahogany and satinwood crossbanded sofa table, the rounded rectangular top above four frieze drawers with brass pull handles on reeded square section end standards inlaid with crossed spears ending in dual splay legs with brass box casters, the whole decorated with ebony and boxwood lines.

61.5in (156cm) wide extended

£3,500–4,500 **L&T**

A Regency gilt metal mounted mahogany and marquetry sofa table, in the manner of George Bullock.

c1820 *60.25in (153cm) wide*

£2,000-2,500 **DN**

A Regency mahogany sofa table, the rosewood banded top over two frieze drawers with sham drawers opposite, raised on standard end supports with sabre legs, brass caps and casters, restorations.

39in (99cm) wide

£900–1,200 **TEN**

A Regency mahogany sofa table, faults.

c1820 *60.25in (153cm) wide*

£3,000-3,500 **DN**

A Regency mahogany sofa table, with an intricately carved pineapple stem, cast lion paw caps and casters, the interior of one drawer bears an armorial wax seal, unextended.

c1820 *37.5in (95cm) wide unextended*

£6,000-8,000 **DN**

A late Regency inlaid rosewood sofa table, the inlaid top with two rectangular flaps flanking two frieze drawers and opposing mock drawers raised on two C-scroll supports with centre stand, united by an ornate turned stretcher and raised on turned bun feet.

55in (140cm) wide extended

£3,000-3,500 **MEA**

ESSENTIAL REFERENCE – PEMBROKE TABLES

The Pembroke table is a small, typically elegant occasional table, with four legs, usually on castors, one or two frieze drawers and two drop leaves supported by wooden brackets on hinges, known as 'elbows'. It was typically placed in the drawing room or the boudoir, where it could be used to take meals, play cards, write, or for needlework.

- According to Thomas Sheraton's pattern book 'The Cabinet Directory' (1803), the form takes its name "from the name of the lady who first gave orders for one of them": the Countess of Pembroke.
- Pembroke tables were produced in England from the mid-18th century.
- Table tops (which may form a rectangle, square, oval or octagon, etc) were often elaborately inlaid with satinwood, ebony and boxwood. Legs could be of cabriole or straight-tapered shape, and of round or square section.
- Pembroke tables had largely been replaced in fashionable drawing tables by the sofa table, which was an extended version of the type. Brass inlay was popular on both forms, and in the late 19th and early 20th centuries they were often painted in revival styles.

A George III inlaid and crossbanded mahogany Pembroke table, with two D-shaped flaps, flanking one mock and one frieze drawer raised on square tapering legs.

32.5in (83cm) wide

£1,000-1,300 **MEA**

FURNITURE

A George III mahogany and satinwood banded Pembroke table, faults.

c1800   *43.25in (110cm) wide*

£500-600   **DN**

A late George III mahogany, satinwood and tulipwood-crossbanded Pembroke table, of small proportions, the rounded rectangular well-figured top with single frieze drawer and ivory pull handles opposed by a simulated drawer, on a slender ring-turned pillar and four downswept reeded legs ending in brass socket casters, the whole inlaid with box and ebony lines.

24.5in (62cm) wide

£3,500-4,500   **L&T**

An amboyna and sabicu oval Pembroke table.

c1810   *39.25in (100cm) wide*

£1,000-1,200   **DN**

A George III satinwood and rosewood crossbanded Pembroke table, faults.

c1810   *34.75in (88cm) wide*

£1,800-2,200   **DN**

A George III mahogany Pembroke table, later painted with ribbons, paterae and swags, the oval top over a bowed frieze drawer and sham drawer opposite, on square tapered legs and casters.

31.75in (81cm) wide

£900-1,200   **TEN**

An American, probably New York, Federal carved mahogany and mahogany veneer drop-leaf table, with working and faux drawers, old refinish.

c1815-20   *34.75in (88cm) wide*

£1,700-2,500   **SK**

An Edwardian rosewood Pembroke table, the rectangular top over a frieze drawer to each end, on square tapered legs with casters, joined by rising X-stretcher with rectangular galleried undertier, labelled 'John and Appleyards, Manufacturers and Merchants, Sheffield'.

30in (76cm) wide

£600–800   **TEN**

A walnut card table.
c1740 and later *31.5in (80cm) wide*
£1,300-1,500 **DN**

CLOSER LOOK

Common to the majority of card tables, the top of this piece has a hinged fold at the centre, allowing the table to be opened out for play and closed for storage against a wall when redundant.

The first half of the 18thC is considered the 'age of mahogany', the wood lending itself perfectly to the elegant carved decoration that epitomised early Georgian furniture.

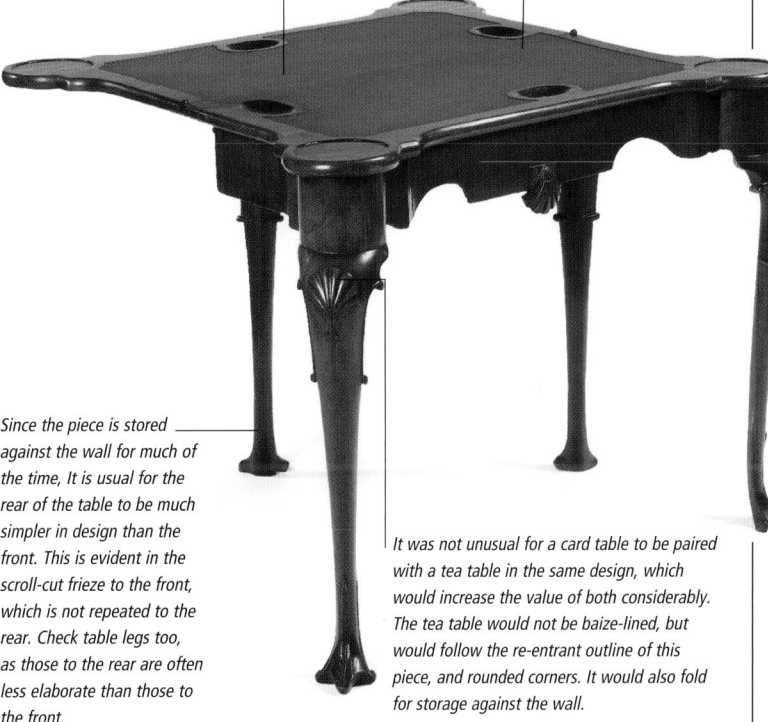

Since the piece is stored against the wall for much of the time, It is usual for the rear of the table to be much simpler in design than the front. This is evident in the scroll-cut frieze to the front, which is not repeated to the rear. Check table legs too, as those to the rear are often less elaborate than those to the front.

It was not unusual for a card table to be paired with a tea table in the same design, which would increase the value of both considerably. The tea table would not be baize-lined, but would follow the re-entrant outline of this piece, and rounded corners. It would also fold for storage against the wall.

A George II, probably Irish, mahogany card table, the folding top opening to reveal a baize-lined surface with money and candle slots, above a plain wide frieze flanked with projecting rounded corners on cabriole legs terminating in webbed pad feet.
37in (94cm) wide
£2,500-3,500 **MEA**

A George II mahogany card table, the top of re-entrant outline with projecting corners, enclosing a baize inset bounded by counter wells, the scroll-cut frieze centred by a scallop shell, on four shell and scroll-carved cabriole legs ending in trefoil-carved pad feet.
35in (89cm) wide
£5,000-6,000 **L&T**

A George II mahogany card table, the lobed rectangular top with counter wells, the shaped frieze on lapetted turned legs with pad feet, restoration and repairs.
30.75in (78cm) wide
£800-1,000 **TEN**

A 19thC George III style rosewood and satinwood crossbanded folding card table, the D-shaped top above a crossbanded frieze and on turned tapering legs, damage, repair.
36.25in (92cm) wide
£550-750 **DN**

A George III satinwood and crossbanded card table, of D-shaped breakfront outline, inlaid with ebonised stringing, the foldover top revealing a green baize inset, on square tapered legs ending in spade feet.
38in (97cm) wide
£1,700-2,000 **L&T**

FURNITURE

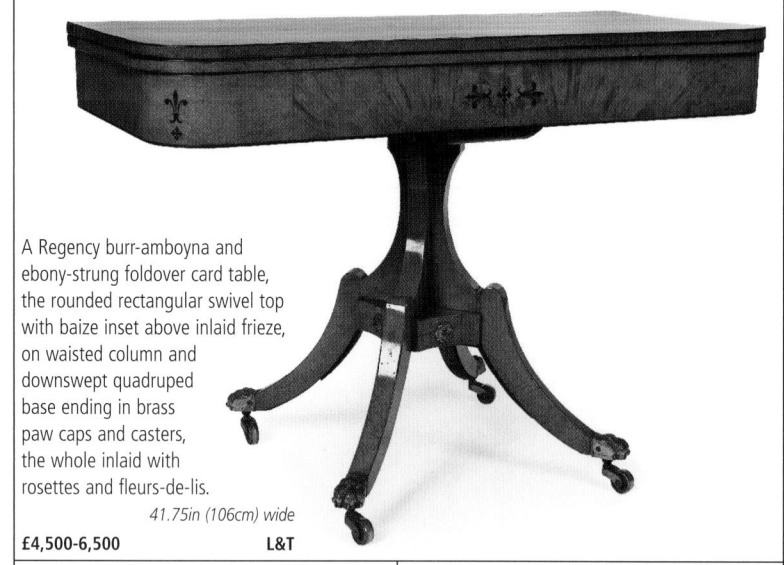

A Regency burr-amboyna and ebony-strung foldover card table, the rounded rectangular swivel top with baize inset above inlaid frieze, on waisted column and downswept quadruped base ending in brass paw caps and casters, the whole inlaid with rosettes and fleurs-de-lis.

41.75in (106cm) wide

£4,500-6,500   L&T

An American Classical carved mahogany and mahogany veneer card table, mid-Atlantic states, the rectangular top with rounded corners with band inlay, the conforming apron with panels of figured mahogany on turned posts and shaped platform on four cornucopia and leaf-carved scrolled supports, shaped base raised on four feather and paw carved feet, on casters.

£1,500-2,000   FRE

An American, probably Massachusetts, Federal carved mahogany and mahogany veneer card table, refinished, imperfections.

c1815-20   *35.5in (90cm) wide*

£2,200-2,800   SK

A Regency rosewood and brass marquetry card table.

36.5in (93cm) wide

£1,000-1,200   DN

A George IV inlaid mahogany rectangular top card table, the top crossbanded in rosewood above a fielded frieze, raised on a spiral-turned centre pillar, leaf-carved and gadroon quadruped base with brass paw toecaps and casters.

36in (91.5cm) wide

£700-1,000   ADA

A George IV mahogany and crossbanded card table, the D-shape swivel top enclosing a green baize-lined interior, above a plain frieze on turned column support united by quadruped scrolling supports and platform base, raised on scrolling legs, brass claw feet and casters.

35.5in (90cm) wide

£650–750   TEN

A William IV rosewood mahogany card table, T. & G. Seddon, bearing paper label 'Manufacturers to her Majesty T & G SEDDON, No. 6466, GRAYS INN ROAD, LONDON'.

c1830   *32.25in (82cm) wide*

£2,700-3,200   DN

A George IV mahogany card table, the reeded edge hinged, and swivel D-shape top to a plain frieze centred with a rectangular tablet, on a turned stem to four hipped and reeded supports terminating in brass sabots and casters.

36in (91cm) wide

£550-650   WW

A Victorian rosewood card table, the rectangular rounded top enclosing a green baize-lined interior above a moulded frieze, supported by a plain column and carved leaf collar, on circular moulded base raised on three claw feet and casters.

35.5in (90cm) wide

£800-1,000   **TEN**

A 19thC possibly Austro-Hungarian walnut and marquetry card table, of square envelope form with kingwood banding, the swivel top with panels depicting landscape and figure scenes within strapwork borders, similar frieze with small drawer, raised on baluster and wrythen-turned tapering legs with bun feet joined by shaped cross stretchers with central finial.

25.25in (64cm) wide

£800-1,000   **HT**

A 19thC Louis XVI-style walnut card table, of oblong serpentine form, the folding top with circular baize, shaped frieze with carved foliage, on shell and leaf-carved cabriole legs with peg feet.

33.5in (85cm) wide

£350-550   **HT**

A Victorian burr-walnut card table, with rectangular hinged swivel top, decorated with ebonised banding, boxwood stringing and foliate motifs, the top opening to reveal a green baize lining, raised on turned and fluted tapering legs with curved understretchers.

38in (96.5cm) wide

£1,000-1,200   **A&G**

An Edwardian rosewood and marquetry envelope card table, inlaid with etched bone urns and foliate arabesques, the square top opening to reveal a tooled baized playing surface with outer counterwells, above a drawer and square tapered legs joined by an undertier and ending in ceramic casters.

22in (56cm) wide

£700-1,000   **L&T**

TEA TABLES

A George II mahogany foldover tea table, the rectangular top with floret-carved edge above a plain frieze, on boldly hipped acanthus-carved legs ending in claw-and-ball feet.

33.5in (85cm) wide

£3,000-3,500   **L&T**

A George III mahogany folding tea and games table, repair.

c1760   *31in (79cm) wide*

£1,800-2,200   **DN**

A George III mahogany folding tea table, repair.

c1790   *37.5in (95cm) wide*

£500-700   **DN**

A pair of early George III mahogany and satinwood crossbanded tea tables, inlaid with stringing and rosewood banding, the demi-lune foldover tops on square tapered legs, rear central legs sliding out to reveal drawers to support each top, legs reduced on one table.

39.75in (101cm) wide

£3,500–5,500   **L&T**

CLOSER LOOK – A KILLARNEY GAMES TABLE

Killarneyware was first made in the 1820s when the Irisih town became a tourist attraction for visiting English aristocrats.

The distinctive style includes architectural marquetry of local tourist sites and inlay of local fauna and flora, and Irish symbols.

A visit from the Queen Victoria and Price Albert in 1861 established Killarney's reputation.

Popular subjects depicted on Killarneyware include nearby historical sites such as Muckross Abbey (pictured here), Glena Cottage, Muckross House and Ross Castle.

A 19thC Killarney yew marquetry and parquetry fold-over games table.

31in (79cm) wide

£15,000-20,000   MEA

An American Philadelphia Chippendale carved mahogany games table, the folding top overhanging a drawer and gadrooned apron, and cabriole legs ending in carved claw and ball feet, old replaced brasses, old refinish and minor imperfections.

c1770-80   *36in (91.5cm) wide*

£16,000-20,000   SK

An American New England Chippendale mahogany diminutive games table, the serpentine top over a frame with a single drawer supported by square moulded legs.

c1785   *29in (73.5cm) wide*

£4,000-5,000   POOK

An Irish George III mahogany games table, the double folding top carved with ribbon and rosette border opening to reveal an inlaid backgammon board on stop-fluted legs surmounted by leaf motifs and with club feet.

24.75in (63cm) wide

£4,000-5,000   ADA

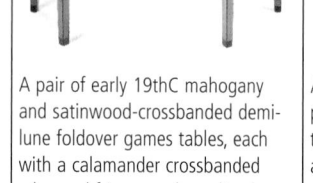

A pair of early 19thC mahogany and satinwood-crossbanded demi-lune foldover games tables, each with a calamander crossbanded edge and frieze on ebony-lined square tapering legs, ending in toes of contrasting veneer.

35.75in (91cm) wide

£3,000-4,000   L&T

A mid-19thC Anglo-Indian carved padouk and ebonised games table, the top with turned ivory balustrade above a gadrooned edge and candleslide, enclosing a detachable chessboard, the central column on a cabriole base, ending in scroll feet.

17.25in (44cm) wide

£1,000-1,500   L&T

An early 18thC country yew wood and crossbanded dressing table, the rectangular top with banded 'strips' and broad crossbanded and moulded edge above a shaped apron enclosing three short cockbeaded drawers, on cabriole legs with pad feet.

29.5in (75cm) wide

£4,500-6,500   L&T

An American Delaware Valley Chippendale walnut dressing table, the rectangular top overhanging a case with one long and three short drawers supported by cabriole legs terminating in ball-and-claw feet.

c1770   *32in (81cm) wide*

£8,000-10,000   POOK

A mid-18thC American Massachusetts or New Hampshire Queen Anne tiger-maple dressing table, the top with notched front corners above the case with flat-headed arches in the front and on the sides, above the cabriole legs ending in pad feet on high platforms, old brass, old refinish, minor imperfections.

33.25in (84.5cm) wide

£10,000-12,000   SK

A George III mahogany gentleman's dressing table, by Gillows, stamped 'GILLOWS, LANCASTER'.

Gillows (founded in Lancaster, c.1727) was the leading furniture manufacturers outside the capital in the 18thC/19thC. Its success was largely due to good quality and workmanship, combined with a wise choice of middle-of-the-road designs that appealed to the provincial middle classes. In 1900, Gillows merged with S.J. Waring & Sons to become Waring & Gillow.
c1790

£1,000-1,200   DN

FURNITURE

A Victorian George II-style carved mahogany tripod table, the circular dished top with a flowerhead and dart-carved edge, the acanthus leaf-carved cabriole legs with claw feet.

22in (56cm) diam

£1,800-2,500   **L&T**

A George III mahogany pedestal table, the circular tilt-top with a moulded pie-crust edge, birdcage undersection, fluted and carved column, on tripod legs, carved and scrolled knees, talon feet.

29.25in (74cm) diam

£6,000-8,000   **L&T**

A George III mahogany tilt-top table, the circular top with birdcage gallery above a spirally-reeded baluster column, on floret-centred leaf-carved cabriole tripod base with scroll feet.

30.75in (78cm) diam

£2,000-2,500   **L&T**

A George III mahogany snap-top supper table, the shaped circular top with pie-crust rim, raised on a baluster centre pillar and leaf-carved tripod base with dolphin head feet.

36.75in (85.5cm) diam

£3,000-3,500   **ADA**

A George III mahogany tip-top occasional table, the plain circular top above a fixed birdcage and turned column platform, a bulbous vase and ring-turned post continuing to tripod cabriole legs ending in pad feet.

27.5in (70cm) high

£1,000-1,200   **TEN**

A Regency yew wood and specimen wood occasional table, the circular rosewood-veneered top with star-inlaid centre and chevron-banded edge on a ring-turned yew wood column and downswept tripod base, decorated with various exotics including snakewood, partridgewood, coromandel and olive wood.

17in (43cm) diam

£2,500-3,500   **L&T**

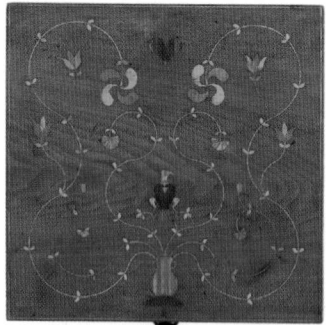

A late 18thC American Pennsylvania walnut tripod table, the square top profusely inlaid with a striped urn emitting vines with tulips and philflots centring on an eagle, over a circular birdcage and baluster standard supported by cabriole legs terminating in pad feet.

28.5in (72.5cm) high

£50,000-60,000   **POOK**

A Pennsylvania Chippendale walnut tea table, the dish top above a birdcage and suppressed ball standard, supported by cabriole legs terminating in claw-and-ball feet.

c1770   33.5in (85cm) wide

£10,000-15,000   **POOK**

A late 18thC American Pennsylvania tiger-maple tea table, the tilt-top above a reeded standard, supported by cabriole legs terminating in pad feet.

29.5in (75cm) wide

£3,500-4,000   **POOK**

CLOSER LOOK – KETTLE STAND

Pierced fretwork galleries were common on kettle stands and their accompanying china tables. Tea-making paraphernalia was costly and the gallery prevented the pieces falling to the floor.

Along with the tea table (to sit at) and the china table (to display cups and saucers), the kettle stand became an important domestic furniture form during the 18thC, as tea and coffee drinking became more fashionable, socially.

The column of this stand has Neoclassical style stop-fluting, while the carving to the knop, the cabriole legs and the claw-and-ball feet are more readily associated with the Rococo style. This is typical of Thomas Chippendale.

A George III mahogany kettle stand, in the manner of Thomas Chippendale, the octagonal pierced fretwork gallery with caddy moulded top rail above a stop-fluted baluster column with a leaf-carved knop, on a rocaille-carved cabriole tripod base with tied acanthus sprays, ending in talon-and-ball feet.

29in (73cm) high

£20,000-25,000   **L&T**

A Pennsylvania Queen Anne walnut candle stand, with a small round dished top, suppressed ball standard, a tripod base with pad feet, retaining an old dry surface.

c1760   *17in (43cm) diam*

£5,500-6,500   **POOK**

An 18thC Queen Anne mahogany candle stand from Philadelphia, moulded circular top on birdcage, tapering stand on suppressed ball and arched legs ending in pad feet.

£1,500-2,000   **FRE**

A late 19thC olive wood tilt-top candle stand, Jerusalem, octagonal top with printed identifications of locations and the seven woods of the Holy Land used, spiralled base, on scrolled feet.

30.5in (77.5cm) high

£600-800   **SK**

FURNITURE

An early 19thC Federal carved bird's-eye maple and bird's-eye maple veneer work table, New Hampshire, the top with ovolo corners, the tops carved with circular fans, above two cockbeaded drawers and skirt joining the quarter-engaged vase and ring-turned legs tapering to feet, original brass pulls, old finish, minor imperfections.

29.25in (74.5cm) high

£7,500-8,000 SK

A Regency mahogany and ebony-strung octagonal work table.

c1815 *21.5in (55cm) wide*

£1,000-1,500 DN

An American Classical mahogany and mahogany veneer work table, Boston or Salem, Massachusetts, the square top with flanking recessed sides and rounded dropleaves with brass supports on conforming table centring an ormolu-mounted drawer with compartmented interior flanked by small drawers and bag drawer below, on ring-turned tapering columns and waterleaf-carved sabre legs continuing to lion-paw feet joined by arched medial stretcher, refinished.

c1815 *22.75in (58cm) wide*

£3,500-4,000 SK

A Regency Pembroke work table.

c1820 *14.25in (36cm) wide*

£900-1,200 DN

A Regency mahogany Pembroke work table, the rectangular top with moulded edge and rounded corners incorporating a pair of hinged flaps, above a deep drawer and a further drawer, on square section tapering legs brass caps and casters, damage.

29in (74cm) high

£1,100-1,300 DN

A George IV rosewood work table, attributed to Gillows, the drop flap rectangular top with rounded corners above two drawers and two opposing dummy drawers, the lower drawer compartmented with four removable trays and a pin cushion, above a sliding pleated work bag, on reeded turned tapered legs ended in brass caps and casters, the bottom of the top drawer bears the name 'Barrow' faintly in pencil.

Barrow was the surname of a family of cabinet makers working for Gillows in Lancaster around 1820.

19.75in (50cm) wide

£2,500-3,500 L&T

A George IV mahogany and chevron-banded work table, of cartouche shaped outline, the inlaid top above a pull-out slide, frieze drawer and a wool drawer below, on splayed square section legs united by a shaped undertier.

30in (76cm) high

£1,800–2,200 L&T

A Biedermeier part-ebonised fruitwood work box on stand, the hinged lid with needlework, panelled and fitted interior, base with frieze drawer, medial shelf with small yarn basket, with splayed legs.

c1825 *18.5in (47cm) wide*

£500–800 SK

A William IV style mahogany box table, of rectangular form, with hinged lid with gadroon border above twin false drawer fascia, raised on a turned tapering centre pillar and concave platform with scroll feet inset with brass casters and applied with brass rosettes.

22.5in (57cm) wide

£450-550 ADA

A classical carved mahogany work table, from Albany, New York, the veneered top with crossbanded veneer in outline above two drawers, the top one with divisions, flanked by veneered and brass-inlaid dies above waterleaf-carved legs ending in paw feet, old refinish, imperfections.

1830-40 *20.75in (53cm) wide*

£650-750 SK

A mid-19thC French rosewood work table, the canted rectangular hinged top with kingwood crossbanding and a large inlaid ornate central cartouche, the interior with an arrangement of open and lidded compartments, upheld on double C-scroll supports and a faceted column, the quatreform base with short scroll feet.

22.75in (58cm) wide

£2,000-3,000 L&T

A mid-19thC Victorian burr walnut and marquetry work table.

23.5in (60cm) wide

£1,200-1,400 DN

A 19thC Killarney yew ladies work table, the rectangular top profusely inlaid with scrolling shamrocks around a rectangular plate, centred with an abbey ruin, the top opening to reveal a fitted compartment and the underside inlaid with harp and shamrocks above a wool box on octagonal stem and circular base with scroll legs.

22in (56cm) wide

£4,000–4,500 MEA

A Victorian walnut work table, the burr walnut top over a fitted drawer with sliding workbox under, on carved and pierced end supports with scrolled feet, joined by a turned stretcher.

22in (56cm) wide

£800–1,000 TEN

A Victorian burr-walnut work table, the hinged top decorated with inlaid scrolls and stringing, opening to reveal a leather-lined writing surface and pen tray, single drawer to the frieze, with wool drawer under, on turned columns with carved splay legs ending in ceramic casters.

24.5in (62cm) wide

£600-800 A&G

A late Victorian mahogany work table, satinwood-banded and inlaid stringing, the twin-hinged top revealing a divided interior and silk-lined compartment, above drawers and a pull-out bag on square tapering legs united by an X-stretcher on spade feet.

15.5in (39cm) wide

£350-400 WW

An Edwardian inlaid mahogany work table, decorated with inlaid boxwood stringing, the serpentine hinged top opening to reveal a lift-out tray above a wool box, raised on square tapering legs with spade feet and understretchers.

19in (48cm) wide

£400-500 A&G

FURNITURE

ESSENTIAL REFERENCE – DRESSERS

The dresser is a piece of case furniture consisting of a rack of shelves to display or store pewter or ceramics over a base of drawers and a cupboard, or an open base with a pot board.

● The term is derived from the French 'dressoir', used in the Middle Ages as a sideboard for displaying plates or serving wine, preparing food, and storing dishes.

● The fashion for tin-glazed earthenware (dating from c1650) gave rise to the delft rack – a set of shelves on which delftware could be displayed – which was soon integrated into the basic form. By c1790 the dresser had been reinvented for the country home, where it became an important item of furniture. Designs tend to be traditional and conservative, which can make dating difficult.

● Many different regional types were developed over the years. For example, break-front dressers with closed racks above drawers and cupboards are associated with North Wales, in contrast to the dressers with open racks and bases of South Wales.

● Most dressers were made from oak, but fine examples are known in elm, ash, fruitwood, yew, chestnut and walnut. Pine examples were made in Scotland, Ireland and South-West England. These were often painted.

An early 18thC joined oak low dresser, the moulded top over three filed-front drawers and a bold base moulding, on turned baluster forelegs.

75.25in (191cm) wide

£4,500-5,000   **TEN**

A mid-18thC and later George II oak and crossbanded dresser, with two rows of three short drawers, later gallery.

89.25in (227cm) wide

£1,800-2,200   **DN**

A George III oak low dresser, the moulded top over three frieze drawers and a shaped apron, on slender baluster legs joined by a potboard, on block feet, possibly reduced in height.

66in (168cm) wide

£3,000-3,500   **TEN**

A George III oak dresser base.

c1760   *86.5in (220cm) wide*

£1,200-1,800   **DN**

A George III oak dresser base.

c1780   *61.25in (155.5cm) wide*

£2,400-2,800   **DN**

A George III oak high dresser.

c1780   42.25in (133cm) wide

£3,000-3,500   DN

An 18thC and later walnut high dresser.

72.5in (184cm) wide

£1,800-2,200   DN

A large George III joined oak dresser, the rack with a diaper-inlaid frieze over three shelves, the base in two sections with a row of four short drawers over four panelled doors, on bracket feet.

89.5in (227cm) wide

£3,500-4,500   TEN

A George III oak dresser, the later rack with a coved cornice and waved frieze over three shelves between tiered niches, the inverted breakfront base with a moulded top over two banks of three short drawers flanking a central arched cupboard, on bracket feet.

80in (203cm) wide

£4,500-5,500   TEN

A George III oak dresser, the rack with a moulded cornice over three shelves between fluted pilasters, the base having a moulded top over three frieze drawers and two doors flanking a central panel, on bracket feet.

68in (173cm) wide

£4,500-5,000   TEN

An 18thC and later oak dresser, the delft rack with moulded top, fret-cut frieze, side shelves above small cupboards and spice drawers, the base with moulded edged drawers, shaped apron on three baluster turned front legs and two rear stile supports.

73in (185.5cm) wide

£1,500-2,000   HT

A George III oak Montgomeryshire high dresser, crossbanded mahogany, the open shelf rack flanked by a single two-panel cabinet door to each side, the base with an arched apron above an open pot board with four short baluster front supports, feet reduced.

78in (198cm) wide

£2,000-4,000   HALL

FURNITURE

A late 17th/early 18thC Jacobean oak two-part cupboard, with moulded cornice and three panelled doors, lower section with three drawers and two panelled doors, on block feet.

56in (142cm) wide

£2,500-3,500   **SK**

An oak tridarn, the moulded cornice above an open shelf with shaped slatted sides and turned column supports, the middle section with a pair of panelled doors above cupboard doors below, on moulded feet, handles and locks replaced.

44in (112cm) wide

£1,800-2,200   **WW**

An early 19thC oak Deuddarn, the cavetto cornice over three ogee-arched panelled doors, three short frieze drawers with two twin-panel cabinet doors to the base, raised on shaped bracket feet, fitted with later brass knob handles.

43.75in (111cm) wide

£1,000-1,500   **HALL**

ESSENTIAL REFERENCE – CUPBOARDS

A cupboard is a piece of closed storage furniture with doors to the front. The earliest cupboards were open sets of shelves, called court (from the French, court meaning 'short') cupboards. These cupboards were first made in England in the late 16thC, usually in oak, and in America and the rest of Britain in the 17th centuries. They were widely imitated in the 19thC.

● The earliest type of closed cupboard or aumbry with one door was soon adapted into new forms with two doors, two storeys with four doors. From the 16thC the cupboard became increasingly elaborate, with carved columns and cornices.

● Variations on the cupboard include two distinctive forms of the press-cupboard developed in Wales in the 17thC. The cwpwrdd deuddarn (two-piece cupboard) was relatively common from early 17thC. It was usually seen in the hall or kitchen of a farmhouse and was used to keep food and utensils.m The cwpwrdd tridarn (three-piece cupboard) was made in the late 17thC and 18thC, principally in Caernarfonshire. It has an open, canopied upper section for display and offering cover and protection in rooms that were dominated by a smoky hearth.

● 17thC/18thC German 'Schrank' and 'Nasenschrank' (cupboards) were typically restrained in their decoration, focusing on geometrical raised panelling on the doors or rich figuring of the veneer.

A large late 17th/early 18thC northern German oak and walnut Schrank, the cornice and frieze centred by a carved tableau of the judgement of Solomon, over two doors each centred by an oval wreath surmounted by a bishop's mitre/crown and with spandrels carved with Old Testament scenes, between pilasters carved with tiered allegorical figures of the seven Liberal Arts and two others, the base with two drawers between plinths carved with figures, all on turned feet.

Bears a printed label on the back: 'From Street & Son Antique Furniture Warehouse, Brewer Street, Golden Square, London'. Street & Son are recorded at the Brewer Street address in Pigot's 'Directory' for 1839. They were described as dealers in 'old oak carvings' in a letter from William Burn to O. Tyndall Bruce, 4th May 1842.

£8,000-10,000   **TEN**

CLOSER LOOK – A DUTCH KAS

The large-scale cupboard became a seminal furniture form in Europe from the 17thC onwards. Commonly comprising an upper section with two doors above a lower section with drawers, designs were typically architectural, with moulded cornices and, later, pediments.

Intended for the storage of household linen, the upper section of such pieces was most often shelved across its entire width.

This Dutch example is typical of pieces made in the lowlands at this time, its defining characteristic being the prolific floral marquetry that covers the panelled cupboard doors and the drawer fronts of the lower section.

A George II mahogany linen press, the broken pediment with egg-and-dart rocaille and key fret mouldings flanking a central pine cone finial above a blind fret-carved frieze, the panel doors enclosing hanging space, the lower section with leaf-carved edge and two simulated short drawers above two long drawers, on carved apron and bracket feet.

52in (132cm) wide

£6,000-8,000   **L&T**

An 18thC Dutch marquetry inlaid mahogany kas, with foliate-carved and moulded cornice above a pair of doors enclosing a shelved interior with drawers, lower section with two short and two long drawers, on stemmed bracket feet, with bird and foliate inlaid.

61in (155cm) wide

£6,500-8,500   **SK**

A George II mahogany linen press, with a moulded top and blind-fretted frieze, over two panelled doors enclosing trays, with brass carrying handles to the sides, the base with two short drawers over one long drawer, on bracket feet.

51.25in (130cm) wide

£1,800-2,200   **TEN**

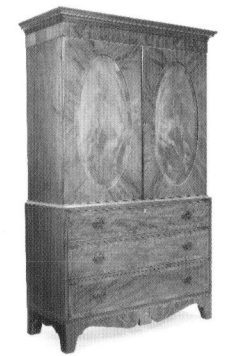

A Georgian mahogany linen press, the projected moulded cornice over a plain frieze above crossbanded oval panelled doors and three graduated long drawers with shaped apron, raised on bracket feet.

50.75in (129cm) wide

£2,000-2,500   **L&T**

A, probably New York, Federal cherry inlaid linen press, in two sections with inlaid stringing, quarter fans and urns, replaced brasses, refinished, imperfections.

c1790-1800   *44in (112cm) wide*

£2,500-3,500   **SK**

An early 19thC Dutch walnut wardrobe, the cornice with gilt-metal ram's masks above a pair of re-entrant framed doors carved with ribbon-tied drapes, the lower part with drawers with lion-stamped brass oval handles, on block feet.

63.75in (162cm) wide

£800-1,200   L&T

A large Regency mahogany breakfront linen press, having two panelled doors enclosing trays, drawers below, flanked by full-length shelved cupboards to each side, all between reeded baluster pillars, on a conforming plinth.

This press is similar in form and detail with furniture made by Gillows of Lancaster, but it is not stamped or otherwise marked.

96.5in (245cm) wide

£1,000-2,000   TEN

A Regency mahogany linen press, the coved cornice over two panelled doors enclosing trays, the base with three long drawers, on tapered bracket feet.

51.25in (130cm) wide

£1,500-2,000   TEN

A late Georgian mahogany linen press, the arcaded cornice above a pair of fielded panel doors enclosing sliding shelves, with two short and two long graduated drawers below with fitted turned knob handles, raised on splay bracket feet.

51in (129.5cm) wide

£800-1,000   A&G

A mahogany wardrobe, the moulded cornice and arcaded frieze over two oval-panelled doors with sham drawers below, enclosing hanging space, a long drawer to the base, on swept bracket feet.

46in (117cm) wide

£700-800   TEN

A Biedermeier satin-birch armoire, the shaped cornice with carved gilt-leaf decoration against a cream ground, the armoire with twin panelled doors and three half-round columns with gilt capitals, on block feet.

70.5in (179cm) wide

£3,500-4,500   DUK

An Edwardian satinwood and kingwood-banded breakfront wardrobe, having a moulded dentil-inlaid cornice and fluted frieze over a bowed centre with two doors enclosing trays, with two short and two long drawers under, flanked on each side by coved doors enclosing full-length hanging space, all on turned feet.

78.75in (200cm) wide

£1,800-2,200   TEN

ESSENTIAL REFERENCE – COFFERS AND CHESTS

The earliest movable storage furniture was a hollowed-out log, which now lends its name to the word 'trunk' (travelling container). In the Medieval period these logs were replaced by chests

- A coffer is the simplest form of chest, made from the 13thC onward. The wood could be covered with leather and banding, with a lid for storage. As coffers were designed for travelling, they often have carrying handles and a domed lid to throw off water. They do not generally have feet.
- Chests (sometimes refered to as coffers) had flat hinged lids and feet and were designed for use inside buildings: the feet kept the contents away from damp floors. They were primarily made of oak in Northern Europe, with walnut used in the South.
- Chests were made by the joiner, whereas portable coffers were made by the cofferer, who also made coffins, but who was primarily a leather worker.
- Panelled and framed chests were developed during the 15thC, and were produced in large quantities during the 16thC. They were often decorated with carvings, which became more elaborate as a way of exhibiting wealth and social status. Contrasting inlays of wood, bone or mother-of-pearl was also used, particularly on the German 'Nonsuch' chests.
- By the 17thC coffers and chests were made in large numbers both in Britain and the USA. The Jacobean style was typical in Britain throughout the 17thC.
- Around the mid-17thC, the coffer evolved into the mule chest, with a drawer at the base to make it easier to gain access to items at the bottom.

An early 17thC Continental walnut coffer, the long rectangular top moulded with a thumbnail edge above a carved front panel worked to show putti masks, iron handles to the sides.

67in (170cm) wide

£2,000-3,000   FRE

A panelled oak chest, with profusely carved panel front,
c1670 and later.   *54.25in (138cm) wide*
£500-700   DN

An early 17thC oak chest.
c1620
£600-700

44in (112cm) wide
DN

A Charles II panelled oak chest, repair, faults.
c1680   *54.25in (138cm) wide*
£600-800   DN

A Charles II boarded chest of small proportions, probably Welsh, the lid having aged worm, now with short length of chain attached to the front centre over a front carved with stylised leaves and facing dragons on a matt ground, on cut-out ends with front mouldings and corner brackets.
30.75in (78cm) wide
£2,000-3,000   HALL

A Charles II oak coffer, the twin-plank top above a triple-panel front with a fluted frieze and applied central lion's head mask flanked by a pair of cushion-moulded lozenges, on stile feet.
52.5in (133cm) wide
£1,000-1,200   L&T

FURNITURE

A 17thC joined oak chest, the panelled lid over a fluted frieze and three carved panels, between moulded muntins and stiles, on stile feet.

50in (127cm) wide

£400–600   TEN

A 17thC oak coffer, with panelled hinged lid and later carved panelled front and plain sides, raised on block feet.

53in (134.5cm)

£500-600   A&G

A 17thC and later oak coffer, with heavy plank top, three moulded front panels, plain stiles and sides.

52.5in (133.5cm) wide

£400-600   HT

A 17thC and later Italian carved walnut and bone-marquetry inset coffer seat, later marquetry panels and backrest, adapted.

51.25in (130cm) wide

£1,800-2,200   DN

A late 17thC Italian giltwood cassone, faults.

The cassone was an important piece of furniture in Renaissance Italy, and often, but not always, a marriage piece. Many were decorated with intricate inlay (intarsia). Others were painted with mythological or figurative designs, or decorated with pastaglia (gold painted gesso). Important marriage cassoni were often made in pairs and decorated with heraldic devices. More humble examples could be used told hold the linen and household textiles that constituted the bride's dowry. Some were carved with the initials of the married couple and the date of their wedding. Many examples were handed down through the family.

67in (170cm) wide

£1,500-2,000   DN

A very small possibly Scottish Queen Anne oak panelled coffer, the twin-plank moulded top above a front decorated with stylised tulips, and stile end supports.

24in (61cm) wide

£1,200-1,800   L&T

An early George III oak coffer bach.

c1760   *27.5in (70cm) wide*

£1,500-1,800   DN

A 19thC painted and decorated sea chest, with moulded rectangular lid on conforming case painted green and decorated with roping, the case decorated with barquentine, with macramé becket handles.

49in (124.5cm) long

£1,200-1,500   FRE

ESSENTIAL REFERENCE – CHESTS-OF-DRAWERS

From the mid 16thC, chests were fitted with drawers in the base, underneath the main large compartment accessible. Generally used for holding money or other precious goods, these drawers were called 'drawing-boxes' (from which the modern word is derived), or 'tills', denoting a draw where money was kept: a term still used today for cash registers.

- The chest-of-drawers assumed its modern form in the 17thC, although the system of graduated drawers (deepest at the bottom, shallowest at the top) was only reached at the end of the century. It was at about this time that the chest-of-drawers superseded the chest as the principal item of furniture for storage.
- Early chest-of-drawers were made by joiners, and the marks of construction were clearly visible. By the end of 17thC, cabinet-makers had taken over, and drawers became secured by hidden dovetailed joints.
- At this time, efforts were made to enrich the visible surfaces. Veneering with burr woods, oyster veneering, and seaweed and floral marquetry were particularly fashionable, with parquetry becoming popular in Louis XV's France. In contrast, the majority of George II and George III chests-of-drawers are simple and plain.
- 19thC chests-of-drawers were decorated in a variety of styles, revived from previous centuries.
- Native woods were used for carcases in most countries in Europe. For example, France and The Netherlands used oak.
- Some variations have acquired special names, such as the bureau, chiffonier, chiffonnière, the tallboy and its American variations, the highboy and lowboy.

A late 17thC oyster olive wood chest-on-stand, the top with interlaced white stringing and banding over two short and two long drawers, the stand with a long drawer on spiral turned legs joined by a waved flat stretcher, on ball feet.

38.5in (98cm) wide

£10,000-12,000   **TEN**

A late 17thC William & Mary oyster-veneered burr-walnut and marquetry chest-of-drawers, repair, faults.

38.25in (97cm) wide

£9,000-12,000   **DN**

A George I walnut and featherbanded bachelor's chest, the foldover top with caddy-moulded edge enclosing quarter-veneered interior above four long graduated drawers with brass ring handles and escutcheons, on bracket feet.

33in (84cm) wide

£10,000-12,000   **L&T**

A George I walnut chest-of-drawers, with oak side panels.

c1720   *37.5in (95cm) wide*

£3,500-5,500   **DN**

A George II walnut and featherbanded chest-of-drawers.

c1735   *30in (76.5cm) wide*

£12,000-15,000   **DN**

FURNITURE

A George II walnut chest-of-drawers.

c1740   *36.5in (93cm) wide*
£1,500-2,000   DN

A George II walnut chest-of-drawers, inlaid with stringing, the moulded top above three short and three long graduated drawers, on later bracket feet.

36.25in (92cm) wide
£4,000-4,500   L&T

A George II walnut and burr-walnut chest-of-drawers, inlaid with featherbanding, the quarter-veneered crossbanded top above a brushing slide and four long graduated drawers, enclosed by rounded corners, on shaped bracket feet.
41.25in (105cm) wide
£2,500-3,500   L&T

A mid-18thC George II walnut and herringbone crossbanded chest-of-drawers, some later elements.
39.5in (100cm) wide
£2,500-3,500   DN

A mid-18thC George II mahogany chest-of-drawers, with slide.

30.75in (78cm) wide
£2,400-2,600   DN

A mid-18thC early George III mahogany chest-of-drawers, with slide.

31in (79cm) wide
£1,200-1,500   DN

A small 18thC Dutch marquetry chest, the foliate and ancanthus leaf decorated serpentine top over four long graduated drawers decorated with flowers and fitted applied and gilt-metal handles and lock escutcheons, raised on a cut-away plinth base, repairs, some veneer missing.

32.75in (83cm) wide
£1,500-2,000   A&G

A George III mahogany serpentine-fronted chest-of-drawers.

c1780   36.5in (93cm) wide

£3,500-4,500   DN

A George III mahogany serpentine chest-of-drawers, the moulded top above four long graduated drawers, on ogee bracket feet.

43in (109cm) wide

£5,000-6,000   L&T

A George III mahogany bachelor's chest, the fold-over top above a single frieze drawer and two short and two long further drawers, all applied with brass drop handles and key escutcheons, raised on bracket feet.

31in (79cm) wide

£4,500-6,500   TOV

An 18thC Dutch Rococo rosewood crossbanded mahogany bombé chest-of-drawers, the rectangular top above a case fitted with a brushing slide, two short and three long graduated drawers, on ogee bracket feet.

40.5in (103cm) wide

£3,500-4,500   SK

CLOSER LOOK – A SECRÉTAIRE CHEST

A rather fine piece, the rectilinear form, light-coloured wood veneers and small dimensions of this secretaire make it desirable to today's antique buyer.

The design of the piece particularly stands out, with the inlaid decoration to the top and the beautifully crafted fitted interior.

A number of elements help to date the piece to the turn of the 19thC, primarily the brass ring handles, the splayed bracket feet and the oval inlay – common features of the Neoclassical style that dominated the period.

You should check pieces like this for damage or restoration to fall-front, or similar, mechanism, which can often fail owing to wear and tear.

A George III harewood, satinwood and crossbanded secrétaire chest, faults.

c1790   31.75in (81cm) wide

£10,000-12,000   DN

A George III mahogany serpentine chest-of-drawers, the oval-inlaid top with a moulded edge over four crossbanded long drawers, between inlaid canted stiles, on bracket feet.

41in (104cm) wide

£10,000-12,000   TEN

FURNITURE

CLOSER LOOK – A NEO-CLASSICAL CHEST

The austerity of this design is particularly associated with Italian cabinet-makers of the early-19th century.

The drawer fronts are flush with the top of the piece: a design pioneered by Giuseppe Maggiolini.

The design of the chest is known as 'sans traverses', where the front of the piece is treated as a whole, decoratively, and the urn pattern ignores the division between the two drawers. The practice dates back to early-18th-century French commodes, so the Neoclassical motif is useful when it comes to dating the piece.

Square, tapering feet became a feature of smaller case pieces like this as the Neoclassical style developed. They were a particular feature of Continental European pieces, while British equivalents favoured bracket or lion's paw feet.

An early 19thC Italian Neo-classical inlaid and penwork-decorated walnut two-drawer chest, rectangular top and case, decorated with large Classical urns, on panel-inlaid square, tapered legs.

45.5in (115.5cm) wide

£6,000-7,000   **SK**

Check decorative details carefully for signs of damage or restoration. Penwork is easily touched up and the lines may be less refined as a result; make sure the wear to any penwork, i.e. cracks in the ink, are consistent with the age of the piece.

ESSENTIAL REFERENCE – CAMPAIGN FURNITURE

Made from the 18thC to the early 20thC, campaign furniture, could be easily assembled and dismantled for ease of transport. Typical pieces included chairs, writing chests, chests-of-drawers, washstands and beds.

- **It was usually made of hardwoods such as teak or mahogany, with brass fittings to protect corners from bumps and knocks. Instead of ordinary joining methods, campaign furniture often used screws.**
- **The Wellington chest, named after the Duke of Wellington, was one of the most popular early pieces. It featured a hinged, lockable bar, which extended from the frame to secure the drawers and was available in a variety of sizes. The Wellington chest was succeeded by the Victorian brass-bound chest-of-drawers, which was composed of two parts and had brass handles for easy carrying.**

A George IV camphorwood campaign chest, the rectangular top above one deep frieze drawer, two short and two further long drawers, raised on turned feet.

38.6in (98cm) wide

£2,500-3,500   **L&T**

A pair of small 19thC mahogany and crossbanded library chests, each with an ebony line-inlaid top above a plain frieze and five long graduated drawers between turned column uprights, on plinth bases.

27.5in (70cm) wide

£6,500-8,500   **L&T**

An early 19thC mahogany and brass campaign chest, made in two portable sections, the central frieze drawer with bird's-eye maple interior.

39.25in (100cm) wide

£3,500-4,000   **L&T**

A hardwood and brass-mounted campaign secrétaire chest-of-drawers.

c1835   *43in (109cm) wide*

£2,400-2,800   **DN**

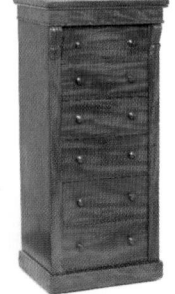

A William IV mahogany Wellington chest, with six drawers between locking stiles headed by scrolled trusses, on a plinth with casters.

49.5in (126cm) high

£2,000-2,500   **TEN**

A late 19thC Victorian hardwood campaign chest-of-drawers.

39in (99cm) wide

£1,000-1,200   **DN**

ESSENTIAL REFERENCE – COMMODES

The term 'commode' was first used in France in the late 17thC to describe a low chest with deep drawers, so called because it was a more convenient piece of storage furniture than a chest. Its height corresponded with the dado rail, and did not therefore interfere with the decoration of walls above.

- Variations evolved, such as the commode en console, with long legs and one shallow drawer, and the commode à vantaux, with doors over drawers.
- In the mid-18thC French furniture became fashionable in Britain. British commodes were highly decorative, low chests of drawers in curving forms that evolved in the Rococo style. They are typically classified by the form of their front, e.g. bombé, break-front, or serpentine.
- In 19thC England, the term 'commode' was also used to describe a close stool or pot-cupboard.

A mid-18thC late Regence gilt-bronze mounted kingwood and parquetry-inlaid commode, with rouge royale marble top with slight bowfront above a conforming case fitted with three drawers, fluted corners to case, foliate cast mounts.

50in (127cm) wide

£3,000-3,500   SK

A mid-18thC Regence ormolu-mounted kingwood and marble top commode, with brown and grey veined marble top above a slightly bowfronted case fitted with two short and two long drawers flanked by fluted pilasters, with foliate cast mounts.

45in (114.5cm) wide

£4,500-6,500   SK

A Louis XV serpentine kingwood and rosewood bombé commode, by Delorme, applied with gilt-bronze mounts, the serpentine grey marble top above two short and two long drawers, on splayed feet.

Adrien-Faizelot Delorme became master furniture maker in 1748.

c1750   *47.25in (120cm) wide*

£6,500-8,500   SOTH

A George III mahogany serpentine commode, with a moulded top over four graduated long drawers between canted stiles carved with trailing flowers and foliage on fluted, leaf-carved bracket feet.

30.7in (78cm) wide

£25,000-30,000   TEN

CLOSER LOOK: AN ITALIAN COMMODE

Commodes of this period were often enriched with parquetry or marquetry, using fruitwoods and exotic woods, particularly tulipwood. Marquetry is a type of decorative veneer, in which small pieces of wood and/or materials such as ivory, bone or mother-of-pearl, are laid out in a pattern and then applied to the carcass of a piece of furniture.

The Neo-classical style, which took over from the more elaborate Rococo style, can be seen in the Classical figures, and the basic form of the commode, which is refined, plain and linear.

Marquetry, which had been out of fashion in the early 18thC, was revived in the 1760s and 1770s.

A late 18thC North Italian rosewood, tulipwood and marquetry commode, the later rectangular top over four marquetry-decorated drawers, between sunk panelled pilasters, on tapered square feet.

50.5in (128cm) wide

£50,000-60,000   TEN

CLOSER LOOK – A GEORGE II CHEST-ON CHEST

This is a particularly fine example of the chest-on-chest form that became popular from the mid-to-late 18th century, particularly in Britain and the United States. The elegant proportions of the piece and the beautiful figuring of the walnut are both telltale signs of its superior quality.

Examples with a row of smaller drawers at the top of the upper section and a pullout brushing slide at the top of the lower section are an indication of the cabinet-maker's skill. Such elements are likely to increase the value of a piece.

It is unusual for a piece from this period to have survived wholly intact, so check for likely signs of wear or restoration: for example, damage to the bracket feet, obvious holes inside the drawers to suggest replacement handles and/or escutcheons; and poorly running drawers or brushing slide.

Beware of 'marriages' when looking at pieces like this – a top chest being sold with a non-matching bottom chest. Obvious differences will be the brass fittings or the surface decoration, such as featherbanding or inlays, although it is not unusual for such elements to be adapted.

A George II walnut chest-on-chest, with a coved cornice over three short and three long drawers, between ovolo corners, the base with a slide over three long drawers, on bracket feet.

41.25in (105cm) wide

£10,000-11,000   **TEN**

A George I walnut matched chest-on-chest, the upper section fitted with three short drawers and three long drawers, the lower section fitted with a brush board over three long drawers, raised on bracket feet.

42in (106.5cm) wide

£2,500-3,000   **FRE**

A mid-18thC early Georgian inlaid walnut chest-on-chest, the lower section with a brushing slide above three long drawers, lowermost inlaid with a mariner's compass in a concave indention, on bracket feet.

45.5in (115.5cm) wide

£7,000-10,000   **SK**

A George III mahogany chest-on-chest, the dentil-cut cavetto-moulded cornice above a blind-fret frieze and two short and three long graduated drawers, the lower section with a brushing slide and three long drawers, on bracket feet.

44in (112cm) wide

£3,200-3,500   **L&T**

A George III mahogany chest-on-chest, the broken pediment carved with rocaille open trelliswork and blind fretwork, above drawers with rocaille cast handles, on a gadrooned apron with relief-carved inscrolling ogee bracket feet.

47.25in (120cm) wide

£7,000–9,000   **L&T**

A George III mahogany chest-on-chest, with a pierced dentil cornice over a blind-fretted frieze, and top and bottom parts with drawers all between canted blind-fretted corners, on ogee bracket feet.

With original receipt, dated 1951, purchased from Greenwood & Sons, Harrogate, for £295.

48.75in (124cm) wide

£8,000-9,000   **TEN**

A late 18thC George III mahogany chest-on-chest, with Greek key cornice.

45.25in (115cm) wide

£2,500-3,000   **DN**

An unusual George II, probably Irish, mahogany chest-on-stand, the cavetto cornice above eight drawers, graduated in pairs, the shaped stand with a central carved shell and acanthus-leaf-carved cabriole legs ending in claw feet.

32.25in (82cm) wide

£10,000-15,000   **L&T**

A George III mahogany chest-on-chest, with moulded dentil cornice and blind fret-carved frieze, fitted with two short and three long drawers between fluted angled corners, the lower section with three graduated long drawers raised on bracket feet.

72in (183cm) high

£3,500-5,000   **ADA**

An 18thC and later walnut and crossbanded chest-on-chest.

38.5in (98cm) wide

£1,500-2,000   **DN**

A Queen Anne walnut escritoire, the upper section with a moulded cornice above a long-lined convex-fronted drawer, the fall with elaborate pierced brass key escutcheon within featherbanding enclosing a fitted interior, the lower section with conforming featherbanding, on compressed bun feet.

45in (114.5cm) wide

£5,000-7,000   **DUK**

A late 17th/early 18thC Italian walnut, mother-of-pearl and bone marquetry secrétaire cabinet, the interior with an arrangement of drawers, lacking elements and with wear overall.

44in (112cm) wide

£7,000-8,000   **DN**

A George II walnut secrétaire chest-on-chest, the cornice over three short and three long drawers, the base with a secrétaire drawer and two further drawers, with a sunburst, on bracket feet.

41.75in (106cm) wide

£5,500-7,000   **TEN**

A George III mahogany secrétaire chest-on-chest, the moulded cornice with Greek key pattern above a plain frieze over drawers, the lower section with secrétaire drawer, enclosing an interior fitted with drawers and pigeonholes, above drawers, on bracket feet.

50.25in (128cm) wide

£2,000-3,000   **L&T**

A Pennsylvania Chippendale applewood secretary, the moulded cornice over two recessed panel doors, resting on a lower section with fall enclosing a fitted interior with carved drawer-front above four drawers supported by bracket feet.

c1790   *38.75in (98.5cm) wide*

£4,000-5,000   **POOK**

An early 19thC Dutch marquetry inlaid secrétaire chest-of-drawers, with concave-fronted frieze drawer over five graduated drawers elaborately inlaid with flowers within string lines, the side panels decorated with urns, flowers and butterflies, on tapered square short legs.

43in (109.5cm) wide

£2,000-2,500   **TEN**

A Biedermeier fruitwood secrétaire à abattant, with a frieze drawer above a drop-front writing compartment enclosing cupboard, drawers and shelves, and two cupboard doors below raised on square block legs.

35in (90cm) wide

£1,000–1,500   **MEA**

CLOSER LOOK – A SECRÉTAIRE LIBRARY BOOKCASE

Cabinetmakers emulating the style of Gillows of Lancaster sought to bring elegant architectural proportions to their designs, and made use of well-figured mahogany veneers.

The construction of the glazed doors can be helpful when dating a piece like this. Glazed panels made of small panes held together by glazing bars are earlier technologically (pre-1800); large sheets of glass with applied wooden moulding first appeared in the early 19thC.

The central 'drawer' is, in fact, a fall-front door, opening onto an arrangement of drawers and pigeonholes – the secretaire element of the piece.

The colour and figuring of the mahogany are both indicative of the superior quality of this piece. More desirable pieces will have 'flame' (richly figured) veneers, in particular 'matching' them in a number of panels so that they have almost identical markings.

A Regency mahogany secrétaire library bookcase, in the manner of Gillows.
c1820   67in (170cm) wide

£7,000-9,000   **DN**

An American, possibly Massachusetts, Federal mahogany bowfront secrétaire bookcase, with swan-neck cresting surmounted by a carved eagle, above a pair of glazed doors, a beaded secrétaire drawer enclosing a fitted interior, and two further cockbeaded drawers, on turned tapering legs.

50.5in (128cm) wide

£4,500-6,500   **L&T**

A Scottish Regency mahogany and rosewood-crossbanded secrétaire bookcase, the quadrant-beaded and flame-figured cupboard doors enclosing slotted shelves, the lower part of inverted breakfront form with a quadrant-beaded secrétaire drawer above cupboard doors between reeded pilasters and volute scroll capitals, on short turned and gadrooned legs.

46in (117cm) wide

£2,000-3,000   **L&T**

A Victorian mahogany secrétaire library bookcase, with four glazed doors split by fluted pilasters over a fitted drawer, two short drawers and four panelled cupboard doors on plinth base.

100in (254cm) wide

£4,500-5,500   **GORL**

FURNITURE

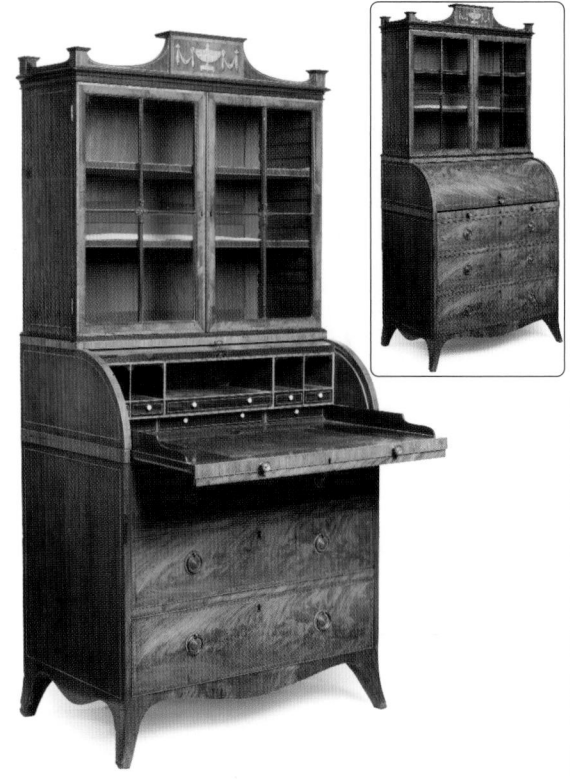

A George III mahogany bureau bookcase, with concealed lock mechanism for two of the blind-fret-decorated interior drawers, repair.

c1780   89.75in (228cm) high

£4,500-5,000   **DN**

A George IV mahogany cylinder-front bureau bookcase, with rosewood banding and stringing, the pediment with painted entablature, astragal glazed panelled doors to the upper section, with Prince of Wales feather ties, the cylinder front enclosing a fitted retractable interior with a hinged writing surface, on splayed bracket feet.

34.25in (87cm) wide

£3,000–5,000   **L&T**

BREAKFRONT BOOKCASES

A late George III figured mahogany breakfront library bookcase cabinet, four glazed doors astragal moulded with lancet arches and enclosing adjustable shelves, the base fitted with a central secrétaire compartment above a double cupboard, flanked by two drawers and further cupboard doors, raised on a plinth base.

85in (216cm) wide

£12,000-18,000   **TOV**

A George III mahogany inverted breakfront library bookcase, adapted from a large bookcase, the moulded dentil-cut cornice above a Neo-classical frieze with ribbon-tied harebell festoons, above four glazed doors with interlaced ogee astragals, raised on a plinth base.

104.5in (265cm) wide

£4,000–5,000   **L&T**

A George III mahogany breakfront bookcase.

c1810   78.75in (200cm) wide

£3,000-4,000   **DN**

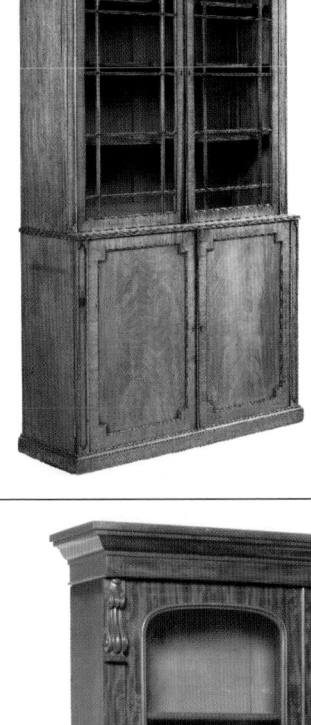

A Regency mahogany library bookcase, the projecting beaded cornice above Gothic quatrefoil sunken field frieze and conforming uprights flanking a pair of reeded astragal glazed doors enclosing adjustable shelves, the lower section with a pair of panelled doors with beaded quadrant decoration, on plinth base.

55in (140cm) wide

£1,800-2,500 **L&T**

A George III style mahogany library bookcase, the pierced rosette-carved cornice with key pattern and blind fretwork carved frieze above a pair of astragal glazed doors, the undercabinet with reeded top with blind fret frieze above a pair of flame-figured panel doors, on cut plinth base.

50.75in (129cm) wide

£3,000-4,000 **L&T**

An early 19thC mahogany bookcase cabinet, the detachable cornice above a pair of astragal glazed doors enclosing adjustable shelves, the base with a pair of panelled doors enclosing a shelf, on turned feet, restoration and replacements.

48.75in (124cm) wide

£1,200-1,800 **WW**

A Victorian mahogany bookcase, with a moulded cornice and plain frieze over two arched glazed doors enclosing adjustable shelves, between stiles with scroll-carved trusses, the base with a square-edged top over two arched-panel doors enclosing shelves, between stiles with scrolled trusses, on a plinth.

56.25in (143cm) wide

£1,500-2,000 **TEN**

A George IV olivewood bookstand, the revolving superstructure with three graduated tiers on spiral-turned supports, the octagonal base with a conforming shaft and a quadriform base with scroll feet.

53in (135cm) high

£1,800-2,500　　DUK

A William IV mahogany waterfall open bookcase, the shell-crested S-scroll back above four shells, raised on half-reeded fluted legs.

47.75in (121cm) wide

£1,500–2,000　　MEA

A William IV mahogany open bookcase, with stylised lappet capitals.

c1835　　*33.75in (86cm) wide*

£2,500-3,000　　DN

A William IV rosewood breakfront dwarf bookcase, with a brass-galleried shelf on pillar supports backed by mirrored panels, the base with a beaded edge to the top over a pair of brass-grill and silk-pleated doors, enclosing shelves, flanked by open adjustable shelves to each side, on carved paw feet.

52.25in (133cm) wide

£2,500-3,000　　TEN

A Victorian mahogany open bookcase, the oblong top above three adjustable shelves flanked with flat pilasters on a plinth base.

49.5in (126cm) wide

£2,500-3,000　　MEA

ESSENTIAL REFERENCE – EMPIRE STYLE

The Empire style, sometimes considered the second phase of Neo-classicism, is an early 19thC design movement. It is named after the period during which Napoleon I ruled France, and was specifically intended to idealise Napoleon's leadership and the French state.

- The style combines antique forms and ornaments with motifs closely associated with Napoleon, such as bees, giant Ns surrounded by laurel wreaths and eagles, as well as Egyptian-influenced forms, which gained a new significance in the wake of Napoleon's Egyptian campaign of 1798-1801.
- Draperies were always used: plain or simply-patterned fabrics were looped over pelmets and bed frames to create lavishly draped rooms.
- Furniture was typically made of a single wood, (usually mahogany) with a sparing use of gilt-bronze enrichment, to geometrically simple designs, often adapted from the Antique, e.g. sabre legs, curule-like stool. This made it much easier to mass-produce furniture. Jacob-Desmalter, the period's most celebrated furniture maker, was the owner of a factory, rather than a craftsman.
- The style spread across Europe in the wake of Napoleon's armies and remained popular after his final defeat. It was revived in the late 19thC.

A 19thC Empire-style mahogany and gilt-metal-mounted open bookcase.

41.25in (105cm) wide

£1,200-1,800　　DN

A late 17thC William & Mary walnut and brass-mounted cabinet on stand, repair, later elements.

48.5in (123cm) wide

£3,500-4,500   DN

An early 18thC Sri Lankan Dutch Colonial ebony and satinwood cabinet, with a canted top and moulded cornice with frieze drawer, over two panelled doors enclosing small drawers, the stand on turned legs joined by a cross stretcher.

39.25in (100cm) wide

£1,800-2,500   TEN

A Louis XV style tulipwood and Sèvres-style mounted bonheur du jour, with three-quarter brass gallery, and decorated overall with foliate and figural mounts, porcelain plaques painted with foliage and birds, on cabriole legs.

c1880   *28.5in (72.5cm) wide*

£3,500-4,000   SK

ESSENTIAL REFERENCE – CABINETS

Cabinets, which are distinct from cupboards because they have drawers and pigeon-holes, and from chests-of-drawers because they have doors, are intended for storage or display. They were particularly fashionable in Louis XIV's France and Restoration England.

- **The form originated in 16thC Italy, where cabinets were often inlaid with architectural decoration. At this time they stood on tables, rather than on stands, which became popular in the 17thC.**
- **Many cabinets-on-stands were decorated in elaborate veneer and marquetry. Oriental lacquer cabinets (and European imitations) were very popular in Northern Europe from the late 17thC. They were set on carved and gilt-wood stands made in The Netherlands, Britain and Germany.**
- **Cabinets made from rare woods and embellished with materials such as ivory and pietre dure were often the most elaborate pieces of furniture in European households up until the late 17thC. Consequently, the term 'cabinet-maker' came to be applied to superior types of joiner from 1681 onwards.**
- **The display cabinet had largely replaced the cabinet-on-stand by the 19thC.**

A satinwood, harewood and tulipwood bonheur du jour, in the manner of George Seddon, with two cabinet doors backed by pleated silk enclosing shelves, and a fold-out writing slope inlaid with a conch shell, on inlaid square tapering legs.

George Seddon (1727-1801) was an important English cabinetmaker working in the Neo-classical style. His London-based furniture-making business, George Seddon & Sons (est. 1785), was hugely successful.

31in (79cm) wide

£400-600   L&T

A mid-19thC Anglo-Chinese amboyna, ebony and ivory-inlaid writing cabinet, with two cupboard doors enclosing a fitted interior, the lower section with a sliding top, opening to reveal a compartmented interior with trays and a ratchet-adjustable writing surface, above three dummy frieze and six real drawers, raised on squat bun feet.

42in (107cm) wide

£6,000–9,000   L&T

A late George III Moorish-style burr-maple and rosewood crossbanded collector's cabinet, the chamfered pediment above a pair of glazed doors with cusped 'mihrab' arches enclosing drawers and pigeon-holes, the stand with a crossbanded frieze, on box and ebony line-inlaid square tapering legs united by an inswept undershelf.

27.5in (70cm) wide

£1,000-1,500   L&T

FURNITURE

A Victorian satinwood inlaid and gilt-metal bonheur du jour, the superstructure with a covered top over two doors inset with oval porcelain plaques, enclosing velvet-lined shelves, the base with a shaped frieze drawer raised on slender cabriole legs joined by a shaped undertier.

35.5in (90cm) wide

£3,000-3,500   TEN

An Empire style gilt and patinated metal Connemara marble mounted cabinet, of recent manufacture, with marble top, above grille doors enclosing shelves, over a base with marble insert and two drawers.

44in (112cm) wide

£1,200-1,800   DN

CLOSER LOOK – A SPANISH CABINET-ON-STAND

This piece epitomises the Baroque-revival style that became fashionable in Europe from the middle of the 19thC. Typical features include the use of exotic materials, such as tortoiseshell and ivory, and the painted scenes on the drawer fronts.

Grandiose, architectural elements are typical of original Baroque pieces, seen here in the pierced balustrade, the decorative columns and the squared, tapering baluster legs of the stand.

Given the age of such pieces it is not unusual for the two pieces to become separated over time, through loss or damage, and for a cabinet to be sold with a different stand. Though not undesirable, this 'marriage' should be reflected in the price.

A late 19thC Spanish ivory, tortoiseshell, rosewood, ebonised and gilt-metal-mounted cabinet-on-stand.

70.75in (180cm) wide

£20,000-25,000   DN

An early 18thC walnut cabinet-on-chest, with moulded cornice and cushion-like frieze drawer over two glazed doors enclosing shelves, the base with two short and two long drawers, on ball feet.

43.25in (110cm) wide

£4,000–5,000   **TEN**

A George III mahogany display cabinet.

c1770   *57.75in (147cm) wide*

£5,000-7,000   **DN**

An 18thC Dutch walnut and marquetry china cabinet, the arched cornice centred by a scrolling acanthus, over two glazed doors enclosing shelves, between glazed canted sides, the bombé base with three drawers over a shaped apron, between canted trusses, on claw feet.

70.75in (180cm) wide

£7,000-8,000   **TEN**

A George III mahogany standing corner cabinet, the moulded cornice above two astragal glazed doors, above a drawer and two further doors, on bracket feet.

c1790   *45.25in (115cm) wide*

£1,500-2,000   **DN**

A George III oak and elm glazed corner cupboard.

c1790   *39.75in (101cm) wide*

£1,300-1,600   **DN**

A late 18thC Dutch walnut bombé display cabinet, the cornice with a central rosehead, shell and wreath cresting, above two glazed doors, the lower section with canted corners above a moulded apron, on claw-and-ball feet.

55in (140cm) wide

£1,200-2,000   **L&T**

An unusual 18thC and later mahogany cabinet, with covered caddy top and dentilled cornice over a glazed door modelled as a Serlian window with key-fret architrave supported on Tuscan pillars with a Vitruvian scroll plinth, enclosing drawers marked A–Z, probably originally part of a larger piece.

41in (104cm) wide

£3,000–3,500   **TEN**

A late 18thC Dutch mahogany and floral marquetry display cabinet, feet reduced, truncated elements.

56.75in (144cm) wide

£3,000-4,000   **DN**

FURNITURE

A North European mahogany and glazed side cabinet.

c1860   52.75in (134cm) wide

£700-900   DN

A Victorian walnut, marquetry and gilt-metal-mounted display cabinet.

c1880   41.5in (105.5cm) wide

£2,000-2,500   DN

A late 19thC Dutch walnut cabinet on bombé chest, the cornice with a central carved scroll and foliage surmount above a burr-walnut frieze and a pair of astragal glazed doors, the base with drawers, fitted later cast brass handles, flanked by angled scrolls on carved paw feet.

75in (190.5cm) wide

£1,800-2,200   WW

An inlaid Victorian mahogany and satinwood display-case cupboard, on a plinth base.

61in (155cm) wide

£1,200-1,800   L&T

An inlaid mahogany cabinet, by Shapland & Petter, the locks stamped 'S. & P.'

43in (109cm) wide

£3,000-4,000   A&G

A late 19thC Louis XV style kingwood vitrine, probably Whytock & Reid, Edinburgh, with brèche d'Alep marble top, the quarter-veneered lower panels above shaped aprons and cabriole legs, the whole applied with gilt brass rocaille mounts and sabots.

Edinburgh-businessman, Richard Whytock founded his company in 1807. In 1876, cabinet-maker John Reid joined, forming Whytock and Reid. The company received two royal warrants, the first in 1838.

70in (178cm) wide

£10,000-12,000   L&T

A pair of George III mahogany and yew-banded breakfront side cabinets, faults.

49in (124.5cm) wide

£17,000-20,000   **DN**

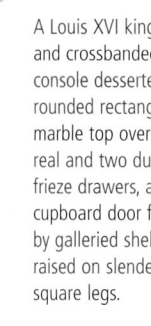

A Louis XVI kingwood and crossbanded console desserte, the rounded rectangular marble top over one real and two dummy frieze drawers, above a cupboard door flanked by galleried shelves, raised on slender square legs.

c1785   *32in (81.5cm) wide*

£1,200-1,500   **FRE**

A late 18thC Italian carved walnut side cabinet.

32.25in (82cm) wide

£1,000-1,200   **DN**

A Louis XVI brass-mounted mahogany and marble-top side cabinet, rectangular with rounded corners above a conforming case fitted with two panelled doors and a shelved interior, on toupee feet.

49.5in (125cm) wide

£2,200–2,800   **SK**

CLOSER LOOK – REGENCY SIDE CABINETS

The quality of these cabinets is evident in their detail: the reverse breakfront top, panelled frieze, and elaborately carved pilasters and feet are the hallmarks of an accomplished cabinetmaker.

The cabinets epitomise the exuberant Neoclassical style that arose during the Regency period at the beginning of the 19thC, influenced by the Empire style that was prevalent in France at the same time: highly figured veneers, such as rosewood, elegant brass mounts, protruding pilasters and lion's paw feet are all telltale features.

The brass grilles are particularly associated with Regency furniture.

It is almost always the case that an identical pair will be considerably more valuable than a single piece. Check for consistencies between the two to make sure the pairing is authentic.

A pair of Regency rosewood and brass-mounted side cabinets, each with a crossbanded inverted breakfront top above a panelled frieze and a pair of brass trellis doors, backed by burgundy silk, enclosing a shelf between stiff-leaf-carved pilasters with oval capitals, on boldly carved front-facing paw feet.

32in (81cm) wide

£10,000-15,000   **L&T**

A George IV mahogany bowfront side cabinet, adapted, later elements.

c1825　　　　　　　　　　　　　　　　63.75in (162cm) wide

£1,000-1,200　　　　　　　　　　　　　　　　　　DN

A small George IV rosewood side cabinet, of breakfront form, the white marble top above a glazed panel door enclosing adjustable shelves and enclosed by bowed glazed cupboard doors with shelves, the whole divided by reeded pilasters and raised on reeded tapered bun feet.

30.25in (77cm) wide

£3,000-4,000　　　　　　　L&T

A George IV mahogany collector's cabinet, the two doors opening to an arrangement of fourteen drawers.

c1825　　　　　　　29.5in (75cm) wide

£1,200-1,400　　　　　　　DN

An early 19thC mahogany bowfront side cupboard.

24.5in (62cm) wide

£800-1,000　　　　　　　DN

A William IV mahogany pier cabinet, with gadrooned breakfront top above three frieze drawers with rope moulding and central panelled cupboard flanked by spiral-turned pillars and raised on tassel feet.

38.25in (97cm) wide

£600-1,000　　　　　　ADA

A mid-19thC Continental Neo-classical parcel-gilt and ebonised wood side cabinet, the rectangular case with carved frieze drawer and two doors, flanked by blackamoor maidens, on paw feet.

40in (101.5cm) wide

£3,000–3,500　　　　　　　SK

A pair of satinwood, ebonised and parquetry standing corner shelves, adapted, formerly part of a larger item.

c1860　　　　　　30in (76cm) wide

£2,400-2,800　　　　　　　DN

A Victorian figured walnut breakfront credenza, applied with patinated bronze plaques, with a moulded top and central panelled door with glazed cupboards to each side, flanked by pilasters headed by caryatids, on a conforming plinth, stamped 'Lamb Manchester'.

69.75in (177cm) wide

£2,000-3,000   **TEN**

A Victorian ebony, ebonised, amboyna and gilt-brass-mounted credenza, the moulded top over an inlaid frieze and door centred by an oval Wedgwood plaque, between columns backed by mirrored plates and flanked by glazed cupboards, on a conforming plinth and turned feet.

67in (170cm) wide

£1,600–2,000   **TEN**

A late Victorian ebonised, cut brass and porcelain-mounted credenza, the frieze with Sèvres-style porcelain panels above a boulle marquetry door with cut brass arabesques around a porcelain panel, flanked by glazed doors divided by four uprights, on plinth base with shallow disc feet.

86.5in (200cm) wide

£2,500-3,500   **L&T**

A Victorian figured walnut and inlaid credenza, of bow-breakfront form, the top with a gilt-metal edge over an inlaid frieze and panelled door, flanked by glazed quadrant cupboards enclosing shelves to each side, on a plinth.

61in (155cm) wide

£1,800-2,200   **TEN**

A Victorian figured walnut, amboyna-banded and metal-mounted credenza, the moulded top over an inlaid frieze and two central glazed arched doors, enclosing velvet-lined shelves with a mirror back, flanked by detached columns and glazed quadrant cupboards, on a conforming plinth.

37.75in (96cm) wide

£2,000-2,500   **TEN**

A late Victorian ebonised, parcel-gilt and thuya wood side cabinet, by Gillows of Lancaster, the central doors with carved panels, enclosed by fluted and carved terminals, the bowed and glazed cupboards enclosing shelves, on plinth base, one door stamped 'GILLOW & CO 197'.

72.25in (186cm) wide

£600-1,000   **L&T**

CHIFFONIERS

A Regency rosewood chiffonier, with grille doors.

c1815   *42in (107cm) wide*

£1,500-2,000   **DN**

A Regency mahogany chiffonier, in the manner of John Mclean.

c1815   *37in (94cm) wide*

£2,000-2,500   **DN**

An early 19thC Regency rosewood crossbanded mahogany chiffoniere, the upper section with three-quarter gallery and two small drawers, the projecting lower section with two drawers and two doors, on short sabre feet.

36in (91.5cm) wide

£1,400-1,600   **SK**

A Regency rosewood chiffonier, the top with pierced brass three-quarter gallery above a pair of cockbeaded frieze drawers and a pair of pleated silk-lined brass trellis doors, on turned feet.

35.75in (91cm) wide

£1,600-2,000   **L&T**

A pair of late 18thC Dutch Neo-classical amaranth, sycamore, kingwood and mahogany marquetry sideboards, each with a front housing a single panelled door, inset with japanned lacquer panels suspended from a ribbon and hung with tassels, chamfered corners, raised on square tapering legs on brass ball feet.

35.5in (90cm) high

£25,000-30,000   SOTA

A George III mahogany and inlaid sideboard, of serpentine breakfront outline, with trellis-pierced brass back rail above a frieze drawer flanked by two deep drawers, panelled as four, on 'Gothic dot-and-line' inlaid square tapering legs ending in spade feet.

71.75in (182cm) wide

£6,000–8,000   L&T

A George III mahogany and marquetry sideboard, later elements.

c1790   *72in (183cm) wide*

£1,200-1,800   DN

A George III serpentine mahogany and marquetry sideboard, with brass gallery.

c1790   *71.75in (182cm) wide*

£5,500-7,500   DN

A George III mahogany and kingwood-crossbanded demi-lune sideboard, the central drawer flanked by a divided cellaret drawer and a further deep drawer, on six square tapered legs.

72in (183cm) wide

£2,500-3,500   L&T

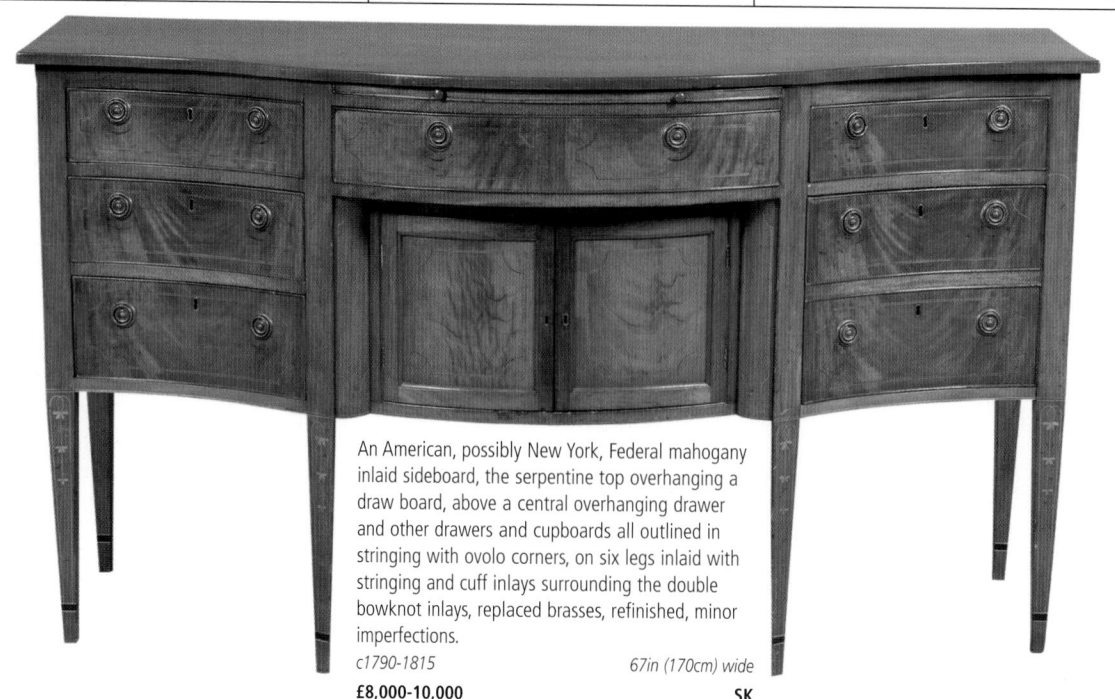

An American, possibly New York, Federal mahogany inlaid sideboard, the serpentine top overhanging a draw board, above a central overhanging drawer and other drawers and cupboards all outlined in stringing with ovolo corners, on six legs inlaid with stringing and cuff inlays surrounding the double bowknot inlays, replaced brasses, refinished, minor imperfections.

c1790-1815   *67in (170cm) wide*

£8,000-10,000   SK

A Scottish William IV breakfront sideboard, inlaid with eboniised stringing, the central drawer above a deep baize-lined drawer, flanked by a deep cellaret drawer and a drawer above a cupboard door, on spiral turned supports.

78.5in (199cm) wide

£1,500-2,000   **L&T**

A William IV mahogany sideboard, with deep bowfront drawers, one drawer bearing remnants of the trade label for William Dow, Cabinet Maker & Upholsterer, decorated with panels of floral motifs, on turned and reeded tapering legs.

87in (221cm) wide

£1,500-2,000   **A&G**

A Victorian walnut pedestal sideboard, with a scrolling fruit and foliate-carved mirror back, above a shaped top with a single central drawer, each pedestal with a panelled door, scrolling claw supports, plinth base.

94in (239cm) wide

£2,000-3,500   **JA**

CLOSER LOOK – SIDEBOARD

The sideboard is decorated with vignettes of Reynard the Fox (a poem in twelve cantos), based on a character originally thought to have featured in medieval European folklore.

Their quality of the vignettes suggests they might be by, or from, the studio of H. Leutemann, the artist who created the original steel engravings for an English version of the tales in 1852.
T

Painted pieces like this were, on the whole, made of pine. Many of them originated in rural areas, allowing cabinetmakers of lesser skills to make nevertheless desirable pieces.

A Victorian painted ledge-back sideboard, of inverted breakfront form with three recessed frieze drawers and three graduated drawers flanked by a pair of panelled doors with ceramic handles, on plinth base.

74.5in (189cm) wide

£2,400-2,800   **L&T**

A late 19th/early 20thC George III style satinwood marquetry and kingwood crossbanded demi-lune sideboard, the top with radiating veneers centred by a fanburst, on square section tapering legs and spade feet, damage.

54.25in (138cm) wide

£1,100-1,300   **DN**

A 19thC carved oak sideboard, with terms and capitals from the 17thC, incorporating a central Flemish panel, the inverted breakfront top above three drawers on spiral-twist front supports, the rear with fluted terminals, on a plinth base.

95.25in (242cm) wide

£1,000-1,200   **L&T**

An early 20thC Edwardian fruitwood and harewood-inlaid and crossbanded mahogany sideboard, with bowfront, above four short and one long drawer, on square tapered legs ending in spade feet, inlaid with bellflowers and foliage.

72in (183cm) wide

£3,000-3,500

FURNITURE

A George III mahogany bowfront serving table, the brass-galleried back with urn finials and twin outscrolling branches above three frieze drawers carved with drapery swags and bellflowers, raised on square tapering legs surmounted by further ribbon-tied trailing bellflowers, terminating in gaitered feet.

76.75in (195cm) wide

£3,000-3,500   L&T

An early 19thC Southern states hard pine huntboard, with a scrolled backsplash and two drawers supported by square tapering legs.

48in (122cm) wide

£4,500-5,500   POOK

A late George III mahogany and crossbanded bowfront serving table, faults.

c1790   43in (109cm) wide

£4,000-4,500   DN

A 19thC mahogany and brass-mounted sideboard suite, comprising a sideboard table with a serpentine top and frieze applied with guilloche paterae, swags and urns, on square tapered legs with spade feet, and a pair of pedestals, each with a moulded top and frieze drawer applied with swags, over a door centred by a brass patera within a lozenge panels, shelves and drawers within, on curved feet mounted with anthemia.

43.25in (110cm) high

£4,000-5,000   TEN

BEDSIDE CABINETS

A George III mahogany night table, faults.

c1770   21.75in (55cm) wide

£500-700   DN

A George III mahogany night commode.

c1780   20in (51cm) wide

£500-700   DN

A George III mahogany bedside cupboard.

c1780   23.25in (59cm) wide

£350-450   DN

A George III mahogany bedside cupboard, with tambour slide.

c1780   19.75in (50cm) wide

£400-450   DN

A George III mahogany serpentine bedside chest.

c1780   23.5in (60cm) wide

£700-900   DN

A George III mahogany washstand or bedside table.

c1790   30in (76cm) high

£600-700   DN

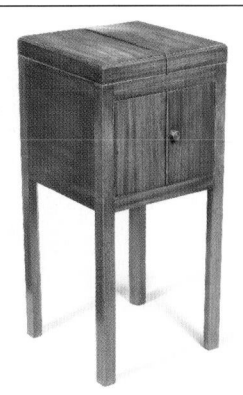

A late 18thC George III mahogany enclosed wash stand, with twin hinged covers.

14.75in (37.5cm) wide

£250-350　　　　　　　DN

A George III mahogany tray top night-time bedside commode, with a frieze drawer over two cupboard doors and a pull out seat compartment on square legs.

22.5in (57cm) wide

£1,200-1,500　　　　　MEA

A matched pair of late 18th/early 19thC Dutch walnut and floral marquetry commodes, of small proportions, each of serpentine bombé outline with two drawers inlaid sans travers with floral scrolls, tulips and summer flowers, one slightly larger and inlaid with box and ebony lines, both on slender tapering cabriole legs.

Largest 27.5in (70cm) wide

£3,500-4,000　　　　　L&T

An early 19thC George III mahogany and ebony-strung washstand or whatnot.

15.25in (39cm) wide

£200-300　　　　　　　DN

A Victorian mahogany pot cupboard, of cylindrical form, the moulded top with white marble inset above a panel door and raised on a circular plinth base, stamped 'Strahan'.

30in (76cm) high

£1,200-1,500　　　　　ADA

A 19thC Sheraton-style satinwood and marquetry pot cupboard.

38.75in (98.5cm) high

£700-800　　　　　　　DN

A late 19thC French rosewood and kingwood petit commode, the moulded-edge brèche d'Alep marble top above three drawers, the top one with a metal plaque 'KG 7203', with gilt-metal mounts.

17.25in (43.5cm) wide

£500-600　　　　WW

A pair of late 19th/early 20thC Continental walnut and marquetry bedside tables.

15.75in (40cm) wide

£1,000-1,200　　　　　DN

A George II walnut double-sided kneehole desk, with false drawer fronts to the reverse and green leather inset, repair.

c1735   40.25in (102cm) wide

£4,500-6,500   **DN**

A George II walnut and featherbanded kneehole desk.

c1740   30.75in (78cm) wide

£7,000-9,000   **DN**

A George II crossbanded and herringbone-inlaid walnut kneehole desk, the quarter-veneered top with re-entrant corners above a brushing slide with two inset brass ferrules, the whole raised on high scroll-cut bracket feet.

33in (83.5cm) wide

£3,500-4,500   **L&T**

A George III mahogany desk, the top with a gadrooned edge over a narrow frieze drawer fitted for writing, over nine drawers above the kneehole cupboard, on ogee bracket feet, restorations and repairs.

48in (122cm) wide

£5,000-7,000   **TEN**

A George III mahogany serpentine kneehole desk.

c1790   53.5in (136cm) wide

£2,500-3,000   **DN**

A Continental rosewood and marquetry desk, the superstructure with small drawers and pigeon holes over an inlaid top and five drawers about the shaped kneehole, on slender cabriole legs, alterations.

46.5in (118cm) wide

£4,000–5,000   **TEN**

An Edwardian rosewood, satinwood-crossbanded and arabesque-inlaid Carlton-House-style writing desk, the whole decorated with Neo-classical urns and vignettes of putti playing musical instruments.

48in (122cm) wide

£2,500-2,000   **L&T**

An Edwardian freestanding satinwood and painted Carlton House desk, painted throughout with Neo-classical motifs, on square tapered legs ending in casters.

57.5in (146cm) wide

£2,000-3,000   **L&T**

An Edwardian satinwood and painted Carlton House desk, the wrap-around stage back with drawers and drop-hinged stationery cupboards, above a gilt-tooled tan skiver with forward sliding action, painted overall with peasant girls and Neo-classical decoration.

55in (140cm) wide

£3,000-5,000   **L&T**

CLOSER LOOK – CARVED MAHOGANY PEDESTAL DESK

The design of this piece is based on the library table that Chippendale made for Nostell Priory, in Yorkshire, in the 1760s. At the time, it was said to have cost £72 and 10 shillings.

The addition of, in this case tooled, leather as a writing surface was commonplace on pieces like this – a practice that had been in use since the Renaissance. Make sure the state of the leather is in keeping with the age of the piece – genuine scratches or ink spills – as the leather is often replaced.

Desks like this one were often called 'partner's' desks, their generous depth allowing for two people to sit opposite each other. Each side of the desk would be carved in exactly the same way and would have a drawer above the kneehole and cupboards either side, in the pedestals. The cupboards may also have been fitted with shelves or sliding trays for storing documents.

The quality of this piece is evident in its being made from solid mahogany (like the original). The carved elements are typical of the Neoclassical style that began to prevail during the second half of the 18thC, and which featured in Chippendale's Director: paw feet, swags and garlands, grotesques and paterae.

A 20thC George III style carved mahogany pedestal desk, based on a model by Thomas Chippendale, carved with pendant husks, fluting and paterae and with carved husk-shaped reserves on paw feet.

79in (200.5cm) wide

£12,000-14,000   **SK**

A George III mahogany tambour-top desk, faults.

c1790   43.25in (110cm) wide

£2,200-2,800   **DN**

A late 19thC mahogany roll-top pedestal desk, by Gullachsen & Son Ltd., Newcastle, the tambour fall-flap enclosing pigeon holes and two small drawers, raised on plinth base.

55in (139.5cm) wide

£1,000–1,500   **A&G**

A Victorian mahogany cylinder desk, the desk a pull-out slope with ratcheted central desk and well, all raised on pedestals with three drawers in each, on plinths with casters.

56.25in (143cm) wide

£1,200-1,800   **TEN**

A French lady's mahogany and painted cylinder desk, with Vernis-Martin-style painted panels, the cylinder fall enclosing fitted drawers above a pull-out slide and full-width frieze drawer, on tapering legs ending in toupie feet.

c1900   31in (79cm) wide

£1,500-1,800   **L&T**

An Edwardian mahogany cylinder desk, the tambour fall enclosing a fitted interior with pull-out leather-lined writing slide with well, raised on square tapered and gaitered legs, on casters.

41.75in (106cm) wide

£1,400-1,600   **TEN**

A 19thC satinwood, tulipwood and purpleheart parquetry bureau plat, attributed to Donald Ross, the top with a tooled green leather skiver within a crossbanded and trellis parquetry border, the corners inlaid with flowerheads, the similarly inlaid frieze enclosing two drawers, one stamped with the serial number '06174', on turned and fluted tapering legs ending in brass casters, the whole decorated with foliate cast gilt-metal mounts.

Donald Ross's London workshop specialised in finely inlaid furniture during the second half of the 19thC. He became particularly celebrated for his use of 'dot and trellis' parquetry, strongly influenced by the work of French ébénistes, particularly Jean-Henri Reisener. Ross was also a client of, and supplier to, the firm of Edwards and Roberts who made and retailed fine furniture in the French taste from their premises in Wardour Street in London.

44.75in (114cm) wide

£9,000–12,000   **L&T**

A Louis XVI style mahogany and gilt-brass-mounted desk, the frieze drawer flanked by a fitted deep drawer and two short drawers, on fluted legs ending in brass toupie feet.

59in (150cm) wide

£2,500-3,000   **L&T**

A Victorian walnut kingwood-crossbanded and gilt-metal-mounted bonheur du jour, the arched back with a fret-pierced gallery centred by a Sèvres-style porcelain plaque and a mirrored plate, with further inset porcelain panels to frieze, raised on square cabriole legs ending in sabots.

46.75in (119cm) wide

£3,000-4,000   **L&T**

A William IV mahogany architects' desk, the rectangular panel top with a centre section on ratchet, above an arrangement of two long and two short drawers, raised on ring-turned baluster legs.

47in (120cm) wide

£1,500–2,000   **MEA**

A Victorian rosewood bureau plat, of slender serpentine outline, with five dummy drawers and one real lateral drawer, the tapered cabriole legs with foliate scroll and cabochon gilt-brass mounts.

42in (107cm) wide

£1,500-2,000   **L&T**

A Victorian kingwood and burr-walnut bonheur de jour, with gilt-brass mounts and Sèvres-style floral porcelain plaques, on square tapered cabriole legs with ornate mounts ending in sabots.

48.75in (124cm) wide

£2,000-4,000   **L&T**

An ebonised coromandel, brass marquetry and gilt-metal-mounted bureau plat, with five drawers around the central kneehole, opposed by five false drawers, faults.

c1880   *65in (165cm) wide*

£7,000-9,000   **DN**

A late Victorian burr-walnut and arabesque-inlaid bonheur de jour, the arched mirror back with drawer flanked by glazed cabinets, the fall enclosing fitted interior, all decorated with Rococo cast gilt-metal mounts, on cabriole legs.

32.75in (83cm) wide

£1,500-2,000   **L&T**

FURNITURE

A pollard oak serpentine-front desk, stamped 'Maple & Co LD', probably formerly a dressing table with later leather inset.

c1890   *51.5in (131cm) wide*

£550-750   **DN**

A walnut writing desk, in the manner of Howard & Sons, one drawer stamped '35536', faults.

c1900   *36.25in (92cm) wide*

£400-600   **DN**

An early 20thC Edwardian mahogany and marquetry kidney-shaped desk, in the manner of Edwards and Roberts.

38.5in (98cm) wide

£1,000-1,200   **DN**

A George I walnut and featherbanded bureau, in two sections, the crossbanded fall front revealing a stepped fitted interior, above four drawers framed by ovolo mouldings, the skirted base on bracket feet.

42.5in (108cm) wide

£2,500-3,500   **L&T**

An early 18thC walnut and chevron-banded bureau, the fall enclosing a fitted interior with a well, short drawers and pigeon-holes, on ogee bracket feet.

33in (84cm) wide

£1,000-1,200   **L&T**

A George II yew bureau, repairs.

c1740   *36.5in (93cm) wide*

£1,200-1,800   **DN**

A mid-18thC George II walnut and crossbanded bureau, with fitted interior and well, repairs.

36.25in (92cm) wide

£500-700   **DN**

A mid-18thC George II mahogany bureau, profusely decorated with 19thC marquetry landscapes and hunting scenes.

39in (99cm) wide

£1,500-2,000   POOK

A George III mahogany bureau, damage, repairs.

c1770   *36.5in (93cm) wide*

£400-600   **DN**

A George III mahogany bureau, repairs.
c1780 41.25in (105cm) wide
£700-900 DN

A late 18thC Portuguese Colonial hardwood bureau, with pressed metal handles, the fitted interior with concealed spring-locked central door.
39in (99cm) wide
£1,000-1,500 DN

CLOSER LOOK – MAHOGANY ROLL-TOP DESK

This desk is typical of the Neoclassical style that emerged from the 1760s. Key characteristics include the predominantly rectilinear form, inlaid decoration, square tapering legs, and round brass handles.

The tambour front rolls back into its case to reveal an interior fitted with pigeonholes and drawers.

Expensive, pale woods, such as satinwood and harewood, were used mostly as veneers. They brought an elegance to the more delicate pieces made in the Neoclassical style.

The decorative inlays are typical of the Neoclassical style, with motifs inspired by ancient Greek and Roman forms, which include scrolling foliage.

A George III satinwood and harewood-inlaid mahogany roll-top desk, with tambour enclosing fitted interior, inlaid with scrolling foliage and pendant bell flowers, on square tapered legs on casters.
c1780 37in (94cm) wide
£2,500-3,500 SK

FURNITURE

ESSENTIAL REFERENCE – SHERATON

Thomas Sheraton (1751-1806) gave his name to the last phase of 18thC English furniture. No furniture made by Sheraton has ever been identified, so his fame rests on his books of designs.

- The furniture of this post-Hepplewhite and pre-Regency phase of the 1790s was elegant and sophisticated. Sheraton's designs had a remarkable stylistic unity: simple outlines combined with elaborate flat (painted or inlaid) decoration.
- The designs emphasise the qualities of the wood, and the grains of veneers are carefully delineated.
- Like Robert and James Adams, Sheraton used antique ornaments, such as urns, paterae, vases and swags.

A George III burr-yew wood and tulipwood-crossbanded cylinder bureau, after a design by Thomas Sheraton, the cylinder fall above a slide with leathered slope, on square tapering gaitered legs and casters, the whole inlaid with boxwood lines.

32.75in (83.5cm) wide

£12,000-15,000　　L&T

A late 18thC French kingwood and rosewood-banded free-standing cylinder bureau, with white marble top, parquetry-veneering and gilt-brass mounts, on rosewood and satinwood-strung tapered legs ending in brass feet, locks later.

39.5in (100cm) wide

£10,000-15,000　　L&T

A late 19thC Dutch walnut and floral marquetry cylinder bureau, the fall enclosing a fitted interior and pull-out slide above a shaped apron with frieze drawer, on cabriole legs with gilt-metal mounts and sabots.

37.75in (96cm) wide

£1,000-2,000　　L&T

An Edwardian satinwood and rosewood-crossbanded cylinder bureau, painted with foliate swags, garlands and musical trophies, the roll top revealing an interior with pigeon holes, drawers and a sliding leather insert, on tapered legs.

35.5in (90cm) wide

£1,500-2,000　　L&T

FURNITURE

A William IV bird's-eye maple davenport, the top with three-quarter gallery and slope front, hinged and enclosing four drawers on a pedestal with four conforming side drawers, and with two turned supports.

20in (51cm) wide

£1,000–1,500　　　MEA

A William IV rosewood and marquetry davenport, the sloping top flanked with two candle slides and a pen and ink drawer with four drawers and four opposing mock drawers raised on bun feet.

24.5in (63cm) wide

£3,500–4,000　　　MEA

A mid-Victorian burr-walnut piano-top davenport, the pop-up letter compartment with a pierced fretwork gallery above a hinged flap revealing a pull-out writing surface, raised on fluted supports and a plinth base fitted with ceramic casters.

£2,200-2,800　　　TOV

A 19thC walnut davenport, the serpentine writing slope with skiver, enclosing drawers and writing compartment, carved cabriole legs terminating in C-scrolls, raised on plinth base with bun feet and ceramic casters.

Presented to Alexander Simpson Esq. Dundee by the Directors of The Kinnaird Hall in acknowledgement of services rendered at the inauguration of the organ, October, 1865.

28.5in (72cm) wide

£600-900　　　L&T

A Victorian figured-walnut davenport, the sliding desk enclosing a fitted interior with pen drawer to the side, on a plinth with casters.

21.75in (55cm) wide

£1,200-1,800　　　TEN

A Victorian oak piano-top davenport, the rise and fall stationery compartment over a four-drawer pedestal, with a cabriole leg to each front corner terminating in hoof foot, raised on a flat platform on compressed bun feet.

The Davenport is a small desk first made from the early 19thC, purportedly for a Captain Davenport. It comprises a hinged sloping top above a chest-of-drawers, in which the drawers were set at right-angles to, rather than aligned with, the top.

21.5in (54.5cm) wide

£800-1,000　　　HALL

A Regency rosewood music canterbury, the top with four X-shaped divisions with laurel wreath decoration, above two small drawers with small turned and carved handles, on splayed bracket feet.

23in (58.5cm) wide

£2,000-2,500   **DUK**

A Regency mahogany canterbury, five concave dividers, blocked uprights with finial surmounts above a single frieze drawer, on baluster-turned legs with brass caps and casters.

17.75in (45cm) wide

£2,500-3,000   **TEN**

A Regency mahogany canterbury, faults.

c1820   *20.5in (52cm) wide*

£800-1,000   **DN**

A William IV rosewood canterbury, of three cross-framed divisions united by lotus-carved wreaths

19.75in (50cm) wide

£1,000-1,200   **L&T**

A William IV mahogany canterbury, having five folio dividers arranged radially on a rectangular base with gadrooned edge and drawer, on turned and reeded legs with casters.

19.25in (49cm) wide

£1,500-2,000   **TEN**

A Victorian walnut canterbury, of three-division arched form with tapered baluster spindles, the leaf-carved turned corner supports with knopped finials above a concealed apron drawer, on short turned legs with ceramic casters.

20in (51cm) wide

£1,200-1,800   **L&T**

A Victorian figured walnut and gilt-metal-mounted canterbury, with a domed lid enclosing two compartments, on carved cabriole feet with casters.

21.25in (54cm) wide

£1,500-1,800   **TEN**

A William and Mary walnut and marquetry cushion wall mirror, later mirror plate.

c1680   37.5in (95cm) high

£550-750   **DN**

A 17thC-style carved and giltwood framed wall mirror.

45.25in (115cm) high

£900-1,200   **DN**

One of a pair of late 19thC William & Mary style brass and marble mirrors, the wood frame with cast brass panels accented with central multicoloured marble roundels, with cherub mask detailing.

18.75in (45.5cm) high

£1,200–1,800 PAIR   **SK**

A late 17thC carved giltwood picture frame, now with an oval mirror plate within the flower-carved and moulded frame with raffle leaf outer border.

35.75in (88cm) high

£600-800   **TEN**

A late 17th/early 18thC carved giltwood picture frame, now with an oval mirror within an ogee-moulded frame fringed with scrolling acanthus, paired putti to the top and a winged cherub to the base.

47.25in (120cm) high

£1,000-1,200   **TEN**

An early 18thC Queen Anne burl veneer looking glass, with scalloped crest, bolection-moulded frame and copper-wheel engraved and cut-glass plate.

22in (56cm) wide

£2,000-2,500   **POOK**

A Queen Anne style carved giltwood wall mirror, the bevelled plate with re-entrant corners, within a shaped pounced ground frame, surmounted by a Prince of Wales plume cresting, the apron centred by a shell motif.

54.75in (139cm) high

£2,800-3,200   **L&T**

A Queen Anne black japanned wall mirror, the divided shaped bevelled plate engraved with a palm tree, within a reeded slip and chinoiserie decorated arched moulded frame, later decoration.

55in (140cm) high

£3,000-5,000   **L&T**

A George I mahogany looking glass, with scalloped crest and base, retaining its original mirror plate and old dry surface.

c1720   38in (96.5cm) high

£3,500-4,000   **POOK**

A 19thC Regence-style giltwood mirror, tablet-shaped mirror plate in frame topped by rocaille shell over two cherub masks, the frame with C-scrolls and three further cherub masks.

28.5in (72.5cm) high

£1,000–1,500　　　　SK

A George I style walnut, veneered and giltwood wall mirror, the swan neck pediment with central urn finial, over a rectangular mirror plate, flanked by pierced scrolling leaves, over a shaped apron.

28in (71cm) wide

£600-800　　　　HALL

A George II mahogany looking glass, with scrolled crest and stepped and bevelled mirror plates, retaining an old dry surface and original mirrors. *c1730*

£3,000-3,500　　　　POOK

A mid-18thC giltwood pier glass, in the manner of Thomas Johnson, the frame pierced and carved with foliage, vines and rocaille beneath a ho ho bird cresting, the lower flanks with cluster columns issuing fronds, the diptych mirror plate with a hand-cut bevel at the margin.

64.5in (164cm) high

£5,500-7,500　　　　L&T

A George II mahogany wall mirror, the dentilled broken-arch pediment with a central carved foliate spray above a cushioned frieze, below is a mirror plate within a banded moulded surround with outset corners.

53.25in (135cm) high

£7,000-8,000　　　　L&T

A mid-18thC giltwood 'sea-phantasy' pier glass, the architectural 'stipple' textured frame with broken triangular pediment and central scallop shell above a sunken field re-entrant decorated frame around a silvered plate of thin gauge.

55in (140cm) high

£800-1,200　　　　L&T

An early George III mahogany and parcel-gilt wall mirror.

c1760　　　　*49.5in (126cm) high*

£1,800-2,200　　　　DN

An early George III giltwood wall mirror.

c1760　　　　*41.25in (105cm) high*

£800-1,000　　　　DN

FURNITURE

CLOSER LOOK – A TRIPTYCH OVERMANTEL MIRROR

Chinoiserie is particularly associated with the early 18thC, popularised by Thomas Chippendale's Director; archetypal Chinese-inspired motifs make the style easy to identify – look for pagodas, oriental figures, birds and flowers.

The intricate nature of the design makes it vulnerable to damage – chips to the gilding, but also breaks in the pierced frieze

A 19thC giltwood triptych overmantel mirror, in the Chinese Chippendale style, the pierced frieze with pagoda and bell flower cresting flanked by ho ho birds to each corner, with a similarly carved and pierced rocaille apron.

47.25in (120cm) wide

£5,000-6,000   **L&T**

The triptych design is in keeping with similar pieces that were made during the 18thC; because glassmaking technology was yet to develop, large pieces of glass were rare and big mirrors had to be made of several sheets held in an elaborate giltwood frame.

An 18thC-style Rococo carved giltwood overmantel mirror, of arched cartouche-shaped design, the cresting and uprights profusely carved with acanthus leaves and trailing foliage, the margin plates with similarly carved astragals.

69in (175cm) wide

£2,500-3,000   **L&T**

An 18thC French verre eglomisé pier glass, the diptych plate with a painted fleur-de-lys to arch within a border of red and gilt marginal plates, the frame and inner slip made in foliate moulded gilt-metal.

67.25in (171cm) high

£3,000-4,000   **L&T**

A late 18thC George III carved giltwood framed wall mirror, with foliate carved openwork cresting and apron, losses, mirror plate later.

52.75in (134cm) high

£1,200-1,800   **DN**

A 20thC 18thC-Continental-style giltwood and gesso overmantel mirror.

84.25in (214cm) high

£1,000-1,500   **DN**

A George III mahogany and parcel-gilt fret-frame wall mirror, with a rectangular bevelled plate and moulded cusp-cornered frame with a ho-ho bird to the cresting and a shell to the base.

41.75in (106cm) high

£1,000-1,200   **WW**

A Regency giltwood and gesso convex wall mirror, the circular mirror within a reeded slip and ball-moulded frame, surmounted by an eagle crest and flanked by twin flaming torch scroll candle sconces.

26.25in (67cm) wide

£1,800-2,200   **L&T**

A Regency giltwood convex mirror, the moulded cavetto frame applied with orbs, reeded ebonised slip, carved eagle surmount flanked by foliate scrolls, moulded fan-shaped base.

42in (106.5cm) high

£500-600   **HT**

A small Regency giltwood and gesso convex mirror, the eagle cresting above a ball-moulded outer edge enclosing a reeded slip and mirror plate, with leaf scroll apron.

30in (76cm) high

£1,000-1,200   **L&T**

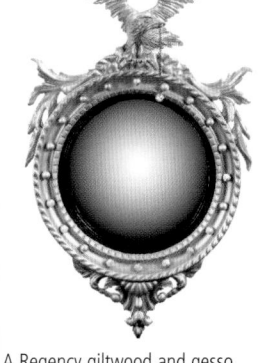

A Regency giltwood and gesso convex wall mirror, surmounted by an eagle, a chain and gilt ball in its beak, flanked by acanthus leaf scrolls, with ball decoration to the circular frame, applied carved leaf decoration to the base.

28in (71cm) high

£1,000-1,200   **A&G**

A Regency giltwood and gesso overmantel mirror, the moulded cornice above a trellis frieze and rectangular plate, flanked by cluster columns with Doric capitals.

65.75in (167cm) wide

£3,500-4,000   **L&T**

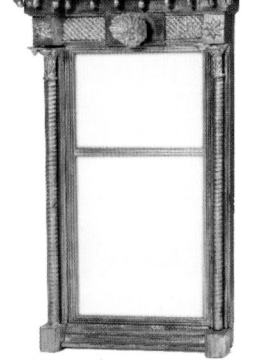

A pair of 19thC brass oval wall mirrors, with Rococo-style pierced and scrolling frame and a three-arm candelabra applied to the base leading from a lion mask.

17in (43cm) high

£450-650 PAIR   **FRE**

A Regency giltwood and gesso pier mirror, the inverted breakfront ball-moulded cornice above a reverse-glass-painted panel depicting a galleon, over a bevelled mirror plate enclosed by leaf-decorated reed Corinthian pilasters.

46.5in (118cm) high

£500-700   **L&T**

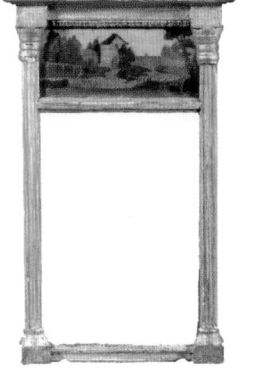

A Regency reverse-painted and giltwood-framed wall mirror.

c1815   *20.75in (53cm) high*

£300-400   **DN**

A Regency gilt mirror, inverted breakfront moulded cornice above a central shell frieze and two mirror plates, flanked with bead-turned pilasters, each with leaf capital.

36in (92cm) high

£1,200-1,800   **MEA**

A Regency giltwood and gesso overmantel mirror, the ball-moulded concave cornice above a scene with a lion-drawn chariot, the central bevelled plate flanked by a pair of outer plates and reeded Corinthian pilasters, re-gilt.

54.75in (139cm) wide

£1,000-1,200   **L&T**

FURNITURE

A Regency mahogany cheval mirror, the rectangular plate between turned and reeded supports with adjustable candle branches, on splayed reeded sabre legs with brass caps and casters.

A Regency mahogany cheval mirror, with reeded legs.

c1815   62.25in (158cm) high

£900-1,200   DN

40.65in (160cm) high

£2,000-2,200   TEN

An early 19thC French Empire-style mahogany and gilt-metal-mounted cheval mirror.

75.75in (190cm) high

£600-700   DN

DRESSING MIRRORS

A mid-18thC late George II mahogany dressing table mirror, the base with three-frieze drawer.

20.5in (52cm) high

£150-200   DN

A late 18thC George III mahogany dressing table mirror, the base with serpentine front.

£200-300   DN

A George III mahogany dressing table mirror, the serpentine box base fitted with three drawers, on ogee bracket feet, losses to stringing and veneers, replacements to feet.

22.5in (57cm) high

£450-550   WW

A Regency mahogany breakfast dressing table mirror.

c1820   24in (61cm) high

£150-200   DN

A George IV mahogany dressing table mirror, the uprights with brass sconces, the base with two drawers.

c1825   29.5in (75cm) high

£200-300   DN

An early 19thC, probably Colonial, rosewood dressing table mirror, with ring-turned supports and a rectangular box base with two frieze drawers, having turned bone handles on turned flattened bun feet.

23in (58.5cm) high

£300-350   WW

A 19thC, possibly Scottish, mahogany dressing table, the rectangular bevelled plate to nulled scroll supports, the box base with inlaid stringing and two curved drawers, on carved paw feet.

21.25in (53.5cm) wide

£200-250   WW

A Regency mahogany four-tier whatnot, the four graduated shelves with raised borders between turned uprights, with brass casters.

50in (127cm) high

£1,000-1,200   DUK

A Regency rosewood three-tier whatnot, with shaped three-quarter gallery above open shelves with block and ring-turned supports, base drawer and turned feet, on casters.

c1820   45in (114.5cm) high

£1,500-2,000   SK

A George IV goncalo alves étagère, the rectangular top with lobed corners and inlaid ebony stringing, the tiers supported by fluted columns, on turned legs to brass caps and casters stamped 'Cope & Collinson Patent'.

24in (61cm) wide

£4,500-5,000   WW

A William IV rosewood four-tier étagère, by John Howard & Son, the top with hinged reading slope on a ratchet support, with stencilled maker's name verso.

50in (127cm) high

£2,500-3,000   L&T

An early Victorian rosewood corner whatnot, of three graduated quadrant tiers with fret-cut galleries, on scrolling supports, on carved cabriole feet.

44in (112cm) high

£700-900   TEN

An early Victorian Gillows mahogany whatnot, of three round-cornered rectangular tiers on tapered pillar supports and brass-railed ends, on gadrooned bun feet with casters bearing stamp 'Gillows, Lancaster'.

32.75in (83cm) high

£3,000-3,500   TEN

A Victorian mahogany whatnot, faults.

c1860   35.5in (90cm) wide

£450-650   DN

A late 19thC French kingwood parquetry and gilt-metal-mounted étagère.

25.5in (65cm) wide

£3,000-3,500   DN

A Victorian rosewood three-tier whatnot, the foliate-pierced, three-quarter-galleried top on spiral twist supports, the lower tier with a drawer and short turned legs with brass caps and casters.

23.25in (59cm) wide

£400-600   L&T

A Victorian satinwood étagère, the top with replaced brass lifts, on open supports with ebonised roundels, on scroll legs to brass casters, the underside with printed label for 'Wills & Bartlett, Upholsterers, Cabinet Manufacturers and Paper Hangers, Kingston-on-Thames'.

27.5in (69cm) wide

£900-1,200   WW

A pair of brass and painted wood two-tier étagères, inset with agate tablets.

c1900   22.75in (58cm) high

£1,800-2,200   DN

FURNITURE

A Victorian mahogany buffet.

c1865   46.75in (118.5cm) wide

£500-700   **DN**

A Victorian mahogany rectangular three-tier dumb waiter, raised on end supports and splayed ball feet joined by a turned stretcher.

£400-500   **ADA**

A Victorian mahogany buffet, of three rectangular tiers, the shaped upright supports with carved and moulded brackets raised on moulded platform bases with brass casters.

47.25in (120cm) wide

£450-650   **TEN**

CLOSER LOOK – A DUMB WAITER

A popular piece from which to serve side dishes, cheese and desserts, the dumb waiter has a number of tiers – three is normal, and you may see examples with four, but never more –raised on a tripod base.

Check that the tiers graduate – smallest at the top, largest at the bottom – and that the diameter of the largest is slightly wider than that of the base. Awkward proportions may suggest that the piece has been altered in some way

In many such designs, the tiers revolved around the central column, to make selection easier. If this is the case, make sure each one still functions well.

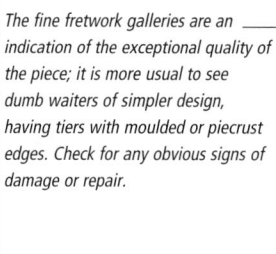

The fine fretwork galleries are an indication of the exceptional quality of the piece; it is more usual to see dumb waiters of simpler design, having tiers with moulded or piecrust edges. Check for any obvious signs of damage or repair.

The condition of the piece and rich colour of the wood is another indication of quality, as is the sparing use of carved decoration.

A George III mahogany dumb waiter, each tier with a pierced Gothic open-fretted gallery on a stop-fluted and spirally knopped column above an acanthus-carved cabriole tripod base ending in pad feet.

45.25in (115cm) high

£12,000-15,000   **L&T**

A Regency rosewood teapoy, by J.D. Maclean, Dundee, of sarcophagus form, the base of one canister stamped twice 'JD MACLEAN'.

32.5in (83cm) high

£900-1,200   L&T

A Regency mother-of-pearl inset rosewood teapoy, the caddy of sarcophagus form, with twin subsidiary caddies within.

c1815   *18.5in (47cm) wide*

£400-500   DN

A 19thC Killarney yew and marquetry teapoy, the top inlaid with shamrock sprays and chequer string, with slotted interior, the body supported by a spiral stem with conforming platform and scroll legs.

31in (80cm) wide

£4,000-4,500   MEA

A Regency mahogany teapoy, with fitted interior containing a Chinese blue and white bowl.

c1815   *32.25in (82cm) high*

£400-600   DN

A Regency mahogany teapoy, interior later lined to be used as a humidor with hygrometer inscribed 'Dunhill'.

c1820   *24in (61cm) wide*

£900-1,200   DN

A Victorian walnut and brass adjustable music stand, faults.

52.75in (134cm) high

£200-300   DN

FURNITURE

A George III mahogany and brass-bound wine cooler.

c1790   *29.5in (75cm) wide*

£3,000-4,000   **DN**

A George III mahogany and brass-bound oval wine cooler, the moulded top enclosing metal liner and drain tap, flanked by lion mask handles, on a squat turned pedestal and four hipped sabre legs ending in brass box casters.

28in (71cm) high

£3,000-4,000   **L&T**

A Regency oval mahogany and bronze-mounted wine cooler, the moulded hinged lid enclosing a lead-lined interior above tapered sides with twin cast handles and castellated apron, raised on a moulded plinth base with brass casters.

35.5in (90cm) wide

£4,500-5,000   **L&T**

CLOSER LOOK – A REGENCY MAHOGANY WINE COOLER

The sarcophagus form is one of several motifs (alongside the urn and lion's head) that became ubiquitous in the late-Neoclassical style.

The sarcophagus form was revived during the late-19th and early-20thC, although such pieces tend to be inferior in quality.

Many wine coolers of this period have had their lead linings removed. That this one has not increases its value.

Being made of solid mahogany, pieces like this might show wear at the hinges to the heavy lid, with them becoming either loose or warped over time.

A Regency mahogany sarcophagus wine cooler, the coffered top with gadrooned handle and gadrooned edge enclosing a divided lead-lined interior, raised on four massive hairy lion paw feet with recessed brass casters.

32.25in (82cm) wide

£10,000-12,000   **L&T**

A Regency mahogany wine cooler, by Holland & Sons, of ogee sarcophagus form, the top with leaf knop and egg-and-dart carved edge, the sides with carved escutcheons, with scrolling acanthus-carved canted uprights, base stamped 'HOLLAND & SONS'.

33.75in (86cm) wide

£9,000-12,000   **L&T**

A Regency 'plum pudding' mahogany cellaret, of sarcophagus form, the hinged lid with a reel-moulded edge and enclosing a lined interior, with mahogany loop side handles, raised on block feet with concealed casters.

31in (79cm) wide

£4,500-5,500   L&T

A George IV mahogany cellaret cabinet.

c1825

£350-550   DN

A 19thC mahogany brass-bound and satinwood-crossbanded octagonal wine cooler, the top with inlaid fan patera enclosing a divided lead-lined interior, on splayed square tapering legs ending in casters.

27.5in (70cm) high

£3,000-4,000   L&T

An early 19thC oak cylindrical wine cooler.

21.25in (54cm) diam

£2,000-2,500   DN

PAILS

A late 18thC George III mahogany and brass-banded plate bucket, with swing handle.

16.25in (41cm) high

£1,500-2,000   DN

A pair of 18thC-style Irish mahogany and brass-bound peat buckets, of spirally reeded tapering form with wrythen-twist swing handles and detachable liners.

£2,800-3,200   L&T

A George III brass-banded mahogany peat bucket, with copper swing handle and later zinc liner.

c1800   *12.75in (32.5cm) high*

£2,000-2,500   DN

A large Regency-style mahogany peat bucket, with removable liner, brass bands and twin loop carrying handles, the spiral-reeded sides with applied shell mouldings.

22.5in (57cm) high

£1,800-2,200   L&T

FURNITURE

A Regency rosewood combined occasional and jardinière table, with oval cover above the recessed zinc liner.

c1815 *19in (48cm) wide*
£500-700 DN

A William IV mahogany wine cooler or jardinière, the beaded moulded top enclosing a metal liner on a spiral reeded and turned stem on a platform with three spiral supports and a scroll tripod base.

34in (87cm) wide
£1,500–2,000 MEA

An early 19thC painted toleware jardinière stand.

37.5in (95cm) high
£500-600 DN

A William IV rosewood jardinière stand, faults.

c1835 *43in (109cm) high*
£700-900 DN

TORCHÈRES

A pair of late 19th/early 20thC Venetian blackamoor figures, the standing figures in gilt-enriched polychrome painted costume, each holding a torch in one hand, raised on octagonal bases, fitted for electricity.

33in (84cm) high
£4,000-6,000 L&T

A pair of carved giltwood and painted torchères, the ornate stylised Corinthian quadriform capitals with leaf and berry decoration and upheld by conformingly decorated pillars.

62.5in (159cm) high
£2,500-3,000 L&T

A Black Forest carved bear card stand, the bear with glass eyes, with out-stretched front legs supporting a carved vine leaf tray, on a naturalistic carved plinth, on four wood turned feet.

c1910-20
£2,500-3,000 WEB

A pair of 19thC carved and painted blackamoor figures.

57.5in (146cm) high
£7,500-9,000 POOK

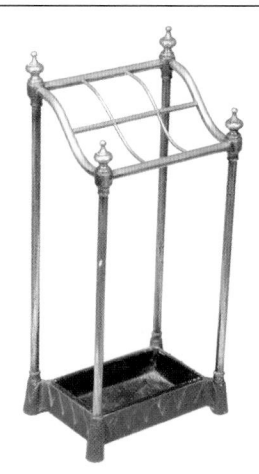

A mid-19thC Victorian brass and iron stick stand, incorporating a shaped top with six divisions.

13in (33cm) wide

£500-600 **DN**

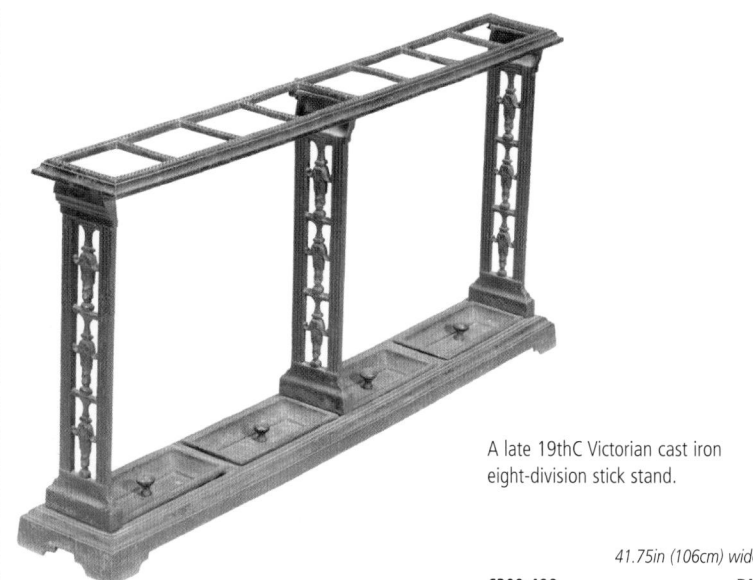

A late 19thC Victorian cast iron eight-division stick stand.

41.75in (106cm) wide

£300-400 **DN**

A late 19thC Victorian brass stick stand, of demi-lune form with urn finials.

24.5in (62cm) high

£400-450 **DN**

A late 19thC mahogany and brass hall stand, the metal tray inset bearing maker's initials 'WR'.

25.25in (64cm) wide

£450-550 **DN**

A late 19thC Victorian black-painted cast iron stick stand, with eight circular apertures above a lift-out tray.

17.75in (45cm) wide

£300-400 **DN**

A late 19thC Victorian painted and parcel-gilt leather shell case, adapted as a stick stand, decorated to one side with the Royal Arms.

24in (61cm) high

£450-550 **DN**

A late 19thC Victorian mahogany revolving snooker cue stand.

53.5in (136cm) high

£700-900 **DN**

FURNITURE

A George III brass-banded mahogany oval tray, with raised handles at each end, old repairs.

c1780   *20.75in (53cm) wide*

£250-350   **DN**

A satinwood and banded oval tray on low stand in George III style, of recent manufacture, the gallery tray with two silvered metal handles, the stand with a crossbanded frieze on square-section moulded legs.

29.5in (75cm) wide

£450-650   **DN**

A large George III mahogany tea tray, of serpentine outline, the moulded top rail on a balustraded gallery with inlet handles, the base with moulded edge 'LONDON LA 147'.

29in (74cm) wide

£3,000-3,500   **L&T**

A Regency japanned metal tray, decorated with an Anglo-French battle scene.

c1815   *28.75in (73cm) wide*

£400-500   **DN**

A large early 19thC gilt polychrome-painted papier-mâché tray, the scallop-edged tray centrally painted with a peacock, on a green-painted ground, highlighted with gilt, repairs, cracks.

32in (81cm) wide

£2,000-2,500   **SK**

An early 19thC papier-mâché tea tray, of cartouche shape with a raised wavy border and all-over gilt decoration with a central scene of Chinese figures among buildings.

27in (68.5cm) wide

£200-300   **DUK**

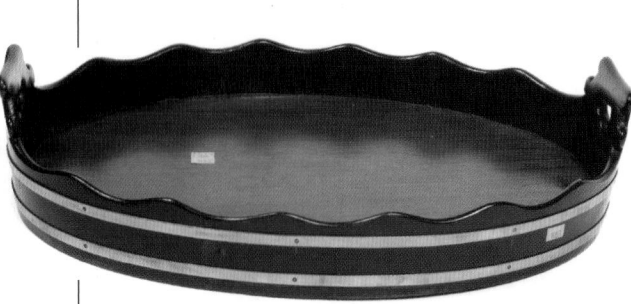

A 19thC oval brass bound mahogany serving tray, with cut out handles and wavy edge.

19in (49cm) wide

£900-1,200   **MEA**

A graduated set of three Victorian oval black japanned metal trays, with parcel-gilt and painted floral decoration.

c1875   *Largest 30in (76cm) wide*

£200-300   **DN**

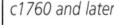

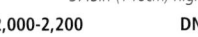

A carved mahogany pole screen.

c1760 and later
57.5in (146cm) high
£2,000-2,200 DN

A mid-19thC Victorian needlework upholstered and burl walnut firescreen, the panel depicting figures in a landscape, with foliate cresting and tripod base with gadrooned body and shaped legs.

54in (137cm) high
£300–400 SK

A William IV rosewood polescreen, with a floral silkwork panel.
c1835 *55.5in (141cm) high*
£200-300 DN

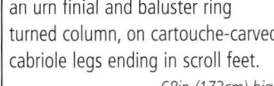

A Victorian walnut adjustable firescreen, the needlework panel within a carved frame, the pole with an urn finial and baluster ring turned column, on cartouche-carved cabriole legs ending in scroll feet.

68in (173cm) high
£600-900 L&T

A George III mahogany pole screen, the elaborate needlework panel with bouquet of flowers, above a heavily-carved tripartite base with claw-and-ball feet.

c1760 *64in (162.5cm) high*
£4,500-5,000 POOK

A Victorian giltwood firescreen, the shaped screen with a needlework panel of a family departing for a hunt, within a scrolling and spiral-turned frame, on downswept legs with scroll feet.

31in (79cm) wide
£300-500 DUK

A Victorian carved mahogany and part-gilt firescreen, the rectangular glazed needlework panel within a frame carved as palm leaves, with carved cabriole legs and scrolled toes.

44in (112cm) high
£500-600 TEN

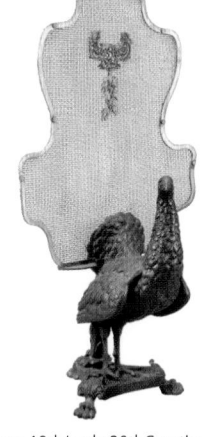

A late 19th/early 20thC patinated and gilt-metal and wire mesh firescreen, modelled as a peacock.

33.5in (85cm) high
£300-400 DN

A late 19thC French Rococo Revival gilt-metal and mesh firescreen.

26.25in (67cm) high
£250-350 DN

A 20thC painted wood and metal-mounted dummy board stick stand, decorated with a girl in Dutch dress.

38.25in (97cm) high
£500-700 DN

FURNITURE

A 19thC embossed leather and gilt four-fold screen.
72.75in (185cm) high

£1,000-1,200   **DN**

A probably 17thC Gothic Revival walnut and tapestry-mounted three-panel floor screen, the central panel with carved scrolling foliage, the two side panels with tapestry fragments.
75in (190.5cm) high

£3,000–3,500   **SK**

A late 19th/early 20thC Indian polychrome-painted four-fold screen, Rajastan, each fold centred by full length portraits of ladies and gentlemen, damage.
73.25in (186cm) high

£300-400   **DN**

BEDS

An American southeastern Pennsylvania William & Mary daybed, with a banister back and boldly turned legs joined by medial stretcher, retaining an old black over green surface.
c1730

£3,000-4,000   **POOK**

An American mid-18thC Pennsylvania painted pine and poplar tall-post bed, with claw-and-ball front feet and bottle-turned rear legs, retaining an early 19thC red and black grained surface.
77.5in (197cm) long

£25,000-30,000   **POOK**

A Portuguese carved and turned rosewood bed, incorporating a 17thC Indian footboard, with spiral-turned spindles and finials and pierced carved decoration depicting birds in scrolling foliage and centred by putti.
c1800   *96in (244cm) long*

£20,000-25,000   **SOTH.**

An American 19thC Federal mahogany tall post bed, each post with a reeded top above foliate and swag carving.
92in (233.5cm) high

£2,500-3,500   **POOK**

An American Pennsylvania Sheraton painted tall-post bed, retaining its original yellow and red canopy.

c1830   81in (205.5cm) long

£2,500-3,000   POOK

A mid-19thC Anglo-Indian carved and ebonised hardwood four-poster bed.

83.5in (212cm) long

£3,000-3,500   DN

A 19thC Dutch mahogany and floral marquetry lit en bateau, with panelled sides between scrolled ends with curved head- and footboards, a fitted box base within the rails, on turned feet with casters, with mattress.

82.75in (210cm) long

£1,500-2,000   TEN

One of two single four-poster beds, each with an arched canopy and octagonal and baluster-turned posts.

80in (203cm) long

£700-900 PAIR   WW

MISCELLANEOUS

One of a pair of Victorian satinwood and rosewood corner-hanging wall shelves, in the manner of Holland and Sons, each with mirrored backs, the shelves flanked by turned columns.

66in (167.5cm) high

£4,000-5,000 PAIR   DUK

A late 18thC painted pine hanging pewter shelf, with scalloped sides.

37in (94cm) wide

£900-1,200   POOK

A set of George IV mahogany bed steps, incorporating a control sliding lidded commode step, the bowfront moulded treads each with a gilt-tooled green leather inset, on short turned tapered legs.

31.5in (80cm) deep

£500-800   L&T

An early 19thC set of mahogany library steps, of three stairs, the underside bearing an armorial frontispiece titled 'D.D. Inglis Esq.'

19.75in (50cm) high

£2,800-3,200   DN

A mid-18thC American painted poplar dry sink, from Lancaster County, Pennsylvania, the deep well with moulded base, above a lower shelf supported by boldly scalloped sides, terminating in cutout feet, retaining its original red painted surface.

48in (122cm) wide

£40,000-50,000   POOK

A late 19thC Gothic-style oak pew.

The design of this pew can be attributed to Thomas Allom, who completed the saloon at Highclere Castle after the death of Sir Charles Barry. Design elements of the pew are echoed in the staircase and saloon at Highclere Castle.

62.25in (158cm) high

£250-350   DN

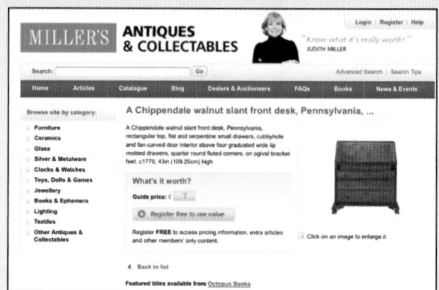

A mid-18thC Colonial padouk tea caddy, with silver metal mounts and side carrying handles, the hinged top with a gadrooned edge and enclosing three steel canisters, raised on scroll feet.

10.5in (27cm) wide

£4,000–4,500   L&T

A George III red tortoiseshell and ebony tea caddy, of cube form with a sarcophagus lid, white metal handle, each of the two-section interior with a sarcophagus lid, on ogee bracket feet.

5in (13cm) wide

£5,500-6,000   L&T

A George III ivory decagonal tea caddy, with tortoiseshell stringing and banding, the hinged lid with mother-of-pearl disc inlay, the interior void and front with an inlaid vacant cartouche.

4.25in (11cm) wide

£1,500-2,500   L&T

A George III satinwood and marquetry tea caddy, of straight-sided oval form, decorated with meandering foliage, the front with an oval inset rosewood panel, the lid similarly decorated.

6.25in (16cm) wide

£1,000-1,200   L&T

A George III harewood and marquetry tea caddy, of oval straight-sided form, the lid and front decorated with flowers and foliage with ribbon ties, interior with inlaid cover.

6in (15cm) wide

£900-1,200   L&T

A George III harewood, crossbanded and marquetry tea caddy, of oval section.

c1800   *5.75in (14.5cm) wide*

£900-1,200   DN

A George III satinwood and marquetry tea caddy, of oval straight-sided form, formal scroll and fleur-de-lys motif to the lid, floral spray with a ribbon tie to the front, small ivory escutcheon.

6in (15cm) wide

£900-1,200   L&T

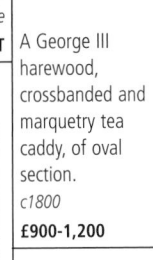

A George III harewood and marquetry tea caddy, of oval straight-sided form, the lid with an oval foliate rosette surrounded by beading, the front with crossed flowers.

6in (15cm) wide

£800-1,000   L&T

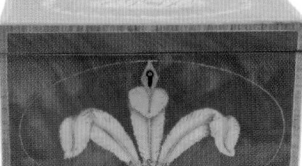

A George III mahogany and satinwood tea caddy, the front inlaid with the Prince of Wales feathers and the lid entitled 'PDC', enclosing two lidded canisters.

8in (20.5cm) wide

£1,300-1,500   GORL

BOXES

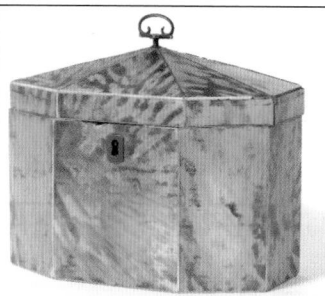

An early 19thC tortoiseshell-veneered two-division tea caddy, of hexagonal form, the panelled and gently sloping lid with pewter wire stringing for a C-shape centre handle, internally with two hexagonal flat pull-off lids.

5.5in (14cm) high

£1,200-1,500 TEN

A Regency rosewood tea caddy, of sarcophagus form, the lid opening to an associated cut glass bowl and a Continental white metal caddy spoon.

c1820 *12.5in (32cm) wide*

£120-180 DN

A Regency rosewood sarcophagus form tea caddy, with a rectangular top with broad carved handle, the interior fitted with twin, shaped, lidded tea compartments and central vacant recess, on gilt animal paw feet.

14in (35.5cm) wide

£150-300 DUK

A Regency tortoiseshell tea caddy, of sarcophagus form, with ivory banding and silver stringing, the cavetto-moulded hinged lid enclosing a twin-lidded interior.

6.75in (17.5cm) wide

£800-1,000 L&T

An early 19thC thuya and ebonised tea caddy.

7.5in (19cm) high

£200-300 DN

A George IV rosewood sarcophagus-shape tea caddy, with boxwood line edging, the interior with a pair of hinged lidded canisters and a silver mounted mixed bowl, with later side handles, London.

1820 *12.5in (32cm) wide*

£250-350 WW

A large George IV rosewood and brass-inlaid tea caddy, with hallmarked silver handle, the lid revealing a large removable canister flanked by a pair of smaller canisters, on an ebonised plinth base.

16.25in (41cm) wide

£300-400 L&T

A tortoiseshell veneered concave-fronted two-division tea caddy, with pewter wire stringing, ivory veneered inner rim framing two flat-lidded compartments, one with finial lacking, on bun feet.

c1840 *8.75in (22.5cm) wide*

£800-1,000 TEN

A tortoiseshell and mother-of-pearl inlaid two-division tea caddy, of bowfronted sarcophagus form, with pewter stringing, the cover and front panel decorated with inlaid mother-of-pearl and wirework leaf scroll, raised on bun feet.

c1840 *7.75in (20cm) wide*

£1,200-1,500 TEN

A 19thC and later rosewood tea caddy, of sarcophagus form with moulded top, two interior canisters flanking a bowl recess, no bowl, mother-of-pearl escutcheon, embossed brass ring handles.

13in (33cm) wide

£120-180 HT

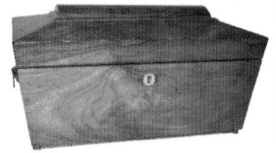

A Victorian tortoiseshell and mother-of-pearl inlaid bombé tea caddy, decorated throughout with scrolling foliage, the hinged lid enclosing lidded compartments with turned ivory handles, raised on bun feet.

8.25in (21cm) wide

£1,000-1,500 L&T

A late 17thC William and Mary oyster laburnum veneered lace box, losses.

17in (43cm) wide

£600-700   DN

A George III tortoiseshell work box, of oblong form with canted corners, the sarcophagus lid with gilt-metal beading, ivory outlines with white metal divisions, the well-fitted interior with compartments, part silk lining.

11in (28cm) wide

£1,500–2,000   L&T

An 18thC/early 19thC Anglo-Indian Vizagapatam work box, veneered in tortoiseshell and inlaid with engraved ivory, the lid inset with painted and printed panels of flowers and enclosing a fitted interior, the front with a drawer.

16in (40.5cm) wide

£500-700   DUK

A Georgian paint-decorated octagonal fruitwood nécessaire box, the lid with painted border and oval scene of figures before a country house, side lifting handles, the paper-lined interior with removable divided compartment.

10.5in (26.5cm) wide

£700-1,000   SK

An early 19thC rectangular straw work box, decorated with river and boat scenes within decorative banding, enclosing three divisions enclosed by a pair of uphinged lids.

11.75in (30cm) wide

£350-400   TEN

An American early 19thC flame-birch and mahogany veneer sewing box, probably New England, the bow lid centred with an inlaid bone and ebony heart, hinged lid opening to interior compartments and lower drawer.

9.25in (23.5cm) wide

£1,200-1,800   SK

A 19thC pollard oak sarcophagus sewing casket, raised on four bun feet with gadrooned borders and twin ring handles, opening to fitted tray to interior.

11.75in (30cm) wide

£350-450   FLD

A French rosewood and marquetry work box, of sarcophagus form.

c1840   *23.75in (60cm) wide*

£400-600   DN

A 19thC Chinese export lacquer work box, decorated with scrolling foliage, the hinged lid enclosing an ivory fitted interior, above a drawer enclosing a hinged writing surface and pen wells.

17in (43cm) wide

£1,000-1,500   L&T

A Victorian papier mâché needlework cabinet, decorated with monastic ruin scenes, the domed lid opening to divided compartments above two doors enclosing five graduated drawers, large section of lid damaged.

19in (48.5cm) high

£500-600   WW

BOXES

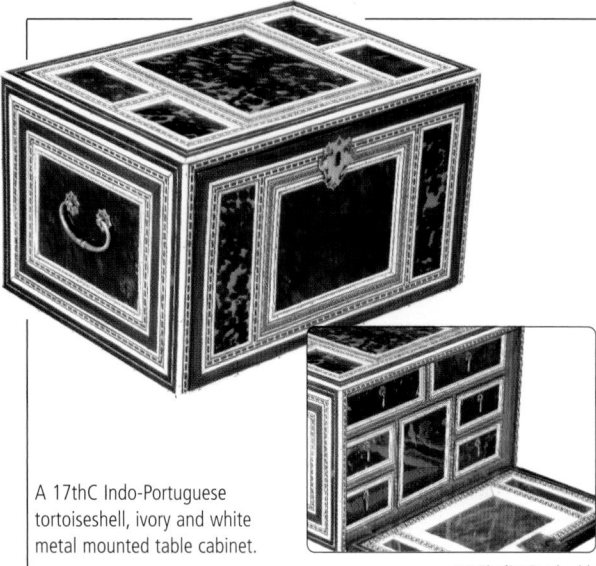

An early 17thC Persian sadeli-worked table cabinet, probably Sindh Province, restoration.

14.25in (36cm) wide

£2,000-2,500 DN

A 17thC Indo-Portuguese tortoiseshell, ivory and white metal mounted table cabinet.

£8,000-10,000

13.5in (34.5cm) wide

DN

An early 18thC Indo-Portuguese tortoise shell and ivory table cabinet, the panelled lid and sides with twin carrying handles, opening to reveal a fitted interior with an arrangement of eight drawers.

10.5in (27cm) wide

£7,000-10,000 L&T

A small German Directoire mahogany and brass moulded table cabinet, in the manner of David Roentgen, with sliding trays over a brass-ribbed drawer enclosed by a tambour slide.

David Roentgen (1743–1807) was one of the most innovative and commercially driven cabinetmakers of the 18thC. He perfected the standardisation of parts of his elegant furniture, enabling it to be taken apart, shipped to clients and then easily reassembled.

21.5in (55cm) wide

£4,000-4,500 TEN

An 18thC American Chester County walnut spice box, with compass star inlaid door enclosing nine small drawers, resting on turned ball feet.

15.75in (40cm) high

£50,000-80,000 POOK

An American New England Federal mahogany spice chest, with two flame-maple doors enclosing an interior with five herringbone-inlaid drawers supported by French feet.

c1805   *12.75in (32.5cm) wide*

£3,000-3,500 POOK

A Continental table cabinet, covered entirely with old silk petit point floral needlework, the coved top over two doors enclosing satin-fronted drawers with cedar linings, on bracket feet.

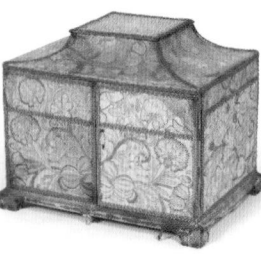

25.5in (65cm) wide

£600-800 TEN

A Charles II oak Bible or desk box, the front carved with initials 'M B' flanked by scrolls and lozenge motifs, dated, repair.

1692   27in (68.5cm) wide
£200-300   DN

A mid-18thC walnut table-top bureau, with serpentine front, faults, formerly with a mirror section.

16.75in (42.5cm) wide
£700-900   DN

A George IV rosewood and foliate cut brass inlaid rosewood writing slope, with fully fitted interior.

c1830   19.75in (51cm) wide
£450-550   DN

A William IV rosewood and brass-bound writing slope, with stringing and sunken side handles, the interior with replaced leather and inkwells, secret drawers, restored.

14in (35.5cm) wide
£200-250   WW

A painted faux malachite papier mâché and brass mounted writing slope.

c1870   15in (38cm) wide
£250-300   DN

A 19thC Anglo-Indian teak and bone inlaid writing slope, with geometric foliage patterns, ebonised and with brass banding, the interior with hinged slopes and partitions with two hidden drawers.

19in (48cm) wide
£350-450   WW

A late 19thC Italian rosewood and parquetry writing slope, with pierced scroll fretwork, an ink bottle and lidded compartments, the chequer and star-inlaid fold opening to reveal a green leather writing surface and three small drawers.

18in (45.5cm) wide
£150-250   L&T

A 19thC burr-walnut folding table writing desk, with interior fittings, including two glass ink bottles with gilt-metal covers.

14in (35.5cm) wide
£150-200   A&G

A late Victorian oak stationery box, the hinged lid revealing a leather pen holder above shaped divisions for letters, a pen tray and a leather-lined folding writing slope, stamped 'Rd 173369', side carrying handles missing.

13.5in (34cm) wide
£200-250
WW

An early 20thC tortoiseshell desk set, by William Coymns, London, comprising covered letter rack and writing pad, decorated with foliate scrolls and panels of Classical scenes.

1915   11.5in (29cm) wide
£1,500-2,000   L&T

A William IV brass-inset rosewood dressing case, the fitted interior with glass jars with silver-plated tops.

c1835   *12.25in (31cm) wide*

£150-200   **DN**

An early Victorian rosewood and brass-inlaid travel box, of rectangular form, with hinged lid and recessed handles to the sides, and the interior fitted with an enclosed pouch.

11in (28cm) wide

£250-300   **ADA**

A Victorian silver mounted dressing table set and box, London, the brass-bound coromandel case fitted with twelve silver mounted bottles, with a concealed drawer containing nail scissors and other things, maker's mark 'JV'.

1859   *7.5in (19cm) high*

£900-1200   **TEN**

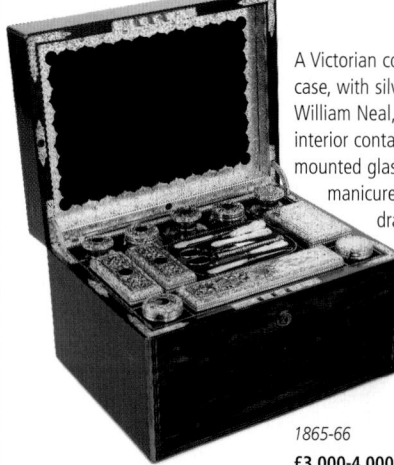

A Victorian coromandel dressing case, with silver mounted fittings, William Neal, London, the fitted interior containing glass jars, silver mounted glass boxes and a manicure set, and two 'secret' drawers, one fitted with a writing slope, the other plain.

1865-66   *13in (33cm) wide*

£3,000-4,000   **L&T**

A Victorian silver mounted dressing table set and box, the brass-bound coromandel case fitted with eleven silver mounted accessories, with a concealed drawer containing shaving and manicure implements, all initialled, maker's mark 'JV', London.

1866   *7in (18cm) high*

£700-900   **TEN**

A Victorian coromandel and brass mounted lady's dressing box, by W. Leuchars, Piccadilly, London, inside of lid with a cracked mirror and document folder, interior with lidded boxes, implements tray and storage space, with a now-locked lateral drawer, key lacking.

11.75in (30cm) wide

£500-1,000   **L&T**

A Victorian kingwood, ebony and brass inlaid toilet box, the hinged lid enclosing an interior fitted with various cut glass jars and containers, the lock stamped 'I. BRAMAH 194 PICCADILLY', losses.

12in (30.5cm) wide

£250-300   **WW**

A Continental travelling dressing set, with marks for Belgium, maker Sergeni and Aine, contained within a mahogany brass-bound and strung case with hinged flush carry handles and elaborate scroll cartouche to lid.

Case 18.75in (48cm) wide

£600-800   **L&T**

DECANTER BOXES

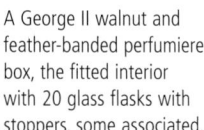

A George II walnut and feather-banded perfumiere box, the fitted interior with 20 glass flasks with stoppers, some associated.

c1740   *16in (40cm) w*

£800-1,000   **DN**

A late George III flame-mahogany domed decanter box, with strung edges and ebonised mouldings, the hinged lid revealing a lined divided interior with six gilt painted decanters, lobed stoppers mainly associated, with key.

10.5in (26.5cm) wide

£800-1,000   **L&T**

ESSENTIAL REFERENCE – KNIFE BOXES

- Usually supplied in pairs to sit at either end of a sideboard, knife boxes were decorative cases with an interior fitted with slots for storing cutlery.
- They were introduced in the 18thC, in the reign of George II. The basic form, with a serpentine front, remained mostly unchanged until the 1780s. The earliest were often covered in silk-velvet or shagreen, rather than veneered. From the 1760s knife-boxes in mahogany were made and often had bow-fronted form, hinged slope with drop-handles, and shaped bracket or claw-and-ball feet.
- Decoration became increasingly lavish in the 1770s, with crossbanding and featherbanding, ebony-inlaid star parquetry to the slopes and green-stained shell inlay.
- The vase-form knife-box was introduced in the 1780s.
- Knife-boxes became increasingly redundant during the early 19thC as sideboards had fitted drawers for cutlery.

A George II shagreen cutlery box and fittings, London, complete with twelve-piece sets of table knife and fork and dessert knife and fork, knives with maker's mark 'TS' and forks with 'SD', all leaf-capped pistol grips, crested, with later steel blades and tines.

c1739-55   15in (38cm) high

£3,500-4,000   **TEN**

A pair of George III mahogany cutlery boxes, of casket form, with baize-lined interiors, formerly fitted, inlay of a later date, on brass claw-and-ball feet.

16.25in (41cm) high

£2,000-3,000   **L&T**

A Shagreen knife-box, retaining a 24-piece pistol-grip set of knives and forks marked 'IH'.

c1740   Box 12.75in (32.5cm) high

£4,500-5,500   **POOK**

A set of three George III mahogany cutlery urns, inlaid with stringing, the domed lids revealing stepped interiors fitted for cutlery, the spreading moulded feet on quarter-veneered square bases.

Largest 26.75in (68cm) high

£6,000-8,000   **L&T**

A matched pair of George III mahogany and kingwood crossbanded cutlery urns, London, of square tapered vase form with concave corners, enclosing cutlery apertures, each raised on a socle and square plinth base, silver mounts hallmarked.

1805   25in (63cm) high

£3,500-4,500   **L&T**

A pair of 19thC mahogany serpentine-fronted knife boxes, one with original fittings, the other fitted for stationery, each with brass carrying handles to the sides.

14.25in (36cm) wide

£600-800   **A&G**

A late 18thC New England mahogany pipe-box, with scalloped sides and heart cut-out back, retaining an old mellow patina.

20.75in (52.5cm) high

£4,500-5,500   **POOK**

BOXES

A William and Mary boarded elm box, the moulded-edge top with later hinges to an interior with a lidded till, the front carved with foliage and 'IC 1693', with conforming sides.

22.5in (57cm) wide

£200-250   **WW**

A Victorian, probably Welsh, slate and black- and gilt-painted casket, the cavetto moulded lid above sides painted with scenes from north Wales, on a plinth base with squat feet, signed 'R Williams'.

9.5in (24cm) high

£500-700   **L&T**

A miniature longcase clock pocket watch holder, boxwood stringing to the borders, inlaid plinth upon ogee feet, top of back board with hinged door to locate pocket watch.

c1840   *13.75in (35cm) high*

£600-700   **TEN**

A Regency mahogany artist's box, by Windsor & Newton, with named paint blocks, ceramics, mixing trays and accessories above a drawer with brass handle, with label to underside of the lid.

9.25in (23.5cm) wide

£400-500   **L&T**

A Victorian Scottish penwork games box, decorated with scenes of everyday life, the interior with tray and four boxes, on embossed brass feet, bears paper label for Smith and Co., Aberdeen.

The penwork scene decorating the lid of this box is adapted from Sir David Wilkie's 1807 painting 'The Rent Day'.

11in (28cm) wide

£2,500–3,500   **L&T**

An American late 18thC Pennsylvania painted pine slide-lid candle box, by John Drissel, inscribed on lid 'Johannes Stauffer Anno 1797, John Drissel, his hand'.

9in (23cm) wide

£35,000-40,000   **POOK**

A small 19thC Swedish inlaid steel casket, the lid centred by a lion-supported coat of arms within flowering rose stems, internally lined in blue silk, the panels of the base decorated with further roses, upon flattened bun feet.

3.25in (8.5cm) wide

£350–450   **TEN**

A mid-19thC brass bound coromandel desk box, lid with engraved brass presentation shield and banner, dated, with marblised-paper-lined interior and singled drawer.

11in (28cm) wide

£200-300   **SK**

A Victorian oak country house letter box, of cylindrical form with faceted and foliate moulded top above letter flap and door with rate card, the circular base with one apron drawer.

14.5in (37cm) high

£2,000-2,500   **L&T**

A 19thC carved oak box, applied throughout with sections of 17thC oak and walnut carving, including rosettes, cherubs, scroll cartouches and masks on chevron-inlaid low bracket feet, currently locked.

25.5in (65cm) wide

£500-700   L&T

A Victorian gilt-metal mounted coromandel jewellery box, with a hinged, bowed rectangular lid centred by a blue jasperware medallion, fitted interior, Gothic revival mounts.

12.25in (28.5cm) wide

£400-600   JA

A Victorian Gothic Revival walnut bijouterie box, of rounded rectangular form, the Gothic gilt hinges with Florentine pietra dura roundels and blue fitted interior.

11in (28cm) wide

£400-500   L&T

A small 19thC Eastern rosewood and brass mounted trunk, decorated with foliage and stars, the fitted interior with rails to the cover and lift-out tray and compartments with hinged covers, side carrying handles.

22.5in (57cm) wide

£400-500   WW

A 19thC mahogany, rosewood and straw-work dressing box, the hinged cover above two faux short drawers and two other small drawers, on bun feet, with decoration of house and buildings to sides and to fitted interior. 1

1in (28cm) wide

£150-250   L&T

A Victorian oak and glazed letter box, the central hinging lid with brass letter aperture, above a bevelled glazed panel and narrow pull-out tray, sides with space for letters.

18.25in (46cm) wide

£600-700   L&T

A late 19thC Victorian oak, glazed and brass mounted domestic posting box.

10in (25.5cm) wide

£400-450   DN

A Victorian ebonised and brass mounted casket, with a velvet-lined interior.

10.75in (27.5cm) wide

£250-350   WW

A late 19thC burl wood and inlaid cigar box, with serpentine front, inlaid with brass outlining and cartouches, with ebony and mother-of-pearl accents, interior fitted with four cigar slides and a drawer.

10.75in (28.5cm) wide Est

£300-400   SK

A late 19thC Anglo-Indian carved ebony work box, Ceylon, the profusely carved exterior with hinged cover, with a lift-out lidded tray.

16.5in (42cm) wide

£450-550   WW

A late 19thC French burl wood veneered and inlaid cordial box, inlaid with brass, mother-of-pearl and abalone cartouches, interior with a pair of etched glass decanters, and six cordial stems.

Box 11.25in (28cm) wide

£350-400   SK

BOXES

A Stobwasser papier mâché snuff box, painted with 'wanderde Komediganten' inscribed in red inside the lid and numbered 'f.77' inside the base.

4in (10cm) high

£800-1,000   GORL

A matched pair of 19thC timber snuff boxes, modelled as ladies' shoes, both with sliding covers, and pique work to the exterior.

4in (10cm) long

£350-500   FRE

A 19thC Scottish carved and stained wood snuff box, the lid carved in high relief with three Scottish figures seated, with various animals carved to thumb-lift and side panels.

By tradition, snuff boxes of this type are attributed to 'Blind Jack' of Edinburgh, and the scene may be taken from the literature of Robert Burns.

6.5in (16.5cm) wide

£400–500   TEN

TREEN

An early 18thC French boxwood tobacco rasp, carved in relief with boor hunters and St Hubert above a coat of arms, the opensided back with head of a nobleman over the original rasp and open-mouthed head terminal.

c1730   *7.5in (19cm) high*

£4,000-5,000   GORL

A George II carved walnut cribbage board, decorated with a rose and other floral motifs, some old worm damage and losses to bottom corners, dated.

1734   *11.5in (29cm) high*

£2,000-2,500   GORL

A George III two compartment mahogany cheese coaster, of curved form on a plinth with four small roller casters.

17in (44cm) wide

£1,000-1,500   MEA

An early George III mahogany cat, the upper section revolving, restoration.

c1770   *13.75in (35cm) high*

£200-300   DN

A late 18th/early 19thC American carved oblong burl bowl.

19.5in (49.5cm) wide

£2,500-3,000   SK

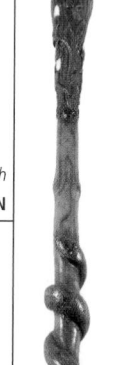

A 19thC carved holly, mother-of-pearl and bone inset walking stick, with two serpents in relief, lacking ferrule.

35.5in (90.5cm) high

£500-600   DN

A George III mahogany cheese coaster, losses.

c1780   *18.75in (48cm) wide*

£150-200   DN

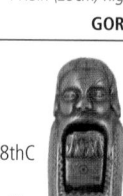

A late 17th/early 18thC boxwood lever nutcracker, carved with a bearded man's head above an armorial.

4.75in (12cm) high

£2,500-3,000   GORL

A Victorian carved coconut cup, the carved half-coconut bowl with a seated figure of Queen Victoria, with Highland figures and Scottish emblems, on a slender stem and a plain foot.

3.5in (9cm) diam

£250-300   L&T

A 19thC Polish silver mounted coconut etrog container, coconut resting on a realistically cast leaf, hinged lid, marked '12'.

6.5in (16.5cm) wide

£2,500-3,000   SK

A 19thC Bavarian carved wooden inkwell in the form of a bulldog head, with glass eyes to the hinged cover and with leather collar.

4in (10cm) high

£500-600   ADA

A 19thC oak and fruitwood Selsey-type mousetrap, the circular welled base with a notched platform (bait nibbler) and a pair of supports and a solid drop weight.

10in (25.5cm) high

£450-550   WW

CARVINGS

A 19thC American carved and gilded wooden phoenix figural plaque.

32in (81cm) wide

£8,000-9,000   SK

A large 19thC carved giltwood hanging hunting trophy, the ribbon-tied surmount with trailing oak leaves and acorns above an entwined game bird, bugle, sword, flask and gun, below is a fruit basket and bird and further oak leaves.

118in (300cm) high

A Spanish polychrome carved wooden sculpture of a saint, reading.

34.5in (87.5cm) high

£2,500-2,800   ADA   £5,500-6,500   L&T

A 19thC Austrian carved timber pipe, the horned shaped mouthpiece leads to a carved timber head moulded as a bearded gentleman with headdress in a fitted case.

6in (15cm) long

£150-250   FRE

A large carved pine panel, probably Swiss or German, carved in high relief with two cherubs amidst floral blooms, above a harp and trumpet, the whole within moulded rectangular frame.

45.75in (116cm) wide

£2,500-3,500   L&T

A large carved pine panel, probably Swiss or German, carved in high relief with a war trophy, surrounded by a floral and fruiting wreath, the whole within moulded rectangular frame.

46.5in (118cm) wide

£2,000-3,000   L&T

CLOCKS, BAROMETERS

CLOCKS, BAROMETERS AND SCIENTIFIC INSTRUMENTS

As has been the trend in recent years, good-quality clocks by important makers are currently performing well, regardless of the type of clock. London makers still have the edge here, with many collectors believing that their work represents the very best quality available. However, good-quality pieces from regional makers are now also realising comparable prices. For example, John London from Bristol, who specialised in lantern and longcase clocks with character and striking engraving, is currently highly rated, as are Joseph Finney and the Condliff family from Liverpool, both of whom made exceptional pieces for a wealthy clientele. At the other end of the scale, more ordinary clocks continue to see waning interest, and this is reflected in current prices that make them good value for money.

Twenty to thirty years ago, the clock and barometer market consisted of purists who were unwilling to pay a premium for restored pieces. In recent years, however, buyers have been more willing to accept restored pieces, considering their aesthetics to be just as important. Early clocks with the best proportions – as long as they have all their original components – are currently sought after. Since most clocks of this age will have undergone some restoration, this should not affect the value if the work has been carried out honestly and sympathetically.

The longcase clock market has struggled a little in the last twelve months. The most desirable English examples from the late 17th and early 18th centuries, by names such as Thomas Tompion, Joseph Knibb, Henry Jones and Daniel Quare continue to sell well. However, mid-18th century clocks with larger proportions are performing badly, as few modern homes can accommodate them. Later 18th century mahogany examples are also struggling, unless made by sought after makers such as Mudge & Dutton.

Recent trends have seen a growth in interest in lantern clocks, in particular those that have been conserved and not over-polished, and these are currently achieving the best prices. There are many fake lantern clocks, however, so it is important to remain vigilant.

Any carriage clock made prior to 1680 sells for a premium, while those by renowned makers such as Garnier, Jacot, Drocourt, Le Roy, Margaine and Soldano remain desirable. In general, collectors are looking for examples that retain their original escapement and, if possible, original leather-covered travelling case and key. Pieces with complicated movements such as those with moon phase, especially spherical moon phases, are also desirable, as they are considered quirky by today's buyers.

A good quality barometer by a sought after maker such as Daniel Quare or John Patrick will command high prices due to its rarity, originality in design and historical importance. Late 19th century examples by makers such as Adie and Dollond are doing well. Royal Polytechnic and Fitzroy barometers are commanding good prices and aneroid barometers are performing well. There has been a surge of interest in barographs. In early 2008 a good example would fetch £300-400, however by the end of 2009 they could command £600-800.

Left to right: late 17th century walnut and floral marquetry longcase clock by Andrew Broun, Edinburgh, £5,800 at Lyon & Turnbull; mahogany mercury wheel barometer by J. Spelzini, London, c1840, £680 at Dreweatt's.

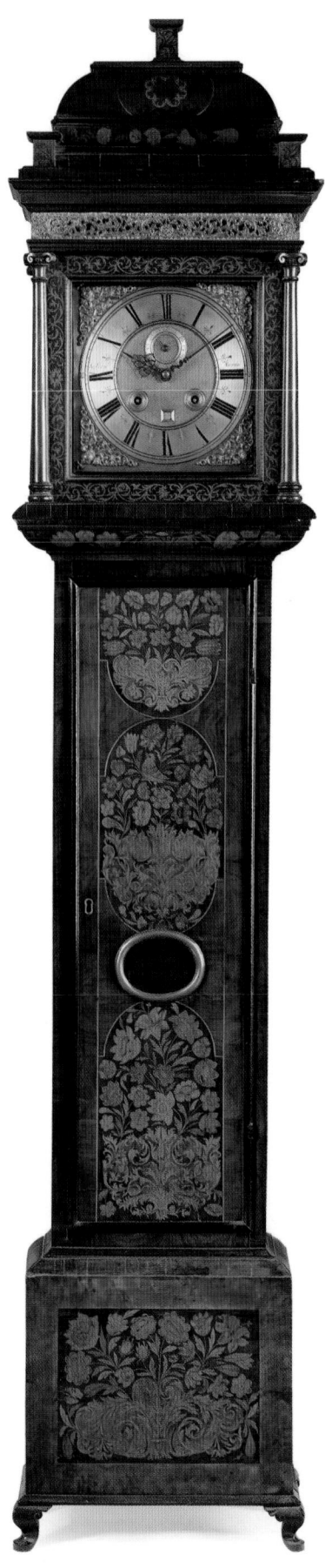

CLOCKS

A stained burr-maple eight-day longcase clock, Mark Hawkins, Bury St Edmunds, the 12in (30.5cm) brass dial with signed silvered chapter ring, seconds dial and date aperture, five-pillar movement with anchor escapement and rack striking on a bell, later seatboard.

c1715   81in (206cm) high

£4,000-5,000   TEN

A George I walnut eight-day longcase clock, James Stevens, London, with five-finned pillar rack and bell-striking movement.

James Stevens is recorded as working in London c1710.

c1725   85.75in (218cm) high

£3,000-4,000   DN

A George II inlaid walnut eight-day longcase clock, William Newman, Norwich, five-finned pillar rack-striking movement, the case with break-arch cornice and integral pilasters above parquetry lunette-decorated break-arch long door flanked by reeded canted angles to trunk.

c1730   84.75in (215cm) high

£2,000-2,500   DN

A George II walnut eight-day longcase clock, Edward Greatrex, Birmingham, with penny moon, the four-pillar rack and bell-striking movement, the plinth-base case with alterations.

Edward Greatrex is recorded as working in Birmingham c1750.

c1745   87.5in (222cm) high

£2,000-3,000   DN

A red and gilt chinoiserie lacquer longcase clock, Henry Thornton, London, 12in (30.5cm) break-arch engraved brass dial, the movement with five knopped, finned and ringed pillars playing six tunes on nine bells with hourly striking on a further single bell, with Vauxhall plate mirror door.

c1730   108in (274cm) high

£45,000-55,000   ASC

A rare George II red japanned eight-day longcase clock, Joseph Herring, London, five-pillar rack and bell-striking movement, in a polychrome- and raised-gilt-decorated case with Oriental scenes, original decoration with wear and losses to finish.

c1750   90.25in (229cm) high

£3,000-4,000   DN

An 18thC mahogany eight-day longcase clock, William Mitchell, East Burnham, the five-pillar rack and bell-striking movement with 12in (30.5cm) brass break-arch dial with calendar aperture, signed 'William Mitchell East Burnham' to the lower edge.

82.25in (209cm) high

£1,800-2,200   DN

An 18thC ebonised longcase clock, the 12in (30.5cm) brass dial with equation of time aperture and silvered plaque signed 'Wm Scafe, London', strike/silent and rise/fall dials, the six-pillar movement with anchor escapement and striking on a later bell, case associated.

94.5in (240cm) high

£10,000-15,000   TEN

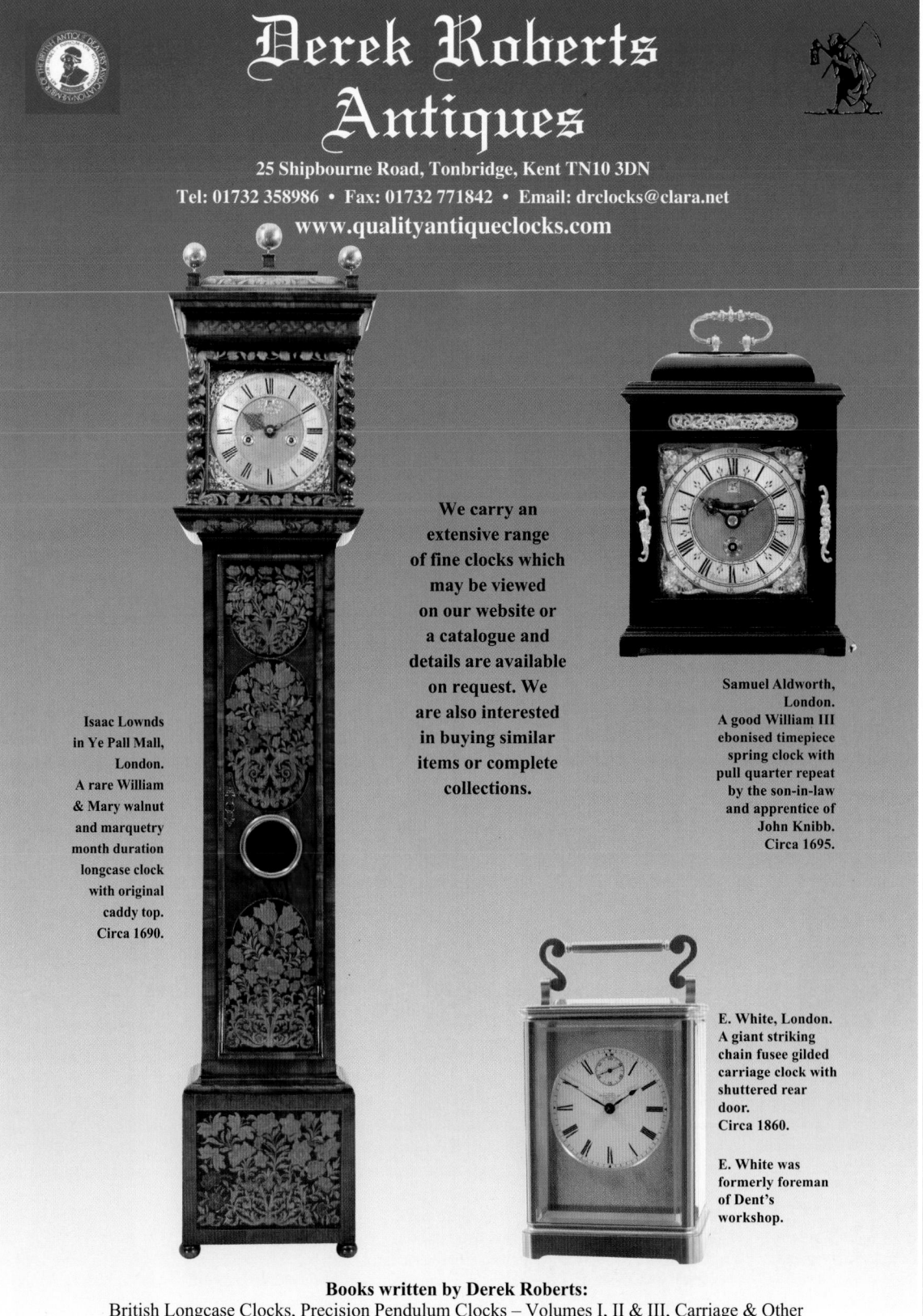

A mid-18thC oak longcase clock, the brass dial with silvered chapter ring, with subsidiary seconds dial and date apertures, fitted eight-day movement striking on a single bell, with Roman numerals inscribed 'Hen Simcock, Daintree'.

84in (213cm) high

£2,000-2,500   A&G

A mid-18thC mahogany longcase clock, the month going six-pillar movement striking on a bell, with a 12in (30.5cm) arched brass dial, the arch with a silvered boss inscribed 'John Neale, Leadenhall Street, London'.

93in (236cm) high

£7,000-9,000   WW

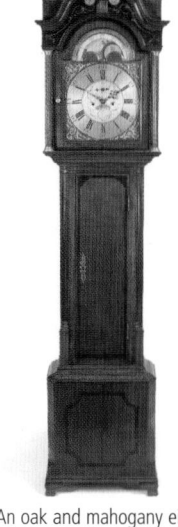

An oak and mahogany eight-day longcase clock, David Collier, Gatley, a 13.25in (33.75cm) arched brass dial below moon disc for lunar scale and maker's signature, four-pillar movement with anchor escapement and rack striking on a bell.

c1770   86.5in (220cm) high

£3,000-4,000   TEN

A George III mahogany eight-day longcase clock, Edward Bilbie, Chew Stoke, four-pillar rack and bell-striking movement.

The use of single-sheet dials by some Chew Valley clockmakers predates the general fashion by around 20 years. The earliest known example by a member of the Bilbie family is on a thirty-hour longcase clock by William Bilbie, who died in 1767.

c1775   90.25in (229cm) high

£3,000-4,000   DN

A George III figured-mahogany eight-day longcase clock, Charles Penton, London, the five-pillar rack and bell-striking movement in a break-arch case, on plinth base with moulded skirt incorporating bracket feet.

c1775   87.5in (222cm) high

£3,500-4,500   DN

An oak and mahogany eight-day longcase clock, James Butler, Bolton, the 13in (33cm) square brass dial with maker's signature, four-pillar movement with anchor escapement and rack striking on a bell, later seatboard.

James Butler was born in 1757 and worked as a clockmaker in Bolton, Lancashire until his death in 1809.

c1780   87.75in (223cm) high

£2,000-3,000   TEN

A mahogany eight-day longcase clock, Clements, London, the 12in (30.5cm) arched brass dial with maker's signature and with strike/silent, five-pillar movement with anchor escapement and rack striking on a bell.

c1780   84.25in (214cm) high

£12,000-15,000   TEN

An oak eight-day longcase clock, Lawson, Leigh, the 13in (33cm) square brass dial with silvered chapter ring, inner date ring and maker's signature, four-pillar movement with anchor escapement and rack striking on a bell, dial foot broken.

c1780   85.5in (217cm) high

£1,200-1,800   TEN

A mahogany longcase clock with automata in the arch, Richard Collins, Margate, above the dial decorated with a painted rural scene, at the hour when the clock strikes the sails of a windmill turn and a figure appears, the eight-day striking movement with a repeat cord to trip the automata, striking at will.

Richard Collins is recorded as working in Margate between 1780 and 1827.

c1790   90.25in (229cm) high

£15,000-18,000   DR

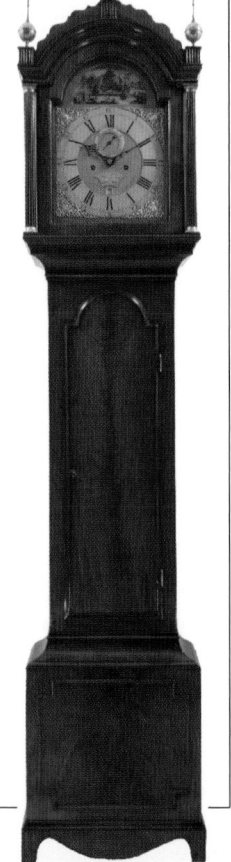

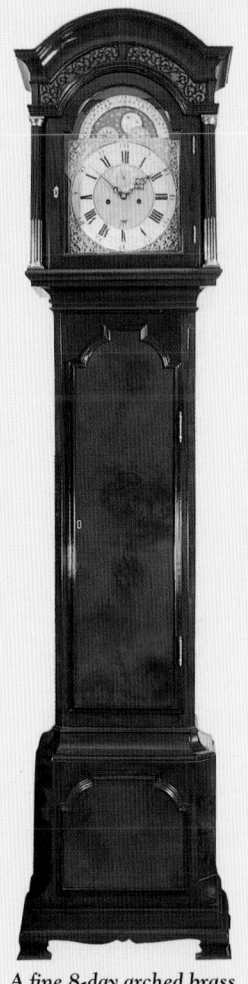

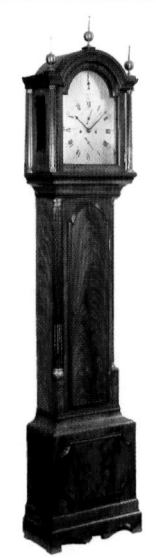

A George III mahogany eight-day longcase clock, John Grant, London, five-pillar rack and bell-striking movement.

The nephew of clockmaker Alexander Cumming, John Grant worked in Fleet Street, 1786-1810.

c1790   87.5in (222cm) high

£5,000-7,000   DN

A mahogany eight-day longcase clock, Webster, Whitby, the 13in (33cm) signed dial with chapter ring and dummy date ring, four-pillar movement with anchor escapement and rack striking on a bell, possibly later seatboard.

c1790   84.5in (215cm) high

£2,000-3,000   TEN

An unusual George III oak mahogany-banded longcase clock, the oval face with a 12in (30.5cm) dial and marked 'Bickerton, Ellesmere', with a subsidiary second dial and painted maiden, with eight-day twin-train bell-striking movement.

87.5in (222cm) high

£4,000-5,000   L&T

A George III mahogany, satinwood-banded and ebony-strung longcase clock, by William Breakenrig, Edinburgh, the twin-train movement striking the hours on a bell, with a Rococo cast-brass dial, seconds dial and calendar aperture.

90.5in (230cm) high

£2,500-3,500   L&T

A George III mahogany longcase clock, the arched 11.5in (29cm) dial with steel chapter ring and subsidiary seconds dial and marked 'Geo. Goodall, Tadcaster', the three-train eight-day movement striking on a bell.

88.5in (225cm) high

£3,000-5,000   L&T

CLOSER LOOK – GEORGE II LONGCASE CLOCK

Exceptional quality movements, or mechanisms, command high prices. This example shows top-quality craftsmanship to the five-pillar movement and has a particularly well-executed gear-driven moonwork.

Brass hands retain their original gilding.

The regulator deadbeat escapement in this clock ensures increased accuracy of timekeeping.

The Classical-style case is a good example of its type. It is well-proportioned with crisp mouldings to the trunk door and base panel.

A flame mahogany longcase clock, Thomas Dobson, Chiswell Street, London, 12in (30.5cm) painted dial with maker's signature, with moonphases to arch, five-pillar movement with deadbeat escapement, maintaining power, tee-shaped front plate to take the gear-driven moonwork and regulator-style suspension for the wood rod pendulum.

The maker, Thomas Dobson, may be one of several Thomas Dobsons at Chiswell Street in the late 18thC.

c1800   92in (234cm) high

£20,000-23,000   ASC

A rare English musical steeple clock, the Gothic case enclosing a three-train movement with eleven bells, lower cylinder and pipe organ mechanism, the side plate engraved 'French Royal Exchange, London', signed on the face and engraved on the backplate 'James McCabe Cornhill London 1806'.

68.25in (173.5cm) high

£30,000-35,000   POOK

An early 19thC George III mahogany eight-day longcase clock, S. Gill, Rye, with four-pillar rack and bell-striking movement.

The clock was probably made by a relative of Daniel Gill who is recorded as working in Rye c1797.

83in (211cm) high

£1,500-2,500   DN

A small ebonised bell-top bracket clock, Robert Henderson, London, the brass dial with silvered chapter ring and strike/silent dial in the arch, the eight-day fusee movement with original verge escapement, strikes on a bell and with trip repeat, maker's signature.

Robert Henderson is recorded as working in St Martin's Court between 1768 and 1805.

c1780   14in (36cm) high
£18,500-22,500   **DR**

A mahogany quarter-chiming bracket clock, John Taylor, London, the 8in (20.5cm) composite-brass dial engraved 'John Taylor, London', strike/silent dial in the arch, eight-day, three-train fusee movement chiming quarters on nine bells, verge escapement and fully-engraved backplate, restoration.

24in (61cm) high

£8,000-12,000   **SK**

A George III ebonised bracket clock, by Benjamin Wilson, London, the silvered arched dial with subsidiary strike/silent dial to the arch, maker's name, date aperture and engraved arabesques, the domed top with a brass loop handle and later pine finials.

£4,000-5,000   **L&T**

A George III mahogany bell-striking bracket clock, the face with winding holes and a painted pastoral scene, the twin train-anchor movement striking on a bell, the caddy-moulded case with glazed sides.

20.5in (52cm) high

£1,000-1,500   **L&T**

A large ebonised and brass-bound bell-top clock, Benjamin Tolkien, London, the signed eight-day twin chain fusee movement has deadbeat escapement and strikes on a bell, both the dial and movement are engraved '2471'.

Benjamin Tolkien is recorded as working in London from 1805 and is best known for being in partnership with William Gravell, who was Master of the Worshipful Company of Clockmakers.

c1800   12.5in (57cm) high

£10,000-15,000   **DR**

An ebonised striking bracket clock, Allam & Caithness, London, the 7in (18cm) silvered arched dial with maker's signature and strike/silent, twin fusee movement with anchor escapement and striking on a bell.

c1805   15in (38cm) high

£5,000-6,000   **TEN**

CLOCKS

A 19thC French boullework, ebonised and gilt-bronze mounted bracket clock and bracket, the 10in (25.5cm) dial with individual ceramic numerals, with a twin-train eight-day movement striking on a bell, stamped 'HPA' to rear.

59.75in (152cm) high overall

£5,000-6,000   L&T

A Dutch walnut-veneered and inlaid bracket clock, by T. Ratsma, Harlingen, the 9.5in (24cm) composite-brass dial with applied name boss in the arch, eight-day brass fusee five-pillar movement with verge escapement, 'Dutch striking' calendar and alarm.

£5,000-6,000   SK

24.75in (63cm) high

A George IV mahogany and brass-inlaid bracket clock, the twin fusee movement striking on a bell, an enamel dial, the case with ebonised mouldings and recessed panels, the sides with glazed and pierced Gothic panels, ring side handles, on ball feet.

22.25in (56.5cm) high

£1,500-2,000   WW

A Regency brass-mounted mahogany bracket clock, the five-pillar twin fusee bell-striking movement with anchor escapement, signed 'Dawson & Peene, London' to backplate, the 7.5in (19cm) dial inscribed 'Hales & McCulloch, Cheapside, London'.

c1825   *22.5in (57cm) high*

£2,500-3,000   DN

A Regency mahogany bracket clock, the 6in (15cm) steel dial with twin winding apertures, strike/silent switch and marked 'Ellicot London', the eight-day train fusee movement striking on a bell, backplate with inscribed maker's cartouche.

9.5in (24cm) high

£6,000-8,000   L&T

An early 19thC Regency brass-inlaid ebony bracket clock, French, London, with 8in (20.5cm) cream painted dial, the five-pillar twin fusee rack and bell-striking movement with anchor escapement and engraved backplate signed 'French, Royal Exchange, London'.

Santiago James Moore French is recorded as working from Royal Exchange, London, c1810-40.

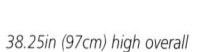

38.25in (97cm) high overall

£2,500-3,000   DN

A Regency brass-inlaid mahogany bracket clock, McMaster, Dublin, the double fusee movement with a circular painted convex dial signed 'McMaster, Dublin', and with Roman numerals.

21in (54cm) high

£3,500-4,500   MEA

A Regency mahogany repeating bracket clock, the twin fusee movement striking on a bell, the shaped plates with an engraved border and inscribed 'Roberts, Sat. James's', the case with gilt-brass mounts and pierced scale panels.

16.25in (41cm) high

£3,500-4,500   WW

A Regency mahogany and brass-inlaid bracket clock, by J. Steele, Oxford, together with a wall bracket, the white painted dial with a striking twin-train movement with anchor escapement.

17.25in (44cm) high

£5,000-7,000   L&T

A Regency ebonised striking bracket clock, Urquhart & Hart, London, the 8in (20.5cm) circular painted dial signed, twin fusee movement with anchor escapement and striking on a bell, engraved movement backplate, later seatboard.

17in (43cm) high

£2,000-2,500   TEN

A William IV mahogany bracket clock, Richard Widenham, London, the five-pillar twin fusee bell-striking movement with keyhole-shaped plates and anchor escapement, signed to backplate, the 8in (20.5cm) engraved brass dial also signed and with strike/silent switch, with original wall bracket.

Richard Widenham was recorded as working at Lombard Street by 1835 and began trading as 'Widenham and Adams' in 1840.

c1830

24.75in (63cm) high overall

£2,000-2,500 DN

A Victorian quarter-chiming bracket clock, by Benson, London, with burl-walnut veneer case, dial signed 'Benson, 26 Old Bond Street, London', slow/fast subsidiary dial in the arch, eight-day chain-driven fusee movement.

22.75in (58cm) high

£2,000-3,000 SK

A large quarter-repeating bracket clock, the eight-day movement striking on eight bells and four gongs, with walnut case surmounted by gilt-metal urns and swags, regulator, chime silent and chime selector dials.

28in (71cm) high

£2,500-3,500 A&G

MANTEL CLOCKS

A late 18thC French gilt-metal and carved giltwood mantel clock, by Cesar Bte., A Lorient, the enamelled dial with maker's signature, the eight-day movement with silk suspension and single bell-strike stamped 'Bolviller a Paris.

22in (56cm) high

£800-1,200 L&T

A George III Scottish mahogany and brass-mounted eight-day table clock, by Alexander Dickie, Edinburgh, the twin-wire fusee movement with five pillars and verge escapement striking on bell, strike/silent and regulator to arch.

c1790

19.75in (50cm) high

£6,000-8,000 L&T

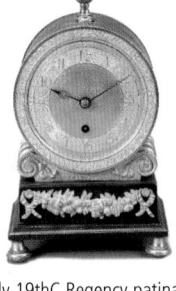

A late 18thC French bronze mantel clock, with two-train, half-striking movement with pull alarm, bell placed horizontally above body, with enamel dial, acorn finials, on pointed feet, movement marked Fumey.

11.75in (30cm) high

£2,000-3,000 SK

An early 19thC Regency patinated and gilt-brass fusee drum-head mantel timepiece, the circular single train fusee movement with anchor escapement and engine-turned circular gilt Arabic numeral dial within a repeating anthemion bezel.

8.5in (21.5cm) high overall

£1,000-1,500 DN

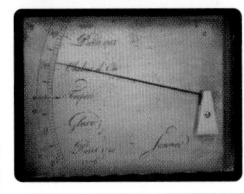

An 'Audience' clock, by Antide Janvier, Paris, no. 332, with 5.5in (14cm) signed dial, the spring-powered movement with signed backplate and regulated by a 10.5in (26.5cm) pendulum suspended on a silk thread, above a thermometer with single hand and silvered plate.

A gifted astronomer and mathematician as well as clockmaker, Antide Janvier was Mechanical Clockmaker by Appointment of King Louis XVI from 1784-91. He produced the most complicated and ingenious clocks of his time.

c1802

12.5in (32cm) high

£12,000-18,000 SK

A bronze and ormolu figural mantel timepiece, F. Baetens, Gerrard Street, London, a bronze figure on a pedestal next to the clock, the eight-day timepiece chain fusee movement signed in two places.

c1820

12in (31cm) high

£4,000-5,000 DR

CLOCKS

A boulle striking mantel clock, the case with applied gilt-metal, glazed side windows, front door missing glass, 5.5in (14cm) cast dial with twelve Roman enamel cartouches, twin-barrel bell-striking movement, backplate numbered '31261'.

c1880   19.25in (49cm) high

£1,000-1,200   TEN

A French ormolu mantel clock, fitted eight-day striking movement, Japy Frères, surmounted by a Paris porcelain urn, with painted porcelain dial inscribed 'Whytock & Sons, Paris', flanked by female masks and acanthus leaf scrolls.

13in (33cm) high

£900-1,100   A&G

A French gilt-bronze mantel clock, having an eight-day bell-striking movement, with a white enamel Roman and Arabic numeral dial, mounted in a classically decorated fluted case surmounted by an urn.

12.25in (31cm) high

£2,000-2,500   JA

A gilt-metal and porcelain-mounted striking mantel clock, porcelain dial with Roman numerals, twin-barrel movement with outside countwheel striking on a bell, backplate stamped 'Grohe, Paris' and numbered '3876', missing pendulum.

c1880   17in (43cm) high

£1,200-1,500   TEN

A late 19thC French ormolu mantel clock, Aubert and Klaftenberger, 157 Regent St, London, with perpetual calendar and centre seconds dial, the eight-day two-train gong-striking movement with hammer-shaped pendulum and visible brocot escapement to the recessed centre of the dial.

18in (46cm) high

£7,000-10,000   DN

A late 19thC French black marble and gilt-bronze-mounted mantel clock, with 4.5in (11.5cm) polished steel dial, the black marble case with a bronze lion surmount, raised on scroll feet, with twin-train cylinder movement.

23.75in (60cm) high

£1,000-1,200   L&T

A late 19thC French bronze, gilt bronze and marble mantel clock, the 4in (10cm) engine-turned steel dial housed within a bronze figure of a Grecian maiden with attendant greyhound, the twin-train eight-day barrel movement striking on a bell.

29.25in (74cm) high

£1,000-1,500   L&T

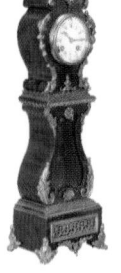

A late 19thC French figural bronze and marble mantel clock of a 'Seated Sappho', by Jean-Jacques Pradier, the black marble base with two-train, half-striking Japy Frères movement, surmounted by a figure of a seated classical poetess.

18.75in (47.5cm) wide

£800-1,200   SK

A French brass-mounted tortoiseshell mantel clock, in the form of a miniature longcase clock, the eight-day gong-striking movement with white enamel Roman numeral simulated thirteen-piece cartouche dial.

c1900   19.25in (49cm) high

£1,000-1,200   DN

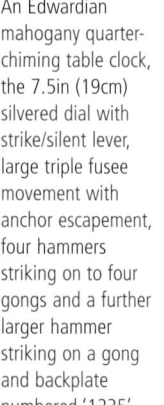

An Edwardian mahogany quarter-chiming table clock, the 7.5in (19cm) silvered dial with strike/silent lever, large triple fusee movement with anchor escapement, four hammers striking on to four gongs and a further larger hammer striking on a gong and backplate numbered '1235'.

23.25in (59cm) high

£1,000-1,500   TEN

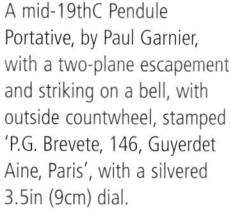

An early petite sonnerie striking carriage clock, Le Roy & Fils Hgers Du Roi à Paris, the eight-day movement striking the quarters on two bells, in a gilded case with a rear door, stamped with maker's details and numbered '3876'.

c1845   *5.5in (14cm) high*

£4,000-5,000   **DR**

A 19thC French gilt-brass oval carriage clock, the platform lever escapement striking on a bell, to an enamel dial, the base stamped 'A Cottin'.

7.5in (19cm) high

£1,000-1,500   **WW**

A mid-19thC Pendule Portative, by Paul Garnier, with a two-plane escapement and striking on a bell, with outside countwheel, stamped 'P.G. Brevete, 146, Guyerdet Aine, Paris', with a silvered 3.5in (9cm) dial.

Paul Garnier (1801-69) was a key figure in the semi-mass-production of carriage clocks. This clock is a more stylish example of the brass-cased carriage clock. Although not entirely suitable for travelling, examples are known with travelling cases.

9in (23cm) high

£3,500-4,500   **WW**

An English fully-engraved striking and repeating carriage clock, Dent, 82 Strand, London, the silvered dial with engraved centre and signed cartouche, the eight-day chain fusee movement signed and numbered '482' and with a strike/silver lever on the backplate.

c1840   *6in (15cm) high*

£16,000-18,000   **DR**

A 19thC French gilt-brass carriage clock, by Margaine, with platform level escapement striking on a gong with AM and beehive trademark, numbered 13932, to a silver chapter ring, inscribed 'Jas Ramsay, Paris', in original leather travel case.

9in (23cm) high

£3,500-4,500   **WW**

A mid-19thC English gilt-brass carriage clock, with a platform lever escapement and a single fusee movement, the backplate inscribed 'Phillips, 23 Cockspur St London, 1926', enamel dial with same inscription, numbered winding key.

8.25in (21cm) high

£4,000-5,000   **WW**

An English striking and repeating carriage clock, Noyer, London, the eight-day movement with a chronometer escapement signed 'Noyer, London', with alarm and calendar work in a gilt-chased and engraved case, numbered '692'.

c1870   *5.5in (14cm) high*

£9,500-11,500   **DR**

A fully-engraved gorge-cased carriage clock, Joseph Soldano, Paris, the eight-day gong-striking movement stamped 'J.S. Paris 4701' and the lever platform escapement numbered '736'.

c1875   *6in (15cm) high*

£7,000-9,000   **DR**

CLOCKS

A late 19thC French gilt-brass gorge-cased carriage clock, with repeat and alarm, with a platform lever escapement and striking on a gong, the backplate inscribed 'Repassee par Leroy & Fils, Palais Royal 13 & 15 Paris, 8562, 6659'.

7in (18cm) high

£2,000-2,500   **WW**

A late 19thC French gilt-brass carriage clock, with repeat, the platform lever escapement striking on a gong, number 5382, with an enamel dial with painted numerals, with remains of retailer's name, within a gorge case.

5.5in (14cm) high

£1,000-1,500   **WW**

An early 20thC lacquered brass combination carriage timepiece with aneroid barometer and compass, the barometer with enamel register indistinctly inscribed 'By Special Appointment to H.M. the King', set beside carriage timepiece with platform lever escapement and conforming enamel dial, in case with circular escapement aperture and conforming silvered compass beneath handle.

3.5in (9cm) high excluding handle

£400-500   **DN**

LANTERN CLOCKS

A William & Mary gilt brass lantern clock, William Reeve, Spalding, the posted countwheel bell-striking movement with original verge escapement and pendulum swinging within the frame behind the trains, with bell supported in a domed bearer above.

William Reeve of Spalding appears to be unrecorded, but the frame design and dial engraving stylistically date this clock to around 1690. It is reminiscent of the work of Thomas Power of Wellingborough. The gilding to the frame is unusual and appears to have been done early in the clock's life or at the time of its manufacture.

c1690   *15.25in (39cm) high*

£5,000-6,000   **DN**

An 18thC brass lantern clock case, Henry Lintott, Farnham, the 6.25in (16cm) dial with signature, original movement replaced with single-barrel platform lever movement stamped 'Smiths Astral'.

15in (38cm) high

£350-550   **TEN**

A 20thC brass lantern clock, the single fusee striking movement to an engraved dial with silver chapter ring.

15.25in (38.5cm) high

£500-800   **WW**

A brass thirty-hour lantern clock, Henry Baker, Malling, four-posted movement with anchor escapement and countwheel striking on a bell, together with associated oak bracket.

Henry Baker is recorded as working in Malling from 1768-84.

c1770   *11in (28cm) high*

£1,400-1,800   **TEN**

A 20thC late 17thC-style brass lantern clock, Paul Evans, Romsey, the posted weight-driven movement with verge escapement and countwheel striking on a bell.

14.5in (37cm) high

£500-800   **DN**

A 20thC brass lantern clock, with an eight-day striking movement, to an engraved dial, inscribed 'Thomas Mudge', with chapter ring, with adapted strike.

15.5in (39cm) high

£400-800   **WW**

A pair of almost identical English skeleton clocks, Evans, Handsworth, the timepiece chain fusee movement with wheel work with six crossings and an ebony and pewter pendulum.

In 1805 Boulton & Watt of the Soho Foundry, Handsworth, Birmingham, handed the clock-manufacturing side of the business over to their foreman, John Houghton. The new business flourished, and Houghton's son-in-law, William Frederick Evans, soon joined him. Houghton retired in 1843, leaving Evans to run the business.

16.25in (41cm) high excluding dome

£8,500-10,500 DR

A brass skeleton timepiece, T. & J. Ollivant, Manchester, the single fusee movement with anchor escapement, with signed 4.25in (11cm) silvered dial, glazed dome cracked.

Thomas and John Ollivant are recorded as working in Manchester between 1828-85.

c1850　　　　10.5in (27cm) high

£600-800 TEN

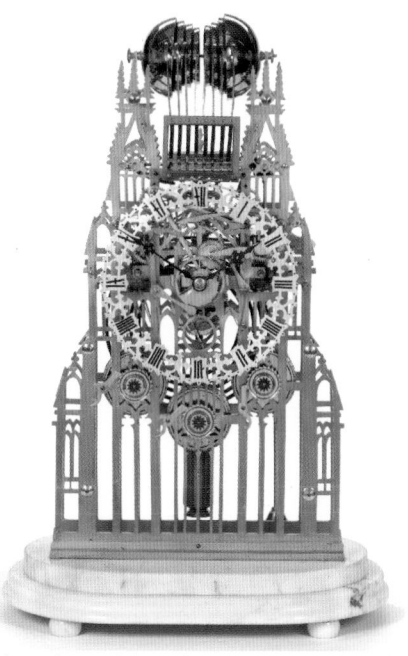

A Cathedral brass chiming skeleton clock, the triple chain driven fusee movement with anchor escapement, six spoke wheels, chiming the quarters on eight bells and striking the hour on a large spiral gong, with pendulum.
c1880　　　　23.5in (60cm) high

£25,000-30,000 TEN

ESSENTIAL REFERENCE – SKELETON CLOCKS

- Skeleton clocks evolved in France in the mid-18thC, probably because the great clockmakers of the time were looking to show off their skill. They were also made in Austria in the same period.
- They were first introduced in Britain in c1820, where they were produced in large numbers by specialised manufacturers from the mid- to late 19thC, with production reducing significantly in the early 20thC.
- The pierced or fretted brass frame reveals the mechanism, which typically features cut and pierced brass plates secured by screws. Dials often have the centre cut out. Fine skeleton clocks were often modelled on famous buildings.
- The base is usually made of marble or wood, with a glass dome cover to protect the exposed clock movement from dust. An original dome increases the value; broken domes are difficult to replace.
- Clocks with elaborate designs and complicated mechanisms command the highest prices.

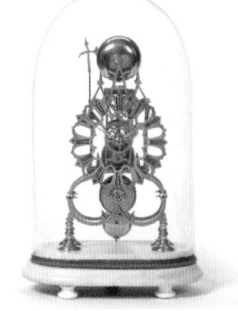

A brass skeleton mantel clock, the single fusee movement with anchor escapement and passing strike on a top-mounted bell, four spoke wheels, and a 6in (15cm) dial.
c1890　　16.25in (41cm) high

£500-700 TEN

A brass skeleton clock, with a single fusee movement and deadbeat escapement, the pierced silvered dial with subsidiary seconds and hour dials, with moon phase.

16.5in (42cm) high

£1,000-1,500 WW

A chiming skeleton mantel clock, Sinclair Harding, no. 998, triple chain-driven fusee movement with anchor escapement, backplate signed and numbered.
2003　　14.5in (37cm) high

£7,000-10,000 TEN

CLOCKS

A gilt-metal and painted-porcelain-mounted striking mantel clock with garniture, 3.25in (8.5cm) painted porcelain dial, twin barrel movement with outside countwheel striking on a bell, backplate numbered '1367', with a pair of matching candelabra.

Clock 15.25in (39cm) high

£900–1,200 TEN

A mid-19thC ormolu and painted-porcelain-mounted mantel clock, with eight-day bell-striking movement, stamped 'Japy Frères', pendulum and winding key, repaired, and a pair of lidded vases.

Clock 19.5in (49.5cm) high

£3,500-4,500 WW

A 19thC French marble and bronze clock garniture, dial marked 'Massot Bayonne', the twin-train movement striking on a bell, with winder and pendulum, together with a pair of urns.

12.25in (31cm) high

£400-600 L&T

An ormolu and white-metal striking mantel clock with garniture, twin barrel bell-striking movement, backplate stamped 'Japy Frères' and numbered '298' and case with registration mark for 1871, with matching candelabra.

1871   Clock dome 19.25in (49cm) high

£3,000-4,000 TEN

A late 19thC French white marble and gilt-bronze clock garniture, the clock modelled as an ebonised globe upheld by putti, twin-train bell-striking movement, with matching candelabra.

Clock 17in (43cm) high

£1,000-1,500 L&T

A marble four-glass striking mantel clock with garniture, with twin barrel gong-striking movement stamped 'AD Mougin' and numbered '508 411', twin-tubed mercury pendulum, together with matching garniture.

c1890   Clock 11in (28cm) high

£500-800 TEN

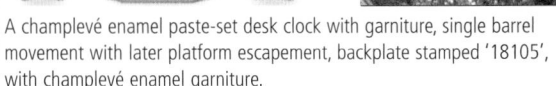

A champlevé enamel paste-set desk clock with garniture, single barrel movement with later platform escapement, backplate stamped '18105', with champlevé enamel garniture.

c1900   Clock 8.25in (21cm) high

£300–400 TEN

A gilt-brass striking mantel clock with garniture, 4in (10cm) dial, two-barrel movement striking on a gong, backplate stamped 'Marti' and '4333 52', together with pair of matching gilt brass and bronzed urns.

c1900   Clock 13in (33cm) high

£500-600 TEN

A three-piece Egyptian marble and gilt-brass-mounted mantel clock garniture, the clock with a dial signed 'J.W. Benson, Ludgate Hill', together with a pair of conforming tazzi.

Figures 12in (30cm) high

£900-1,200 MEA

A mahogany-cased hooded striking wall clock, Alexander Cumming, London, the engraved silvered 10in (25.5cm) dial signed and with strike/silent, the eight-day gut fusee bell-striking movement has substantial plates and anchor escapement.

Alexander Cumming (1732-1813) was a Fellow of the Royal Society of Edinburgh and in 1781 became an Honorary Freeman of the Clockmakers' Company.

c1790   26in (66cm) high

£15,000-18,000   DR

CLOSER LOOK – A LATERNDLUHR

The Laterndluhr, meaning 'small lantern clock', is a type of clock that was made in Vienna in the first half of the 19thC. Miniatures are fairly rare, and examples in good condition command high prices.

The shape of the case is in the style of the Austrian clockmaker Ferencz Lobmayer, who worked between c1795-1850.

It is rare to find the movement and escapement fully glass-enclosed in such a small clock.

The unusual full-length, one-piece door enables the whole of the pendulum to be viewed.

A rare early 19thC Regency Gothic Revival gilt-brass and ebonised miniature wall timepiece, Thomson, Princes St, Edinburgh, the four-pillar single train movement with long pendulum and standing barrel wound via a pulley linked to a pull cord and dummy weight hanging below the clock, the 2in (5cm) dial with maker's signature.

Several makers with the surname Thomson are recorded as working in Edinburgh during the early 19thC. This clock was most likely supplied by either John Thomson, who is recorded as working from 1794-1814, or Archibald Thomas, from 1794-1836.

5.5in (14cm) high

£1,000-1,200   DN

A month-duration timepiece Dachluhr in a light cherry case, the movement with deadbeat escapement, a small driving weight and a pendulum.

c1830   36in (92cm) high

£8,500-10,500   DR

An early miniature Laterndluhr, signed Lobmayer Ferencz Nagy Szombatban, the enamel dial enclosed behind a glazed and gilded bezel with signature, the eight-day movement with weight drive via the main barrel and a subsidiary drive from a main spring, with a deadbeat escapement, walnut case.

Instantly recognisable as Lobmayer as he is the only maker to have produced these small clocks in this style.

24in (61cm) high

£14,500-17,500   DR

BAROMETERS

ESSENTIAL REFERENCE – BAROMETERS

The barometer – an instrument for measuring atmospheric pressure – became popular in the 17thC following the discovery of the connection between alterations in the pressure of the air and the weather. It was invented by the Italian philosopher and mathematician Evangelista Torricelli in 1643-4.

- Barometers made in the late 17th and early 18thC are very rare and valuable today. The most sought-after early barometers are probably those by the clockmaker Daniel Quare (1649-1724), who used ivory, fine woods and silver as his materials.
- Stick barometers were the most common type of barometer in the 18thC. The earliest designs following clock fashions, and later designs following furniture fashions. The similar angle (or signpost) barometer was

introduced in the 1670s, but was never widely popular because of its expense and unweildy shape.

- Wheel barometers became widespread in the late 18thC.
- In the late 19thC, the wheel barometer was superseded by the accurate and easily portable aneroid ('liquid-free') barometer. Pocket versions were produced from c1860.
- The style of the case, the maker, and the quality of materials are the main indicators of price. Earlier barometers followed clock styles, but from the 18thC onwards the main influence was furniture design.
- To avoid damaging the fragile glass tubes and spilling mercury, barometers should always be kept upright and never tipped or laid flat.

A George II mahogany cistern tube stick barometer, James Verrier, Somerset, with silvered double scale titled 'SOMMER', 'WINTER' and inscribed 'Fair if rise', 'Foul if fall'.

c1750   1.25in (105cm) wide

£2,000-2,500   DN

A mid-18thC mahogany bulb cistern tube stick barometer, Thomas Benbow, Newport, Shropshire, with moulded case and silvered register annotated for 'Summer' and 'Winter' with simple brass pointer.

35.5in (90cm) high

£1,500-2,000   DN

A rare George III mahogany double tube barometer, possibly Dominico Sala, with boxwood scale inscribed 'The Great Double Barometer' above a siphon tube and an oil-filled tube alongside a scale with sliding pointer.

c1760   42in (107cm) high

£2,000-2,500   DN

A George III mahogany cistern tube stick barometer, Nairne & Blunt, London, with arched top silvered scale with vernier, set into a full-width caddy moulded case.

c1785   35.5in (90cm) high

£2,000-2,500   DN

A George III mahogany stick barometer.

c1785   38.5in high

£1,000-1,200   POOK

A George III mahogany cistern tube stick barometer, with shaped pediment above inset brass vernier scale signed 'Nairne & Blunt, London', the moulded trunk with exposed tube.

c1785   38.5in (98cm) high

£800-1,000   DN

A George III mahogany stick barometer, the pediment with ivory urn finial, with silvered plate inscribed 'Dollond, London', with vernier scale and thermometer, the base with adjuster.

39.5in (100cm) high

£3,000-5,000   WW

A rare George III mahogany multiple-tube barometer, Peter Rabalio, London, with two columns filled with mercury and a third with coloured oil, against a scale calibrated 01-6.5in, with thermometer.

c1790   23.25in (59cm) high

£1,300-1,500   DN

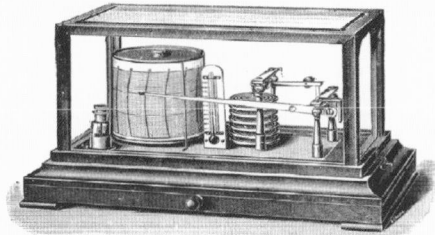
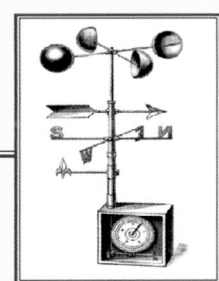
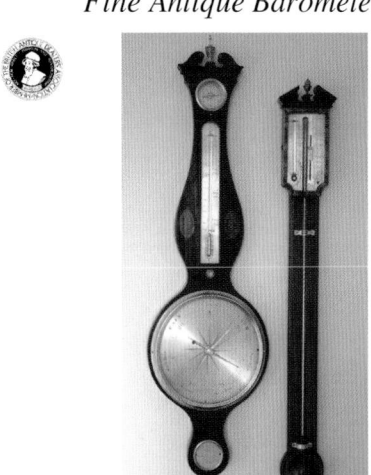

BAROMETERS

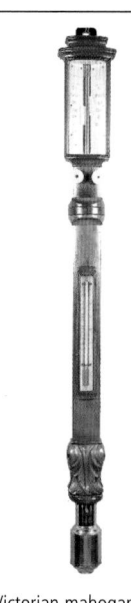

A Victorian mahogany bowfronted marine stick barometer, C. G. Brander & Son, London, double vernier scale inscribed '10A.M. TODAY', '10A.M. YESTERDAY', mercury thermometer.

c1865   37.5in (95cm) high

£2,000-3,000   DN

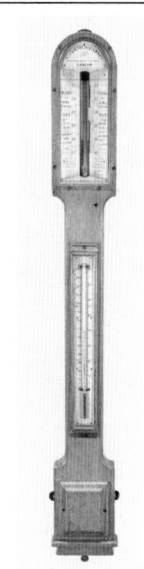

A Victorian oak cistern tube stick barometer, Negretti & Zambra, London, with glazed ivory scale with vernier and annotated with predictions, and Fahrenheit scale mercury thermometer.

c1865   40.5in (103cm) high

£600-900   DN

A Victorian oak cistern tube 'Admiral Fitzroy's Storm Barometer' with double vernier scale, Negretti & Zambra, London, with glazed-front ceramic scale, above vernier setting discs and thermometer.

c1865   40.5in (103cm)

£900-1,200   DN

A Victorian oak cistern tube stick barometer, James Henry Steward, London, the ivory scale with vernier and Fahrenheit mercury thermometer, trunk with exposed tube.

c1875   35.75in (91cm) high

£300-400   DN

A Victorian oak cistern tube stick barometer, James Steward, London, with ivory double scale with vernier inscribed with Admiral Fitzroy's observations, and Fahrenheit scale mercury thermometer.

c1875   36.5in (93cm) high

£500-800   DN

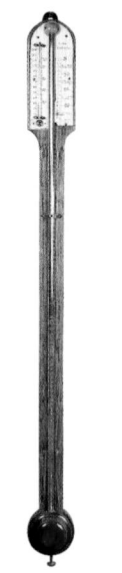

A Victorian oak cistern tube stick barometer, James Hanny, Shrewsbury, with ivory vernier scale with Fahrenheit mercury thermometer above slender trunk with exposed tube.

c1875   35in (89cm) high

£300-400   DN

A carved oak Admiral Fitzroy's Barometer, John G. Murdoch & Co. Ltd, London, with pediment incorporating timepiece with eight-day lever movement and Roman numeral dial, above scales and thermometer.

c1885   48.5in (123cm) high

£500-800   DN

An early 20thC gilt-brass and ebonised cistern tube pillar barometer, unsigned, in the style of Daniel Quare, with canted silvered scale above adjustable setting collar calibrated in inches and labelled 'Yesterday'.

35.5in (90cm) high

£700-900   DN

An early 20thC black japanned mercury marine stick barometer, H. Hughes & Sons Ltd, London, the silvered vernier scale calibrated in inches above Fahrenheit scale mercury thermometer.

37in (94cm) high

£800-1,000   DN

A brass-mounted ebonised cistern tube pillar barometer, Adams, London, in the style of Daniel Quare, the break-arch top with three ball finials, the left turning to operate the pointer, above a glazed silvered scale.

c1925   40.5in (104cm)

£700-1,000   DN

ESSENTIAL REFERENCE – WHEEL FORM

The wheel barometer was invented by Robert Hooke (1635-1703) in 1663. It features a U-shaped tube with one long and one short arm. A float on the mercury in the short arm is attached to a lighter counterweight by a thread over a pulley wheel, which is connected to a pointer on the dial. The movement of the mercury in the tube raises or lowers the float, rotating the pointer.

- The wheel barometer became popular in Britain after the 'banjo' form was introduced in c1770. This consisted of a dial and thermometer in a banjo-shaped wooden case. The silvered-brass dial had a blued-steel indicating-hand, and a brass fixed-hand for recording the reading.
- Many wheel barometers feature a spirit level to ensure they are hung vertically, because if they are not level, the float jams. Hygrometers, which indicate humidity (which, like temperature, can affect the height of mercury), were also often fitted. These often consisted of a beard of oats (later cat gut), which curled and uncurled with changes in air moisture, and moved a needle set on a dial with indications from 'moist' ('damp' from c1800) to 'dry'.
- Before c1825 most cases were veneered in mahogany, satinwood, maple or pearwood. 'Onion' or 'tulip top' cases became popular from the mid-19thC, and were inlaid with mother-of-pearl, tortoiseshell and brass. Solid, carved oak was used in the late 19thC.

A George III inlaid mahogany wheel barometer, John Merry Ronketti, London, the silvered register beneath ivory setting pointer adjustment disc and brass-bordered thermometer flanked by oval fan inlaid paterae, the rounded pediment with hygrometer, the conforming base with spirit level.

c1795   39in (99cm) high

£1,500-2,000   DN

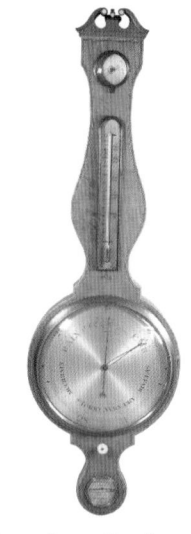

A rare George III satinwood mercury wheel barometer, Tagliabue & Torre, London, the silvered register beneath thermometer and hygrometer, the rounded base with spirit level and ivory setting pointer adjustment disc.

c1805   44.5in (113cm) high

£1,000-1,500   DN

A Regency mahogany mercury wheel barometer with timepiece, the circular silvered register beneath circular white Roman numeral clock dial, arched Fahrenheit scale alcohol thermometer, the rounded base with spirit level signed 'Hudson, Greenwich' and setting pointer adjustment disc.

c1820   43in (109cm) high

£500-800   DN

A Regency mahogany mercury wheel barometer with timepiece, Matthew Woller, Birmingham, the circular silvered register beneath ivory setting pointer adjustment disc, white enamel Arabic numeral clock dial and arched Fahrenheit scale mercury thermometer, with hygrometer to base.

c1820   45.75in (116cm) high

£700-1,000   DN

A wheel barometer and clock combination, D. Gugeri, Boston, the silvered brass barometer dial and convex enamelled clock dial above and below a thermometer, hygrometer and signed spirit level, the eight-day fusee timepiece movement with long rectangular plates and a starter lever at the front.

Dominic Gugeri is recorded as a maker of watches, clocks and barometers, as well as a silversmith and jeweller, working at Market Place, Boston, Lincolnshire from 1835-42. It is believed that he was actually trading from about 1815 to 1845. A 'J. Gugeri' is also listed as working in Boston, possibly a brother.

c1830

49in (125cm) high

£7,000-9,000   DR

An unusual mahogany mercury wheel barometer, the high position silvered register with landscape to centre, beneath hygrometer, the base with spirit level signed 'J. Laffrancho, Ludlow' beneath rectangular mirror and thermometer.

c1840   38.5in (98cm) high

£600-900   DN

An ebony and box-strung mahogany mercury wheel barometer, John Schalfino, Taunton, the silvered register calibrated in inches, beneath convex mirror, thermometer and hygrometer, the base with spirit level and setting pointer adjustment disc.

c1840   38.5in (98cm) high

£500-800   DN

BAROMETERS

A Victorian oak mercury wheel barometer, the register beneath a small roundel engraved 'Made from the wreck of the Royal George sunk, August 29th 1782' and a convex mirror, thermometer and hygrometer, the base with spirit level signed 'Mansford, London'.

c1845   43.25in (110cm) high

£600-900   DN

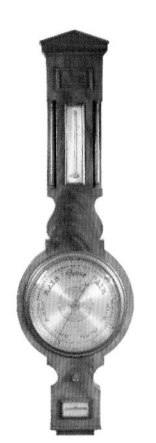

A Victorian mahogany mercury wheel barometer, the silvered register beneath rectangular Fahrenheit scale mercury thermometer flanked by turned column uprights and panelled gable pediment, the moulded square base with spirit level signed 'McDowall, Edinburgh'.

c1845   44in (112cm) high

£700-1,000   DN

A Victorian pewter-inlaid rosewood mercury wheel barometer, the silvered register beneath Fahrenheit scale bowfronted thermometer and hygrometer to the swan-neck pediment with foliate finial, the base with spirit level signed 'Barrett Blandford'.

c1850   43.75in (111cm) high

£500-800   DN

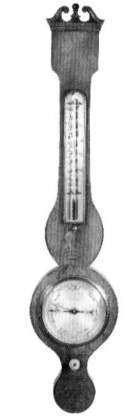

A mid-19thC mahogany mercury wheel barometer, the circular silvered register signed 'Adie & Son Opticians, Edinburgh', beneath arched Fahrenheit scale alcohol thermometer and swan-neck pediment, the rounded base with ivory setting pointer adjustment disc.

36.5in (93cm) high

£600-900   DN

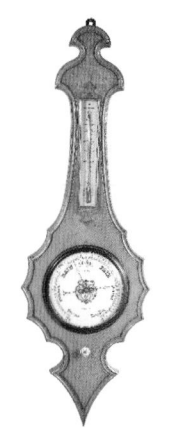

A Victorian carved oak mercury wheel barometer, R. Howse, Marlborough, the circular ceramic register signed to the scroll-decorated centre, beneath Fahrenheit and Réaumur scale mercury thermometer, with ivory setting pointer adjustment disc to base.

c1865   41.25in (105cm) high

£350-450   DN

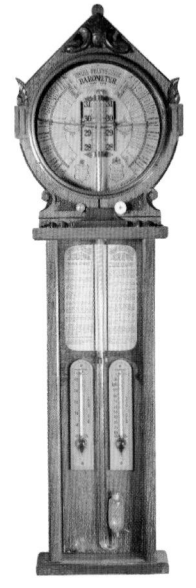

A Victorian mother-of-pearl inlaid rosewood mercury wheel barometer, the circular silvered register signed 'HODSON, Worcester' to the centre beneath Fahrenheit scale mercury thermometer beneath foliate spray to the scroll pediment.

c1860   41in (104cm) high

£250-350   DN

A carved oak Royal Polytechnic Barometer, Joseph Davis & Co., London, with gabled pediment above a glazed circular paper register with brass pointers, the glazed lower section with 'Special Remarks' papers above two thermometers.

c1885   41in (104cm)

£600-900   DN

A mid-19thC aneroid barometer, the silvered calibrated in inches to upper section, mounted with alcohol thermometer with Centigrade and Réaumur scales, opposing mercury Fahrenheit thermometer to lower section, inscribed 'Salon and Co. Makers'.

6.75in (17cm) diam

£250-350   DN

A brass-cased Naudet pattern aneroid barometer, with carved oak mantel stand, E. G. Wood, London, the circular silvered register to upper section, and with alcohol thermometer with Centigrade and Réaumur scales, opposing mercury Fahrenheit thermometer.

c1865   12in (30cm) high

£350-450   DN

A late 19thC aneroid wall barometer in Swiss carved beech case, the circular open-centered paper register calibrated in inches, with brass pointer to glass within lacquered brass bezel set into carved case with mercury tube thermometer and game bird applied crest.

25in (63cm) high

£80-120   DN

A late 19thC cast iron combination wall clock and barometer, the clock with eight-day bell-striking movement and white enamel Roman numeral dial, with mercury thermometer to upright and aneroid barometer with paper register signed 'J.J. Wainwright and Co. Birmingham' with brass setting pointer to glass.

26.5in (67cm) high

£150-250   DN

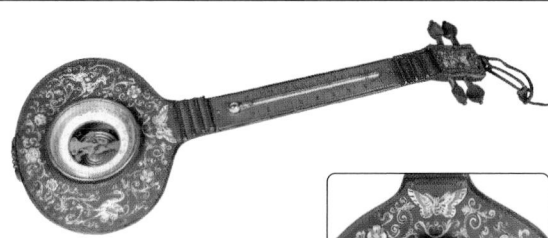

A late 19thC Continental novelty aneroid wall barometer with thermometer in the form of a mandolin, with white paper scale and brass setting pointer to glass within brass bezel, mounted onto polychrome decorated ovoid metal plate beneath simulated fingerboard applied with mercury thermometer.

18.5in (47cm) high

£50-80   DN

A late 19thC carved oak case aneroid barometer, the circular ceramic register with Admiral Fitzroy's observations, with brass setting pointer to glass within brass bezel and ropetwist-carved surround.

9in (23cm) diam

£80-100   DN

An early 20thC brass-cased marine aneroid bulkhead barometer, John Barker & Co. Ltd, Kensington, the ceramic register with Admiral Fitzroy's observations, the glass with brass setting pointed within moulded brass bezel, in cylindrical case.

9.25in (23.5cm) diam

£120-150   DN

OTHER BAROMETERS

A lacquered brass aneroid pocket barometer, Negretti & Zambra, London, the circular silver register calibrated in inches and with altimeter scale up to 10,000 feet with rotating bezel and steel pointer.

c1870   *3in (7cm) diam*

£120-150   DN

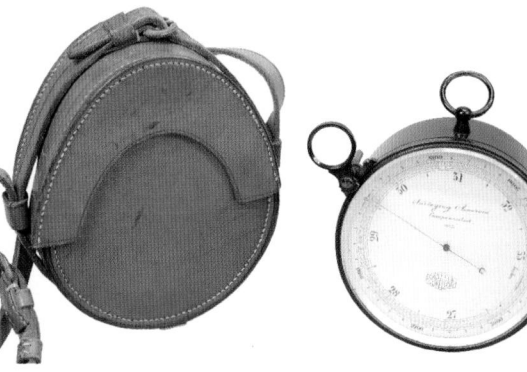

A brass compensated aneroid surveyor's barometer, Casella, London, the silvered register with rotating altimeter scale and milled bezel mounted with a pivoted magnification lens to circumference.

c1890   *4.75in (12cm) diam*

£250-350   DN

An early 20thC gilt-brass aneroid pocket barometer, Negretti & Zambra, London, the 2.5in (6.5cm) circular silvered register calibrated in inches within rotating brass bezel with steel pointer, the rear with altitude adjustment.

19in (7.5cm) diam

£150-200   DN

A late 19thC gilt-brass aneroid pocket barometer with altimeter scale and compass, Eardley B. Norton, Manchester, the circular silvered register calibrated in inches with rotating altimeter scale calibrated to 10,000 feet, the other side with mother-of-pearl compass with locking lever to bezel, in two-part gilt-brass cylindrical case.

2in (5cm) diam

£350-450   DN

A late 19thC ship's drum-shaped barometer, with mercury thermometer, by G. L. Casella.

7.5in (19cm) diam

£100-150   N

A Victorian novelty ship's wheel barometer, Folkard & Son, Brighton, the silvered dial with curved mercury tube within a beaded bezel and spoked outer frame, on a spreading surbase with maker's cartouche and an onyx plinth base.

13.5in (34.5cm) high

£500-800   L&T

SCIENTIFIC INSTRUMENTS

An early 19thC mahogany cased two-day marine chronometer by MacLachlan, London, the glazed two section cover with recessed brass carrying handles enclosing a gimbal-mounted silvered dial with roman numerals, signed on the dial.

6.75in (17cm) wide

£1,500-2,500   L&T

An early 20thC rosewood two-day marine chronometer, the silvered dial with subsidiary second and up/down dial, within a brass bound rosewood case bearing ivory plaque, signed on the dial 'H. G. Blair & Co, Cardiff'.

7in (18cm) wide

£2,000-3,000   L&T

A Charles Frodsham eight-day marine chronometer, London, in a two-tiered rosewood box with brass mounts and ivory name boss, 4.5in (11.5cm) silvered dial engraved 'Charles Frodsham, 84 Strand, London, No. 2718'.

Box 8in (20.5cm) high

£10,000-12,000   SK

A two-day marine chronometer, by Wm. Weichert, Cardiff, no. 2359, the 4in (10cm) silvered dial with gold hands, engraved Royal Coat of Arms, Golden Arms, Paris 1867 medals and maker's credit, brass bezel with rim engraved 'By Special Appointment to H.M. the Emperor of Austria', the fusee movement with damascened plates and compensated bi-metallic balance, in brass gimbal.

7in (18cm) high

£2,500-3,000   SK

A two-day marine chronometer, Victor Kullberg, London, the ebony case with an ivory plaque with maker's name, the 4in (10cm) silvered dial signed and with two plaques inscribed 'To H M The King of Norway and Sweden' and 'Prize Medal Award 1860 1862 1864', single fusee movement numbered '3972'.

Victor Kullberg (1824-1890) was one of the most successful horologists of the 19thC and made some of the finest chronometers of his day.

1878   *7.25in (18.5cm) high*

£5,500–6,500   TEN

A mahogany two-day marine chronometer, the 4in (10cm) silvered dial signed 'Henry Taylor Meltham No. 3009 auxiliary H compensation', fusee movement with Harrison's maintaining power, Earnshaw's spring detent chronometer escapement, temperature compensation balance, diamond endstone.

c1880   7.75in (20cm) high

£2,000-2,500   TEN

A rare coromandel wood eight-day marine chronometer, Victor Kullberg, London, no. 4656, 4.75in (12cm) silvered dial with maker's signature, single fusee movement, Earnshaw's spring detent escapement, Harrison's maintaining power, Kullberg's mid-range temperature compensation balance movement contained within a gimbal.

This chronometer was commissioned by Captain Townley Parker and delivered by Kullberg on 23rd October 1887. Kullberg's day book shows the sale, listing the delivery time of six months, at a cost of £60.

c1887   *9in (23cm) wide*

£14,000-16,000   TEN

An English lacquered brassCulpeper-type microscope,with rack-and-pinion focusing, circular stage signed 'Smith, Royal Exchange', sprung slide-holder, threaded eyepiece, and reflector on compass joint, on mahogany base, with accessories, parts missing.

14.5in (37cm) high retracted

£2,500-3,000   **SK**

A 19thC brass monocular microscope, with lenses and bone slides, in a fitted mahogany box with ebonised and brass inlay.

9.75in (24.5cm) high

£200-250   **WW**

A 19thC brass Gould-type microscope, with lenses and bone slides attaching to a fitted mahogany box.

5in (12.5cm) wide

£450-550   **WW**

A mid-19thC brass field microscope, Cary, London, the detachable tube mounted via an armature to the vertical limb signed 'Cary, LONDON', with accessories. Telescope

6.5in (16.5cm) high constructed

£400-500   **DN**

A 19thC mahogany and brass pocket microscope, the cylindrical shaft with height-adjustable detachable stage and objective lens screw-mounted onto the small mahogany case containing a spare objective lens.

4.5in (11.5cm) wide

£200-250   **DN**

A 19thC brass monocular microscope, Charles Baker of London, 244 High Holborn, London, with brass lens case, 19 glass slides, contained in mahogany case with interior fittings.

£250-350   **A&G**

A lacquered brass and ebonised monocular microscope, by R & J Beck, London, no. 5177, the tube, stage and mirror pivoting on a triangular base, with two eyepieces and three lenses, in a mahogany case.

14in (35.5cm) high

£150-200   **WW**

A monocular microscope, in a box, a slide rule, cased, drawing instruments by Aston & Mander, cased, and a pocket aneroid barometer, 'Greenslade & Co, Weston S. Mare'.

8in (20cm) high

£200-300   **WW**

A lacquered brass monocular microscope, stamped 'Swift & Son, 81 Tottenham Ct Rd, London, W.C.'

12in (30.5cm) high

£80-120   **WW**

A late 19thC lacquered and patinated brass monocular microscope, the tube with focus adjustment above circular opaque glass, inset stage and pivoted mirror, signed 'SWIFT & SON, 81 TOTTENHAM CTR'D, LONDON W.C'.

9in (23cm) high

£150-200   **DN**

An early 20thC brass monocular microscope, J. B. Dancer, Optician, Manchester, with a collection of microscope slides by various makers, contained in a stained and fitted mahogany case.

£600-700   **A&G**

An early 20thC mahogany-cased brass and black-lacquered monocular field microscope, with two lenses.

9.5in (24cm) high

£80-120   **FLD**

SCIENTIFIC INSTRUMENTS

A single-drawer 1in (2.5cm) reverse-tapered spyglass, with faceted decagonal 24in (61cm) mahogany tube, turned-brass rings and eyepieces with dust-slides, signed 'J Gilbert, Tower Hill, London', object lens cracked.

£700-1,000 SK

A 2.75in (7cm) library telescope, Dollond, with 43in (109cm) tapering mahogany tube with original finish and later gilt grain-painting, rack-and-pinion focusing, lacquered brass fittings, eyepiece tube, three eyepiece lenses and object lens cap, on brass pillar and folding cabriole feet.

Case 45in (114.5cm) long

£2,500-3,000 SK

An early 19thC brass and mahogany 2.75in (7cm) refracting telescope, with rack and pinion focusing and mahogany-bound tube signed 'DOLLOND, LONDON' to eyepiece end, on columnar stand with folding tripod legs, some damage.

52.75in (134cm) long unextended

£250-350 DN

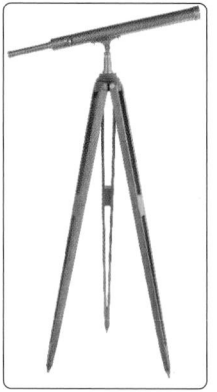

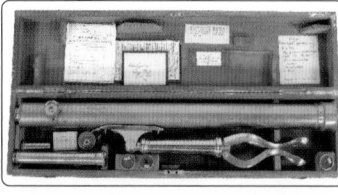

A 19thC 2.75in (7cm) brass telescope, by Cary, the 31in (79cm) tube stamped 'CARY, Optician, 181 Strand, London', with day tube and eyepieces, on a folding tripod, in a fitted mahogany box and a large folding oak and brass tripod.

£1,800-2,200 WW

A late 19thC brass 2in (5cm) draw telescope, W. Bruce, London, with brass folding stand engraved 'J.H. STEWARD, 406 STRAND, LONDON'.

41.25in (105cm) long extended

£400-450 DN

A large brass 4.5in (11.5cm) telescope, mounted in cast iron and brass armature with mahogany tripod stand, with spare lenses.

c1900 72.5in (184cm) long unextended

£2,000-3,000 DN

SUN DIALS

A late 18thC 15in (38cm) horizontal plate sundial, the bronze circular plate engraved 'A Adie Edinburgh', with outer hour scale reading to one minute, gnomon lacking.

£500-700 TEN

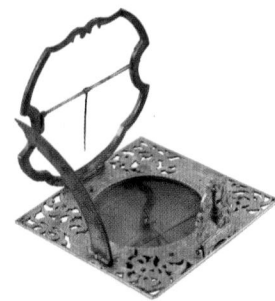

An Augsburg-Pattern Universal Equinoctial dial, Johann Vogler, with gilt-brass base plate, silvered compass, folding chapter ring, hinged latitude arc, and compass box with engraved number and latitudes of 14 European cities/islands, in original leather case.

3in (7.5cm) diam

£700-1,000 GORL

An early 18thC brass analemmatic dial, Thomas Tuttell, with horizontal eight-point compass dial beneath a hinged gnomon and elliptical dial, a 'perpetuall almanacke' verso for 1700-61.

A very similar dial by instrument maker Thomas Tuttell is in the National Maritime Museum Collection, London.

6.25in (16cm) wide

£6,500-7,000 GORL

A 19thC lignum vitae Potter pattern pocket sundial, with pivoted calibrated card mounted with brass gnomen within turned case with equation of timescale to inside of the domed cover, lacking internal glass cover.

2.25in (6cm) diam

£100-150 DN

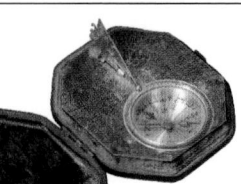

A silver-plated Butterfield sundial, with inset compass well, double horary scale, folding engraved bird gnomon, the underside engraved with thirty European cities and their latitudes, engraved 'Butterfield a Paris', in velvet-lined leather-covered pasteboard case.

2.5in (6.5cm) long

£2,500-3,000 SK

An early 20thC rectangular mahogany-cased barograph, Frank Moore Ltd, Southampton, with five glass panels, on moulded base with drawer, enclosing spare charts.

14in (36cm) wide

£600–800　　MEA

An early 20thC oak-cased aneroid barograph, Callaghan, New Bond Street, London, the mechanism with concealed vacuum chamber operating inked pointer for the rotating drum lined with a paper scale, with maker's signature.

14.5in (37cm) wide

£350-450　　DN

A Thatcher's calculating instrument, no. 1740, serial no. 773, marked 'W.F. Stanley, London, 1882', in mahogany case with label of 'Keuffel & Esser Co., Manufacturers of Mathematical & Surveying Instruments, 127 Fulton St. & 42 Ann St., New York', patd. by Edwin Thatcher, 1st November 1881.

1881

£900-1,200　　SK

An 18thC German brass and silvered-brass perpetual calendar, engraved 'Immerwehrender Calender', with days to the edge, the reverse with zodiacal symbols, date and length of night and day, with fishskin case.

1.25in (3cm) diam

£800-1,000　　GORL

A surveyor's mahogany plane table compass, Benjamin Martin, depicting the globe with continents labelled, except Australia, Roman chapter ring, primary and secondary points, brass compass ring, with mahogany box, missing glass and needle.

8.5in (21.5cm) long

£1,200-1,800　　SK

A 'Tell Tale' Mariner's compass, Robert King, New York, the 6.25in (16cm) brass case with brass ring hanger, printed compass card, maker's signature.

A 'Tell Tale' compass was hung over a sea captain's bunk to allow him to view the direction of the ship while lying in bed.

£2,000-2,500　　SK

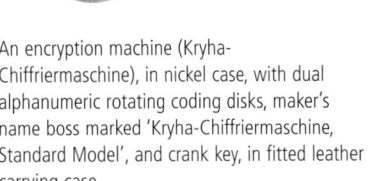

An encryption machine (Kryha-Chiffriermaschine), in nickel case, with dual alphanumeric rotating coding disks, maker's name boss marked 'Kryha-Chiffriermaschine, Standard Model', and crank key, in fitted leather carrying case.

10in (25.5cm) high

£3,000-3,500　　SK

A late 19thC Victorian brass and iron kaleidoscope, the faux-leather-covered tube printed 'NEW PATENT JEWEL KALEIDOSCOPE, LONDON STEREOSCOPIC COMPANY' to the end panel, on gilt finish fluted upright with spreading leafy foot.

16.5in (42cm) high

£400-500　　DN

A mid-18thC ebony and brass navigational quadrant, the ebony frame with T-shaped bracing, inset ivory scale and engraved pivoted radius arm initialled 'J.C.' to scale aperture, with pinhole sight and prism, filters and mirror lacking, distressed.

17.25in (44cm) diam

£200-300　　DN

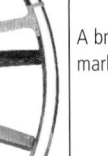

A brass transit on wood tripod, marked 'T.H. Temple Maker Boston'.

£1,200-1,800　　FRE

A brass surveyor's level.

7.5in (19cm) high

£150-250   WW

A German level, stamped 'Hildebrand-Wichmann-Werke Freiberg (SA.) – Berlin Nr. 172094'.

13.5in (34cm) long

£50-80   WW

A mid-19thC cased oval magnifying glass, mounted in a silver frame, in an engine-turned and handcarved black hard rubber case.

4in (10cm) wide

£100-150   PC

A lacquered brass paper scale, by F. Leunig & Co., with silvered scale and adjustable stem, the base printed 'Standard,… F. Leunig & Co, Paper Makers, Scales Manufactures 68 Upper Thames Street, London', in fitted box, distressed.

7.25in (18.5cm) high

£120-180   WW

A bronze sunshine recorder, Gregory, London, with glass sphere supported within vertical arc and horizontal curved scale with channels to take calibrated record card, mounted on marble base applied with maker's name.

c1900   *11.5in (29cm) high*

£600-800   DN

A 19thC cased surgeon's set, by John Weiss & Sons, London, the brass-bound mahogany case opening to reveal a fitted interior with ebony-handled stainless steel tools, with inset plaque with maker's name.

17.75in (45cm) wide

£2,000-3,000   L&T

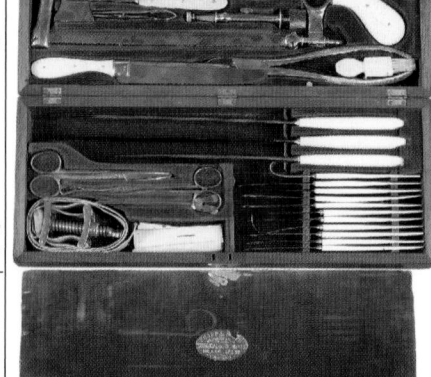

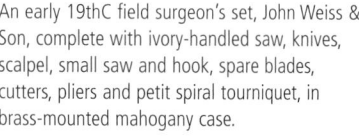

An early 19thC field surgeon's set, John Weiss & Son, complete with ivory-handled saw, knives, scalpel, small saw and hook, spare blades, cutters, pliers and petit spiral tourniquet, in brass-mounted mahogany case.

16in (40.5cm) high

£2,500-3,500   GORL

An American Civil War bone-handled field amputation set, by Sharp and Smith, Chicago, in brass-bound walnut case with fitted velvet-lined interior, with maker's label and indistinct gilt lettering on the lid 'D.H.L.H.'.

16in (40.5cm) wide

£7,000-10,000   SK

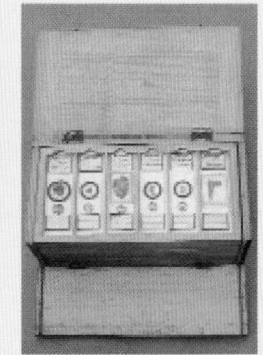
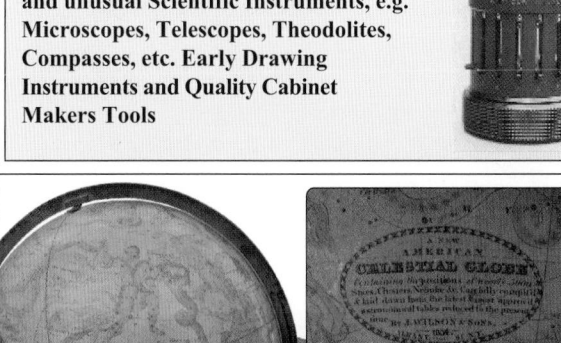

A Wilson 13in (33cm)
celestial globe, made up
of twelve engraved and
hand-coloured gores and
two calottes laid to the
celestial poles of a
plaster sphere, minor
wear to rim.

18in (46cm) high

£5,000-6,000   SK

A 13in (33cm) terrestrial
globe, J. Wilson & Son,
New York, made up of
twelve engraved gores on
plaster sphere, on probably
later cabriole mahogany
stand with original horizon
ring, some damage.

29in (73.5cm) high

£4,500-5,000   SK

An early 19thC celestial globe, John
& William Cary, London, the stand
with ring-turned pedestal upright
issuing three cabriole supports with
glazed compass suspended
between, the stand cleaned or
possibly later.

Globe 12in (30.5cm)

£450-550   DN

A mahogany and brass Armillary
library sphere, on an associated
19thC stand with baluster column
and inlaid splayed tripod base
ending in brass paw caps and
casters, adapted.

*Armillary spheres were used to
track the path of the sun for any
given day of the year.*

35.75in (91cm) high

£2,200-2,800   L&T

ESSENTIAL REFERENCE – MUSIC BOXES

Mechanical music boxes take a number of forms, with the two main forms being cylinder and disc music boxes.

- Cylinder music boxes that use a revolving cylinder. These cylinders are covered with pins arranged so that they pluck metal teeth on a 'comb'. The different lengths of the teeth produce different tones when struck. Most have a fixed cylinder, although some rare examples have interchangeable cylinders. Good manufacturers include B.A. Bremond, Paillard and particularly Nicole Frères. This form was popular from the mid-19thC to the 1890s.
- Disc musical boxes, which use a steel disc with punched holes that leave a protruding tab, that strikes the comb. These reached the height of their popularity from the 1890s to the first decade of the 20thC. Well known manufacturers include Symphonion. Phonographs, developed by Thomas Edison, and wind-up gramophones, developed by Emile Berliner in 1887, are also included.

- Condition is a major consideration when choosing a musical box and assessing its value. Torn or missing tune sheets, lifting veneers or cases damaged by woodworm are some of the more obvious defects that hardly need further comment. Also note that original tune sheets, and more complex and finely detailed inlaid decoration on lids will add desirability and, often, value.
- The musical mechanism needs careful scrutiny. Careful inspection of the cylinder will reveal any bent pins, which may impair the music and repinning the whole cylinder is the solution. Look for pitting to the surface of the comb, missing teeth, tips and badly repaired sections. Corroded tuning weights (suspended beneath the comb) will be indicated by a fine white deposit around the affected area. Should a whisper, click or grating noise be heard whilst playing, a worn comb, dampers that are badly aligned or missing will be the likely cause.

A cylinder music box by George Bendon, six bells with automaton strikers, playing eight airs, the box with original Swiss finish.

9.5in (24cm) wide

£4,500-5,500　　　　　　　　　　　KEMB

An Overture-format Mandoline musical box, by Bremond, no. 7965, playing 'Norma' in two revolutions and four other airs, with small groups of up to four mandoline teeth, flat-topped winding lever, and inlaid rosewood veneered case.

21.5in (54.5cm) wide

£6,000-9,000　　　　　　　　　　　SK

A key-wind three-overture musical box, by Nicole Frères, no. 24531, with brass bedplate, instant stop, tune sheet, walnut case with red interior, recent repairs.

17.5in (44.5cm) wide

£5,000-6,000　　　　　　　　　　　SK

A late 19thC Mermod Frères Ideal Soprano cylinder music box, together with four cylinders.

31in (79cm) wide

£3,000-4,000　　　　　　　　　　　POOK

A 19thC Mermod Frères Ideal Soprano cylinder music box, with an oak case and six cylinders.

39in (99cm) wide

£8,000-10,000　　　　　　　　　　　POOK

A rare American Style C Capital Cuff musical box, no. 186, by F. G. Otto & Sons, New Jersey, patd. dates to 1889, oak case with cuff storage compartment and six 7.5in (19cm) cuffs.

The firm F. G. Otto & Sons was established by Frederick G. Otto in Jersey City in 1875 as manufacturers of surgical instruments and batteries. The design for a self-playing American-made instrument that incorporated attributes of both cylinder and disc musical boxes led to the creation of the Capital Cuff Box, intended as a direct competitor for New Jersey's other major musical export, the Regina. Its American roots are reflected in its large repertoire of popular and patriotic music, solid casework in oak or mahogany, and American eagle emblem emblazoned on the gold lacquered cuffs.

26.5in (67.5cm) wide

£4,500-6,000   **SK**

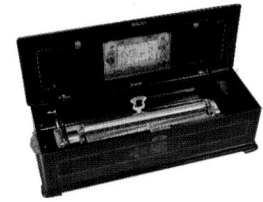

A Sublime Harmony musical box, playing twelve popular and operatic airs including 'Boccacio Serenade', 'La Norma' and 'Mikado Chorus', in grained case with ormolu handles and inlaid lid, and 'Harlequin' tune sheet.

34in (86.5cm) wide

£2,000-2,500   **SK**

A Sublime Harmony interchangeable musical box, by Mermod Frères, no. 17340, with three six-air cylinders playing popular and operatic airs, two tune sheets, and bookmatched burl-walnut veneered case.

33.5in (85cm) wide

£3,500-4,500   **SK**

An early 19thC key-wind cylinder musical box, with three external control levers, playing four airs, with original tune sheet, the fruitwood case with original finish, movement restored.

32in (81.5cm) long

£1,500-2,000   **KEMB**

A Swiss cylinder musical box, playing eight airs, the rosewood case with ornate inlay, mechanism restored.

22.75in (58cm) wide

£3,500-4,500   **KEMB**

A Sublime Harmony piccolo interchangeable musical box on table, no. 4082, with six cylinders playing eight airs each, in bookmatched burl-walnut veneered case with boxwood stringing and ebonised borders, on matching table.

52in (132cm) wide

£6,000-8,000   **SK**

A Swiss Allard-Sandoz orchestral music box, with seven engine-turned bells, drum and castanet, with double comb encased in an ebonised and burr-walnut case on a matching table with single drawer containing six cylinders.

c1870   *52in (132cm) wide*

£9,000-12,000   **POOK**

An early 17thC silver verge watch, Le Grand, Rouen, with engraved octagonal case, monogrammed 'H.B.', the engraved gilt-brass dial with applied silvered Roman chapter ring, the signed gilt-brass three-wheel train movement with ratchet set-up, round baluster pillars and gut-line fusee.

c1630   1.75in (4.5cm) long

£20,000-25,000   **GORL**

A late 17thC pair-cased verge pocket watch, Charles Burgis, silver and champlevé dial, full-plate gilt verge movement, pierced, engraved balance cock, divided tulip pillars, in silver and red tortoiseshell case.

c1685   2.25in (5.5cm) diam

£7,000-8,000   **GORL**

A late 17thC pair-cased verge pocket watch, Henry Godfrey, full-plate gilt verge movement, pierced, engraved balance cock, tulip pillars, silver dial, sector aperture, silver inner case, signed.

2in (5cm) diam

£7,500-8,500   **GORL**

A silver pair-case verge hour repeating alarum clock watch, Phillip Graet of Lintz, full-plate gilt movement with pierced, engraved cock, Egyptian pillars, engraved case, monogrammed 'GPR', signed.

c1730   3in (7.5cm) diam

£6,500-7,500   **GORL**

An early 18thC English white metal pair-cased verge pocket watch, Thomas Gorsuch, gilt movement with Egyptian pillars and winged cock within semi-circular aperture, Salop dial with single hand.

£3,500-4,500   **FLD**

An 18thC hallmarked silver verge pocket watch, Alex Mackay, London, with faux tortoiseshell case decorated with pheasants and heather.

1766

£700-800   **FLD**

A late 18thC gilt metal verge movement pocket watch, London, back plate engraved 'Geo Light', case decorated with blue, white and gilt enamel details.

£800-1,000   **FLD**

An 18ct gold pocket watch, Johnson, Grays Inn Passage, London, no. 1180, gilt fusee movement, later converted to lever escapement, three-armed steel balance, diamond endstone, inscription to case back.

1800   2in (5cm) diam

£400-500   **TEN**

A William IV hallmarked silver pair-cased verge pocket watch, engraved 'Keep me clean and use me well – and I to you the truth will tell' to border, back plate engraved 'R. Tyler', Melton No 524, Birmingham 1830'.

1830'.

£450-500 FLD

An 18ct gold open-face pocket watch, no. 6156, Marten & Bishopp, Bunhill Row, London, gilt-plate English lever movement with gilt Roman dial having floral engraved centre.

c1855 *1.5in (4cm) diam*

£150-200 RTC

An Auguste Saltzman, Chaux de Fonds, 18ct gold full-hunting cased single-push chronograph pocket watch, no. 1287, with independent quarter flying seconds, the nickel-plated two-train lever movement with 30 ruby jewels, bimetallic compensation balance with blued overcoil hairspring.

c1860

£1,200-1,800 TEN

A Joseph Sewell 18ct hallmarked fusée open-face pocket watch, Liverpool, with Roman and Arabic numerals to white enamelled dial, marked 'Chester 1863'.

1863

£300-350 FLD

A Charles Frodsham 18ct gold open face lever pocket watch, London, with power indication, no. 03398 ADFmsz, lever movement, bimetallic balance, diamond endstone, case engraved, maker's mark 'JWS CF'.

1866

£2,000-2,500 TEN

A J. Vassalli, Scarboro 18ct gold open face chronograph lever pocket watch, no. 20081, frosted-gilt finish lever movement, gold-coloured dial, slide-to-operate chronograph hand, case with maker's mark 'HB'.

1866

£500-600 TEN

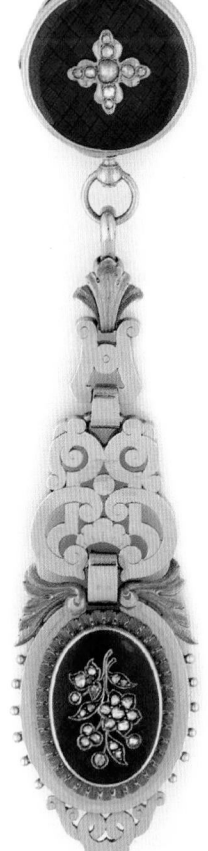

A Victorian 18ct gold open face fob watch, Charles Frodsham, with key-wound fusée movement, foliate-engraved bezel and engine-turned case with central vacant cartouche, dial and case signed.

1.25in (3.5cm) diam

£400-500 L&T

An 18ct gold half-hunting cased chronograph keyless lever pocket watch, retailed by B. Danyiger & Co, Johannesburg, gilt-finished lever movement, bimetallic compensation balance, maker's mark 'IJTN'.

1881

£700-900 TEN

A Continental 14ct gold full hunter cased pocket watch, the case with engine-turned decoration, keyless wind movement unsigned, inscribed to dust cover 'ANCRE LIGNE DROITE LEVEES VICIBLES SPIRAL BERGUET 17 RUBIS CHATON'.

£300-350 L&T

A Victorian gold, enamel and diamond-set fob watch with chatelaine, Bablin & Cie, frosted gilt bar cylinder movement, case and chatelaine decorated with enamel and set with diamonds, back fitting converted to brooch pin.

1in (2.5cm) wide

£600-800 TEN

A 14ct gold open-face pocket watch with enamel portrait, frosted gilt-finish lever movement, bimetallic compensation balance with blued overcoil hairspring, enamel portrait of soldier, signed 'JE Reymond'.

2in (5cm) wide

£1,800-2,200　　　**TEN**

An 18ct gold full-hunting case chronograph quarter repeat pocket watch, gilt finished lever movement, bimetallic compensation balance with blued overcoil hairspring, plain polished case numbered '6033'.

c1900

£900-1,200　　　**TEN**

A lady's 18ct gold, enamel and diamond-set fob watch, frosted gilt-finished lever movement, bimetallic balance, case decorated with guilloche enamel guilding, together with an associated bow brooch.

c1900　　　*1in (2.5cm) wide*

£600-800　　　**TEN**

A 14ct gold open-face single push chronograph keyless lever pocket watch, gilt finish lever movement stamped 'Anker', numbered '12752', bimetallic compensation balance with blued overcoil hairspring, plain case.

c1900　　　*2in (5cm) wide*

£400-500　　　**TEN**

A lady's 18ct yellow gold open-face watch pendant, the bezel set with demantoid garnets and 16 old European cut diamonds, porcelain dial, Swiss 15 jewel nickel movement.

1in (2.5cm) diam

£300-350　　　**RTC**

An 18ct gold full-hunting cased keyless lever pocket watch, Birmingham, nickel-finished lever movement with temperature compensation and blued overcoil hairspring, engraved polished case.

1924　　　*2in (5cm) wide*

£600-700　　　**TEN**

A 9ct gold full-hunting cased minute repeating chronograph keyless lever pocket watch, London, lever movement with compensation balance, hammers repeating on gong, maker's mark 'HEM', '389'.

1925

£1,500-2,000　　　**TEN**

A German Lange & Sohne lever deck watch with power reserve indication, no. 200962, lever movement with compensation balance and blued overcoil hairspring, micrometer regulation.

c1940

£1,700-2,200　　　**TEN**

WRISTWATCHES

A Baume & Mercier stainless steel calendar chronograph wristwatch, self-winding level movement, dial with three subsidiary dials, case with stepped bezel snap-on back, associated strap, boxed.

c1990

£900-1,200　　　**TEN**

A Baume & Mercier steel and gilt calendar chronograph wristwatch with moonphase, mechanical lever movement, case with a stepped gilt coloured bezel, snap-on back, leather strap with gilt buckle.

c1985　　　*1.25in (3.5cm) wide*

£600-800　　　**TEN**

A Carrera Heuer gentleman's stainless steel wristwatch, the silvered dial with baton numerals and date aperture, with subsidiary dial and stopwatch hand to outer dial, with original black leather strap with Heuer clasp.

£600-800　　　**L&T**

A Cartier diamond set platinum and gold rectangular wristwatch, rose-cut diamond-set platinum bezel and crown, the 18ct gold case back and deployant platinum-capped buckle on black grosgrain and leather strap.

c1930

£5,000-6,000　　　**RTC**

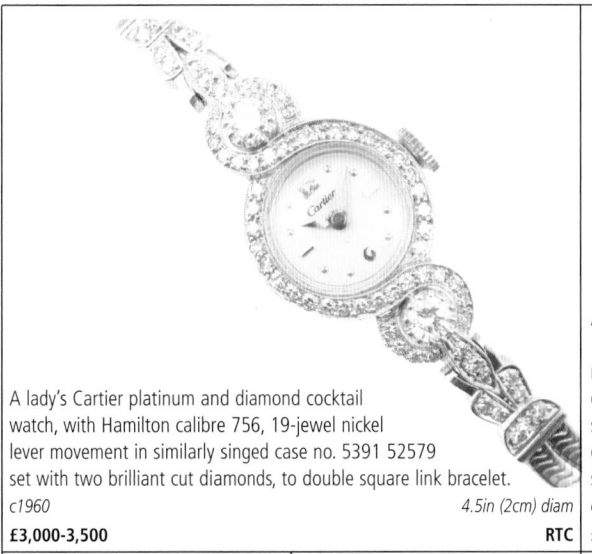

A lady's Cartier platinum and diamond cocktail watch, with Hamilton calibre 756, 19-jewel nickel lever movement in similarly singed case no. 5391 52579 set with two brilliant cut diamonds, to double square link bracelet.
c1960   *4.5in (2cm) diam*
£3,000-3,500   **RTC**

A lady's Cartier Bagnoire 18ct gold wristwatch, mechanical lever movement, dial with Roman numerals and secret signature at '7', oval-shaped case numbered '780949119', cabochon set winding crown, Cartier strap, with box.
c1990   *1in (2.5cm) wide*
£1,200-1,500   **TEN**

A 1930s American Hamilton Raleigh Plain white-gold-filled wristwatch, with some brassing to the case.

£70-90   **ML**

A Jaeger-LeCoultre 18ct gold wristwatch, nickel finish lever movement, silvered dial, case with down turned lugs, screw back numbered '765072', Jaeger-LeCoultre guarantee.
c1960
£700-900   **TEN**

A Jaeger LeCoultre 9ct gold wristwatch, calibre P480, nickel finished lever movement number '349810', case with snap-on back and maker's mark 'DTE'.
c1958   *1.25in (3.5cm) wide*
£300-400   **TEN**

A Kelek stainless steel chronograph wristwatch, mechanical lever movement, case with rounded sides and screw back.
c1970   *1.75in (4.5cm) wide*
£200-300   **TEN**

An Art Deco Longines 18ct gold rectangular wristwatch, nickel finish lever movement no. '5223645', bimetallic compensation balance and blued overcoil hairspring, micrometer regulator, case with a faceted front, hinged back.
c1932
£800-1,200   **TEN**

A Longines 18ct gold rectangular wristwatch, retailed by Tiffany & Co., mechanical lever movement, bimetallic compensation balance, rectangular case with snap on back, maker's mark 'DS&S'.
1949   *0.75in (2cm) wide*
£1,000-1,500   **TEN**

A Longines 18ct gold rectangular-shaped quartz wristwatch, quartz movement, white dial with applied dagger marks, subsidiary seconds, rectangular case with snap-on back, Longines 18ct gold bracelet with double deployant clasp.
c1995
£1,200-1,800   **TEN**

A gentleman's Omega Seamaster Aqua Terra co-axial chronometer wristwatch, the 27-jewel movement adjusted to five positions and numbered '81129923', with metal and leather bracelet, boxed.

£1,800-2,200   **GORL**

An gentleman's Omega 9ct gold wristwatch, the ivory dial with baton numerals and Arabic numbers to the cardinal points, with brick-link bracelet strap.

Omega was founded in 1848 by Louis Brandt (1825-1879), a young watchmaker based in Le Chaux-de-Fonds in Switzerland. His watches were sold throughout Europe and the company achieved great success, adopting the name 'Omega' in 1894. In the 20thC the success continued, and Omega became the official timekeeper for the Olympic Games, and supplied watches to both American and Russian astronauts.

£250-350　　　　　　　　　　　　L&T

An Omega Speedmaster stainless steel automatic chronograph wristwatch, self-winding lever movement, dial with chronograph hand, black tachymetre bezel, snap-on back no.'5691 1069', stainless steel bracelet, with warranty.

c2002　　　　1.25in (3.5cm) wide

£1,000-1,200　　　　　　　　TEN

A gentleman's Patek Philippe Jumbo Nautilus steel wristwatch, the 36-jewel movement heat/cold adjusted to isochronism and five positions, numbered '1305710', lacks winder, case numbered '536515, 3700/1'.

c1978

£8,000-9,000　　　　　　　GORL

A gentleman's Patek Phillipe 18ct gold wristwatch, the silvered dial with baton numerals and subsidiary dial, on 18ct gold mesh bracelet.

£4,000-5,000　　　　　　　GORL

A Rolex Oyster stainless steel wristwatch, ref. 6044, 15 jewel lever movement, overcoil hairspring, silvered dial with Arabic numerals, subsidiary seconds, case with super oyster winding crown, screw back.

c1945　　　　1.25in (3.5cm) wide

£500-700　　　　　　　　　TEN

A Rolex Oyster Perpetual 18ct gold centre seconds wristwatch, ref. 6050, certified chronometer, nickel finish self-winding lever movement, tonneau case with Rolex winding crown, 18ct gold bracelet.

c1950

£2,000-2,500　　　　　　　TEN

A lady's Rolex gunmetal ball watch, 15-jewel lever movement signed 'Rolex' with compensation balance, globe-shaped case with polished blue surface, together with marcasite set bow brooch.

1in (2.5cm) wide

£800-900　　　　　　　　　TEN

A Rolex Oyster Perpetual stainless steel automatic calendar centre seconds wristwatch, chronometer certified, ref. 1500, calibre 1570, 26-jewel self-winding lever movement, overcoil hairspring, steel bracelet.

c1975

£350-450　　　　　　　　　TEN

A gentleman's Rolex 18ct gold Oyster Perpetual day-date watch, ref. 18038, serial no. 6157927, 18ct (.750) Calibre 3055, 27-jewel rhodium-plated nickel lever movement, 'President' bracelet.

1979

£3,000-4,000　　　　　　　RTC

A gentleman's Rolex Oyster Perpetual 18ct gold day-date chronometer, no. 18038, the gold-coloured dial set with diamonds in place of numerals, the bezel fully set with 44 diamonds, and 18ct flexible bracelet.

£4,500-5,500　　　　　　　HT

A gentleman's Rolex gold Oyster Perpetual datejust watch, ref. 15037, serial 9674487, 14ct (.585) Calibre 3035, 27-jewel nickel-lever movement, gilt dial, water resistant case with fluted bezel and screw down crown, 'Jubilee' bracelet.

£3,000-4,000　　　　　　　RTC

A gentleman's Rolex stainless steel and gold Oyster Perpetual datejust watch, ref. 16013, serial 6666005, 18ct (.750) Calibre 3035, 27-jewel nickel-lever movement, water resistant case, 'Jubilee' bracelet.
1980

£1,300-1,800 RTC

A Rolex Oyster Precision stainless steel centre seconds wristwatch, ref. 6426, 17-jewel lever movement, case with screw down winding crown and screw back, stainless steel oyster bracelet, guarantee.
1.25in (3.5cm) wide

£800-1,200 TEN

A lady's Rolex Oyster Perpetual stainless steel automatic centre seconds wristwatch, ref. 76094, self-winding lever movement, screw-down winding crown, Rolex stainless steel 'Jubilee' bracelet.
c2006 *1in (2.5cm) wide*

£900-1,200 TEN

A Tag Heuer, Monza stainless steel automatic calendar chronograph wristwatch, self-winding lever movement, boxed with guarantee.
c2005

£800-1,200 TEN

A Swiss Universal Geneva wristwatch, with stainless steel case, white dial and Swiss-made 17-jewel movement, probably made for United Nations military service.

£70-100 ML

A Vacheron & Constantin 18ct yellow gold gentleman's wristwatch, no. 6452, movement no. 578110, with certificate and boxed.

£1,800-2,200 LT

A 1970s Rolex gentleman's stainless steel wrist watch, the black circular dial with silver coloured baton numerals and hand and date aperture, stamped ROLEX OYSTER PERPETUAL DATEJUST, SUPERLATIVE CHRONOMETER OFFICIALLY CERTAIFIED, fitted to a black leather strap.
Face 1.5in (3.5cm) wide

£2,000-3,000 L&T

ESSENTIAL REFERENCE – ROLEX

Rolex is currently the largest luxury watch brand, producing about 2,000 watches per day.
- **The company (then known as Wilsdorf & Davis) was founded in London in 1903 and became known as Rolex in 1915. Rolex moved to Switzerland in 1919, as British taxes and export duties on gold and silver were driving costs up.**
- **Rolex had made no attempt to enter the automatic wristwatch market until 1929 when the Harwood watch company, went bankrupt. Up to that point Harwood's many patents had prevented or restricted other companies from creating automatic watches. Rolex had designed the waterproof Oyster case in 1927 and in the early 1930s the company designed a silent 360° self-winding movement. The motor was very large, so these watches (launched in 1934) had domed case-backs, which became known as 'Bubble Backs'. This became the foundation of Rolex's current success.**
- **Rolex SA currently has three watch lines: Oyster Perpetual, Professional and Cellini.**

A rare Rolex Oyster Perpetual Submariner British Royal Navy stainless steel automatic wristwatch, ref. 5513/5517, cal.1520 nickel lever movement, mono-metallic balance, 26 jewels, stainless steel Oyster case, back engraved with the broad arrow, Royal Navy store number, issue number and year, the case, dial and movement signed.

This became an official Military issue model in 1968, after the British Royal Navy commissioned a series of Submariners with specific adaptations. The dial was marked with an encircled 'T' to indicate the use of the luminous material tritium. The large, high-visibility sword hands and diamond-tip seconds hand are unique to this model. The watches were also fitted with a hacking feature that allowed the easy synchronisation of time, an especially useful function for troops on operations.
c1972

£80,000-100,000 SOTH

A diorama of the schooner yacht 'Atlantic' at the Kaiser Cup Challenge 1905, by Erik A. R. Ronnberg, Jr.

In the spring of 1905, at the invitation of Kaiser Wilhelm II, eleven vessels crossed a starting line off Sandy Hook, New Jersey, on a race for England. The three-masted schooner 'Atlantic' won the race, finishing in 12 days, four hours, one minute, and 19 seconds, indicating an average of well over 200 miles per day for the entire trip.
1997   *38in (96.5cm) wide*
£1,500-1,800   **SK**

An American cased diorama of the schooner 'Fair Wind', signed and dated 'Perk 1925' at lower left stern, mounted on a wooden base, in a case with painted background, with the Portland, Maine lighthouse and a distant steamer.
                              56in (142cm) wide
£1,000-1,500   **SK**

A late 20thC diorama entitled 'Getting Away, New England Sword Fishermen c1920', by Rex Stewart, Southbridge, Massachusetts, in a glazed, moulded mahogany frame.

                              39.5in (100cm) long
£400-600   **SK**

A late Victorian marine diorama.
                    46.5in (118cm) wide
£700-900   **DN**

A shipping diorama titled 'Shanghai Bound: British Tea Clipper Ship c.1860', by Erik A. R. Ronnberg, Sr., signed lower right, minor stains and craquelure to background sky, in a glazed moulded mahogany frame.
1986   *36in (91.5cm) wide*
£800-1,000   **SK**

PAINTINGS

Antonio Nicolo Gasparo Jacobsen (American/Danish, 1850-1921), shipping scene, signed 'ANTONIO JACOBSEN 1917' lower right, oil on canvas, the clipper and schooner carrying American flags, in a moulded wood frame, relined, retouched.
                              30in (76.2cm) wide
£7,000-10,000   **SK**

George Emerick Essig (1838-1926), 'Cat Boat off Barnegat Light', oil on canvas, signed and dated 'G.L. Essig 1872', framed.

                              36in (91.5cm) wide
£5,000-6000   **FRE**

Raffael Corsini (Turkish, active 1830-1880), 'Barque Juniata, Capt. Joseph Cheever, at Smyrna 1852', signed, gouache on paper, in original walnut veneer frame.

Corsini is well known for his watercolours and gouaches.
                              23.75in (60.5cm) wide
£8,000-10,000   **SK**

Antonio Nicolo Gasparo Jacobsen (American/Danish, 1850-1921), painting of the Joy Line steamship 'Larchmont', signed and dated 'A. Jacobsen 1902 31 PALISADE AV West Hoboken, NJ 1904', oil on canvas, in later frame, relined, minor retouches.
                              36in (91.5cm) wide
£17,000-20,000   **SK**

19thC English School, Portrait of the S.S. Calabria, oil on canvas, unsigned, lined and framed.
                              30in (76cm) wide
£2,000-3,000   **FRE**

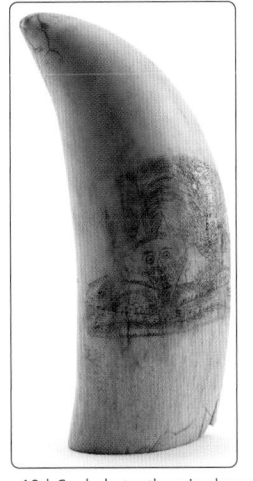

Two 19thC whale tooth scrimshaws depicting antipodean animals, one with a of a Wallaby with its young inside its pouch within a verdant landscape, another depicting a horned, prowling Tasmanian Devil.

Largest 6.25in (16cm) high

£900-1,000   **L&T**

An early 19thC scrimshaw powder horn, decorated with numerous wild fowl and small game, signed 'John C. Hennick'.

11.5in (29cm) long

£1,800-2,200   **POOK**

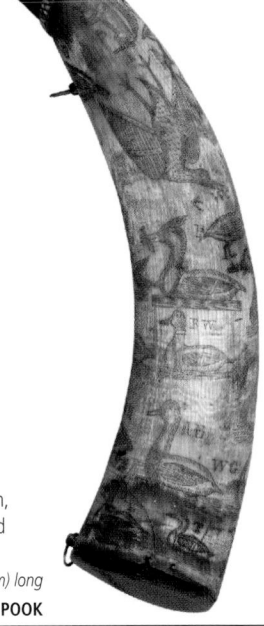

CLOSER LOOK – SCRIMSHAW POWDER HORN

Scrimshaw is a decorative technique where a design is carved into the surface using a pin or knife, then soot is rubbed into it, highlighting the design.

This is an early piece, designed for use not decoration, which makes it a rarity, as do the initials carved onto it. The image of a woman is also unusual.

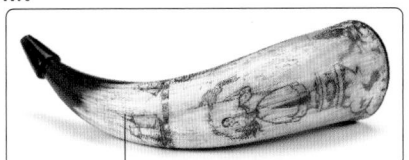

The American flag and eagle make it highly collectable. The political message refers to trade embargoes and war in America, and is also an unusual feature.

An American scrimshaw decorated powder horn, with depictions of ships at sea and a woman holding an American flag and an eagle with arrows, inscribed 'Free Trade and States Rights', bearing the initials 'W.H. and E.W.', the wooden end of the horn impressed 'Heller'.

c1830

17in (43cm) long

£10,000-15,000   **FRE**

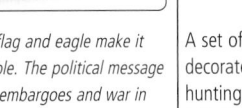

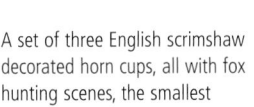

A set of three English scrimshaw decorated horn cups, all with fox hunting scenes, the smallest initialled 'S+P'.

c1800   *tallest 4.5in (11.5cm) high*

£1,400-1,600   **POOK**

An unusual Greenock dock pass, the oval brass medallion with ship in full sail with 'BOATMAN 24 GREENOCK', with integral suspension and leather strap.

The function of this pass is uncertain, but it seems likely it was a pass for a crew member to get back into the docks once he had left and to show his official status in the area. Passes of this type are well recorded for Royal parks, roads, operas and so on.

3.25in (8.5cm) high

£300-350   **L&T**

A late 19th/early 20thC brass and glazed maritime oil lantern.

15.75in (40cm) high

£40-60   **DN**

A mid-19thC sailor's woolwork picture, worked with a three-masted ship of the line in long and short stitch, with raised, padded sails, black cotton rigging.

Mounted 15.75in (40cm) wide

£400-500   **KT**

THE METALWARE MARKET

The last year has been a good one for silver, with increased prices seen throughout the market. As silver bullion prices haven risen during the economic downturn, this field represents an attractive area for antique buyers, as any purchase is a good investment as well.

In general terms, the lower end of the market remained steady, the middle section of the market was largely flat, while the quality and collectors' sections performed significantly better than in previous years. The demand for fine silver is greater than ever and high prices are being reached for, in particular, pre-1830s silver. Items such as tea sets and salvers have seen an increase in value, and continue to find buyers among established collectors.

Also very strong, is the 'collectables' market: small and novelty items such as snuffboxes, vinaigrettes, wine labels and caddy spoons. Many record prices have been set for rare and unusual examples. An Asprey & Company (of London) Butt marker, hallmarked Chester 1922, of a known and relatively standard form reached a £2,700 hammer price (estimate £1,200–1,500), while a very fine Irish silver-gilt presentation snuff box by James England of Dublin c. 1800, brought a hammer price of £7,500 (estimate £1,800–2,500).

An area that has seen good growth over the last 12 months is post-war silver, which is becoming more popular among younger collectors. Leaders in this field include the names Gerald Benney, Stuart Devlin, Christopher Lawrence and Rod Kelly. These and other modern and contemporary silversmiths who do not fall into the 'Decorative Arts' category (see pages 577-586) are proving to be a field worthy of watching. Sales of other metals – bronze sculptures, for example – have been dominated by high-end items and buyers could take advantage of the resulting drop in price of mid-range pieces.

As with all markets, buyers and collectors should always be mindful of quality, condition and rarity when buying. For many years these have been the factors demanded by the market and no doubt this will not change for the future.

A George II silver chamber stick, by Edward Feline, London, the large circular base with flared rim and engraved crest and initials, with central reeded socket and with single C-scroll handle with raised thumb piece.

1731	6in (15cm) diam 15oz
£1,500-2,000	L&T

A pair of George III silver chambersticks, John Scofield, London, the circular pans with flying scroll handles and vase-shaped nozzles with detachable sconces and conical snuffers, beaded borders throughout, crested.

1780	5.25in (13.5cm) diam 18oz
£1,200-1,800	TEN

A small George III silver chamberstick, John and Thomas Settle, Sheffield, circular form, crimped edge, scrolling thumbpiece, dish base.

1817	3.25in (8.5cm) diam
£150-200	WW

A pair of late George III silver chambersticks, Paul Storr, London, the bases with cast leaf and gadrooned border, shell and moulded handle, the lobed centre engraved with a crest and with an urn-shaped sconce with reeded and gadrooned edge.

1819-20	5.75in (14.5cm) diam
£4,000-5,000	L&T

A pair of William IV silver chambersticks, T. J. & N. Creswick, Sheffield, the circular bases rising to campana-shaped nozzles with detachable sconces, flying leaf-capped scroll handles, crested, one with matching conical snuffer.

1837	3.5in (9cm) high 15oz
£700-1,000	TEN

A small Victorian silver chamberstick, Yapp & Woodward, Birmingham, with a border of leaves, detachable nozzle, conical snuffer.

1848	3.75in (9.5cm) diam 2.25oz
£350-450	WW

A pair of Victorian silver circular chambersticks, Edward Hutton, London, with gadrooned borders, detachable nozzles and conical snuffers, crested.

c1880	5.75in (15cm) diam 20oz
£1,200-1,800	WW

A pair of George III silver candlesticks by John Parsons & Co., Sheffield, with reeded borders and part fluted vase-shaped capitals, tapering columns and round bases.

1791   *11.5in (29.5cm) high*

£1,200-1,800   **DN**

A pair of George II silver candlesticks, Paul de Lamerie, London, bases with inturned corners, cast leaf detail and chased shells, the dome with applied and cast shells in cartouches on a matted ground, a tapering square baluster stem with shell detail, scale pattern to the sides, foliate clasped socket, the base engraved with a rose crest.

The crest of the rose is probably for Sir Theodore Janssen (1658-1748), a Dutch merchant who settled in England c1680 and was a founder director of the Bank of England. He was created a baronet 1714, a very successful financier with a reputed wealth of £300,000. He was implicated in the South Sea Bubble scandal and was heavily fined by the House of Commons committee in 1721.

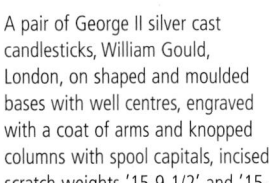

1737-38   *7.75in (19.5cm) high 22oz each*

£50,000-60,000   **L&T**

A George II silver taperstick, John Cafe, London, cast shell and scroll pattern, initialled 'B' over 'HM'.

1745   *5in (12.5cm) high 4oz*

£400-500   **TEN**

A set of four George II silver cast candlesticks, Georges Wickes, London, on shaped bases with 'well' centres and knopped columns, decorated with ropework and gadrooning and leaf capping, detachable nozzles, the bases crested, the undersides with incised scratchweights '21-1', '21-8', '19-6' and '20-15', numbered 'No. 6', 'No. 3', 'No. 8' and 'No. 7'.

1745   *8.75in (22cm) high 82oz*

£10,000-12,000   **WW**

A pair of George II silver cast candlesticks, William Gould, London, on shaped and moulded bases with well centres, engraved with a coat of arms and knopped columns with spool capitals, incised scratch weights '15-9 1/2' and '15-15 1/2'.

7in (17.5cm) high 30oz

£1,800-2,200   **WW**

A pair of George II silver candlesticks, John Quantock, London, with turned and lappet stems, with engraved armorial on hexafoil foot.

1752   *9.25in (23.5cm) high 41oz*

£2,500-3,500   **GORL**

A set of four George II silver table candlesticks, John Cafe, London, of typical multiple knopped design, the flared shaped square nozzles with shells at the angles and engraved with the horse crest of Fingall, the indented and shaped square cast bases engraved with a further similar crest.

1752   *9.5in (24cm) high*

£8,000-10,000   **TEN**

A pair of French Louis XVI-style silver candlesticks, Andrew Debain, each with an infant holding aloft a torchere issuing a foliate-cast nozzle, raised on a shaped square base cast with cartouches and foliate scrolls.

c1900   *13in (33cm) high*

£1,800-2,200   **FRE**

METALWARE

ESSENTIAL REFERENCE – CANDLESTICKS

Before the advent of mass-production, silver candlesticks were used predominantly by the church and the wealthy. Surviving examples from before the mid-17thC are rare, because they were often melted down after being damaged, or were converted to coin, but they were widely recorded. The earliest silver candlesticks had tripod feet and a pricket (metal spike) to hold the candle: sockets and sconces were introduced in the 15thC. Candlesticks were also made from less valuable materials, such as pewter.

- Most 17thC British silver candlesticks were raised from thin hammered sheet metal. In the 1690s candlestick making was revolutionised by the newly arrived Huguenot silversmiths, who began casting candlesticks in solid silver. These examples were generally elegant and simply patterned.
- The baluster shape was popular during the early and mid-18thC, with Rococo style decoration. In the 1740s detachable nozzles were added to to save dripping wax. The Neo-classical style was favoured in the 1750s and 60s.
- By the late 18thC, huge numbers of loaded-sheet silver candlesticks were being made using mechanised production in Sheffield and Birmingham. Plate candlesticks, which have visible seaming lines where the sheet or plate has been joined, were primarily intended for the newly prosperous middle classes. The best candlesticks were still cast. Both were decorated in the Victorian taste.

A set of three George III silver candlesticks, George Ashworth & Co., Sheffield, the fluted oval bases rising to flared stems supporting vase-shaped nozzles with detachable oval sconces, reeded borders.

One 1793, two 1797   12in (30.5cm) high

£2,000-3,000   **TEN**

A set of four George III silver-gilt candlesticks, Paul Storr, London, each on serpentine square base, elaborately cast with shells, scrolls and four masks, each representing the seasons: Neptune amid rocaille and shells, Flora amid flowers, Pomona amid fruit, Bacchus amid grapevines, the square tapering stem with pendant husks and stylised ornament under a border of acanthus, rising to a circular flute socket with similar band, the removable nozzle engraved with a crest.

Engraved with the Ducal coronet above a crest within the Garter for Lt. Col. Sir William Lowther, 1st Earl of Londsdale.

1811-12   *9in (23cm) high*

£80,000-90,000   **L&T**

A set of four George III silver table candlesticks, Paul Storr, London, base with a C-scroll and acanthus clasped border, with four grotesque masks each with a rose above, knopped stem with clasping to the upper knop, leaf clasped sconce and each with a removable drip pan, each engraved with a crest.

1815-16   10.25in (26cm) high 112oz

£20,000-25,000   **L&T**

A set of four cast late George III table candlesticks, William Elliot, London, serpentine bases with stepped edge, C-scroll base with floral detail, a lion's head, sea monster and an eagle, stems modelled as an eagle, floral sconces, the removable drip trays with cast eagle, shell, floral and C-scrolls to the top.

1819-20   13.5in (34cm) high 320oz

£30,000-40,000   **L&T**

A pair of George IV silver candlesticks, by J Watson & Son, Sheffield, the fluted and tapered stems with scroll-knopped details and sconce, the shaped circular base with C-scroll and foliate design.

1826   8.25in (21cm) high

£600-800   **L&T**

A pair of George IV sterling silver Rococo revival candlesticks, Waterhouse, Hodson & Co., Sheffield, the stems cast with floral bands and scrolls, weighted.

1829   10.5in (26.5cm) high

£2,000-3,000   **FRE**

A pair of late Victorian silver dwarf Corinthian column candlesticks, Harrison Brothers & Howson, Sheffield, on stepped square bases, with bead borders.

1899   *5.75in (14.5cm) high*

£300-400   **WW**

A set of four Edwardian sterling silver candlesticks, Thomas Bradbury & Son of Sheffield, London, of baluster form with urn form candle nozzles and acanthus clad square bases, weighted.

1910/11   *11in (28cm) high*

£1,800-2,200   **FRE**

CLOSER LOOK – A REGENCY SILVER CENTREPIECE

There is a strong similarity to the design by Flaxman for a candelabrum presented to The Marquess of Salisbury, with the Classical figures replacing the Highlanders, the stags replacing the deerhounds which are part of the crest.

It is mounted with three standing kilted Highlanders by a palm trunk, rising to a canopy of openwork leaves from which spread three tiers of foliate scroll reeded branches.

The base is applied with three couchant deerhounds on whose backs rests an upper plinth applied on each side with arms and coronets.

The triform base sits on four massive lion's leg supports which are linked by openwork foliage, inscribed in English and Gaelic below a band of palm and acanthus.

A Regency silver ten-light 'Huntly Testimonial' candelabrum centrepiece, Paul Storr for Rundell, Bridge & Rundell, London, fully marked, and stamped with London signature of Rundell, Bridge and Rundell.

General George Gordon, GCB (1820), Col., Royal Scots Fusiliers and Governor of the Castle of Edinburgh, eldest son of the 4th Duke of Gordon was summoned to Parliament as Lord Gordon of Huntly with the courtesy title of Marquess of Huntly.

1814-15   *39.75in (101cm) high 847oz*

£80,000-90,000   **L&T**

A pair of George III Royal three-light candelabra, Benjamin Smith II, London, stepped circular base with gadroon detail, fanned ribbed platform with a rising socle, the stems formed as vase-shaped columns with four pairs of feet and with four Classical female heads with fruit head dresses, the detachable branches formed as stylised scroll dolphins, part covered in acanthus and with a clasped rosette motif, the sconces of Roman lamp form, stems with an applied coat of arms and an engraved crest in garter.

1807-08   *23.25in (59cm) high 290oz*

£80,000-120,000   **L&T**

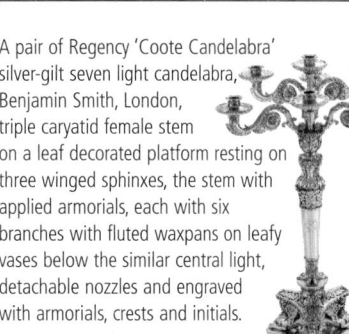

A pair of Regency 'Coote Candelabra' silver-gilt seven light candelabra, Benjamin Smith, London, triple caryatid female stem on a leaf decorated platform resting on three winged sphinxes, the stem with applied armorials, each with six branches with fluted waxpans on leafy vases below the similar central light, detachable nozzles and engraved with armorials, crests and initials.

1812-13   *35.75in (91cm) high 932oz*

£150,000-200,000   **L&T**

ESSENTIAL REFERENCE – JEAN-BAPTISTE-CLAUDE ODIOT

Jean-Baptiste-Claude Odiot (1763-1850) was a French silversmith, who worked predominantly in the Empire style. He produced work similar to that of Biennais, but more massive and obviously Classically influenced.

- **He came from a family of silversmiths and took over his father's workshop in 1785. He was subsequently hailed as a master by the Paris Corporation.**
- **Odiot worked for Napoleon, and after the Restauration became orfèvre (goldsmith) to Louis XVIII.**
- **When he retired in 1827, the firm taken over by his son, Charles.**

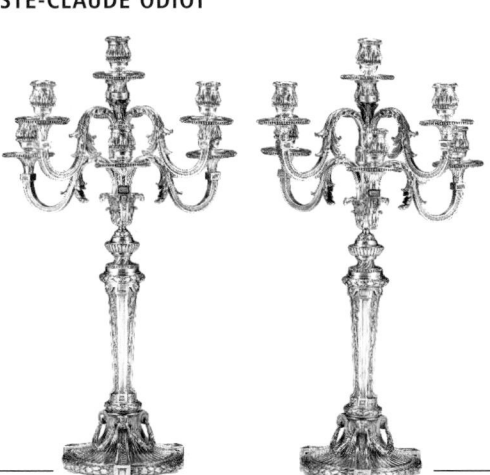

A pair of French silver seven-light candelabra, Jean Bapiste-Claude Odiot, Paris, with a tapered torchère standard, with a wreath cast base with two tiers of three curved candle arms and a single stiff candle arm, with acanthus leaf decoration, beaded drip pans and leaf-cast beaded nozzles, the fluted base with supports chased with guilloche and ribbon-tied laurel garlands, on square scrolled feet.

c1830   *27.5in (70cm) high*

£30,000-40,000   **FRE**

METALWARE

A pair of mid-19thC Italian silver four-light candelabra, Fillipo Pansi, base with embossed border, knopped stem, scrolling braches, foliate drip trays.

c1840   18.25in (46.5cm) high 70oz

£2,000-3,000   **WW**

A Victorian Neo-classical-style silver five-light candelabrum, Fordham & Faulkner, London, square base, stop-fluted Corinthian column with detachable scroll arms and nozzle.

1897   26in (66cm) high

£1,000-1,500   **TEN**

A pair of late Victorian silver five-light candelabra, by Hawksworth Eyre & Co Ltd, Sheffield, knopped stem, quatrefoil base, four scroll branches, shaped pan and sconces.

1899   19in (48cm) high

£6,000-7,000   **L&T**

One of a pair of Edwardian silver three-light candelabra, Hawkesworth, Eyre & Co., Sheffield, the scroll branches with vase shaped capitals and urn finials.

1903   15.5in (39cm) high 30oz

£1,200-1,800 PAIR   **WW**

A pair of Edwardian 18thC-style silver candelabra, Fordham & Faulkner, Sheffield, with shaped square bases, knopped baluster stem and twin-branch detachable arms.

1905   19.5in (49.5cm) high

£2,000-3,000   **TEN**

A sterling silver five light candelabrum, B. G. & Co., Birmingham, the columnar standard issuing four scrolling candle arms and a single stiff candle arm, each with a Corinthian capital nozzle and beaded drip pan, raised on a stepped, square base.

1926   18.75in (47.5cm) high

£2,000-3,000   **FRE**

SILVER CUPS

A Charles I silver communion cup, London, together with a matching paten, maker's mark 'RP', mullet below.

The paten only fits the cup as a cover with its 'foot' downwards.

1640   Cup 6in (15.5cm) high 11oz

£3,500-4,500   **WW**

A Charles II silver tumbler cup, London, initialled 'DD'.

1684   2.5in (6cm) high
                           4.1oz

£700-800   **WW**

A Queen Anne silver tankard, William Andrews, London, slight tapering with a skirted base and flattened, domed cover, with a broad brim, the large handle pricked 'B' over 'EF', volute thumb piece.

1705   7.25in (8cm) high 28oz

£3,000-4,000   **WW**

A George I plain silver tapering mug, Joseph Ward, London, scroll handle, the base inscribed 'EX DONO EW & WR to NW'.

1716   4in (10cm) high 9oz

£250-350   **WW**

A Boston, Massachusetts silver tankard, of tapered cylindrical form with a domed lid topped by a bell finial, bearing the touch of John Coburn and the cipher 'TD'.

c1755   8.25in (21cm) high 27.1oz

£6,500-7,500   **POOK**

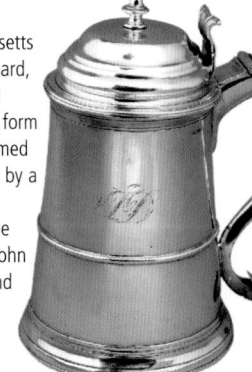

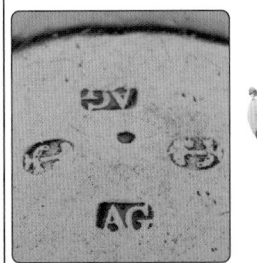

A pair of early George II silver mugs, Adam Graham, Glasgow, the baluster body with S-scroll handle and acanthus leaf thumbpiece, on stepped foot rim, marked 'AG' twice, Glasgow town mark twice.

c1765   4.5in (11.5cm) high 12oz

£3,500-4,500   **L&T**

A rare George III Scottish silver provincial two handle-cup, James Erskine, Aberdeen, of vase form, decorated with a frieze of drapery and foliate festoons below the reeded rim, two vacant oval cartouches, struck with three castles, 'E', hand and dagger under foot.

c1795   10in (25.5cm) high 20oz

£1,500-2,000   **WW**

A set of three George III silver communion cups, possibly by J. Gray, Edinburgh, bowls with slightly everted rim, raised on a baluster and knopped stem on a stepped circular foot, marked 'IG'.

1807-08   9.75in (25cm) high 20oz

£1,600-2,000   **L&T**

A rare early 19thC Chinese tapering mug, with reeded hoops around the body, initialled 'MJR 1823' and 'CMD 1918' pseudo marks (for Messrs Eley, Fearn & Chawner, London 1810).

3.25in (8cm) high 8oz

£500-600   **WW**

An early 19thC Philadelphia silver presentation mug of nautical interest, bearing the touch of Edward Lownes, inscribed 'From Thos. & Mary Ann Evans to Capt. Geo. Robinson ...'

5.25in (13.5cm) high 11.3oz

£1,500-2,000   **POOK**

An early Victorian silver mug, John S. Hunt, London, with a naturalistic handle, tapering body, decorated in relief with fruiting vines on a matt ground, initialled, gilt interior.

1846   3.25in (8cm) high 7oz

£350-450   **WW**

A Victorian silver christening mug, Edward Ker Richards, London, the diaper-work chased body with scroll handle and collet foot.

1865   4in (10cm) high 7oz

£250-350   **TEN**

A small Victorian silver mug, Hilliard & Thomason, Birmingham, with bead borders, floral engraving, scrolling handle.

1871   3.25in (8cm) high 3.3oz

£120-180   **WW**

An Edwardian silver wager cup, Neresheimer & Co. of Hanau, Import Agent Bertholdt Muller, Chester, in the form of a woman in 16thC costume holding a foliate chased cup above her head.

1906   10.5in (26.5cm) high 10oz

£500-600   **TEN**

An early 20thC German silver Kiddush cup and underdish, cast with foliate detail and Hebrew text, with conforming underdish, both marked '800' with crown and moon.

4.75in (12cm) high

£500-600   **SK**

A Queen Anne silver-gilt cup and cover, Pierre Platel, London, one side engraved with mirror cipher within baroque cartouche, the other with a later elaborate coat of arms and similar cartouche.

1712   12in (30.5cm) high 100oz

£20,000-25,000   **L&T**

A George III Irish silver bright cut two handled cup and cover, Richard Sawyer, Dublin, the domed cover with an urn finial, with circular moulded and stepped base.

c1813   12in (30cm) high 28oz

£800-1,200   **MEA**

METALWARE

A George IV silver gilt cup and cover, John Edward Terry, London, the square base rising to a foliate chased pedestal support to a baluster body chased with panels of quatrefoils and two acanthus cartouches, one with an armorial, the other inscribed 'STEWARDS The Right Honorable LORD GREY and COL YATES 1825', with foliate chased scroll handles and conforming domed cover, retailer's inscription to the base 'MICAH FURNISS MANCHESTER'.

c1825   16in (40.5cm) high 111oz

£4,000-5,000   **TEN**

A late Victorian silver trophy cup and cover, by Job Frank Hall, London, the domed cover with embossed floral and scroll borders and with St George slaying the dragon finial, on original turned wooden stand.

Cup 1895 Cover 1894

16.25in (41cm) high 110oz

£2,000-3,000   **L&T**

A silver 'goliath' trophy cup and cover, London, the deep tapered bowl with reeded girdle and moulded circular cartouche, the cartouche with removable centre, with twin S-scroll handles with leaf-capped detail, raised on knopped stem with stepped circular foot, the domed pull-off cover with moulded rim and urn-type finial.

1913   31.5in (80cm) high 375oz

£10,000-15,000   **L&T**

SILVER TEAPOTS

A George II silver bullet teapot, James Kerr, Edinburgh, Assay Master Archibald Ure, with band of simple chased decoration to upper rim with scroll and shell detail, the cover with applied hinge and bun finial, the whole resting on a simple domed stepped foot.

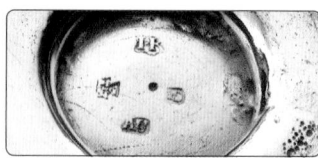

1734-35   6in (15.5cm) high 22oz

£1,200-1,800   **L&T**

A George III silver teapot, Milne and Campbell, Glasgow, of tapered vase form, with swan-neck spout and simple C-scroll handle with acanthus caps and running acanthus garlands, resting on a simple domed foot with beaded border, marked 'M&C' twice, Glasgow town mark.

c1765   9in (23cm) high 25oz

£700-1,000   **L&T**

A George II silver bullet teapot, James Mitchell, Edinburgh, Assay Master Edward Lothian, of compressed spherical bullet form, with semi-fluted scroll spout and S-scroll handle with acanthus leaf thumbpiece and reeded border.

There has long been confusion with the attribution of the maker's marks of John Main and James Mitchelson. It is now firmly ascribed to James Mitchell whose marks, along with James Welsh, are the only maker's marks in Scotland to include a figure within the punch. It has long been debated what these figures are holding: a bag of coinage, precious metal, or tool of the craft? There seems little doubt it does signify a connection with the craft and trade. The maker's mark struck to this piece is a particularly clear example of this mark, which is often seen badly or mis-struck.

1742-43   5.5in (14cm) high 23oz

£2,000-3,000   **L&T**

A George III silver teapot, John Payne, London, of drum form with a flush fitting cover with a turned wooden handle, beaded borders throughout, crested.

1775   5in (12.5cm) high 16oz

£400-500   **TEN**

SILVER TEAPOTS - DATES AND SHAPES

George III bombé Rococo, UK

George III shaped oval, UK

George III shaped oval, UK

George III classical vase-shaped, UK

George III oval oblong, UK

George IV oblong, UK

George IV compresses round, UK

Victorian circular tapered, UK

Mid 19thC Victorian oval straight-sided, UK

A George III teapot and stand, D. Smith and R. Sharp, London, both pieced with engraved crest of a dragon facing left, duty head lacking.

1784   *4.75in (12cm) high*

£1,000-1,500   **L&T**

An unusual George III silver teapot, by Charles Aldridge, London, faceted tapering body with floral bright cut detail, hinged cover with bright cut border and wood leaf finial, wood handle.

1789-90   *12.25in (31cm) wide 21oz*

£2,500-3,500   **L&T**

A George III shaped silver oval teapot, London, with vertical sides, a straight, tapering spout and frieze of bright-cutting, maker's mark 'BM'.

1789   *15oz*

£400-500   **WW**

A George III silver barge-shaped teapot, Timothy Renou, London, on ball feet, with reeded frieze and a cast serpent knop.

1808   *21.5oz*

£450-550   **WW**

A George III silver teapot, Rebecca Emes and Edward Barnard, London, of rounded rectangular form engraved leaf and anthemion bands, stained wood handle, slender curved spout, all on ball feet.

1809   *6.5in (16.5cm) high 21oz*

£300-400   **L&T**

An early 19thC Russian silver oviform teapot, probably Alexander Yarshinov, St. Petersburg, plain with a hinged cover and knop finial, the base numbered '1-50', gilt interior.

5.5in (13.5cm) high 20.5oz

£800-1,200   **WW**

A William IV silver teapot, Paul Storr, London, foliate chased throughout, initialled 'HD' for Hugh Delamere, 2nd Baron Delamere, stamped 'Storr & Mortimer'.

1833   *5in (12.5cm) high 26oz*

£1,000-1,500   **TEN**

A Victorian teapot, by William Hattersley & William Hewit, embossed with scrollwork design, hinged cover with inscription 'To Mr. John Bates, Clerk of the Parish Church of Morpeth, 1841', scroll feet.

5.5in (13.5cm) high 23.25oz

£400-600   **A&G**

METALWARE

A George II silver coffee pot, by Edward Feline, London, the body of plain tapered cylindrical form on stepped foot rim, with domed hinged cover with urn finial, S-scroll wooden handle and facetted swan-neck spout.

1740   *10in (25cm) high 24.5oz*

£1,500-2,000   **L&T**

A George II silver kettle on stand, London, the inverted pear-shaped body with a scroll spout, domed cover with a pine cone finial and a swing handle, all supported on three cast scroll legs.

1746   *14in (35.5cm) high 73oz*

£2,000-3,000   **TEN**

A George II silver provincial coffee pot, Isaac Cookson Newcastle, tapering with a tucked-in base, decorative spout and a double-domed cover with a pine cone finial, the base scratched 'H' over 'R.E.'

1752   *8.75in (22cm) high 20oz*

£1,200-1,800   **WW**

An early George III silver baluster-shaped coffee pot, London, the body profusely chased with flowers, cartouches and scrolls, on a circular domed stem and foot, applied with scrolling handle, domed and hinged cover with a spiral reeded knop finial.

c1763   *10in (25.5cm) high 22oz*

£1,500-2,000   **MEA**

A George III silver baluster coffee pot, Thomas Whipham & Charles Wright, London, with gadrooned borders, domed cover and a knop finial.

1765   *11.5in (29cm) high 31oz*

£1,000-1,500   **WW**

A George III silver tea urn, by J. Scofield, London, the urn of tapered conical form with fluted bottom section and reeded rim with twin hinged loop handles, the pull-off domed cover with semi-fluted section and reeded ball finial, on a waisted stem.

1792   *12.25in (31cm) high 45oz*

£1,000-1,500   **L&T**

A George III silver coffee pot of cylindrical form, London, with hinged lid, together with a matched George III silver heater base, on tripod legs.

Pot 1799   *11.25in (28.5cm) high*

£300-400   **TOV**

A George IV silver coffee pot, by Robert Garrard, London, the hinged slightly domed cover with flower finial, swan-necked fluted spout, resting on a simple foot rim chased with foliate and shell borders.

1825   *9in (23cm) high 27oz*

£400-500   **L&T**

A William IV silver coffee pot, Charles Fox, London, of baluster form, chased with scrollwork, shells and foliage with a scroll handle and a domed cover with cast foliate finial, crested.

1833   *11in (28cm) high 35oz*

£650-850   **TEN**

A late Victorian silver coffee pot stand and burner, by W & J Barnard, London, the coffee pot of bellied circular outline with fluted upper section, the everted rim with gadrooned and shell border, with simple C-scroll wooden handle, resting in a circular frame with reeded border with three strap work legs on paw feet, with circular support to base enclosing burner.

1891   *9.5in (24cm) high 42oz*

£450-550   **L&T**

A George III four piece silver tea service, William Burwash & Richard Sibley, London, with part-fluted, circular bodies and gadrooned borders comprising a teapot, milk jug, sugar bowl and hot water jug on stand with burner, crested.

1812   *97oz*

£2,500-3,500   **WW**

A George IV silver three piece tea service, Robert Gray & Sons, Glasgow, comprising teapot, twin-handled sugar bowl and a cream jug, each of circular outline with tapering bodies, all with convex fluted lower sections with upper gadrooned rims and simple circular foot rims with simple borders.

1821-22   *Teapot 6.25in (16cm) high*

£1,000-1,500   **L&T**

A George III silver coffee and tea service, Paul Storr, London, comprising a large spirit samovar, a coffee pot, a teapot and a twin handled sugar bowl, each of circular form with scrolling floral and rosette border with flower head details to rim and gadrooned fluting to lower section, the handles of all with Classical mask socket mounts and curved scroll handles, together with a matched hot milk jug in a similar style.

1816-17   *Coffee pot 10.5in (27cm) high 262oz*

£25,000-30,000   **L&T**

A matched five piece tea and coffee set, tea and coffee pot Sheffield, water jug London, of pear form, the domed lids, with spreading foot.

Teapot 1829   *Set 86oz overall*

£1,000-1,500   **HT**

A George IV three-piece silver-gilt tea service, by Paul Storr, London, stamped 'Storr & Mortimer', comprising a teapot, a milk jug, a twin-handled sugar bowl, bellied bodies, with scalloped everted shell detailed rims, S-scroll handles.

1828-29   *Teapot 7in (18cm) high 56oz*

£5,000-6,000   **L&T**

A William IV silver three piece tea service, Elder & Co., Edinburgh, J. Hamilton & Co., comprising teapot, milk jug and sugar bowl.

1832-35   *Teapot 7in (18cm) high*

£1,000-1,500   **L&T**

A Victorian four piece silver Rococo Revival tea service, Elkington & Co. Ltd, Birmingham, comprising teapot, coffee pot, sugar basin, milk jug.

1893   Coffee pot 11in (27.5cm) h 92oz

£1,200-1,800   **TEN**

An American sterling silver three-piece chocolate set, by Arthur Stone, with chased detail, stamped 'A STONE STERLING T'.

Chocolate pot 9.5in (24cm) high

£6,000-7,000   **DRA**

An American sterling silver faceted coffee set, Kalo, with pot, creamer and sugar, stamped 'STERLING ... KALO', 'J.M.G. 18 February 1939'.

Coffee pot 10in (25.5cm) high

£2,000-3,000   **DRA**

METALWARE

A George III silver hot water jug, Charles Wright, London, the pedestal foot supporting a vase-shaped body chased with husk swags, with a wickered scroll handle and domed cover with button finial, crested.

1773   11in (28cm) high 24oz
£700-1,000   **TEN**

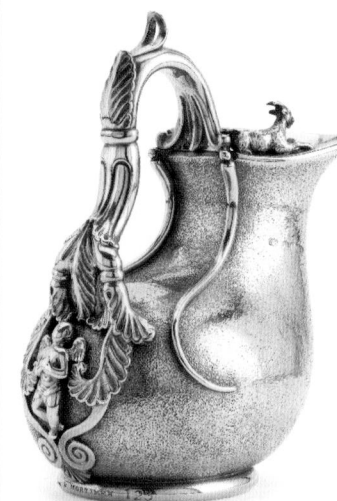

A William IV silver ewer, Paul Storr, London, 1835-36, of ascos form, in a modern fitted case.

The ascos jug follows an ancient Greek prototype used as a receptacle for the oil burnt in lamps, Its unusual form is derived from early examples which were fashioned from leather.

1835-36   8.75in (22cm) high 32oz
£5,000-6,000   **L&T**

An early Victorian Scottish novelty silver claret jug, James Howden & Company, Edinburgh, naturalistically formed as a seated fox with paw raised on a branch.

1844-45   11.75in (30cm) high 54oz
£10,000-15,000   **L&T**

A Victorian silver gilt ewer, Edward Barnard & Sons, London, the body chased with rinceau bordering two strapwork cartouches, one vacant, the other chased with a horse race, the domed cover with a horse and jockey finial.

1868   12in (30.5cm) high 40oz
£2,000-3,000   **TEN**

A pair of Victorian Grecian-style silver ewers, by Francis Boone Thomas, London, in the form of Grecian winged sphinxes, on rectangular bases, with engraved side panels depicting male and female figures, the trumpet-shaped silver-gilt rim also engraved with Grecian figures, loop pattern handles.

1875   9.75in (25cm) high
£5,500-6,500   **A&G**

An early Victorian silver-gilt bottle stand with an associated green glass hock bottle and stopper, Paul Storr, London, the matt body finely chased with pierced panels of trellis-work and quatrefoils alternating with bands of flowering foliage, applied with a scrolling cartouche with mirrored cipher 'H de G' below a coronet.

1837-38   Stand 5.25in (13.5cm) h 11oz
£4,000-5,000   **L&T**

An early Victorian silver-gilt mounted claret jug, Reilly and Storer, London, the rich green bulbous glass body with a silver-gilt vine leaf handle, the hinged cover with vine leaves and grapes, the whole body clasped with vine branch tendrils, the front with socket for a wine label, all on a simple circular foot.

1849-50　　　　*11.75in (30cm) high*

£2,500-3,500　　　　　**L&T**

A pair of Victorian silver-gilt mounted frosted glass claret jugs, John Samuel Hunt, London, the silver-gilt handle of natural branch form onto a vine branch clasping the neck, with hinged plain domed cover with vine and grape finial, the lower part of the body with vine leaf and grapes, the base with a solid rim and further branch detail with leaves.

John Samuel Hunt was the nephew of the famous silversmith Paul Storr. From 1810 he worked for Storr & Co. as a silversmith, and in 1826 he was taken on as the third partner, along with Paul Storr and John Mortimer. He remained with the company, which was known as Mortimer & Hunt from 1838, and Hunt & Roskell from 1843.

A George II silver cream boat, by Paul de Lamerie, London, the baluster body with chased floral garlands and foliate detail, the scalloped rim and large curved lip with finely chased scroll and foliate details, with simple s-scroll naturalistically formed handle.

1744-45　　　　*3in (7.5cm) high 4.5oz*

£4,500-5,500　　　　　**L&T**

1852-53　　　　*13.75in (35cm) high*

£13,000-18,000　　　　　**L&T**

A George II silver helmet cream jug, Robert Innes, London, with a heavy gadrooned rim, a cast serpent handle, a circular foot and embossed decoration, crested.

1752　　　　*4in (10cm) high 5.5oz*

£450-550　　　　　**WW**

A George III silver baluster cream jug, Thomas Shepherd, London, embossed with pastoral scenes and a swimming swan, below a punch beaded rim, central cartouche, crested.

1778　　　　*4.5in (12cm) high 3.5oz*

£250-350　　　　　**WW**

A silver repoussé creamer, Andrew Ellicot Warner (1786-1870, Baltimore, Maryland), the sides chased and embossed with chinoiserie motifs including pagodas, boat scenes and dense scrolled foliage, the shield-shaped cartouche below spout, angled ribbed handle with grape cluster terminals, marked 'A.E. Warner' in serrated rectangle, and '11' and an underlined '8'.

5.75in (14.5cm) high

£1,500-2,000　　　　　**SK**

METALWARE

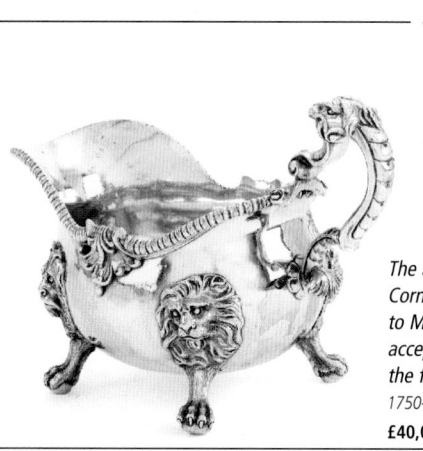

A pair of George II sauceboats, Paul de Lamerie, London, with scrolling shell detail and engraved armorial under the spout, with muscular S-scroll handle and lion mask terminal, raised on four claw and ball feet with large sweeping lion mask terminal, one with engraved scratch weight of 23=5 in contemporary script to side of base.

The arms of Richard, 1st Baron Edgcumbe of Mount Edgcumbe, Devonshire and Cotehele, Cornwall. M.P. for Cornwall, he was created a peer in 1742, he died in 1758. The family moved to Mount Edgcumbe in the 17thC, but they continued to own Cotehele until 1947 when it was accepted by the treasury in payment of death duty and given to the National Trust. This was the first property in Britain to be acquired by Trust via the 'in lieu of death duty' route.
1750-51   *9in (23cm) wide 42oz*
£40,000-50,000   **L&T**

A pair of George II oval sauceboats, Peze Pilleau, London, with moulded rims, leaf-capped scroll handles, raised on stepped oval bases.
1758   *9in (22.5cm) wide 35oz*
£1,800-2,200   **WW**

A pair of Irish provincial silver sauceboats, Carden Terry, Cork, bellied with flying scroll handle, bead border, crested, on three feet.
c1780   *6.75in (17.5cm) long*
16.2oz
£3,000-4,000   **WW**

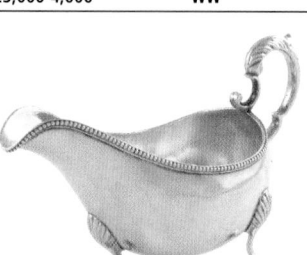

A George III Irish silver sauceboat, M. West, with bead borders, scrolling handle, crested.

1789   *7in (8cm) long 10oz*
£550-650   **WW**

A Classical coin silver presentation pitcher, John B. Jones, Boston, the pitcher with double scroll case handle, rectangular in section with applied leaf on top, bands of gadrooning on rim, middle and base, marked 'J.B. Jones' on base, the side engraved with the names of five generations of men by the name of Dexter residing in or around Boston, Massachusetts.
1782-1855   *9.75in (25cm) high*
£800-1,200   **SK**

A George III silver cow creamer, John Schuppe, London, the body with hair detail, the cover engraved floral spray border with a bee, engraved to the haunch 'JhC' and engraved date beside the hallmark '1757'.
1757-58   *6in (15cm) long 4.5oz*
£4,000-5,000   **L&T**

A George III silver cow creamer, John Schuppe, London, the body with hair detail to the neck and back, the cover with chased floral spray border with a bee.
1757-58   *5.75in (14.5cm) long 4oz*
£4,500-5,500   **L&T**

A George III cow creamer, John Schuppe, London, modelled with hair detail to the body, traditional bee to the cover and engraved floral border.

1761-62   5.75in (14.5cm) long 4oz

£5,000-6,000   L&T

ESSENTIAL REFERENCE – COW CREAMERS

From the late 17thC, two sorts of tea were available in Europe: a green unfermented tea, and a cheaper, black fermented variety, which could be taken with milk or cream, and sugar. Tea accessories, such as cream jugs and sugar bowls, were widely made in silver, pottery and porcelain. The earliest silver cream jug was plain and pitcher-shaped. But by the mid-18thC more elaborate vessels were being produced, such as cream-boasts (smaller versions of sauceboats) and cow creamers, which memorably feature in P.G. Wodehouse's 1938 novel 'The Code of the Woosters'.

- Cow creamers have a covered opening on their back, which allows the vessel to be filled with cream. The cow's mouth forms the spout, and the tail looped over the back as a handle. Some examples have hair detailing, whilst others are smooth, and many have bees perched on their backs.
- The cow creamer enjoyed only brief popularity, and it seems likely that none were produced from c1770. True Georgian examples are, therefore, rare and collectable. A century later, the Dutch revived the form for tourist souveniers.
- Silver cow creamers were created almost exclusively by one London-based silversmith, John Schuppe (active 1753-73), who was possibly of Dutch origin.
- Cow creamers were also made in porcelain and pottery.

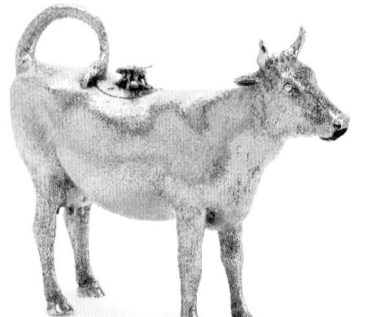

A Victorian silver cow creamer, George Fox, London, modelled with hair detail to the body, traditional bee finial to the cover.

1865-66   6.25in (16cm) long 6oz

£3,500-4,500   L&T

SILVER BOXES

A late Victorian scroll presentation casket, Edwards & Sons, Glasgow, with applied sporting emblems, domed section with finial of a sportsman with gun and dog, original case.

Inscription to border cartouche reads 'Presented to Captain John Gilmour ... 22nd May 1888'.

1887-88   10.25in (26cm) wide

£1,500-2,000   L&T

A late 19thC/early 20thC silver musical bird table box, the lid embossed with a putti band with birds, scroll and flower background, the hinged cover opening to reveal an animated bird with pierced scroll grill, stamped to base '800', together with bird finial key.

4.25in (10.5cm) wide

£2,000-3,000   L&T

A presentation casket, probably by J. Forrest, Glasgow, retailed by Whytock & Sons Dundee, panels decorated with official buildings and coats of arms, with inscription and Dundee coat of ams as finial, in fitted case.

The inscription reads 'Presented by, The City of Dundee, to The Right Honourable Sir John Gilmour Bart ...10th October 1928'.

1928-29   11.75in (30cm) wide

£2,000-2,500   L&T

A George III silver tea caddy, probably Charles Wright, London, with engraved borders of intertwined branch and garlands with star motifs between, with bright cut oval cartouche to centre below key hole with a crest of a pelican in piety, with well formed branch foliate and flower head finial.

1774   3.75in (9.5cm) diam 10oz

£2,500-3,500   L&T

A George III silver oval tea caddy, William Vincent, London, with bead borders and engraved floral bands around the body, vase shaped finial, crested.

1783   5in (13cm) wide   12.5oz

£650-750   WW

METALWARE

A George III silver octagonal tea caddy, by Walter Tweedie, London, the domed hinge lid with carved ivory knop finial, the body engraved with foliate garlands between foliate bands.

1784   *5.5in (14cm) high*

£1.000-1,500   **TOV**

A George III silver tea caddy, Hester Bateman, London, of cylindrical oval form with bright engraved fleur-de-lys and flowerhead borders, the centre of the body engraved with a canted rectangular cartouche with stylised flower head borders, with crest of a dragon looking left, the flush hinged cover with green stained carved ivory pineapple finial.

1785-86   *4.25in (11cm) wide*

£3,500-4,500   **L&T**

A Victorian silver tea caddy, Reilly and Storer, London, of serpentine bombé form, with floral finial to the Chinoiserie decorated pull off cover, one side with a coat of arms and motto 'Benefictorum Memorum' (mindful of favours), all within a C-scroll and floral cartouche, engraved to the underside 'From Mrs. Temple to her niece Mrs. Kelham'.

1851-52   *5.25in (13.5cm) high 14oz*

£1,500-2,000   **L&T**

SILVER CADDY SPOONS

A George III silver caddy shovel, Samuel Davenport, London, with a green-stained ivory handle, crested bowl.

1791

£80-120   **WW**

A George III silver mounted natural shell caddy spoon, Matthew Linwood, Birmingham, with a bifurcated, Thread pattern stem, maker's mark.

c1800

£1,500-2,000   **WW**

A George III silver vined leaf caddy spoon, London, with a coiled wire handle.

1801

£100-150   **WW**

A George III silver engraved leaf caddy spoon, Elizabeth Morley, London, with a wire tendril handle.

1802

£150-200   **WW**

A Victorian silver naturalistic caddy spoon, Hilliard & Thomason, Birmingham, with a host of embossed shells in the bowl and applied lily leaves up the stem.

c1852

£400-500   **WW**

A Victorian silver caddy spoon, Francis Higgins, London, with gilt shell bowl, shaped scrolling stem, oval cartouche, monogrammed.

1855   *4.25in (10.5cm) long*

£150-200   **WW**

A Victorian silver caddy spoon, George Unite, Birmingham, openwork tendril handle, gilt shell-shaped bowl.

1859

£150-200   **WW**

A late Victorian silver spoon, J.N. Mappin for Mappin & Webb, London, with an openwork handle and a plain scoop bowl.

1894   *4.5in (11cm) long 1oz*

£120-180   **WW**

CLOSER LOOK – SILVER ENTRÉE DISHES

Benjamin Smith II was active from 1791-1822 and was one of the most innovative silversmiths of the period.

From 1802-7, in partnership with the designer Digby Scott, he directed the workshops of the royal silversmiths Rundell Bridge & Rundell. The company, which was based in Greenwich, south London, made silverwares for the royal family and other wealthy patrons.

Smith was renowned for making smaller pieces of silverware such as salvers, trays, teasets and these entrée dishes.

A set of four George III 'Rutland Marine Service' silver entrée dishes, covers and liners, Benjamin Smith II, London, the body with a band of peacocks alternating with anthemion and wheat ears, the cover with a cast band of palmettes and flowers on a matted ground, the finial formed as four dolphins above a cast band of grapevine and Bacchanalian masks, engraved on each side with a crest within a garter motto beneath a Duke's coronet, the cover engraved on each side with a Duke's armorials, numbered 1-4.

His work typically features delicate decoration such as the bands of peacocks, anthemion and wheat ears, palmettes and flowers, and grapes and masks seen on the covers.

1807 12.5in (32cm) long 523oz

£100,000-150,000 **L&T**

One of a pair of George III soup tureens, covers, liners and stands, Paul Storr, London, with gadrooned border with acanthus and shell details and reeded loop handles with shell points, the lower section raised on four scroll feet with acanthus terminals, and fluted shell feet, on an integral shaped oval stand, the upper level of stand with engraved crest of a squirrel within foliage, each with domed cover with reeded loop handle with lion mask terminal.

1807-08 17.25in (44cm) wide 406oz

£80,000-100,000 PAIR **L&T**

A George II silver tureen and cover, by Paul de Lamerie, London, of oval form, the stepped cover with fixed shell and leaf clasped handle on a scrolled fish scale decorated ground, the cover engraved with a crest and coronet, the serpentine oval base with bold scroll handles, engraved with armorials and raised on lion's legs with well modelled lion's head capitals.

1747-8 14.5in (37.5cm) wide 116oz

£50,000-60,000 **L&T**

A George III Warwick vase tureen and cover, Benjamin Smith II & Benjamin Smith Jnr III, London, of shallow kantharos form, body with a calyx of acanthus banding, typical masks, handles formed as intertwined vine leaves, domed cover with engraved armorial, oak leaf and acorn border, rising platform with a figure of a lion, finial part marked for Benjamin Smith.

Engraved with the shield of the Lancashire family of Peel, who included Sir Robert Peel (1788-1850), who twice served as Prime Minister.

1817-18 16.5in (42cm) high overall 242oz

£30,000-40,000 **L&T**

METALWARE

ESSENTIAL REFERENCE – SALVERS

Salvers – flat, handleless dishes used to serve food or drink – are typically silver or plated. If a salver has a single foot or pedestal it can be known as a tazza or 'footed salver'.

- The earliest salvers, dating from the mid-17thC, were made from thin-gauge metal, raised on a central foot. They were used as stands for porringers or caudle cups, and the finest were gidled and chased in the Dutch Baroque style. Heavier-gauge metal was used c1680-c1720.
- From the 1720s the central foot was generally replaced by three or four small cast (usually bracket) feet. Moulded and applied rims of convex and concave curves were common.
- Salvers dating from the 1740s are typically circular or five- or six-sided, and are often centrally engraved with armorials. They also feature strapwork and interlacing scrolls.
- From the mid-18thC, asymmetrical Rococo designs were used, with elaborate borders sometimes cast separately. At this time, salvers were greatly in demand for carrying tea and coffee services. Smaller versions, known as 'waiters' (less than 8in or 20cm in diam) were made, and sets of two or more salvers were common.
- The Neo-classical period saw more restrained borders on salvers. The Regency period produced large, heavy, often silver-gilt examples, with paw feet. During the 19thC, salvers in 18thC styles were popular, thought the decoration is more elaborate in these later examples.

One of a pair of George II silver waiters, Paul de Lamerie, London, of shaped circular outline with reeded border, scroll and shell points, the flat finely chased with a border of scroll and shell detail, flanked by cartouches of cross hatched fine stipple chasing, the centre engraved with detailed armorial, all raised on four acanthus bracket feet.

Original scratch weights engraved to underside, 'No 1, 13 = 4' and 'No 4, 13-0'. The arms are those of Lamb of Higham, Sussex.

1738-39   *7.5in (19cm) diam 26oz*

£30,000-40,000 PAIR   L&T

A pair of George II silver salvers, John Tuite, London, with a shell and scroll rim, raised on four leaf-capped scroll feet, inscribed 'No 1 33=15' and 'No 2 35=12'.

1739   *12in (30.5cm) diam 61oz*

£2,000-3,000   TEN

A George II silver salver, James Kerr, Edinburgh, Assay Master Edward Lothian, with everted scroll and shell detail border, the centre engraved with a crest and motto, raised on four scroll and hoof feet.

The crest and motto are for Murray.

1743-44   *8.75in (22cm) diam 14oz*

£800-1,200   L&T

A pair of George II 'Anson Service' silver circular serving dishes, Paul de Lamerie, London, with bold gadroon rims with leaves at intervals, the borders engraved with contemporary arms.

Engraved to rear with scratch weights: 42=19 and 45=7. The arms are those of Anson quartering Carrier for George Anson (1697-1762), 1st Baron Anson, the famous Admiral who circumnavigated the globe in four years and acquired Spanish Treasure to the value of approximately half a million pounds, from 1751 till his death in 1762 he was First Lord of the Admiralty.

1746-47   *12.5in (31.5cm) diam 86oz*

£25,000-30,000   L&T

A George III silver salver, John Scofield, London, with a beaded rim on four bracket feet, crested.

1780   *22in (56cm) long 130oz*

£4,000-5,000   TEN

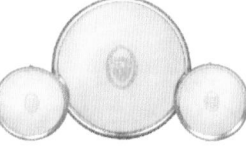

A suite of three George III silver salvers, Thomas Hannam & John Crouch, London, on large and two smaller, circular, with bead borders and beaded bracket feet, engraved coat of arms.

1784-5   *Largest 15.75in (40cm) diam 84oz*

£6,000-8,000   WW

A Royal Presentation silver-gilt tray, to H.R.H. Ernest Augustus, Duke of Cumberland, Digby Scott and Benjamin Smith, London, of oval form, raised on four substantial mask, scroll and crouching satyr supports, the central engraved armorial within a scrolling foliate border, the rim boldly cast with vine leaves, grapes, tendrils and fruit, ribbon tied berried laurel rim, the handles formed as rytons flanking a panther mask.

1805 *29.5in (75cm) wide*
250.5oz

£140,000-160,000 **L&T**

A pair of George III silver-gilt tazza, Digby Scott and Benjamin Smith, London, of circular form, the circular foot with chased band of oak leaves and acorns, the dish with a border of open work vine leaves and bunches of grapes, engraved to the centre with a coat of arms and motto.

1805 *12.5in (31.5cm) diam 104oz*

£60,000-80,000 **L&T**

A named Lloyds Patriotic Fund vase and cover, Benjamin Smith, London, with the original fitted oak case with inset brass name plaque and trade label to the lid interior.

1807-08 *15.25in (39cm) high 123oz*

£40,000-50,000 **L&T**

A George III Warwick vase and stand, Paul Storr, London, the twin-handled vase of shallow kantharos form, the body chased with a calyx of acanthus banding to the lower half and with typical masks, lion pelts, clubs and spears, the handles formed as intertwined vine leaves.

1815-16 *20in (51cm) high 352oz*

£40,000-50,000 **L&T**

A silver oval sweetmeat basket, William Plummer, London, with fret work body embossed with swags, swing handle.

1774   6in (5.5cm) long 3.8oz
£250-350   WW

A George III silver cake basket, William Plummer, London, with a swing handle and bead borders, the sides pierced and embossed with foliate festoons and paterae, pierced foot and engraved coat of arms.

1776   13.75in (35cm) long 31oz
£1,800-2,200   WW

A George III silver basket, by William Abdy, London, oval with a bright cut and pierced border of classical ornament, with a swing handle, beaded borders throughout, crested.

1780   14in (35.5cm) long 30oz
£1,800-2,200   TEN

A George III silver swing handled sugar basket, William Vincent, London, of navette outline with a wavy rim and pedestal base, crested.

1789   6.25in (16cm) wide 9oz
£300-350   WW

A George III Irish silver bright cut sugar basket, Richard Sawyer, Dublin, the boat-shaped body with an oval stem foot, and swing handle.

1806   9oz
£1,500-2,000   MEA

A Victorian silver sugar basket, D.C. Hands, London, with a vine leaf and grape decorated swing handle, the basket with well-pierced and reticulated sides with game birds in tree branches, a cartouche engraved with a crest, the base of small open scrolls, with a blue glass liner.

1853-54   7in (18cm) high 8oz
£500-600   L&T

A pair of Victorian comports, Charles S. Harris, London, the baskets with embossed and chased floral decoration with pierced details, with spreading oval foot with reticulated and pierced floral decoration.

1888   7.5in (19cm) wide 8oz each
£350-450   L&T

A small Charles II silver porringer, London, chased with a frieze of stylised leaves below the pricked initials 'W.P', base chased with grapes, maker's mark 'IC'.

1675   2.75in (7cm) high 3.5oz
£1,800-2,200   WW

A small Queen Anne silver porringer, London, with reeded scroll handles, the body embossed with part-fluting, a moulded rope girdle and stamped with rows of repeating leaf motifs, with a large circular cartouche on one side, crested.

1713   3in (8cm) diam 2.75oz
£500-600   WW

A Philadelphia silver baptismal bowl, Joseph Richardson, Sr, marked 'IR' on base and inscribed 'Presented to Howard D. Potts, by His Mother Jan. 14th, 1875'.

c1760
£3,500-4,500   POOK

CLOSER LOOK – JOHN BRIDGE DESSERT BOWL

John Bridge came to the notice of George III and found such favour that the company, Rundell & Bridge, est. 1785, became Jewellers and Goldsmiths to the King.

Drawing on the Greek Classics, the shell shaped bowl makes a natural container for food.

The design is thought to have been inspired by the Marine Service, supplied to Frederick, Prince of Wales in the 1740s.

A similar set of four silver-gilt dessert bowls with covers were made for the Royal Collection by John Bridge 1826-27.

A George IV silver dessert bowl, by John Bridge for Rundell, Bridge and Rundell, London, the large clam shell with a surmount of a twin-tailed triton blowing a conch, the shell supported by three hippocamps in a wild sea setting and supported by three groups of clam shells, coral and turtles.

1824-25   *16.5in (42cm) wide 343oz*

£100,000-150,000   **L&T**

A George III Royal silver-gilt cream pail and ladle, Paul Storr, London, the pail of coopered form, simple loop handle, engraved with a coronet and monogram, also with an engraved initial in an oval to the underside, the ladle modelled as a smaller pail, similarly coopered and with an upright handle of shaped form.

1795-96   Pail 4.75in (12cm) high

£7,000-9,000   **L&T**

A George III silver and wood quaich, Peter Aitchison, Edinburgh, the turned wooden bowl with silver mounts chased with a border of thistles, the lug handles inset with wood.

By repute, the wood comes from a holly tree that Queen Mary sat under in the gardens of Holyrood Palace.

c1810–20   *4.5in (11.5cm) long*

£900-1,200   **TEN**

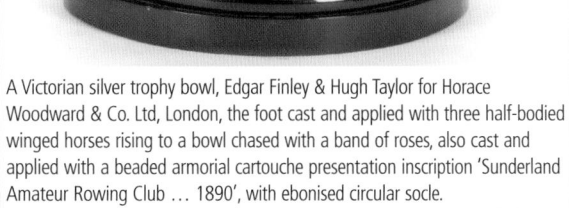

A Victorian silver trophy bowl, Edgar Finley & Hugh Taylor for Horace Woodward & Co. Ltd, London, the foot cast and applied with three half-bodied winged horses rising to a bowl chased with a band of roses, also cast and applied with a beaded armorial cartouche presentation inscription 'Sunderland Amateur Rowing Club … 1890', with ebonised circular socle.

1889   *12.5in (31.5cm) high excluding plinth 106oz*

£5,000-6,000   **TEN**

A large silver and silver gilt rose bowl, Goldsmith & Silversmith Co., London, the half reeded body profusely chased with scrolling foliage on a domed stem base.

1895   10in (25.5cm) high 28oz

£1,500-2,000   MEA

A late Victorian silver monteith, by W, J, M, S Barnard & R Dubock, London, with lion mask and angular ring handles, concave fluted lower section, the cartouches engraved with scene of a Church, the base engraved with retailer's mark for 'James Aitchison Edinburgh'.

1896   12.25in (31cm) diam 94oz

£3,500-4,500   L&T

A large Edwardian silver Monteith, Carrington & Co., London, with lion mask, shell and scroll handles with inscription relating to the 'Griff Colliery Co.'

1905   12in (30.5cm) high 72oz

£2,000-3,000   GORL

ESSENTIAL REFERENCE – PAUL DE LAMERIE

French-born Paul de Lamerie (1688-1751) was one of the most prominent silversmiths in 18thC Britain. He produced some of the best English Rococo pieces, but his output was large and not all his pieces are outstanding.

- **In 1703 he began his apprenticeship in London under Pierre Platel, the well known Huguenot silversmith, and in 1713 he registered his first mark at Goldsmiths' Hall.**

- **He was appointed goldsmith to George I in 1716 with offices in Windmill Street, St James's, later transferring to Gerrard Street, Soho in 1738. At this time he worked in the stark Queen Anne style, and the heavy cast Huguenot style.**

- **By the 1730s he was producing an individual version of the Rococo style, combining it with earlier styles.**

A set of four George II silver cauldron salts, Paul de Lamerie, London, with gilt interiors, the bodies applied with four shell motifs between scroll terminals on scroll legs with hoof feet and beaded rim, engraved to the underside with a crest with coronet above.

1741-42   3in (7.5cm) diam 5.5oz each

£8,500-10,500   L&T

A set of four George II silver open salts, by Edward Wood, London, the simple shallow bowls with moulded rim and on reeded and knopped squat stem, the stepped foot rim with moulded edge.

The bowls engraved with a later crest of a lion rampant.

1731   3in (7.5cm) diam Combined weight 12oz

£700-900   L&T

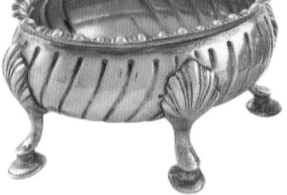

A pair of George III silver salts, R & D Hennell, oval outline, swirled fluted bodies, gadrooned borders, gilt interiors, on four stepped feet.

1769-71   5.3oz

£120-180   WW

A pair of Victorian silver figural salts, John S. Hunt, London, modelled as a standing boy and girl dressed in country dress, both with wicker baskets, he with a bunch of grapes, she with a rose, cartouche with a crest and on circular disc feet, engraved to foot rim 'Hunt & Roskell late Storr and Mortimer' and numbered '2776'.

1864   *7.25in (18.5cm) high 44oz*

£10,000-12,000   **L&T**

A set of four Victorian cast silver and parcel gilt figural salts, Robert Garrand, London, each cast as a group of three mermaids supporting a shell and raised on a naturalistic rockwork base.

1853-54   *10.5in (27cm) high 145oz*

£40,000-50,000   **L&T**

A Victorian standing silver figural salt, Charles Frederick Hancock, London, the central figure of a standing lady dressed in 19thC cycling clothes, with a flared skirt, trousers and a tightly buttoned tunic, carrying a small barrel on a strap, her hat tied in a bow, she is flanked by a pannier to each side, all on a rocky outcrop.

1866   *8.25in (21cm) high*

£3,000-4,000   **L&T**

A pair of George III cruet frames, by Paul Storr, London, the bases with heavy cast foliate and shell border with integral twin foliate scroll handles, raised on four large foliate bracket feet with shell detail to centre, the frame with four foliate bracket supports with simple ring housing for bottles, the crystal bottles with diamond-cut upper panels and faceted lower section.

1816-17   *12.25in (31cm) high Heavier 74oz*

£40,000-50,000 PAIR   **L&T**

ESSENTIAL REFERENCE – BARNARD & SONS

Barnard & Sons is one of Britain's oldest silversmiths, with origins that can be traced back to Anthony Nelme's company founded in c1680.

- In 1829 Edward Barnard I, who had worked for the firm from the late 18thC, became the proprietor, with his son Edward Barnard II, John Barnard and William Barnard. They traded under the name Edward Barnard & Sons and registered their mark later that year.
- Barnard & Sons also produced electroplate and even supplied silvered plates for daguerreotypes.
- Their key sales items were formal dining ware and commemorative pieces.
- After the retirement of Edward Barnard I in 1846, the company continued under Edward II, John and William.
- Edward II was the father of the artist Frederick Barnard. William Barnard was grandfather to the artist Elinor M. Barnard.
- The firm became a limited liability company in 1910.
- In 1977 Edward Barnard & Sons Limited became a subsidiary of Padgett & Braham Ltd.
- Much of the company's archieve was recently donated to the Victoria and Albert Museum in London.

A large early Victorian silver Warwick cruet, Edward I, Edward II, John and William Barnard, London, the frame of four eagle's masks, acanthus and claw and ball feet, with central baluster handle and reeded shell, scroll handle, the front with a foliate scroll and diaper work cartouche, engraved with a coat of arms, fitted with three octagonal lidded casters, two silver-mounted cut glass bottles.

The arms are those of Darby with grant in pretence for Francis Darby Esq., of Sunniside House, Coalbrookdale, Shropshire, and his wife Hannah, only daughter of John Grant. Francis Darby was the son of Abraham Darby who, with John Wilkinson, designed and constructed the Iron Bridge over the River Severn at Coalbrookdale.

1838-39   15.25in (39cm) high 110oz

£15,000-20,000   **L&T**

SILVER DESKSTANDS

A George I silver desk stand, Courtauld, London, the tray engraved with armorial to opposing sides, centrally applied with simple raised stand with pull-out drawer and applied with three moulded stands for chalk pot, inkwell and table bell, all engraved with crest with coronet above.

Drawers in inkstands are unusual. Engraved scratch weight to underside of tray 80-10. Engraved with the Arms of Thomas Howard, 8th Duke of Norfolk, the boxes and bell with the crest and Ducal coronet for the Dukes of Norfolk.

1721-22   12.25in (31cm) wide 76oz

£18,000-20,000   **L&T**

A George IV silver gilt travelling inkwell, John Reily, London, square with cast and applied foliate borders, an oval cover with hinged cast shell thumbpiece, engraved 'AR' beneath a baronial coronet.

1824   2.5in (6.5cm) long 6oz

£600-800   **TEN**

A Victorian silver partners' desk stand, by Henry Wilkinson & Co, Sheffield, with two faceted glass baluster bottles, one inkwell and other powder pot, with foliate scroll borders and central chamber stick on stand.

1853   13in (33cm) wide

£1,000-1,500   **L&T**

A mid-Victorian silver partners' desk stand, by C T Fox & G Fox, London, with glass inkwells with simple hinged circular covers, the centre with a chalk pot with engraved arched decoration with flower head detail.

1856   12.25in (31cm) wide

£800-1,200   **L&T**

A Victorian silver inkstand, Lamberts, London, the circular base with a cast openwork trellis border and gadrooned rim, supporting a spherical glass well with pierced and engraved mounts.

1897   7in (18cm) diam

£300-400   **TEN**

An Edwardian novelty silver inkwell, by Samson Mordon & Company, London, formed as a sedan chair, the front hinged to reveal a moulded glass inkwell within, on four scroll feet.

1906   3.75in (9.5cm) high

£800-1,200   **L&T**

A George III/IV silver provincial wine label, James Barber & William Whitwell, York, of waisted oblong outline, with an embossed border of roses and other flowers, incised 'CLARET'.
1820
£400-500   **WW**

A George IV silver decorative wine label, with a border of roses, thistles, shamrock, grapes and two inverted leopard masks, pierced 'MADEIRA' marks partially lost in piercing, London.
c1825
£400-500   **WW**

A George IV Irish silver wine label, Dublin, of rounded oblong form with a bright-cut border, incised 'PORT', maker 'JS'.
1825-1830
£250-300   **WW**

A George IV silver cast wine label, Edward Farrell, London, in the form of a scallop shell, pierced 'MADEIRA'.
1827
£800-1,200   **WW**

CLOSER LOOK

Used to hang around the neck of a bottle or decanter to identify the contents, wine labels are also known as 'bottle tickets'.

The stamped floral motif is typical of the designs used on drinking accessories: grapes and vines are also commonly found.

The embossing is highly decorative and desirable.

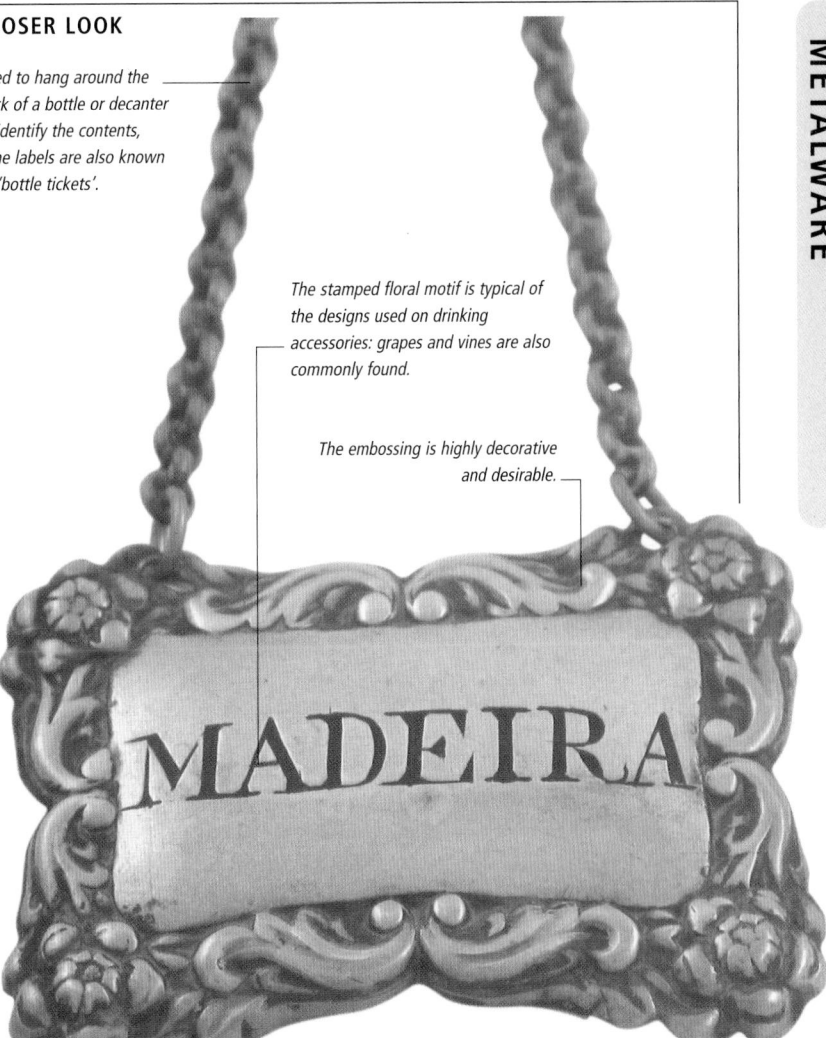

The thistle mark was used by Edinburgh assay office from 1759 to 1975.

The additional marks indicate Peterhead regional assay office.

A rare George IV Scottish silver provincial label, W. Ferguson, Peterhead, with a stamped floral scroll border, incised and infilled 'MADEIRA', with additional Edinburgh marks.
1826
£3,000-4,000   **WW**

METALWARE

A Scottish provincial mustard pot, William G. Jamieson, Edinburgh, everted scalloped rim, with S-scroll handle and hinged domed lid, raised on three shell terminal scroll feet, marked 'W. G. J. ABD'.

1898-99   2.75in (7cm) high 2oz

£180-220   **L&T**

A silver dish ring, Nathan & Hayes, Chester, of typical form with pierced and chased decoration of wading birds, foxes and dolphins amidst reeds and vines, and a vacant Rococo cartouche.

1911   8.5in (21.5cm) diam 17oz 1dwt

£500-600   **TEN**

A Scottish silver provincial mustard pot, A McLeod, Inverness, the reticulated sides with arched design with engraved detail and border of pierced alternating circles and diamonds, with a light blue glass liner, with an angular S-scroll handle, the lid with engraved scroll and cross hatched border and simple scroll thumbpiece, marked 'A.MC', 'INS' device stuck four times.

The marks struck to this piece are a newly recorded maker's punch for Alexander McLeod of Inverness previously recorded with maker's mark 'AML', 'AML' (M&L conjoined) or 'AMcL'. The maker's punch struck to this piece is also known struck 'A.MC, LEOD'. With the device mark struck four times this seems to suggest the maker is the same Alexander McLeod or a continuation of his firm.

                                    3in (7.5cm) high 3.5oz

£1,800-2,200   **L&T**

A George III silver pap boat, London, with reeded borders, maker's mark worn.

1807   5.25in (13cm) long 2oz

£80-120   **WW**

An Edwardian silver jewellery box, Goldsmiths & Silversmiths Co. Ltd., London, in the form of a bow-ront toilet mirror, with shield shaped mirror, velvet lined pull-out frieze drawer, on four feet.

1903   7.5in (18.5cm) high

£700-800   **WW**

A William and Mary silver chinoiserie toilet mirror, Anthony Nelme, London, with a wooden easel back, flat-chased with fruiting foliage and ho ho birds, with an applied fruiting leaf in each corner, the detachable cresting with a moulded scroll border and flat-chased scene with native figures, birds, foliage and the central feature of a viaduct with towers above a small building.

1690   20in (51cm) high

£20,000-30,000   **WW**

A life-size silver model of a standing owl, by Edward Charles Brown, London, well-modelled and detailed, inset with large glass eyes, the removable head revealing a gilt interior.

1869-70   13.5in (34.5cm) high 45oz

£15,000-20,000   **L&T**

A late Victorian silver owl table ornament, the owl of naturalistic form with embossed and engraved feathers and hinged wings, sitting on a simple branch-formed perch, on a domed naturalistic base with running lizard, with London import marks.

c1880   10.25in (26cm) high 17oz

£1,000-1,500   L&T

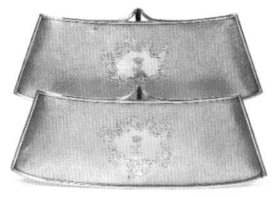

A pair of William IV silver rectangular lampshades, T J & N Creswick, Sheffield, with a matted ground, crested within a foliate reserve.

1837   15in (38cm) long 30oz

£550-650   TEN

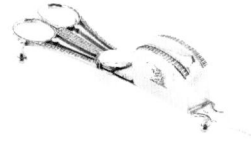

A pair of George III silver candle trimmers, William Bateman, London, the edges with feathered detail, engraved crest to the rear, all on three small circular feet.

The crest of Clavering Savage of Elmley Castle, Worcestershire.

1807-08   7in (17.5cm) long 3oz

£300-400   L&T

An 18thC German silver plaque, chased with military figures and horses within a woodland scene, engraved 'CZAPARY 1684', maker's mark 'CL, Danzig', in an ebonised and tortoiseshell frame.

10in (25.5cm) wide

£800-1,200   TEN

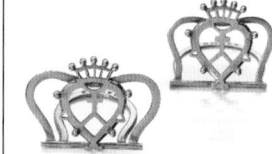

A cased pair of Victorian luckenbooth silver menu holders, J. M. Talbot, Edinburgh, the scroll base with scalloped scroll upright with applied conjoined luckenbooth hearts with simple crown above, contained within fitted case.

1900-01   1.25in (3cm) high 0.5oz

£200-300   L&T

A silver mounted ceremonial mallet, the bulbous wooden head applied with chased silver pendants and a plaque depicting two religious figures, the tapering silver handle chased with scrolling foliage.

c1880   9in (23cm) high

£300-400   TEN

A George IV silver-gilt table bell, John Edward Terrey, London, the cast body chased with shells, flowers and foliage, the handle formed as four plumes rising to a cushion knop surmounted by a finial formed as a marquess's coronet.

1820-21   5in (12.5cm) high 13oz

£4,500-5,500   L&T

A William IV silver toast rack, probably William Esterbrook, London, monogrammed below an ornate handle, shell border, with acanthus capped claw feet.

1831   7in (17.5cm) wide 15 oz

£700-1,000   RTC

A Victorian silver novelty pepperette, C. Saunders & F. Shepherd, Chester, in the form of a miniature side-handle coffee pot.

1896   1.75in (4.5cm) high

£120-180   WW

METALWARE

A brass bucket, of tapering form, with a swing handle.

19.5in (49.5cm) high

£200-250 **WW**

A Dutch copper and brass log bin, embossed with a pastoral scene, foliage and a crest, with lion mask ring handles, on tripod paw feet.

14in (35.5cm) high

£300-400 **WW**

A 19thC brass adjustable dog collar, engraved 'Lion, Arthur Manners', of plain cylindrical form with five piercements for adjustment.

6.5in (22cm) diam

£800-1,200 **TEN**

A large late 19thC brass ram's head wall mount, the head within an acorn leaf, berry and trailing ribbon surround.

29in (73cm) wide

£800-1,000 **L&T**

A brass bell, possibly by A.W.N. Pugin, of hemispherical form with trefoil-shaped circular section handle surmounted by a shaped finial above a fleur de lys section, the bell housing pierced with flowerheads above six bells mounted on a frame.

11.5in (29cm) high

£1,000-1,500 **TEN**

An 18thC pewter communion flagon, inscribed 'Auchtermuchty'.

1786 *11in (28cm) high*

£1,000-1,500 **L&T**

A late 18thC Scottish pewter tappit hen, of typical form.

11in (28cm) high

£350-450 **L&T**

A late 18thC Scottish pewter tappit hen, with indistinct initials lid.

11.5in (29cm) high

£500-600 **L&T**

A late 18thC Scottish pewter tappit hen, 'KWDG' and touchmarks.

11.75in (30cm) high

£250-350 **L&T**

A late 19thC Victorian black japanned, painted, parcel gilt and mother-of-pearl inset tea canister.

18in (46cm) high

£400-500 **DN**

A 19thC Pennsylvania tôleware coffee pot, with rare decoration of a yellow bird perched on a floral branch, all on a black ground.

11in (28cm) high

£2,500-3,500 **POOK**

A 19thC tôleware coffee pot, with yellow fruit decoration and ivory band.

10.75in (27.5cm) high

£2,200-2,800 **POOK**

THE GLASS MARKET

The glass market has changed little over the last year. An interest in rare and early drinking glasses continues as it has for several years. Of particular interest to collectors is the heavy baluster – a seminal form of the early 18th century – a trend that started earlier this year and that, at the time of writing, sees no signs of abating. As to their price, there has been a gradual increase as demand has steadily risen, but nothing spectacular.

Also in demand are rummers and early 19th century decanters. Decanters should have their original stopper; check that the design and decoration fit with that of the decanter itself and that the stopper fits the neck properly. The value of a decanter lacking its original stopper will be around half that of one retaining its original stopper.

Collectors continue to look for pieces that exhibit a high level of craftsmanship in their manufacture: the introduction and manipulation of air; colour and mercury twists within fragile stems; crafted knops and balusters; and drawn-out bowls and feet tend to be popular with collectors. Such pieces required a level of skill and craftsmanship that meant that they were made in small numbers and sold as luxury items in their day. They remain desirable and valuable pieces and continue to find buyers willing to pay for their longevity and beauty.

Early 19th century coloured glass represents particularly good value for money, especially Bristol green and blue examples. High prices continue to be paid for mid 19th century paperweights by factories such as Baccarat, St Louis and others, and original enamelled 'Mary Gregory' glasses.

Mid to late 19th century Bohemain glass continues to do well. Buyers are looking for pieces in excellent condition that show exceptional craftsmanship in every area of design and creation: from the blowing and casing of the glass to the level of detail in the cutting and polishing of the decoration. Running a thumb over the surface of the glass will show how deep the cutting is: the deeper and finer this is the better the quality of the piece is likely to be. Any engraving should add fine detail to the subject matter and create a sense of realism.

When buying glass, any damage should be avoided, as it will almost always lower value. Repairs are costly and will not increase value significantly.

An English heavy baluster wine glass, waisted bucket bowl with solid base, with cusp knop over teared inverted baluster and base knops, folded foot.
c1710-20   5.75in (14.5cm) high
£1,800-2,200   JH

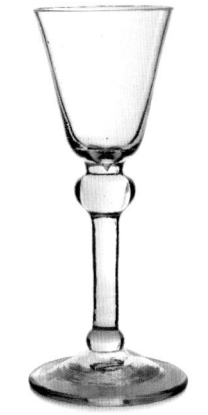

An English balustroid wine glass, the round funnel bowl over shoulder- and base-knopped stem.
c1730   6.75in (17cm) high
£450-550   JH

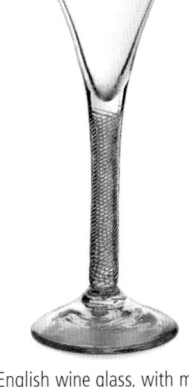

An English wine glass, with multi-spiral drawn trumpet bowl, and air-twist stem.
c1745   6.25in (15.5cm) high
£250-300   JH

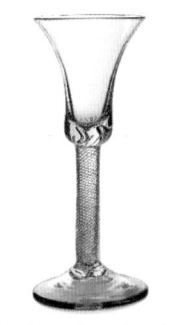

A bell-bowl two-piece wine glass, with multi-spiral air-twist stem emanating from the base of the bowl.
c1745   6.25in (16cm) high
£300-350   JH

An English wine glass, the bell bowl on a multi-spiral air-twist stem with shoulder and centre knops.
c1745   6.5in (16.5cm) high
£500-600   JH

GLASS

A round funnel bowl wine glass, on double series opaque twist stem with thick central core surrounded by two tapes.

c1755   5.75in (14.5cm) high

£250-300   **JH**

An 18thC wine glass, the rounded funnel bowl on hollow baluster short stem linked to an inverted bell-shape bowl with internal bell clapper.

c1750   10.25in (26cm) high

£550-750   **TEN**

A mid-18thC Jacobite-style wine glass, the straight-sided bowl engraved with a thistle and a six-pointed star, raised on a thick plain stem.

6in (15.5cm) high

£600-800   **WW**

A set of six possibly late 18thC similar green glass rummers, with round bowls on prunted hollow stems and conical feet.

4.5in (11.5cm) high

£300-400   **DN**

A small ovoid bowl wine glass, on double series opaque twist stem, pair of flat tapes surrounded by two multi ply bands, on an unusual tavern foot.

c1765   4.25in (10.5cm) high

£300-350   **JH**

An ogee-bowl wine glass, the bowl with polished circle and star band and petal-cut base, the diamond cut stem with central swelling knop.

c1765-75   5.75in (14.5cm) high

£250-300   **JH**

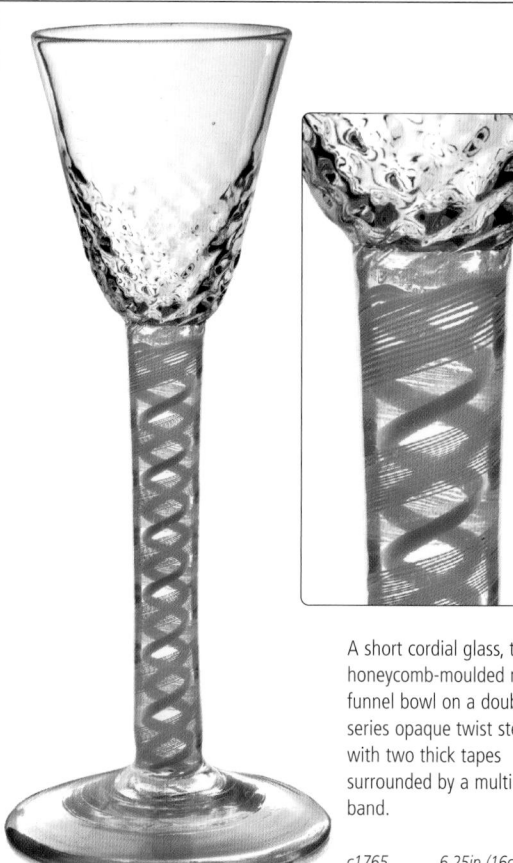

A late 18thC Bristol blue wine glass, possibly decorated by James Giles (1718-1780), enamelled and gilded with Neo-classical decoration, with small chip to rim.

4in (10cm) high

£250-300   **SWO**

A rare facet stem cordial glass, the ogee bowl with cutting to form a flower effect when looking into the bowl, rare shield-cut stem with central knop.

c1760   6.5in (16.5cm) high

£700-900   **JH**

A short cordial glass, the honeycomb-moulded round funnel bowl on a double series opaque twist stem, with two thick tapes surrounded by a multi ply band.

c1765   6.25in (16cm) high

£800-1,000   **JH**

An English gin glass, the bell bowl over a triple knop stem, on a folded foot.

c1730   *4.5in (11.5cm) high*
£250-300   **JH**

A gin glass, the trumpet-shaped bowl above a teadrop and multiple knopped stem, raised on a folded foot.

c1730   *5in (13cm) high*
£600-800   **WW**

An English hexagonal jelly glass.

c1760-70   *3.5in (9cm) high*
£70-100   **JH**

An English syllabub glass, with pan top.

c1760-70   *4.25in (10.5cm) high*
£70-100   **JH**

A British thistle-shaped rummer, the bowl engraved with a band of roses, thistles and shamrocks, over heavy diamond cutting, annulated knopped stem, on a star-cut foot.

c1810-20   *5.5in(14cm) high*
£150-200   **JH**

CLOSER LOOK – ENGRAVED GOBLET

This goblet was engraved to commemorate the opening of the Sunderland High Level Bridge. Made as souvenirs, the quality of these types of glasses varies greatly.

Look for finely detailed engravings which convey a sense of perspective, such as this very good example. The building is unusual and detailed.

The elaborate star-cut base is a feature common to late Georgian and Regency drinking glasses.

The quality, shape and size of the body count toward value. Designed for display rather than use, this large glass would have been a specially made.

An English ale glass, the elongated round funnel bowl engraved with hops and barley, over a double series opaque twist stem.

c1765   *7.25in (18.5cm) high*
£400-500   **JH**

An English rummer, the bucket bowl engraved with a view of the Sunderland Bridge, the reverse engraved with an initialled cartouche, on a bladed knop stem.

c1830   *5.25in (13.5cm) high*
£350-400   **JH**

An early 19thC Sunderland Bridge engraved goblet, the rounded bucket bowl engraved on one side with a named view 'Sunderland Bridge', three sailing vessels beneath the span, on the opposite side a titled view of 'The Exchange', and with oval reserve enclosing initials 'JJH' beneath a basket of flowers, upon square 'lemon squeezer'.

7.75in (20cm) high
£3,000-3,500   **TEN**

GLASS

A large goblet, the rounded bowl engraved 'Nagshead JAS 1861' within a frame of fruiting hops and barley, on a short concave-sided stem, star cut circular foot.

1861   *9.25in (23.5cm) high*

£350-450   **TEN**

A Bohemian glass graduated tankard, engraved with a stag in a woodland scene.

c1880   *4.5in (11.5cm) high*

£80-120   **JH**

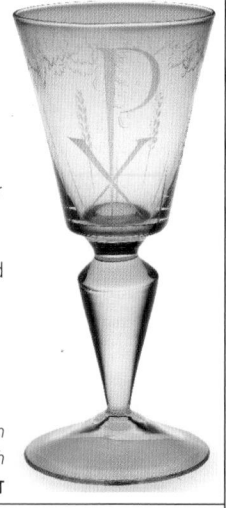

An etched communion chalice by Laurance Whistler for the Crafts Council with chi-rho and fruiting vine and barley frieze.

1965   *9in*
                 (23cm) high

£400-600   **LT**

DECANTERS

An Indian club-shaped decanter, with engraved floral swags and scale cutting, and vesica-cut stopper.

c1790   *11.25in (28.5cm) high*

£300-340   **JH**

A decanter, three neck rings, slice-cut shoulders, flute-cut base, radial-cut mushroom stopper.

c1800-10   *9.5in (24cm) high*

£180-220   **JH**

A pair of Austro-Hungarian parcel gilt cased decanters, each with gilt line edged shoulders over a double headed eagle motif, with possibly later associated cork stoppers with ovoid amber bead finials.

c1800   *13in (32.5cm) high*

£650-850   **TEN**

A pair of Cork Glass Co. decanters, of mallet form the base and lower quarter of each, moulded with a band of ribs, the neck with triple rings, with bull's-eye stopper, with moulded circular mark.

c1800   *10.5in (26.5cm) high*

£700-1,000   **BE**

A pair of George III slice-cut decanters and stoppers and five wine glasses en suite, the decanters with flattened oval stoppers, on slice-cut panelled shoulders, basal collar, slice cut and acid-etched around the waist with two shields enclosing anchor motifs, the glasses similarly engraved on panelled stems and circular feet.

c1800   *Tallest decanter 12.75in (32.5cm) high*

£700-1,000   **TEN**

A decanter, with three triple-bladed neck rings, over blaze and flute cutting, with mushroom stopper.

c1810-20   *10.25in (26cm) high*

£180-220   **JH**

A pair of early 19thC Bristol green spirit decanters, the shaped lip above a short neck and large hollow faceted cuts, engraved with a band of sun, star and moon motifs, flutes from the base, with cockade stoppers.

7.75in (20cm) high

£600-800 ADA

A decanter, three neck rings, slice, diamond and flute cut body, and mushroom stopper.

c1820 *9.5in (24cm) high*

£150-180 JH

A straight-sided decanter, with step-cut neck, flat-cut body, and blown mushroom stopper.

c1830 *10.25in (26cm) high*

£150-180 JH

A 19thC blue glass decanter, of tapered cylindrical form, with stylised heart-shaped stopper and plain body.

12in (30.5cm) high

£400-500 ADA

One of a large pair of late 19thC decanters and stoppers, each to hold six bottles, engraved with a coronet and the motto of the Order of the Garter, the other side with the initials 'JR', damage to one stopper.

£5,000-7,000 PAIR WW

A Netherton Furances engraved claret jug and two matching wine glasses, the ovoid jug with shaped neck and angular handle, engraved 'Presented to Mr G Turner by his Dudley & District friends March 30th 1882', with 'Perfect Amity and Friendship' motto, with Christ and figures, on the reverse a view of Netherton Furnaces and Dudley Castle, and two glass similarly decorated.

1882 *Jug 10.25in (26cm) high*

£900-1,200 TEN

A Victorian silver mounted claret jug, by Rupert Flavell & Co., London, the cut glass ovoid body with a slender loop handle and foliate-chased collar mounted with a domed cover and pineapple finial.

1887 *11in (28cm) high*

£500-700 TEN

A Victorian silver-mounted claret jug, by R. Favell & H. Elliot, London, the glass body with spreading mount with simple quatrefoil hinged cover spout, the cover engraved with a crest of a bull with motto 'CAVE TAURUM' above.

1888 *9in (23cm) high*

£650-850 L&T

A Victorian silver mounted claret jug, John Round & Sons, Sheffield, tapering cylindrical cut glass body with an angular handle and plain silver collar with domed cover and ball finial, crested.

1890 *13in (33cm) high*

£400-500 TEN

GLASS

A Lithyalin glass beaker vase, with a faceted body, the green metal with yellow and orange marbling.

5.75in (14.5cm) high

£300-400   **WW**

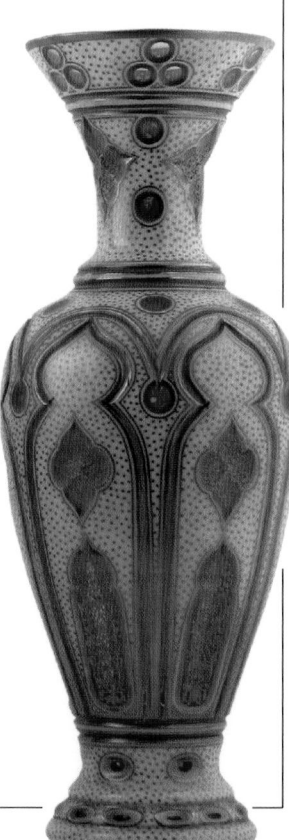

An American Meridan Cut Glass Co. Alhambra cut glass vase, with Greek key bands at top and bottom.

21in (53.5cm) high

£4,500-5,500   **POOK**

A pair of 19thC Continental marbled glass vases, the shoulders decorated with a stylised design in pink, blue and green enamels, highlighted with gilding.

8.75in (22.5cm) high

£250-350   **WW**

A pair of late 19thC Islamic-style opaque glass bottle vases, with knopped neck, signed base.

11in (28cm) high

£200-300   **L&T**

A 20thC Baccarat cut glass vase and cover, with ormolu fittings, its handles inset with cut beads.

The Baccarat glassworks in northern France was founded in 1765 and became famous for its tableware and mid-19thC paperweights.

19in (48cm) high

£1,200-1,800   **DRA**

BOHEMIAN GLASS

A mid-19thC German amber stained clear glass beaker, of waisted form transparently enamelled with a narrow band of flowers and a continuous frieze containing a castle and figures above a slice cut and fretted band.

5in (13cm) high

£400-500   **BE**

A mid-19thC Bohemian ruby overlay glass vase, with nine-sided bucket bowl over a knopped stem and scalloped foot, with etched design of deer in a woodland setting, with an associated cover.

11.5in (29cm) high

£600-800   **L&T**

CLOSER LOOK – BOHEMIAN GLASS VASES

For centuries, Bohemia has been known for its enamelled and hand-gilded art glass. The pieces are typically decorated with heraldic or naturalistic patterns.

Casing coloured glass in opaque white is particularly challenging, and many hours of skillful cutting and gilding went into the production of these pieces.

These vases are typical of the high Victorian style, displaying a mix of Moorish and Gothic influences that were popular at the time.

The large size and the fact that this is a pair adds to the value.

A pair of large 19thC Bohemian glass vases, overlaid in white with six gothic panels, highlighted with gilding.

20in (51cm) high

£4,000-5,000   **WW**

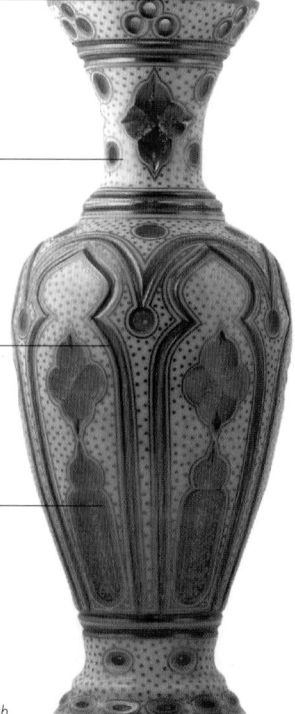
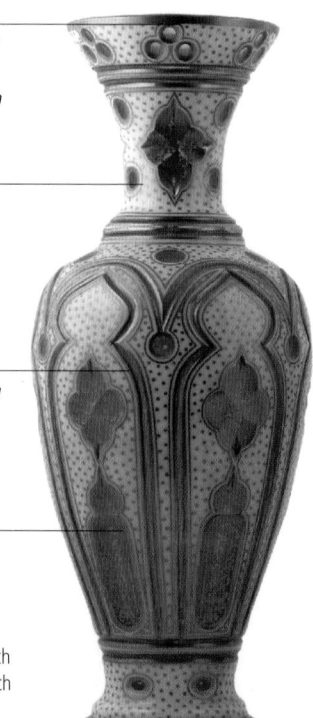

A late 19thC Bohemian flashed ruby glass cup and cover, the ogee body finely carved with a scene showing deer in a forest setting, with thumbnail cut surrounds, the conforming cover terminating in a faceted finial.

19.75in (50cm) high

£900-1,200   **JA**

A pair of late 19th/early 20thC Bohemian ruby flash glass trumpet vases, each deeply engraved with a scene of stags in a woodland within stylised geometric borders, on circular bases.

16in (40.5cm) high

£1,800-2,200   **GORL**

A pair of late 19thC Bohemian white-cased and cranberry flashed cut glass fruit coolers, bodies with central printed and painted portrait busts of ladies, with gilt enamel scrolling, on trumpet bases, one with large repair.

11in (28cm) high

£1,500-2,000   **SK**

A pair of 19thC Bohemian green glass footed beakers, each with central panel painted with a portrait of a maiden flanked by floral decorated panels, within white and gilded borders.

7in (18cm) high

£650-850   **GORL**

A late 19thC German enamel decorated green glass vase, enamel decorated with the 'Stages of Man' from birth to age 100, and with central scene of Adam and Eve in the Garden of Eden, with gilt grapevines.

13.5in (34cm) high

£1,000-1,500   **SK**

A pair of early 20thC Bohemian amethyst glass and enamel vases, of elongated oval form, the glass from amethyst to clear and decorated in enamels with poppies.

13.5in (33cm) high

£1,200-1,800   **FRE**

BOWLS AND SALTS

A George III silver-gilt mounted cut glass skep and dish, by Richard Cooke, London, the hobnail cut body, cover and dish with simple silver-gilt mounts with chased foliate detail, the cover with a cast gilt bee.

1800   *5.25in (13.5cm) high*

£1,200-1,800   **L&T**

A shallow glass fruit bowl, with elongated diamonds above flute cutting, scallop-cut rim and star-cut base.

c1810   *12in (30cm) long*

£100-150   **JH**

A small glass fruit bowl, with flute cutting over leaf cuts, on hollow pedestal stem.

c1810   *7in (17.5cm) high*

£250-300   **JH**

A glass fruit bowl, spirally pillar-cut on bladed stem, with diamond cut foot.

The bowl appears to be moulded but it is entirely hand cut.

c1820   *8in (20.5cm) diam*

£250-300   **JH**

GLASS

A glass fruit bowl, strawberry- and diamond-cut panels, with diamond-cut foot.

c1825-30   7.5in (19cm) diam

£250-300   JH

An amethyst glass sugar bowl, with hollow trumpet stem and folded foot.

c1830-40   4.5in (11.5cm) high

£150-200   JH

A set of four 19thC amethyst glass salts, faceted on square bases, and two smaller oval salts on rhomboid bases.

3.25in (8.5cm) high

£200-250   WW

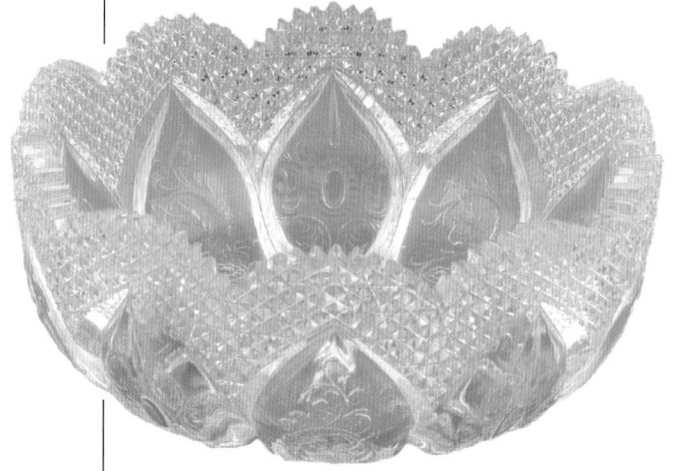

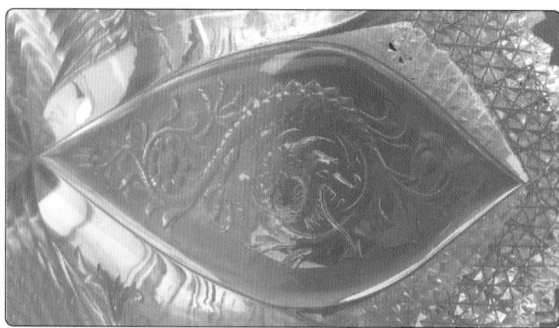

A rare American T. G. Hawkes & Co. engraved and cut glass bowl, by Edward Palme, with dragon decoration, signed on interior with Hawkes trademark and on underside 'E. Palme'.

In 1880 Thomas G. Hawkes set up a cutting shop in Corning, New York, using blanks from the Corning Glass Co. By 1886 the company was making glass for the White House. From 1895, all Hawkes pieces were marked with two hawks, making pieces easily identifiable.

9in (23cm) diam

£2,500-3,500   POOK

LUSTRES AND CENTREPIECES

A pair of late 19thC Victorian opaline glass table lustres, with prism drops.

10in (25.5cm) high

£250-350   DN

A pair of late 19thC Continental white opaline glass mantel lustres, with ogee scalloped rim with quatrefoil gilt enamel accenting, on balustroid stem and spreading foot, hung with long colourless cut lustres.

1.5in (4cm) high

£300-400   SK

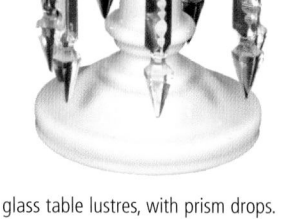

A pair of late 19th/early 20thC glass tazze, with etched Greek key motifs and cranberry border.

9.5in (24cm) diam

£200-300   LOC

A Baccarat miniature paperweight, close-packed with gridel canes.
1845-60   1.75in (4.5cm) diam
£1,000-1,500   **SBG**

CLOSER LOOK – MOUNT WASHINGTON PAPERWEIGHT

Mount Washington paperweights of this date are not as common as those by other manufacturers.

This is a particularly fine example, and would have been very expensive when it was made.

The lamp-worked rose is lifelike and complex, with many detailed petals and leaves, and two buds in different colours.

Until the mid-19thC, many paperweights were made in France. When many French makers went to the US, it lead to a second flourishing of paperweight-making there.

A Mount Washington large pink rose paperweight, with a yellow and a white bud.
c1880   4.25in (11cm) daim
£8,000-12,000   **DCP**

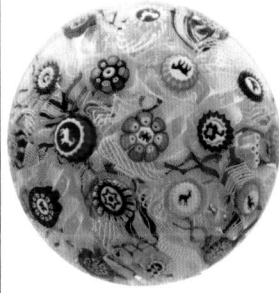

A Baccarat paperweight, with spaced millefiori on muslin, silhouettes of a dog, horse, deer, monkey, dove, goat, squirrel, rooster and butterfly, 'B1848' date cane.

The Baccarat factory in Lorraine, France, first made paperweights in c1845. Baccarat paperweights often feature millefiori containing silhouettes of animals. The General Manager of Baccarat, Jean-Baptist Toussaint, is credited with introducing animals in 1846. The weights also often contain 'signature' canes featuring the letter 'B', or the date from 1846-49.
1848   3in (7.5cm) diam
£2,500-3,000   **SBG**

A Baccarat Garlanded Pompon Dahlia paperweight.
      2.75in (7cm) diam
£2,000-2,500   **SBG**

A Bacchus close concentric paperweight.
c1848   3.5in (7.5cm) diam
£5,000-7,000   **DCP**

A Bigaglia spaced millefiori paperweight, with silhouette canes, dated.
1845   2.5in (6.5cm) diam
£4,000-5,000   **DCP**

A Clichy paperweight, chequered with white, pink and turquoise roses.

Founded in 1837, Clichy began making paperweights in 1846. From 1852 production of paperweights was greatly reduced, and the factory closed down in 1885. Distinctive canes in Clichy paperweights include the 'Clichy Rose' a pink cane cut across to resemble an open rose, and a cane with the letter 'C'.
1845-60   2.5in (6.5cm) diam
£2,500-3,000   **SBG**

A Patin pink rose on white ground paperweight.
c1878   3in (7.5cm) diam
£5,500-7,500   **DCP**

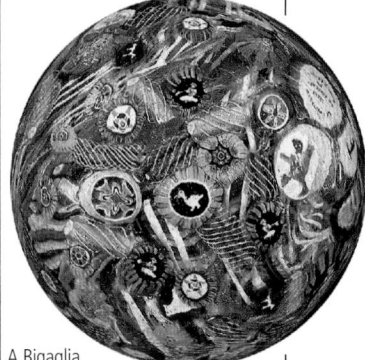

JEWELLERY

The jewellery market has made headlines over the past year, primarily owing to the increase in gold prices during the economic downturn. However, quality of design and craftsmanship from the main jewellery houses such as Cartier, Boucheron and Van Cleef & Arpels continue to attract the discerning buyer. Significant trends developing this year include renewed interest in late-20th century silver jewellery from names such as George Jensen, and a revival of high-quality costume jewellery.

In terms of jewellery types, traditional earrings have seen a revival, particularly the pendant or chandelier forms, where five-figure prices are not unusual. Gentlemen's jewellery has also picked up this year, with traditional cufflinks a typical buy. Ranging in price from £150 to £2,400 for a pair, all manner of designs are sought after in most combinations. Watches are also becoming more popular and traditional makes such as Rolex always attract eager buyers.

There is a tendency for large multi-stone set pieces of jewellery that are impressive, but which do not have great design or craftsmanship, to be bought in order to break up to remake into smaller pieces of jewellery that are profitable. The trade is also tending to prefer purchasing one or two good items rather than a larger number of mediocre, lesser value pieces.

The buoyancy of vintage and antique costume jewellery sales can, in part be explained by the economic climate; perhaps there is a desire for buyers to want to cheer themselves up, or maybe there is a reluctance to spend large amounts on 'precious' jewels. Whatever, the reason, this market has seen an increase in new collectors. Among the designer names that have held their value well are high-quality pieces from the 1950s by designers such as Miriam Haskell and Christian Dior. These have always been strong and require an investment mentality. Long pendant necklaces by makers such as Goldette, Sarah Coventry and Stanley Hagler, are especially sought after and are currently undervalued. There is also considerable interest in European costume jewellery from the 1980s by firms such as Givenchy, Chanel, Christian Dior and Yves Saint Laurent. With the exception of the ever 'in demand' Chanel, the majority of these were severely undervalued in the middle parts of 2009, but not so now, as prices are rising remarkably quickly.

While no particular area of costume-jewellery collecting has diminished in price, the more traditional 1940s Trifari, Corocraft, Hattie Carnegie and Pennino Bros – the mainstay of collecting for over 20 years – have been static in value, with top-end quality pieces still commanding good money. Good named pieces signed by well-known fashion houses are increasing in collectability, as are good, signed jewels from the 1950s, 1960s and 1980s. Designer, accompanied by signature, condition and look are vital to any purchase bought as a long-term investment.

Clockwise from top left: flower pin by Kramer for Dior c1960 £60-100 private collection; Van Cleef & Arpels necklace c1950 £13,500 at N. Bloom & Son; Art Deco diamond pendant earrings £15,000 at Lyon & Turnbull.

ESSENTIAL REFERENCE – JACOBITE JEWELLERY

James II (and VII of Scotland), the Catholic brother of Charles II, took the throne in 1685. As a Roman Catholic himself, James attempted to introduce religious tolerance between Catholics and Protestants, and this made him extremely unpopular with the Anglican establishment. They gave their support to William of Orange, husband of James's daughter Mary. William and Mary were crowned in 1689, but many Catholics, Episcopalians and Tory royalists, particularly in Scotland, still supported James and his young son, Charles (later Bonnie Prince Charlie) even after both had fled to France.

- Many Scottish traditions were outlawed by the victorious English monarchs, with reprisals for supporting the Jacobite cause including death. Those who backed James and Charles had to find secret ways to show their support. This resulted in poetry and songs, in which neither James's nor Charles's names were ever uttered. This theme was often present in the applied arts, such as silver, carvings, glass and jewellery.

- Many Jacobite rings and brooches featured hidden symbols that proclaimed their allegiance. Some, such as the ring currently on display at the Clan Cameron Museum at Achnacarry, could be opened by a secret spring, to reveal a portrait of one of the exiled monarchs.

- In 2008 an apparently plain Jacobite ring was sold for £12,200 at Lyon & Turnbull in Scotland. Rather than being plain, the ring was was marked with the cipher ' CR III 1766' underneath the stone. 1766 was the year James II and IV, and Charles began to style himself King Charles III, the rightful King of Scotland, rather than Prince of Wales. This ring acted as a ' signature' to be used on Charles's correspondence. No document could carry Charles's real signature or seal without the bearer being put to death if found in possession of such papers. The ring would therefore accompany Charles's messenger to show that documents had originated from him, allowing ' Bonnie Prince Charlie' to keep all his loyal supporters abreast of his plans and movements.

A portrait ring of James II of Scotland, with central glazed painted portrait, with accompanying hand-written letter.

The letter reads ' The small ring with a picture in miniature of King James 2nd which was given to those of this party who had subscribed to his support and has a claim for five hundred pounds for them the Stewart family if they shall recover the throne of England' [sic].

£3,000-4,000   L&T

An early Georgian memorial pendant, set with a colourless gem atop a hair scroll, within a blue enamelled garter inscribed 'HONI SOIT QUI MAL Y PENSE', with simple surmount, inscribed to reverse 'H BEAUFORT OBt 24 MAY 1714 AEt 30'.

1.25in (3cm) long

£1,200-1,800   L&T

A Georgian gold long chain with amethyst pendant, the chain of textured belcher links, the pendant claw set with a large oval cut amethyst within a bead and wirework surround.

Chain 38.5in (98cm) long

£1,800-2,200   L&T

An early 19thC diamond brooch/pendant, claw set throughout with graduated old mine-cut diamonds, with outer scrolling border set with rose-cut diamonds.

1.5in (4cm) wide

£700-1,000   L&T

An early 19thC diamond set ring, claw-set with five graduated old mine cut diamonds, flanked above and below by rose-cut diamond border.

£1,500-2,000   L&T

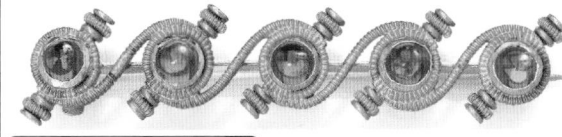

A Renaissance Revival brooch, by John Brogden, of scrolling design, collet-set with five circular-cut ruby cabochons, stamped to reverse 'JB', tests as gold.

1.5in (3.5cm) wide

£500-700 **L&T**

A Victorian sapphire and diamond-set bar brooch, with central floral cluster, set throughout with circular-cut sapphires and old European-cut diamonds.

1.5in (4cm) wide

£400-500 **L&T**

A Victorian diamond -et brooch pendant, with central floral cluster, set throughout with graduated old European and rose-cut diamonds, with detachable brooch fitting.

1.5in (4cm) wide

£400-500 **L&T**

An alexandrite and diamond pendant/brooch, prong-set with a cushion-cut alexandrite, framed by old European-cut diamonds, gold mount.

Diamond 6.20ct 1in (2.5cm) diam

£90,000-110,000 **SK**

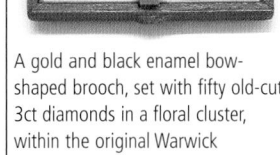

A gold and black enamel bow-shaped brooch, set with fifty old-cut 3ct diamonds in a floral cluster, within the original Warwick Jewellers of Regent Street box.

£1,000-1,500 **GHOU**

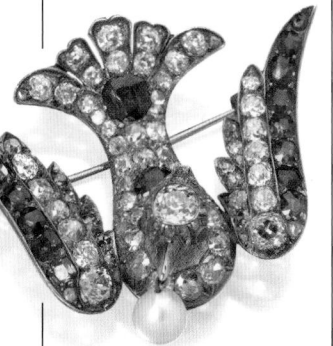

A 19thC multi-gem set brooch/pendant, set throughout with graduated old mine-cut diamonds, cushion-cut sapphires to wings, circular-cut bright red garnets to body, circular-cut ruby cabochon eyes and an old European-cut yellow diamond to the head, also suspending a baroque pearl from the beak, with detachable brooch fitting.

2.25in (5.5cm) wide

£5,000-7,000 **L&T**

CLOSER LOOK – GIULIANO BROOCH

In 1874, Giuliano established a shop in Piccadilly, London, which won the patronage of Queen Victoria and became popular amongst the artistic community.

A caduceus is a symbol of healing, widely used by the medical profession, and demonstrates Giuliano's interest in interpreting antique sources to create jewellery reflecting 19thC Eclecticism.

Carlo and Arthur Giuliano made technically superb enamelled gold pieces which used gems for their colour rather than value.

Signed pieces by Giuliano are much sought-after by collectors.

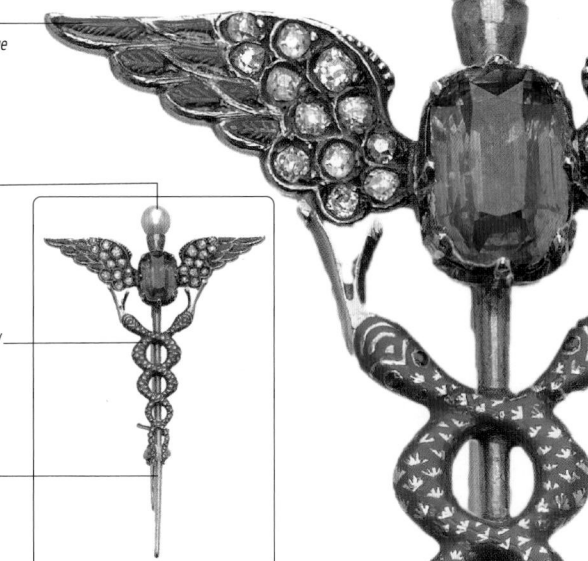

A Giuliano sapphire and diamond -t caduceus brooch, the terminal set with a pearl surmounting a claw-set oval-cut sapphire, flanked by rose-cut diamond-set and blue enamel entwined serpents, signed 'C&AG' for Carl and Arthur Giuliano.

2in (5.5cm) long

£2,500-3,500 **L&T**

JEWELLERY

A multi-gem set coronet brooch, set with borders of rubies, emeralds and rose cut diamonds, with graduated pearls to the terminals, contained in a fitted case.

1.5in (4cm) wide

£600-800   **L&T**

A late Victorian ruby and diamond-set crescent-form brooch, of open design, alternately set with graduated circular-cut rubies and old European-cut diamonds.

1.75in (4.5cm) long

£500-700   **L&T**

A late Victorian sapphire and diamond-set brooch, the central, claw-set, circular-cut sapphire within a surround of round, brilliant-cut diamonds, flanked to either side by similarly set scrolls.

1.5in (4cm) long

£400-500   **L&T**

A late Victorian diamond-set star brooch/pendant, of slightly domed twelve-pointed design, set with graduated old European- and rose-cut diamonds.

1in (2.5cm) diam

£700-1,000   **L&T**

A late Victorian diamond-set brooch, set throughout with old European-cut diamonds, with detachable diamond-set bale and brooch fittings.

1.25in (3cm) diam

£1,200-1,800   **L&T**

A 19thC carved ivory and jet oval brooch, the ivory carved and pierced with flowers, fruit and foliage on a jet oval panel.

Cameo jewellery was particularly popular in 19thC and 20thC. It takes the form of a hardstone, shell or gem carved in relief to depict a range of subjects including classical groups, landscapes and mythological deities. The colour of the subject may contrast with the background if the original carved material has two differently coloured layers.

£350-450   **BE**

A late 19thC oval shell cameo brooch, the carved shell depicting Hebe and the eagle within a foliate engraved gold frame.

2.5in (6.5cm) long

£500-700   **BE**

A late 19thC French hardstone cameo circular brooch, with central layered agate cameo depicting a young woman wearing a high neck lace collar, claw-set within a foliate frame of seed-pearls and rose cut diamonds.

1.25in (3cm) diam

£1,500-2,000   **BE**

A Renaissance-style multi-gem set pendant, set with an oval-cut open cabochon, surmounted by two reclining figures, the surround set with pearls and rubies, suspending a pearl drop, with French control marks.

2in (5cm) long

£300-400   **L&T**

A late 19thC multi-gem set and enamelled pendant, set to the front with graduated turquoise cabochons, within a black and white enamelled surround, with old European-cut, diamond-set bale.

2.5in (6.5cm) long

£1,500-2,000   **L&T**

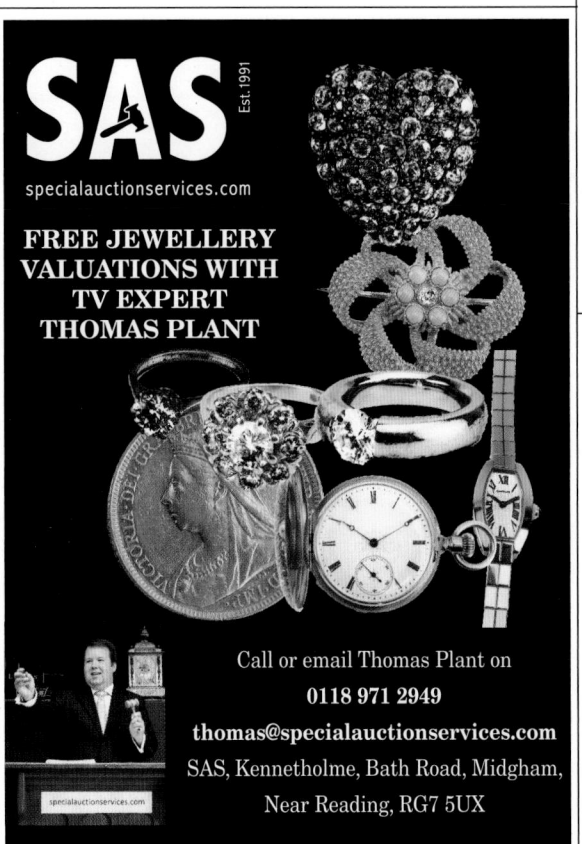

A Victorian garnet and diamond-set brooch/pendant, composed of a garnet cabochon within a surround of diamonds, with a glazed oval panel to reverse, suspending a further garnet cabochon and diamond-set drop.

3.25in (8cm) long including bale

£2,000-2,500   L&T

A Victorian diamond three-stone ring, claw-set with graduated old mine-cut diamonds, interspersed by rose-cut diamonds, with scroll pierced gallery.

Diamonds 4.00cts total

£7,000-10,000   L&T

JEWELLERY

A late 19thC gold, opal and diamond eleven-stone cluster ring, with three graduated oval opals, separated by rows of graduated old brilliant-cut diamonds in a scroll-pierced setting.

£450-550   BE

A Victorian 18ct yellow gold enamel and pearl slide bracelet, the flexible bar link with a cobalt blue enamel buckle slide, decorated with possibly natural pearls.

32g

£1,200-1,800   RTC

A late 19thC gold, opal and diamond mounted hinged bangle, with nine graduated oval opals separated by pairs of brilliant cut diamonds.

£900-1,200   BE

A late 19thC enamelled gold and freshwater split pearl hinged bangle, with five freshwater split pearls, white enamel and engraved decoration.

£900-1,200   BE

A late 19thC enamelled gold split pearl and diamond mounted hinged bangle, with central circular cluster between blue enamelled fan-shaped motifs, on a similarly decorated tapering bangle.

£900-1,200   BE

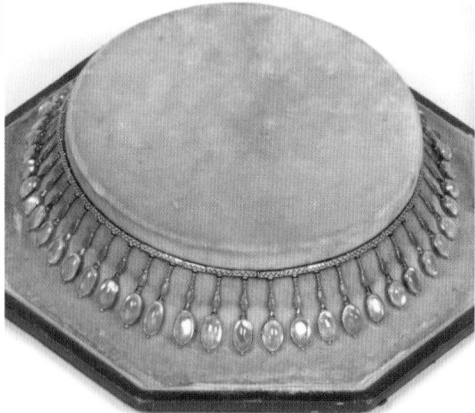

An Archaeological Revival enamel and moonstone fringe necklace, by Carol Giuliano, blue enamelled tubes suspend drops enamelled in green, red and blue, each terminal featuring a cabochon moonstone, signed 'G. G.' in an oval, in a fitted case marked 'C. Giuliano, 115 Piccadilly, London'.

1874-1895
£17,000-20,000   TEN

A late Victorian enamelled parure, comprising a necklace, bracelet and earrings.

Necklace 15.25in (39cm) long

£1,000-1,500   L&T

A pair of Victorian pendant earrings, the circular drops set with a garnet carbuncle, applied with a rose-cut diamond-set star, within enamelled, ropetwist and bead borders, with wire fittings.

c1860   1.5in (3.5cm) long
£1,800-2,200   L&T

A late 19thC Persian painted ivory panel belt, with 20 rectangular links including nine with variously figured scenes and contained in a wooden box with sliding lid.

£300-400   BE

A Belle Époque-style natural pearl and diamond-set pendant, composed of diamonds and bouton pearls, suspended from a trace link chain, with accompanying report that the pearls are natural.

Pendant 2in (5cm) long

£1,500-2,000   **L&T**

An Art Nouveau gem set scroll-form brooch/pendant, claw-set to the centre with an old European-cut diamond, within a pierced surround millegrain set with further diamonds and pearls.

2.25in (6cm) wide

£1,000-1,500   **L&T**

A German plique à jour enamel and paste pendant, with green enamel palmettes and drops, stamped '900' 'Depose' and unidentified maker's mark.

The plique àjour technique was developed during the 17thC in Russia, and was used widely by Art Nouveau jewellers. The stained glass window effect is produced by supporting translucent enamel in an unbacked framework.

14.5in (37cm) long overall

£500-700   **DN**

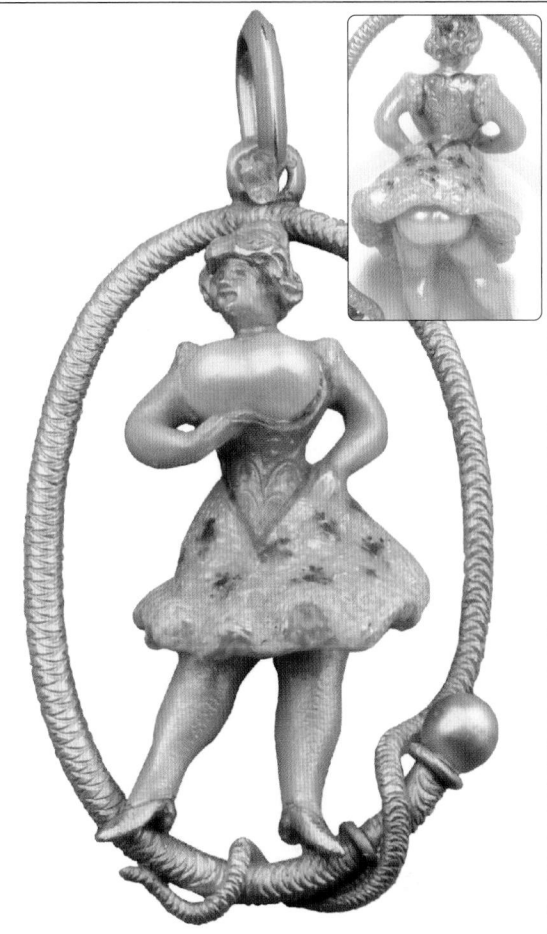

An Art Nouveau erotic enamel and pearl pendant, the burlesque figure of a voluptuous woman with bodice, enamel gown, pearl bosoms and derrière, framed by an engraved horsewhip with pearl terminal, gold mount, within fitted box, Continental hallmark.

1.5in (4cm) high

£7,000-10,000   **SK**

A sterling pendant with two enamelled medallions, by Ramsden & Carr, one as a blue-green jewel, the other painted with a Pre-Raphaelite maiden, later upper chain, hairline to enamel, stamped 'R.N & C.R.', with lion passant, panther, and 'k' hallmarks.

The Pre-Raphaelite Brotherhood was a group of English painters, poets, and critics, founded in 1848 by William Holman Hunt, Everett Millais, and Dante Gabriel Rossetti. They believed that the Classical poses and compositions of Raphael had corrupted art, and wanted instead to return to the intense colours and detail of 15thC Italian and Flemish art, hence the name "Pre-Raphaelite".

1905   *4.75in (12cm) high*

£2,000-3,000   **DRA**

An early 20thC 18ct gold, sapphire and diamond pendant-brooch.

Pendant 1.5in (4cm) high

£1,000-1,500   **TDG**

An early 20thC enamelled gold, citrine and cultured pearl pendant, with central rounded rectangular citrine within a white and black dot enamelled frame highlighted with round citrines and suspending a single cultured pearl drop.

£1,000-1,500   **BE**

JEWELLERY

An early 20thC platinum and diamond-mounted pendant, of openwork foliate design with single pearl drop, later converted to be worn as a brooch.

£1,500-2,000   BE

An Edwardian 15ct gold necklace, set with amethysts and seed pearls.

16.25in (41cm) long

£1,000-1,500   L&T

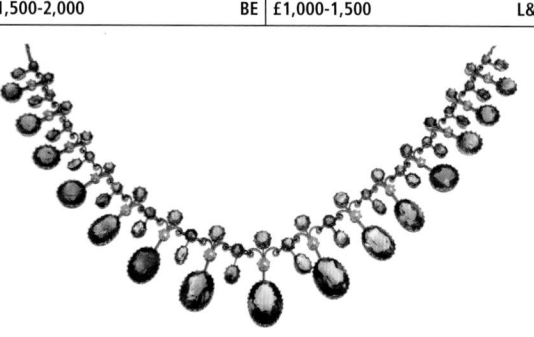

An early 20thC gold, amethyst and split seed pearl fringe necklace, of milligrained scrollwork links claw-set with graduated oval and circular amethysts and projected single amethyst drops, in fitted tooled leather case.

£2,500-3,000   BE

An early 20thC diamond set bar brooch, claw-set with graduated old European-cut diamonds, to a knife bar.

2in (5cm) wide Principal diamond 1.25cts

£2,000-2,500   L&T

An early 20thC black opal and diamond-mounted bar brooch, with single oval black opal in millegrain setting, within a frame of six similarly set round old brilliant-cut diamonds.

£2,000-3,000   BE

An early 20thC enamelled gold and seed pearl dragonfly brooch, with red enamelled abdomen, split seed pearl-set wings and thorax with cabochon ruby eyes.

£550-750   BE

A Belle Époque emerald and diamond set ring, millegrain collet set to the centre with a trap-cut emerald flanked above and below by similarly cut emeralds, within a shaped oval surround of single cut diamonds.

0.75in (2cm) high

£1,200-1,800   L&T

An Edwardian Scottish 18ct gold mounted diamond single-stone ring, claw-set with an early round brilliant-cut diamond, with scroll details to the shoulders.

Diamond 2.02cts

£4,000-5,000   L&T

An Edwardian gold, opal and diamond hinged bangle, claw-set to the front with eleven graduated oval cut opal cabochons, interspersed by borders of rose-cut diamonds, with snap fastening and safety chain.

2.5in (6.5cm) diam

£1,800-2,200   L&T

An Art Deco red spinel and diamond-set ring, the central claw-set square trap cut spinel of an intense red hue, flanked to either shoulder by two diamonds.

In mineralogy, spinel classifies a group of related minerals, of which only a few are of gem quality. The origin of the name is uncertain, possibly derived from the Greek word for spark or Latin for thorn. Gem quality spinel occurs in all colours, the most highly prized being a ruby-like red. It is also quite rare to find gem quality spinel of this size.

Spinel 6.25cts

£3,000-4,000   L&T

An Art Deco platinum-mounted diamond-set ring, the central claw set early round brilliant-cut diamond flanked by tapering stepped shoulders set with small single-cut diamonds.

Principal diamond 0.75cts

£1,800-2,200   L&T

An Art Deco diamond-set necklace, the panels set with round brilliant single, and square-cut diamonds, fringed by diamond drops, on a trace link chain, with fitted case stamped 'BROOK & SON, EDINBURGH'.

15.25in (38.5cm) long

£5,500-7,500   L&T

A pair of 1920s/1930s Art Deco paste and metal earrings.

2in (5cm) long

£150-200   TDG

A diamond, onyx and coral brooch, the open circle of onyx with diamond set coral batons.

1.5in (3.5cm) long 0.75ct total

£1,000-1,500   DN

An Austro-Hungarian multi-gem set novelty brooch, designed as a carved agate terrier, with single cut diamond set collar and eye, with post-1922 control marks.

1.25in (3cm) long

£900-1,200   L&T

A pair of Cartier Art Deco cufflinks, decorated with overlapping black enamelled circular motifs, within an outer border of diamonds, 'CARTIER PARIS LONDON NEW YORK' to the edges, conjoined by belcher links.

Cartier was founded in Paris by Louis-Francois Cartier in 1847, and turned into a worldwide brand name by his grandsons, Louis, Pierre and Jacques. As well as jewellery created for the royal families of Europe, Cartier is credited with producing the first wristwatch in 1904. It was designed by Louis Cartier, who was also responsible for the company' s ' Mysterious Clocks' and the ' Tutti Frutti' jewellery.

0.5in (1.5cm) diam

£3,600-4,600   L&T

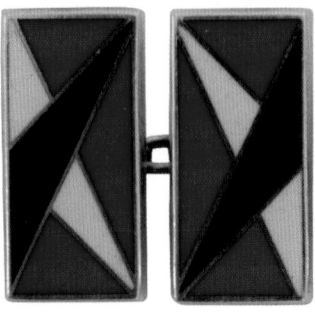

A pair of Art Deco silver and enamel rectangular chain-linked cufflinks, decorated with abstract red, black and white enamel.

£400-500   FLD

ESSENTIAL REFERENCE – GEORG JENSEN

Danish designer George Jensen (1866-1935) was one of the most important silversmiths of the 20thC.

- After training as a goldsmith in Copenhagen, he travelled to France and Italy. On returning to Denmark, he started a small porcelain factory, which failed, before turning to silver and jewellery. He opened his own workshops in 1904.
- Jensen adhered to the principals of the Arts and Crafts movement, which were based on the ideal of a craftsperson taking pride in their handiwork.
- In 1907, he began his association with the painter Johan Rohde (1856-1935), with whom he developed the simple, striking style that was to make him famous. Jensen's tea wares typically have graceful curves, decorated finials and elongated handles.
- Jewellery, and some of the early silver, is Art Nouveau in style: taking inspiration from nature. His jewellery often incorporates semi-precious stones.
- His vessels often have the famous Jensen satiny surface, produced by annealing the piece, immersing it in sulphuric acid and then buffing it, allowing slight oxidisation to remain.
- Many of his designs are still produced today by the Georg Jensen company, which now has stores all over the world.

A Georg Jensen 18ct gold brooch, designed by Arno Malinowski, model no. 1320, stamped marks.

1.75in (4.5cm) wide

£700-1,000   WW

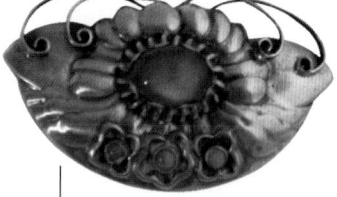

A Georg Jensen silver and moonstone brooch, cast in low relief with flowers, applied tendrils, stamped marks.

2.25in (5.5cm) wide

£250-350   WW

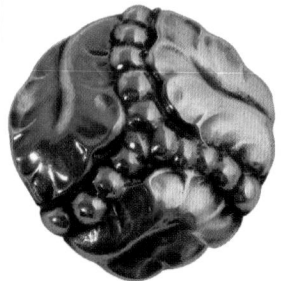

A Georg Jensen silver brooch, model no. 82A, circular form, stamped marks.

1.25in (3cm) wide

£150-200   WW

A Georg Jensen silver brooch, model no. 251, designed by Arno Malinowski, cast with two leaping dolphins, stamped marks.

1.5in (3.5cm) wide

£250-300   WW

A Georg Jensen silver brooch, model no. 217, cast as a bunch of hanging grapes, stamped marks.

2.5in (6.5cm) long

£220-280   WW

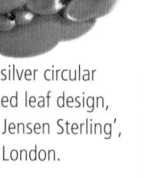

A George Jensen silver circular brooch, of entwined leaf design, stamped 'George Jensen Sterling', 20' hallmarks for London.

1952

£250-300   BE

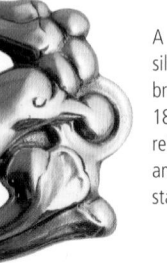

A Georg Jensen silver and enamel brooch, model no. 187, cast in low relief with a bird amongst foliage, stamped marks.

1.5in (4cm) wide

£350-450   WW

A Georg Jensen silver and enamel brooch, designed by Henning Koppel, model no. 307, stamped marks.

2.25in (6cm) wide

£600-800   WW

A pair of Georg Jensen silver earrings, designed by Nanna Ditzel, model no. 126, stamped marks.

1.25in (3cm) long

£120-180   WW

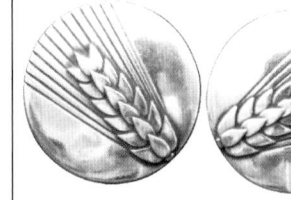

A pair of Georg Jensen silver dress clip earrings, model no. 246, cast in shell form, stamped marks.

1.25in (3cm) long

£120-180   WW

A pair of George Jensen silver earrings, model no. 127B, stamped marks.

0.75in (2cm) diam

£180-220   WW

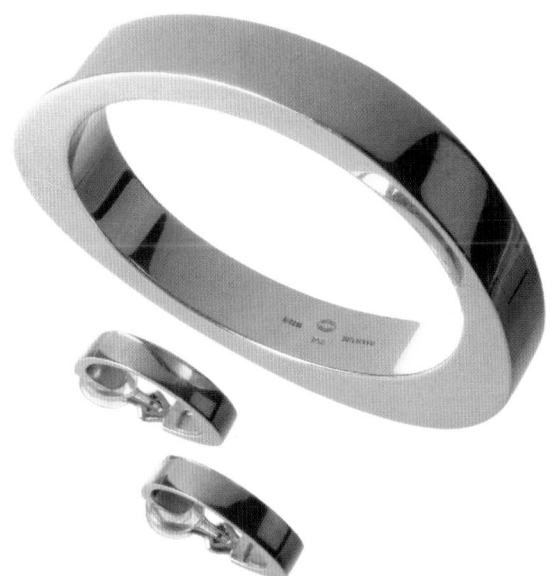

A Georg Jensen silver bracelet, model no. 133A, stamped marks.

6.75in (17.5cm) wide

£500-700   WW

A Danish gold-coloured bangle and matching earrings, by Georg Jensen, design numbers 1422B and 1422, of square section and rounded triform outline, bangle signed 'Georg Jensen' with post-1945 stamped marks.

Bangle 4in (8cm) wide 91g (gross)

£1,200-1,800   DN

A Georg Jensen silver and amethyst link bracelet, model no. 11, stamped marks.

5.25in (13.5cm) long

£350-400   WW

A Georg Jensen silver bangle, model no. 211, stamped marks.

2.75in (7cm) wide

£400-500   WW

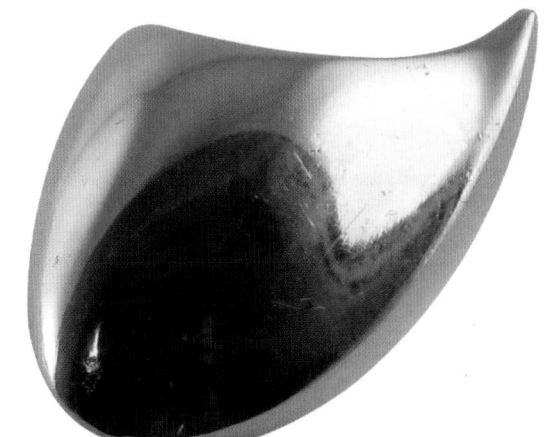

A Georg Jensen silver ring, designed by Nanna Ditzel, model no 91, stamped marks.

1.25in (3cm) long

£120-180   WW

A Georg Jensen silver ring, model no. 148, stamped marks, size J.

0.75in (2cm) wide

£220-280   WW

JEWELLERY

ESSENTIAL REFERENCE – GEMSTONES

Some gemstones can be identified by colour or hardness, but many need to be examined for factors such as carat weight, colour brilliance and cut to establish their authenticity.

- Colour is the least reliable means of identification, as many stones are of similar colours, and others exist in a range of colours. Additionally some stones are heat-treated to improve their colour. Natural colour depends on the natural impurities dispersed throughout the stone.
- Most natural gemstones have inclusions, which reduce their brilliance and are therefore removed (as much as possible) by a gem-cutter. Synthetic stones, and paste and glass imitations, typically lack inclusions, although paste will sometimes contain bubbles.
- The different facets of a cut stone alter the amount of refracted light escaping from it, and so gemstones are cut to increase their clarity and brilliance. The different styles of cut include brilliant-, rose-, old- and eight-cut. Heavily flawed stones are typically cabochon-cut, which creates an un-facted but polished surface.
- Desirable gemstones include amethyst, aquamarine, diamond, emerald, garnet, lapis lazuli, opal, peridot, ruby, sapphire, topaz and turquoise.

A violet sapphire and diamond-set brooch, designed as a bow-tied ribbon, suspending a detachable tapering drop set with a sapphire and diamonds.

1.75in (4.5cm) long Sapphire 3.12cts

£1,500-2,000   L&T

An aquamarine and diamond brooch, comprising three large oval cut aquamarine set within borders of mixed size brilliant-cut and baguette cut diamonds, in white gold setting.

£6,500-8,500   HT

An 18ct gold mounted diamond single-stone ring, claw-set with an early round brilliant cut diamond, to a tapering shank.

Diamond 2.80cts

£2,000-3,000   L&T

A ruby and diamond-set giardinetto ring, the curved two-colour front collet-set with a large rose-cut diamond amidst a surround of smaller similarly cut diamonds and graduated oval-cut rubies, unmarked, tests as gold.

0.75in (2cm) high

£700-1,000   L&T

An 18ct gold and platinum mounted pearl and diamond cluster ring, the central pearl within a claw-set surround of round brilliant-cut diamonds.

0.75in (2cm) high

£2,000-3,000   L&T

A pair of 1970s 18ct gold earrings and a matching ring, by John Donald, set at intervals with old European-cut diamonds, oval and circular-cut sapphires.

John Donald established his reputation as a leading jewellery designer in the 1960s. Working in London, he created jewellery designs that were baroque and essentially organic in form. Often mounting uncut precious gems, he also experimented with molten gold in water, producing textured designs reminiscent of nature, as in this example.

Ring 1in (2.5cm) high

£2,000-3,000   L&T

An all-diamond cluster ring, with a central invisibly set border of baguette-cut diamonds, flanked above and below by claw-set round brilliant cut diamonds, mount stamped '18K 750 D302'.

0.5in (1cm) high

£2,500-3,500   L&T

A pair of 18ct white gold solitaire diamond ear studs.

3.03cts

£5,000-7,000   GORL

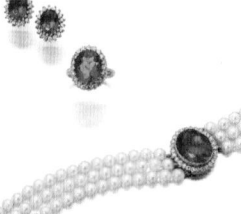

A fire opal, diamond and cultured pearl set suite, the necklace of three rows of pearls, centrally set with an opal, the earrings and ring matching, also ten additional loose pearls.

14in (35.5cm) long

£1,800-2,200   L&T

A Czechoslovakian Art Deco Egyptian Revival glass and metal necklace.

c1925   18in (46cm) long

£1,500-2,000   **TDG**

An Art Deco Egyptian Revival scarab beetles and foiled glass on metal necklace.

c1925   17in (43cm) long

£250-350   **TDG**

An Art Deco plastic necklace.

c1925   22in (56cm) long

£180-220   **TDG**

A 1920s/1930s Art Deco metal and glass sautoir.

28.75in (73cm) long

£300-400   **TDG**

A 1950s Weiss Austrian crystal brooch.

Albert Weiss (1942-71) set up his New York jewellery-making company, Weiss, in 1942 having worked at the famous Coro Company during the 1930s. His jewellery is typically set with Austrian crystal rhinestones, which display exceptional purity of colour. A variety of floral, foliate, fruit, figural, and geometric designs were produced. All pieces produced after 1943 are marked either ' Weiss' , ' Albert Weiss' or ' AW Co.'

2.25in (6cm) wide

£120-180   **TDG**

ESSENTIAL REFERENCE – YVES SAINT LAURENT

In 1957, at the age of 21, Yves Saint Laurent (1936-2008) became the chief designer at the House of the Dior, following the death of Christian Dior. His first couture collection, featuring the Trapeze line, was very successful, but later collections were less popular with buyers, press and Dior executives.

- Conscripted to the army in 1961, returning in 1962 after suffering a nervous breakdown, Dior refused to take Saint Laurent back. Pierre Bergé, Saint Laurent' s partner, successfully sued for breech of contract and the two started their own fashion house with the settlement money.
- Saint Laurent introduced many of the trendsetting designs of the 1960s, including the tunic dress with large-scale Mondrian-style designs and the ' Le Smoking' tuxedo for women. By the 1980s, his designs had become a fashion classic.

A 1950s paste and metal necklace.

18in (46cm) long

£150-200   **TDG**

A 1950s glass bead necklace.

17in (43cm) long

£100-150   **TDG**

An Yves Saint Laurent chunky 'gem' set necklace, Rive Gauche, the large irregular stones in gilt metal clawed mounts.

1987   10in (25.5cm) diam

£1,500-2,000   **KT**

OBJETS DE VERTU

ESSENTIAL REFERENCE – NATHANIEL MILLS

Nathaniel Mills & Sons was a 19thC company of Birmingham silversmiths, well-known for high-quality silver boxes, vinaigrettes, snuff boxes and card cases.

- Nathaniel I (1746-1840) first registered his mark in 1803 when he was a partner in jewellers Mills & Langston. He registered his own mark from a new address in Caroline Street, Birmingham.

- He was succeeded in his business by his sons Nathaniel II (1811-73), William and Thomas, who were partners in the company. It was under their direction that the business took off and most collectable Nathaniel Mills & Sons boxes were made in this period. Many pieces made c1840-53 were made by William or Thomas, rather than Nathaniel II.

- Nathaniel II introduced many new techniques, such as engine-turning, stamping and casting, and became known for successfully adapting them to the industry.

- Nathaniel Mills & Sons was one of Britain's most prestigious makers of 'castle top' boxes, which were repoussé or die-stamped with pictures of famous (or sometimes obscure) buildings and landmarks. Some were produced as souvenirs for tourists, since their popularity coincided with the opening of passenger railways in Britain.

- When Nathaniel Mills II died, he left £30,000 in his will.

An early Victorian silver rectangular castle-top card case, Nathaniel Mills, Birmingham, embossed in relief with Abbotsford and with Windsor Castle verso, each framed by scroll foliate embossing.

1837   *3.75in (9.5cm) high 3oz*

£1,000-1,500   DN

A Victorian silver castle-top card case, Nathaniel Mills, Birmingham, chased with a view of St Paul's Cathedral.

1842   *4in (10cm) high*

£1,200-1,800   TEN

A Victorian silver rectangular castle-top vinaigrette, Nathaniel Mills, Birmingham, chased in relief with York Minster from the south within a foliate border, the sides engine turned with a conforming base engraved 'C.P. died May 29th 1861', the gilt interior with a scroll pierced grille.

1842   *1.75in (4.5cm) wide*

£3,000-4,000   DN

A Victorian silver castle-top vinaigrette, Nathaniel Mills, Birmingham, of shaped rectangular form, engraved with a view of the Royal Exchange, initialled 'MAJ' and dated '1864'.

1844   *1.5in (4cm) wide*

£800-1,200   TEN

A Victorian silver rectangular castle-top vinaigrette, by Nathaniel Mills, Birmingham, chased in relief with Gloucester Cathedral within a foliate border, the sides engine turned with a conforming base, the gilt interior with a scroll pierced grille.

1844   *1.75in (4.5cm) wide 1.25oz*

£4,000-5,000   DN

A Victorian silver castle-top card case, Nathaniel Mills, Birmingham, chased with a view of the Houses of Parliament.

1846   *4in (10cm) high*

£1,000-1,500   TEN

A Victorian silver Castle Top card case, Nathaniel Mills, Birmingham, engraved with a view of Norwich Cathedral.

1849   *4in (10cm) high*

£3,500-4,500   TEN

A Victorian silver castle-top vinaigrette, Nathaniel Mills, Birmingham, rectangular shape, engraved with a view of St Paul's Cathedral, initialled 'MAB'.

1850   *1.5in (4cm) wide*

£1,000-1,500   TEN

CLOSER LOOK – A SILVER CASTLE-TOP CARD CASE

Pieces by Alfred Taylor are comparatively rare. This example is of high quality and in good condition, and is therefore likely to be desirable.

The Royal Pavilion (sometimes called the Brighton Pavilion) was built in the early 19thC for the Prince Regent (later George IV).

The decorative scrollwork is particularly attractive.

Most of these 'castle-top' boxes feature castles, hence the name. Boxes using images of the Royal Pavilion are extremely rare.

A Victorian silver shaped rectangular castle-top card case, David Pettifer, Birmingham, embossed in relief with the Royal Exchange, London, framed by scroll foliage on a matted ground, engraved with an armorial and embossed with scroll foliage verso.

1848   4in (10.5cm) high 2oz

£1,500-2,000   **DN**

A Victorian silver castle-top card case, Alfred Taylor, Birmingham, chased with a view of the Royal Pavilion, initialled.

1854   4in (10cm) high

£5,000-6,000   **TEN**

A Victorian silver-shaped rectangular castle-top card case, Hilliard & Thomason, Birmingham, embossed in relief with Westminster Abbey framed by scroll foliate chasing, the verso with conforming foliate chasing.

1868   3.75in (9.5cm) high 2oz

£1,000-1,500   **DN**

A Victorian snuff box, F. Marsden, Birmingham, rectangular shape with foliate engraving throughout, presentation inscription.

1872   2.75in (7cm) wide 2oz

£200-500   **TEN**

A Royal Presentation silver cigarette case, Alfred Clark, London, applied with the cipher of King George V and Queen Mary in blue and red enamels, inscribed 'XMAS 1920', in original fitted case.

1918   3.25in (8cm) long 4oz

£1,200-1,800   **TEN**

ESSENTIAL REFERENCE – PAUL STORR

Paul Storr (1771-1844) was England's most celebrated 19thC silversmith. From the very beginning of the 19thC, Storr produced silver in a revived version of the Rococo style: in direct contrast to the strict Neo-classical style favoured at the time, his pieces were encrusted with shell-work and rock-work, and sometimes incorporated sea-horses. It is unknown how much of the silver Storr made himself.

- He was apprenticed to Andrew Fogelberg, a Swedish-born silversmith working in the Adam style, in Soho, London. In 1792, he entered into a short-lived partnership with William Frisbee, which lasted until 1796, when Storr entered his first mark alone.
- By 1807, styled as Storr and Co. and now having registered his fourth mark, he began producing a lot of work for the Royal Goldsmiths, Rundell, Bridge & Rundell. In 1811 he formed a sub-partnership with them. He used this time to make contact with some of the most eminent sculptors and artist-craftsmen of the period (including John Flaxman). The partnership between Storr and the Royal Goldsmiths ended in 1819, when Storr took premises in Clerkenwell, London.
- He went into partnership with John Mortimer in 1822, benefitting from Mortimer's retail premises in New Bond Street. He recruited various excellent craftsmen who had worked for Rundell, as well as his own nephew, John Samuel Hunt, as a chaser. Storr retired in 1838.

A Japanese Meiji period shibayama card case, decorated with quail beneath chrysanthemum, flowers and insects, the reverse with cranes beneath bamboo.

4.5in (11.5cm) long

£2,000-3,000   **TEN**

A Victorian wood, ivory and tortoiseshell card case, all-over decorated with a triangle mosaic design.

4in (10cm) high

£60-80   **LT**

An Indian lacquer visiting card case, overlaid with ivory arabesques, the central oval cartouche engraved in black with an Indian deity.

4.25in (11cm) high

£50-80   **LT**

OTHER BOXES

A William III silver snuff box, London, with canted corners, the cover engraved with a cupid amidst scrolling foliate, stylised leaf engraved borders throughout, maker's mark 'DS' crowned struck twice.

c1700   *2.25in (5.5cm) long*
1oz

£160-220   **TEN**

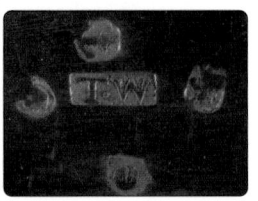

A George III silver oval nutmeg grater, Thomas Willmore, Birmingham, engraved with a vacant tablet and arcaded bands, the grater with a damaged hinge.

1802

£450-550   **DN**

A George IV silver seal box, Paul Storr, London, of typical circular form, the hinged cover chased with the Royal arms, the borders with an oak leaf and acorn border.

1817   *6.75in (17cm) diam 20oz*

£3,000-5,000   **L&T**

A George IV glass medallion mounted silver box, John Riley, London, with a titled glass paste portrait medallion of 'Lord Frederick Campbell Lord Register of Scotland', signed, dated 'Henning F. Edin, 1809', frosted glass ground, gilt interior.

John Henning Senior (1771-1851) was raised in Scotland. After training under his father as a builder, he tried wax portraiture but, in 1803, after seeing the Elgin Marbles in London, he turned to sculpture. For more than a decade he carved a copy of the frieze, selling plaster copies at a reduced size. He also produced wax portraits, and small portraits for reproduction at Wedgwood. Later, he made plaster copies of the Raphael Cartoons at South Kensington. He exhibited at the Royal Academy in the 1820s, at the British Institution and the Royal Scottish Academy.

1823   *3.25in (8.5cm) diam*

£700-1,000   **DN**

A Victorian silver gilt vinaigrette, marked GW/WS, London, bright cut engraved scrolled decoration, engraved crest, engraved grille.

1840   *1.5in (4cm) wide 1oz*

£450-550   **L&T**

A Victorian silver vinaigrette, Nathaniel Mills, Birmingham, of watch case form with foliate pierced circular grille, cast foliate border and suspension ring, presentation inscription 'To Miss Hellen Glass … Edinburgh, Ladies Institution for Southern District'.

1843   *1.5in (4cm) diam*

£300-400   **TEN**

A Victorian silver snuff box, William & Edward Turnpenny, Birmingham, rectangular with engine turned incurved sides, the cover inscribed within a C-scroll cartouche '… To Mr JOHN-BEEDLE Tide Surveyor Cleveland Port, … Oct 1848'.

1845   *3in (7.5cm) wide 2oz*

£450-550   **TEN**

A Victorian table snuff, Charles Rawlings & William Summers, London, rectangular with incurved side and cast foliate thumbpiece and rim, interspersed with thistles, roses and shamrocks, engraved throughout with arabesque strapwork cartouches adorned with flowers, presentation inscription 'Presented to Captain Wiltshire, Ship Newcastle by the Passengers who sailed from England, July 1860, as a mark of their esteem'.

1861   *4in (10cm) long 9oz*

£1,200-1,800   **TEN**

A Victorian silver novelty vinaigrette flask, of horn shape, with engraved diaper ground, hinged cover, screw end terminal.

4in (10cm) long

£250-350   **L&T**

A late 19thC Russian silver-coloured metal gilt trompe l'oeil table cigar box, Heinrich Lassas, St Petersburg, assay master 'AF', 84 zolotniks, engraved with trompe l'oeil wood graining and with facsimiles of Imperial tax bands.

1883   *7.75in (20cm) wide 27.5oz*

£1,800-2,200   **DN**

A German silver musical bird box, chased with scrolls and song birds throughout, the hinged back concealing the key.

c1890   *4in (10cm) wide*

£1,500-2,000   **TEN**

A late 19thC Russian silver-coloured metal trompe l'oeil table cigar box, Moscow, assay master A. Romanov, 84 zolotniks, frosted and engraved with trompe l'oeil Imperial tax bands and tobacconist's marks, maker's mark 'GK'.

1891   *4.25in (11cm) wide 8.5oz (245g)*

£600-800   **DN**

A Victorian vesta case, Chester, chased in high relief with a horse race.

Vesta cases were small box with snapshut covers, used for holding vestas (short matches) and keeping them dry. Vesta cases were widely available from c.1890 to 1920, coinciding with the rapidly increasing popularity of smoking. The high value of this case is most likely due to the racing subject matter.

1895

2in (5cm) 18dwt

£700-1,000   **TEN**

A Continental silver cigarette box, rectangular with chased laurel leaves amidst trellis-work, all framed by a blue enamel border.

c1900

3.5in (9cm) wide

£100-150   **TEN**

A Scottish Ballater provincial snuff box, William Robb, Edinburgh, of plain oval outline, the hinged lid set with a panel of moss agate with scalloped thumbpiece, marked 'ROBB BALLATER' in triangular punch.

1913-14

3in (7.5cm) widest

£1,000-1,500   **L&T**

A George V silver shooting marker, Adie Bros Ltd, Birmingham, with engine-turned sides, the interior fitted with eight ivory and silver pegs numbered 1–8.

1927

2in (5cm) high

£1,200-1,800   **TEN**

A French gold snuff box, Paris, with engine-turned panels bordered by scrolling foliage on a matted ground, maker's mark '(?)H'.

1803-09

3in (7.5cm) long 2oz

£2,000-3,000   **TEN**

A Swiss gold snuff box, with engine-turned decoration enclosing a central three colour gold floral spray.

c1820

3.25in (8cm) long 2oz

£3,500-4,500   **TEN**

A George III gold vinaigrette, Giles Loyer, London, with engine-turned decoration bordered by a laurel chased rim.

1809

1in (2.5cm) diam

£1,000-1,500   **TEN**

A circular gold skippet box, George Unite, Birmingham, with engine-turned decoration throughout and beaded borders, with folding loop handle and safety chain.

1922   2.5in (6.5cm) diam 2oz

£500-600   TEN

A George III gold and semi-precious stone snuff box, A. J. Strachan, London, with engraved turned sides enclosed by chased foliate borders on a matted ground, the base inset with an agate panel, the cover with bloodstone.

1803   2in (5cm) diam

£2,000-3,000   TEN

An early 19thC gold piqué tortoiseshell circular box.

2.75in (7cm) diam

£400-600   GORL

A George IV mourning gold-mounted tortoiseshell snuff box, rectangular with incurved sides and plain gold mounts, cast foliate thumbpiece and memorial cameo applied to the cover within an oval cartouche.

The portrait is probably that of Philip Rundell.

c1880–1925   3in (7.5cm) long

£600-800   TEN

INKSTANDS

A Regency ormolu inkstand, the detachable cover surmounted with two running horses, and three monopodia winged griffins.

8.75in (22cm) high

£300-500   GORL

A Louis Philippe green serpentine marble and gilt-metal mounted inkstand, the square section glass well with engine milled mounts, damage.

c1830   7.5in (19cm) wide

£150-250   DN

A Victorian ebonised timber, coromandel and enamelled ink stand, of square form, inset with cut glass square inkwell with brass hinged lid decorated with polychrome enamel flowers, on a brass and enamelled plinth with stepped timber base.

7.25in (18.5cm) high

£500-800   ADA

A late 19thC French gilt-metal ink stand, of rectangular form, with a hinged pierced lid, revealing two quill troughs, and four ink bottles with gilt-metal covers, the base applied with handles over bracket feet.

12in (30.5cm) wide

£250-350   FRE

An olivewood and electroplated-metal mounted presentation ink stand, inscribed 'Mr Jas. Ln Graham, from the Journeymen and Apprentices in the Finishing Shop', dated, plating rubbed overall.

1892   5.5in (14cm) wide

£250-350   DN

A presentation desk ink stand, Elkington & Company, Birmingham, the socle side base with presentation legend in Arts and Crafts style script, the side and back with chased scenes of Glasgow buildings, the hinged figural clasp with lion rampant, saltire and thistles, the slightly domed hinged cover with applied Glasgow coat of arms, the interior fitted with two inkwells and pen tray, the whole raised on four sea creature feet, on fitted stepped wooden stand and with original presentation box and scroll.

The legend to front of the stand reads 'Presented to the Rt Hon Sir John Gilmour Bt Pd DSO/ MP L.L.D' on his Majesty's principal Secretaries of/ State… Glasgow 7th May… 1929'. The presentation parchment details Sir J. Gilmour's admission as a Burgess and Guild Brother of the city and Royal Burgh of Glasgow.

1928-29   10.5in (27cm) wide

£1,500-2,000   **L&T**

A 19thC rosewood and boulle desk set, comprising a pen and ink stand fitted with two glass ink bottles, two circular taper holders, a stationery box with domed cover, engraved crest and initials, a letter balance with semi-nude figure mount, and an oblong vesta box inset striking plate.

12in (30.5cm) wide

£1,500-2,000   **A&G**

A curly horn snuff mull, of typical curled form, the rim with collar mount engraved in script 'William MacKay' with collar mount below, the hinged domed cover with wriggle work border and engraved to centre in foliate script 'WMK', the well curled horn with applied shield cartouche engraved with the arms to body and to curl with simple oval thumbpiece engraved '1800'.

The engraved arms to shield cartouche are those of MacKay, Baron Reay.

4in (10cm) long

£700-1,000   **L&T**

A ram's head snuff mull, of traditional form, the black-faced ram's head with well curled horns with thistle mounts to terminal and collet set smoky quartz, the head with central box with hinged domed cover set with moss agate cabochon, together with tools suspended from belcher link chains, ebony and ivory mallet, ivory pricker, rake and rabbit paw.

£1,000-1,500   **L&T**

A Jacobean banded baluster snuff mull, composed of sixteen alternating staves of ebony and ivory, with a simple girdle to the lower section and reeded silver rim, a collar mount to the rim with engraved hare bell border and applied silver hinge of a thistle to base and crown to cover with engraved detail, the matching ebony and ivory lid with applied oval cartouche engraved with a flower.

2.25in (6cm) high

£3,500-4,500   **L&T**

A Scottish provincial silver gilt table snuff box, possibly by Peter Ross, the hinged domed lid with foliate and S-scroll border, the base with ovolo and S-scroll foliate rim, marked 'PR' struck twice.

The style and construction of this box was intended to resemble the high quality examples being produced in Birmingham, by such prolific makers as Nathaniel Mills. The proportions and decoration, while a close copy, do not have the refinement. There has been some debate over the origin of this box and particularly the maker's marks. Items struck with maker's mark 'PR' only (struck twice or thrice) are not rare within Scottish flatware, and are attributed to Peter Ross of Aberdeen. Only with the find of this box has this rule been questioned. Ross, while a prolific maker, is not known for larger wares and a box of this accomplished nature would stretch his skill. The other candidate is Patrick Robertson of Edinburgh. It is extraordinary that he would have been the manufacturer of the extant body struck with a maker's mark only, when he was so well regarded. His work would have been under much closer control from the Assay office.

3.25in (8.5cm) wide

£450-550 L&T

An early Victorian silver snuff box, James Nasmyth, Edinburgh, the box with all over engine engraved design, the pull off cover with inset Highland Agricultural Society of Scotland medallion, awarded to 'Roderick Grand Esq, Peterhead, 1837', with engraved border around medallion to cover, fitted leather box.

1838-39 *4.8oz*

£2,000-2,500 L&T

A 19thC French silver cast novelty snuff box, of oval form, modelled as a winged cherub and a lamb, gilt interior.

1.75in (4.5cm) wide 2oz

£500-800 L&T

A late 19thC Italian micromosaic mounted snuff box, the round horn box mounted to centre with a micromosaic roundel of a dog, interior with rose gold lining.

3.5in (9cm) diam

£3,500-4,500 SK

A late 18thC gold and ivory box inset with miniatures of Peregrine, Duke of Ancaster and Kestevin and his wife, the box of ovoid form with gold hinges, the cover with two oval miniatures set with gold.

General Peregrine Bertie, Third Duke of Ancaster and Kestevin (1714-78) inherited the title of Duke on the death of his father in 1742 and also became Lord Great Chamberlain, Lord Lieutenant of Lincolnshire, and a member of the Privy Council. The other miniature is of his second wife Mary Wynn Panton.

c1760

£450-550 L&T

An early 19thC gold and shagreen circular vinaigrette, cover with a ruby-centred four-petal flower, the sides with green-stained shagreen, the grille pierced as a scroll flowerhead, in a later case from Harman & Lambert, New Bond St.

1in (2.5cm) diam

£1,000-1,500 DN

A Scottish gold and bloodstone vinaigrette, the faceted semi-precious stone base and cover with cast foliate gold mounts, the grille finely pierced and engraved with thistles.

c1825 *1.25in (3cm) wide*

£1,000-1,500 TEN

A gilt-metal bee skep jewellery casket, retailed by Howell James & Co., Regent St., London, of naturalistic design with twisted loop handle, button push release, knob lacking, flanked by two applied bees with banded agate cabochon abdomens, raised upon a branch effect square stand.

c1870 *8.75in (22.5cm) high*

£450-550 TEN

A German silver and enamel cigarette case, depicting four racehorses and jockeys over a water jump.

c1890 *3.5in (9cm) wide*

£800-1,200 TEN

A Bilston enamel snuff box, of circular outline with waisted base, the sides decorated with scenes of buildings and country scenes, the domed hinged cover with gilt ormolu mounts, painted to the cover with standing figures of a Highlander in full dress and a portrait of Bonnie Prince Charlie to the interior.

2.25in (6cm) diam

£1,500-2,000   **L&T**

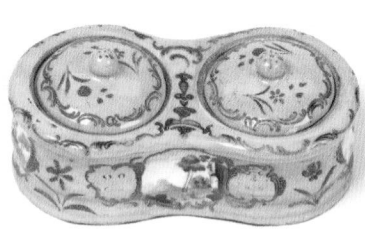

An enamel double inkwell, South Staffordshire, of hourglass section, painted with four landscape cartouches within gilt scrolls against a duck-egg blue ground, enclosing two semi-ovoid ink receptacles with ropetwist rims, the shallow domed covers with compressed sphere knops.

c1765   *5in (13cm) wide*

£500-800   **TEN**

A pair of 18thC enamel candlesticks, painted with colourful sprays of flowers on a white ground, damage and restoration.

11in (28cm) high

£400-600   **WW**

A Napoleon III gilt bronze and cloisonné enamel tripod vase, Ferdinand Barbedienne, the body and three spade-form handles decorated with scrolling foliate designs, raised on the monopodia panthers, united by a stretcher, signed 'F. Barbedienne'.

13.25in (33.5cm) high

£1,500-2,500   **L&T**

A late 19thC gilt and champlevé enamel carriage-shaped dish, of scrolled Rococo design.

10.5in (27cm) wide

£150-200   **L&T**

A French gilt metal and enamel jewellery box, probably Limoges, the hinged lid decorated with figures seated in a garden, the sides with riverside landscape views, opening to reveal a plush lined interior and raised on bracket feet.

c1900   *8.25in (21cm) wide*

£1,000-1,500   **L&T**

A late 19thC Medieval-style enamel triptych of a king and courtiers, the king enthroned under a canopy with three courtiers, the flanking pieces each with a further courtier in front of an arcade, in a painted wooden frame.

6.75in (17cm) high

£500-800   **DN**

An 18thC German carved ivory and silver-mounted stein, one litre oval shape, carved hunt scene with wild board, lion and stag, figural handle, fluted to cover and footrim, German hallmarks.

8.5in (21.5cm) high

£8,000-10,000   **SK**

An 18thC German carved ivory and gilt-silvered mounted stein, half litre cylindrical shape, carved mythological scene with boar hunting, handle with a satyr grasping for a nude nymph, Pan finial, scrolled foliage to silver foot, thumbrest and hinged cover, German hallmarks.

11in (28cm) high

£10,000-15,000   **SK**

A late 17th/18thC probably French carved ivory oval relief panel depicting Saint Joseph with the Infant Christ, in a profusely carved oval frame.

11in (28cm) high

£650-750   **DN**

A late 19thC Continental carved ivory plaque, depicting Empress Elizabeth of Russia in full court regalia, within laurel and oak borders accented with scrolls and cornucopia, over a double-headed eagle.

6in (15cm) high

£5,000-7,000   **SK**

An 18thC Spanish ivory and tortoiseshell veneered crucifix, the ivory corpus with loosely draped perizonium, with traces of original polychrome, mounted on ebony and tortoiseshell veneered cross with stepped hexagonal base.

25.5in (65cm) high

£800-1,200   **L&T**

An early 19thC Italian carved ivory crucifix, with white metal mounts.

24.5in (62cm) high

£5,000-6,000   **ADA**

A pair of epergnes, each elephant ivory tusk section body with simple scalloped silver-plated mounts, with scroll support for the moulded glass epergne, on a black turned wooden base.

29.5in (75cm) high

£1,500-2,000   **L&T**

A late 19thC Continental carved ivory figure of Napoleon, the figure standing in full military dress, hands crossed across chest, with four cannon balls stacked at base, on turned ebonised wooden base.

Overall 12.5in (32cm) high

£1,800-2,200   **SK**

A late 19thC Continental carved ivory triptych figure of Napoleon, carved as a standing figure of Napoleon in Imperial garb, holding fleur-de-lys staff, his robe opening on hinges to a triptych scene of the marriage of Napoleon and Josephine, on turned ebonised wood base.

Overall 9.75in (25cm) high

£2,000-3,000   **SK**

A pair of 19thC Continental ivory figures, each modelled as a standing cavalier, raised on later carved oak pedestal base.

Tallest 7.5in (19cm) high

£2,500-3,500   **L&T**

A 19thC ivory tusk, excellent patina, uncarved strong convex form, over wood stand.

35in (89cm) high

£600-800   **FRE**

A pair of 19thC colonial ivory tusks, of slight convex form, beautifully carved to show royal figures and animals, on wood stands.

Tusk 50in (127cm) high

£2,500-3,500   **FRE**

OBJETS DE VERTU

ESSENTIAL REFERENCE – PRISONER OF WAR WORK

During the Napoleonic Wars (1792-1815) about 100,000 French prisoners were captured by the British. They were held in moored hulks and in prisons. Under extremely difficult conditions the captives performed the laborious task of producing bone and ivory ship models.

- The calibre of their craftsmanship is apparent in the intricate examples that they produced. These artisans produced these models from scratch, using any materials available to them, without the aid of any official designs on which they could base their works. They must have had a good knowledge of shipping and fleets.
- Their diet of mutton or beef stew, with the bone, proved to be a vital source of raw material. In addition, materials such as animal and human hair, clothing, jewellery or wood, were used to make these masterpieces.

A gold mounted ivory toothpick case, the cover carved with three entwined branches labelled 'England', 'Scotland' and 'Ireland' bound by the words 'Mutual Interest', 'Harmony' and 'Union'.

c1810   *3in (7.5cm) long*

£550-650   TEN

A mid-19thC American carved and inlaid ivory and bone yarn swift, the ivory swift topped with a covered yarn cup, on a turned shaft inlaid with red and black wax, the clamp inlaid with abalone and wood, the bone slats joined with red and blue silk ribbons, inlaid with wood dots and engraved with floral vines, imperfections.

16in (40.5cm) high

£4,500-5,500   SK

A 19thC Prisoner-of-War model ship, contained in a glazed display case.

31in (79cm) wide

£6,000-8,000   ADA

MINIATURES

A rare 17thC Dutch locket, enclosing eight miniature portraits of a family, each painted on one side of five oval leaves.

£8,000-10,000   POOK

An 18thC English School group of four portraits, depicting a gentleman, a woman and two children.

£6,000-8,000   POOK

An oval portrait miniature of two children holding a squirrel, by Thomas Chubbard, signed with initials 'TC' on obverse, in an oval gold frame with plaited hair at reverse.

c1770   *1.5in (3.5cm) wide*

£1,200-1,800   DN

An English school portrait miniature gentleman, wearing a black coat, a white vest and a red waistcoat, in a gilt metal oval frame, with brown plaited hair and blonde plaited hair in the form of a bow to the reverse.

By repute the sitter is from a Belgian family of Braxtead Hall.

c1790   *1.75in (4.5cm) high*

£400-600   DN

An English school portrait miniature of a gentleman in profile, attributed to Isabella Beetham, wearing a coat and a lace cravat, his hair tied in a pigtail, silhouette painted on the reverse of convex glass, reverse with broken Beetham's trade label no 5, in a turned pearwood frame.

c1790   3.5in (9cm) high
£300-500   DN

A portrait miniature of Colonel Milnes of the Grenadier Guards, by Charles Sheriff, wearing a blue uniform with red facings and gold epaulette, in an oval gold frame, the reverse with bright cut border.

c1790   2.25in (5.5cm) high
£4,000-5,000   DN

A portrait miniature of a gentleman in profile, by John Field, the sitter wearing a coat and a lace cravatte and his hair tied in a pigtail, bronzed silhouette painted on ivory, signed 'Miers' under truncation in an oval gold locket frame, with hair locks tied with gold wire to the reverse.

c1795   1.75in (4.5cm) high
£600-800   DN

An English school portrait miniature of a gentleman facing right, wearing a brown coat, a white shirt and a stock, with plaited hair an inner blue glass and seed pearl locket to the reverse, in a plain oval frame.

c1800   2.75in (7cm) high
£250-350   DN

An English school portrait miniature of a gentleman, wearing a blue coat with a black collar, a blue and white striped waistcoat and a red vest, in an oval pierced gilt-metal scroll brooch mount.

c1800   2.5in (6.5cm) high
£250-350   DN

A pair of portrait miniatures a young girl and young chorister, by Joseph Tassy, one signed on the obverse, both signed on the reverse, with the address 'Rue Cauebiere 25, Marseille'.

Joseph Tassy painted portrait oils and miniatures in Paris, and participated in the Paris Salon of 1791. He very rarely signed his work, and is thus an almost unknown artist.

1807   2.25in (5.5cm) wide overall
£300-500   DN

An early 19thC memorium miniature, of oval form, decorated with an urn with inscription commemorating the deaths of John and Hannah Marsden in 1800 and 1807, under a willow tree constructed out of hair, with inscription to border, in a gilt frame, with glass to front and back.

3.25in (8.5cm) high
£250-350   L&T

A 19thC oval portrait miniature painting of Napoleon II as Duke of Reichstadt, by Forster, watercolour on ivory, of the Duke in white tunic, inscribed to verso 'Herzog v. Reichstadt', in a large square rosewood and ebonised frame.

2.75in (7cm) high
£300-500   L&T

A miniature portrait painted porcelain plaque, depicting a woman, the reverse of the plaque with inscription 'Agnes Wheler Aged 16 years Painted by Wm Corden 1822. Given to me by my aunt H Mari Fitzherbert, 14 August 1899', signed 'W Fitzherbert'.

1822   5.5in (14cm) high
£1,000-1,500   TEN

An English school portrait miniature of a young red-haired woman, seated half length, a portfolio of drawings under her right arm, holding a pen in her right hand and wearing a lace-trimmed claret dress, in a crushed Morocco folding frame with inner ormolu milled slip frame.

c1830   3in (7.5cm) high
£350-550   TEN

An early/mid-19thC American school watercolour on ivory miniature portrait, of a gentleman in a blue jacket.

2.25in (5.5cm) high
£600-800   POOK

A portrait miniature of a young lady, by Moritz Michael Daffinger, the sitter wearing a brown-trimmed green stole and a white dress, a pink rose at her corsage and a similar rose in her hair.

c1835   4in (10cm) high
£650-850   DN

OBJETS DE VERTU

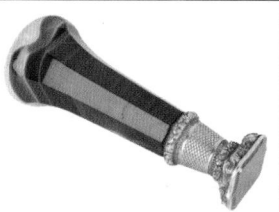

A Victorian banded agate-handled desk seal, the un-engraved table with a scroll chased and engine turned mount.

2.5in (6cm) long

£450-550   DN

A 19thC gold mounted bloodstone seal, the vase-shaped bloodstone handle with claw mounts at either end set with a seal-engraved white agate and an intaglio bloodstone.

2.25in (5.5cm) long

£550-650   DN

An unusual faceted blue glass double-ended scent bottle, the caps with chased foliate borders and figures of bears standing on all four paws.

6in (15cm) long

£300-500   DN

A late 19thC blue flash cut glass double-ended scent bottle, with plain caps, one engraved with a monogram.

5in (12.5cm) long

£120-180   DN

A George IV silver child's rattle, James Henry Daniel, London, chased overall with flowering scroll foliage, with a whistle, a suspension loop, eight spherical bells hung from a leafy corona and with a coral teether.

1826   *4.75in (12cm) long*

£400-600   DN

A Victorian silver child's rattle, Hilliard & Thomason, Birmingham, chased with flowers and foliage, with a whistle, a suspension loop, six bells hung from a spherical knop and with a coral teether, engraved 'ADP 1864'.

1863   *5.25in (13.5cm) long*

£400-600   DN

An Argyll & Sutherland Highlanders' dress sporran, the badger mask body with six white horse hair tassels suspended from gilt bullion knotted ropes, with red leather backing.

15.75in (40cm) long

£600-800   L&T

A Scottish provincial Balmoral Highlanders' sporran, William Robb, Edinburgh, marked 'ROBB BALLATER', also inscribed 'ERI (in monogram) 1904', white horse hair body with three black horse hair tassels suspended from oval belcher.

1903-04   Cantle 7.25in (18.5cm) wide

£2,000-3,000   L&T

A 19thC white and grey marble Moorish-style pavilion, the stepped and fluted cornice above a faux dentil frieze, on four ribbed columns supporting trefoil carved and pierced arches, on moulded plinth base, some significant losses to marble at the corners.

22.5in (57cm) high

£400-500   L&T

A late 19thC alabaster plaquette of the Alhambra with two ogee arches before a painted garden scene, the upper portion decorated with Kufic script highlighted in gold, blue and red, the lower part rendered as mosaic tiling, inscribed 'No9 - Enrique Linares. Es propiedad' within a crenellated walnut frame.

15.25in (39cm) high

£600-800   L&T

A 19thC Indian miniature painting of the Taj Mahal.

4in (11cm) wide

£150-250   DN

A pair of 19thC alabaster relief plaques, in the manner of Gislebertus, carved as Adam and Eve, copies of 12thC lintel carving from Autun.

The original Eve is now in the museum in Rolin, the Adam is now thought to be lost.

12.75in (32.5cm) wide

£350-550   GORL

A Victorian double-sided sailor's shell valentine, in a folding octagonal mahogany case, comprising various coloured shells in segmented radial arrangement, bears motto 'REMEMBER ME'.

9in (23cm) wide

£1,500-2,000 **L&T**

A mid-Victorian velvet casket, set with a memoriam locket of Mary Queen of Scots' hair, the rectangular casket with rounded corners, and brass lock escutcheon, the slightly domed cover set to centre with oval glass panel with hair beneath with applied brass engraved Scottish royal corn above and ribboned garter below inscribed 'A LOCK OF QUEEN MARY'S HAIR WHICH BELONGED TO THE LATE LADY BELHAVEN', the interior of the casket simply lined with watered cream silk.

The lock of hair contained with this casket was part of a larger find by the 8th Lord of Belhaven in his position of High Commissioner of Scotland. The main of the lock was subsequently gifted to Her Majesty Queen Victoria and formed part of her collection of Queen Mary Stewart relics. The lock was found within his official residence in Holyrood in a secret drawer of her bureau in an envelope with the hand-written note saying 'a lock of my own hair' signed 'Mary R'. The signature was later authenticated as that of Queen Mary Stuart, believed to have been compared with original documents held in the Royal Collections. When its importance was realised the bequest by Lord Belhaven to Queen Victoria was made and the lock split in two.

6in (15.5cm) wide

£7,000-10,000 **L&T**

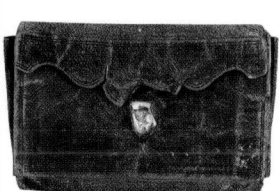

A Philadelphia leather wallet, inscribed 'The Gift of Hen Drinker to Caspar Wistar June 30th 1760'.

7.25in (18.5cm) wide

£1,500-2,000 **POOK**

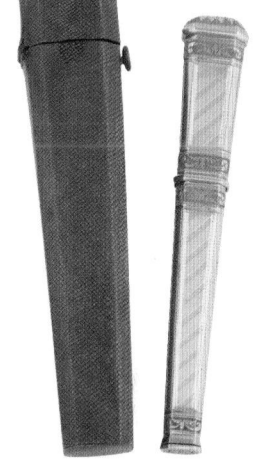

A French gold bodkin case, Paris, of rectangular tapering form, finely machine engraved panels between foliate borders on a matted ground, initialled 'CH' to the base, in fitted shagreen case.

1798–1809 *4in (10cm) long*

£1,000-1,500 **TEN**

A George III shagreen tapered oblong draughtsman's drawing instrument case, printed label 'Carpenter Best Skin Case London', with fittings.

6.5in (16.5cm) high

£250-350 **DN**

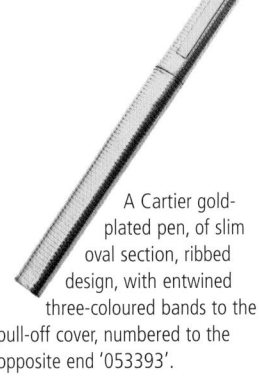

A Cartier gold-plated pen, of slim oval section, ribbed design, with entwined three-coloured bands to the pull-off cover, numbered to the opposite end '053393'.

5in (13cm) long

£100-200 **L&T**

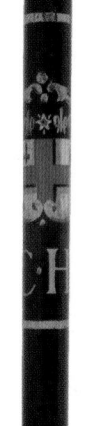

A late 19thC Victorian painted parcel gilt and ebonised wood tipstaff, decorated with the Arms of Christ's Hospital.

70.75in (180cm) high

£350-450 **DN**

OBJETS DE VERTU

A large 19thC bottle whimsy, probably American, large blown cylindrical glass bottle topped with carved acorn-shaped finial the interior fitted with a carved wooden revolving two-tier skein winder on a stand, wound with silk embroidery threads.

14.5in (37cm) high

£1,200-1,800   SK

A 19thC Italian ormolu crucifix, with suspension ring to the top, the back of the cross worked in relief with Christ's face and symbols of the Passion, contained in the original olivewood orange velvet-lined case.

11.5in (29cm) high

£300-400   TEN

A hand-painted and printed paper fan, hand-painted with flowers, in original box with inscription 'A Spanish Fan-Present from H.A. W. Royce (Albion) to her mother A Wells-(New Hartford) August 18th 1852 Price $2.00.'

c1850   10.5in (26.5cm) long

£70-100   FRE

A Regency ivory mounted silk purse, with a four piece sewing set, all with initials 'KJB', comprising tape measure, two pin cushions and needle case, with acorn-shaped pin box and one other ivory box.

£550-650   GORL

A modern commemorative egg, by Stuart Devlin, London, the textured gilt egg with applied silver male and female figures, hinged and opening to reveal a male and female figure standing beneath a tree beside a rough bright green crystal on a naturalistic base.

1974   2.95in (7.5cm) high

£450-550   L&T

A silver mounted coconut, Sheffield, with gadroon edge and stem base.

c1938

£250-350   MEA

A large Jurassic period Moroccan limestone Mantelliceras Ammonite, on a black limestone plinth, with Orthoceras specimens.

Orthoceras are fossilised squid shells.

22in (56cm) high overall

£1,500-2,000   TEN

A 9ct gold gem set thimble, with alternately set border of seed pearls and circular cut turquoise cabochons.

1in (2.5cm) high 5.5g

£150-200   L&T

A Russian silver-gilt and cloisonné enamel kovsch, Grachev Brothers, St Petersburg, of traditional form, the flat handle with a vacant cartouche.
1908-1917   *13.25in (33.5cm) long*
£45,000-55,000   **L&T**

A Russian silver-gilt and enamel kovsch, Vasili Agafonov, Moscow, with shaded cloisonné foliage, flowerheads set with cabochon hardstones.
1899-1908   *8.5in (22cm) long*
£25,000-30,000   **L&T**

A Russian silver-gilt and cloisonné enamel kovsch, Moscow, in the form of a peacock, the head set with red cabochons, the tip of the openwork tail similarly set with cabochon stones.

1899-1908   *9in (23m) long*
£35,000-45,000   **L&T**

A Russian silver-gilt and cloisonné enamel tea-glass holder, Konstantin Skvortsov, Moscow, decorated with stylised polychrome floral scrolling with panels enclosing geometrical motifs, maker's mark.
1908-1917   *4.75in (12cm) high*
£10,000-15,000   **L&T**

A Russian silver-gilt and cloisonné enamel tea-glass holder, Nikolai Alexeev, Moscow, the lobed body decorated with swans and flowerheads, maker's mark.
1896-1908   *3.5in (9cm) high*
£10,000-15,000   **L&T**

A Russian silver-gilt and shaded cloisonné enamel three-handled loving cup, Feodor Rückert, Moscow, the lower part of the baluster shaped cup with lobed cartouches supporting mythological sirens and swans amidst stylised polychrome floral decoration, within twisted ropework borders, the stylised handles similarly decorated, the underside of the base with engraved inscription in English 'To my esteemed friend Frank Johnson after 27 years of business association J.C. Hoagland March 15th 1899', scratched inventory number '7590'.

The scratched inventory number suggests this cup was retailed by Fabergé.
c1890   *7.75in (19.5cm) high*
£200,000-250,000   **L&T**

RUSSIAN ANTIQUES

A Russian silver-gilt and cloisonné enamel tazza, Gustav Klingert, Moscow, the bowl supported on a baluster stem, with foliate scrolls on a turquoise ground, extensively decorated with gilt filigree.

1895 *5.25in (13.5cm) high*

£3,000-4,000 **L&T**

A Russian silver-gilt and cloisonné enamel two-handled tazza, Orest Kurliukov, Moscow, extensively decorated with scrolling foliage.

1896-1908 *15.75in (40cm) wide*

£120,000-180,000 **L&T**

A Russian silver-gilt gem-set and cloisonné enamel two-handled tray, Orest Kurliukov, on four bun supports, with vacant heart-shaped central cartouche.

c1900 *10.5in (27cm) wide*

£55,000-65,000 **L&T**

A Russian silver-gilt and shaded cloisonné enamel dish, Fedor Rückert, Moscow, on three ball supports.

1896-1908 *4in (12cm) diam*

£20,000-30,000 **L&T**

A Russian silver-gilt and shaded cloisonné enamel swing-handle cake-basket, Nikolai Alexeev, Moscow, the bowl decorated with a flying swallow amongst stylised flowers.

c1890 *5.25in (13.5cm) diam*

£10,000-15,000 **L&T**

CLOSER LOOK - CLOISONNÉ JEWELLERY BOX

A Russian silver-gilt and cloisonné enamel casket, Gustav Klingert, Moscow, the gilt interior engraved 'Souvenir Amiseul de la Famille Matimor 1897'.

1896 *5.25in (13.5cm) wide*

£5,000-6,000 **L&T**

The image is 'The Unveiling of the Bride' after the painting by Konstantin Makovsky (1838-1915). His historical paintings often show an idealised view of Russian life.

Fedor Ruckert was a Fabergé workmaster and his chief supplier of enamelwares. He was of German origin, and born in Moscow, where made articles in cloisonné enamels.

Often Fabergé's Moscow signature obliterates Rucket's initials. Rucket also sold his cloisonné objects independently, and consequently several of his pieces, such as this one, have no Fabergé marks.

A Russian silver-gilt cloisonné and en-plein enamel jewellery box, Fedor Rückert, Moscow.

1908-1917 *5.5in (14cm) wide*

£200,000-250,000 **L&T**

A Russian silver-gilt cloisonné and plique-à-jour enamel box, Antip Kuzmichev, Moscow, the hinged lid with plique-à-jour stylised foliage, with hinged clasp.

1891 *4.75in (12cm) wide*

£15,000-20,000 **L&T**

A Russian silver-gilt and cloisonné enamel card case, Fedor Rückert, Moscow, decorated with the King of Spades and the Queen of Diamonds, the top of the hinged cover with a medallion beneath the Imperial eagle, decorated with the pious pelican and with Russian inscription 'For the benefit of the Imperial Foundling School', gilt interior with two compartments, scratched number 2410.

c1890 *3.75in (9.5cm) high*

£100,000-150,000 **L&T**

A Russian silver-gilt and shaded enamel coffee service, Pavel Ovchinnikov, Moscow, comprising a coffee pot, covered sugar basin, cream jug, sugar-tongs, and twelve coffee spoons, all within the original silk-lined wooden case, the interior of the lid with the manufacturer's stamp beneath the Imperial Warrant.

A gift from Nicholas II to the father of a previous owner during one of his trips to Russia in 1905.
1899-1908   *Coffee pot 6.5in (16.5cm) h*
£150,000-200,000   **L&T**

A Russian silver-gilt and cloisonné enamel three-piece tea set, Moscow, comprising teapot and cover, sugar basin and cover, and milk jug.
1892-3   *4.75in (12cm) high*
£20,000-25,000   **L&T**

A silver-gilt and red enamel four-piece tea-service, Pavel Ovchinnikov, Moscow, the egg-shaped teapot cast and chased with flowers and applied with a bee, the hinged lid cast with the figure of a lizard, the sugar basin and cover and the milk jug applied with insects, the lid with an open flower and a bee, the tray cast and chased with a spider in his web.
1883-1885   *Tray 10.75in (27.5cm) wide*
£40,000-50,000   **L&T**

A silver-gilt and cloisonné enamel and silver vodka set, Pavel Ovchinnikov, Moscow, comprising vodka flask, stopper and stand and six small charki.

1899-1908   *Tray 11.25in (28.5cm) wide*
£45,000-50,000   **L&T**

A Russian silver-gilt and shaded cloisonné enamel tea-caddy, Fedor Rückert, Moscow, with stylised flowerheads and floral scrolls on a dark-brown ground, the shovel with identical decoration and with maker's mark 'N.P., Moscow'.

1908-1917   *5in (13cm) high*
£70,000-80,000   **L&T**

A large Russian silver-gilt and cloisonné enamel bowl, Pavel Ovchinnikov, Moscow, chased and engraved with gryphons, scroll handles set with cabochon stones, one missing, maker's mark beneath Imperial Warrant.

1899-1908   *12.5in (31.5cm) wide*
£100,000-150,000   **L&T**

A Russian silver-gilt and shaded cloisonné enamel two-handled vase, Vasili Naumov, Moscow, with four circular reserves of stylised scrolling polychrome foliage.

1908-1917   *5in (13cm) high*
£90,000-110,000   **L&T**

A pair of Russian silver-gilt and champlevé enamel candlesticks, Pavel Ovchinnikov, Moscow, the design based on elements of Russian vernacular architecture, the collars with pierced flanges hung with enamel pendants.

1878   *8.75in (22cm) high*
£10,000-15,000   **L&T**

A Fabergé silver-gilt and shaded enamel kovsch, Moscow, the sides decorated with enamel foliage, each side supporting a siren, the front and back with a lion, the pierced flat-shaped handle with flowers.

1908-1917   14.5in (37cm) long

£90,000-120,000   L&T

ESSENTIAL REFERENCE – FABERGÉ

Master craftsman, Peter Carl Fabergé (1846-1920) designed and made jewellery and objects d'art. He is best known for creating 57 beautiful Imperial eggs, the first of which was commissioned by Tsar Alexander III of Russia for his Empress in 1884.

- He served his apprenticeship in Frankfurt, Germany, after which he returned to Russia and took over the family business in 1870. It soon became the leading jewellery firm in St. Petersburg, and received the Imperial appointment in 1881. Fabergé won the Gold Medal at the Pan-Russian Exhibition in 1882.
- Over the next 30 years, he established shops in several Russian cities and in London, and gained the patronage of many royal houses.
- At its height, Fabergé's company employed more than 500 assistants, designers, modellers, gem-cutters, golds-miths and enamellers, with Fabergé himself largely directing artistic and commercial policy, rather than designing.
- The company produced a wide range of objects, such as dinner- and tea-services, cigarette cases, pen rests, picture frames, cigar lighters, hard-stone statuettes of animals, and sprays of flowers with gold stalks and jewelled petals.
- Following the Revolution of 1917, the House of Fabergé was nationalised by the Bolsheviks and Fabergé fled Russia in 1918. He died in Lausanne, Switzerland in 1920.

A Russian Fabergé parcel-gilt and guilloché enamel kovsch, St. Petersburg, workmaster probably Anders Nevalainen, workmaster's initials indistinct, scratched inventory number 15475.

3.25in (8cm) long

£15,000-20,000   L&T

A Fabergé jewelled silver and enamel charka, Moscow, chased with panels of stylised leaves, with reserves of matt-green enamel, the rim set with four cabochon stones, gilt interior.

1908-1917   4.25in (10.5cm) wide

£15,000-20,000   L&T

A late 19thC Fabergé silver-gilt and enamel-mounted gem-set agate dish, Moscow, the handle in the form of a stylised anthemion set with a Catherine II gold rouble 1776, the portrait embellished with red enamel, the terminal set with two diamonds flanking a cabochon sapphire, marked 'K. Fabergé' beneath Imperial Warrant, the foot marked with initialled 'K.F.'

4in (10cm) wide

£18,000-22,000   L&T

A late 19thC Fabergé silver-mounted sandstone vesta-holder, Moscow, marked 'K. Fabergé' beneath Imperial Warrant, scratched inventory number 4687, 88 standard.

4.75in (12cm) high

£20,000-25,000   L&T

A Russian Fabergé silver, gold and enamel scent bottle, engraved with the stock number '4602' to the neck of the bottle, in fitted case, Imperial Warrant to the lining of the case.

c1887-90   1.25in (3cm) long

£22,000-26,000   TEN

A Fabergé gold Easter egg, by Erik Kollin, the egg decorated with a star set pearl on each side, opening to two birds facing each other with ruby eyes, with initials for Erik August Kollin and 56 standard marks for St. Petersburg.

Erik August Kollin (1836-1901), became a Fabergé master in 1868, then became head goldsmith 1870-1886. His works are relatively rare. After 1886, he worked independently but continued to produce occasional pieces for Fabergé.

0.75in (2cm) high 14ct

£7,500-8,500   **RTC**

A Russian silver-mounted jade vase, the mounts 1st Silver Artel, Moscow, the celadon-green vase in the form of an early Chinese bronze, with Fabergé mark beneath Imperial Warrant.

1908-1917   7.5in (19cm) high

£12,000-18,000   **L&T**

A pair of Fabergé silver Rococo-style candlesticks, workmaster Julius Rappoport, St Petersburg, cast and chased with foliate scrolls and garlands, rocaille shells and foliage, marked 'Fabergé' and with workmaster's initials, 88 standard.

1908-1917   6in (15cm) high 36oz

£14,000-18,000   **L&T**

A Fabergé silver-mounted guilloche enamel wood photograph frame, workmaster Karl Gustav Armfeldt, St Petersburg, marked Fabergé, with workmaster's initials, 88 standard.

1896-1908   9.75in (25cm) high

£40,000-45,000   **L&T**

OTHER RUSSIAN ANTIQUES

An unusual late 19thC Russian gold-mounted lapis lazuli hand seal with three matrices, Samuel Arnd, St Petersburg.

3.75in (9.5cm) long

£8,000-12,000   **L&T**

CLOSER LOOK RUSSIAN SILVER WINE COOLERS

These wine coolers are possibly inspired by the great Parisian goldsmiths, Thomas Germain and Jacques Roettiers. But these are very far from copies. The way in which the krater-like vase has been completely enveloped by the living vine could only be Victorian, but the craggy rocky base which supports the vase reinvents a Roettiers centrepiece of the 1740s, while the vine handles recall those of a Germain wine cooler of 1727.

The rims of the detachable liners are cast with vines.

The handles are realistically modelled as scrolling fruiting vines rising from bases in the form of rock promontories.

The bowls are cast, repoussé, chased and engraved with huntsmen with hounds pursuing deer and rabbits through woods.

Carl Tegelsten supplied silver to the famous St Petersburg silver retailers Englishmen Nichols and Plinke, known as the Magazin Anglais, active between 1829 and 1870. The Russian aristocracy and the Imperial Court were its main clients.

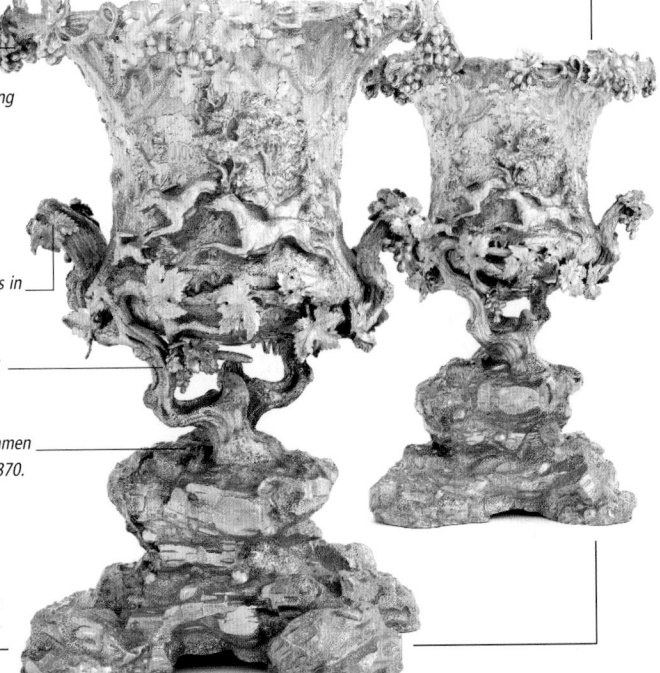

A pair of mid-19thC Russian silver wine coolers, Carl Tegelsten, St. Petersburg.

1849   16.5in (42cm) high

£60,000-70,000   **L&T**

RUSSIAN ANTIQUES

A Russian Gardiner porcelain equestrian figure, depicting a boy riding bareback, with red printed mark.

8.25in (21cm) high

£1,700-2,200   **SK**

A late 19th/early 20thC Russian porcelain figural inkwell, formed as a man in red coat and top hat, carrying a basket, the lid removing to small inkpot and sander.

7.75in (20cm) high

£1,000-1,500   **SK**

A large Russian porcelain plate, from the Lomonosov Porcelain Manufactory, St Petersburg, painted with an elaborate cliff top castle being approached by a ship, titled in Russian with 'Struggle Breeds Heroes', painted mark and dated.

1921   *13in (33.5cm) diam*

£1,000-1,500   **WW**

A 19thC Russian 'Virgin of Joy' icon, painted in egg tempura on gold leaf with a depiction of the Virgin Mary holding the infant Christ and sceptre, overlaid with an embossed brass frame, signed 'A. Reznikov', with a certificate of authenticity.

13.25in (33.5cm) high

£900-1,200   **JA**

A 19thC Russian icon, painted in egg tempura with a representation of St Nicholas, within an ornate foliate embossed gold leaf surround, signed 'A. Reznikov', with a certificate of authenticity.

12.25in (31cm) high

£1,300-1,800   **JA**

A Russian icon, ornately painted with a depiction of Christ's Resurrection, shown in twelve panels, the central panel with a detailed representation of the Easter theme, with embossed gilt and jewelled borders, signed 'A. Reznikov', with a certificate of authenticity.

£1,800-2,200   **JA**

A 19thC Russian icon, depicting the intercession, with Saint Peter and Alexandra, painted in egg tempura on gold leaf gesso, signed 'A. Reznikov', with a certificate of authenticity.

7in (18cm) high

£700-1,000   **JA**

A 19thC Russian icon, depicting Saint Michael Arkhistrategos, panted in tempura on gesso, signed 'Sergei Agafonov', with a certificate of authenticity.

11.75in (30cm) high

£1,200-1,800   **JA**

An early 18thC Russian boxwood cross, carved with exposition windows of the life of Christ, inscribed in Cyrillic, with brass frame pendant mount and fishskin case.

5.25in (13.5cm) high

£2,000-2,500   **GORL**

A late 19thC Russian malachite veneered black marble plate.

8.25in (21cm) diam

£350-450   **DN**

An early 19thC Russian fiddleback mahogany and metal mounted dome-top dressing table casket, bearing paper retailer's label to interior 'Nichols and Plincke, Magazin Anglais, ST. PETERSBOURG', with bun feet, one lacking.

10in (25.5cm) wide

£700-1,000   **DN**

A 17thC north European brass candlestick, raised on a bell base with drip panel and a baluster stem, with a socket pierced with extraction holes.

6.25in (16cm) high

£200-300   WW

A pair of early 18thC probably English brass baluster candlesticks, with slightly flared panelled sconces and multi-knopped stem to dished hexagonal bases, each sconce pierced.

6in (15cm) high

£250-350   TEN

A pair of early 18thC brass hexagonal candlesticks, with domed bases and knopped stems.

6.5in (16.5cm) high

£400-450   WW

A pair of George II brass candlesticks, with hexagonal bases and baluster stems.

7in (18cm) high

£200-250   WW

A pair of early George III brass candlesticks, with shaped and welled square bases and knopped stems.

7.25in (18.5cm) high

£100-150   WW

An 18thC brass tinder box, with a pierced sconce and handle.

3.75in (9.5cm) high

£150-200   WW

A pair of 18thC brass tapersticks, of typical form with multiple knopped stems and on multiple moulded rounded square bases.

4.75in (12cm) high

£600-700   TEN

A pair of early 19thC-style gilt-brass candlesticks, the loaded circular bases with shell, leaf and tracery stems, ribbed sconces with detachable leaf nozzles.

8.5in (21.5cm) high

£180-220   WW

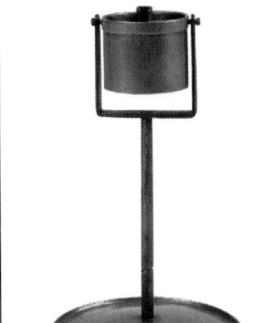

A mid-19thC American brass and iron gimballed fat lamp, Pennsylvania, impressed 'John Derr'.

9.25in (23.5cm) high

£2,000-2,500   POOK

An American Peter Derr brass and wrought iron fat lamp, the shaft impressed 'P.D. 1850'.

6in (15cm) high

£3,500-4,000   POOK

A pair of late 19thC large Victorian brass candlesticks.

21.5in (54.5cm) high

£300-400   DN

A late 19thC set of six brass candlesticks with knopped shafts and square bases.

8in (20.5cm) high

£500-700   DN

A late 19thC pair of Louis XV-style gilt-bronze and crystal candelabra, with urn-form turned stems, and seven branches hung with pear-shaped drops and faceted cut-crystal swags, fitted for electricity.

27.75in (70.5cm) high

£2,500-3,000 **FRE**

A pair of similar Louis XVI-style gilt and patinated bronze cassolettes, the domed lids with pineapple and naturalistic finials lifting to reveal a candle nozzle, raised on three ram's mask scroll supports, terminating in a stepped circular base.

Tallest 10.25in (26cm) high

£800-1,200 **L&T**

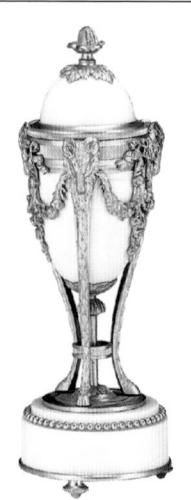

One of a pair of Louis XVI-style gilt-bronze and marble cassolettes, oviform, the lid with finial reversing to a candle nozzle, raised on trefoil legs, on a stepped circular, beaded base.

12in (30.5cm) high

£500-800 PAIR **FRE**

A pair of late 19th/early 20thC Louis XVI-style parcel-gilt bronze figural eight-light candelabra, the candle arms formed as flower stems, supported on cherub-form standards and white marble bases, electrified.

30.25in (77cm) high

£3,500-4,500 **SK**

A pair of possibly Irish cut-glass candlestick lustres, with hollow vase-form stems cut with repeat lozenge motifs to the shoulders, with elongated nozzles within separate six-point collars supporting slice-cut almondine drops.

c1800 *8.75in (22.5cm) high*

£500-600 **TEN**

A pair of French Empire-style bronze and ormolu three-branch four-light table candelabra, each with a central raised campana nozzle with flambeau finial insert, within three acanthus scroll branches.

18.25in (46.5cm) high

£900-1,200 **TEN**

A pair of early 19thC Empire parcel-gilt bronze four-light candelabra, the stems formed as winged Classical maidens, holding four scrolled candle arms ending in eagle's heads, drilled and electrified.

26in (66cm) high

£7,000-10,000 **SK**

A pair of early 19thC gilt-bronze candelabra, the ornate scroll four-branch candle arms and upper candle nozzles upheld by standing putti, on naturalistic bases, fluted socles and garland and leaf scroll feet.

21.75in (55cm) wide

£1,800-2,200 **L&T**

A pair of French bronze and sienna marble candelabra, after Clodion, modelled as a seated cherub and a young bacchus, supporting two out-scrolling naturalistic branches terminating in candle nozzles, raised on fluted sienna pedestal bases.

19in (48cm) high

£3,000-5,000 **L&T**

A pair of ormolu-mounted Sèvres-style porcelain three-light table candelabra, each with ovoid painted porcelain vase body, with two S-scroll branches flanking a central raised light with rocaille pans.

c1870   *21.75in (55.5cm) high*

£2,200-2,800   **TEN**

A pair of 19thC French ormolu-mounted bronze four-light candelabra, each with vine cast branches supported by a satyr and his putto companion, standing on plinth bases with canted corners, converted to electricity.

21.75in (55cm) high

£4,000-4,500   **TEN**

A pair of French Neo-classical parcel-gilt bronze pedestal vases, each baluster vessel with entwined serpent shoulder handles beneath upswept candle nozzles, with a frieze of dancing maidens, on plinths and ebonised wood bases.

c1870   *22in (56cm) high overall*

£1,500-1,800   **TEN**

A pair of 19thC French ormolu table candelabra, in the form of Bacchanalian cherubs holding aloft cornucopias issuing flower stems, each with three lights and beaded nozzles on pedestals with Sèvres-style panels, on plinth bases.

29.5in (75cm) high

£1,000-1,500   **L&T**

A pair of French gilt-metal five-light candelabra, the sconces as flower heads arranged among foliage, on fluted plinths.

c1880   *22in (56cm) high*

£500-600   **DN**

A pair of late 19thC Baccarat two-branch figural candelabra, the decagonal panelled campana nozzles over everted pans hung with diamond-faceted lancet drops, on upswept branches, each with moulded mark 'Baccarat'.

18.75in (47.5cm) high

£1,000-1,200   **TEN**

A pair of late 19thC Lithyalin glass and ormolu-mounted candlesticks, with tulip-shaped sconce with pair of angular handles, on panelled glass stem, and flaring octagonal base, with sienna, black and green swirled glass.

10in (25.5cm) high

£300-400   **SK**

A pair of 19thC French bronze novelty candlesticks, one modelled as a pug in naval officer attire, the other as a terrier as captured pirate with bound wrists, on stepped circular bases.

11.25in (28cm) high

£550-750   **L&T**

A pair of 19thC Italian carved wood polychrome and parcel-gilt figural candle holders, in the form of sculptures of angels, kneeling on octagonal bases.

12.25in (31cm) high

£2,500-3,000   **ADA**

A pair of Continental gilt-bronze and grey marble-mounted figural candle holders, the stems as Bacchantes.

c1900   *6.25in (16cm) high*

£100-150   **DN**

A pair of late 19th/early 20thC Continental gilt-bronze and marble-mounted models of amorini, fitted for electricity.

15.75in (40cm) high

£550-750   **DN**

LIGHTING

A pair of French ormolu two-branch candelabra, of fluted columnar form with pineapple finials, the outscrolled acanthus-sheathed branches with leaf-decorated campana sconces, on white marble bases with toupie feet.

c1900   9.5in (24cm) high

£350-450   TEN

A pair of French gilt-metal and porcelain mounted candlesticks, stamped 'P.H. Mourey', later fitted for electricity.

12in (30.5cm) high

£200-300   WW

A pair of electroplated altar candlesticks, the turned stems with applied decoration, surmounted by deep bowl-form drip-pans, raised on tapered circular bases ending in paw feet.

55in (140cm) high

£2,000-2,500   L&T

A pair of ornate bronze and ormolu four-light candelabra, with scrolling sconces on a plain column with leaf-moulded base and dolphin pattern triform base, raised on a stepped plinth.

21.5in (54.5cm) high

£500-700   A&G

An early 18thC brass six-light chandelier with knopped stem and scrolling branches.

22in (56cm) wide

£1,500-2,000   DN

A 20thC Louis XVI-style gilt-metal and opaque glass electrolier the upper circlet with ram masks and bell-flower swags.

20.75in (53cm) high

£150-200   DN

An early 20thC Empire-style twelve-light chandelier, with a cascade of graduated crystalline glass beads to a wreath-cast frieze mounted with trumpet-shaped sconces, the lower strings of drops upswept to a central boss.

41.25in (105cm) high

£1,800-2,200   L&T

A 20thC Louis XV-style gilt-bronze and glass-hung chandelier.

37in (94cm) high

£1,800-2,200   DN

A probably late19thC Regency-style gilt-metal eight-light chandelier, damage, losses.

22.5in (57cm) high

£1,800-2,200   DN

A late Victorian or Edwardian brass, copper and glass-hung ceiling light, the copper circlet with a shield to one side, with opaque glass rods hung below, three writhen supports above.

c1900   *69.25in (176cm) high overall*

£300-500   DN

An English Arts and Crafts-style polished brass three-arm ceiling light, with replacement white glass bell shades.

c1900-1920   *21.25in (54cm) diam*

£350-450   EAL

A pair of mid-20thC Rococo-style nine-light chandeliers, of open cage form with undulating arms and urn nozzles alternating with faceted obelisks in tiers of faceted drops and flowerheads in glass and rock crystal.

33in (84cm) high

£2,000-2,500   FRE

A 20thC Venetian coloured-glass five-light chandelier, with an upper tier of decorative scrolling flowers and leaftips, the lower tier with scrolled arms, shaped drops and scrolling leaves.

36in (91.5cm) high

£1,800–2,200   SK

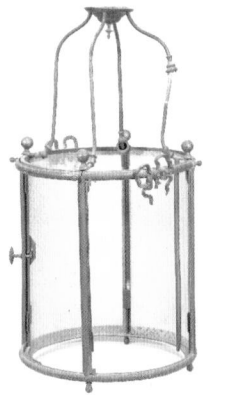

A late 19thC George III-style brass and glazed cylindrical lantern, lacking two glass panels.

29.25in (74cm) high

£200-300   DN

A 19thC wrought iron Gothic hall lantern, of faceted form decorated with pierced trellis work on twelve scrolling 'spike' uprights, the leaf-embossed surmount with ring hook above conforming pendant.

59in (150cm) high

£2,800-3,200   L&T

An English copper lantern, with original frosted glass shade.

1900-1910   *16.5in (42cm) high*

£300-350   EAL

A Continental wrought iron globe four-light electrolier, decorated with palmettes, fitted for electricity.

28in (71cm) high

£500-600   WW

ESSENTIAL REFERENCE – OSLER

F. & C. Osler was founded by Thomas Osler in Birmingham in 1807, and rose to prominence in the mid-19thC. A glasshouse was opened in Freeth Street in 1849. It closed in 1922.

- **A.F. Osler, son of the founder, developed a method of building up solid glass around a metal core, enabling him to make large and complex pieces. Osler subsequently became world-famous for its ornate chandeliers and massive glass furniture, such as tables and thrones.**

A bronze and gilt-bronze three-light hall lantern, in the manner of Osler, the ovoid body with six elongated apertures for now-missing curved glass panels, surmounted by acanthus cresting, the pendant draped with laurel swags.

c1900   *70.75in (108cm) high*

£1,000-1,500   L&T

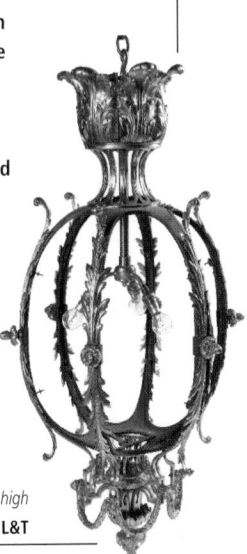

LIGHTING

A large pair of gilt-bronze lanterns, each of inverted bell form with leaf-cast supports and ribbon-tied panels, stamped 'LH'.
c1900   *32in (81cm) high*
£10,000-15,000   **FRE**

A gilt-brass and glazed cylindrical hall lantern, decorated with classical swags, faults.

31in (79cm) high
£1,000-1,500   **DN**

A late 20thC gilt-metal and glazed hall lantern, of hexagonal section, lacking one pane of glass.

£500-600   **DN**

A set of four late 19thC gilt-brass five-light candle wall appliqués, each with split half-baluster stems with ring finials, supporting a central scroll-supported upraised campana nozzle over four further spreading swept branches.

18in (46cm) high
£500-800   **TEN**

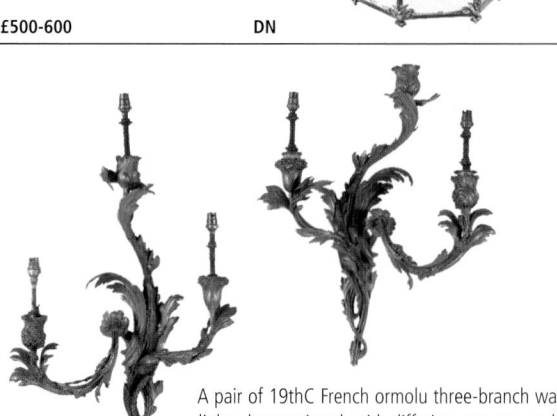

A pair of 19thC French ormolu three-branch wall lights, later painted, with differing sconces, and another matching the left one, drilled.

20.5in (52cm) high
£600-700 SET   **WW**

A set of four ormolu single-branch wall lights, the leaf-domed plates issuing acanthus leaf and scroll branches with conforming drip pan, sconce and ribbed detachable nozzle.

12in (31.5cm) high
£700-900 SET   **WW**

A pair of early 20thC gilt-bronze three-light Rococo Revival wall appliqués, with raised centre light flanked by S-scroll branches, from leafy backplates.

24.5in (62cm) high
£350-500   **TEN**

A pair of early 20thC Louis XV-style gilt-bronze two-light wall sconces, with torch-form backplate centred by a lion mask, flanked by two flatleaf and husk candle arms.

20in (51cm) high
£1,500-1,800   **SK**

A pair of gilt-brass twin-branch wall appliqués, of tied cornucopia form, with pineapple finials.

12.25in (31cm) high
£200-250   **ROS**

A 19thC pair of Louis XV-style marble and gilt-bronze mounted urns, with angel-mask handles and cast socle bases with toupie feet, converted to lamps.

33in (84cm) high

£7,000-10,000   **FRE**

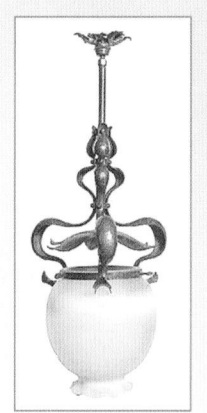

A pair of 19thC Baroque-style giltwood newel-post lamps, in the form of cherubs holding aloft fronds, each with one leg raised above a Rococo C- and S-scroll carved plinth, with flame glass shades.

24.75in (63cm) high

£1,200-1,800   **L&T**

A pair of 19thC French polished zinc lamps, each with a brass plaque 'PAR BREVET D'INVENTION / LAMPES HYDROSTATIQUE / DE THILORIER & SERRUROT / RUE DU BOULOY No.4' and numbered '17980' and '81'.

23.25in (59cm) high

£2,500-3,000   **L&T**

An Art Nouveau wrought iron table light, with period iridescent glass shade.

c1900-1910   *15.75in (40cm) high*

£300-400   **EAL**

A George III carved pine fire surround, with stepped shelf above an elaborately carved frieze, above an egg-and-dart slip, flanked by scrolling upright corbals with pendant festoons.

73.25in (186cm) wide

£5,000-6,000   **ADA**

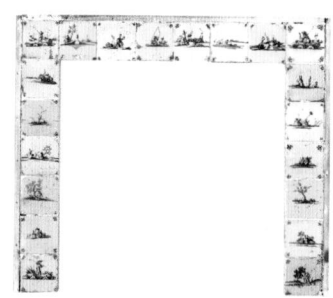

An 18thC Delft tile fireplace surround.

40.5in (103cm) wide

£800-1,000   **POOK**

A late 19thC Neoclassical style carved oak triple breakfront chimneypiece, with foliate tablet and frieze, on jambs with Ionic columns.

81.75in (208cm) wide

£1,500-2,000   **DN**

A Neoclassical Adam-style white and verde antico marble chimney piece, the fluted frieze and uprights with verde-antico marble inset, brass register and brass and steel grate.

72in (183cm) wide

£7,000-9,000   **ADA**

A 19thC Neoclassical style white and sienna marble chimney piece, carved with a swagged urn above an egg-and-dart border and with reeded scroll corbals surmounting the uprights.

73.25in (186cm) wide

£2,000-3,000   **ADA**

A large Jacobean style carved oak fire surround.

c1880   *112.25in (285cm) wide*

£3,000-3,500   **RMAA**

GRATES

A George III polished steel basket grate, the arched fireback above a serpentine basket, the inswept pierced frieze between high obelisk-shaped andirons with pierced and engraved decoration, each on four columnar uprights and ogee-cut plinth bases.

c1760   *33in (84cm) wide*

£10,000-12,000   **L&T**

A George III Irish brass and iron register grate, in the manner of George Binns, Dublin, with engraved decoration, the bowed railed basket above a pierced and engraved brass apron.

c1770   *27.25in (69cm) wide*

£2,000-3,000   **L&T**

A George III Irish register grate, in the manner of George Binns, Dublin, the frame with three applied roundels, the basket with brass urn finials above a fret pierced apron.

c1770   *39.5in (100cm) wide*

£3,500-4,500   **L&T**

A George III-style steel and cast iron fire-grate.

29in (74cm) wide

£500-600   DN

A George III 'Howsham Hall' polished steel basket grate, Maurice Tobin, Leeds, the arched backplate above a basket with three urn finials, the apron on columnar uprights tapering to fluted obelisks surmounted by urn finials, signed with a stamp on left capital.

Maurice Tobin was hailed by his contemporaries as one of the finest 'whitesmiths' of the period. Fine grates by Tobin, often working in conjunction with Carr & Adam, were supplied to many great country houses, including Nostell Priory, Newby Hall and Harewood House in Yorkshire, and thus rarely appear on the market.

c1778   *32.25in (82cm) wide*

£15,000-25,000   L&T

A Victorian tiled cast iron grate, recently restored.

c1880   *38.25in (97cm) wide*

£600-800   RMAA

A pair of late 17thC English cast and wrought iron andirons, with dramatic turned shaft and trestle base.

13.75in (35cm) high

£600-800   **POOK**

A pair of early 18thC English iron and brass andirons, with turned finials and two brass bosses, supported by brass legs with octagonal penny feet.

17.75in (45cm) high

£3,500-4,000   **POOK**

A pair of early 18thC American wrought iron andirons, with large brass finials and penny feet.

23in (58.5cm) high

£3,000-3,500   **POOK**

A pair of American Newport, Rhode Island brass andirons, with ball finials and baluster shafts, above a circular boss supported by cabriole legs terminating in ball-and-claw feet.

c1760   *17in (43cm) high*

£3,000-3,500   **POOK**

A pair of 19thC Louis XVI-style gilt-bronze chenets, each with flambeau urn finial, lacking elements.

15.25in (39cm) high

£500-600   **DN**

A pair of American New York Federal brass andirons, stamped 'R. Whittingham New York'.

21.25in (54cm) high

£1,500-2,000   **POOK**

A pair of early 19thC American Massachusetts Federal brass andirons, stamped 'J. Davis Boston'.

15.25in (38.5cm) high

£550-650   **POOK**

A pair of Gothic silver-plated brass andirons, each arched and traceried column andiron surmounted by a seated griffin, each enclosing a shield, linked by square section knopped bar.

32.5in (83cm) high

£4,000-5,000   **TEN**

A pair of Victorian Neoclassical brass andirons, modelled as two-handled vases on square section bases cast with musical instrument trophies, on pillar supports and front pairs of cloven feet.

c1880   *18.75in (47.5cm) high*

£450-550   **TEN**

A set of large Arts and Crafts andirons, complete with poker and bar and full set of fireplace tools on original stand.

Each 30in (76cm) wide

£6,000-7,000   **DRA**

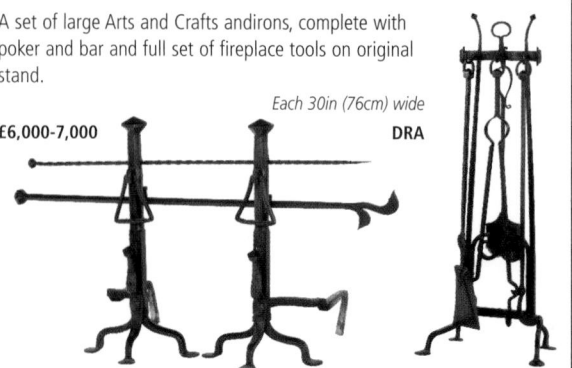
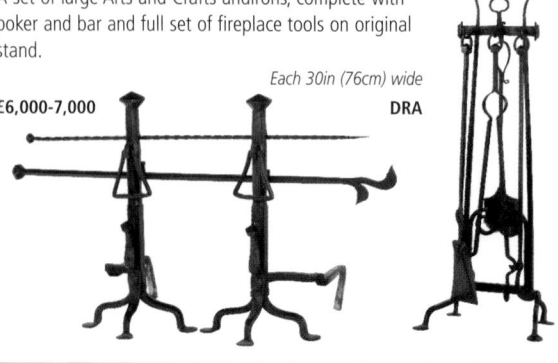

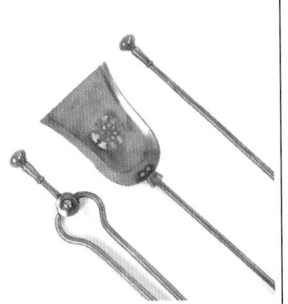

A set of three polished-steel fire tools, with turned flattened knop handles, lacquered.

£300-400   WW

A set of early 19thC polished-steel fire irons, with facet-cut handles and knopped shafts, comprising a shovel, poker and pair of tongs, the shovel with a shaped bowl pierced with a floral design.

Shovel 28.75in (73cm) long

£600-800   WW

A set of three steel fire irons, with brass handles, raised foliated ornamentation and ball finials, comprising a shovel, tongs and poker.

£800-1,200   A&G

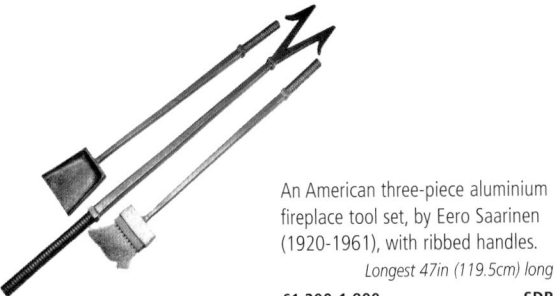

An American three-piece aluminium fireplace tool set, by Eero Saarinen (1920-1961), with ribbed handles.

Longest 47in (119.5cm) long

£1,200-1,800   SDR

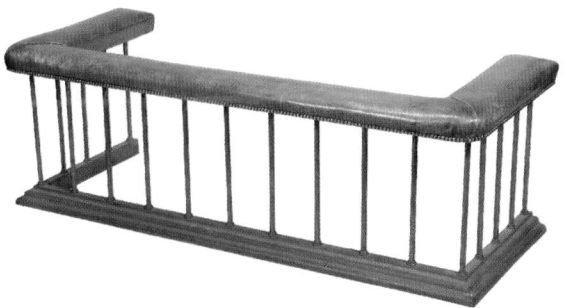

An early 20thC steel and leather upholstered club fender.

63.5in (161cm) wide

£900-1,200   DN

A brass curb, the arched ends and front with copper applied ribbons, festoons and foliage.

56.5in (143.5cm) wide

£400-500   A&G

ARCHITECTURAL ANTIQUES

An Art Deco gilded plaster ceiling sculpture, by Émile-Jacques Rhulmann (French 1879-1933), with stylised flowers, from the Bon Marche department store.

47in (119.5cm) high

£2,500-3,500   DRA

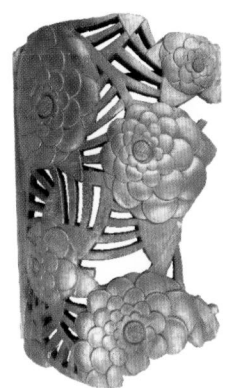
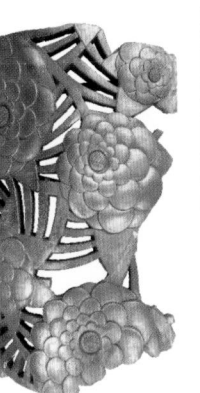

A gilt-bronze lift panel, 'The Wind', cast from a model by C. A. Llewellyn-Roberts for the lift of Selfridges, London.

16.75in (42.5cm) wide

£600-800   WW

A large copper log basket, with a swing iron handle.

21.25in (54cm) high

£1,500-2,500   WW

A pair of 19thC Coalbrookdale cast iron garden benches, with pierced floral backs and arms and central circular panel with armorial shield on standard end supports, seat slats differ.

60in (152.5cm) wide

£3,500-4,500   GORL

A 19thC Victorian cast iron tilt-top garden table, probably Coalbrookedale, the top with openwork designs of foliage and the signs of the zodiac, on a base with moulded decoration of C-scrolls.

29.75in (75.5cm) diam

£900-1,200   SK

A set of cast iron bench supports modelled as winged sphinxes, SLB Foundry, Sittingbourne, Kent, lacking wooden slats.

c1880   £1,500-2,000   DN

A Liberty & Co. terracotta jardinière and tray, designed by Archibald Knox, probably Compton Pottery, cast in low relief with Celtic Knot motif, impressed marks.

17.25in (44cm) high

£1,200-1,800   WW

ESSENTIAL REFERENCE – LIBERTY & KNOX

Liberty & Co. was established in London by Arthur Lasenby Liberty (1843-1917) in 1875, and the store produced and commissioned furniture, fabrics, jewellery and metalware.

● Archibald Knox (1864-1933) began designing for Liberty in 1899, designing many Celtic Revival pieces, including the 'Cymric' (silver) and 'Tudric' (pewter) ranges. As well as metalwork and jewellery, Knox designed, terracotta garden ornaments, carpets, wallpaper and fabrics for Liberty & Co. In 1917 he was commissioned to design the headstone for Arthur Lasenby Liberty's grave.

A Liberty & Co. terracotta planter, designed by Archibald Knox, probably Compton Pottery, cast in low relief with Celtic Knot motif border.

21.25in (54cm) diam

£1,200-1,800   WW

A Liberty & Co. 'Siegfried' terracotta jardinière and stand, designed by Archibald Knox, probably by Compton Pottery, cast in low relief with Celtic Knot, impressed 'Liberty mark'.

42.5in (108cm) high

£3,000-4,000   WW

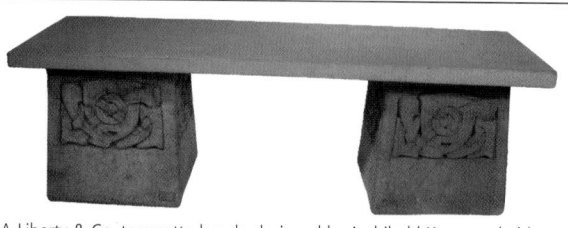

A Liberty & Co. terracotta bench, designed by Archibald Knox, probably Compton Pottery, tapering square section cast with entrelac panels, with simulated terracotta top, stamped marks to both bases.

53in (135cm) wide

£1,800-2,200   WW

A pair of 19thC cast iron garden urns, the bodies with grapevine and putti decoration and ram's head handles.

27.5in (70cm) high

£800-1,000   POOK

A pair of 19thC Garnkirk terracotta garden urns, the gadrooned bowls above turned socles on wreath-cast pedestals, with moulded plinth bases.

50in (127cm) high

£2,000-3,000   **L&T**

A pair of Grecian Revival silvered bronze and champleve enamel urns, by Elkington & Co., the necks with anthemion-and-dart decoration, above tapered sides with Classical panels, on inswept surbases with lion paw feet.

c1875   *12.25in (31cm) high*

£2,500–3,500   **L&T**

A set of six late 19thC cast iron garden urns, each with an egg-and-dart rim, above a wreath-decorated body with lion's-head handles, resting on square bases.

41.5in (105.5cm) high

£2,500-3,500   **POOK**

A French terracotta urn, decorated with fairies, with stone base.

1830-1850   *35in (89.5cm) high*

£550-750   **RMAA**

A pair of modern carara marble spinxes on rectangular plinth bases, modern.

30.25in (77cm) deep

£5,000-7,000   **L&T**

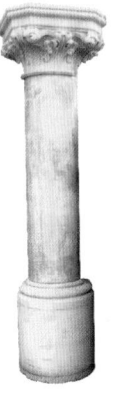

A set of eight 19thC marble and stone columns, the turned stepped bases and cylindrical pilasters with Corinthian capitals, two with outset tops supported by further slender cylindrical pilasters.

106.25in (270cm) high approx

£8,000-10,000   **L&T**

A Gothic arcaded oak door, some remains of green and ochre coloured painting, faults, now fixed to a modern panel for standing.

c1540   *73.5in (187cm) high*

£1,000-1,500   **DN**

A late 19thC copper, glazed and wrought iron mounted wall lantern, of square, tapering form.

52in (132cm) high overall

£450-550   **DN**

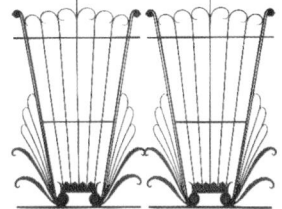

A pair of 1920s iron window grates, by Walter Kantack.

Designed for the AT&T Building, New York.

68in (173cm) high

£2,000-3,000   **SDR**

A pair of Art Deco wrought iron gates, with stylised floral and vine motif in the manner of Edgar Brandt, signed 'Edgar Brandt'.

51.5in (131cm) high

£4,000-5,000   **DRA**

ESSENTIAL REFERENCE – WEATHER VANES

The earliest weather vanes (or wind vanes) were simply arrows, and they were made all over Europe, and the US. From the 18thC onwards, most weather vanes (or windvanes) were balanced with a larger motif to help them to point upwind. Such motifs include cocks, ships, and figures.

● The hollow-bodied iron or copper weathervane became one of the most popular forms of American folk art from the mid-19thC. These were cast from wooden patterns and hammered in a variety of imaginative forms, before possibly being possibly gilded or painted. If left as plain copper, they turn a weathered green (verdigris) which is extremely desirable.

A late 19thC copper pointing finger and banner weather vane, with cast iron directionals, J. W. Fiske Co., New York, old gray-green surface with traces of gilding, including black metal base.

65.5in (166.5cm) total height

£5,000-7,000   **SK**

A cast and sheet iron cockerel on ball weather vane, attributed to Rochester Iron Works, Rochester, New Hampshire, the body cast in two sections and joined together with pierced sheet iron tail, painted yellow, including a metal stand.

47.74in (121.5cm) high

£20,000-30,000   **SK**

A late 19thC American moulded copper gilded 'Hamburg' cockerel weather vane, with flattened full-bodied figure, mounted on a copper rod, gilded surface.

28in (71cm) long

£10,000-15,000   **SK**

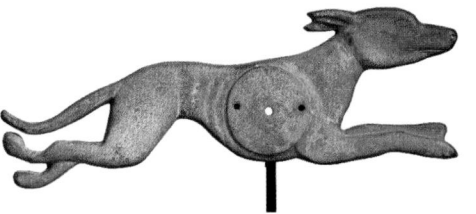

A late 19thC American yellow-painted cast iron leaping dog target, including stand.

26in (66cm) long

£8,000-12,000   **SK**

A late 19th/early 20thC American moulded sheet copper cockerel weather vane, including copper directionals, weathered surface with traces of paint, verdigris and earlier gilding, dents.

30in (76.2cm) long

£4,000-6,000   **SK**

A late 19thC American moulded sheet copper and zinc running horse weather vane, the surface with yellow sizing and traces of gilt, including black metal stand, minor losses.

28in (71cm) wide

£6,000-8,000   **SK**

A rare late 19thC American moulded sheet copper and cast Iron 'Lexington' standing horse weather vane, flattened full-body figure with cast iron head, copper ears, and embossed sheet copper tail, yellow sizing and verdigris surface with traces of gilt, repairs.

32in (81.2cm) wide

£15,000-20,000   **SK**

An early 20thC American large molded sheet copper and cast iron horse and jockey weather vane, green-painted surface, no stand, imperfections.

57in (145cm) long

£5,000-7,000   **SK**

CLOSER LOOK – A CIGAR STORE FIGURE

A British drum maker's trade sign, inscribed '1st Battn. The Lancashire Fusiliers', with brass tack decoration.

c1840   46in (117cm) high

£2,000-3,000   POOK

Samuel A. Robb opened his Canal Street wood-carving shop in 1886 in New York. It was the largest shop of its kind in the city at the time.

Punch figures, and Robb's more well-known cigar store Indians, are advertising figures, which were placed on the pavement to catch the attention of those passing by and let them know tobacco was sold inside. The average 19thC American smoker couldn't read, so these cigar store figures pointed the way.

Punch's raised forefinger and dirty leer coaxed buyers into the shop.

As these figures were placed outside, many have signs of damage. That Punch is in such good condition greatly contributes to his value.

An 18thC painted wooden 'T. Doty' double-sided tavern trade sign, from Canton, Massachusetts.

Overall 71.5in (181.5cm) high

£15,000-20,000   SK

A late 19thC carved and painted Punch cigar store figure, attributed to the shop of Samuel Robb in New York (1851-1928), the original base inscribed 'Cigars Tobacco/Havana Cigars/Smoker's Articles'.

75in (190.5cm) high

£80,000-120,000   POOK

A 19thC Philadelphia painted Friendship Fire Co. parade hat, the front depicting a young woman, the reverse inscribed 'Engineer F.E.', bearing the label of James Remick.

13.5in (34cm) diam

£7,000-10,000   POOK

A late 19thC Ohio molded stoneware planter and stand, attributed to The Robinson Clay Products Co., with applied blue glazed trailing grapevines in deep relief, flanking a panel with figures in a landscape.

28.5in (72.5cm) high

£8,000-12,000   POOK

A paint-decorated leather fire bucket, 'STEPHEN B. IVES ACTIVE 1824', polychrome decoration, depicting Mercury blowing a trumpet, the bottom impressed 'W.OSBORN', wear.

11.75in (30cm) high

£2,000-3,000   0 SK

A tin advertising sign for the 'National Federation of Hairdressers', damage to one side.

17.75in (45.5cm) wide

£60-80   RMAA

An Afghan runner.

153.5in (390cm) long

£300-400   **DN**

An Afshar rug, the dark brown field abrashed to dark blue, with three dazzler medallions.

c1890   *68.75in (175cm) wide*

£800-1,200   **SOTA**

An Afshar rug, the dark blue field with a 'Boteh' trellis.

c1900   *65in (165cm) wide*

£1,500-2,000   **SOTA**

A late 19hC Bakhtiyari corridor carpet, southwest Persia.

188in (477.5cm) long

£2,000-3,000   **FRE**

A late 20thC Bakhtiyari carpet, the field with allover polychrome tree and foliate lattice, within red tree border between indigo bands.

187in (475cm) long

£1,000-1,500   **L&T**

A late 19thC Belouch rug, northeast Persia.

60in (152.5cm) long

£500-750   **FRE**

A late 19thC Bakshaish carpet, northwest Persia.

185in (470cm) long

£10,000-15,000   **FRE**

A late 19thC Belouch rug, northeast Persia.

106in (269cm) long

£1,000-1,500   **FRE**

A Bidjar throw rug, with a red medallion on a navy field within multiple borders.

c1920   *84in (213cm) long*

£1,200-1,500   **POOK**

A late 19thC Fereghan carpet, west Persia.

198in (503cm) long

£3,000-4,000   **FRE**

A late 19thC room-size Fereghan rug, with central navy medallion on an ivory field with multiple borders.

140in (355.5cm) long

£5,000-8,000   POOK

A Hamadan rug, the central blue lozenge decorated with foliate motifs in red and ultramarine tones, madder spandrels within a polychrome decorated cream borders.

132.75in (337cm) wide

£250-350   DN

A Heriz carpet, the red field with central stepped indigo and rose medallion suspending pendants, similar spandrels within red turtle palmette, rosette and foliate vine border between cream bands.

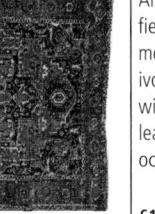

151.5in (385cm) long

£3,000-4,000   L&T

An early 20thC Heriz carpet, the red field with central indigo and ivory medallion suspending pendants, ivory, red and ochre spandrels, within indigo rosette and serrated leafy vine border between blue and ochre bands.

144in (366cm) long

£1,000-1,500   L&T

A room-size Heriz rug, with central medallion on a red field with ivory corners and blue borders.

c1920   208in (528.5cm) long

£5,000-6,000   POOK

A mid-20thC Heriz carpet, northwest Persia.

226in (574cm) long

£1,500-2,000   FRE

A mid-20thC Heriz carpet, northwest Persia.

189in (481cm) long

£3,000-3,500   FRE

A late 19th/early 20thC Isfahan rug, central arabesque medallion with double pendant, indigo spandrels.

84.25in (214cm) long

£700-900   L&T

An Isfahan rug.

95.75in (243cm) long

£1,600-2,000   DN

TEXTILES

A mid- to late 20thC Isfahan carpet, the cream field with allover palmette and scrolling vine pattern, within cream palmette and scrolling vine border between similar bands, signatures to the corners.

175.5in (446cm) long

£1,000-1,200   L&T

A Kashan partial silk prayer rug, central Persia.

c1930   *80in (203cm) long*

£600-800   FRE

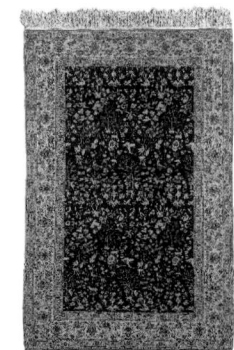

A part-silk Kurk Kashan rug, the royal blue field with allover pattern of deer, birds and butterflies amidst trees, within cream palmette, deer, bird and scrolling foliate vine border between cream bands.

92.5in (235cm) long

£1,500-2,000   L&T

A Kashan carpet, central Persia.

c1930-40   *206in (523cm) long*

£3,000-5,000   FRE

A Kazvin carpet, northwest Persia.

c1930   *209in (531cm) long*

£4,000-5,000   FRE

A Khamseh rug.

82.75in (210cm) long

£300-400   DN

ESSENTIAL REFERENCE – KIRMAN CARPETS

Following the Safavid conquest of Persia in the 16thC, four royal workshops for weaving textiles and carpets were established in the cities of Isfahan (now Esfahan), Kashan, Kirman and Tabriz.

- **The city of Kirman, now in southeast Iran, is known especially for its 'vase' carpets made from the mid-16th to the late 17thC. Vase carpets have a distinctive weave structure and often feature Chinese-style vases on a trelliswork of vines, palmettes and leaves. Floral patterns are typical.**
- **These patterns were widely copied in the 19th and 20thC. Designs were influenced by European tastes due to the flourishing export market to the West. Floral designs with elaborate borders were popular.**
- **Most Kirman carpets are woven in silk with the asymmetric Persian knot. The high density of weave allows smooth curvilinear shapes in the design.**
- **The palette of antique Kirman carpets features deep red and rich blue. More recent Kirman carpets tend to include pastel colours.**

A Persian Kirman carpet with flower pattern on violet ground.

c1930   *211.75in (538cm) long*

£10,000-12,000   SOTA

A late 19thC Kurdish rug, northwest Persia.

69in (175.5cm) long

£700-1,000   FRE

A late 19thC Kurdish runner, northwest Persia.

154in (391cm) long

£1,500-2,000   FRE

A Mahal carpet.

156in (396cm) long

£1,000-1,200   DN

An early to mid-20thC Quashqa'i Khordjin, southwest Persia.

44in (112cm) long

£500-600   FRE

A Quashqa'i carpet.

22.75in (312cm) long

£600-800   DN

A Qum rug.

84.25in (214cm) long

£600-800   DN

An early 20thC Sarouk Fereghan carpet, west Persia.

336in (853.5cm) long

£45,000-55,000   FRE

A Sarouk rug, the madder field centred by an ivory lozenge and flowerhead medallion, within a flowerhead decorated brown border, red and blue guard stripes.

74.75in (190cm) wide

£1,000-1,500   DN

A Persian Sarouk room-size rug, with indigo and mustard floral sprays on a cranberry field.

c1920   160in (406.5cm) long

£2,500-3,500   DRA

A Sarouk carpet.

141.75in (360cm) long

£500-600   DN

A west Persia Senneh region rug.

c1920   70in (178cm) long

£350-450   WW

TEXTILES

A large early 20thC Sparta Serapi-style carpet, woven in set pattern with main carpet flanked by runners and a kelleh, the main cream field with allover foliate lattice, within indigo border.

216.5in (550cm) long

£1,500-2,000 L&T

A Serapi room-size rug, with a blue medallion on a mustard field with red corners and navy border.

c1970 *218in (554cm) long*

£13,000-15,000 POOK

A Shiraz rug, the navy field with twin central ivory lozenge medallions, within ivory borders and multiple polychrome guard stripes.

76.5in (194cm) wide

£180-220 DN

A Shiraz rug, some wear.

58in (147.5cm) long

£50-80 DN

A southwest Persia Shiraz rug, Fars province.

c1950 *117.5in (297cm) long*

£220-280 WW

CLOSER LOOK: A SULTANABAD CARPET

Sultanabad carpets with bold curvilinear designs of floral and foliate motifs are highly sought after.

The best examples of their type command the highest prices. The design is a harmonious combination of blue, soft green, dark red and ivory, which are typical of the Sultanabad palette.

The vibrant colours, made using natural dyes, are still strong.

Carpets with a fine weave remaining in good condition always sell well. Some wear is acceptable but it shouldn't be excessive

A Sultanabad carpet, worn.

In the 19thC a flourishing export market of Persian goods to the West led to European and American companies setting up carpet factories in cities such as Sultanabad, now Arak, in northwest Iran. Traditional Persian designs were adapted to suit European tastes and became very popular. They remain highly collectable.

146.75in (373cm) long

£20,000-30,000 DN

A large late 19thC Sultanabad carpet, the rust red field with allover stylised radial rosettes and foliate vine pattern, within indigo turtle palmette and foliate vine border between ivory, blue and green bands.

254in (645cm) long

£4,000-6,000 L&T

A Persian Sultanabad room-sized rug, with a repeating palmette and lattice pattern in cinnabar and indigo on a black field, surrounded by a turtle palmette border.

c1910 *178in (452cm) long*

£1,800-2,200 DRA

A northwest Persia Tabriz carpet, the ivory field with a terracotta reserve enclosing an ivory medallion, all with small herati, walnut main border of rosettes and serrated leaves, multiple minor borders.

c1890   *153.5in (390cm) wide*

£2,500-3,000   **SOTA**

A late 19thC Tabriz carpet, the faded rust mihrab field with cypress tree and foliate pattern, cream spandrels and castellated bar, with cream, tree and floral vase border between lemon cartouche bands, faded.

147.5in (375cm) long

£3,500-4,500   **L&T**

A late 19th/early 20thC Tabriz carpet, the cream field with allover polychrome palmette and foliate lattice, within red turtle palmette and stylised vine border between cream and blue bands.

130.75in (332cm) long

£1,300-1,800   **L&T**

A late 19th/early 20thC Tabriz carpet, the blue field with birds and animals amidst foliate vine, central cusped rose medallion, with indigo palmette, bird and scrolling vine border between camel bands.

145in (368cm) long

£1,000-1,500   **L&T**

A Tabriz throw rug, with figures hunting on an ivory field within a cobalt border.

c1915   *72in (183cm) long*

£1,000-1,500   **POOK**

A Tabriz hunting rug, the ivory field decorated with seven equestrian figures in polychrome, within a bird and flower decorated border.

102.25in (260cm) wide

£300-400   **DN**

A Tabriz, possibly Hadji Jelali, carpet, torn into two parts.

312in (792.5cm) long

£25,000-35,000   **DN**

A Tabriz-style woven carpet.

248in (630cm) long

£750-1,000   **DN**

A Tabriz carpet, northwest Persia.

c1940   *38in (97cm) long*

£2,000-3,000   **FRE**

A late 19thC northwest Persian corridor carpet.

240in (609.5cm) long

£10,000-15,000   **FRE**

One of a pair of late 19thC northwest Persian rugs.

86.5in (220cm) long

£2,500-3,500 PAIR   **L&T**

TEXTILES

A Gendje Caucasian rug, the brown field with allover lattice and star pattern, within ivory serrated leaf and wine glass border.

87in (221cm) long

£800-1,200   L&T

A 19thC south-west Caucasus Karabagh runner, worn, with a kink.

121in (307cm) long

£500-600   WW

A late 19thC Karabagh runner, south Caucasus.

149in (378.5cm) long

£800-1,200   FRE

A late 19thC Karabagh rug, south Caucasus.

123in (312.5cm) long

£1,500-2,000   FRE

A late 19thC Karabagh rug, south Caucasus.

95in (241.5cm) long

£1,500-2,000   FRE

A 19thC Moghan Kazak throw rug, with ten medallions on an ivory field with multiple borders, retaining a full rich pile.

84in (213.5cm) long

£2,500-3,500   POOK

A late 19thC Karatchopf Kazak long rug, the green field with ivory square and red and brown shaped medallions, mihrab-style end bars.

102.5in (260cm) long

£800-1,200   L&T

A late 19thC Kazak rug, the indigo field with three polychrome stepped lozenge medallions, within ivory wine glass and serrated leaf border.

89.75in (228cm) long

£700-1,000   L&T

An Armenian southern Caucasus Kazak prayer rug, the madder field surrounding three dog figures within conjoined diamond designs on navy blue and camel grounds, accented by lesser diamonds in polychromic checkerboard designs.

c1890 57.5in (146cm) long

£3,500-4,500   RTC

A late 19th/early 20thC Kazak rug, the red field with three polychrome hooked lozenge medallions.

35.5in (140cm) long

£500-800   L&T

A late 19th/early 20thC Sewan Kazak long rug, two polychrome lobed medallions, between red and blue skittle bands.

120.5in (306cm) long

£800-1,200   L&T

A Kazak rug, south-west Caucasus, the indigo field with central ochre hooked lozenge medallion flanked by two similar red medallions.

78.75in (200cm) long

£800-1,200   **L&T**

A Kazak rug, the turquoise field with four polychrome hooked octagonal medallions, within ivory hooked bar border between blue bands.

70in (178cm) long

£600-900   **L&T**

A Caucasus Kazak area rug, with a ruby medallion on indigo field, surrounded by a cherry dovetail pattern border.

c1930   *72in (183cm) wide*

£500-800   **DRA**

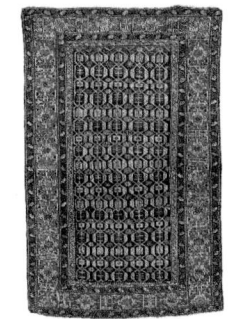

A late 19thC Konakgend Kuba rug, east Caucasus.

66in (167.5cm) long

£1,500-2,000   **FRE**

A Kuba Leshgi rug, east Caucasus.

c1900   *56in (142cm) long*

£1,500-2,000   **FRE**

A 19thC Perepedil double niche prayer rug, east Caucasus.

67in (170cm) long

£3,500-4,500   **FRE**

A late 19th/early 20thC Seychour rug, the ivory field with three indigo and brown X medallions.

70.75in (180cm) long

£700-1,000   **L&T**

A late 19thC Shirvan prayer rug, east Caucasus.

57in (145cm) long

£3,500-4,500   **FRE**

A late 19th/early 20thC Shirvan rug, the indigo field with allover polychrome rosette lattice, within cream linked hexagon border between multiple red and green bands.

77.25in (196cm) long

£1,000-1,500   **L&T**

A Shirvan rug, from the Azerbaijan region of the south-east Caucasus, the indigo field with central ivory star medallion, flanked by two similar red medallions, yellow hooked lozenges between, dated 1330 AH.

1912   *83.5in (212cm) long*

£600-1,000   **L&T**

A Soumak carpet, centred by three lozenge medallions.

113.5in (288cm) long

£350-450   **DN**

A south Caucasus long rug, the abrash indigo field with central column of five polychrome medallions, flanked by blue medallions and ivory arabesques, within polychrome octagon border between skittle and outer red bands.

124in (315cm) long

£1,700-2,000   **L&T**

An Anatolian kelim, the cream field with three large polychrome hooked hexagonal medallions, within red and brown hooked side borders, cream serrated hexagonal ends.

146.5in (372cm) long

£400-600   **L&T**

An early 19thC Beshir prayer rug, south Turkestan.

82in (208.5cm) long

£3,000-4,000   **FRE**

An Ersari Turkman soumak woven carpet, Turkmenistan.

c1900   *109in (277cm) long*

£300-400   **WW**

A late 19th/early 20thC Tekke main carpet, the rust red field with four columns of 18 guls between striped poles with hooked lozenge motifs, within ivory hooked pyramid border between S and striped bands.

130in (330cm) long

£1,000-1,500   **L&T**

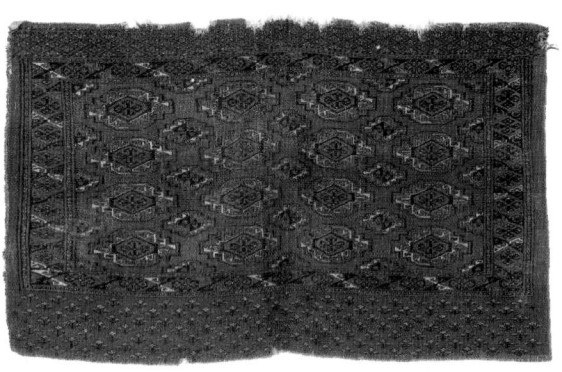

A 19thC Saryk Turkoman chuval, east Turkestan, cotton highlights.

61in (155cm) wide

£2,000-3,000   **FRE**

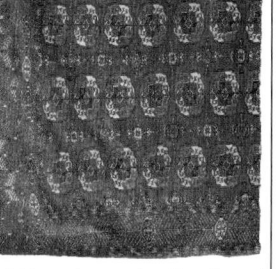

A Tekke main carpet section, the red field with four columns of six and a half guls, cruciform motifs between, within part red starburst octagon border between bands, one half of original carpet.

90in (229cm) square

£800-1,200   **L&T**

A Tekke rug, damaged.

63.75in (162cm) long

£100-150   **DN**

A Tekke prayer rug, the field with two main columns of guls between multiple red, indigo and cream columns, tapered to one end.

52in (132cm) long

£700-1,000   **L&T**

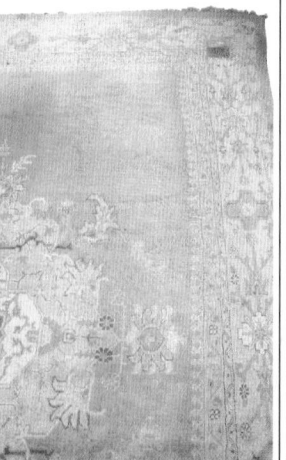

An Ushak carpet.

151.5in (385cm) long

£1,000-1,500   **DN**

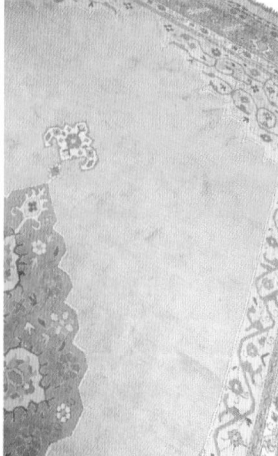

An Ushak carpet, with faults and repairs.

198.75in (505cm) long

£2,000-3,000   **DN**

An Ushak carpet.

151.5in (385cm) long

£1,000-1,500   **DN**

A late 19thC Ushak carpet, the faded red field with serrated palmette and foliate vine pattern, within turquoise stylised vine border between red and ochre bands.

157.75in (401cm) long

£4,000-6,000   L&T

A large late 19thC Ushak carpet, the blue field with allover red palmette and foliate vine lattice, within red lozenge, tulip and stylised vine border between ochre bands.

212.5in (540cm) long

£5,000-8,000   L&T

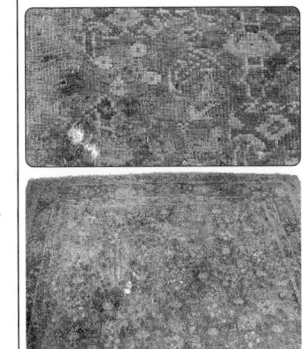

An Ushak carpet, the madder field decorated throughout with polychrome with abstract and foliate motifs, within a conforming navy border and guard stripes, damage, repair.

175.25in (445cm) wide

£700-1,000   DN

An Ushak long rug, the madder field centred by three lozenge medallions within polychrome abstract motifs, with a yellow ochre border and multiple guard stripes, damage.

126in (320cm) wide

£200-300   DN

ESSENTIAL REFERENCE: ANATOLIAN CARPETS

Rug-weaving was well established in Anatolia (Asian Turkey) by the 13thC, and Anatolian carpets have been sought for centuries. Today, 'antique' rugs, over 100 years old, command the highest prices, and 'old' rugs, over 50 years old, are in demand.

- **The main centres of production in Anatolia are Ghiordes, Hereke, Istanbul, Ladik, Konya and Ushak.**
- **Village and nomadic rugs mostly feature geometric patterns woven in wool. Town-made pieces often have formal, curvilinear designs possibly with floral elements. The best quality examples are made from silk on a wool foundation. Colours vary from bright, vibrant jewel colours to subdued pastel shades. Poor examples feature harsh, garish colours.**
- **When buying a rug, consider condition, harmony of colour and the fineness and interest of the design.**

A large Ushak carpet, the slate blue field with stylised palmette and foliate angular lattice pattern, within salmon small rosette, tulip and stylised vine border between blue, pink and brown bands.

214.5in (545cm) long

£17,000-22,000   L&T

A modern Uzbeki susani, the cream field with central rosette medallion issuing floral diagonals, within cream floral and serrated leaf border between similar bands.

72in (183cm) long

£400-600   L&T

A 19thC Yomud Turkoman asmalyk, west Turkestan.

47in (119.5cm) wide

£3,500-4,500   FRE

A mid- to late 19thC Yomud chuval, west Turkestan.

43in (109cm) wide

£800-1,200   FRE

A late 19thC Yomud asmalyk, west Turkestan.

45in (114.5cm) wide

£800-1,200   FRE

A Yomud engsi, the brown field with cruciform pattern, with lozenge-filled panels, within brown serrated lozenge border between ivory bands, stepped hooked half gul elems.

67in (170cm) long

£400-600   L&T

TEXTILES

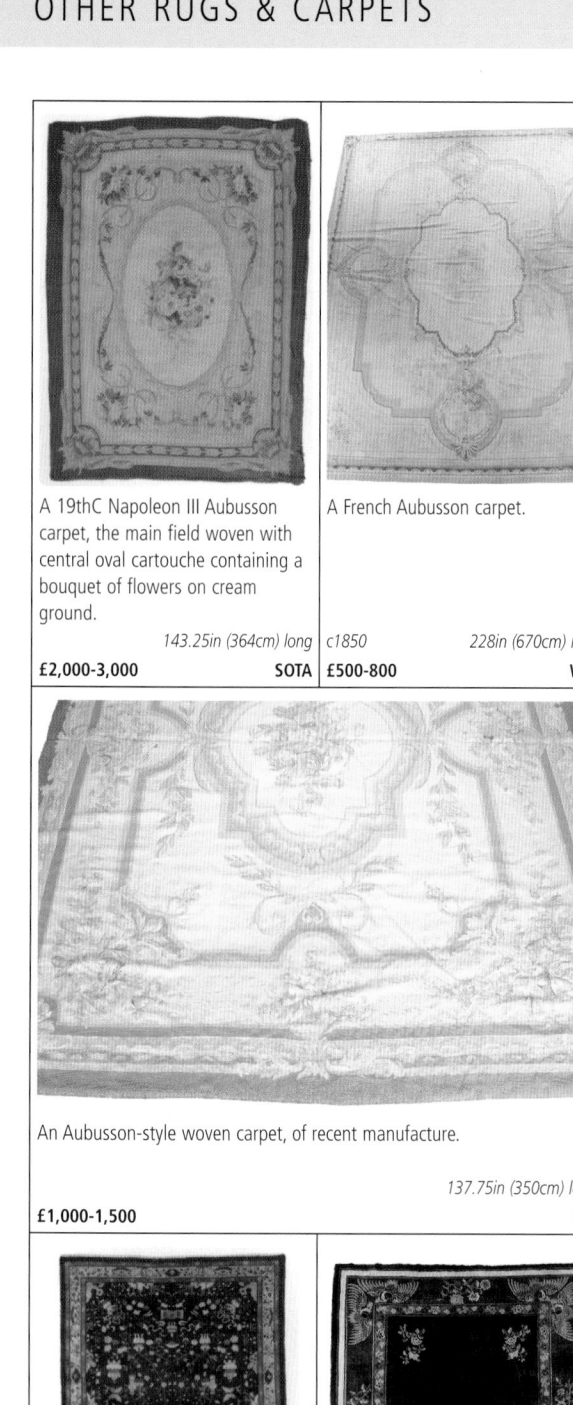

A 19thC Napoleon III Aubusson carpet, the main field woven with central oval cartouche containing a bouquet of flowers on cream ground.

143.25in (364cm) long

£2,000-3,000   **SOTA**

A French Aubusson carpet.

c1850   228in (670cm) long

£500-800   **WW**

A 20thC Aubusson rug.

108in (274cm) long

£800-1,200   **WW**

A French Aubusson-style woven carpet, worn, damaged.

198.5in (504cm) long

£2,000-3,000   **DN**

An Aubusson-style woven carpet, of recent manufacture.

137.75in (350cm) long

£1,000-1,500   **DN**

An Indian carpet.

c1900   176in (447cm) long

£2,000-3,000   **FRE**

A probably Indian 17thC Damascus-style woven rug.

67in (170cm) long

£1,500-2,000   **DN**

A large Chinese carpet, probably Peking.

c1900   229.5in (583cm) long

£9,000-10,000   **SOTA**

A north Chinese Tianjin carpet.

c1930-1950   138in (350.5cm) long

£650-850   **WW**

A Peshawar Serapi room-size rug, with a terracotta and mustard geometric medallion on an ivory field, buff spandrels, surrounded by a terracotta border.

140in (355.5cm) wide

£1,000-1,500   **DRA**

A large Donegal carpet, with simple flower and tree border on a green ground.

177.25in (450cm) long

£1,200-1,800   **WW**

A German hunting tapestry, after 'Les chasses de Maximilien', by Bernard van Orley (1488-1541), depicting a hunting party in pursuit of the stag into the lake, and representing the month of September, with monogram MG.

98in (249cm) high

£3,500-4,500 SOTA

CLOSER LOOK

By the 18thC, France was the European centre for silk-manufactory and weaving, making work from Spain and Italy, once major producers, more unusual.

Tapestries are woven on a loom and each panel of colour is built up separately, following a paper design known as a cartoon.

The one female musician holds tambourine decorated with a flaming pierced red heart, which symbolises religious ardour is an attribute of Venus in secular art.

The pastoral scene with musicians in classical garden landscape, was a popular subject matter.

A rare 18th/19thC Spanish pastoral tapestry, depicting a group of musicians and ladies with flowers and small children in a landscape, within a ribbon twisted husk border with escutcheon corner motifs.

109in (277cm) long

£35,000-45,000 SOTA

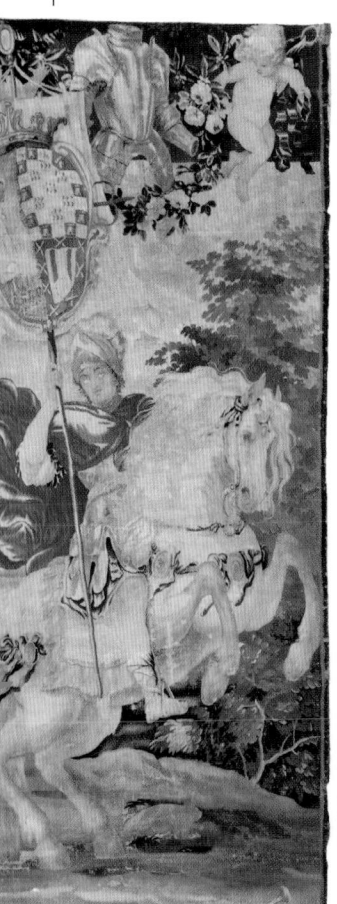

A small 17thC woven tapestry picture, with couched metal purl and crimped steel, bullion threads, chenille threads and moss work, applied with seed pearls and glass beads, depicting King Charles II and Queen Henrietta, in a later ebonised and gilt frame.

18.5in (47cm) high

£1,200-1,800 TEN

A late 17thC tapestry fragment, depicting flowers, birds, insects and animals, with a plush mount and a rosewood moulded frame.

Tapestry 20.5in (52cm) wide

£600-800 WW

A late 17thC Flemish wool tapestry, depicting a sculpted garden with fountains and peacock, with a wooden terrace, and a mansion in the distance, within decorative borders centred at top by double coat and arms, and at a lower section with entwined monogram roundel, muslin backed.

52.5in (133cm) wide

£20,000-30,000 SK

A late 17thC Flemish equestrian armorial portieres, Brussels workshop, woven with an equestrian figure holding a pendant enclosing family coat of arms of Velasco of Castile.

138.75in (352cm) wide

£20,000-25,000 SOTA

An early 18thC probably Brussels tapestry, depicting a view from a woodland toward a formal country house garden, within a border of ribbon-tied fruits and flowers inhabited by birds and animals.

165in (419cm) wide

£7,000-10,000 TEN

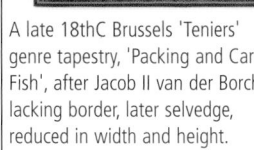

A late 18thC Brussels 'Teniers' genre tapestry, 'Packing and Carting Fish', after Jacob II van der Borcht, lacking border, later selvedge, reduced in width and height.

82.75in (210cm) high

£3,000-4,000 SOTA

A 17th/18thC Flemish verdure wool tapestry, depicting trees and foliage in a wood, within foliate borders.

120in (305cm) long

£5,000-7,000 SK

TEXTILES

An embroidered picture, by Adriana Smith, the satin ground worked with two central figures in tent stitch, the costumes adorned with couched silver threads and sequins.

1629   *20.75in (53cm) wide*

£1,500-2,000   **KT**

A 17thC embroidered panel fragment, worked with a shepherd playing his hurdy gurdy beneath a tree with animals gathered, the background worked with silver thread with initials 'K. C.', in a modern frame.

11.25in (28.5cm) wide

£1,500-2,000   **SWO**

A Charles II embroidered needlework, depicting knights in battle.

21in (53.5cm) wide

£6,000-8,000   **POOK**

A Pennsylvania silk- and paint-on-silk embroidery, attributed to Folwell, depicting a young lady and child in a pastoral setting with a cottage and monument inscribed 'Friendship'.

Embroidered needle paintings became popular in the late 18thC, worked in silk or chenille threads with the more detailed or delicate areas of painted silk. Pastoral and Neo classical themes were popular subject matter. Samuel Fowell (1764-1813) was an artist who, with his wife Elizabeth, set up a needlework school in Philadelphia.

c1805   *20in (51cm) wide*

£7,000-10,000   **POOK**

An early 19thC silk and woolwork picture of a cat on a cushion, later mounted, framed and glazed.

24.5in (62cm) high

£250-350   **DN**

An American early 19thC Pennsylvania Moravian silk-on-silk embroidery, depicting a basket of flowers.

6in (15cm) high

£900-1,200   **POOK**

A pair of early 19thC French colonial silk and chenille needlework pictures, each in giltwood frame, one depicting a gentleman arriving at an island colony, retrieving a child, the other depicting the man arriving at a city port, the child running to a woman nearby, with painted faces.

21in (53.5cm) high

£3,000-4,000   **SK**

An early 19thC coloured silk needlework, of musicians under a tree surrounded by farm animals, in a carved pine frame.

22.75in (58cm) wide

£400-500   **SWO**

An American wool- and paint-on-silk stumpwork and embroidered needlework picture, Lancaster, Pennsylvania, depicting a young woman, in original frame, old label on reverse inscribed 'Picture by Lydia Klin*** Lancaster, Pa'.

c1820-30   *16in (40.5cm) wide*

£900-1,200   **POOK**

An American silk-on-gauze needlework blessing, wrought by Eleanor Goss, with central script surrounded by elaborate floral vine border, dated.

1821   *15.5in (39.5cm) wide*

£1,000-1,500   **POOK**

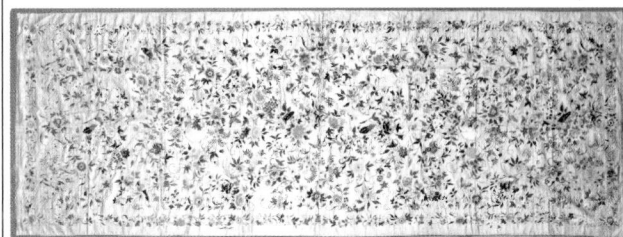

An American Pennsylvania silk-on-linen show towel, wrought by Magdalena Staufer, with lovebirds, potted tulips and figures, dated 1842.

68in (173cm) long

£350-450   **POOK**

A 19thC American silk-on-linen cross stitch show towel, by 'Barbara Mark', Pennsylvania, with profuse pink and blue decoration of peacocks, potted flowers and figures.

63in (160cm) long

£1,200-1,800   **POOK**

One of a pair of late 19thC embroidered wall hangings, of pale blue satin densely embroidered with myriad blossom, butterflies and birds.

134in (340cm) long

£3,000-4,000 PAIR   **KT**

WOOLWORK EMBROIDERIES

A late 17thC William & Mary framed wool needlework picture, rendered in gros and petit point, depicting a regal couple with a serving woman, a cherub and an angel in a wooded landscape with a city in the background.

Picture 16in (40.5cm) high

£700-1,000   **SK**

An early 18thC gros and petit point needlework panel, with a seated lady and doves below Chinese pots.

14in (36cm) square

£350-450   **DN**

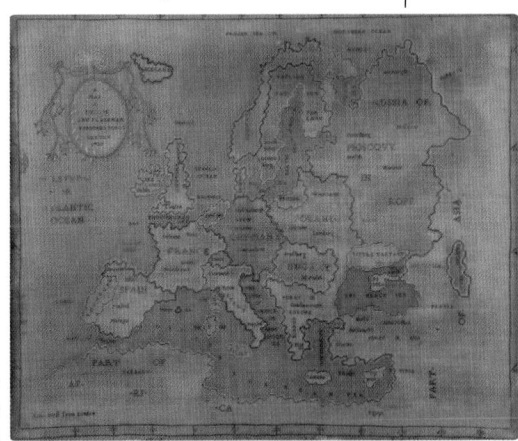

A George III embroidered map of Europe, framed and glazed, inscribed 'ANN FLASHMAN, B. MOORES SCHOOL, EXETER'.

1785   *27.25in (69cm) wide*

£150-200   **DN**

An early 19thC embroidered woolwork panel, by William Beckford, apparently depicting his estate in Jamaica, with two figures walking in a wooded gorge with waterfall, within a Rococo carved gilt-gesso frame.

Sir William Beckford (1709-1770), twice Lord Mayor, was the son of a wealthy Jamaican sugar planter and owned more than 22,000 acres at his Rosehall Estate in Jamaica. His son, William Beckford the younger (1760-1844) was left a vast fortune on his father's death, and built a Gothic folly at Fonthill Abbey in Yorkshire. He also wrote the Gothic novel, 'Vathek'.

Overall 31.5in (80cm) wide

£400-500   **L&T**

An American Reading, Pennsylvania wool needlework, wrought by Louisa Kitting, with central courtyard scene with figures within a floral vine border.

1840   *28in (71.5cm) wide*

£3,000-4,000   **POOK**

A mid-19thC Berlin woolwork and beadwork picture of a recumbent spaniel, later mounted, framed and glazed.

24.25in (64cm) wide overall

£700-1,000   **DN**

A mid-19thC woolwork picture of a golden pheasant, later framed and glazed.

31.5in (80cm) high

£350-450   **DN**

A Berlin woolwork embroidery of a Newfoundland dog, after Landseer, worked in wools in tent stitch.

29.5in (75cm) wide

£600-800   **KT**

A 19thC sailor's woolwork picture, depicting a three-masted sailing ship in full sail, on a calm sea, the cloudy sky filled with birds.

14.25in (36cm) wide

£1,000-1,500   **BE**

One of a pair of mid-19thC framed Continental needlework pictures, in silk and metallic threads on silk ground, depicting Louis IX of France in royal and saintly garb and pose.

Picture 15.5in (39.5cm) high

£550-750 PAIR   **SK**

A large Victorian woolwork picture of HMS Eurydice, wrecked off Dunnase, Isle of Wight, March 24th 1878, by G G. Baldie R. A., in a maple frame.

33in (84cm) wide

£2,000-3,000   **GORL**

A Victorian woolwork panel of HMS Bombay, on fire, 'December 22nd 1864', framed.

20.5in (52cm) wide

£700-1,000   **GORL**

A woolwork picture of R.M.S. Lusitania.

The British ocean liner R.M.S. Lusitania was launched 6th June 1906 and torpedoed by a German U-boat 7th May 1915.

23.25in (59cm) wide

£350-450   **WW**

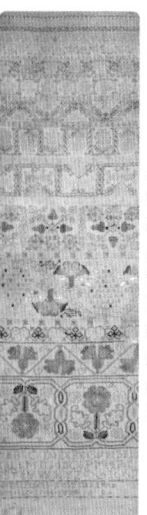

A 17thC band sampler, worked by Elizebeth Erlysman on a linen ground and silk threads, incorporating into the design embroidered acorns, stylised flowers and appliquéd flowerheads, later framed.

1652   *26.5in (67.5cm) high*

£1,500-2,000   **TEN**

ESSENTIAL REFERENCE – SAMPLERS

The earliest samplers were, as their name suggests, samples: a record of stitches and patterns used by professional and amateur needleworkers. 16thC samplers included border patterns and spot motifs, such as flowers, animals and insects, worked in coloured silks on linen. Few of these examples survive today.

- By the 17thC samplers were used primarily to show the embroiderer's skill, as their original function had been superseded by printed pattern books. Samplers still included border patterns and spot motifs, but these were joined by whitework, drawn thread work and needlelace techniques, as well as the occasional name and date.
- Alphabets, inscriptions and pictorial elements gradually began to appear until they became ubiquitous on 18thC samplers. Many of the most detailed examples were stitched by young girls, who were taught needlework as a vital skill for employement or accomplishment.
- Initially samplers were likely to be long rectangles that were easy to roll. This changed in the 18thC, when square samplers began to predominate.
- The pictorial element became increasingly dominant in the 19thC. The variety of stitches also decreased, with many examples only featuring cross stitch.
- Sampler-making became less important as education for women became more common. By the 20thC, it had became primarily a leisure activity.

An embroidered sampler, worked in the year of the Great Fire of London, worked by Elizebeth Short 'her sampler ended the first day of June, 1666', the upper section worked with three foliate bands in coloured silks, above alphabet test, white work, pulled and drawn threadwork, small section of hollie point, and reticella.

1666   *31.75in (81cm) long*

£3,500-4,500   **KT**

A George III cross-stitch sampler, depicting a central three-masted schooner, surrounded by motifs of buildings, flowers and animals, with 'May peace and plenty of our nation smile, and trade with commerce, bless the British Isles', and signed 'Mary Anne Dundas Finished this Sampler, June 12, 1797, Aged 8 Years', in burlwood frame.

c1797   *16in (40.5cm) high*

£1,200-1,800   **SK**

A silk-on-linen sampler, with a pot of flowers, figures and a house, dated.

1809   *21.5in (54.5cm) high*

£1,800-2,200   **POOK**

An early 19thC American silk-on-linen needlwork, Pennsylvania, inscribed 'Mary Barnes sampler aged 8 years. Marilla Keeler Ins', with facing birds and potted flowers above an alphabet and poem within a strawberry vine border.

16.25in (41.5cm) wide

£1,200-1,800   **POOK**

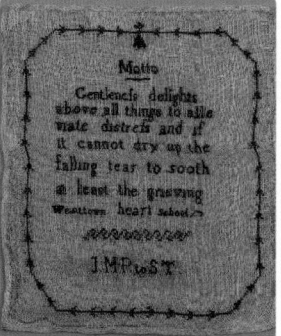

A early 19thC Pennsylvania Westtown School motto sampler, from Chester County, wrought by JMP to ST (Sarah Thomas).

8.25in (21cm) high

£1,500-2,000   **POOK**

An early 19thC Pennsylvania silk-on-linen sampler, from Chester County, wrought by Phebe Downing.

11.5in (29cm) high

£1,500-2,000   **POOK**

An Adam and Eve needlework sampler, worked in silk threads on a loosely woven wool ground, signed and dated 'Mary Ann Barnes worked this sampler in the 10 year of her age 1815', in a later moulded wood frame.

1815   *16in (40.5cm) high*

£900-1,200   **SK**

TEXTILES

A needlework sampler, by Rebekah Mayfield, St. Lawrence County, with a pious verse and the inscription 'Rebekah Mayfield finished this work Dec 20 1822 aged 9 years', in wool threads.

1822   *15in (38cm) high*

£6,000-8,000   **FRE**

CLOSER LOOK – PENNSYLVANIA SAMPLER

Samplers of this box-border design are typical of Leah Meguier's students.

Personal details, such as the maker's name and the date, greatly increases desirability

The overall design is well balanced and finely stitched.

A Harrisburg, Pennsylvania silk-on-linen sampler, wrought by Sarah Dougherty at Mrs Leah Meguier's School, with a large central scene of a young man and woman within a blocked border with vignettes of eagle, moon and children.

1819   *19in (48.5cm) wide*

£30,000-40,000   **POOK**

An early 19thC needlework sampler, worked with alphabet, religious verse and heraldic distinctions and English crests and crowns, by 'Elizabeth Chappell aged six years April AD 1833' in blue cotton on a linen ground, mainly in cross stitch within a glazed maple frame.

1833   *20.5in (52cm) wide*

£1,800-2,200   **TEN**

A William IV needlework sampler, by Elizabeth Redman, worked with a palace, tree, figures and birds below and idyllic country setting, dated.

1834   *16in (40.5cm) wide*

£2,000-3,000   **GORL**

An early 19thC needlework sampler, woven with a verse tablet inscribed 'Helen McEwen Allan 1836', above floral urns, trees and a grand house flanked by thistles and trees, floral border, framed and glazed.

1836   *20in (51cm) high*

£1,000-1,500   **L&T**

A school girl sample book, 'Specimens of Needlework', by Letitia Mercer, Derrylee School, Northern Ireland, including examples of patchwork button holes, darning, silk-on-linen samplers and doll dresses, approximately fifty pieces.

c1863

£2,500-3,500   **POOK**

An early 19thC English silk-on-linen sampler, wrought by Ann Parkinson (b1803), with central verse mounted by birds and flowers, above a lawn with figures and animals.

22.5in (57cm) wide

£1,500-2,000   **POOK**

A mid-18thC fan, the leaf decorated with a pastoral scene, with pierced and stained ivory sticks carved with military trophies and young gallants, similarly decorated guards, in a giltwood glazed scalloped-shaped display case.

10.25in (26cm) long

£550-750 BE

A late 18thC ivory fan, the leaf painted with a scene depicting 'The Apotheosis of Ephiginia', the ivory guards decorated with painted chinoiserie scenes of figures and pagodas, contained in a giltwood and glazed display case.

8.5in (22cm) long

£300-400 BE

A Continental painted fan, the vellum leaf painted with a fête champêtre with numerous figures, the reverse with Venus and putti, the mother-of-pearl and parcel gilt sticks pierced with a mythological scene, the guards carved and pierced with feathery guilloche, signed 'A Soldé'.

c1840–50 *20.5in (52.5cm) wide*

£1,500-2,000 TEN

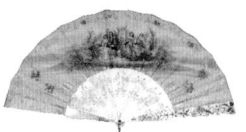

A mid-19thC fan, the printed paper and over painted leaf depicting a goat-drawn carriage, to the reverse a seated courting couple, heightened in gilt, with pierced and inlaid mother-of-pearl sticks and guards.

10.5in (27cm) long

£300-400 BE

A 19thC chinoiserie fan, the hand-painted leaf depicting a bird amongst foliage and a seated figure, with ivory sticks, the guards decorated with mother-of-pearl.

9.75in (25cm) long

£200-300 BE

A 19thC Continental fan, the hand-painted paper leaf depicting four figures in 18thC dress, signed 'Eugene? Andre', heightened in gilt, with mother-of-pearl sticks and guards, in a tan leather case.

10.5in (27cm) long

£400-500 BE

A late 19thC fan, the Belgium lace leaf extensively decorated with flowers and the name 'Augusta' below a coronet, with mother-of-pearl sticks and guard.

10.5in (27cm) long

£250-350 BE

TEXTILES

A 19thC Amish wool pieced quilt, in a centre diamond pattern, with a grey back, brick border, and purple and dark aqua centre.

Amish quilts are typically characterised by plain, dark fabrics and strong geometric patterns.

82in (208cm) long

£4,000-6,000   POOK

An early 20thC Amish pineapple pattern quilt, with red, blue, brown and green borders.

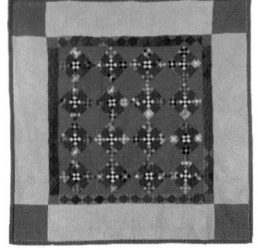

80in (203cm) square

£3,000-5,000   POOK

An Amish rayon and wool double nine patch quilt, with triangular border.

80in (203cm) long

£2,000-3,000   POOK

An early 20thC Amish nine patch in a nine patch quilt.

80in (203cm) long

£1,800-2,200   POOK

An early 20thC pieced feather quilt, with sawtooth border.

86in (218.5cm) long

£2,000-3,000   POOK

ESSENTIAL REFERENCE – QUILTS

Quilting probably arrived in Europe from the East in the 12thC, with decorative quilting increasing in the 14thC.

- By the 18thC quilted bed covers or 'quilts' were widespread. Quilts with centre panels and surrounding borders, known as 'medallion quilts' were popular. Some incorporated appliquéd detail and printed cotton into their designs. Patchwork became more common in the 19thC, and the two techniques were often combined.
- Quilting techniques were taken to America by European settlers in the 17thC. There bed quilts served a decorative and practical purpose, as well as becoming an integral part of the social life of the women who worked them: as the 'quilting bee' became a social ritual. Initially, patterns were based on English and Welsh designs, but gradually American forms emerged, such as the 'block' pattern.
- Album, autograph or friendship quilts were worked extensively in America, including the famous mid-19thC 'Baltimore album' quilts.

An Amish pieced quilt, the centre diamond pattern in purple, blue and maroon.

79in (200.5cm) long

£1,800-2,200   POOK

An early 20thC Amish, probably Lancaster County, green and red sawtooth centre diamond quilt.

80in (20.5cm) long

£4,000-6,000   POOK

An early 20thC Amish, probably Lancaster County, centre diamond quilt.

79in (200.5cm) square

£4,000-6,000   POOK

An early 20thC Amish bar quilt.

80in (203cm) long

£2,800-3,300   POOK

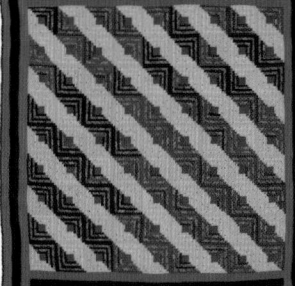

A 20thC Amish log cabin quilt, with brown and black borders.

77in (195.5cm) square

£1,200-1,800   POOK

An early/mid-20thC Amish postage stamp crib quilt.

34in (86.5cm) long

£1,000-1,500   **POOK**

A New York appliqué friendship quilt, wrought by Rosina Jobes, with twenty five squares depicting an eagle, cat and other images.

1849   *68in (172.5cm) wide*

£1,200-1,800   **POOK**

An American crazy quilt, probably New York state, dated '1884', a green plush velvet border enclosing squares of silk and velvet patches with anchor, artist palette, horse shoe and ladies' boot appliqués, initialled 'E.D.F.'

1884   *67in (170cm) wide*

£400-600   **FRE**

A 19thC pieced Ohio star crib quilt.

34in (86.5cm) square

£1,800-2,500   **POOK**

A late 19thC pieced Pennsylvania quilt with flying geese pattern.

90in (229cm) long

£400-600   **POOK**

A 19thC pieced quilt, Pennsylvania, with central diamond pattern star on a blue field with orange corners and quilted birds within a repeating star border with quilted hearts.

85in (216cm) wide

£2,000-3,000   **POOK**

A late 19thC pieced Pennsylvania quilt with Star of Bethlehem pattern.

95in (241cm) wide

£600-1,000   **POOK**

A pieced and appliquéd cotton Star of Bethlehem quilt, from Trexlertown, Pennsylvania, with large central eight-point star constructed of small calico printed fabric diamonds.

Included with the quilt is The Quilt Engagement Calendar 1889, in which this quilt is illustrated for January of 1890.

c1890   *80in (203cm) square*

£700-1,000   **SK**

An early 20thC Lancaster County, Pennsylvania cross-stitch wonder quilt.

This quilt was winner of the 1950 Lititz Community Show.

84in (213.5cm) long

£2,500-3,500   **POOK**

TEXTILES

A 17thC Italian framed 'Reticalla' needlelace sampler, cutwork and needwork lace with blocks of various design, upper right edge stiched 'Luca', damask ground, burl walnut frame.

Lace 15.5in (39.5cm) high

£1,800-2,200   **SK**

An American woolwork purse, probably Chester County, Pennsylvania, inscribed 'Samuel Garven', initialled 'PB' and dated 1767, with elaborate central potted floral vine on a green background.

1767   *10.5in (26.5cm) high*

£6,500-8,500   **POOK**

A rare early 19thC Lord Chancellor's burse, with stumpwork arms of England, pearls, gold and silver threadwork, owned by John Lord Eldon, Lord Chancellor of England 1751-1838.

The burse (purse) is traditionally used to carry the Great Seal, kept by the Lord Chancellor.

£9,000-12,000   **GORL**

A pink and white striped moiré ball gown, the short bodice trimmed with white bugle beads and lace, over elongated, oval shaped skirt.

c1865

£3,000-4,000   **KT**

A Matisse Mandarin robe, for Diaghilev's Ballet Russes 'Chant du Rossignol', of brilliant yellow satin adorned with crudely outlined painted black flowerheads centred by gold lamé discs daubed with curls, neck opening with domed glass buttons, quilted muslin lining.

The Ballet Russes (French for the 'Russian Ballet') was founded in 1909 by Russian impresario Serge Diaghilev (1872-1929). The vitality of colour and movement of Russian ballet created a sensation in Western Europe, and the influence of the Ballet Russes can be seen in almost every area of the arts in the Art Deco period.

1920   *Chest 62in (158cm)*

£40,000-50,000   **KT**

A French beaded flapper dress, the orange georgette ground embroidered in floss silk, silver thread, white, silver and orange bugle beads, oval metal beads in an oriental inspired pattern of swirls and clouds, matching slip.

c1924–25   *Bust 40in (101cm)*

£650-850   **KT**

A late 1930s/early 1940s Schiaparelli mauve satin bolero and extra-long evening gloves, plastered with opalescent sequins and large pastel coloured stones, matching gloves, printed black and white Paris label.

Gloves 27.5in (70cm) long

£2,000-3,000   **KT**

A late 1930s Worth gold cloqué evening gown, with figure-hugging bodice over bias cut skirt, the full sleeves with padded shoulders, zip fastened, labelled.

Bust 34–36in (86cm)

£1,500-2,000   **KT**

An early 1930s Maggy Rouff cream moss crêpe gown, with gently cowled neckline, ruched bands over bosom, keyhole back, pointed trained hem, labelled 'Av. des Champs-Elysées, 136, Paris 136' and indistinctly numbered.

Maggy Rouff opened her own couture house in 1929. This is a very early example of her work.

Bust 32in (81cm)

£1,500-2,000   **KT**

A late 1950s Jean Desses black draped chiffon cocktail dress, no. 3332, the corsetted bodice overlaid with graduated horizontal chiffon bands which fall in deep swags to the skirt front, white satin label.

Bust 34in (86cm)

£1,500-2,000 **KT**

CLOSER LOOK – PACO RABANNE MINI DRESS

Paco Rabanne (1934-) became well knwon in the 1960s for creating strange and influential clothes made from unusual, non-woven materials such as plastic and aluminium

Rabanne is perhaps best known for designing the costumes for the 1968 film, Barbarella starring Jane Fonda.

At the time he seemed to be embracing the futuristic styles favoured by his contemporaries, such as Pierre Cardin, but Rabanne's designs also harkened back to medieval armour and chain-mail.

Rabanne's designs have inspired today's avant-garde designers, including Yohji Yamamoto and Helmut Lang.

.

A rare Paco Rabanne chain-linked armour-plate mini dress, the dress formed from square metal plates which elongate down the skirt, linked by metal loops, black label pasted to interior.

1967 *Chest 32in (81cm)*

£10,000-12,000 **KT**

A Madame Grès 'Cabochard'-print evening gown, the dress bearing the black cross-hatched print incorporating the words 'Grès, Paris' as a design repeat, with broad swathe of fabric to bateau neckline, side split, zip-fastened.

This dress was reputedly made for the launch and press campaign of the Cabochard perfume, Mme Grès's first perfume, introduced in 1959. The box for the perfume is covered in this same design.

c1959 *Bust 34in (86cm)*

£1,000-1,500 **KT**

A Balenciaga satin evening coat, double-breasted with large buttons, short sleeves inset into the side seams, vented pocket to the front sides, lined in ivory satin and interlined in wool, labelled and indistinctly numbered.

c1959–61

£5,000-7,000 **KT**

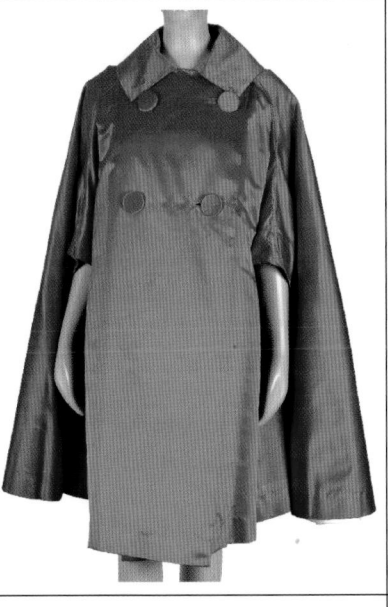

A late 1960s/early 1970s Madame Grès ivory chiffon gown, the satin-backed crêpe inner gown with plunging back, the front with demure double panel of chiffon and with asymmetric trained panels falling from each shoulder, labelled pencilled model tag and metal duty tags.

Bust 34in (86cm)

£4,500-5,500 **KT**

A 1960s Madame Grès black velvet and silk jersey evening gown, open down one side with empire line asymmetric bodice, with matching full-length jersey petticoat, woven satin label.

Bust 34–36in (86–92cm)

£3,000-4,000 **KT**

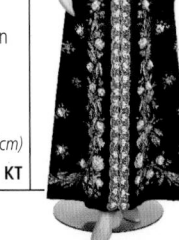

A Pierre Balmain evening gown, no. 124747, embroidered by Lesage with three dimensional flower sprays and leaves in chenille and floss silk, silver friesé strip and silver thread, and decorated overall with crystal beads, with matching organza backed satin stole, labelled.

This gown was worn only once to a reception at the Elysees Palace.

1960 *Bust 34–36in (86–92cm)*

£6,000-8,000 **KT**

A Loris Azzaro rose-pink jersey jewelled evening dress and cape, the bodice inset to centre-front and cuffs with 'barbaric' jewels wrapped with gilt wire, the hooded cape with simple ties to neck.

c1970 *Bust 32in (81cm)*

£900-1,200 **KT**

COUTURE

An Ossie Clark/Celia Birtwell for Quorum 'Marilyn' dress, in a figure hugging bias-cut, the low back with cross-over straps, revealing flounced front panels, labelled.

c1974   *Bust 34in (86cm)*

£1,500-2,000   KT

A mid-1980s Roberto Capucci black velvet flamenco-style ball gown, the plain, fitted black bodice exploding into tiers of acid green, hot pink and bright turquoise silk flounces.

Bust 34in (86cm)

£4,000-5,000   KT

A late 1980s/early 1990s Jean Paul Gaultier Femme black vinyl and dark wine jersey evening dress, with integral vinyl bustier, labelled 'GB size 8'.

Gaultier experimented with rubber and vinyl in his 'Forbidden Gaultier' collection in which he combined the traditional and technological.

Bust 32in (81cm)

£700-1,000   KT

A 1980s Jacqueline de Ribes emerald green paper taffeta cocktail dress, the swathed, strapless gown punctuated with bows to front and back, matching stole, labelled 'Paris–New York'.

Bust 30in (76cm)

£700-1,000   KT

A 1980s Jacqueline de Ribes fluorescent pink silk halter-neck evening gown, the bodice split to the waist with large plastic buckle, the short skirt revealed at the front within full-length over-skirt, labelled 'Paris–New York'.

Bust 34in (86cm)

£1,200-1,800   KT

A 1980s Roberto Capucci bronze silk faille ball gown, of simple classic construction with V-neckline over full skirt, broad belt, labelled.

Bust 34in (86cm)

£5,000-7,000   KT

A Jean Paul Gaultier Dominatrice dress, 'Women among Women' collection, shirred sleeves with zip fasteners, with elongated train to the rear that culminates in a buckle, and central band of corset-like hook and eye fasteners, Femme labelled.

1989–90   *Bust 36in (91cm)*

£3,500-4,500   KT

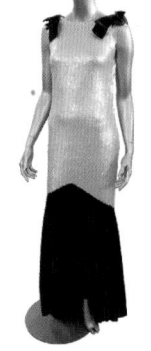

An early 1990s Chanel sequined evening gown, the column of white sequins above gently flared black sequined hem, camelias and bows to the shoulders.

Bust 34in (86cm)

£2,500-3,500   KT

A 1990s Thierry Mugler 'safari' suit, comprising raffia trimmed short sleeved jacket and matching knee length skirt, together with pink full length figure-hugging skirt with 'grass skirt' hem, labelled.

Bust 38in (96cm)

£900-1,200   KT

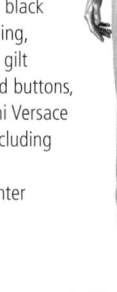

A Gianni Versace mint green silk and black leather 'bondage' dress, the bodice criss-crossed with black leather banding, applied with gilt Medusa-head buttons, with a Gianni Versace catalogue including this dress, Autumn–Winter 1992–3.

Bust 34in (86cm)

£1,200-1,800   KT

ESSENTIAL REFERENCE – HERMÈS

Hermès International, S.A. is a French fashion house, established by Thierry Hermès (1801-1878) in 1837 in Paris, France, with the aim of producing finely wrought harnesses and bridles carriages belonging to European noblemen. The first bag was introduced in 1900.

- Clients include Jackie Kennedy, Ingrid Bergman, Lauren Bacall, and Grace Kelly, after whom the 'Kelly' bag (previously the Sac à dépêches bag) was renamed in 1956.

A late 1950s/early 1960s Hermès brown crocodile handbag, lined in soft kid, with mirror and purse, gilt-brass circular closure, wide front flap, stamped in gold to the interior front pocket with maker's name and '24, Fg St Honoré'.

10in (25cm) long

£550-750   KT

A 1960s Hermès black suede clutch, press stud fastened, leather interior with zipped pocket, gilt floral appliqués to the front flap, stamped 'Hermès, Paris' to the interior.

8.75in (22cm) long

£350-450   KT

A 1930s black alligator handbag, resembling a small doctor's bag, with etched brass top closure, two rolled loop handles, lined in soft kid leather, unmarked.

£450-550   FRE

A 1950s French Strater 'Lite-On' black crocodile handbag, US patent, the engraved gilt metal interior 'guaranteed 24 carat gold finish', grey leather lining, magnetised lipstick and perfume holders, comb, cigarette compartments, photo holder, automatic internal lights, complete with instruction booklet.

9.5in (24cm) wide

£200-300   KT

A 1960s Hermès black leather vanity case, with gilt-brass lifter claps, the lid with inset mirror lined in red leather, the base lined in red satinised waterproof cotton, leather strap for holding containers, both stamped 'Hermès Paris'.

11.5in (29cm) long

£650-850   KT

A 1960s Chanel brown jersey quilted bag, with gilt stamp to the interior, gilt chain and hardware.

10in (25.5cm) wide

£150-250   KT

A 1960s burgundy crocodile transportable jewellery/vanity case, the upper section detaching to form a handbag, the lower compartments quilted for jewellery and with compartments for jars and cosmetics.

18.5in (47cm) high

£900-1,200   KT

A Chanel mini chain handle purse, black quilted kidskin with logo turn-clock closure on the front flap, with long chain handle, lined in burgundy leather and embossed 'Chanel' and 'Made in France' on the interior.

£550-750   FRE

A Hermès midnight blue crocodile clutch bag, navy kid interior with zipped pocket, stamped in gold to the inner flap 'Hermès Paris'.

c1970   *8.75in (22cm) long*

£700-1,000   KT

COUTURE

A 1980s Judith Leiber brushed gold and crystal minaudiere, eight sides, with triangles of pavé rhinestones alternating with etched gold sections, the lift-lid with triangular amethyst cabochon latch, cushioned gold leather bottom and interior with coin purse and comb, attached chain.

£250-350   FRE

A Hermès black crocodile Constance bag, with gilt-brass 'H' lifter clasp, lined in black leather, stamped in gold under flap.

c1970   *9in (23cm) wide*

£1,200-1,800   KT

A late 1970s Hermès brown leather Kelly bag, stamped with maker's name under front flap, with three interior pockets and detachable long strap.

12in (31cm) wide

£700-1,000   KT

A modern Hermès tan leather Kelly bag, with gilt brass hardware padlock, and two keys, with orange flannel storage bag.

11in (28cm) long

£600-800   KT

A modern Hermès Birkin of blue-jean toga leather, with white metal hardware and lock with two keys, with original box, all original packing materials, rain protector, orange cotton storage bag.

14in (36cm) long

£6,000-8,000   KT

TRUNKS

An early 20thC Louis Vuitton wood-strapped and leather-covered streamer trunk, serial no. '123 323', with brass fittings, leather straps, ends stencilled 'M.K. Young, New York'.

Established in 1854, Louis Vuitton Malletier is a French fashion house, well known for its iconic LV monogram. Originally the company was a trunks and luggage retailer, moving in to fashion and acquiring its legendary status in the mid-20thC.

39.5in (100.5cm) wide

£2,000-3,000   SK

A large Goyard travelling trunk.

La Maison Goyard was founded in 1853 by François Goyard (1828-1890) to make hand-made cases, trunks, luggage and handbags. Edmond Goyard (1860-1937), son of the founder later developed a natural, resistant and waterproof canvas, which could be used to cover the trunks. Edmond's original weaving method is still used today.

41.25in (105cm) wide

£4,500-5,500   DN

A set of three Goyard suitcases.

Largest 31.75in (81cm) wide

£700-1,000   DN

A Louis Vuitton black leather trunk, bearing leather label 'Louis Vuitton, Paris 70 Champs Elysees, Nice 4 Jardin Public, model depose', stamped '773720'.

33.5in (85cm) wide

£150-250   DN

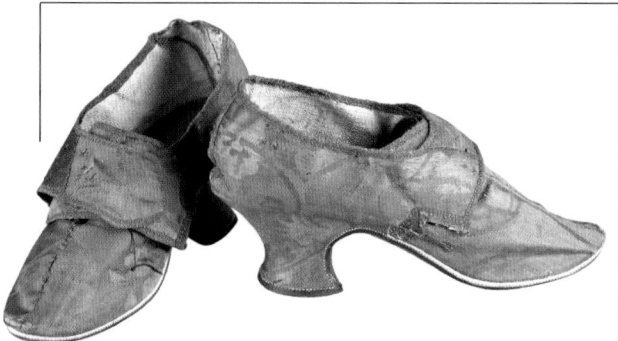

A pair of ladies' green damask shoes, with rounded toe, curved heel with steep arch, white leather rand.
c1740–60

£900-1,200   KT

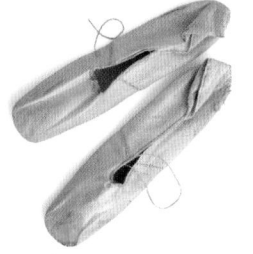

A pair of mid-19thC straight-soled kid sandal-slippers. The shoes could be worn on either foot, and so several pairs were bought at a time and replaced individually as they wore out.

£50-100   LDY

A pair of mid-19thC slippers, the black kid leather uppers embroidered, with pleated ribbon trim and with lace and ribbon rosettes.

£200-500   BZ

A pair of black satin shoes, embroidered with flowers and with multiple loop bows.

By the 1860s shoe designs were inspired by those of the 17th and 18thC. These bows – similar to the 'Fenelon' bows popular after 1863 – were popular in Europe and the US, where the shoes were known as 'Marie Antoinette slippers'.

c1860

£500-1,000   BZ

A pair of mid-19thC slippers, the fabric uppers embroidered with a basket of flowers and with pleated red ribbon trim.

£200-500   BZ

A child's beaded shoe, dark red velvet with multicoloured floral design.
c1880

£50-100   BZ

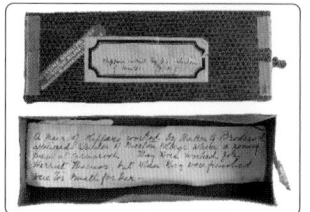

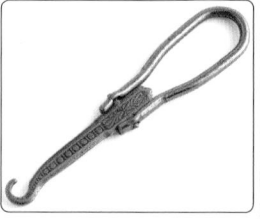

A 19thC pair of child's Berlin woolwork embroidered slippers. A note in the box reads: 'A pair of slippers worked by the Hon G Borderick [1831-1903], afterwards warden of Merton College, where a young man at Carnabrook. They were worked for Harriet Thomas but when they were finished were too small for her.'

£200-500   BZ

A 19thC pair of button boots, green and cream leather uppers.

Boots were popular after c1860 because they were warmer and more modest when worn under huge crinoline skirts. The buttons were done up and undone using a boot hook, and although this method made any adjustments during the day awkward and impractical, boots remained fashionable – possibly because many ladies employed maids to attend to such things.

£200-500   BZ

TEXTILES

A pair of black silk and gold leather shoes, with paste buckle decoration.

c1930

£200-500   BZ

A pair of black silk shoes, with jewelled straps, buckles and heels, marked 'S. Appleby, Station Bridge, Harrogate'.

c1930

£200-500   BZ

A pair of black suede court shoes, with suede and satin buckle detail, marked 'Made by Bally in Switzerland exclusively for Russell & Bromley. A Toby Shoe.'

c1930

£100-200   PC

A pair of 1930s black nubuck suede shoes, with leather lattice panel, marked 'Selberite Arch Protector shoes by Manfield & Sons Ltd'.

£50-100   CANS

A rare pair of 1930s terracotta suede Bally shoes, with ankle straps and diamanté-inset buckles.

£20-100   CANS

A pair of 1930s brown nubuck lace-ups, with diamond-woven leather panels, printed 'Made in Belgium especially for Regent Shoe Stores 31 Wardour St Shaftesbury Avenue London W1'.

£100-200   CANS

A pair of 1940s brown suede and snakeskin court shoes.

£50-100   GCHI

ESSENTIAL REFERENCE – SALVATORE FERRAGAMO

Salvatore Ferragamo (1898-1960) was born in Bonito, Italy and made his first pair of shoes at the age of nine, from materials he borrowed from the local cobbler. At age 16 he moved to California, set up a business and became shoemaker for the stars of Hollywood, inventing the cage heel and developing the wedge. Throughout the 1940s and 50s his styles filled the pages of the world's top fashion magazines.

- Ferragamo's first job in America was in a boot factory, but he soon set up his own shop in Santa Barbara, California and started to make cowboy boots for actors in Westerns.
- As his reputation grew, he moved on to create bespoke shoes for other Hollywood stars. His client list included Mary Pickford, Pola Negri, Clara Bow and Rudolph Valentino.
- Ferragamo was keen to perfect the comfort of his footwear, and took a course in anatomy to help him develop a steel arch support that was inserted into the instep of his shoes.
- By 1927, overwhelmed by demand for his custom-made creations, Ferragamo moved his business to Florence, Italy where he was able to combine the city's traditional leather craftsmanship with American mass-manufacturing techniques.
- The shoes he made often featured unorthodox materials, from hummingbird feathers to mosaics of coloured glass.
- Ferragamo is probably most famous for the cork wedge and his innovative 'cage' heel, made from filigree brass.
- When Ferragamo died in 1960, his business was taken over by his wife and children, and continues to be a leading footwear, fashion and luxury goods company.

A pair of 1940s Salvatore Ferragamo 'Ferrina Aquilaire 2' brown suede shoes with buckles.

£50-100   CANS

A pair of 1940s Salvatore Ferragamo blue lace shoes.

£200-500   LDY

An English and Latin New Testament Bible, printed by James Nycolson, Southwark, second edition of Coverdale's diglot testament, 18thC panelled calf, lacking two leaves, some early annotations, upper cover detached, light spots and stains.

Myles Coverdale's (1488-1569) Bible comprises the Vulgate text of the New Testament printed side by side with Coverdale's English translation. It was first published in London in 1538 by Southwark-based publisher James Nicolson, but Coverdale was unhappy with the result, finding it full of errors, and published a second edition in November of the same year with French printer Francis Regnault. Nicolson, however, also published a second version towards the end of 1538 with many of the errors corrected, which, according to the title-page in some of the copies but not others was 'Faythfullye translated by Johan Hollybushe'.

1538

£9,000-12,000   **L&T**

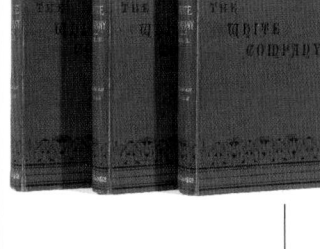

Dickens, Charles, 'A Tale of Two Cities', first edition, published by Chapman and Hall, London, 16 plates by H.K. Browne, publisher's green cloth, covers stamped in blind, spine lettered in gilt, bindings in unusually fine condition.

1860

£6,000-8,000   **BLNY**

Arthur Conan Doyle, 'The White Company', first edition, three volumes, 8vo, original brown cloth, some light foxing and slight rubbing to spines, otherwise an unusually good set.

1891

£3,000-4,000   **BLO**

Doyle, Sir Arthur Conan, 'The Hound of the Baskervilles', first edition, first impression, first state, very light ownership inscription on front pastedown, original gilt and black pictorial red cloth, minor rubbing to corners.

1902

£1,100-1,300   **BLO**

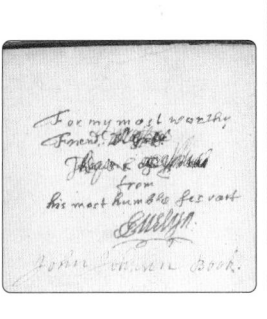

Evelyn, John, 'Acetaria, a discourse of sallets', London, ink inscription 'For my most worthy friend [name scored out] from his most humble servant J. Evelyn', blank, folding table, contemporary calf, rebacked retaining original gilt backstrip, some splitting to hinges, foxing throughout.

1699

£2,000-3,000   **L&T**

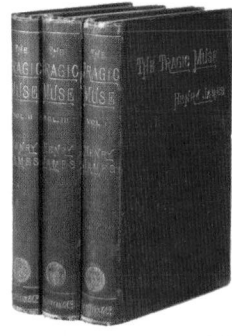

Henry James, 'The Tragic Muse', first English edition, in three volumes, 8vo, original cloth, rubbed and cocked, spines faded, vol. 3 with small split to head of lower joint, in modern drop-back box.

This example is one of only 500 sets printed.

1890

£1,000-1,500   **BLO**

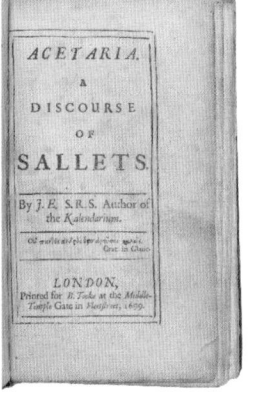

Rackham, Arthur, watercolour over pen-and-ink for 'The Valiant Little Tailor' in the expanded 1902 reissue of 'The Fairy Tales of the Brothers Grimm', signed and dated.

Rackham often added new pictures to reissues of old books or reworked earlier drawings with watercolour for exhibition. In this example Rackham has pasted an ornamental border to the drawing.

1906

£14,000-16,000   **BLNY**

Twain, Mark, 'The Adventures of Huckleberry Finn,' first American edition, published by Charles L. Webster, New York, illustrations by E. W. Kemble, original cloth, in collector's box, minor wear to spine, damp flecks to boards.

Inscribed and dated by its first owner in early April 1885, this is one of the earliest inscribed copies to appear at auction.

1885

£2,500-3,500   **L&T**

Baum, L[yman] Frank, 'The Wonderful Wizard of Oz, first edition, second printing, published by Geo. M. Hill Co, Chicago and New York, illustrated by W.W. Denslow, inscription dated 'December 25, 1902', pictorial endpapers, hinges cracked, light soiling, spine tips worn, in clamshell case.

This first edition is one of the most heavily designed children's books ever published with 24 colour plates and many textual pictures in varying colours.
1900

£1,800-2,200   **BLNY**

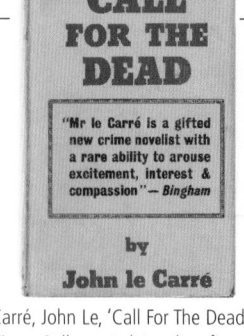

Burroughs, Edgar Rice, (1875-1950), 'The Outlaw of Torn', first edition, A.C. McClurg and Co., Chicago, original red cloth, in publisher's dust jacket, staining, mild soiling, small chips, some offsetting to endpapers, two small tape repairs to verso.
1927

£2,000-3,000   **BLNY**

Carré, John Le, 'Call For The Dead', Victor Gollancz Ltd, London, first edition, original red cloth and yellow dustwrapper, protective cellophane wrapper, slight dustmarking and chipping to edges, interior clean.
1961

£3,500-4,500   **L&T**

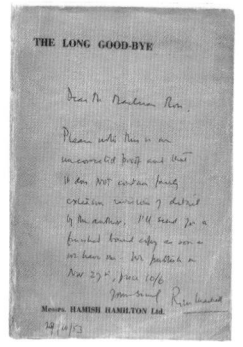

Chandler, Raymond, 'The Long Good-bye', uncorrected proof copy for the first edition, Hamish Hamilton, inscribed on the upper cover by the editor, Roger Machell, original printed wrappers, minor repair to spine end.
1953

£2,500-3,500   **BLO**

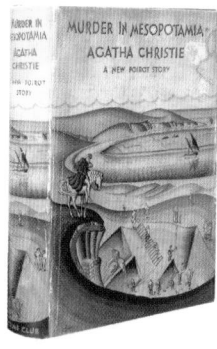

Christie, Agatha, 'Murder in Mesopotamia', first edition, first impression, original upper panel of jacket mounted onto front pastedown, original cloth, dust jacket, restoration to spine ends, some marking, soiling, rubbing and crease marks.
1936

£1,500-2,000   **BLO**

Dahl, Roald, 'Charlie and the Chocolate Factory', first edition, published by Alfred A. Knopf, New York, illustrated by Joseph Schindelman, original cloth, in dust jacket.

This American edition preceded the English by three years.
1964

£4,500-5,500   **BLNY**

Wheatley, Dennis, 'The Devil Rides Out', Hutchinson, first edition, first impression, inscribed by author, publisher's advertisements at end, map endpapers, original cloth, dust jacket, original publisher's wrap around and book guild 'Black Magic Story', sticker, minor rubbing to corner tips.
1935

£5,500-7,500   **BLO**

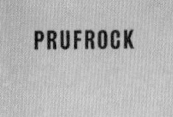

Eliot, T. S., 'Prufrock and other Observations', first edition, published by The Egoist Ltd, London, one of only 500 copies, original wrappers, in half morocco and blue cloth slipcase, very slightly rubbed.

Contains the much-anthologised 'Love Song of J. Alfred Prufrock', a poem of alienation and indecision within a stifling metropolis.
1917

£14,000-16,000   **BLNY**

Eliot, T. S., 'The Confidential Clerk', first edition, published by Faber and Faber, London, presentation copy inscribed to Eliot's brother-in-law 'to Maurice Ahme Haigh-Wood/ from T. S. Eliot/ 6iv54', original cloth and dust jacket, slight rubbing.
1954

£1,600-1,800   **BLNY**

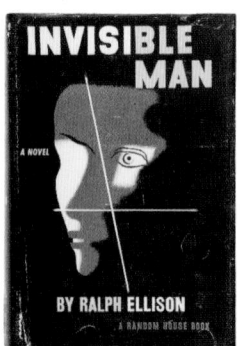

Ellison, Ralph, 'Invisible Man', first edition, first printing, published by Random House, New York, publisher's cloth, in dust jacket, spine a bit rubbed, minor professional repairs.
1952

£1,000-1,500   **BLNY**

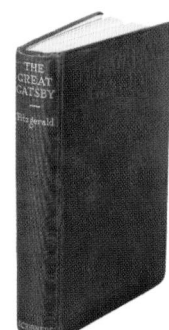

Fitzgerald, F. Scott, 'The Great Gatsby', first edition, first issue, published by Charles Scribner's Sons, New York, original green cloth stamped in blind, gilt spine title, a trace of rubbing to spine ends.
1925

£2,500-3,500   **BLNY**

Fitzgerald, F. Scott, 'Tender is the Night', first edition in a first issue jacket, Charles Scribner's Sons, New York, original green cloth, partially restored.

1934

£5,500-7,500   **BLNY**

Fleming, Ian, 'Casino Royal', first edition, first impression, ownership stamp on front free endpaper, bookseller's small sticker on rear pastedown, original boards, light marking visible to foot of upper cover, first state dust jacket, rubbed.

1953

£6,000-8,000   **BLO**

Golding, William, 'Lord of the Flies', first edition, signed by the author, ink stamp of Ealing Studios' Scenario Department, original cloth, shelf lean, dust-jacket, rubbed at corners, a few minor closed tears, slight spotting.

1954

£3,200-3,800   **BLO**

Greene, Graham, 'England Made Me', first edition, original cloth, dust jacket by Youngman Carter, frayed at spine ends and corners.

'England Made Me' was one of Greene's early novels, which caused the New Statesman to compare him to Malraux, Faulkner and Hemingway.

1935

£12,000-18,000   **BLO**

ESSENTIAL REFERENCE – HEMINGWAY

Ernest Hemingway (1899-1961) is one of America's most famous novelists. His writing is characterised by economy and understatement, and stoical male protagonists.

- **In 1953 Hemingway received the Pulitzer Prize for 'The Old Man and the Sea', and in 1954 he was awarded the Nobel Prize in Literature.**
- **He had great successes with 'A Farewell to Arms' (Scribner, 1929), set during WWI, and 'For Whom The Bell Tolls', set in the Spanish Civil War (Scribner, 1940). These famous, iconic titles are prized, but in general first edition books written at the height of an author's power are worth less than early/less-well received books, as fewer were published.**
- **In a recent list of most valuable first editions, three Hemingway titles featured in the top 15: 'The Sun Also Rises' (Scribner, 1926) valued at £30,000+, 'Three Stories & Ten Poems' (Contact Publishing, 1923) valued at £25,000+, and 'In Our Time' (Three Mountains Press, 1924), at £25,000+.**

Lee, Harper, 'To Kill a Mockingbird', first edition, published by JB Lippincott and Co., Philadelphia, original green cloth and brown boards in dust jacket with author photo by Truman Capote, rubbed at spine ends, folds and bottom edge of front panel.

1960

£6,000-8,000   **BLNY**

Heller, Joseph, 'Catch-22', first edition, first impression, signed by the author, on preliminary blank, original cloth, dust jacket, slight abrading to spine, small chip from top edge of lower panel.

1961

£1,800-2,200   **BLO**

Hemingway, Ernest, 'A Farewell to Arms', published by Charles Scribner's Sons, New York, from an edition of 10 signed by the author, original half vellum and boards.

The only work by Hemingway issued in a signed limited edition.

1929

£7,000-10,000   **BLNY**

Hemingway, Ernest, 'A Farewell to Arms', published by Charles Scribner's Sons, New York, first edition, first issue, original cloth with dust jacket, shelfworn, slightly rubbed jacket with spine panel lightly faded.

1929

£1,800-2,200   **BLNY**

Huxley, Aldous, 'Brave New World', first edition, published by Chatto & Windus, London, original cloth, dust jacket, very minor wear to bottom edge of spine faint spotting to jacket verso.

1932

£5,500-7,500   **BLNY**

Joyce, James, 'Ulysses', first edition, published by Shakespeare and Co., Paris, contemporary morocco, spine in six compartments, original wrappers bound in at rear, binding rebacked but spine preserved, corners rubbed.

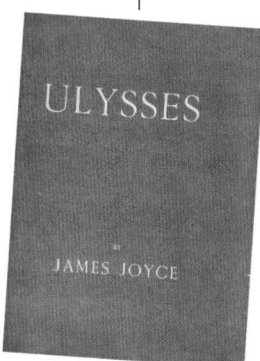

This example is one of only 150 copies.

1922

£16,000-18,000   **BLNY**

Kesey, Ken, 'One Flew Over the Cuckoo's Nest', first edition, published by the Viking Press, New York, signed 'Ken Kesey' on front endpaper, original green cloth, in dust jacket, custom half morocco folding case, spots of slight rubbing.
1962

£5,000-7,000   BLNY

Michell, Margaret, 'Gone with the Wind', first edition, published by The Macmillan Company, New York, original grey cloth in dust jacket, custom cloth folding case, rear panel lightly smudged, very minor rubbing along folds.
1936

£5,000-7,000   BLNY

CLOSER LOOK AT A FIRST EDITIONS OF THE HOBBIT

This is one of only 1,500 copies printed in the small initial print run published in September 1937 and sold out by December. Tolkien revised the text in two later editions to reflect new developments in his mythology of Middle Earth.

The condition is good with only light restoration to folds and spine ends.

The endpapers are maps drawn by Tolkien. Originally these were to be the only illustrations in the book, but the staff at Allen & Unwin were so taken with the author's drawings that he was invited to supply further illustrations.

This is the rare, original dust jacket, designed by Tolkien.

Tolkien, J. R. R., 'The Hobbit, Or There and Back Again', first edition, published by George Allen & Unwin Ltd, original pictorial green cloth, in dust jacket, custom folding case, light spotting to fore-edge.

'The Hobbit', was only published after Stanley Unwin's young son Rayner, aged 10, was asked to read the manuscript and assess its appeal for children. He liked it. 'The Hobbit' has since come to be regarded as rare feat of imagination.
1937

£30,000-40,000   BLNY

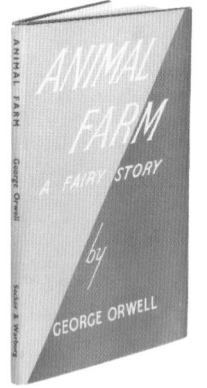

Orwell, George, 'Animal Farm', first edition, published by Secker & Warburg, original green cloth, green and grey dust jacket, custom folding cloth case, trace of rubbing.
1945

£6,000-8,000   BLNY

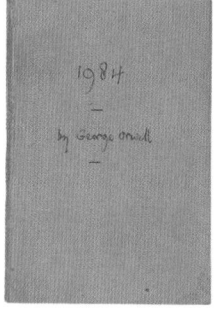

Orwell, George, '1984', published by Secker & Warburg, London, rare uncorrected proof, original plain blue wrappers with author and title in blue ink to upper wrapper and spine, black cloth chemise and slipcase, edges lightly spotted, some faint browning.
1949

£11,000-13,000   BLNY

Rand, Ayn, 'Atlas Shrugged', first edition, published by Random House, New York, original green cloth, in dust jacket, minor rubbing to spine.

1957

£500-700   BLNY

Rowling, J.K., full set of Harry Potter books, each with author's signature, 'Harry Potter and the Half Blood Prince' and 'Harry Potter and the Deathly Hallows' first editions, all original boards with dust jackets, the first five in a single five volume publisher's card slipcase, split at lower bottom.

£7,000-10,000   L&T

Stapledon, Olaf, 'Star Maker', first edition, first impression, small stamp/sticker to foot of front pastedown, original cloth, dust jacket, some light staining, and rubbing and browning to spine.

This novel is considered a sci-fi classic.
1937

£2,000-2,500   BLO

Steinbeck, John, 'Of Mice and Men', first edition, published by Covici-Friede, New York, with tipped-in signature 'For Miss Wilkes, John Steinbeck, Dec. 1962', publisher's cloth, original dust jacket with light wear, light thumbsoiling.
1937

£2,500-3,500   BLNY

Wodehouse, P.G., 'The Clicking of Cuthbert', first edition, first impression, original sage green cloth, minor rubbing, dust jacket, light soiling, tears at corners and head of spine with slight loss.

1922

£2,500-3,500   BLO

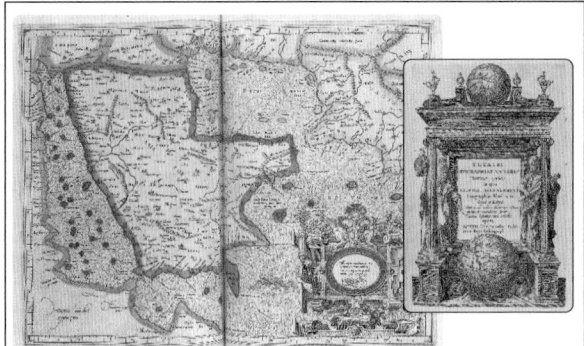

Berthius, Petrus, 'Theatri Geographiae Verteris', published by Isaac Elzevir and Jodocus Hondius, Leiden and Amsterdam, first edition, 47 double-page engraved maps, 30 hand-coloured in outline, 18thC mottled calf gilt, red morocco label, some damp staining.
1618-19

£6,500-8,500   L&T

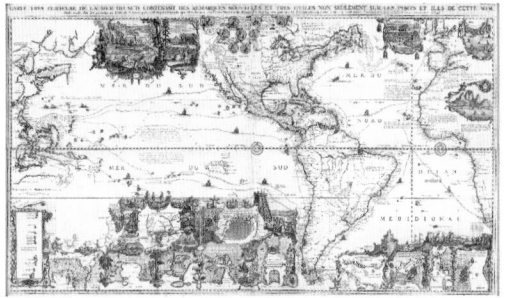

Chatelain, Henri Abraham, hand-coloured engraved map, 'Carte tres Curieuse de la Mer due Sud', in four joined sheets mounted to board, minor chipping to edges, negligible paper loss, old colour, possibly cleaned.

Henri Abraham Chatelain (1684-1743) published the 'Atlas Historique' in seven volumes in the early 18thC. The atlas contained a selection of maps accompanied by a range of information from topography and cosmography, to heraldry and costumes of the world. Amongst other maps it contained the vast 'Carte tres Curieuse de la Mer due Sud', which features North and South America and the Pacific and Atlantic Oceans, along with medallion portraits of New World explorers including Columbus, Vespucci, Magellan, Drake, La Salle and Dampier, and views of New World cities.

56.5in (143.5cm) wide

£7,000-10,000   FRE

Harris, J., 'New Map of America', published in 1721 by John Senex, London.

21.75in (55cm) wide

£1,500-2,000   POOK

Cook, Captain James - Anderson, George William, 'A new, authentic and complete collection of voyages round the world', Alex Hogg, London, folio, 37 maps, 114 plates, contemporary calf gilt, rebacked, later endpapers, corners worn, light water stains.

£1,200-1,800   L&T

A hand-drawn map of the United States, copied by Caleb Wall, titled 'Map of the United States of America Laid Down from the best authorities Agreeable to the Peace of 1783', ink on paper, framed.
1795   *42.5in (108cm) wide*

£1,300-1,500   FRE

BOOKS AND PRINTS

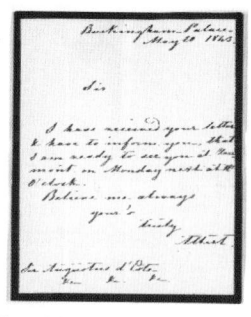

Albert, Prince Consort, three autograph letters, two on mourning stationery with contemporary docketing and envelopes, Buckingham Palace and Windsor Castle, 20 May to 27 August 1843, with a signed letter from Sir Robert Peel, Whitehall, 21 May 1843.

£600-800   L&T

Faulkner, William, autograph letter, in Faulkner's hand-addressed envelope, to A.B. Shepperson, chairman, English Department, University of Virginia.
December 1st 1959

£4,500-5,500   FRE

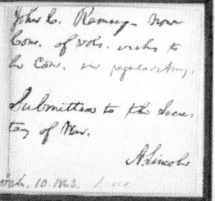

Lincoln, Abraham, short autograph document, trimmed from a large sheet, framed with a mezzotint portrait of Lincoln by William Sartain.
1863

£5,000-7,000   FRE

Washington, George, signed documents, also signed by George Clinton, printed document filled in for sale of land in White's Town York to Samuel Wells, also signed by 'Tobias Lear' and 'D(avid) Humphreys'.

£12,000-15,000   FRE

PHOTOGRAPHS

Doyle, Arthur Conan, signed portrait photograph by 'Elliott & Fry, 55 Baker Street, London', inscribed by sitter in ink on mount 'yours very truly, A Conan Doyle'.

£1,800-2,200   L&T

Two silver printed portraits of Audrey Hepburn, by Angus McBean, two versions of the same image, each signed in the negative 'Angus McBean, London '51', in later frames.
1951   *Largest 15in (38cm) high*

£700-1,000   L&T

An original signed and inscribed photograph of Helen Keller, with her teacher Annie Sullivan, inscribed 'To Billy Fickes from his friend Helen Keller', signed in pencil on the image, matted and framed.
9in (24cm) high

£1,000-1,500   BLNY

A Mark Twain signed photograph, framed silver print of the author standing, pictured from the waist up.
c1904   *10.25in (26cm) high*

£2,500-3,500   BLNY

A late 1960s long-sleeved white England no. 6 international jersey worn by Bobby Moore, with embroidered three lions cloth badge, with a Bobby Moore tribute publication.

Robert 'Bobby' Moore (1941-1993) captained West Ham United football team and the England team that won the 1966 World Cup. Moore subsequently became a British national icon: named BBC Sports Personality of the Year in 1966 and later decorated with the OBE in the New Year Honours List.

£1,800-2,200   GBA

A 15ct Everton FC gold medal presented to the Club Secretary Richard Molyneux from the players in 1898, the obverse engraved with a 'RM' monogram, the reverse engraved with presentation inscription.

£1,500-2,000   GBA

Alex Stepney's Manchester United 1968 European Cup winner's medal, .750 Continental gold, by Peka, inscribed 'COUPE DES CLUBS CHAMPIONS EUROPEENS', the reverse inscribed 'VAINQUEUR, 1968, ALEX STEPNEY'.

Alex Stepney (b.1942) was Manchester United's goalkeeper when the team became the first English club to win the European Cup in 1968, defeating Portuguese champions Benfica 4-1.

1.5in (4cm) high

£25,000-35,000   GBA

Six rare autographed postcards portraying Tottenham Hotspur footballers who played in the first match at White Hart Lane 4th September 1899, each card signed and inscribed in ink.

£3,500-4,500   GBA

An F.A. Cup final programme Arsenal v Cardiff City, 23rd April 1927.

The 1927 F.A. Cup final was won by Cardiff City who beat Arsenal 1-0 to take the F.A. Cup trophy outside of England for the only time. This was also the first ever Cup Final to be broadcast by the BBC.

£1,500-2,000   GBA

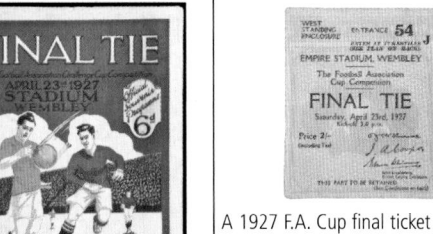

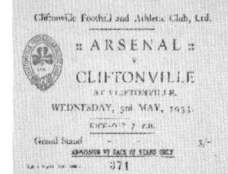

A 1927 F.A. Cup final ticket stub Arsenal v Cardiff City.

£400-500   GBA

A rare pre-War ticket for the Cliftonville v Arsenal match 3rd May 1933.

£300-400   GBA

A Hugh Philip and Allan Robertson longnose playclub, the fruitwood head stamped 'H. Philip' and 'Allan', leather insert to face, horn insert to sole, lead counterweight, hickory shaft, head cracked and sole damaged.

Hugh Philip (died 1856) was a maker of exceptional golf clubs and Allan Robertson (1815-1859) is considered one of the first professional golfers, who also manufactured feathered golf balls and clubs that were exported all over the world.

£9,000-12,000 **L&T**

A Cochranes Ltd. 'Giant' putter, Edinburgh, with dot pattern face, hickory shaft.

£4,000-5,000 **L&T**

A 'The Ocobo 27 1/2' mesh pattern ball, with a white metal girdle band, inscribed 'Hornsey Golf Club, Opening Competition, 1898, Won by R. P. Maw'.

£1,000-1,500 **L&T**

A set of twelve unused Haskell bramble pattern gutty balls, contained in original trade box.

£5,500-7,500 **L&T**

A Tom Morris St. Andrews and Manchester trade postcard, decorated with portraits of the Morris family, including Old Tom.

5.5in (14cm) wide

£1,500-2,000 **L&T**

An early black and white photographic portrait of Walter Hagen, Spring Lake Golf and Country Club.

4.5in (11.5cm) high

£500-700 **L&T**

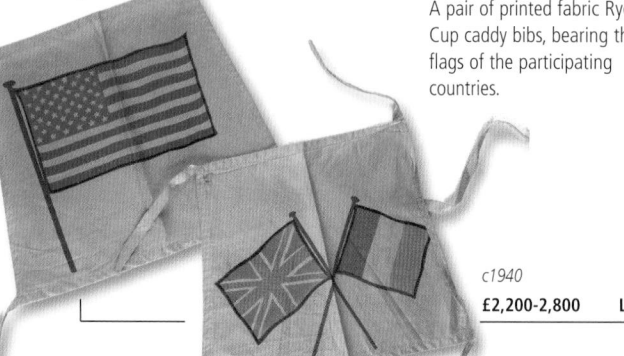

A pair of printed fabric Ryder Cup caddy bibs, bearing the flags of the participating countries.

c1940

£2,200-2,800 **L&T**

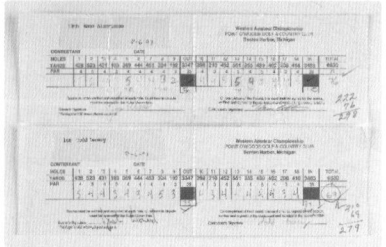

A pair of official Western Golf Association 1993 scorecards, one for the winner, Todd Demsey, signed, the other for Hans Albertsson, signed by him and the scorer Tiger Woods.

This is believed to be the earliest official Tiger Woods-signed scorecard ever auctioned.

£1,000-1,500 **L&T**

A Royal Doulton 'black boy' sugar bowl, titled 'I Wasn't Ready, The All Black Team', cracked and minor chips.

5in (13cm) diam

£220-280   **GBA**

A Victorian Staffordshire bowl, printed in green with two designs of a cricket match with tents and a church beyond, oak leaf decoration to the inside of the rim.

6.5in (16.5cm) diam

£180-220   **GBA**

A Victorian Staffordshire bowl, printed in colours with a repeated design of a cricket match with tents and a church beyond, oak leaf decoration to the inside of the rim.

5in (13cm) diam

£180-220   **GBA**

A Victorian Staffordshire mug, printed in colours with two designs of a cricket match with tents and a church beyond, oak leaf decoration to the inside of the rim, and crossed bats, stumps and balls to handle.

4in (10cm) high

£150-200   **GBA**

A Staffordshire mug, printed in colour with a portrait of Syd F. Barnes at the crease, and inscribed 'SYD F. BARNES, FAMOUS INTERNATIONAL BOWLER'.

4in (10cm) high

£120-180   **GBA**

A Doulton Lambeth Art Nouveau stoneware mug, by John Broad, moulded in relief with figures of Abel, Woods & Mac Gregor.

6in (15cm) high

£550-750   **GBA**

A set of five original artworks for newspaper cartoons featuring cricket, cut and pasted onto backboards, subjects comprising Fred Trueman, West Indies, a 'sleepy' Test at the Oval' and Ted Dexter, signed and dated.

£300-400   **GBA**

A copy of the first printing of the 1788 MCC Laws of Cricket, in a complete edition of 'The London Chronicle' 25th to 28th July 1789, in good condition, with tax stamp.

The Marylebone Cricket Club was formed in 1787 and produced the first official Laws of the Game in 1788. These printed MCC laws end with a section on 'Betts', as the need for an official set of laws arose partly from the practice of betting on matches that often led to violence following disputed results.

£2,500-3,000   **GBA**

SPORTING

The breeches worn by Richard Johnson when riding Looks Like Trouble to victory in the 2000 Cheltenham Gold Cup, signed in red marker pen by Johnson, mounted under glass with a copy of the racecard and a title plaque.

44in (112cm) high

£250-350   GBA

A horsewhip dropped by Richard Johnson at the furlong pole aboard Rooster Booster in the 2003 Martell Cognac Aintree Hurdle, the whip inscribed 'R. JOHNSON', sold together with the cap Johnson was wearing and an official printed fence flag.

£300-400   GBA

A set of green and red Aga Khan silks worn by Walter Swinburn while winning the 1981 Derby Stakes at Epsom.

Owned by H.H. Aga Khan, Shergar ranks high amongst the most famous racehorses of the 20thC. His 10 lengths win in the 1981 Derby remains the longest winning margin in the race's history. In 1983, after retiring, Shergar was stolen and held to ransom. He was never seen again, and presumably killed, and the incident has become one of the most notorious episodes in Turf history.

£9,000-12,000   GBA

Desert Orchid's 1989 Cheltenham Gold Cup winner's coat, in display case, sold with a letter of authenticity signed by Richard Burridge, a photo of Desert Orchid, the signature of David Elsworth, and two further frames containing Desert Orchid's career record and a BBC film about him.

72in (183cm) wide

£5,000-7,000   GBA

A collection of 14 Grand National Meeting 'Blue Riband' posters, for the Grand Nationals of 1947, 1952, 1954, 1956, 1960, 1961, 1962, 1963, 1964, 1968, 1969, 1970 and 1973, plus a black example.

Each 28.25in (72cm) high

£900-1,200 SET   GBA

A silk scarf commemorating the 1901 Derby won by Volodyovski owned by William Collins Whitney.

The 1901 Derby was known as the 'Stars and Stripes' Derby as the winning owner, the trainer and jockey were all American.

£150-250   GBA

ESSENTIAL REFERENCE – PIERRE JULES MENE

French sculptor Pierre Jules Mene (1810-71) was the most successful and prolific Animalier sculptor of his time, modelling over 150 different subjects, which were turned into thousands of bronze casts. His favourite subjects were horses, followed by dogs.

● **His father was a successful metal-turner who taught his son the principles of casting and how to work with metals, but Mene was primarily a self-taught artist.**

● **His first foundry was established in 1837.**

● **Following Mene's death, the foundry was run by his son-in-law, Auguste Cain. It was closed after Cain's death in 1892.**

A French bronze 'Vainqueur du Derby' statue, by Pierre Jules Mene (1810-71), signed 'PJ Mene', rich deep-brown patination.

17in (43cm) high

£4,000-5,000   L&T

Ackermann & Co., 'The race and the road, Epsom, London', folding colour plate.

£1,500-2,000   L&T

Two Muhammad Ali World Heavyweight Championship boxing programs, including v Cleveland Williams at the Houston Astrodome 14th November 1966, and v Joe Frazier at Madison Square Garden 8th March 1971.

£400-500 GBA

An Austrian bronze 'Coup de Main' statue, by Rudolf K. Kuchler (b.1867), rich patination, signed 'R Kuchler', inscribed 'internal fencing fate, Italian exhibition, London, presented by Charles Hancock Esq, Won by Maurice le Maitre'.

22in (56cm) wide

£2,200-2,800 L&T

An Aryton Senna and 1994 Williams Team signed print, signed by Adrian Newey, Frank Williams, David Coulthard, Damon Hill, Patrick Head, framed and glazed.

22in (56cm) wide

£1,200-1,800 GBA

A used set of Barry Sheene Team Suzuki leathers from his 1977 World Championship-winning season, in the colours of team sponsor Texaco-Heron, with all that year's co-sponsors' logos, with two press cuttings.

Barry Sheene (1950-2003) was a British World Champion Grand Prix motorcycle road racer. Handsome and exuberant and with a good interest in business, he was one of the first riders to make a lot of money from endorsements. His 1979 battle with American Kenny Roberts at the British Grand Prix at Silverstone is arguable one of the greatest motorcycle Grand Prix races of the 1970s.

£10,000-15,000 GBA

A 'WELSH RUGBY BY DENNIS BUSHER' lithographic poster, published by the Daily Herald.

The Daily Herald newspaper reached its peak in the 1930s as the world's top selling paper with daily sales of 2m. Circulation wars led to a spiralling decline. It was re-launched as The Sun in 1964.

30in (76cm) high

£200-300 GBA

A USA Olympic team swimming cap worn by Michael Phelps when winning his eighth Olympic gold medal at Beijing 2008, signed by Phelps and with his letter of authenticity, with two scanned copies of photographs of him.

£7,000-10,000 GBA

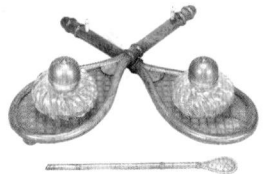

A late 19thC Victorian carved olivewood and glass mounted ink stand, in the form of crossed tennis racquets, the two ink bottles with brass jockey hat cover, with a conforming olivewood pen.

12.25in (31cm) long

£700-1,000 DN

A competitor's diploma for a shooting competition at the 1924 Olympic Games in Paris, awarded to Krikos Agathon, recorded in manuscript.

25.5in (64.5cm) high

£450-650 GBA

A copy of the official report for the 1936 Olympic Games, 'XI Olympiade Berlin 1936', in two German volumes as well as volume I of the rare English version, with a POW history hand-written by the previous owner in the front.

£500-700 GBA

An Armand Marseille black baby doll, mould 341, with solid dome bisque head and composition five-piece bent limb body, in antique silk and lace outfit.

Black dolls of this type are rarer than white examples.

9in (23cm) high

£400-450   BEJ

A 1920s Armand Marseille baby doll, mould 341, with solid dome bisque head and five-piece bent-limb baby body, in vintage outfit.

9in (23cm) high

£200-250   BEJ

A Belton doll, made for the French market, solid dome bisque head on French-type composition jointed body, with original pale blonde mohair wig, wearing an antique cotton outfit.

The solid domed bisque head is characteristic of these dolls.

c1880

£900-1,200   BEJ

A German folk doll, with biscolene head and cloth body, with carefully delineated fingers sewn in, wearing an original brightly-coloured ethnic outfit.

c1930   *13.5in (34cm) high*

£150-200   BEJ

A 1930s all-original composition Googly doll, with one-piece head, body and jointed arms, painted features and full mohair wig.

16in (40.5cm) high

£300-350   BEJ

A mid-1930s Ideal Shirley Temple doll and a paper-covered steamer trunk decorated with pictures of Shirley and opening to fold-out wardrobe containing original costume from 'Bright Eyes' and four other original costumes on card hangers, missing Shirley Temple button.

Doll 13in (33cm) high

£1,000-1,500   SK

A French Bébé Jumeau doll, size 12, with bisque head with large inset glass 'paperweight' eyes, fully-jointed body, in cotton outfit, antique leather slippers and original Jumeau socks with 'Jumeau Diplôme d'Honneur' label to body and red 'Tête Jumeau' stamp to the head.

26in (66cm) high

£4,500-5,000   BEJ

An Emile Jumeau pressed-bisque bébé doll, impressed 'Deposé E 11 J' and red painter's mark 'L', with four floating-ball jointed papier-mâché body with straight wrists, original finish and blue stamp 'Jumeau Medaille d'Or, Paris' on the back.

£5,500-6,500   SK

A Kämmer & Reinhardt 114 bisque 'Gretchen' character doll, impressed 'K*R 114', with closed pouty mouth, blue painted eyes, ball-jointed composition body and period printed lawn dress, some damage.

£2,000-2,500   SK

A Kämmer & Reinhardt character boy doll, mould 126, with bisque head, flirty glass eyes and bent-limb toddler body, in excellent condition.

c1925-30   17in (43cm) high

£800-1,000   BEJ

A Kestner 221 bisque Googly character doll, with closed smiling watermelon mouth, round weighted eyes, mohair wig, and ball-jointed composition body, impressed 211, minor damage.

13.5in (34cm) high

£2,500-3,000   SK

A Kestner bisque pouty child doll, trunk and costumes, impressed '13', some repaint on body, in fitted faux-alligator-covered doll trunk.

Doll 21in (53.5cm) high

£2,000-2,500   SK

A rare Kestner JDK 206 character child doll, with a pink ball-jointed composition body, glass sleepy eyes, wearing a fanciful white cotton lace-like dress, antique pink leather shoes, with original mohair wig with two braids forming buns over her ears.

The firm of Kestner made a series of rare and desirable character dolls, known as the 200 series.

12in (30.5cm) high

£6,000-7,000   JDJ

A Kestner bisque shoulder-head 'Gibson Girl' character doll, impressed '172.5 U Made in Germany', weighted glass eyes, upswept blonde mohair wig on plaster pate, jointed kid body, yellow satin and white net dress, bonnet and white lawn undergarment.

This doll was inspired by the work of American illustrator Charles Dana Gibson (1867-1944). In her book 'America's Great Illustrators', Susan E. Meyer describes his signature 'Gibson Girl' as being 'taller than the other women currently seen in the pages of magazines... infinitely more spirited and independent, yet altogether feminine. She was poised and patrician. Though always well bred, there often lurked a flash of mischief in her eyes'. Kestner's interpretation in doll form captured the spirit of the modern American young woman as made popular by Gibson.

c1910   18.5in (47cm) high

£1,000-1,500   SK

A Kestner 'A.T.' bisque doll, impressed '15', resembling the bébés of French maker A. Thullier, with accented open/closed mouth, weighted glass eyes, mohair wig on plaster pate and early straight-wrist jointed composition body in the original finish, in period outfit, some wear, eyes slightly loose.

23.5in (59.5cm) high

£8,500-9,500   SK

An early 20thC Kley & Hahn 549 bisque head character boy doll, impressed 'K & H 549 6 Germany' with glass sleeping eyes, original short blonde mohair wig, fully articulated composition body in original finish, dressed as a young man, some damage.

18.5in (47cm) high

£1,800-2,200   SK

A British Lucy Peck wax doll, with rare sleeping eyes, composition lower legs with painted socks and shoes, in green silk outfit and several layers of underclothing, with original mohair wig.

c1890   16.5in (42cm) high

£700-800   BEJ

A British Pierotti wax doll, with soft body and wax lower limbs sewn through grommet attachments to the upper legs and arms, glass eyes which can close, with a wire mechanism running through the lower body and up to the head.

c1870   21in (53.5cm) high

£1,200-1,800   BEJ

A British Pierotti wax child doll, with flushed colouring and delicate poured wax lower limbs, with blonde inserted mohair wig and blue glass eyes, in original silk and lace outfit.

16in (40.5cm) high

£1,200-1,700   BEJ

TOYS

A French Pintel & Godchaux bébé doll, with bisque head on composition jointed body, with mohair wig and antique outfit.
c1890   13in (33cm) high
£1,500-1,800   **BEJ**

A French Société Française de Bébés et Jouets 'Laughing Jumeau' doll, mould 236, with sleeping glass eyes, bent-limb body, in antique boy's outfit.
c1910
£800-900   **BEJ**

An English poured wax child doll, with inset brown glass eyes, wax over composition limbs and soft body, in original silk and lace outfit with velvet ribbon trim.
c1880   11in (28cm) high
£850-950   **BEJ**

CLOSER LOOK – A ROULLET ET DECAMPS BOUQUETIÈRE SURPRISE

Bisque heads of this type were commissioned by Roullet et Decamps for use on a series of larger automata, often incorporating a fantasy element, like the Bouqetière Surprise. Her serene expression makes the strange contents of her basket more surprising.

The doll has an open mouth with accented cupid's bow and two rows of teeth, pronounced philtrum, shapely double chin, fixed blue 'paperweight' eyes, finely painted lashes, pierced ears, cork pate, blonde mohair wig, bisque shoulderplate and hands.

The body contains a single-air going-barrel movement.

The doll wears a cream-coloured satin costume, pleated pink satin underskirt with lace overlay, décolleté bodice, and matching bonnet.

A rare Roullet et Decamps automaton of a Bouqetière Surprise, with bisque portrait head stamped in red 'Déposé Tête Jumeau, Bte. S.G.D.G. 8'.
                    25in (63.5cm) high
£18,000-22,000   **SK**

A gold-painted wicker basket with silk flowers is suspended at her waist. When activated, the doll looks from side to side and waves her hand over the basket as though conjuring, and a small bisque doll rises from a papier-mâché rose in the basket. Throwing kisses, she bows to her audience, the small doll descends into the rose, the lid closes over her, and the sequence begins again.

A French Société Française de Bébés et Jouets bébé doll, mould 301, with pale bisque, sleepy eyes and original mohair wig, fully-jointed French bébé body, in antique outfit.
                    18in (46cm) high
£1,000-1,400   **BEJ**

A Simon & Halbig child doll, size 10, with open mouth with four inserted teeth, on a fully-jointed body, with vintage silk and lace dress and cotton underdress.
c1890   25in (63.5cm) high
£750-850   **BEJ**

A Simon & Halbig black child doll, mould 1039, with rarer flirty eyes, moulded eyebrows, on a matched jointed composition body, in cotton antique outfit with inset ribbons and lace trims.
                    17in (43cm) high
£925-1,000   **BEJ**

A German 'Morning Glory' tinted china shoulder-head doll, with closed mouth, painted eyes, moulded dark brown hair, adorned at the neck with sprays of blue, red and pink flowers, on gusseted cream-kid body, dressed in polychrome striped silk taffeta skirt below sage velveteen jacket with lace adorning the lower neckline.
c1850   22.5in (57cm) high
£6,000-7,000   **SK**

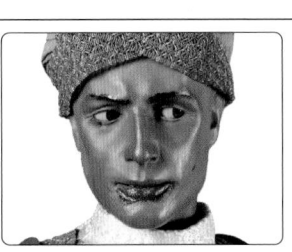

A near life-size magician automaton from the film 'Sleuth', probably by Decamps, his body containing eight-cam electric motor causing the magician to look from side to side and down at the table, he waves his wand and then lifts the cup to reveal a series of four changing items, some damage.

Based on Anthony Shaffer's play, the 1972 film of 'Sleuth' starred Sir Laurence Olivier and Michael Caine. The many automata used in the film served not only as props, but also as amused spectators to the action. The magician appears at appropriate moments, including the final sequence.

c1930   56.5in (143.5cm) high

£30,000-35,000   SK

A rare automaton barrel-piano, by George Hicks, ink-stamped on soundboard 'G. Hicks, Cylinder, Piano Manufacturer, 17 Chapel Street, Caledonian Road, London', with 30-key action, eight-air barrel driving four carved, gilt and polychrome-painted automata figures in mirrored enclosure, some wear.

Signed Hicks barrel pianos are rare, even more so ones with a London address. The scale of this piece suggests a special commission. The Black Forest automata in barrel pianos are often allegorical. In this example, they represent: King Gambrinus, the mythical originator of beer; an ape in jester costume strumming a guitar; a Roman soldier (originally holding a spear); and an Eastern arms-collector depositing a coin into a trough.

37.5in (95cm) high

£13,000-18,000   SK

A rare triple monkey magician automaton, by Phalibois, with central monkey magician, table and two cups flanked by two monkeys playing the violin and the harp, in mainly original costumes.

32in (81cm) wide

£25,000-30,000   SK

A rare Henry Phalibois automaton of a Chinese magician and his vanishing assistant, on panelled base painted to resemble marble, the electric motor driving three pulleys and thirteen boxwood cams, in Chinese robes and hat.

The magician waves his fan and the magic cabinet opens to reveal his assistant. He points into the empty dice cabinet. He beats the gong, and the dice cabinet opens to reveal his assistant, while the magic cabinet is now empty. Both cabinets close. As the magician surveys his audience, the doors open to reveal that his assistant has completely disappeared. The cabinet interiors are illuminated at appropriate moments in the sequence.

c1920   49in (124.5cm) high

£55,000-60,000   SK

A Roullet et Decamps Cambodian dancer automaton, on velvet-covered white-painted wood base with canted corners containing the massive going-barrel motor driving three cams and six-air cartel cylinder movement, in original exotic costume.

With her artistic modelling and exotic origins, the Cambodian Dancer is an example of the automaton as animated sculpture.

40in (101.5cm) high

£180,000-220,000   SK

A rare Roullet et Decamps automaton of the English comedian 'Little Tich', on slatted oak base with large going-barrel movement driving single-air cylinder movement, three cams, a star wheel with two levers, and a sprung axis running through metal tube in figure's left leg that enables his body to rotate left or right while simultaneously moving forwards and backwards.

'Little Tich' was the stage name of Henry Relf (1867-1928), who was four feet tall. He performed pantomime at Drury Lane, vaudeville in New York, and his celebrated 'Big Foot Dance' at the Folies Bergère in Pairs.

29in (73.5cm) high

£62,000-72,000   SK

An unusual Vichy automaton of a gypsy, on later base containing single-air cylinder movement.

Although now playing the role of a matador, this automaton may have been intended as the companion to a breathing Gypsy Lady.

32.5in (82.5cm) high

£5,500-8,500   SK

TOYS

An Epicerie doll's house designed as a confectionery shop, three carved and scalloped pediments mounted on top with paper labels reading 'Bonbons', 'Epicerie' and 'Chocolaterie', a large mirror framed with scalloped trim work and shelf on rear wall, large glass jars of sweets and large scale on shelf, counter holding over 22 boxes of sweets, larger bars of chocolate tied to front inner wall.

29in (74cm) wide

£4,000-5,000   **BER**

CLOSER LOOK – A MOUNT PLEASANT DOLL'S HOUSE

Designed in 1916 by Charles Borie, an architect with the Philadelphia firm of Zantinger, Borie & Medary, who designed the Philadelphia Museum of Art. Made by a skilled carpenter, the doll's house was built as a replica of Mount Pleasant, the Fairmount Park mansion in Philadelphia, built between 1762 and 1765 on the eastern banks of the Schuylkill River.

The multi-paned windows feature hinged casements that can be opened.

The house can be disassembled in three sections, and the front sections open to reveal a detailed interior featuring large rooms with architectural details.

A removable side panel on the left provides access to the kitchen and another chamber above it.

A staircase dominates the centre hallways, rising and turning through both centre hallways to the attic level.

A Mount Pleasant doll's house, with Georgian façade with hand-painted bricks, prominent quoting, Palladian windows in both the front and back and the front entrance with a sweeping stairway leading to an elegant formal entrance, the interior retaining its original painted surfaces with minor wear.

£9,000-10,000   **BER**

A rare Gottschalk red roof doll's house, front façade with curved porches with elaborate railings and columns on both levels, bay windows on both corners, roof with large dormer with flower boxes and a spectacular Dutch gable, open sides and back expose three levels, rooms with inter-connecting doors, walls papered, mahogany staircase that extends all three levels, professionally restored.

C1910   *36in (91.5cm) high*

£2,500-3,000   **JDJ**

A large Lines Bros doll's house, nine rooms, central staircase, original fireplaces with grates and reservoir in the attic supplying water to bathtub and kitchen sink, most of the original wallpapers are covered by old paint, later electric lighting.

c1895   *43in (109cm) wide*

£3,500-4,000   **BER**

A Märklin hand-painted tin doll-sized gazebo, completely railed in ornate posts, red-and-white striped cloth canopy cover, doll on tin swing posed on side decking, steps up to front and rear, with flower boxes.

20in (51cm) long

£8,500-9,500   **BER**

An Edwardian double-fronted doll's house, 'Lanthon Villa 1910', the front opening in three sections to reveal four rooms, hall, landing, with a small assortment of mostly later furniture and furnishings.

39in (99cm) high

£1,000-1,500   **GORL**

ROCKING HORSES

A modern wooden rocking horse, by Haddon, Wallingford, painted dapple grey with horsehair mane and tail, leather saddle and harness, on pine stand.

70.5in (179cm) long

£800-1,000   **A&G**

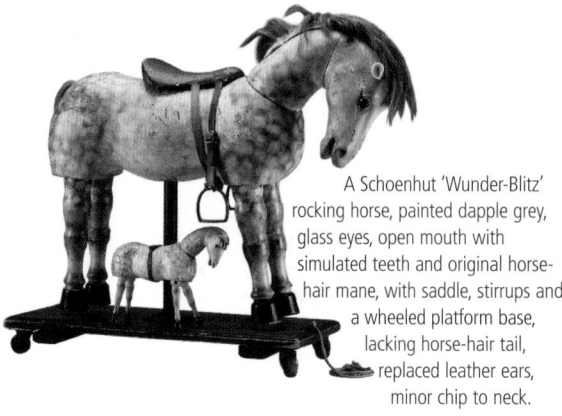

A Schoenhut 'Wunder-Blitz' rocking horse, painted dapple grey, glass eyes, open mouth with simulated teeth and original horse-hair mane, with saddle, stirrups and a wheeled platform base, lacking horse-hair tail, replaced leather ears, minor chip to neck.

£7,000-8,000   **JDJ**

A 19thC rocking horse, covered in calf skin with hair mane and tail, set on wooden trestle-rocker stand with retailer's celluloid label 'Isaac Underwood hairdresser and fancy repository Bradford'.

53.25in (135.5cm) long

£600-800   **SAS**

A 1.5in scale coal-fired Allchin traction engine, single cylinder, Stephensons link valve gear, twin speed gear box, crank shaft, cable drum from axle drive.

This model has been unused for some time and therefore requires a service and minor attention to regulator and feed pipes, overall construction is of a high standard, finished in maroon and black with red wheels.

25in (63.5cm) long

£2,500-3,000   HT

A 1.5in scale Allchin live steam traction engine 'Royal Chester', reg. no. 'CF 4162', based on the engine design by W. J. Hughes, the model finished in pillar-box red livery with cast name plate, transfer label and plaque 'Wm Allchin, Limited, Northampton, England, with spoked red metal wheels, rear wheels.

26in (66cm) long

£4,000-4,500   TEN

A late 20thC Markie precision working model of a steam road locomotive, ref. no. ARG1948, with green-and-black painted boiler and rubber wheels, with original certificate and boiler test certificate.

14in (35.5cm) long

£1,200-1,800   **GORL**

A rare Märklin Live Steam Road Roller, has been fired on a number of occasions, with paint loss around the boiler area, in good condition.

11in (28cm) long

£400-500   **VEC**

DIECAST MODELS

A Corgi Major Toys gift set no. 23, 'Circus Models', comprising six Chipperfields Circus items, Land Rover, international 6x6 crane truck, Bedford giraffe lorry, two animal trailers and an elephant trailer, complete with animals still in packets, contents in very good condition, one tyre missing, box with internal packing.

£350-450   **W&W**

A rare Dinky Supertoys gift set 900, 'Pullmore Car Transporter with Four Cars', Bedford transporter, with mid-blue cab and light-blue trailer, Austin Somerset in red and yellow, Ford Zephyr in green and pale cream, Hillman Minx in apple green and cream, and a Rover 75 in cream and mid-blue, in very good condition, in original box with display insert, complete with load ramp, minor wear to box lid, minor splitting to internal card.

£1,000-1,500   **W&W**

TOYS

A large 1930s British Chad Valley pale gold mohair plush bear, soft-stuffed in parts, label to left foot.

This bear features the typical Chad Valley wide nose.

21in (53.5cm) high

£500-650   BEJ

CLOSER LOOK – A MOHAIR STEIFF TEDDY BEAR

The famous Steiff button-in-the-ear was used from 1904. This bear's underscored 'F' button was used from 1905-50.

This bear's extremely appealing expression probably contributed to its high value.

Cinnamon is one of the rarest colours for Steiff bears, along with white. The colour often fades quickly if exposed to light, so good condition examples are rare.

This bear's long limbs, large spoon-shaped feet, hump, and shoe-button eyes identify it as a very early Steiff bear.

A large Steiff cinnamon mohair teddy bear, with underscored 'F' button in ear, overall fine condition, some damage.

c1905

£14,000-18,000   SK

An American cast-iron mechanical lighthouse bank, a coin of any size up to a quarter can be deposited into the house, the tower can only receive nickels and opens when five dollars has been deposited, lacking base coin plug, paint wear.

c1890 10.25in (26cm) high

£1,300-1,800 SK

A late 19thC cast-iron mechanical 'Novelty Bank', activated by opening the door and placing a coin on tray held by a figure, closing door deposits the coin, paint wear.

6.5in (16.5cm) high

£600-800 SK

An American cast-iron organ grinder and performing bear mechanical bank, manufactured by Kyser & Rex, Philadelphia, activated by winding a turn key and placing a coin in the slot of the organ and moving a lever, which causes the bear to revolve and the organ grinder to turn the crank, depositing the coin, marked 'Pat June 13 82', paint worn.

5.25in (13.5cm) high

£2,500-3,000 SK

An American cast-iron squirrel and tree stump mechanical bank, by Mechanical Novelty Works, New Britain, Connecticut, activated by placing a coin on the acorn and pressing lever at the squirrel's foot, moving the squirrel forward and dropping the coin into the bank, minor paint wear.

c1881 4.5in (11.5cm) high

£3,500-4,500 SK

A cast-iron 'Stump Speaker' mechanical bank, manufactured by the Shepard Hardware Co., Buffalo, New York, activated by placing a coin in the figure's hand and pressing a button lowering the figure's jaw and arm dropping the coin into a satchel, minor paint losses.

c1886 9.75in (25cm) high

£1,500-2,000 SK

A painted cast-iron monkey and coconut mechanical bank, by J. & E. Stevens Co., Cromwell, Connecticut, activated by placing a coin in the monkey's paw and pressing the lever, causing him to open the coconut and drop in the coin while his eyes and mouth move, retouched.

c1886 8.25in (21cm) high

£1,000-1,500 SK

A cast-iron circus elephant and clowns mechanical bank, by J. & E. Stevens Co., Cromwell, Connecticut, activated by placing a coin between the rings held by one clown and moving the ball on the feet of the other, the elephant's trunk strikes the coin, causing it to fall into the bank, while the clown riding the elephant turns at the waist, paint wear.

c1882 6in (15cm) high

£500-700 SK

ESSENTIAL REFERENCE – J. & E. STEVENS CO.

The J. & E. Stevens Company was founded in 1843 in Cromwell, Connecticut by John and Elisha Stevens. By the mid-1860s production was focused almost exclusively on toys.

- J. & E. Stevens's first cast-iron mechanical bank was produced in 1869. The company soon became known for innovatively designed mechanical and still banks.
- Other toys, such as stoves, were also produced until 1928 when production was limited to some cap pistols.
- The company closed during WWII due to the shortage of iron. It was sold to Buckley Brothers of New York in 1950.

A painted cast-iron Two Frogs mechanical bank, manufactured by J. & E. Stevens Co., Cromwell, Connecticut, activated by placing a coin on the flat spot on the stomach of the small frog and pressing the lever, which causes him to kick the coin into the open mouth of the large frog, the large frog lacking glass eyes, minor paint wear.

c1882 4.25in (11cm) high

£1,300-1,800 SK

A painted cast-iron 'I Always Did 'Spise a Mule' mechanical bank, manufactured by J. & E. Stevens Co., Cromwell, Connecticut, activated by placing a coin into the slot under the seated boy and pressing the knob, which causes the mule to kick and knock the boy over as the coin is deposited into the bank, scattered paint wear.

c1897 6in (15cm) high

£900-1,100 SK

A Bassett-Lowke Gauge 1 0-4-0 Tank Loco 'PECKETT TANK', green No. 810, with clockwork mechanism, in near mint condition, with original box.

This locomotive was purchased from Bassett-Lowke's High Holborn, London, shop in April 1927 for a price of £3/5s. The original receipt is included.

£1,500-2,000   VEC

A Bing Gauge 1 4-4-2 'PRECUSOR' Tank L&NWR, black No. 44, with clockwork mechanism, repainted, lined and transferred, in good condition.

£1,200-1,500   VEC

A Bonds O Gauge 4-6-2 Loco and Tender, LMS maroon No. 6247 'CITY OF LIVERPOOL', two-rail electric, in excellent condition with professional repair.

This locomotive was built by Bonds in 1968 for Mr Jack Lewis of Liverpool. It was featured in the 1972 Bonds catalogue.

£1,400-1,800   VEC

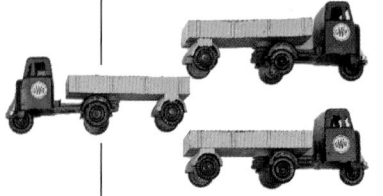

A rare trade pack of three Charbens Scammell scarab articulated railway trucks, in GWR chocolate and cream livery, in very good condition.

£180-220   W&W

A Hornby O Gauge No. 2C Special 4-4-0 Loco and Tender LMS maroon 'COMPOUND' No. 1185, clockwork.

£1,400-1,800   VEC

A Hornby Dublo 3-rail D2 post-war Gresley LNER articulated coach set, complete with centre bogie and corridor connection, in excellent condition, in good condition box, dated '5/48' with Hudson Dobson sticker to one side.

£2,000-2,500   VEC

A Hornby O Gauge 'Coleman's Mustard' Private Owner Van, in good condition.

£1,300-1,800   VEC

A Hornby O Gauge No. 4E 4-4-0 Loco and Tender, Southern green 'ETON' No. 900, 20v electric, in excellent condition.

£2,000-2,500   VEC

A Hornby O Gauge No. 2 Special 4-4-0 Loco and Tender, Great Western green 'County of Bedford' No. 3821, with clockwork mechanism, all driving wheels are missing, in otherwise excellent condition, with original card outer, tender with 'GWR' monogram, in near mint condition.

£1,800-2,200   VEC

A Hornby O Gauge 4-6-2 Loco and Tender, LMS maroon 'PRINCESS ELIZABETH' No. 6201, 20v Electric, all major Mazac metal parts, including driving wheels, bogie and pony wheels, axle boxes have been professionally replaced, in excellent condition, in an original red box.

£2,000-2,500   VEC

A rare large Ives clockwork tin locomotive, hand-painted, eagle mounted at front of boiler, cast-iron spoke wheels, wear to paint, some damage.
c1876   18in (46cm) long

£6,000-7,000   BER

A Märklin HO Gauge pre-war 'R700' 0-4- Loco and Tender, in green, three-rail electric, in good condition.

£1,200-1,800   VEC

A Märklin HO Gauge pre-war HR700 British Outline Pacific 4-6-2 Loco and 8-wheel Tender LNER green, three-rail electric, in near mint condition, in original straw box with retailers label 'Harral Ltd Jewellers and Clock Makers' to the lid and base and a Märklin 'HR700 LNER' stamped label to one end.

£5,000-6,000   VEC

A rare Märklin Gauge 1 4-6-2 Tank Loco maroon 'BOWEN-COOKE', with clockwork mechanism, stamped underneath 'AW GAMAGES HOLBORN LONDON MADE IN GERMANY' in black to the underside of the base, stamped 'T H 1021' in gold to bunker back, in very good condition.

£1,200-1,800   VEC

ESSENTIAL REFERENCE – MÄRKLIN

Gebrüder Märklin (Märklin Brothers) was founded in 1859 by Theodor Friedrich Wilhelm Märklin (1817-1866) in Goppingen. In 1891, the company acquired the Ludwig Lutz tinplate toy factory and combined their handmade techniques with processes of mass-production.

- **At the Leipzig Spring Fair 1891, Märklin introduced simple clockwork trains that ran on rails of standardised sizes.**
- **Trains were made in gauges from 'I' to 'III', using clockwork and steam for power. By 1910 the smaller '0' gauge had taken over and electric trains were also being made. The smaller '00' gauge took over in 1935 and a range of diecast cars, trains and military vehicles were on sale by 1939.**

An unpainted brass O Gauge two-unit US diesel locomotive, class BP-20 'Shark', A&B unit set by NJ Custom Brass, each unit of Co-Co bogie configuration, in very good condition, boxed, some wear and tape repairs.

£280-320   W&W

A Märklin Gauge 1 4-4-0 Loco and eight-wheeler Tender LSWR green No. 310, with clockwork mechanism, with regional transfer to front splasher and running number to cab side, with an 'AW Gamages London Holborn' oval plate to the cab floor, tender with 'LSWR' gold lettering, in excellent condition.

£11,000-15,000   VEC

A Wrenn W2241 AM2 (ins) 4-6-2 LMS lined black Princess Coronation Class Loco No. 6225 'Duchess of Gloucester', fitted with five-pole motor and all-flanged large driving wheels, in mint condition, in near mint condition box.

£2,000-2,500   VEC

A Märklin HO Gauge pre-war 3800 Compound wheel Tender, finished in brown with gold 'LMS' lettering to tender sides, in good condition.

This is one of the rarest tenders in the Märklin range of pre-war British outline locomotives and tenders.

£4,500-5,000   VEC

TOYS

A late 19thC English turned bone Barleycorn pattern chess set, stained red and natural.

Kings 5.75in (14.5cm) high

£500-600   **DN**

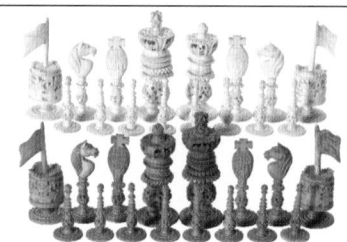

A late 19thC Chinese carved ivory 'Burmese' chess set, the King and Queen as crowns upon multiple knopped and floral openwork carved stems and lotus bases, the pawns as diminutive versions of the same.

King 3.5in (9cm) high

£350-550   **TEN**

A 19thC English turned ivory chess set, natural and stained to simulate tortoiseshell.

Minor chips, three pieces damaged and one or two replaced.

King 3.5in (9cm) high

£600-800   **WW**

A J. Jacques & Son patent chess set, the hinged mahogany case with natural and red-stained ivory pieces, the case stamped 'Status Quo Patent Chess Board' and inset brass name plaque, with release and locking buttons, case warped.

11.5in (29cm) wide open

£200-300   **WW**

A Victorian coromandel-cased games compendium, 'The Royal Cabinet of Games', the hinged lid and double-hinged front enclosing a turned-wood chess set, draughts and leather board, and two removable trays fitted with cribbage, playing cards, dice shakers and lead horses.

£1,400-1,800   **TOV**

A Chinese Export black and gold lacquer games cabinet, containing a carved ivory chess set, the rectangular cabinet decorated on the top, sides and two frontal square doors with extensive pagoda Lakeland landscapes with numerous figures, supporting a red stained and natural ivory chess set, the reds as members of the Manchu court, the other of a European court, a narrow recess below containing a slid-out hinged games board for draughts and backgammon.

c1790   *Cabinet 17in (43cm) wide*

£3,500-4,500   **TEN**

A Thors croquet set, by Slazenger, London, comprising four hickory-shafted mallets, four balls, a peg, six hoops one broken, in a pine box with an applied maker's plaque and label.

£200-300   **WW**

A set of lathe-turned natural ivory and ebony draughts, by the Revd John Henry Holdich, Rector of Bulwick, Northamptonshire, each piece with a different radial pierced pattern, lathe-turned box container with geometric decoration to the lid centred by an ivory medallion, fluted sides, and with conforming dice box with contents.

A paper label adhered to the underside of the lid is inscribed in ink 'The work of the Rev. John Henry Holdich, Rector of Bulwick, Northamptonshire, 1872'. The piece is accompanied by a description of this and other works by Holdich, an extract reading 'He also carved the clock case in Burleigh over the Fiddlers Gallery in the Big Hall out of a section of an oak tree, cut down in Burleigh Park for which he was paid £40'.

1872   *5in (12.5cm) wide*

£1,200-1,500   **TEN**

An unauthorised 'The Wonderful Wizard of Oz: An exciting New ALL-FAIR Game', E.E. Fairchild Corp., Rochester, the folded colour-lithographed playing board of the Land of Oz with four wooden playing pieces, 32 Magic Cards, Colour Move Spinner and rule sheet, some damage.

Based on L. Frank Baum's book, this game includes many characters not in the MGM film, such as the Stork, Mouse Queen, China Dolls, Hammerheads, Animal Kingdom and Monster. It was designed for children aged 7 to 12. Provenance: Fred. M. Meyer collection.

1957

£300-400   **BLNY**

A Britains 'Model Farm' series set no. 152F, comprising farmer, farmer's wife, cow, calf, pony, turkey, sheep, lamb, pig and piglet, tied into box, minor wear, contents in mint condition.

£250-350   W&W

A Britains 'Royal Horse Artillery Gun and Team' set no. 9419, comprising a field gun and limber, plus officer, six horse team, three mounted and four outriders, in very good condition, horses still tied in box, some age wear to box lid.

£350-450   W&W

A rare Britains Military Equipment set no. 2052, 'Anti-Aircraft Unit' with operating crew and eight men, comprising mobile anti-aircraft gun, searchlight, height finger, spotting chair, army range finder and a predictor, in very good condition, tied into original box, some wear to lid.

£300-400   W&W

A rare Britains 'Pilots of the German Luftwaffe' set no. 1895, eight in full dark grey and black uniforms, in mint condition, boxed with insert, 'Armies of the World' label, minor wear/pen mark.

A rare set produced during WWII, 1940-1941.

£450-550   W&W

A rare Britains 'Boy Scouts' set no. 181, comprising Scout Master and 23 Boy Scouts performing various tasks including signalling, wood-chopping and cart-carrying, climbing tree and gate, three trees in leaf, ten fence pieces, six-section trek cart, in mint condition, in two-tier display box.

£2,500-3,500   W&W

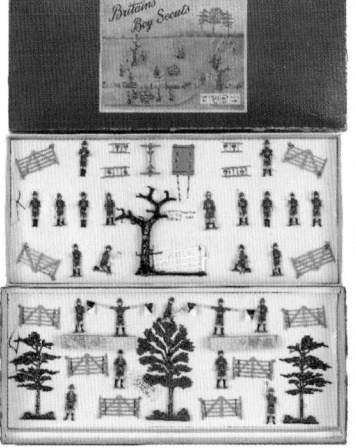
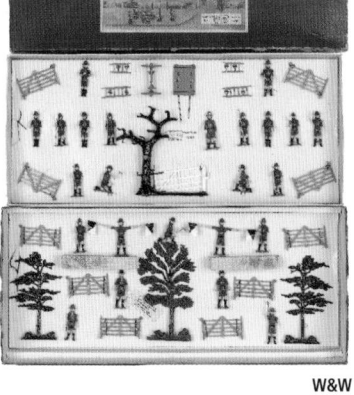

A rare Britains 'Mammoth Circus' series roundabout no. 1439, comprising a gold-painted lead organ and propulsion hub, with a gallopers-style roundabout, attached to a plain card circular base, together with its original square orange paper-covered box, with lift-off lid and original applied label.

Produced in very limited numbers between 1936 and 1939.

£2,500-3,500   W&W

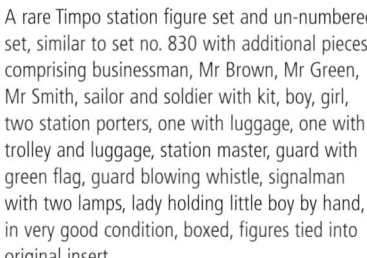

A rare Timpo station figure set and un-numbered set, similar to set no. 830 with additional pieces, comprising businessman, Mr Brown, Mr Green, Mr Smith, sailor and soldier with kit, boy, girl, two station porters, one with luggage, one with trolley and luggage, station master, guard with green flag, guard blowing whistle, signalman with two lamps, lady holding little boy by hand, in very good condition, boxed, figures tied into original insert.

£350-450   W&W

A rare Timpo station figures set no. 830, including station master, two guards, signalman, two porters, Mr Brown, a hiker, in very good condition, tied in original insert, some creasing to lid.

Produced for the American market.

£200-300   W&W

A rare late 1940s Timpo Arctic series, comprising two hunters and sledge driver, sledge with load, five dogs, two seals, two penguins, two polar bears and an igloo, all tied onto original backing cards with Arctic scene banner, boxed with small applied label to lid, in good condition.

£350-450   W&W

TOYS

A Bing enamelled tinplate clockwork limousine taxi, with simple interior, in Prussian blue, lined white and gold, glass windows, high quality clockwork.

c1914   18in (46cm) wide

£7,500-8,500   **L&T**

A German Carette lithographed clockwork limousine, in blue with white striping, with seated chauffeur, passenger, and single head lamp, spoke wheels.

c1919   7in (18cm) long

£2,000-3,000   **BER**

A Chein lithographed tin 'Hercules Mack Ready-Mix' truck, 'C' cab Mack, the drum revolves in mixing motions as the truck is pulled along, in bright orange with black lettering.

c1929   18in (45cm) long

£6,000-8,000   **BER**

CLOSER LOOK – A ROCK & GRANER HORSE-DRAWN SLEIGH

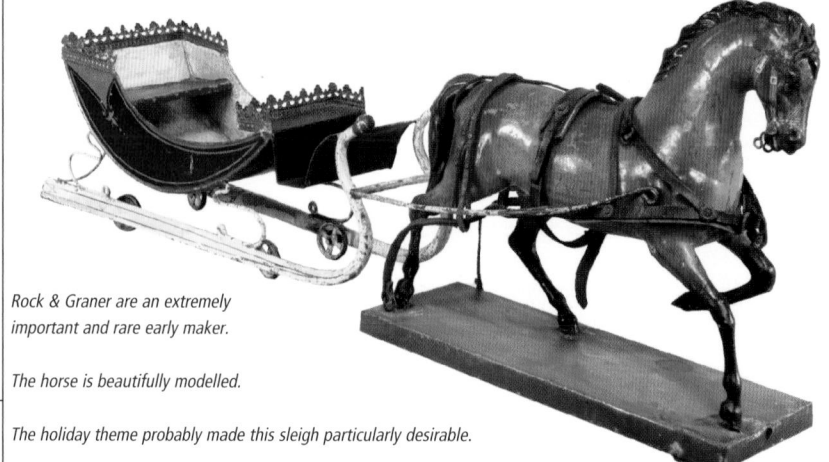

Rock & Graner are an extremely important and rare early maker.

The horse is beautifully modelled.

The holiday theme probably made this sleigh particularly desirable.

A rare Rock & Graner hand-painted tin open sleigh drawn by a detailed horse, sleigh with blue body, pink interior, yellow runner and hitch, with gold filigree trim around seating, red striping to runner, one wheel replaced.

14.5in (37cm) long

£10,000-12,000   **BER**

A German Carette lithographed tin clockwork No. 5 Tonneau, featuring seated drivers and passengers, luggage rack on canopy roof, glass windshield, spoke wheels, rubber tyres and added appointments of head lamps.

8in (20.5cm) long

£3,000-4,000   **BER**

A rare French Citroën clockwork C4 Pole Truck, in green with black roof and running boards, with electric lights, embossed seating and rubber tyres.

18.5in (47cm) long

£1,500-2,000   **BER**

A modern re-issue French Citroën clockwork B14 Taxi, no. 634, in yellow and black, with fold-down windows, opening doors, electric powered lighting, differential axle, nickel grille, plates of authenticity on bottom.

20in (51cm) long

£1,500-2,000   **BER**

A French Citroën clockwork B2 'Cloverleaf' car, in red with boat-tail rear, celluloid windshield, embossed seating.

13in (33cm) long

£1,500-2,000   **BER**

A German lithographed clowns on motorcycle, by Fischer, with driver and rider seated backwards, clockwork action.

9in (23cm) long

£4,000-5,000   **BER**

A JEP clockwork Rolls Royce Phantom, in cream with red trim and running boards, dual windshields, nickel electric lights, complete axle assembly.

19.5in (50cm) long

£3,000-4,000   **BER**

A 1920s Karl Bub lithographed tin clockwork touring car, hand-painted, with glass windows, opening doors, glass head lamps, rubber tyres, with side brake lever.

14in (35.5cm) long

£800-1,200   **BER**

A rare Kellerman no. 353 clockwork touring rider and male passenger, red bike, brown rider, blue and brown passenger, tin wheels, passenger rotates from hips as rider turns, in near mint condition, with good condition full-colour illustrated card box, and original key.

£750-850   **VEC**

An African Bambara carved wood antelope mask, the hollow oval form with four horns projecting from the top, square pierced eyes, and four cowry shell settings, dark patina, old repair.

17in (43cm) high

£400-600 SK

An African Bembe carved wood female figure, the stylised head with turban-style headdress and probably porcelain inlaid eyes, hands to the upper breasts, elaborate scarification marks to abdomen.

11in (28cm) high

£7,000-10,000 SK

An African possibly Bobo carved wood helmet mask, from Upper Volta, with stylized facial features, perforated for attachments at the base, pyro-darkened face and crest, traces of blue and white pigment.

13.5in (34cm) high

£1,000-1,500 SK

An African Dan mask, with pierced rim, the eye sockets damaged, with hand written paper label 'Yakuba, Router de Tonba a Odienne... Siena, 115grs, 5 mai 34'.

9.25in (23.5cm) high

£1,000-1,200 WW

An African Dogon mask, from Mali, with rectangular face and female figural surmount.

43.5in (110.5cm) high

£400-600 WW

An African Ogoni mask, from Nigeria, with horns and slit eye sockets with three beads by each ear, black and white pigment, pierced edges.

12.5in (32cm) high

£400-600 SK

An African Baule carved wood female figure, with hands to the abdomen, finely carved coiffure and scarification marks, standing on a round base, dark glossy patina.

Patina is a fine surface sheen caused by years of handling, with an accumulation of polish and dirt. This results in a softened appearance on silver and furniture, which is often desirable and appealing. A fine patina is a key ingredient looked for in a quality antique.

13.5in (34cm) high

£4,500-5,500 SK

An African Fang polychromed wood mask, with raffia beard, cowrie-shaped eyes, elongated nose and open mouth bearing sharp teeth, with protruding sail-like coiffure, on stand.

21in (53cm) high

£800-1,000 RTC

An African Kongo carved wood Janus figure rattle, the faceted peg surmounted by two seated female figures, both holding relief-carved staffs, traces of kaolin, dark patina, remnant of old tag.

Three million Kikongo speakers live along the Atlantic coast of Africa, including the Vili, Woyo, Beembe, and Yombe and known collectively as the Kongo (meaning hunter) peoples. They are particularly renowned for their nkisi (spirit receptacle) ritual and refined ancestor sculptures. Ivory is used exclusively for prestige objects.

20.25in (51.5cm) high

£10,000-15,000 SK

TRIBAL ART

An African Songye carved wood male figure, with stylised face and hands to the abdomen, standing on a base, dark patina.

10.75in (27.5cm) high

£4,000-6,000   SK

CLOSER LOOK – AFRICAN CARVING

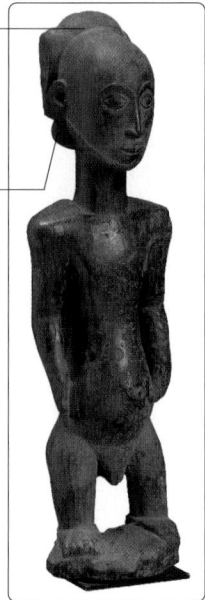

The Hemba people live in plains along the Congo (Zaire) River and produce art similar to that the nearby Luba people. It was only in 1975 that François Neyt identified a distinct Hemba style.

A four-lobed hairdo typical of Hemba figures symbolises the four directions of the universe and the crossroad where spirits meet.

The Hemba carve magnificent commemorative sculptural portraits of their deceased rulers. These customarily avoid distinguishing features, thus stressing the continuity of the royal lineage through a series of rulers.

The figure's serene expression and closed eyes are typical, and can also be found on the sculpture of the Luba. .

An African Hemba carved wood male figure, with long torso and hands to sides, narrow beard and cross-shaped coiffure, partial encrusted patina, severe insect damage to back.

28in (71cm) high

£15,000-20,000   SK

An African Songye Kifwebe mask, with allover grooved decoration and decorated with white and black pigment, pierced to the edges.

Kifwebe are masks used during Songye ceremonies.

19.5in (49.5cm) high

£400-600   WW

An African carved wood kneeling female figure, from Yombe, with mirror inlaid eyes, filed front teeth and blackened coiffure, with hands to the breasts, dark patina.

9.5in (24cm) high

£3,000-4,000   SK

An African carved ivory fly whisk handle, from Yombe, with a seated male figure holding a horn and a remnant root, above a horizontal human figure and large lizard.

8.5in (21.5cm) high

£15,000-20,000   SK

An African Yoruba bronze sceptre, with down-turned beak surmounting cylindrical handle.

13.5in (34cm) high

£700-1,000   SK

An African carved wood and metal adze, from Tanzania, the finial in the form a stylised antelope head with white glass bead eyes and blackened detail.

23.5in (59.5cm) long

£2,000-2,500   SK

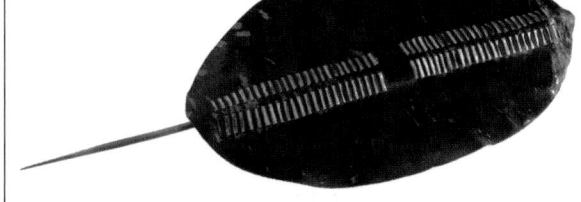

An African Zulu oval hide shield, with spear support.

47.5in (120.5cm) high

£300-400   WW

CLOSER LOOK – INUIT CARVING

A stone 'Polar Bear and Shaman' figure, by Davie Atchealak (1947-2006), E7-1182, from Iqaluit, signed in Roman.

24in (61cm) high

£6,000-8,000　　**WAD**

A stone and ivory 'Inuit Bible class' group, by Ennutsiak (1896-1967), from Iqaluit.

6in (11.5cm) wide

£10,000-15,000　　**WAD**

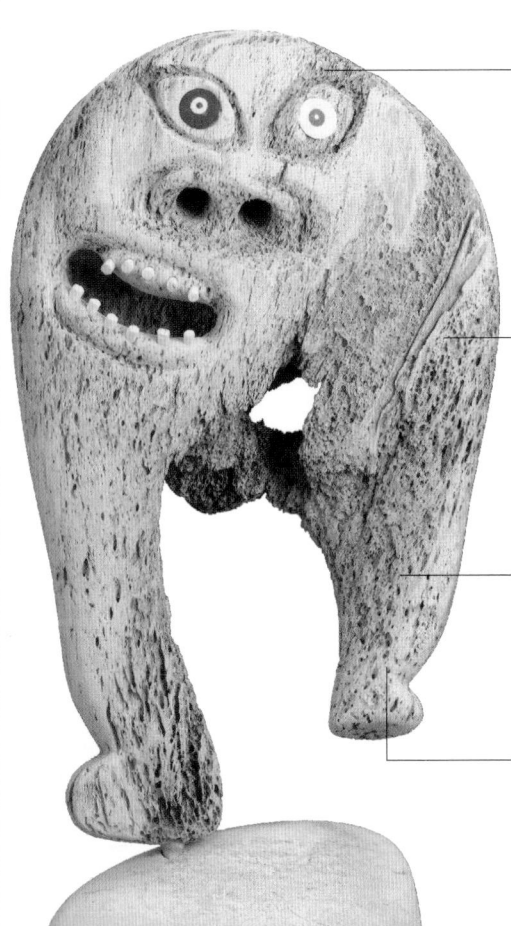

Karoo Ashevak (1940-1974) was one of the most respected and popular Inuit sculptors, and has hugely influenced Kitikmeot artists. Throughout his working life he produced some 250 sculptures that often portrayed grotesque and distorted features in comical and spiritual forms.

He worked mainly in whalebone, with stone, baleen and ivory highlights. He also experimented with antler using it as an inlay for additional detail in his sculptures. His skilled work is highly sought-after by collectors.

Ashevak has been described as the 'Picasso of the North', and this can be seen in the almost Cubist representation of this figure.

This sculpture superbly demonstrates Ashevak's spirituality and his playful and lively imagination. His curiosity and love of life inspired him to create this humourous yet slightly alarming figure.

A bone and stone 'Spirit' figure, by Karoo Ashevak (1940-1974), E4-196, from Spence Bay, signed in syllabics.

15in (38cm) high

£25,000-30,000　　**WAD**

A stone 'Midwives and Child' group, by Ennutsiak (1896-1967), E7-603, from Iqaluit.

6in (12.5cm) wide

£12,000-18,000　　**WAD**

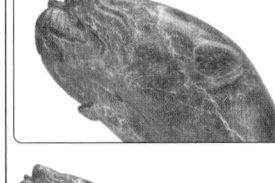

A stone 'Polar Bear with Seal Pup' figure, by Osuitok Ipeelee (1923-2005), E7-1154, from Cape Dorset, signed in syllabics.

c1970　　*19in (48.5cm) long*

£8,000-12,000　　**WAD**

A stone 'Walrus/Shaman' figure, by Osuitok Ipeelee (1923-2005), E7-1154, from Cape Dorset.

1972　　*4in (86.5cm) high*

£6,000-8,000　　**WAD**

TRIBAL ART

ESSENTIAL REFERENCE – OSUITOK IPEELEE

Osuitok Ipeelee (1922-2005) also known as Oshaweetok B, was a sculptor and printmaker, whose work is highly regarded by Inuit and private collectors.

- He came from a family of well-known, skillful carvers. He sold his first piece in the 1940s, which was a miniature ivory fox-trap and had moving parts.
- Ipeelee is known for uniquely delicate green-soapstone sculptures of caribou and birds, which are now extremely sought after. Although he worked primarily in stone, Osuitok he also incorporated other media, such as antler for caribou antlers and ivory for walrus tusks.
- He was an early collaborator with James Houston, the young Canadian artist who was the first to visit the Canadian Arctic with the intention of finding out whether the native art was appealing and could be sold. According to Houston, Ipeelee was instrumental in the conception of the West Baffin Island Eskimo Cooperative.
- In 1959 he was asked to create a sculpture of Queen Elizabeth II, which was presented to the Queen upon her visit to Canada that year.
- In 2004, he was awarded the Lifetime Aboriginal Art Achievement Award.

A stone 'Hawk with Lemming' statue, by Osuitok Ipeelee (1922-2005), E7-1154, from Cape Dorset, signed in syllabics.
c1975   *11in (28cm) wide*
£15,000-20,000   **WAD**

A stone and antler 'Musk Ox' figure, by Kananginak Pootoogook (b.1935), E7-1168, from Cape Dorset.
1991   *28in (71cm) long*
£18,000-22,000   **WAD**

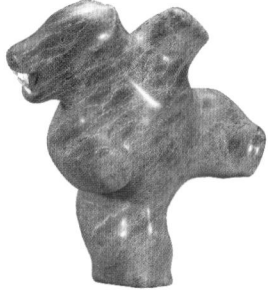

A stone and ivory 'Dancing Bear' figure, by Pauta Saila (b.1916), E7-990, from Cape Dorset, signed in syllabics.
16in (37cm) wide
£15,000-20,000   **WAD**

A set of stone 'Hunter and Wife' figures, by Mannumi Shaqu (1917-2000), E7-824, from Cape Dorset.
c1965   *Tallest 10.5in (26.5cm) high*
£6,500-8,500   **WAD**

A stone 'Mother and Child' figure, by an unidentified artist, signed in syllabics.
c1950   *12in (30.5cm) high*
£10,000-15,000   **WAD**

A limited edition 'Dogs See the Spirits' skin stencil print, by Kenojuak Ashevak (b.1927), E7-1035, from Cape Dorset.
23.75in (60.5cm) wide
£10,000-15,000   **WAD**

A coloured pencil drawing, by Jessie Oonark (1906-1985), E2-384, from Baker Lake, signed in syllabics, framed.
30in (76cm) wide
£5,000-6,000   **WAD**

A limited edition stonecut 'Metiq on Mallik' print, by Pudlo Pudlat (1916-1992), E7-899, from Cape Dorset, from an edition of 80, framed.
32in (81.5cm) wide
£400-600   **WAD**

A limited edition stonecut/stencil 'Owl in Winter Light' print, by Lucy Qinnuayuak (1915-1982), E7-1068.
25in (63.5cm) wide
£700-1,000   **WAD**

A mid-19thC Northeast beaded cloth pouch, with remnant silk edging, partially beaded with multicoloured bilateral floral devices and linear bordering.

5.5in (14cm) high

£400-600   **SK**

Twelve late 19thC Imperial size cabinet photographs depicting the military shortly after The Wounded Knee Battle, Pine Ridge, South Dakota, by the Northeastern Photograph Co., Chadron, Nebraska, in varied conditions.

7in (18cm) wide

£1,800-2,000   **SK**

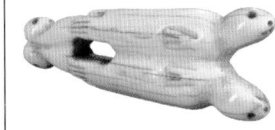

A 19thC Eskimo carved ivory toggle, in the form of two opposing forms possibly giving birth to two small seals, patina of use.

3.5in (9cm) long

£1,500-2,500   **SK**

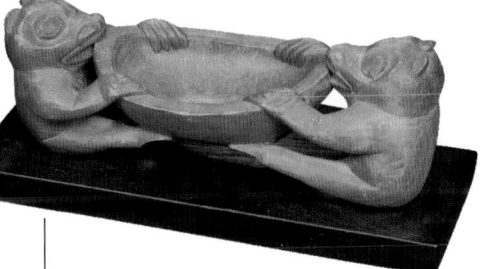

A late 19thC Northwest Coast carved wood bowl, the shallow ovoid cedar form being held by two stylised seated bears.

16in (40.5cm) long

£8,000-12,000   **SK**

A late 19thC Northwest Coast carved two-piece sheep horn ladle, with carved underside depicting a stylised animal flanked by faces, the finial with a man perched on a seated bear.

14in (35.5cm) long

£8,000-12,000   **SK**

A large early 20thC Northwest Coast totem pole, possibly made as a W.P.A. project during the Depression, with various animal and avian totemic devices, weathered surface.

120in (305cm) high

£13,000-15,000   **SK**

A late 19thC Northwest Coast carved and painted wood totem pole, from Nuu-chah-nulth, carved with stylised bird and animal forms, paint loss.

80in (203cm) high

£16,000-18,000   **SK**

A late 19thC Northwest Coast Kwakiutl carved cedar hood mask, pierced mouth overlaid with pounded copper lips, remnants of white, black, blue and red pigments, patina of use, old repairs.

25in (63.5cm) high

£25,000-30,000   **SK**

A 19thC Northwest Coast carved wood raven rattle, with red, black and traces of blue-green pigments, restored tongue, minor wood loss.

11in (28cm) long

£30,000-40,000   **SK**

A Western Mono California coiled cooking basketry bowl, with horizontal and vertical zigzag bands and stepped design.

c1900   *18in (45.5cm) diam*

£3,000-4,000   **POOK**

A Northwest beaded cloth pouch, from Athabascan, beaded fringe, red wool tassels, beaded on one side with a floral pattern, silk lined.

c1900   *12in (30.5cm) long*

£700-1,000   **SK**

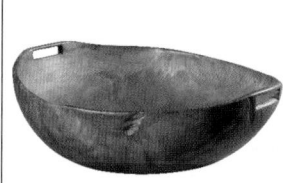

A large 19thC Great Lakes carved probably Elmwood bowl, the raised ends with rectangular slots forming handles, patina of use.

24.5in (62cm) diam

£12,000-18,000   SK

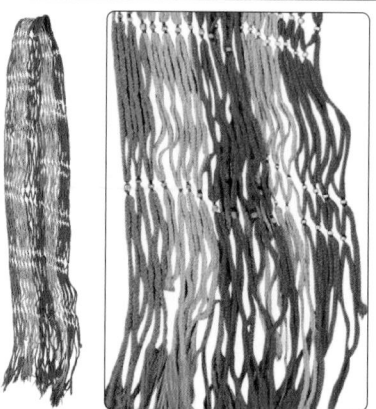

A rare late 18thC Great Lakes finger-woven woodland quilled sash, the braided openwork form in red, green, and yellow ochre, with yellow, black and white quill-wrapped spacers.

82in (208cm) long

£7,000-10,000   SK

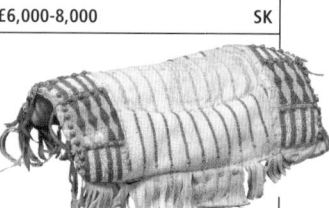

A mid-19thC Western Great Lakes silk appliqué and beaded cloth leggings and pony beaded sash, in red trade cloth, white edge-beading, the sash with bold geometric pattern in white, black.

leggings 24in (61cm) long

£6,000-8,000   SK

A Southern Plains beaded hide woman's dress, from Kiowa, with classic Kiowa designs and colours, yellow and green pigments, with fringe at the sleeves and sides, some restoration.

c1900   *50in (127cm) long*

£6,000-8,000   SK

A mid-late 19thC Central Plains beaded soft hide pipe bag, from Cheyenne, with beaded tabs, tin cone, horsehair danglers and long quill-wrapped fringe, of yellow pigment.

33in (84cm) long

£7,000-10,000   SK

A pair of late 19thC Central Plains fully beaded hide moccasins, from Lokata, with roll-beaded drops from the tongues, the bottoms with a dark translucent blue and white checked design.

10.5in (26.5cm) long

£3,000-4,000   SK

A mid-late 19thC Plains beaded buffalo-hide pad saddle, with fringe, early multicoloured patterns and brass shoe buttons, blue beads, tin cone and horsehair danglers, remnant blue cloth cinch straps.

18.5in (47cm) long

£10,000-15,000   SK

An early19thC Plains quilled ash pipe stem, from Lakota, with dark brown, white, and red plaited quill wrapping at one end, dark patina, minor loss.

38.5in (98cm) long

£15,000-20,000   SK

A Native American Californian Great Plains circular basket, tightly woven, decorated with two rows of figures and geometric motifs.

6.5in (16.5cm) wide

£7,000-10,000   DRA

CLOSER LOOK: TEEPEE LINER

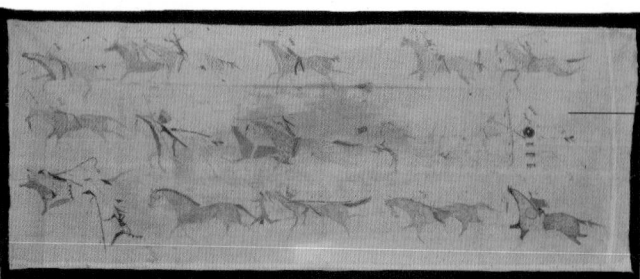

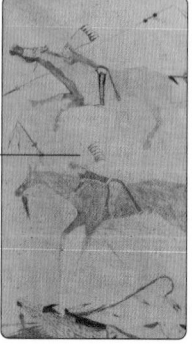

The horse, introduced to the plains people by the Spanish in the 16thC, was vital for hunting, raiding and warfare. It often features in their artwork.

Plains people expressed their artistic talents in three media: porcupine-quill embroidery, beadwork and painting, which was used on almost every surface, including clothing, cooking implements and teepees.

A late 19thC Plains pictorial muslin teepee liner, from Lakota, probably depicting a warrior's exploits, mostly on horseback, wearing feathered bonnets, in red, green, yellow, blue and black.

91in (231cm) wide

£25,000-30,000   SK

An Apache coiled basketry bowl, decorated with human and deer figures, within a stylised flower.

c1900   16.5in (42cm) diam

£2,000-2,500   **POOK**

An Apache coiled basketry olla, decorated with human and deer figures.

c1900   13.25in (35.5cm) high

£3,000-4,000   **POOK**

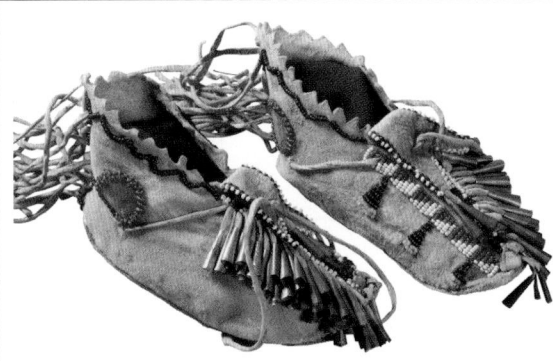

A pair of late 19thC Southwest beaded hide child's moccasins, Apache, with traces of yellow pigment and red pigment detail, partially beaded, with tin cone danglers, fringe at the heels.

The Apache are known to be fierce warriors, though they were also farmers and traders. They spread out over a wide area of Arizona, New Mexico, and into Texas, 'borrowing' from their neighbours. This took the form both of ransacking food and provisions, and peacefully learning their ways. Apache basket designs are similar to those of the Pima. Meanwhile, their beadwork is completely unique.

5.5in (14cm) long

£5,000-7,000   **SK**

A Southwest polychrome carved cottonwood butterfly maiden, from Poli, Mana, Hopi, the female form wearing a shawl with floral designs, a dress and sash, and a large tablita with imagery.

11in (28cm) high

£4,000-5,000   **SK**

A Southwest silver and turquoise cross necklace, from Navajo, a single strand of large hollow beads with eight cross devices, the triple-carinated naja with three turquoise settings, strung on old hide.

c1900   17.25in (44cm) long

£7,000-10,000   **SK**

A Southwest first phase silver concha belt, from Navajo, comprising seven diamond slot round conchas with classic scalloped, stamped, and perforated edge work, stamped buckle, and original commercial leather backing.

c1870   36.5in (93cm) long

£20,000-25,000   **SK**

An early 20thC Southwest natural and synthetic dyed homespun wool pictorial weaving, from Navajo, depicting a single Yei figure flanked by two sun symbols, on a variegated grey-brown background, faded.

£2,000-2,500   **SK**

An early 20thC Southwest coiled basketry tray, from Pima, with a maze pattern.

13in (33cm) diam

£500-700   **SK**

CLOSER LOOK – SOUTHWEST FIGURE

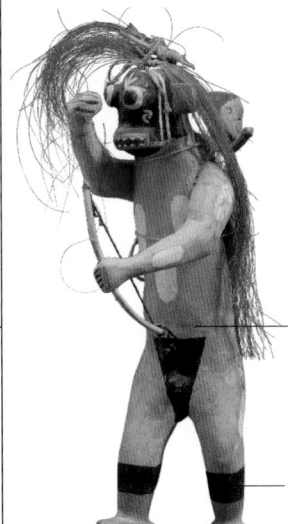

For a thousand years, the Hopi people have lived in stone-built villages surrounded by the Navajo reservation.

The Hopi are a very religious tribe, and the kachina figures, which represent their helper deities, and the kachina carvers are an important part of their religious structure.

There are two main ogre kachinas: the Black Ogre (Nata-aska) and the White Ogre (Wiharu), represented here. Children are taught that the ogre will get them if they are bad.

Kachina dolls are usually carved from a single piece of cottonwood root.

An early 20thC Southwest polychrome carved cottonwood ogre kachina, from Tsaveyo, Hopi, carrying a bow and with a captured child on his back, horsehair attachments, old tag on back.

9in (23cm) high

£6,000-8,000   **SK**

A Pima coiled basketry tray, with concentric zigzag circles.

c1900   15.75in (40cm) wide

£1,000-1,500   **POOK**

A Southwest black on black pottery bowl, from Marie, San Ildefonso, the tapered neck with Avanyu pattern.

4in (10cm) high

£3,000-4,000   **SK**

A Southwest black on black pottery bowl, San Ildefonso, Avanyu pattern band, signed 'Marie'.

10.25in (26cm) high

£1,500-2,000   **SK**

A Southwest polished redware wedding jar, signed 'Helen Shupla Santa Clara Pueblo'.

7in (18cm) high

£1,000-1,500   **SK**

An early 20thC Southwest carved polished blackware pottery bowl, from Santa Clara, with two handles near the rim, imprints at the shoulder, damage.

4.5in (11.5cm) high

£3,500-4,500   **SK**

A Southwest turquoise tab necklace, from Zuni, with two pairs of jaclaw with teardrop-shaped shell pendants, two strands of graduating size stones with heishi spacers.

c1920   18in (45.5cm) long

£2,000-3,000   **SK**

An early 19thC Southeast beaded cloth bandolier bag, from Seminole, with triangular flap, with remnant cotton lining, beaded in early concentric and zigzag devices, damages.

Pouch 8in (20.5cm) long

£12,000-15,000   **SK**

CLOSER LOOK – SOUTHWEST ZUNI OLLA

A Southwest Zuni polychrome pottery olla.

The Zuni or Ashiwi (as the Zuni refer to themselves) are a Native American tribe who live along The Zuni River in western New Mexico.

Clay for pottery is sourced locally and, prior to extraction, thanks are given to the Earth Mother (Awidelin Tsitda). The clay is then grinded, sifted and mixed with water, before being shaped into a vessel or ornament and scraped smooth with a scraper, and covered with a thin layer of finer clay for extra smoothness. The piece is then polished with a stone and painted, using a traditional yucca brush. For hundreds of years the Zuni used sheep dung to fire their pottery, but most contemporary Zuni pottery is now fired in electric kilns.

This piece features traditional motifs, including stylised animals and birds.

Originally pots like this were used to store dry goods and water for use in cooking. Since the arrival of the railroad, much pottery has been made as tourist ware.

17in (43cm) high

£40,000-50,000   **SK**

An early 20thC Chimayo rug, with Vallero design with four pinwheel adornments in red, ivory, soft green, black and tan, all on a teal field.

86in (217cm) long

£700-1,000   RTC

An early 19thC South American Mapuche woven poncho, from Southern Chile, with three panels of concentric stepped cross designs separated by multicoloured stripes on a deep indigo background, fringed ends.

58in (147.5cm) long

£1,500-2,000   SK

A 19thC New Mexican retablo, possibly by José Rafael Aragón (c1795-1862), the tempera and gesso on hand-adzed wood panel depicting the Virgin Mary, with fluted fan at the top.

José Rafael Aragón was an artist working in Spanish New Mexico during the late 18th and early 19thC. He was a wood carver who worked with local woods, and a painter, working in watercolour and tempura. He created mainly religious images for the church and for domestic settings, and was particularly known for his bold colours and decorative motifs.

19.5in (49.5cm) high

£5,000-7,000   SK

An Amazonian wood stool, the dished elliptical seat with incised and punch decoration on scroll supports.

20.25in (51.5cm) long

£400-600   WW

Nine Western Imperial size cabinet card photographs, includes an image of 'Street View of Lead City, Black Hills, D. T.', by F. Jay Haynes.

Largest 8in (20.5cm) wide

£1,000-1,200 SET   SK

A Pre-Columbian Mexican seated female pottery figure, from Nayarit, the skirted form wearing ear and nose ornaments and holding up a bowl in one hand, polychrome geometric decoration, damages.

c100BC-250AD   15.5in (39.5cm) high

£1,000-1,500   SK

A Pre-Columbian Mexican painted pottery female form, from Nayarit, the hollow seated form with hands to the torso, nose and ear ornaments and elaborate body paint.

c100BC-250AD   11in (28cm) high

£1,200-1,800   SK

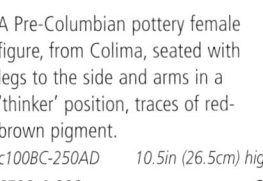

A Pre-Columbian pottery female figure, from Colima, seated with legs to the side and arms in a 'thinker' position, traces of red-brown pigment.

c100BC-250AD   10.5in (26.5cm) high

£700-1,000   SK

A Pre-Columbian painted pottery figure, from Jalisco, the seated male form holding snake-like form, decorated with white on red pigment, re-glued at the neck.

c100BC-250AD   10in (25.5cm) high

£2,200-2,800   SK

CLOSER LOOK – JALISCO WARRIOR FIGURE

Jalisco, named for the modern state, was located in West Mexico along the Pacific coast west of what is now Mexico City. Its sculpture is noted for a hieratic style with stiff postures and staring eyes.

Figures such as this were usually placed in tombs and presumably served a religious purpose.

The bodily proportions – long face, short arms and legs, and a large torso – seem to have been an accepted stylistic convention.

This figure was probably of high rank, symbolised by his multiple items of jewellery and tall headdress.

A Pre-Columbian Mexican pottery warrior figure, from Nayarit, the seated figure in armour, two point helmet, and carrying a mace.
c100BC-250AD   *9.5in (24cm) high*
£2,000-3,000   **SK**

A Pre-Columbian painted pottery warrior figure, from Jalisco, the large seated form wearing basketry armour and holding a mace, with necklace, nose and multiple ear ornaments, remnant geometric painted designs.
c100BC-250AD   *17.5in (44.5cm) high*
£3,000-4,000   **SK**

A Pre-Columbian Mexican pottery couple with child, from Jalisco, emulating the 'Earth Mother' theme and the 'Cycle of Life'.
c100BC–250AD   *9.5in (24cm) high*
£1,500-2,000   **SK**

A Pre-Columbian Peruvian incised blackware stirrup-spout vessel, from Cupisnique, depicting fanged deity heads, accented with red pigment.
c800-200BC   *9in (23cm) high*
£600-800   **SK**

A Pre-Columbian Peruvian stirrup-spout pottery vessel, from Moche, depicting a feline head with a snake in its mouth, orange-slipped with cream paint, broken and repaired.
10in (25.5cm) high
£400-500   **SK**

A Pre-Columbian Peruvian incised polychrome stirrup-spout vessel, from Cupisnique, the detailed feline head with elaborate incised designs and highlights with black pigment.
c800-200BC
£700-1,000   **SK**

A Pre-Columbian Peruvian polychrome effigy vessel, from Chavin de Santa, depicting a seated cargador carrying a large olla on his shoulder, with incised and painted detail.
800-200BC   *9.25in (23.5cm) high*
£1,500-2,000   **SK**

A Pre-Columbian blackware pottery effigy vessel, from Moche, the stirrup-spout form with stylized crab deity, man on his back, with various serpent-like extensions, restoration.
8.5in (21.5cm) high
£1,000-1,500   **SK**

A Pre-Columbian Peruvian stirrup-spout portrait vessel, from Moche the warrior head with large ear plugs and with red, cream and black painted detail.
10.75in (27.5cm) high
£2,500-3,500   **SK**

A Fiji throwing club, with incised zigzag decorated handle inscribed 'Trupeni', remains of faintly inscribed paper label.

15.75in (40cm) long

£400-600   WW

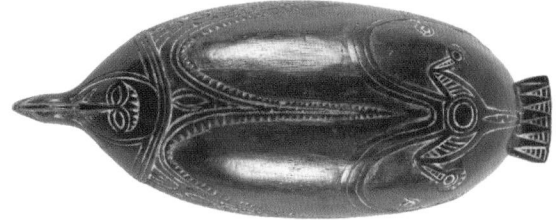

A Papua New Guinea carved ebony oblong bowl, with bird head and fish terminal, the underside with stylised incised and lime filled decoration, with a fin lift.

16.5in (42cm) long

£400-600   WW

A Maori whalebone club/patu paraoa, of spatulate form with circular piercing to the neck and five curved grooves to the butt.

13in (33cm) long

£800-1,200   WW

A Maori carved pedestal figure, one in a series of five, formed as part of a balustrade, the full figure front facing with a tongue poking out.

39.75in (101cm) high

£1,200-1,800   WEB

A Maori carved decorative panel, with a central tiki flanked by two serpentine wheku figures.

61.5in (156cm) long

£1,000-1,500   WEB

A pair of Philippine Ingovat carved wood figures, of a male and a female, each supporting a circular disc with further supports, three missing.

13.5in (34cm) high

£250-300   WW

A Philippine Ingorat carved wood group, of two figures supporting a platform.

14.5in (37cm) high

£200-300   WW

A rare abalone and fishbone fishing lure, with hackles of pale goat hair and a length of old twine, with an old label inscribed in brown italics 'Fishing Hook made and used by Pitcairn Islanders 1829'.

Pitcairn Island was discovered in 1767 by the British and settled in 1790 by the Bounty mutineers and their Tahitian companions. Pitcairn was the first Pacific island to become a British colony (in 1838) and today remains the last vestige of that empire in the South Pacific. In 1789, a famous mutiny took place when Master's Mate Fletcher Christian and about half the crew took control of the HMS Bounty and set the Captain, Lt. William Bligh, adrift in the ship's launch with those crew members who remained loyal to him. Several of the mutineers along with their Tahitian and Tubuan consorts and a handful of native men found sanctuary on Pitcairn. The current population of Pitcairn is 50 from 9 families descended from six of the mutineers and their women.

1829   *4in (10cm) long*

£300-400   L&T

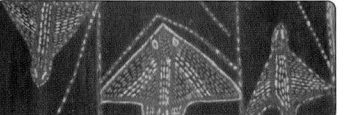

A Polynesian oceanic bark painting.

20.25in (51.5cm) long

£600-800   DN

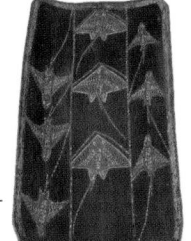

A silver grip flintlock pistol, possibly by Claude Miquet, marked 'London' on frame, with scroll engraving and tapered barrel with ramrod.
c1730-40

£4,000-5,000 SK

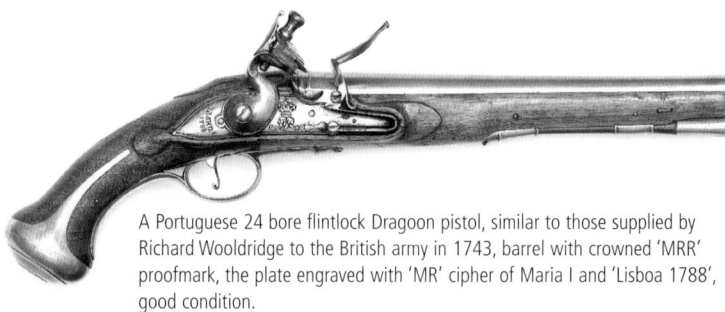

A Portuguese 24 bore flintlock Dragoon pistol, similar to those supplied by Richard Wooldridge to the British army in 1743, barrel with crowned 'MRR' proofmark, the plate engraved with 'MR' cipher of Maria I and 'Lisboa 1788', good condition.

16in (40.5cm) long

£6,500-8,500 W&W

A .65 heavy dragoon flintlock pistol, engraved lock with crowned 'GR' and 'Farmer 1757' across the tail, regulation brass furniture including escutcheon marked '5/19', brass-tipped wooden ramrod, lock re-engraved, stock cracked and restored overall.

18.5in (47cm) long

£1,500-2,000 W&W

A 20 bore flintlock holster pistol, by Wogdon, London, with London proofs, the plate engraved 'Wogdon', walnut fullstock with plain brass mounts, original wooden ramrod, brass tip missing, dark patina.
c1765
13in (33cm) long

£1,000-1,500 W&W

A Scottish all steel flintlock belt pistol, by John Murdoch of Doune, barrel with typical fluted breech and flared octagonal muzzle, the lock engraved 'IO: MURDOCH DOUN', engraved overall, the butt with silver inlay, steel pricker in the butt, and slender steel ramrod, in good condition.
c1770
11.75in (30cm) long

£8,000-10,000 W&W

A cased pair of duelling pistols by Robert Wogden of London, with 10in (25cm) damascus barrels, full stocked and steel mounted, in original case, bearing a rare Riviere label with Oxford Street address.

The pistols date from around 1780, when Wogden's duelling pistols became more austere. The label on the case suggests that the original owner of these pistols, or his descendants, sold them to Isaac Riviere during the period 1810-16 when Riviere was based at his Oxford Street address.

£15,000-20,000 GVI

A 20 bore flintlock holster pistol, by Tow, with London and maker's proofs, engraved 'London' and with maker's name, plain walnut fullstock with brass mounts, brass tipped wooden ramrod, cock and old replacement, slight wear.
c1785
14in (35.5cm) long

£650-850 W&W

A brass flintlock bayonet pocket pistol, Bass, with English proof marks, and a 3in (7.5cm) screw-off barrel.

c1790

£450-550 SK

A .56 Tower short flintlock Sea Service pistol, barrel with Tower proofs, flat lock marked with crowned 'GR' and 'Tower', walnut fullstock with traces of 1806 Ordnance storekeeper's mark, in good condition.

16in (40.5cm) long

£1,200-1,800 W&W

A rare 14 bore Russian model 1809 military flintlock holster pistol, the breech impressed with the Imperial eagle and date '1834', the plate impressed with arsenal name and '1834', the brass mounts with cipher of Nicholas I, in good condition.

16in (40.5cm) long

£2,500-3,500 W&W

MILITARIA

A 52 bore Adams Patent percussion revolver, with octagonal barrel signed 'Wilkinson & Son, Pall Mall, London', the whole fitted to a baize-lined mahogany case with original Wilkinson label, with accessories.

Barrel 6in (15cm) long

£2,000-3,000   **FLD**

A five shot, 54 bore Adams model 1851 self cocking percussion revolver, barrel engraved 'Dooley, 11 Ranelagh St, Liverpool', frame engraved 'Adams' Patent 30760B', London proofs, Adams's '1854' rammer, chequered walnut butt, in good condition, in a refitted oak case with reproduction trade label.

11.5in (29cm) long

£2,500-3,500   **W&W**

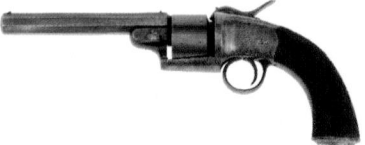

A 56 bore transitional percussion revolver, Joseph Lang, with an octagonal barrel signed 'Joseph Lang, 22 Cockspur St, London', above scroll engraved frame with steel grip cap trap and checkered grip.

Barrel 6in (15cm) long

£700-1,000   **FLD**

A six shot .36 Savage & North second model Navy percussion revolver, the top strap with maker's name and patent dates, reciprocating cylinder, large trigger guard with double triggers, walnut grips, worn and cleaned overall.

14.5in (37cm) long

£900-1,200   **W&W**

A large Nobel Industries Limited cartridge display of Eley and Kynoch sporting and military pattern ammunition, comprising 66 rifle and revolver metallic cartridges from .22 to .450 Express, 80 shotgun cartridges from .22 to four bore, six glass fronted containers of shot, percussion caps and anvils, and sundry wads and printed discs, all contained in glazed oak case.

31in (79cm) wide

£2,500-3,000   **W&W**

A six shot .32 Allen & Thurber self-cocking bar hammer percussion pepperbox revolver, fluted barrels stamped 'Allen Thurber & Co, Worcester', scroll engraved frame, butt with plain walnut grips, slightly worn overall.

7.25in (18.5cm) long

£500-700   **W&W**

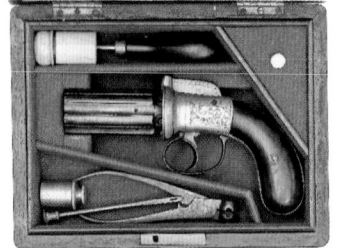

A six shot 160 bore self cocking bar hammer percussion pepperbox revolver, Birmingham proofs, scroll engraved German silver frame and butt strap, plain walnut grips, in fitted brass bound rosewood box.

7.25in (18.5cm) long

£500-700   **W&W**

CLOSER LOOK – COLT PISTOL

Hugely powerful, the gun was revered at the time and would have been retrieved immediately when a Ranger fell in battle.

It retains 40-60% of its finish, and all of its inspector and proof marks, which is of great historical significance, as most of the 1,100 Colt pistols that were produced saw a great deal of action and are in well-used condition.

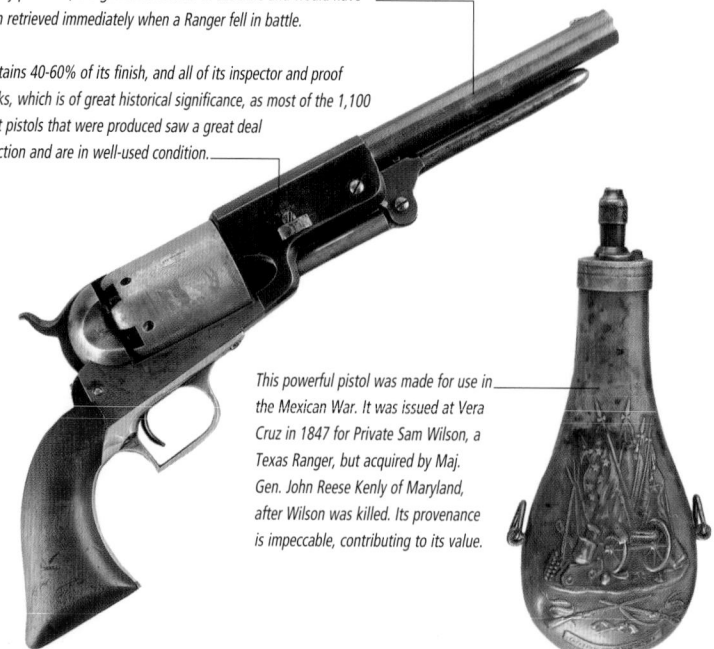

This powerful pistol was made for use in the Mexican War. It was issued at Vera Cruz in 1847 for Private Sam Wilson, a Texas Ranger, but acquired by Maj. Gen. John Reese Kenly of Maryland, after Wilson was killed. Its provenance is impeccable, contributing to its value.

A rare Colt Whiteneyville-Walker pistol, marked 'A Company #210', with original flask issued at Vera Cruz in 1847 to Private Sam Wilson (Texas Ranger), later obtained by Brevet Major General John Reese Kenly of Maryland.

£600,000-800,000   **JDJ**

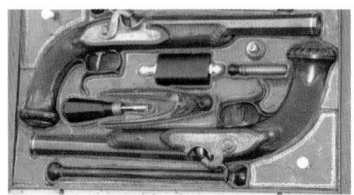

A .577/450 Martini Henry military pattern sporting rifle, by George Gibbs, 39 Carr Street, Bristol, five folding leaf and ladder rear sights, trigger guard engraved 'B2353', steel mounts, lid engraved 'L W Meyer, Ladysmith'.

49.5in (126cm) long

£700-1,000   W&W

A 14 bore Yeomanry percussion carbine, twist barrel, seven groove rifling, fixed sights, flatlock of flintlock form, engraved 'J W Edge'.

Edge had a shop in Manchester c1830-45.

35.5in (90cm) long

£550-750   W&W

A rare .451 military issue Westley Richards 'monkey tail' breech loading percussion carbine, breech no. 'A432', marked with Tower proofs, ordnance inspectors' stamps, maker's name, Birmingham 1861 storekeeper's stamp, '2.1872'.

35in (89cm) long

£1,000-1,500   W&W

A Rheinmetall, Germany FG42 Second Model, SN 04371, calibre 0.25in (7.92mm), 20in (51cm) barrel, unique finned flash hider, spike bayonet, folding bi-pod, flip-up hooded post front sight, flip-up adjustable rear drum sight, original scope, two magazines, from the Stern Collection.

£100,000-120,000   JDJ

A fine Japanese snap matchlock musket, with massive blued octagonal barrel retained by a brass band at the breech, elaborate inlay in silver enriched with gold, solid band of silver at the muzzle, signed in ink beneath the breech, fitted with integral pan with hinged brass pivot-cover, brass lock, brass trigger, stained cherrywood fullstock, now seized, areas of light wear, ramrod missing.

c1870

27.5in (70cm) long

£7,000-8,000   TDM

A 12 bore Holland & Holland Royal side by side sidelock ejector, series no. 25532, 27in (68.5cm) replacement barrels, action with bold royal scroll engraving, hand detachable locks, gold-lined cocking-indicators, in original leather motor case with Holland and Holland trade card.

c1906

27in (68.5cm) barrel.

£6,500-8,500   L&T

A 17thC Highland dirk, the hardwood grip carved with Celtic knotwork above a band of lozenge decoration, the single-edged blade etched 'God Loves King James', the back edge with silver mount with scalloped edge.

20in (51cm) long

£2,000-3,000   L&T

A Georgian Customs Officer's presentation dirk, blued and gilt blade, gilt-copper crossguard, stained ivory grip, copper sheath with roped hanging rings, inscribed 'From Capt Lucas RN to Mr W Carter 1825' with Customs badge.

12in (30.5cm) long

£3,000-4,000   W&W

A rare late 15thC two-handed sword, with long double-edged tapering blade, old repair at tip, with original leather-covered wooden grip, worm damage, slender straight quillons flared at the tip, large globular pommel.

Large double-handed swords were used by Scottish lairds since medieval times, and were symbols of high office for the Barony courts. Not all of the swords are Scottish in origin as trade with the Low Countries and central Europe brought many weapons into the north east of Scotland. This example is possibly from the north east of England.

Blade 46in (117) long

£5,500-7,500   L&T

A mid-17thC English silver-encrusted hunting hanger, the blade stamped with a brass-lined cross and orb mark and a further mark on each side, the steel hilt decorated and with traces of early gilding, the lower portion of the grip with its original woven binding of silver ribband and twisted wire.

17in (43.5cm) blade

£3,500-4,500   TDM

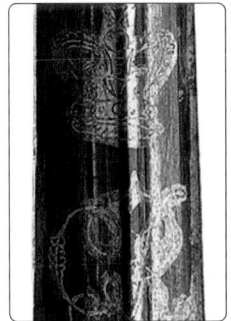

An 18thC silver-hilted small sword, Glasgow, with George III-period London hallmarks to the knuckle guard, the blade with remains of blued and gilt decoration with a 'C' surmounted by a royal crown with a stylised thistle above, with a later black leather scabbard with silver mounts, and the book 'Prince Charlie and the Borderland'.

This sword appears to date from Prince Charles Edward Stewart's time in exile in France after fleeing Scotland in 1746. The Royal Cypher and symbols detailed in gilt to the blade express Charles' belief that he was rightful heir to the Scottish throne. The guard has been fitted in reverse at some period prior to 1929, as it appears in a photograph with the guard reversed.

34.5in (87.5cm) long overall

£20,000-25,000   L&T

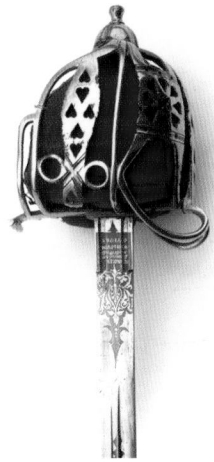

A Victorian officer's basket hilted broadsword, with double-edged 32.25in (82cm) blade, etched with the Queen's crown, 'VR' and maker's name 'Rober Mole & sons, makers War & India office', in its original scabbard.

£1,000-1,500   GVI

A late 18thC Indian sousun pattah sword, with a broad re-curved watered blade, with ornamental reinforcement to parts of the blade edge, the hilt of traditional form, in good condition.

Blade 29in (74cm) long

£700-900   W&W

A 19thC Indian khanjar (dagger), double-edged blade with central rib, pale green soapstone hilt in the form of a ram's head in floral headscarf on ornamental base, in a modern sheath, in good condition.

Blade 10in (25.5cm) long

£450-550   W&W

An early 19thC Coorg ayda katti sword, with a heavy re-curved blade, diced ivory hilt of traditional form, kite-shaped pommel and diced grip, with a heavy oval brass holder with a prominent spike, and a leather and chain shoulder belt, in good condition.

The Croogs are an ethnic group from southeast India. Their origins are uncertain, but they are ethnically and culturally distinct from the other peoples of South India. Their unique weapon, the ayda katti, combines the qualities of a sword and an axe. It is worn at the back of the waist, secured in a belt without scabbard.

Blade 16.5in (42cm) long

£3,000-4,000   W&W

A pair of Japanese Daisho swords, katana Shinto, signed 'Tsuda Echizen No Kami Suke…', wakizashi Shinto blade signed 'Kishu Seki No Ju Nobuyoshi', both swords with repolished blade, in good condition.

Daisho (literally 'large-small') is the name for the pairs of swords carried by the Samurai. The pair comprised the katana, a one-edged long-sword, and the shorter wakizashi, or 'companion sword'.

c1650   *Blade 25.5in (65cm) long*

£6,000-8,000   **W&W**

A Japanese katana sword, after Kotetsu, in new polish, the blade shape (Sugata) a broad shinogi zukuri, the tempering pattern (Hamon) gunome-choji-midare with some togari, the hilt with black binding on white fishskin, the collar and hilt ornaments in shakudo with a floral design in 19thC-style.

Nagasone Kotetsu (c.1597-1678) was a celebrated Japanese sword maker of the early Edo period.

Blade 28in (71cm) long

£3,500-4,500   **W&W**

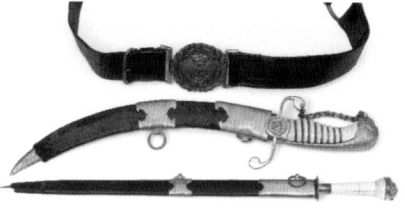

An early 19thC Nepalese kora sword, the heavy blade of traditional form with twin shallow fullers, a red inlaid eye symbol on both sides at tip, plain steel hilt and grip, in good condition.

Blade 19in (48cm) long

£200-300   **W&W**

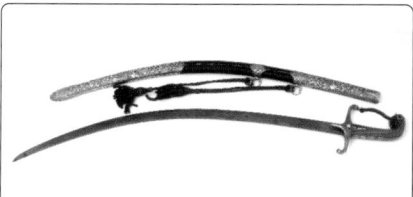

An 18thC Persian shamshir (sword), the blade with gold inlaid maker's mark at forte, one piece crossguard, the central panel decorated with stylised script, unusually shaped bone grips, broad iron strap, in good condition.

£900-1,200   **W&W**

A 19thC presentation shamshir, presented by The Sultan of Turkey to Admiral Sir Charles Napier, KCB, with 31.5in (80cm) curved single-edged blade, the gilt cross-guard with central sunburst medallion inset with a central old brilliant cut diamond with smaller diamonds to the rays, the quillions mounted with further diamonds, the mameluke hilt with polished horn grips, contained in a wooden and leather bound scabbard with gilt metal mounts, together with a naval dirk, with 12.25in (31cm) fullered straight blade, turned ivory grip with gilt brass lion's head pommel contained in a leather and brass mounted scabbard, signed 'W. P. Read, Sword Cutler, Portsmouth', and another Naval dirk with 11.5in (29cm) curved blade, brass crossguard with lion's head medallion and pommel, contained in a leather and brass mounted scabbard, with a naval black leather belt, the brass buckle stamped 'Dudley, Portsmouth'.

Admiral Sir Charles Napier (1786-1860) was a highly controversial character, loved by men in the Royal Navy for his buccaneering spirit. The Sultan of Turkey awarded him the First Class Order of Medjideh with a diamond star and this diamond hilted scimitar for leading 1,500 Turks at the storming of Sidon in the Syrian Campaign of 1839.

£30,000-40,000   **BE**

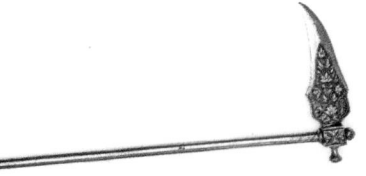

A 19thC Indian all steel axe zhagnal, decorated with applied brass floral spray to both sides, the knopped cube socket with applied brass florets, the shaft with a little copper inlaid decoration, in good condition.

Blade 8in (20.5cm) long

£500-700   **W&W**

A 17thC Netherlandish/German halberd, the head with 13in (33cm) pierced spike, pierced blade and fluke, the knop at the base of the spike decorated with grotesque heads, the fluke stamped with a cross above a 3, later shaft.

81.5in (207cm) long

£450-550   **BE**

A rare WWII Special Forces and OSS clasp knife, with wire cutter, three saw blades and knife blade.

£700-1,000   **W&W**

A complete suit of 18th/19thC Edo period Samurai armour, by Yokohagi Do Tosei Gusoku, the iron plate cuirass with remains of lacquer, leather lacquered skirts, black and red lacquered Zunari kabuto helmet, Mempo face mask, with box and stand.

£2,000-3,000   RTC

An early 17thC heavy breastplate, marked with maker's name 'Braun', with figure '2' above, two studs for shoulder straps, musket ball proof test, the edges perforated with holes for padding attachment.

£650-850   W&W

A heavy breastplate, with distinct medial ridge roped neck and fixed arm cusps, struck with an indistinct maker's mark and a musket ball proof test.
c1660

£2,500-3,500   W&W

An early 18thC Continental siege weight breastplate, with turned-over edges at the shoulders and neck and small steel studs to edges, inspector's marks on each shoulder, hammered finish.

£550-750   W&W

A scarce Elizabethan period open-faced burgonet helmet, heavy skull and high comb formed from one piece of iron, brass-headed rivets backed with brass rosette washers, with armourer's mark 'E H'.

£3,000-4,000   GVI

A cabasset, formed in one piece, pear stalk finial to crown, brass rosettes to rim base, two rosettes missing, in good condition.
c1600

£600-800   W&W

A mid-17thC 'Dutch' lobster tailed helmet, with ribbed skull, four lame lobster tail, pierced ear flaps and sliding nasal bar, in good condition.

£1,200-1,800   W&W

A scarce Fife Light Horse Officer's spiked helmet, of conventional form applied with two-colour badge surmounted by Queen's crown, with curb-link chin strap, contained in original tin box with named brass plate to lid 'J Gilmour Fife Light Horse'.

£2,500-3,500   L&T

A post-1902 officer's blue cloth spiked helmet of The Prince of Wales's Own (West Yorkshire Regiment), gilt mounts, leather and silk lining, in its tin case with name.

£900-1,200   W&W

A Volunteer Vetinary officer's pill box hat, silver lace headband of similar pattern to Army Vetinary Service, silver braided top ornament and purl button, leather lining.

£150-200   W&W

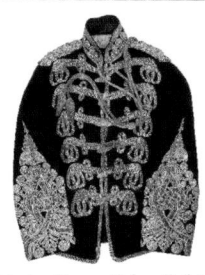

A Victorian Hussar Colonel's full dress tunic, gilt lace edged collar with braided loops, gilt gimp loops to chest and back, heavily braided cuffs, gimp shoulder cords with embroidered crown and two stars, cord cap lines and olivet fastenings, padded silk lining, in good condition.

£650-850   **W&W**

The full dress uniform of Major Edgworth Horrocks, Highland Borderers Light Infantry (Militia), in very good condition, together with a copy of a photograph of Horrocks in full dress uniform of Captain, and photostat family details, with details of his military service.

£2,500-3,500   **W&W**

A late Victorian Second Lieutenant's full dress part uniform of the 2nd Dragoons (Royal Scots Greys), in good condition, one or two surface moth traces to skirts.

£500-700   **W&W**

A Georgian officer's rectangular shoulder belt plate for probably The 29thC (Worcestershire) Regiment, copper with traces of gilt, within a crowned oval Garter on blue enamel, cut off corners, line and chevron border.

3in (7.5cm) high

£2,000-2,500   **W&W**

A Scottish provincial Balmoral Highlander's waist belt plate, by William Robb, Edinburgh, integral clasp to reverse, maker's name and '19 ERI 04', the 2.5in (6.5cm) black leather belt with dirk hanging loops, marked 'ROBB, BLTR'.

1903-4   Plate 3.5in (9cm) wide

£900-1,200   **L&T**

A post 1902 officer's shoulder belt and pouch of the 9th (Queen's Royal) Lancers, red leather pouch with solid frosted gilt flap with 'AR' cipher, the belt of regimental gilt lace on scarlet cloth with frosted gilt buckle, tip and slide, in good condition.

£600-800   **W&W**

An Argyle & Sutherland Highlanders officer's badger sporran, the head with bead eyes mounted over pocket, plain gilt cantle, suspended on the badger fur six goat hair tassels mounted in gilt thistle embossed cups, in good condition.

£900-1,200   **W&W**

A Victorian officers' regimental pattern full dress embroidered pouch of the 7th Queen's Own Hussars, scarlet cloth bearing embroidered Guelphic crown and 'QO' monogram, gilt mounts, red morocco backing, in good condition.

£600-800   **W&W**

A Victorian officer's full dress embroidered sabretache of the 7th Queen's Own Hussars, regimental gilt lace border, embroidered Guelphic crown over QO monogram, in its velvet lined red leather foul weather cover, in very good condition.

£2,500-3,500   **W&W**

A Victorian officer's full dress embroidered sabretache, of the West Yorkshire Yeomanry, blue velvet on blue morocco backing, broad silver lace border, in the centre an embroidered crown, silver plated rose, in very good condition.

c1860

£2,000-2,500   **W&W**

A post-1902 officer's blue cloth shabraque of The 1st Life Guards, embroidered Tudor crown, regimental cipher with battle honour scrolls and badge, khaki kerseyme lining, the pistol holster covers with black bearskin cover, Tudor crowned cipher.

£2,500-3,500   **W&W**

A 17thC Scottish powder horn, of flattened curved cow horn, naively engraved with flowers, thistles and figures and marked 'A*L 1693', the wide end plugged with a simple wooden section, the open pointed terminal with no mounts.

9.75in (25cm) long

£1,800-2,200   L&T

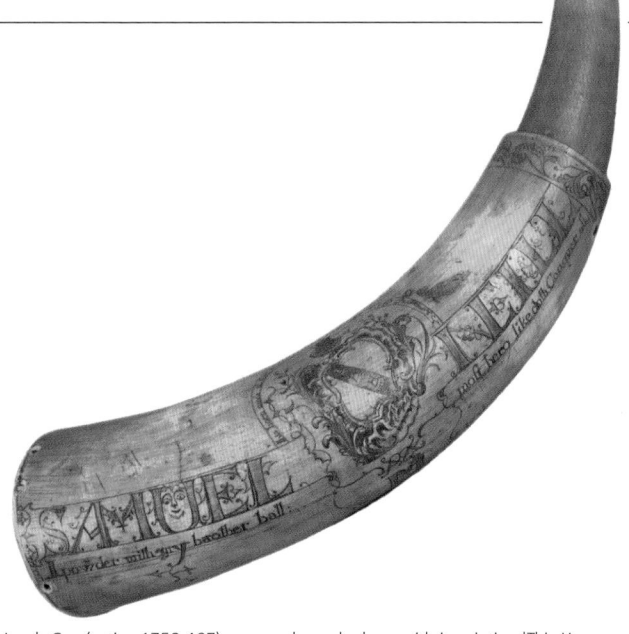

A Jacob Gay (active 1758-187) engraved powder horn with inscription 'This Horn made at Fort Edward May 15, 1758. Samuel McNeill, I powder with my brother ball: most hero like doth conquer all', flanking a cartouche with shell over a family crest.

11in (28cm) long

£25,000-35,000   POOK

An early two-way leather covered pistol powder flask, with plain brass nozzle, hinged cover to compartment containing six lead balls, in good condition.

5in (12.5cm) long

£650-850   W&W

A leather shot flask, by Dixon & Sons, with patent brass top, embossed on one side with a scene of hunting dogs in an oval, the top featuring a spring loaded cover operated by the removal of the scoop.

9in (23cm) high

£150-250   W&W

A small red leather covered pistol flask, with non-adjustable tapered charger, the brass work retaining traces of original lacquer.

3.5in (9cm) long

£800-1,000   W&W

MEDALS

A Military General Service medal 1793-1814, clasps for 'Talavera', 'Busaco', 'Fuentes D'Onor', 'Cuidad Rodrigo', 'Salamanca', 'Vittoria', 'Nivelle', 'Nive', awarded to W. Poulter, Sergt, 3rd Foot Gds.

£3,000-4,000   W&W

A Naval General Service medal, 1793-1840, with original carton inscribed 'List 1-Part 1 867 Medal and 2 clasps, 1 for Lissa 13th March 1811 2 Pelagosa 29 Novr 1811. 'George Haye Lieut. For my son Thos Davey Haye. Recd the 17 Feby 1849', the corners of the carton split, together with the recipient's letter book with copies of letters sent and received during the 1840s.

£12,000-18,000   W&W

A Waterloo medal, awarded to Christopher Bausen, 2nd Regiment Light Dragoons, King's German Legion, June 18th 1815.

£1,800-2,200   LT

A Victorian officer's silver plated elongated Maltese Cross pouch belt badge of The 2nd City of London Rifles, three studs, in very good condition.

£150-250   W&W

A China War medal, awarded to K. Wilson, 55th Regiment, with ribbon, dated.

1842

£450-550   LT

A Military General Service medal, with three bars 'Toulouse', 'Orthes' and 'Vittoria', dated.

1848

£450-550   LT

A Punjab medal, awarded to R. Moss, 1st Battalion 60th R. Rifles, with two bars 'Mooltan' and 'Goojerat', with ribbon, dated.

1849

£450-550   LT

Two sets of medals, the pair for Baltic 1845 and Crimea, no clasps, and the group of three for South Africa 1877-79, Egypt 1882 (1 clasp 'Alexandria 11th July') and Naval Long Service and Good Conduct.

Believed to be a family group of five.

£800-1,000   W&W

An India General Service medal, 1854, one clasp for 'Bhootan', awarded to Lieut C.G. Millet 11th NI, NEF with uneven tone.

Lieut C.G. Millet was killed in action at Chumarchi, January 1865 and is listed, with 14 other officers, on a tablet in St Paul's Cathedral, Calcutta, erected by Bhotan Field Force comrades.

£1,200-1,800   W&W

An Indian Mutiny medal, awarded to Frederek Gordon, 79th Highlanders, with bar 'Lucknow', with ribbon, dated.

1857-58

£350-450   LT

A New Zealand Campaign medal, awarded to William Clarke, A. B., H. M. S. Curacao.

1863-1864

£550-750   LT

A South Africa Campaign medal, awarded to Pte Exter D of E Vol Rifles, with one bar, with ribbon, dated.

1877-8

£350-450   LT

A rare officer's gilt and silver plate 1829 (Bell-top) shako plate of The 13th (First Somersetshire Light Infantry) Regiment, 'Egypt', '13' in strung bugle, on crowned star.

£1,200-1,800 W&W

An officer's gilt 1844 (Albert) pattern shako plate of The 84th York and Lancaster Regiment, in good condition, the gilt fresh, minor distressing to lower three ray tips.

£800-1,000 W&W

An officer's gilt 1844 (Albert) pattern shako plate of The 6th (Royal First Warwickshire) Regiment, silver plated antelope to shield, in very good condition.

£700-800 W&W

A Victorian officer's silver plated elongated Maltese Cross pouch belt badge of The 2nd City of London Rifles, three studs, in very good condition.

£150-250 W&W

A Victorian officer's white metal fur cap grenade badge of a Volunteer Battalion of The Northumberland Fusiliers, applied design on ball, blades and lugs fastening, in good condition.

£150-250 W&W

The Most Eminent Order of the Indian Empire, C.I.E., 1877-86, Companion's first type breast badge with 'India' on the petals, gold and enamels, complete with top suspension brooch, in its R. & S. Garrard & Co. case of issue.

£2,000-2,500 DNW

A Royal Masonic Benevolent Institution, Province of Sussex HM silver and enamelled locket, Birmingham, 1897, with a jubilee medal with bar 14 June 1897 VF, a Founder's jewel Earl of Clarendon Chapter, 3 Masonic Steward jewels 1899-1931 period, two other jewels, and Institute bars covering 1900-1932.

£300-400 W&W

A Scottish silver provincial Balmoral Highlanders' cap badge, William Robb, Ballater, with raised legend 'NEMO ME IMPUNE LACESSIT' and applied lion sergeant to centre, marked 'ROBB/ Ballater' and inscribed 'E.R.I. 1904'.

c1904 *2in (5cm) diam*

£450-550 L&T

A large silver and enamel badge of The Order of St Patrick, possibly for a senior officer's shabraque of 4th Royal Irish Dragoon Guards, seven loop fasteners on reverse, slight chipping to shamrock centre.

9.5in (24cm) high

£700-800 W&W

A Knight Bachelor's badge, HM 1926, EF, in silver gilt and enamel.

3in (7.5cm) high

£300-400 W&W

A rare Third Reich Auxiliary Cruiser badge, appears to be Beadle 141, in good condition.

£250-350 W&W

ANTIQUITIES

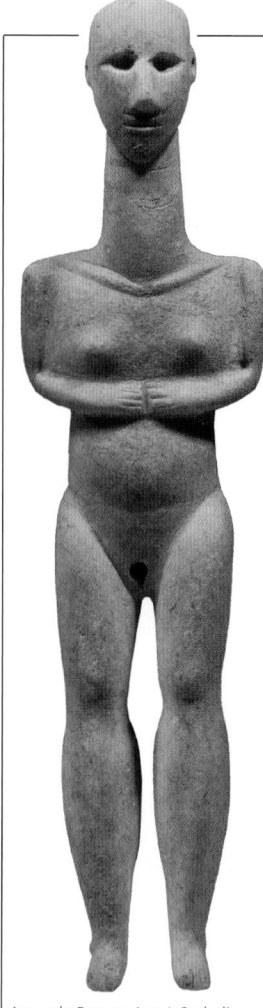

A Bactrian bronze cosmetic vessel, in the form of an animal, perhaps the Saiga antelope or an extinct relative, a pin surmounted by a bird inserted into the vessel's neck.

c1500BC · 5in (12.5cm) high

£70,000-100,000 · **SOTH**

A wood ushabiti of Rameses IX, 20th Dynasty, holding hoes and seed-sack, nine lines of inscription in front, including his prenomen Neferkare-Setepenre.

The mummiform statuette holds the tools the shabti will need to perform its duties. On its forehead is an uraeus or cobra, attribute of kings, queens and several gods. Rameses IX reigned 1131-1112BC.

12in (31cm) high

£350,000-450,000 · **SOTH**

A brilliant blue faience ushabti of Pinudjem II, High Priest of Amun, 21st Dynasty, the overseer holding a whip in his left hand and wearing a kilt and striped wig with diadem, the projecting fold of his garment inscribed, the details painted in black.

c950BC

£25,000-35,000 · **SOTH**

An early Bronze Age I Cycladic marble figure of a man, of Plastiras type, lying with his hands resting on his abdomen, remains of red pigment on neck and face.

c3200-2700BC · 11.5in (29cm) high

£1,000,000+ · **SOTH**

A Ptolemaic period basalt bust of a queen or goddess, wearing a pleated garment leaving her right shoulder bare, long tripartite wig, and fragmentary uraeus, a hole on top of the head for a missing crown.

305-30BC · 13.5in (35cm) h

£800,000+ · **SOTH**

An ancient possibly Egyptian polychrome painted carved wooden figure of a falcon, with diamond painted feather decoration in shades of blue and red.

3.5in (9cm) long

£400-500 · **GORL**

A 2nd/1stC BC Hellenistic/early Roman Imperial Chalcedony portrait head of a deified queen or empress, wearing a veil and diadem decorated with a medallion showing a bust in profile between two stars.

2in (5cm) high

£650,000-750,000 · **SOTH**

A mid-1stC BC late Republican/early Augustan Roman marble portrait bust of a woman, her hair bound in a pointed headcloth with lappet behind, set onto a European marble plinth and socle.

9.75in (25cm) high

£250,000-350,000 · **SOTH**

A Ptolemaic period limestone relief, with the owner standing on the right with raised hands, Osiris in the middle (part erased) wearing a tall crown flanked by feathers, Isis standing in head-dress and holding the ankh sign, hieroglyphs above and below.

c304-30BC · 9.5in (24cm) high

£900-1,200 · **WW**

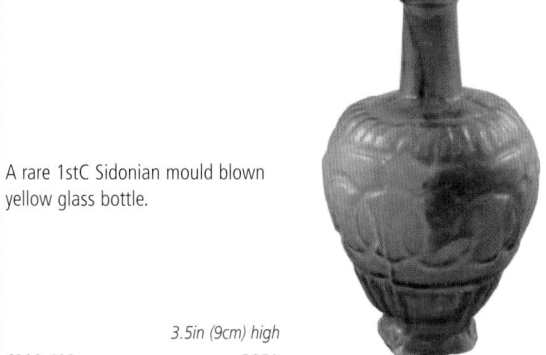

A rare 1stC Sidonian mould blown yellow glass bottle.

3.5in (9cm) high

£300-400   GORL

A 1stC Roman strap handled shouldered blue glass jug.

4.25in (11cm) high

£500-700   GORL

A 1stC Roman purple glass jug.

4in (10cm) high

£700-1,000   GORL

A 3rd/4thC Roman black glass head flask.

2.5in (6.5cm) high

£500-700   GORL

A large 4thC Roman iridescent glass jug, with combed handle, repaired.

8.75in (22cm) high

£600-800   GORL

A 4thC late Roman pale green glass lamp, with blue spot decoration.

5.75in (14.5cm) high

£650-850   GORL

A 4th/5thC Roman two-handled glass jar, with blue zigzag decoration.

3in (7.5cm) high

£200-300   GORL

A 12thC Islamic tall neck bottle, with cut decoration.

7in (18cm) high

£500-700   GORL

A modern Italian violin, by Romeo Antoniazi, Milan, labelled 'ANTONIAZZI ROMEO CREMONESE, FECE A CREMONA L ANNO 1925' and signed, two piece back.

1925   *Back 15in (35.5cm) high*

£18,000-22,000   **SK**

An Italian violin, ascribed to Giovanni Battista Ceruti, labelled 'JO BAPTISTA CERUTI CREMONENSIS, FECIT CREMONAE AN 1809, GBC', two piece back.

Back 14in (35.5cm) high

£35,000-45,000   **SK**

A modern violin, from Garimberti Workshop, branded 'F GARIMBERTI MILANO', labelled 'FERDINANDO GARIMBERTI PARMENSE, FECE IN MILANO 1931 FG', signed.

Back 14in (35.5cm) high

£6,500-8,500   **SK**

An Italian viola, by Giuseppe Nadotti, Placenza, labelled 'JOSEPH NADOTTI, FECIT PLACENTAE 1782', two piece back, with case.

This violin passed through the hands of famous New York violin dealer, Emil Herrmann (1888-1968), and Hungarian-born composer Sandor Salgo (1909-2007).

c1782   *Back 16in (40.5cm) high*

£50,000-70,000   **SK**

An Italian violin, with paper label 'Cav. Raffaelle Calace, Napoli', inscribed '1888', with a two piece back, LOB.

14.5in (37cm) long

£650-850   **WW**

CLOSER LOOK – GAGLIANO VIOLIN

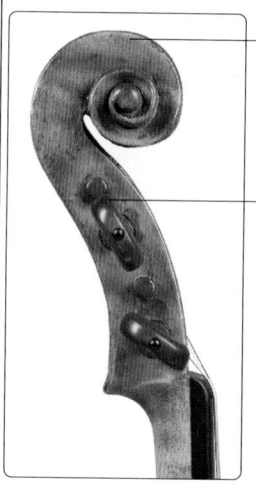

The head is believed to be later, made by Joseph Gagliano.

Gagliano's pieces were finished with a fiery red-gold varnish, adding to their attractiveness.

Later makers were strongly influenced by Gagliano's work, including Gennaro Vinaccia and Vincenzo Sannino.

The violin is finely carved and elegantly proportioned. Such attention to detail contributes to the mellow tone for which Gagliano's work is famed.

An Italian violin, by Alessandro Gagliano, Naples, labelled 'NICOLAUS GAGLIANO FILIUS, ALEXANDRI FECIT NEAP 1754' and '9471', the later head probably by Joseph Gagliano, one piece back, with case.

Alessandro Gagliano was a prominent maker of stringed instruments from c1700-35 in Naples. He started his career in the shops of famous violin makers Nicolo Amati and Antonio Stradivari in Cremona, later going on to found the Neapolitan school. Few examples of his work have survived but some violas, cellos, one double bass and several violins are known.

c1720

£55,000-85,000   **SK**

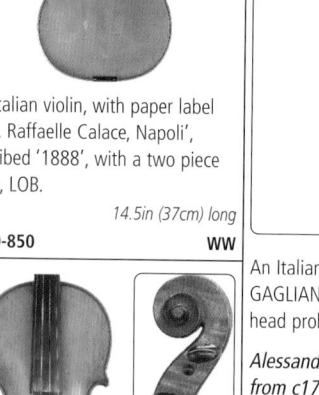

A French Stradivarius copy violin, the jointed back of medium curl with similar wood to the sides and head, the table of a medium grain and the varnish a golden-brown colour.

c1900   *14.25in (36cm) high*

£600-800   **GHOU**

A New York maple violin, labelled by Frederic D. Rich, Yonkers, the scroll with an amusing carved and painted bust of a gentleman, retaining its original ochre grain decorated case.

1829   *23.75in (60.5cm) long*

£3,000-4,000   **POOK**

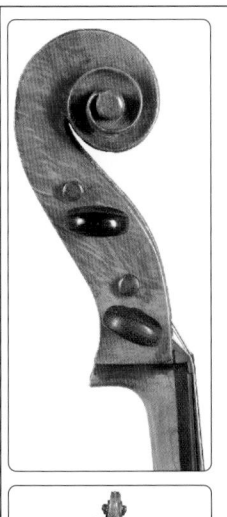

An Italian Neapolitan school violoncello, ascribed to Giovanni Gagliano, labelled 'FERDINANDO GAGLIANO FILIUS, NICOLAI FECIT NEAP 1795', two piece back, with case.

Back 28.75in (75.5cm) high

£100,000-120,000   SK

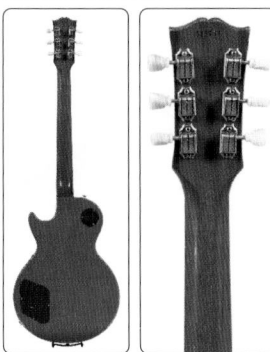

An American Gibson Incorporated electric guitar, Kalamazoo, Model Les Paul, the headstock with 'GIBSON' pearl inlay, silkscreened 'LES PAUL MODEL' and stamped '513763' at the reverse, with original case and hang tag.

1955   Body 17.25in (44cm) high

£25,000-35,000   SK

A Gretsch 1978 Chet Atkins Country Gentleman electric guitar, model 7670, with maple back, sides and neck, ebony fingerboard, gold plated hardware, Bigsby tall piece, Chet Atkins signature on pick guard, within the original Gretsch hard shell case.

£1,200-1,800   GHOU

An American C.F. Martin & Company guitar, Nazareth, style 00-42, stamped 'CF MARTIN & CO, NAZARETH PA', with later case, with original tuning machines.

1922   Back 19.5in (49.5cm) high

£10,000-12,000   SK

DECORATIVE ARTS

While sales in the field of decorative arts in the last twelve months have remained steady, there has nevertheless been a shift in buying trends. In general, the market has seen a retrenchment to more traditional collecting areas during this time, with collectors looking for the reassurance of the big names and avoiding the uncertainties of attributions and lesser followers. The result has been a rise in sales (and prices) of high-end items and stagnation in prices at the mid-to-low end of collecting.

The extreme example of this polarisation was demonstrated when a world-record price was achieved by a pair of armchairs, designed by Eileen Gray circa 1917. These chairs realised just over £20,000,000 in Paris in February at Christie's Yves Saint Laurent-Pierre Bergé sale, proving there is still plenty of money in the market for the right quality and provenance.

There have been considerably fewer exceptional lots offered to the market this year, reflecting a general reluctance on the part of sellers to bring good-quality pieces to auction during the economic downturn. Those that have, however, will have benefited from strong competition from collectors starved of the better quality lots.

The market base, a large group of older, more established collectors, has been devoted to the decorative arts for over a generation and each of the main styles – Arts & Crafts, Art Nouveau and Art Deco – has a strong following. The market for smaller items, including ceramics, woodblock prints, and wrought metal, is considerably more buoyant at the moment, with the best pieces at, or near, the peak levels of two years ago. It's a lot easier to add a vase to a collection, than a bookcase and collectors remain active.

Among the good performers this year have been Arts & Crafts ceramics from the Martin Brothers, William de Morgan and the perennial favourite, Moorcroft, all of which continue to be strong. Named Arts & Crafts pieces continue to be hard to find and prices reflect this rarity. In Art Nouveau glass, big names such as Lalique, Gallé and Tiffany are selling well, and rare Art Deco pieces of Whitefriars glass continue to achieve high prices at auction. High-end Art Deco works, including bronze and ivory figures by the big names such as Ferdinand Preiss and Demètre Chiparus have also performed well. In British Art Deco ceramics, Clarice Cliff continues to sell well – the popularity of her work possibly owing to the supply of fresh pieces that continue to come to market each year – while Wedgwood Fairyland lustre has seen a growth in interest amongst collectors in recent months.

There are still areas of weakness in the middle market, however, particularly for pottery of the Ohio school, including Rookwood and Roseville. There has also been less stability in the prices of furniture, probably because people are not moving to larger houses or building additions. This has particularly been true of mid-range pieces in less than original condition. It remains true that the very best pieces in pristine condition continue to sell at record levels.

Clockwise from top left: Marblehead tile incised by Arthur Baggs, £71,200 at Rago Auctions; Chiparus 'Egyptian Dancer' c1925, £36,100 at Quitttenbaum; Wedgwood Fairyland lustre malfrey pot, £20,500 at James D Julia.

DECORATIVE ARTS

ESSENTIAL REFERENCE – AMPHORA

The company that was later to be known as Amphora was founded in 1892 in Turn-Teplitz, Bohemia (now the Czech Republic) by Eduard Stellmacher, his brothers-in-law Hans and Karl Riessner, and Rudolf Kessel. It was incorporated as Riessner, Stellmacher & Kessel.

- The towns of Turn and Teplitz formed a pottery production centre, with its many companies prospering due to the abundant supplies of kaolin clay (an essential ingredient of porcelain) in nearby riverbeds. The words 'Turn-Teplitz' often appear on the bottom of Amphora ceramics.
- Amphora vessels were made from 'ivory porcelain', a matte yellowish material developed by Eduard's father, Alfred Stellmacher, in the 1870s.
- The company originally imitated the Orientalist and Neo-Baroque styles favoured by Alfred, but quickly developed a unique genre of Art Nouveau ceramics. Amphora's stylistic diversity and quality made it a world leader among industrial manfactuers of Art Pottery.
- The word 'Amphora' consistently appeared on pieces after the late 1890s. After the departure of Eduard Stellmacher, the firm was officially renamed 'Riessner & Kessel Amphora'.
- Common motifs from Amphora's golden age, 1894-1904, include plants (painted and applied flowers and fruit), animals, prehistoric/mythical creatures, portraits in the styles of Klimt and Mucha, biomorphism, and simulated jewelling.

A Reissner, Stellmacher & Kessel Art Nouveau 'Fairy Tale Princess' amphora vase, model '2041', applied with jewels, in colours highlighted in gilt, printed and impressed marks.

11.5in (29.5cm) high

£3,500-4,500   **WW**

An Amphora vase, designed by Paul Dachsel, with gilded ladybirds on indigo and mother-of-pearl floral clusters, stamped 'TURN-TEPLITZ PD/MADE IN AUSTRIA 113 3'.

13in (33cm) high

£6,000-8,000   **DRA**

A tall Art Nouveau Reissner, Stellmacher & Kessel vase, with a delicate maiden in profile beneath reticulated leaves, marked 'Amphora 697 52 750.1029.', red 'RSTK Turn-Teplitz' stamp, wear to gilding.

16in (40.5cm) high

£7,000-9,000   **DRA**

An Art Nouveau Reissner, Stellmacher & Kessel vase, with maidens peering out of water, with reticulated lilies, stamped Amphora Art Nouveau medallion, red 'RSTK Turn-Teplitz' mark and '2007 41', restoration to a single petal.

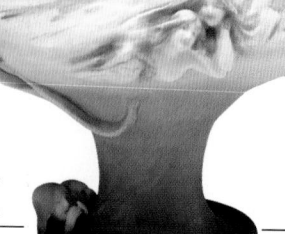

8in (20.5cm) high

£800-1,000   **DRA**

A rare Adelaide Robineau porcelain vase, covered in oxblood and celadon glaze on crackled ground, four iris-carved handles, carved 'AR', '1920', '48', secured firing cracks.

4in (10cm) high

£6,000-7,000   **DRA**

A porcelain kylyx bowl-form, by Adelaide Robineau, with a café-au-lait exterior with fully-blown blue crystals, black handles and a rose-to-brown interior, tight line to rim, restoration to small chip at rim.

8in (20.5cm) diam

£1,000-1,300   **DRA**

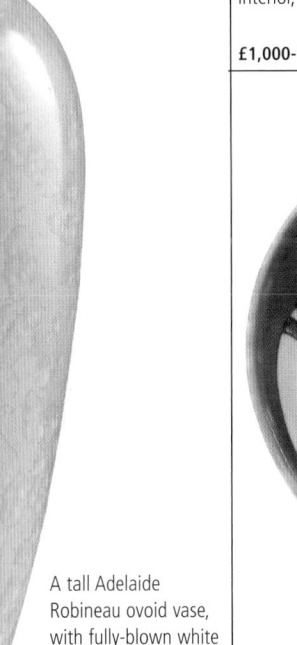

A tall Adelaide Robineau ovoid vase, with fully-blown white crystals on ivory ground, excised 'AR', incised '48'.

10in (25.5cm) high

£12,000-15,000   **DRA**

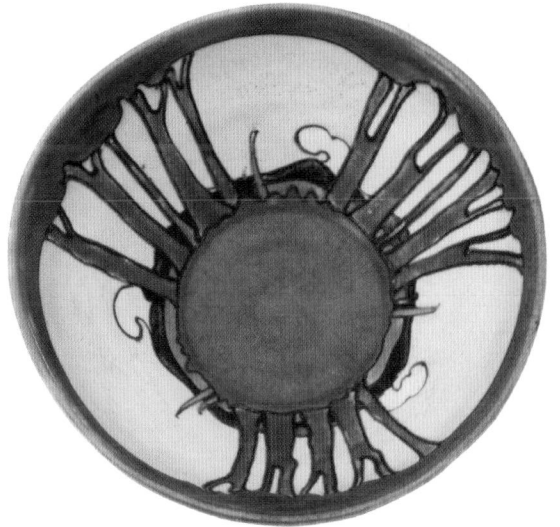

An Arequipa flaring bowl, by Frederick Rhead, the interior decorated in squeezebag with clusters of stylised trees in front of dark mountains and white clouds, with ink mark 'Arequipa California 269'.

6.25in (16cm) diam

£12,000-15,000   **DRA**

An Arequipa ovoid vase, decorated in squeezebag with chains of leaves, minor hairline cracks.

6.25in (16cm) high

£3,000-4,000   **DRA**

An Arequipa squat vessel, decorated in squeezebag with peacock feathers in brown and black on a turquoise ground, with blue ink stamp.

This is an unusual design and technique for this maker.

1912   *4.5in (11.5cm) wide*

£2,500-3,500   **DRA**

A Chelsea Keramic Art Works superlative vase, with an applied 'tableau' painted with two houses, surrounded by ivy, on a free-form vase in mottled blue glaze, stamped 'CKAW', minor nicks to leaves.

8in (20.5cm) high

£1,800-2,300   DRA

A Chelsea Keramic Art Works bottle-shaped vase, applied with clover leaves and blossoms, under glossy and fine vellum glaze, stamped 'CKAW', minute flecks to leaves.

8.25in (21cm) wide

£1,500-2,000   DRA

A rare Chelsea Keramic Art Works crackleware vase, painted with prunus branches, stamped 'CKAW', artists' signatures 'CFD' and 'DPR', two kiln kisses.

6.5in (16.5cm) high

£900-1,200   DRA

A Chelsea Keramic Art Works pitcher, with applied berries and leaves on vines, against a hammered ground, covered in glossy green glaze, stamped 'CKAW'.

7.5in (19cm) high

£1,800-2,300   DRA

A tall rare early Chelsea Keramic Art Works vase, with applied blooming vines and Italian Renaissance masks, in a burnished clay finish, artist's signature 'WFG', stamped 'CHELSEA KERAMIC ART WORKS/ROBERTSON & SONS'.

£2,500-3,000   DRA

A Clewell copper-clad vase, with a good verdigris patina, incised 'Clewell 351-2-9'.

7in (18cm) high

£800-1,000   DRA

A Clewell faceted copper-clad vase, with excellent verdigris patina, incised 'Clewell 438-2-6'.

9.25in (23.5cm) high

£1,200-1,500   DRA

A rare Clewell solid bronze urn, covered in verdigris patina, incised 'Clu Clewell 501-21', filled-in hole on bottom.

9in (23cm) high

£1,600-1,900   DRA

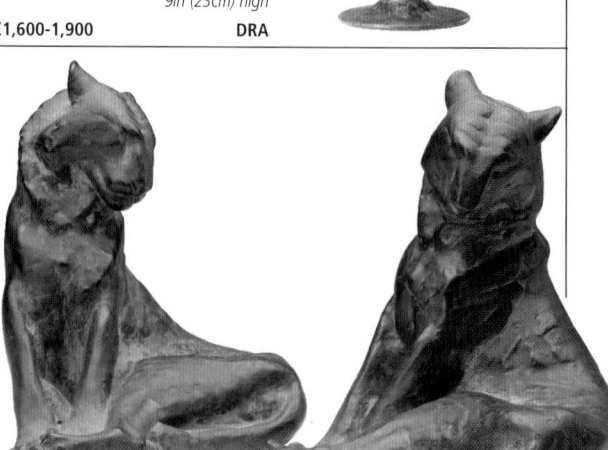

A pair of rare Clewell copper-clad cougar bookends.

8.5in (21.5cm) high

£3,000-4,500   DRA

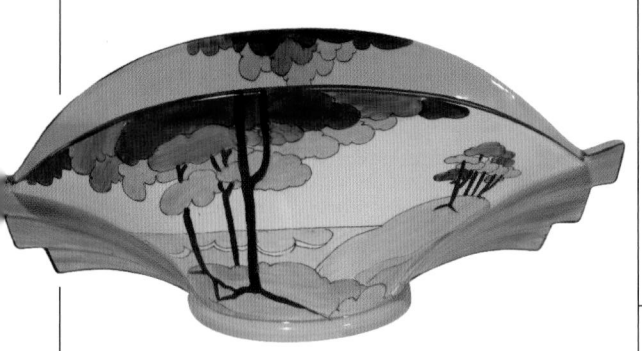

A Clarice Cliff 'Blue Firs' Bizarre Daffodil vase, shape no. 450, painted in colours, printed mark.

Introduced in 1933, Clarice Cliff's 'Blue Firs' pattern features a pen-outlined green landscape with blue fir trees, with a beach in the foreground and sometimes a cottage. Similar patterns include the earliest variation 'Coral Firs' (introduced in 1933) and 'Green Firs' (introduced in 1934).

1933   13.25in (33.5cm) wide
£2,200-2,800   **WW**

A Clarice Cliff 'Applique Lucerne (orange)' Bizarre coffee pot, painted in colours on an orange ground, printed and painted marks, crack to top rim.
1930-31   *7in (18cm) high*
£700-900   **WW**

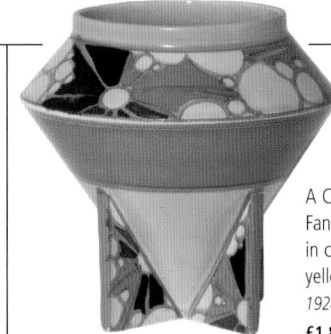

A Clarice Cliff 'Black Broth' Fantasque Bizarre 400 vase, painted in colours between orange and yellow bands, printed marks.
1928   6in (15.5cm) high
£1,800-2,200   **WW**

A rare Clarice Cliff 'Café' miniature vase, designed by Clarice Cliff, painted in shades of red, black and grey, printed mark.
1931   2.25in (5.5cm) high
£3,500-4,500   **WW**

A rare Clarice Cliff 'Autumn Crocus' Bizarre Yo Yo vase, painted in colours between yellow and brown bands, printed and painted mark.

1928   *9in (23cm) high*
£3,000-3,500   **WW**

A Clarice Cliff 'Delecia' vase, designed by Clarice Cliff, shape no. 186, painted in colours, printed factory mark.

1929-30   *6in (15cm) high*

£150-200   **WW**

A Clarice Cliff 'Double V' Bizarre 206 vase, painted in colours between orange and blue bands, printed marks, minor paint loss.

1929   *6in (15.5cm) high*

£350-450   **WW**

A Clarice Cliff 'Erin (orange)' Bizarre Biarritz plate, painted in colours, printed factory mark.

1933   *9in (23cm) wide*

£500-700   **WW**

A Clarice Cliff 'Flowers and Squares' Bizarre Heath fern pot, designed by Clarice Cliff, painted in colours, printed factory mark.

1930   *3in (7.5cm) high*

£180-220   **WW**

A Clarice Cliff 'Forest Glen' single-handled Isis, painted in colours, printed marks.

1935   *10.25in (26cm) high*

£550-650   **WW**

A Clarice Cliff 'Fruitburst' Fantasque Bizarre Conical jug, designed by Clarice Cliff, painted in colours, printed factory mark.

1930   *5.5in (14cm) high*

£300-350   **WW**

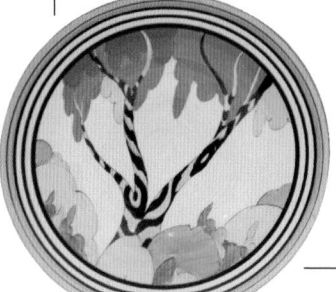

A small Clarice Cliff ribbed charger, in the 'Honolulu' pattern, with a zebra trunk tree with orange, red and yellow foliage within green and black banded borders, printed mark.

12.75in (32.5cm) diam

£800-1,200   **FLD**

CLOSER LOOK – CLARICE CLIFF TEASET

Heavily outlined and stylised designs are typical of Cliff's work, a style she developed in the 1920s, working on blanks in her Newport studio.

The Bizarre range, launched in 1928 as inexpensive domestic pottery, was highly successful. It had a distinctive warm yellow 'honey' glaze.

At the time, Cliff's designs were exuberant, outrageous and hugely popular, flying in the face of drab utility ware.

The visible brushstrokes became a selling point, indicating that the pieces were handpainted.

A Clarice Cliff 'Gibraltar' Bizarre Stamford tea trio, comprising teapot and cover, milk-jug and sugar basin, painted in colours, printed factory mark, Lawleys retailer's mark, small chip to inside of teapot cover.

1931   *Teapot 5in (12.5cm) high*

£3,500-5,500   **WW**

A Clarice Cliff Bizarre charger, 'Latona Red Roses', black printed Newport Pottery mark, black painted 'Latona'

1929-30   13in (33.5cm) diam

£550-650   DN

A Clarice Cliff 'Limberlost' Fantasque Bizarre miniature vase, designed by Clarice Cliff, painted in colours, printed marks.

1932   2.25in (6cm) high

£400-600   WW

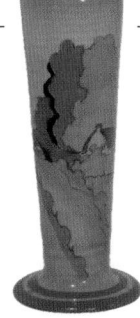

A Clarice Cliff 'Lorna' vase, probably a sample, painted in colours over a Goldstone ground, printed mark, painted feather motif.

1936   10in (25.5cm) high

£300-400   WW

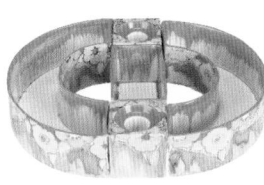

A Clarice Cliff Bizarre table centre, decorated in a variation of the 'Lydiat' pattern, comprising a pair of square-shaped candlesticks, shape 658, an oblong trough, shape 657, and a pair of semi-circular troughs, shape 659.

1933   Candlesticks 2.5in (6.5cm) wide

£200-400   A&G

A rare Clarice Cliff 'May Avenue' Bizarre miniature vase, probably a salesman's sample, painted in colours, printed factory marks.

'May Avenue' was introduced in 1933. The pattern features a pen-outlined avenue of red-roofed houses and spade-shaped trees. Along with 'Appliqué', 'Inspiration', 'Sunray', 'Mountain' and 'Solitude', 'May Avenue' is one of the most rare and desirable patterns.

1933   2.25in (6cm) high

£3,000-4,000   WW

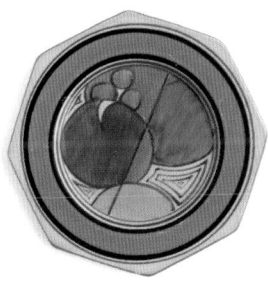

A Clarice Cliff 'Melon' Fantasque Bizarre side plate, designed by Clarice Cliff, painted in colours, printed factory mark.

1930   5.75in (14.5cm) diam

£200-300   WW

A Clarice Cliff 'Original Bizarre' vase, designed by Clarice Cliff, shape no. 265, painted in colours, printed factory mark, small chip to base rim.

1928   6in (15cm) high

£200-250   WW

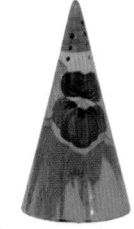

A Clarice Cliff 'Pastel Melon' Bizarre Conical sugar sifter, painted in colours, printed factory mark.

1930   5.5in (14cm) high

£800-1,000   WW

A Clarice Cliff 'Pansies' Fantasque Bizarre Conical sugar sifter, painted in colours, printed and painted marks.

1932   5.5in (14cm) high

£550-650   WW

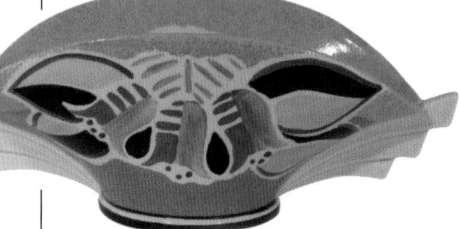

A Clarice Cliff 'Nuage Canterbury Bells' Fantasque Bizarre Daffodil vase, shape no. 450, painted in colours, printed mark.

1932   13in (33cm) wide

£700-1,000   WW

A Clarice Cliff 'Patina Tree Red' Bizarre Globe vase, shape no. 370, painted in colours, painted factory marks.

1932-33   6in (15cm) high

£1,000-1,500   WW

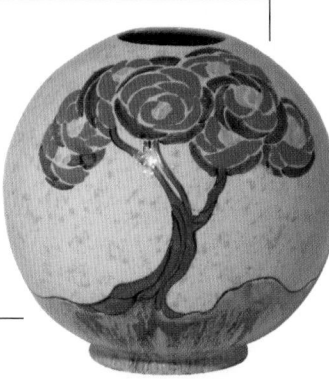

A William De Morgan solifleur vase, with knopped neck, painted with stylised flowers and foliage in ruby lustre on white, impressed tulip mark.

9.75in (24.5cm) high

£1,200-1,800 **WW**

A William De Morgan rice dish, on Staffordshire blank painted in ruby lustre with a frieze of birds, impressed knot, chip to back rim.

11.75in (30cm) diam

£700-1,000 **WW**

A William De Morgan bowl, painted with repeating palmettes, in shades of ruby lustre on a white ground, repaired.

13in (33cm)

£300-400 **WW**

A William De Morgan 'Persian' earthenware vase, by Fred Passenger, shouldered form applied with twin looped serpent handles, decorated with painted fish, painted 'D M Fulham', 'FP' monogram '24', professional restoration.

11.5in (29cm) high

£3,000-5,000 **WW**

A large William De Morgan 'Persian Fan' tile, painted in shades of blue and green with carnation flowers, stamped 'William De Morgan', minor nicks.

8.5in (21.5cm) wide

£1,000-1,500 **WW**

A William De Morgan 'Persian' earthenware charger, painted with a serpent and stylised flowers, painted 'WDM Fulham', minor glaze loss to rim.

11.25in (28.5cm) diam

£1,200-1,800 **WW**

A William De Morgan plate, by Charles Passenger, painted with a bird of prey fighting a lizard, in ruby and sand lustre, painted 'CP'.

8.25in (21cm) diam

£2,200-2,500 **WW**

A William De Morgan 'Mongolian' five-tile panel, impressed 'Sands End Pottery' mark, repairs to one tile and two spacer tiles, framed.

30in (76cm) long

£1,800-2,200 **WW**

A William De Morgan 'Persian' earthenware vase, with knopped neck, painted with mythical birds, impressed mark, minor glaze loss to top rim.

8.25in (21cm) high

£1,800-2,200   WW

A plastic clay William de Morgan tile, decorated with a repeat green, black and blue floral motif in the Islamic taste over cream glazed ground.

6in (15cm) wide

£150-200   FLD

A Wedgwood dust-pressed tile bank, decorated by William de Morgan in ruby lustre with a grid motif detailed with floral sprigs and dodo birds.

6in (15cm) wide

£300-400   FLD

A William de Morgan 'Marlborough' tile, on an Architectural Pottery Co., Poole blank, with moulded mark.

6in (15.5cm) wide

£300-400   DN

A William de Morgan late Fulham 'Cavendish' tile, with impressed 'DM 98'.

6in (15.5cm) wide

£250-350   DN

ESSENTIAL RFERENCE – DOULTON

Initially specialising in useful stoneware, Doulton & Co. was established by John Doulton, Martha Jones and John Watts at Lambeth, South London, in 1815, as 'Doulton & Watts'. It was known as such until 1851 when Doulton's son Henry (1820–97) renamed it Henry Doulton & Co.

- In c1860, the factory began a revival of earlier types of stoneware, notably copies of 18thC stoneware vessels, and salt-glazed wares with blue decoration.
- Doulton began producing art pottery in the early 1870s. These included hand-thrown pieces, that were created and glazed by students of the nearby Lambeth School of Art.
- In 1901 King Edward VII granted Doulton's factory in Burslem, Staffordshire the Royal Warrant. This allowed the business to adopt new markings (which appeared in 1902) and a new name: Royal Doulton.
- Figures were produced from 1913 under the direction of Charles Noke (1858-1941). These figures were all given an individual 'HN' number, after the manager of the painting department, Harry Nixon.
- During the 1920s-1930s, Art Deco functional tablewares, as well as purely decorative pieces and collectable bone china figures, many of which were designed by Lesley Harradine.
- The Lambeth factory closed in 1956, but production continues at Burslem.

A Victorian Doulton Lambeth stoneware vase, by Margaret Aitken, of baluster form, with raised rosette and reeded scroll decoration, signed to the body and to the base, with impressed marks.

11in (28cm) high

£700-800   DUK

A Victorian Doulton Lambeth stoneware vase, by Hannah Barlow, of tapering form, decorated in sgraffito with stags and deer, with blue glaze borders, impressed mark and signatures to the base.

12in (30.5cm) high

£1,000-1,200   DUK

DECORATIVE ARTS

A Doulton Lambeth stoneware vase, by Hannah Barlow and Eliza Simmance, of tapering baluster form, with sgraffito decoration of donkeys and sheep.

20in (51cm) high

£350-550   **DUK**

A pair of Doulton vases, by Hannah Barlow, sgraffito-decorated with a band of horses in a field, within heart-and-scroll decorated borders, impressed marks and monogram.

c1895   16in (40.5cm) high

£900-1,200   **HALL**

A Doulton Lambeth amphora vase, by Frank Butler, supported by winged lions, with scrolling foliage sgraffito decoration, faults.

16.5in (42cm) high

£2,000-3,000   **GORL**

A Doulton Lambeth stoneware vase, enamel decorated and modelled in relief, artist monogram for Mark V. Marshall, impressed mark.

Modelled for the Paris Exhibition of 1900.

c1890   17in (43cm) high

£11,000-13,000   **SK**

A Doulton Lambeth stoneware flagon, of moon flask design, with a raised profile of Toby Philpot, with hallmarked silver rim for Asprey's, impressed mark to base.

9.5in (24cm) high

£1,000-1,200   **DUK**

A Doulton Lambeth stoneware biscuit jar and cover, by Hannah Barlow, no. 664, impressed factory mark, artist's monogram, dated.

1879   9in (23cm) high

£2,000-2,200   **TEN**

A Royal Doulton stoneware jug, by Mark V. Marshall, incised with scrolling foliage design, the handle with mask terminal, in colours, impressed mark, incised 'M.V.M'.

7.75in (20cm) high

£600-900   **WW**

A pair of Doulton Lambeth stoneware jardinières and pedestals, Frank A. Butler, each piece stamped 'Doulton Lambeth 1876', one jardinière inscribed 'FAB', some losses.

1876   Jardinières 19in (48cm) wide

£5,000-6,000   **DRA**

ESSENTIAL REFERENCE – DOULTON LAMBETH

In 1866 John Sparkes, then director of the Lambeth School of Art, asked Henry Doulton to give employment to Lambeth students as an act of philanthropy. George Tinworth (1843-1913) subsequently came to work at the factory, and in 1871 Doulton exhibited art pottery for the first time to great acclaim. The show included 70 pieces, many of them by Tinworth, and some by another Lambeth pupil, Hannah Barlow.

- Hannah Barlow (1851-1916) and her sister Florence (d1909) decorated pieces with sgraffito-style inscribed animals and other scenes. This 'Barlow ware' became extremely popular, and the Barlows were prolific: Hannah worked for Doulton for 40 years, producing up to 1,000 designs a year. Their brother, Arthur also worked for Doulton.
- George Tinworth worked for Doulton until his death. Much of his work was sculptural, with his religious sculptures bringing Doulton world fame in the 19thC. Today, his small, amusing groups of mice and frogs are most popular.
- The success of Doulton's art pottery can be seen in the rapidly increasing number of 'art potters' employed: six in 1873, 44 in 1875, and up to 345 in 1890.

A Royal Doulton stoneware oil lamp, by Edith Lupton, the base incised and enamelled with foliate scrolls, contained within a brass surround, impressed 'Hinks & Sons'.

23.5in (59.5cm) high

£700-800   **HT**

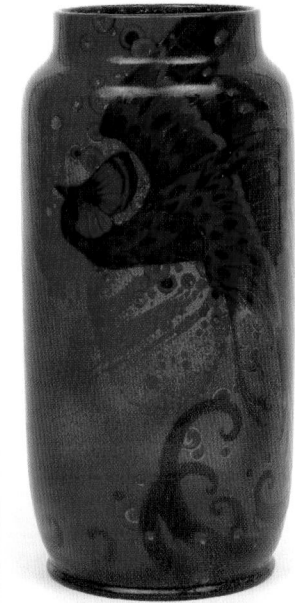

A Doulton Lambeth stoneware plate, by Mark V. Marshall, no. 891, painted with abstract striped forms on a medium blue ground, with impressed mark, with artist's initials.

c1895   *8in (20.5cm) diam*

£700-1,000   **DN**

A Royal Doulton 'Sung Flambé' vase, of cylindrical form, showing a peacock on a marbled pink, yellow and red ground, black factory stamp, model number and 'Sung FLAMBE', signed 'Noke'.

c1930   *8.75in (22cm) high*

£2,500-3,000   **JA**

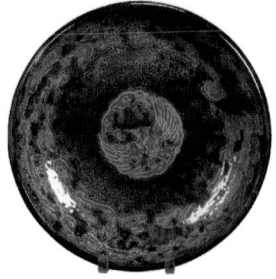

A large 20thC Royal Doulton 'Sung' deep dish, the mottled ground with flambé cloud borders and central bird medallion, the reverse signed 'No. 1A', with printed factory mark.

14.75in (37.5cm) diam

£900-1,200   **SK**

A Royal Doulton 'Sung Flambé' libation cup, moulded in low relief with prunus blossom, covered in a veined flambé glaze, printed mark.

4.5in (11.5cm) high

£400-600   **WW**

A Royal Doulton 'Jade' brush pot, by Charles Noke and Harry Nixon, modelled in low relief with foliage, printed and painted marks, artist monogram and facsimile signature.

6in (15.5cm) high

£1,200-1,800   **WW**

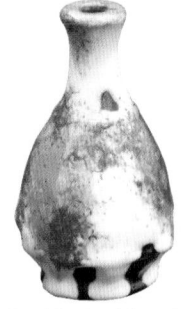

A rare Royal Doulton 'Chang' vase, covered in a running white, red and green glaze over sang-de-boeuf, impressed mark.

3.25in (8cm) high

£400-600   **WW**

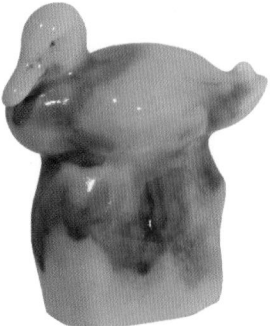

A Royal Doulton 'Jade' duck, designed by Charles Noke, covered in a running green and white glaze, printed factory mark, painted 'Chang' mark.

3.5in (9cm) high

£2,000-2,200   **WW**

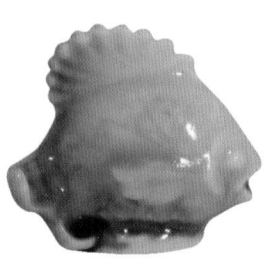

A Royal Doulton 'Jade' fish, designed by Charles Noke, covered in a running green and white glaze, printed mark 'Doulton England', painted 'Jade'.

2.75in (7cm) high

£1,300-1,500   **WW**

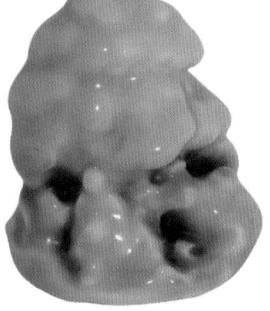

A rare Royal Doulton 'Jade' figure of a sage under a tree, designed by Charles Noke, covered in a running green and white glaze, printed and painted marks, 'Noke' signature.

Doulton's 'Chinese Jade' was designed by Charles Noke (in conjunction with Bernard Moore). It took many years to perfect a glaze that had the same texture and pale green luminescence as real jade, and it was eventually released in 1920. As the glaze was very difficult to make, relatively few 'Chinese Jade' pieces were produced. They are now highly sought after.

3in (7.5cm) high

£2,000-2,200   **WW**

A Royal Doulton 'Moira' figure, HN1347, with Royal Doulton printed mark and hand-painted mark to the base.

6.5in (16.5cm) high

£1,000-1,600   DUK

A Royal Doulton 'Sunshine Girl' figure, HN1344, with printed mark, painted title and 'HN1344', impressed date '3.8.29'.

c1929   5in (13cm) high

£2,500-3,000   DN

A Royal Doulton prototype 'Fortune Teller' character jug, a variation of D6874, with printed factory mark to reverse.

c1900   7in (18cm) high

£1,500-2,000   LT

A Royal Doulton 'The Bouquet' figure, numbered 'HN429' should be HN428, designed by 'G.L.', restored.

This figure was introduced in 1921 and withdrawn in 1936.

£900-1,200   LT

A Royal Doulton 'Lisette' figure, HN1523, designed by 'L.H.'.

This figure was introduced in 1932 and withdrawn in 1936.

£600-800   LT

A Royal Doulton 'Vanessa' figure, HN1838, designed by 'L.H.'

This figure was introduced in 1938 and withdrawn in 1949.

£300-400   LT

A Royal Doulton 'Teresa' figure, HN1682, designed by 'L.H.'

This figure was introduced in 1935 and withdrawn in 1949.

£800-1,000   LT

A Royal Doulton 'Sketch Girl' advertising figure, designed by 'L.H.'

This figure was introduced c1923 and withdrawn c1938.

7in (18cm) high

£1,800-2,200   LT

A Royal Doulton 'Lambeth Walk' figure, HN1881, designed by 'L.H.'

This figure was introduced in 1938 and withdrawn in 1949.

1949

£3,000-3,500   LT

A large early 1960s Royal Doulton 'Gunsmith of Williamsburg' prototype character jug, major modelling differences including tricorn hat, minor colour variation, factory stamp to reverse.

£1,000-1,500   LT

A Royal Doulton veined flambé baluster vase, by Charles Noke, no. 1393, with printed mark, black 'Noke' and 'FM' monogram.

6.25in (16cm) high

£100-150   DN

A Royal Doulton 'Titanian' vase, of baluster form, painted and gilt with a bird of paradise, factory stamp, impressed 'DOULTON' and numbers.

c1930   9in (23cm) high

£800-1,500   JA

A Royal Doulton porcelain vase, of cylindrical form, depicting a country scene, green factory mark and incised number, signed 'H. Morrey'.

16.5in (42cm) high

£1,000-1,200   JA

A rare Dedham crackleware Scottie Dog plate, with 'Indigo Registered' stamp, impressed double rabbits.

1931   8.5in (21.5cm) high
£1,600-1,900   **DRA**

A rare Dedham crackleware cylindrical vase, painted with branches and cherry blossoms, with 'Indigo Registered' stamp, signed 'MEI-CHING-HWA'.
1931   7in (18cm) high
£1,600-1,900   **DRA**

A Dedham experimental vase, by Hugh Robertson, covered in frothy, layered oxblood glaze, incised 'DEDHAM POTTERY HCR', with indigo star and '86'.
6.25in (16cm) high
£1,200-1,800   **DRA**

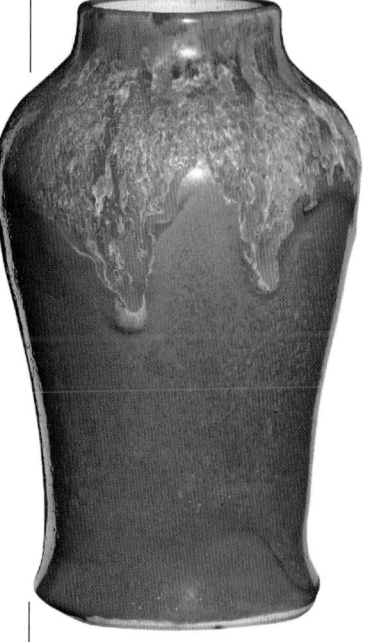

A Dedham experimental vase, by Hugh Robertson, covered in a fine red and emerald lustred oxblood glaze, hairline from rim, incised 'Dedham Pottery HCR'.

7in (18cm) high
£1,500-2,000   **DRA**

A Dedham experimental vase, by Hugh Robertson, covere in an unusual oxblood and bottle-green mottled glaze, volcanic spot to one side, incised 'Dedham Pottery HCR BW'.

7.5in (19cm) high
£1,000-1,300   **DRA**

A Chelsea Keramic Art Works experimental bottle-shaped vase, by Hugh Robertson, covered in a fine apple-green and red orange-peel oxblood glaze, incised 'Dedham Pottery BW HCR', inscribed 'NO 5'.

7.5in (19cm) high
£2,000-2,500   **DRA**

A tall Fulper vase, with flaring neck on squat base, covered in Chinese blue crystalline glaze, vertical ink stamp, touched-up nicks to base.

13.5in (34cm) high
£500-700   **DRA**

A Fulper four-sided flaring vase, for Prang, covered in a fine Flemington Green over blue flambé glaze, with Prang stamp.

8.25in (21cm) high
£500-600   **DRA**

A Fulper squat two-handled vase, with scalloped rim, covered in a thick, frothy Cucumber Matt over mustard crystalline glaze, with vertical mark.
11in (28cm) wide
£1,300-1,700   **DRA**

A Fulper urn, with hammered texture covered in Leopard Skin crystalline glaze, vertical mark.
12in (30.5cm) high
£600-900   **DRA**

A Fulper bullet-shaped blue and ivory flambe vase, tight hairline to neck, vertical mark.
10.25in (26cm)
£200-300   **DRA**

A Grand Feu trumpet-shaped vase, covered in mottled green and brown glossy glaze, marked 'GRAND FEU POTTERY L.A. CAL 154.'

12in (30.5cm) high

£5,000-6,000   **DRA**

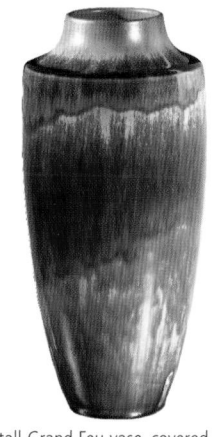

A tall Grand Feu vase, covered in mahogany flambé glaze, stamped 'GRAND FEU POTTERY L.A. CAL. TT', hand-marked '1730 BR'.

13in (33cm) high

£4,000-6,000   **DRA**

A tall Grand Feu porcelain vase, covered in a forest green crystalline glaze, stamped 'GRAND FEU POTTERY L.A. CAL. 70'.

10.5in (27cm) high

£5,300-7,000   **DRA**

A Grand Feu 'Bud' vase, covered in mottled indigo glaze, stamped 'BRAUCKMAN ART POTTERY BG'.

4.75in (12cm) high

£900-1,200   **DRA**

A Grueby gourd-shaped vase, with tooled and applied ribbed leaves, covered in a feathered matte green glaze, stamped 'Grueby', professional restoration to small chip.

9.25in (23.5cm) high

£40,000-50,000   **DRA**

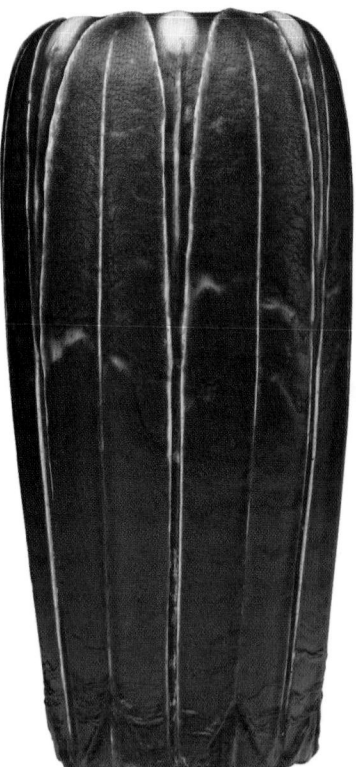

A tall Grueby ovoid vase, with tooled and applied full-height leaves alternating with yellow buds, under a rich, frothy matte green glaze, a circular pottery stamp, very minor nicks.

12in (30.5cm) high

£7,000-10,000   **DRA**

A large Grueby vase, decorated with full-height tooled and applied leaves, alternating with yellow buds, circular Pottery stamp, minor flakes.

22.5in (57cm) high

£10,000-13,000   **DRA**

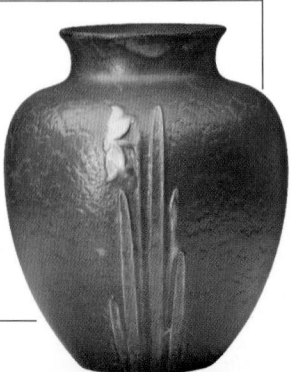

A Grueby bulbous vase, by Ruth Erickson, with three pale yellow daffodils against a rich, curdled green ground, circular Pottery stamp 'RE/ 7/14', restoration.

10.5in (26.5cm) high

£5,000-7,000   **DRA**

A Grueby ovoid vase, by Ruth Erickson, with full-height leaves applied under a rich matte mustard glaze, stamped circular mark, 'RE'.

10.25in (26cm) wide

£1,500-2,000   DRA

A Grueby melon-shaped vase, with full-height leaves alternating with yellow buds, covered in fine leathery matte green glaze, with circular stamp 'RE 36'.

11in (28cm) high

£13,000-17,000   DRA

A rare Grueby vase, by Ruth Erickson, with crisply tooled full-height leaves alternating with amber buds, minor flakes to leaf edge, and circular stamp/artist's cipher.

7.25in (18.5cm) wide

£12,000-15,000   DRA

A Grueby squat vessel, decorated with rounded leaves, under a frothy matte mustard glaze, circular Pottery stamp, illegible incised name or numbers.

6in (15cm) wide

£1,500-2,000   DRA

A low Grueby flower bowl, complete with a rare pierced copper ikebana insert, circular Pottery stamp, small glaze chip to foot and scratches to interior.

9in (24cm) diam

£2,000-3,000   DRA

A Grueby squat vessel, by Marie Seaman, with full-height leaves under matte green glaze, with circular Faience stamp, '155', 'MS', restoration to bottom, nick to edge of leaf.

7in (18cm) wide

£4,000-4,500   DRA

A rare Grueby tile, decorated in cuenca with St George slaying the dragon, in rich matte colours, signed by artist.

8in (20.5cm) wide

£6,000-9,000   DRA

A rare Grueby tile, decorated in cuenca with a rabbit in a lettuce field, set in original metal mount, signed 'CA'.

6in (15cm) wide

£3,000-3,500   DRA

A Grueby 'The Pines' tile, decorated in cuenca, with glazed sides, artist's mark 'EC', nicks to edges.

6in (15cm) wide

£1,500-1,800   DRA

A Grueby advertising tile, with candlesconce and yellow candle, signed 'M.D.', slight clouding of glaze, small glaze chips.

6in (15cm) high

£1,500-2,000   DRA

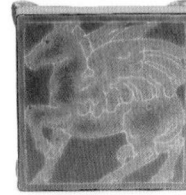

A rare Grueby tile, with winged Pegasus on green ground, in hammered copper footed mount, signed 'M. C.', restoration to two corners.

6in (15cm) square

£2,500-3,000   DRA

A Grueby frieze of two large tiles, depicting a palm tree in an oasis landscape, invisible restoration to two small drilled holes on one tile, and three on the other.

12in (30.5cm) wide each

£6,000-9,000   DRA

A Goldscheider Art Deco figure of a girl, black stamp and incised factory marks to base, signed 'Lorenzl'.

c1930   14.25in (36cm) high

£1,000-1,500   JA

A Goldscheider Art Deco pottery wall mask, in the form of a face and hand holding a bunch of grapes.

12in (30.5cm) high

£600-700   DUK

A Goldscheider wall mask, model 7914, modelled as a stylised woman with a terrier dog, painted in colours, impressed and printed marks.

9.5in (24cm) high

£500-600   WW

A Goldscheider wall mask, modelled as a stylised woman with a tulip flower, glazed in colours, impressed and printed marks, restored hair.

8.25in (21cm) high

£250-350   WW

A Goldscheider figure of a lady in a dancing pose, by Josef Lorenzl, raised to a stepped base, impressed and printed marks, small restoration.

The Goldscheider earthenware and porcelain factory was founded by Friedrich Goldscheider in Vienna in 1885, and continued by his widow and sons until it closed in 1954. In the late 19thC and early 20thC, Goldscheider specialised in figurative subjects and Art Nouveau terracotta figures of maidens. The Art Deco figures and masks for which the factory is now best known were made in the 1920s and 1930s.

15.25in (41.5cm) high

£1,500-1,800   FLD

A Goldscheider terracotta wall mask, model no. 8041, glazed in colours, printed and impressed marks.

9.75in (25cm) high

£900-1,200   WW

A large Goldscheider figure of a dancing lady, by Stefan Dakon, her dress hand-enamelled with blue flowers, on a domed oval black base, impressed and printed marks.

15.75in (40cm) high

£1,250-1,500   FLD

A Goldscheider model of a dancer, no. 7582, by Josef Lorenzl, impressed, printed and painted marks, 'Goldscheider Wien Made in Austria Lorenzl', '7582/13/31', damage to fingers.

13.5in (34cm) high

£700-800   TEN

A Goldscheider figure, no. 7195, by Stephan Dakon, printed and painted marks 'Goldscheider Wien Made in Austria Dakon', '7195/1148/6'.

15.75in (40cm) high

£900-1,200   **TEN**

A Goldscheider figure of a lady in dancing pose, by Presahly, raised to a stepped oval base, impressed and printed marks.

12.5in (32cm) high

£800-1,200   **FLD**

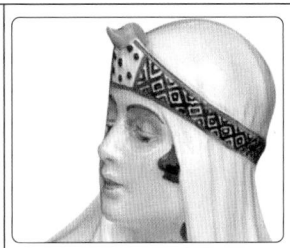

A large 1930s Goldscheider Art Deco figurine of a Harem girl, by Lorenzl, wearing exotic patterned robes, raised to a stepped oval base, signed to the drapes of the dress, with full marks to the base.

7.25in (18.5cm) high

£1,500-1,800   **FLD**

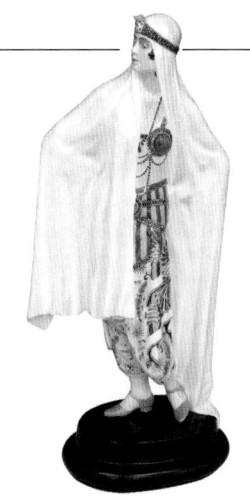

A Goldscheider figure of a girl, in a leaning pose wearing a puff-ball skirt painted with insects.

c1921   *9.75in (25cm) high*

£1,800-2,200   **FLD**

A Goldscheider figure of a dancing girl, by Lorenzl, standing on a drum with a saxophone at her feet.

c1924   *14.5in (37cm) high*

£1,800-2,200   **FLD**

A large Goldscheider 'Captured Bird' figure, by Lorenzl, in walking pose, wearing a batwing dress and raised to a stepped oval base, moulded signature to the base, printed and painted marks.

18.75in (47.5cm) high

£2,500-3,000   **FLD**

CLOSER LOOK – LENCI FIGURE

The figure is naked apart from a beret and has a stiff, slightly 'uncomfortable' pose, both typical features of Lenci figures.

Art Deco figurines typically depict women in carefree, independent poses, literally on top of a world promising adventures. The fashionable hat and dog are also popular motifs at the time.

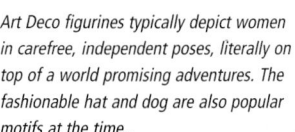

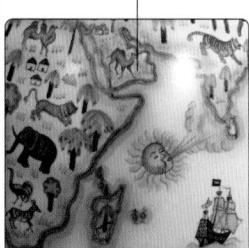

A Lenci 'Sul Mondo' earthenware figure, designed by Mario Sturani and Helen König Scavini, modelled as a young woman seated with a small dog on top of a globe, impressed 'Lenci' to the top of globe, girl restored.

19.25in (49cm) high

£5,500-7,500   **WW**

A pair of Lenci 'Testa Madonna Fiamminga' ceramic wall-hanging masks, Helen König Scavini, painted in polychrome, signed 'Lenci Made in Italy', one marked with treble clef sign, the other '7 XII M'.

11.5in (29cm) high

£2,000-3,000   **SDR**

A Lenci Art Deco ceramic 'Primo Romanzo' figure, by Helen König Scavini, modelled as a young lady in a chair with a book by her side, signed and dated '11/11/36', restored.

9.75in (25cm) high

£5,000-6,000   **FLD**

A Lenci porcelain 'Fanciulla Con Colombi' figure, by Adele Jacopi, modelled as a female in a flower-painted dress with arms outstretched holding two doves, painted marks.

9.25in (23.5cm) high

£600-800   **FLD**

DECORATIVE ARTS

ESSENTIAL REFERENCE – MAJOLICA

A 19thC corruption of the Italian word 'maiolica', the name majolica is used to refer to a type of elaborately modelled earthenware, which is typically covered with thick lead blue, turquoise, green, yellow, orange, black and ground.

● Majolica is also known as Della Robbia ware, faience or Palissy ware.

● It was developed at Minton in Staffordshire, and exhibited at the Great Exhibition at 1851. From 1850-55, models were designed by the French sculptor Carrier-Belleuse, who later worked at Sèvres. Majolica was also produced by Wedgwood, George Jones and T.G. Forester in England; Massier Choisy-le-Roi, Saint-Clément, Sarreguemines and Lunéville in France; Griffen, Smith & Hill of Phoenixville, Pennsylvania; as well as other makers in Europe and the USA.

● Majolica was often used to create large objects, such as jardinières, umbrella stands, garden seats, fountains, birds and figures. Majolica teapots, vases, tureens and dishes were also popular, many of which were decorated with eccentric and bizarre motifs.

● As well as referencing Italian Renaissance pottery, majolica is clearly influenced by the work of 18thC Staffordshire potters Thomas Whieldon and Ralph Wood, and the French Huguenot potter Bernad Palissy, who produced realistically painted wares decorated with three-dimensional reptiles and plant life.

An unusual pair of majolica chinoiserie baluster vases, possibly by George Jones, the body encrusted with Oriental-style decoration and mounted with a dragon and a griffin respectively, on rocaille-moulded circular feet.

28.25in (72cm) high

£2,000-3,000 — L&T

A Minton majolica heron and fish, by Hugues Protat, signed, impressed 'MINTON 1241', date symbol.

French sculptor Hugues Protat was employed at Minton from c1845-58. He was a modelling instructor at Stoke School of Design from 1850-64, and moved to Wedgwood in 1858. He specialised in parian figures, and ornamental wares in porcelain and majolica.

1866   *21in (53.5cm) high*

£1,500-1,800 — TEN

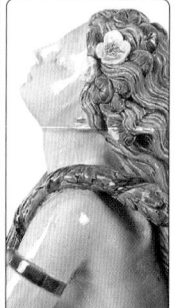

A massive Victorian majolica jardinière, probably Minton, modelled as a conch shell flanked by mermaids, the shell base naturalistically modelled with seaweed on an oval foot.

38.25in (97cm) wide

£7,000-8,000 — ADA

A pair of Minton majolica figural bowls, comprising boy and girl with large yellow baskets, on rustic base, impressed mark.

8in (20.5cm) wide

£700-900 — HT

A Minton majolica centrepiece vase, of Cupid with cornucopia, model no. 1148, impressed marks, date code.

1871   *14.5in (37cm) high*

£900-1,200 — DN

A 19thC Sarreguemines majolica jardinière and stand, supported by high-relief griffons, impressed marks 'B majolica sarreguemines 426'.

15.75in (40cm) diam

£800-1,000 — L&T

A Wedgwood majolica planter, the polychrome enamel decorated with large floral panels, set on three scrolled feet, with impressed mark.

c1870   *16in (40.5cm) diam*

£600-900 — SK

One of a pair of Worcester majolica table candlesticks, the sconces with raised shell decoration, the drip pans in the form of shells, each supported by three dolphins, one impressed mark, firing cracks.

6in (15cm) high

£2,500-2,800 PAIR — A&G

A pair of 19thC majolica planters, on stands, moulded with acorns and oak leaves, on mask scroll feet.

21in (53.5cm) high

£500-700 — GORL

A 19thC majolica cheese bell and stand, moulded with four large roses painted pink and yellow on a dark blue ground, minor enamel wear to the stand.

11.25in (28.5cm) high

£50-150 — WW

A Royal Worcester majolica model of a caparisoned elephant, by James Hadley, with impressed marks, small chips.

c1870

£700-800 — DN

A mid-19thC majolica figure of an elephant, with a castellated howdah on its back, unmarked, the base broken across the front foot and re-glued.

7.75in (19.5cm) high

£150-250 — WW

A 19thC majolica figure of an elephant, with a castellated howdah on its back, restored.

£100-120 — FLD

A large 19thC French majolica two-handled vase, moulded with an elaborate scrolling foliate design with the masks of young girl and a bearded man, some restoration.

15.25in (39cm) high

£300-400 — WW

A Roseville Art-Nouveau-style fine and rare majolica-type jardinière and pedestal set, the jardinière with applied woman's bust to two sides, minor damage, unmarked.

Pedestal 28in (71cm) high

£800-1,000 — CRA

A small Jervis spherical vase, Oyster Bay, incised and enamel-decorated with blue irises on brown ground, incised 'Jervis OB'.

4in (10cm) high

£900-1,200   DRA

An important William P. Jervis vase, decorated in squeezebag with white Queen Ann's lace, signed 'W.P.J.'.

While Jervis supervised the work being done in his studios and participated in most items, this one is actually signed by him.

16in (40.5cm) high

£1,200-1,800   DRA

A 'Briarcliff' faceted covered jar by William Jervis, its lid with oak leaves in squeezebag and topped by an acorn finial, incised 'Briarcliff JERVIS', some glaze chips and scaling.

6.75in (17cm) high

£1,500-2,000   DRA

ESSENTIAL REFERENCE – MARBLEHEAD

The Marblehead art pottery studio was founded in 1904 in Massachusetts as part of a sanatorium, but soon became an independent concern. Director Arthur Eugene Baggs (1866-1947) joined in 1905 and bought the pottery in 1915. It closed in 1936.

- **Marblehead produced simple vases and jars in sober matt colours, including blue, green, pink, brown and grey. These were decorated with incised and painted geometrical patterns, stylised flowers and natural forms.**

A faceted vase, by Arthur Baggs, covered in orange, amber and yellow mottled glaze, with grinding chip, signed 'AEB'.

8.25in (21cm) high

£3,300-4,000   DRA

An early Marblehead geometric decorated vase, with deep brown incised decoration repeating against a rich pea-green ground, impressed ship mark, incised 'N T'.

Probably done within the first several years of Marblehead's production, the quality is typical of this period.

5in (12.5cm) high

£8,500-9,500   DRA

An early Arthur Baggs vase, incised with Native American pattern in black on brown, incised 'AEB 03'.

One of Baggs's earliest efforts, made when he was aged just 17 and a student at Alfred University, under Charles Fergus Binns, this piece is slightly coarse but full of promise. From the collection of his daughter, Mary Trowbridge Baggs Tweet of Tolland, Connecticut.

1903   *5.25in (13.5cm) high*

£2,500-3,200   DRA

An early Marblehead bulbous vase, by Arthur Baggs, incised with a stylised design, incised 'M' with seagull, 'AB', small glaze flake.

This is more Grueby than Marblehead in design.

4.75in (12cm) high

£24,000-30,000   DRA

A Marblehead vase, incised by Arthur Baggs, with brown crabs and green sea plants on an indigo ground, with ship mark, 'AB' and dated.

1915. 9in (23cm) high

£12,000-18,000   DRA

A rare Marblehead vase, carved and painted with panthers and stylised trees in browns on a pale green ground, unusually sharp, ship mark, 'HT'.

7in (18cm) high

£12,000-15,000   DRA

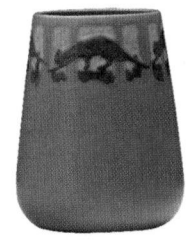

A Marblehead vase, carved by Hannah Tutt, with crouching panthers and stylised trees on matte olive-green ground, stamped ship mark and 'HT', line to rim.

6.75in (17cm) high

£10,000-12,000   DRA

A large Ohio State four-handled vase, by Arthur Baggs, impressed pottery mark, minute nick to base.

1920   *10.25in (26cm) high*

£1,200-1,500   DRA

A Marblehead vase, incised and painted by Arthur Baggs with stylised flowers in yellow and orange against a dark blue and speckled medium blue ground, with ship mark, 'AB', '1915'.

1915   *8.5in (21.5cm) high*

£16,000-19,000   DRA

A Marblehead tile, incised with blue and brown fish under pale blue waves, on a speckled matte grey ground, with ship mark, small nicks to edges.

Complete with original sketch.

6in (15cm) wide

£7,000-9,000   DRA

A Marblehead tile, incised by Arthur Baggs, painted with cedar trees against a cloudy sunset, in the style of Arthur Wesley Dow, minor nicks, mounted in Arts and Crafts frame.

With original preparatory drawing, and page with Baggs's colour designation.

8in (20.5cm) wide

£9,000-12,000   DRA

A Marblehead tile, incised by Arthur Baggs, with a landscape of poplar trees reflected in a pond, ship mark and paper label, with small chips to corners, mounted in an Arts and Crafts frame.

6in (15cm) wide

£70,000-90,000   DRA

A Marblehead tile, with a house and trees, mounted in an Arts and Crafts frame, with ship mark, nicks to corners.

Complete with booklet from Essex Institute Historical Collections, 1977, picturing this tile. From the collection of Arthur Baggs's daughter, Mary Trowbridge Baggs Tweet.

6in (15cm) wide

£6,000-7,000   DRA

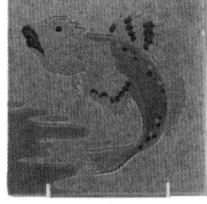

A rare Marblehead tile, incised and glazed in several colours with a flying fish. A few minor flecks to edges, chip to corner, ship stamp, several price and other labels, mounted in Arts and Crafts frame.

6.25in (16cm) wide

£4,700-5,300   DRA

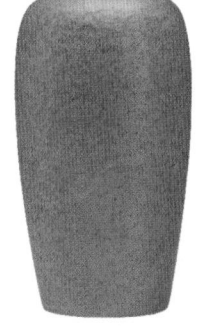

A Merrimac ovoid vase, covered in bright yellow and orange peel matte glaze, mark obscured by glaze.

6.5in (16.5cm) high

£1,300-1,700   DRA

A Merrimac jardinière, carved and embossed with lotus leaves under an excellent feathered microcrystalline matte green glaze, incised 'EB', with abrasion to high points, some glaze flakes.

8.5in (21.5cm) wide

£1,800-2,000   DRA

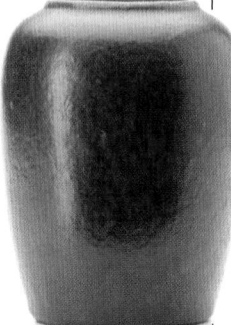

A bulbous Merrimac vase, covered in a rich feathered green and gunmetal glaze, with stamped fish mark.

6in (15cm) high

£1,200-1,500   DRA

A rare Martin Brothers stoneware miniature bird jar and cover, by Robert Wallace Martin, probably modelled as a scent bottle, the base marked 'Angel', and 'R W Martin & Bros, London & Southall', repairs.

3.75in (9.5cm) high

£3,000-5,000   **WW**

A Martin Brothers grotesque bird jar, the head collar with partial original leather liner, signed 'Martin Bros. London + Southall 2-1899', paper label for 'R.W. MARTIN POTTERY'.

1899   11.25in (28.5cm) wide

£23,000-28,000   **DRA**

A Martin Brothers grotesque bird stoneware jar, the base and lid signed 'R. W. Martin Bros. London & Southall 6-1897'.

1897   11.5in (29cm) high

£23,000-25,000   **DRA**

A Martin Brothers grotesque bird stoneware jar, the base and lid signed 'R. W. Martin Bros. London & Southall 6 1903'.

1903   9.5in (24cm) high

£20,000-22,000   **DRA**

A large Martin Brothers grotesque stoneware bird jar, base inscribed 'RW Martin & Brothers London & Southall 1893', head inscribed 'Martin Brothers London + Southall 12-93'.

1893   15in (38cm) high

£35,000-40,000   **DRA**

A Martin Brothers stoneware double-face jug, by Robert Wallace Martin, modelled on both sides with a smiling face, in shades of brown, incised 'R.W. Martin & Bros. London & Southall 8.5.

1910.   7in (17.5cm) high

£2,200-2,800   **DN**

A Martin Brothers stoneware jug, by Robert Wallace Martin, incised with scrolling foliage and stylised round flowers, incised 'R W Martin & Bros, London & Southall, 10-11-84'.

1884   8.75in (22cm) high

£500-700   **WW**

A Martin Brothers stoneware ovoid jug, incised with a horned grotesque mask and scrolling foliage terminating with two gaping leopard heads, incised 'Martin Bros, London & Southall 9.1893'.

1893   9.75in (24.5cm) high

£2,000-2,500   **DN**

A Martin Brothers stoneware vase, by Charles and Edwin Martin, incised and painted with blue flag iris and wild flowers, the neck with bees, incised 'Martin Bros, London & Southall, 4-1893'.

1893   *9.75in (25cm) high*

£1,000-1,500   **WW**

A Martin Brothers stoneware vase, painted with birds flying and standing among tall grasses, incised 'Martin Bros London & Southall, 12-1895', chip and glaze chips to top rim.

1895   *5in (13cm) high*

£400-500   **WW**

An unusual early Martin Brothers stoneware vase, carved with vultures and their young, incised '6-84 Martin Bros, London & Southall *'.

1884   *9.25in (23.5cm) high*

£7,000-9,000   **DRA**

A pair of Martin Brothers stoneware 'Dragon' vases, of slab form with square-section necks, incised 'Martin Bros, London & Southall 11 1899'.

1899   *9in (23cm) high*

£2,500-3,500   **WW**

A pair of early Martin Brothers stoneware vases, by Robert Wallace Martin, incised 'R W Martin London 12-74', 'D37' and 'D38', restored top rims.

1874   *12.5in (31.5cm) high*

£1,000-1,500   **WW**

A Martin Brothers twin-handled stoneware vase, by Robert Wallace Martin, incised with dragons among foliage, incised 'R W Martin & Bros, London & Southall 10-1890'.

1890   *8.25in (21cm) high*

£1,400-1,800   **WW**

A Martin Brothers brown salt-glaze stoneware double-handled vase, Southall, London, with incised green dragons, hand-painted and shaped as a pharmacy jar.

The Martin Brothers produced stone-glazed pottery in Southall from 1877. Robert Wallace Martin (1843-1923) was the modeller, while Walter Frazer Martin (1857-1912) was responsible for throwing, coloured glazes and some incised decoration. Edwin Martin (1860-1915) was the chief decorator, and Charles Martin (1846-1910) assisted with business affairs. They are best known for producing vases with carved or incised decoration, and grotesque birds. The pottery closed in 1914.

10.5in (27cm) high

£2,500-3,000   **RTC**

A Martin Brothers stoneware vase, embossed and incised with fish and sealife, signed '10-11-91, Martin Bros. London + Southall'.

1891   *8.5in (21.5cm) high*

£5,000-5,500   **DRA**

A Martin Brothers four-sided stoneware vase, incised with fish and sealife, incised '9-1913 Martin Bros. London + Southall', restoration to short line at rim.

1913   *6in (15cm) high*

£3,000-3,500   **DRA**

A Martin Brothers stoneware four-sided vase, incised with crabs and anemones, incised '10-1903 Martin Bros. London + Southall'.

1903   *8.75in (22cm) high*

£4,000-4,500   **DRA**

A Martin Brothers stoneware straight-tapered beaker, by Robert Wallace Martin, with a silver-plated collar and interior, a band of flowering plants and a buff ground with an incised foot band, incised 'R. W. Martin Fulham 1 65 74'.

1874   *4in (10cm) high*

£200-300   **DN**

A pair of Martin Brothers stoneware slender bottle vases, by Robert Wallace Martin, incised '225 R W Martin London & Southall' and '226 2.7.79 R W Martin London & Southall'.

1879   *9.75in (24.5cm) high*

£500-700   **DN**

A Martin Brothers table cruet, with impressed patterns and blue glaze decoration, each piece with 'R W Martin London' inscribed to the base, on a silver stand, hallmarked for George Adams, London.

1875

£600-800   **DUK**

A Martin Brothers stoneware 'Judge' inkwell, by Robert Wallace Martin, modelled with gaping mouth, glazed brown, incised 'R W M London', minor chips.

2.75in (7cm) long

£500-1,000   **WW**

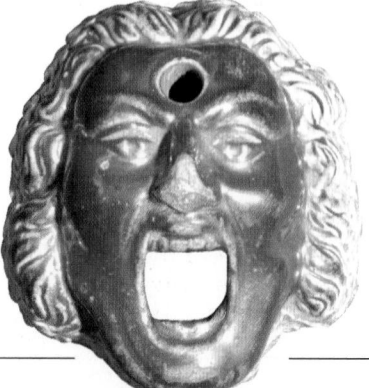

A Martin Brothers stoneware garden stool, by Robert Wallace Martin, deeply carved with Classical foliage and terminals, in shades of blue, ochre and green, stamped 'RW Martin Southall'.

16.25in (41cm) high

£1,000-1,200   **WW**

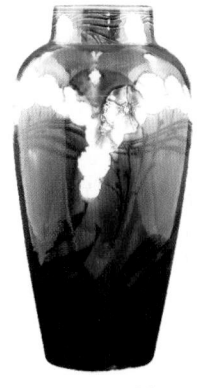

A Minton bone china pseudo-cloisonné vase, Christopher Dresser, the multi-spout vase with bleu-celeste ground, impressed mark.

c1870   10.25in (26cm) high
£3,500-4,500   **SK**

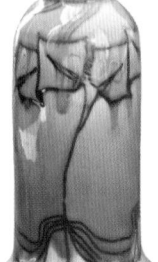

A Minton 'Secessionist' floor vase, by John Wadsworth, decorated in low relief with Art Nouveau flowers, impressed marks, hairline and glaze loss to bruise on top rim.

18.75in (48cm) high
£350-550   **WW**

CLOSER LOOK – MINTON

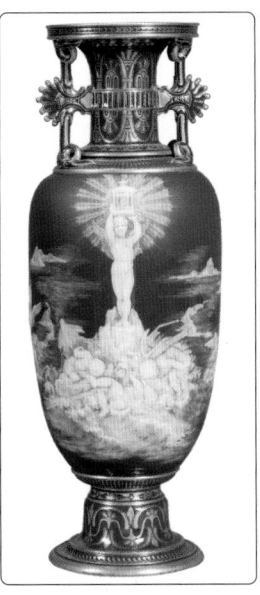

The exquisite pâte-sur-pâte work and skilful gilding indicates that this piece was originally intended for the upper end of the market.

Sèvres introduced the pâte-sur-pâte technique around 1849 but its greatest exponent was Marc Louis Solon, who came to Minton from Sèvres, bringing the technique with him.

The technique involves building up layers of slip against a dark background, to give the illusion of depth, and is ideally suited to Classical Revival motifs.

The piece is signed by a renowned artist, a factor which can increase the value of a piece by 50 per cent.

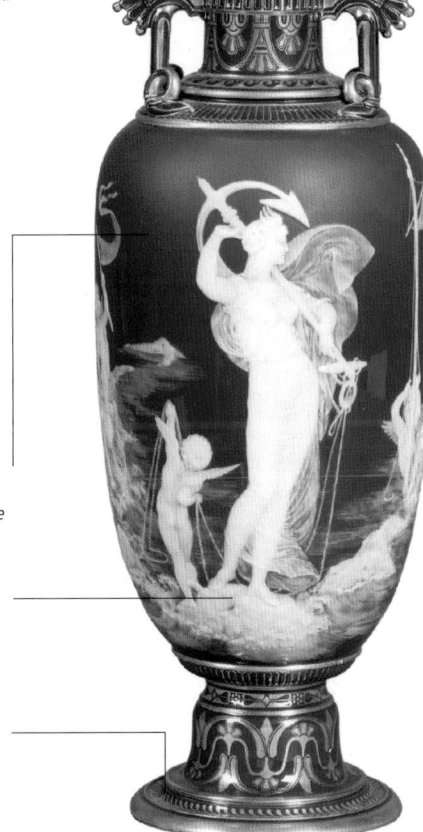

A Minton decorated pâte-sur-pâte vase, by Louis Solon, blue ground with white slip decoration, heavily gilded rim, neck, shoulder, handles and base, artist signed, printed and impressed marks.

1889   20.5in (52cm) high
£30,000-40,000   **SK**

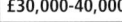

A pair of Minton 'Secessionist' vases, designed by John Wadsworth, bell-shaped, tube-line decorated with ivy in shades of pink and green, printed and impressed marks.

6.25in (16cm) high
£350-400 PAIR   **WW**

A large Minton 'Secessionist' circular tapered vase, no. 3573, limited edition, with stylised flowers on running green glazed ground, impressed mark, slight chip to rim.

18.75in (47.5) high
£500-700   **A&G**

A Minton ovoid vase, decorated in squeezebag with bright yellow and pink peonies and green leaves on a cobalt ground, minor bruise at base, with Minton ink mark.

13in (33cm) high
£400-600   **DRA**

A pair of Minton 'Secessionist' tapering cylindrical vases, by John Wadsworth, with tube-lined swags between olive green vertical lines, painted mark and impressed '3652'.

c1910
£300-400   **DN**

A Minton earthenware jardinière and stand, the polychrome enamel decorated in relief with ferns and hollyhocks bordered with morning glories.

c1870   18.75in (47.5cm) wide

£2,500-3,500   SK

A pair of Minton 'Anacreon' dessert plates, designed by John Moyr Smith, printed and painted in colours, impressed and painted marks.

9.75in (25.5cm) diam

£250-350   WW

A Minton Gothic Revival plate, painted with a heraldic scene of a maiden dreaming of her gallant knight, impressed and painted marks.

15.75in (40cm) diam

£300-400   WW

A Minton Art Pottery Studio earthenware plaque, no. S70, painted with birds on prunus boughs, with printed Kensington Gore mark, impressed and painted marks.

c1871-75   13.5in (34.5cm) diam

£300-400   DN

A Minton Neo-gothic style scalloped circular revolving tray, designed by A. W. N. Pugin, shape no. 799, with a simulated tube-lined radial pattern, impressed marks, date code '1867', rim restored.

1864   18.25in (46.5cm) diam

£500-700   DN

Four Minton 'Aesthetic' tiles, printed in black with elves, impressed marks.

6in (15.5cm) wide

£100-150   WW

Three Minton 'Thomson's Seasons' tiles, designed by John Moyr Smith, comprising Spring, Summer and Winter and three Minton 'Industrial' series tiles, impressed marks.

6in (15.5cm) wide

£150-200   WW

A Minton Hollins & Co. dust-pressed tile, designed by Christopher Dresser, decorated with a repeat Gothic arch motif in maroon, grey, green and lilac.

8in (20.5cm) wide

£150-200   FLD

A Minton China Works dust-pressed block, by A. W. N. Pugin, with a Gothic-inspired vase with stylised lilies within Gothic style borders.

8in (20.5cm) wide

£150-200 FLD

A Minton Hollins & Co. dust-pressed tile relief, by Christopher Dresser, with a palmette motif with daisy heads between banded borders, all in a majolica glaze.

8in (20.5cm) wide

£100-150 FLD

A Minton China Works dust-pressed tile, printed and painted with a repeat border pattern of stylised pomegranates in blue, white and ochre.

6in (15cm) wide

£70-100 FLD

A Minton Hollins & Co. dust-pressed tile relief, in the style of Christopher Dresser, relief-moulded with a stylised flower in blue over celadon ground with dash line borders.

6in (15cm) wide

£80-120 FLD

A Minton 'Secessionist' washstand jug and chamber jug, by John Wadsworth, with tube-lined olive green and yellow stylised flowers on a blue ground, with impressed and printed marks.

c1910   *Jug 14.5in (37cm) high*

£300-400 DN

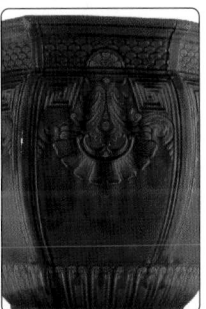

A Minton jardinière and stand, modelled in low relief with panels of foliage, glazed blue, impressed marks, minor damages and loss.

35.5in (90cm) high

£100-200 WW

ESSENTIAL REFERENCE – MOORCROFT

William Moorcroft (1872-1945) became director of the art pottery department at James Macintyre and Co. in Burslem, Staffordshire, in 1898. His first wares for the company, known as the 'Aurelian' ranges, were generally decorated with printed patterns, while the later 'Florian' wares were among the foremost contributions to British Art Nouveau ceramics. Both ranges are typified by their complex Moorish-inspired symmetrical patterns inspired by natural themes.

- **At Macintyre, Moorcroft designed utilitarian wares as well as the now more collectable art pottery pieces.**
- **Moorcroft made inventive use of tube-lined decoration: fine lines of slip applied to the surface of the piece.**
- **After winning a gold medal at the St Louis International Exhibition, Moorcroft insisted on adding his own initials or signature to the pottery he designed.**
- **In 1912, Moorcroft left Macintyre to establish his own ceramics works with the financial backing of Liberty & Co., London. Though still inspired by nature, his new patterns were simpler and bolder, typically with dark grounds, rich and deep colours, and a clear glossy glaze. Patterns include 'Pomegranate', 'Wisteria' and 'Hazeldine'.**
- **Moorcroft was awarded a Royal Appointment in 1929 by Queen Mary, who was a keen collector of his work. In 1946, a second Royal Appointment was granted to the factory, now under the control of William's eldest son, Walter. Many of William Moorcroft's designs were continued and produced throughout the 20thC.**
- **The pottery is still operating today, producing designs that are more exotic, though still based on natural forms, in characteristically rich Moorcroft colours.**

An early Moorcroft 'Florian' vase, with all-over decoration of black-eyed Susans, stamped registration mark, 'W Moorcroft Des' in green, glaze scaling at base, restoration to one handle.

c1902   *10in (25.5cm) high*

£3,000-3,500 DRA

A Moorcroft Macintyre 'Cornflower' vase, of baluster form, decorated with radiating cornflowers against a leafy green background, brown Macintyre factory mark and green painted signature.

c1910   *8.5in (21.5cm) high*

£2,000-2,500 JA

A pair of 18thC William Moorcroft 'Florian' ware pattern vases, McIntyre, decorated with sprays of roses, daffodils and forget-me-nots, against a white ground.

7in (18cm) high

£600-900 PAIR   **GORL**

A Moorcroft Centenary 'Florian Yacht' pattern slender-neck vase, limited edition no. 1358, artist John Moorcroft.

Copyright 1996   9.25in (23.5cm) high

£180-220   **DN**

A pair of William Moorcroft 'Pansy' vases, on white grounds, printed brown factory mark, painted green signature, printed mark 'Made for Townsend & Co, Newcastle on Tyne'.

1911-1912   11.75in (30cm) high

£6,000-6,500   **TEN**

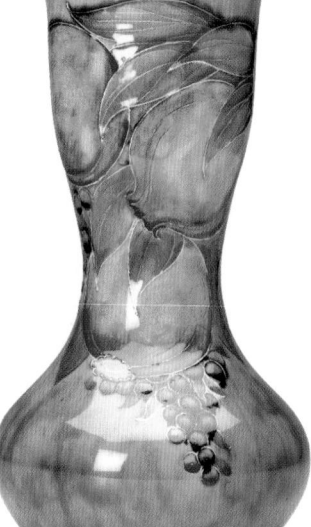

An early tall Moorcroft 'Pomegranate' pattern vase, of unusual shape, green and amber ground, with green ink script signature and '102'.

c 1912   10.75in (27.5cm) high

£4,500-5,000   **DRA**

A James Macintyre & Co. bowl, 'Poppy' pattern, designed by William Moorcroft, printed and painted marks, one handle restored.

11.5in (29cm) wide

£500-600   **FLD**

A Macintyre Moorcroft cylindrical shaped vase, with bulbous base, painted 'Wisteria', green signature, impressed no. '153'.

1912-1914   9.75in (25cm) high

£6,500–8,500   **A&G**

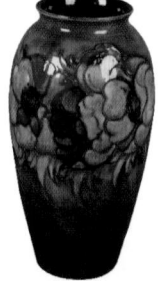

A Moorcroft vase, of tapering form, decorated in pinks and purples with the 'Anemone' pattern, impressed mark and painted signature to the base.

c1949   10in (25.5cm) high

£300-500   **DUK**

A Moorcroft 'Claremont' pattern bowl, with a multicoloured mushroom design on a green ground, green painted signature and impressed factory marks.

1914   10.25in (26cm) diam

£1,500-2,000   **JA**

A Moorcroft Pottery 'Claremont' twin-handled vase, designed by William Moorcroft, with four applied lugs, painted in shades of red, purple, cream and green on a green ground, painted green signature.

Moorcroft's 'Claremont' pattern features toadstools in front of dark mottled grounds, and was probably first produced as Florian ware in late 1902. The pattern was registered in October 1903, and given the name 'Claremont' for sale in Liberty's. In shape and colour it shows stylistic similarities with the 'Hazledene' landscape pattern, produced at a similar time.

8.25in (21cm) high

£5,000-7,000   **WW**

A Moorcroft 'Claremont' pattern bonbonnière, by Shreve, San Francisco, covered by Shreve silver overlay with trefoils, signed in green ink 'W.Moorcroft/Shreve Company San Francisco' and in puce 'R'N'420081'.
c1905   7.5in (19cm) diam
£12,000-15,000   DRA

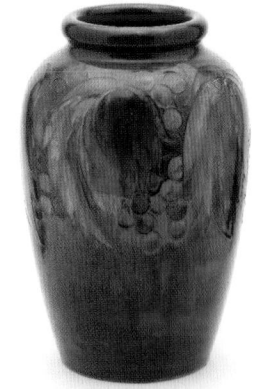

A tall Moorcroft 'Leaves and Fruit' vase, signed in green, stamped signature, 'POTTER TO THE QUEEN, MADE IN ENGLAND', short underglaze line at bottom.
                            13in (33cm) high
£2,500-3,000   DRA

A Moorcroft 'Lily' pattern bulbous vase, stamped 'MOORCROFT MADE IN ENGLAND POTTER TO THE QUEEN', green ink signature, scratches inside rim.
                            9in (23cm) high
£800-1,200   DRA

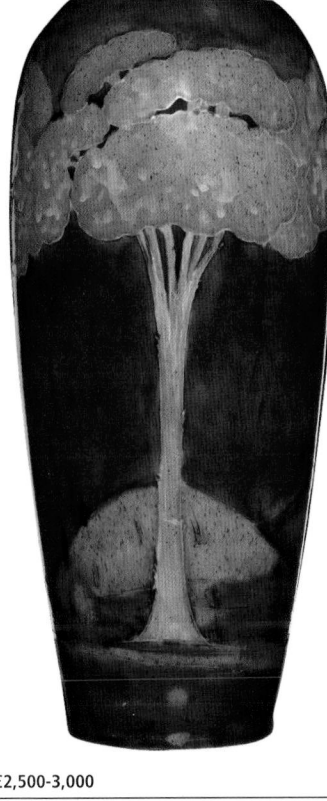

A tall Moorcroft vase, in the 'Moonlit Blue' pattern, green glaze signature, stamped 'MADE IN ENGLAND 101', drilled bottom, and paper label.

Moorcroft created three different colourings for 'Hazeldene', a pattern originally registered in 1902 by James MacIntyre & Co., which Moorcroft took with him when he established his own pottery. Deep blue and green variations are known as 'Moonlit Blue', while versions in rich autumnal colours are known as 'Eventide'. Blue and white salt-glazed pieces are described as 'Dawn'.
                            14.5in (37cm) high
£2,500-3,000   DRA

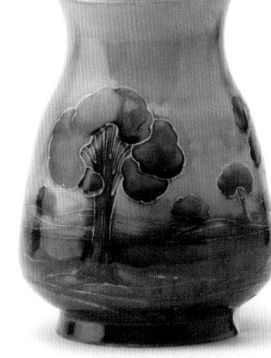

A Moorcroft 'Hazledene' bulbous vase, in blue and green, green script 'W. Moorcroft Des', stamped 'RDNO397964 MADE FOR LIBERTY & CO., P'.
                            5in (12.5cm) high
£3,200-3,500   DRA

A Moorcroft 'Moonlit Blue' pattern squat vase, tube-lined and painted with trees on a blue ground, impressed and painted marks.
                            3.25in (8cm) high
£800-1,000   GORL

A Moorcroft 'Flambé Orchid' pattern vase, of waisted ovoid form, with a continuous pattern of flowering orchids, stamped factory marks and blue painted signature.
c1945   7.5in (19cm) high
£800-1,200   JA

A Moorcroft 'Orchid' vase, of ovoid form, with a repeating pattern of flowering orchids on a green ground, impressed factory stamps and blue painted signature.
c1945   5in (13cm) high
£600-800   JA

A Moorcroft 'Pansy' pattern vase, of compressed ovoid form, decorated with pansies on a deep blue ground, impressed factory marks and model number, green signature.
c1926   5.25in (10.5cm) high
£400-600   JA

DECORATIVE ARTS

ESSENTIAL REFERENCE – BERNARD MOORE

Staffordshire potter, Bernard Moore (1850-1935) is recorded by the British Museum as being the first British potter to produce Chinese flambé glazes on porcelain in 1902.

- He established his own studio in 1905, following the closure of Moore Bros, the factory he had run with his brother.
- He worked as a consultant for a number of potteries, including Doulton, where he helped Charles Noke develop his flambé and sang de boeuf glazes.
- Moore's decorators worked on porcelain blanks made at the Moore Bros pottery, as well as by Minton and Wedgwood.

A Shelley E. R. Wilkes flambé ginger jar and cover, covered in a rich flambé glaze, printed Shelley mark, etched 'E R Wilkes'.

Specialising in flambé glazes, Edward R. Wilkes (1861-1953) was one of the most talented decorators at Bernard Moore's pottery.

9in (23cm) high

£300-350   WW

A flambé vase, by Bernard Moore, of shouldered form, covered in a mottled glaze, painted 'Bernard Moore'.

5.25in (13.5cm) high

£500-550   WW

A Bernard Moore ovoid vase, modelled in low-resist with carp in blue and gilt, over a flambé ground, signed 'Bernard Moore'.

3.25in (8cm) high

£500-600   WW

A Bernard Moore vase, by Annie Ollier, shouldered form painted with perched birds, on a midnight blue ground, incised 'Bernard Moore'.

6.25in (16cm) high

£700-900   WW

A large Pilkington's Lancastrian 'Heraldic' vase and cover, by Richard Joyce, impressed mark and date mark, painted cypher and date mark, restored top rim.

Known as Pilkington's and sometimes Royal Lancastrian (from 1913), Pilkington's Tile & Pottery Co. was founded in 1891 in Manchester. It made architectural goods and, later, domestic wares with distinctive glazes, such as Sunstone (1893), eggshell (1896), lustre (1906), mottled and matt, 'Cunian' (1927/28) and Lapis wares (1928). Ceramics production ceased in 1937, but the factory continues to make tiles today.

1917   *16.5in (42cm) high*

£2,000-3,000   WW

A Pilkington's Lancastrian vase, by Richard Joyce, painted with a deer among cypress trees, in ruby and copper lustre, impressed mark, painted artist cypher.

1914   *6.25in (16cm) high*

£1,000-1,500   WW

A Pilkington's vase, embossed with jaguars on a floral ground in lustred glazes, stamped 'P XII ENGLAND' and artist's signature, missing the lid.

9.25in (23.5cm) high

£700-1,000   DRA

A large Pilkington's Lancastrian Pottery vase, by Gladys Rogers, shouldered form, painted with bands of scrolling flowers and foliage in copper and orange lustre on a mottled red ground, painted bee mark, artist monogram.

16.5in (42cm) high

£400-500   WW

An early Newcomb College bottle-shaped vase, painted by Rebecca Kennon, with stylised trees, marked 'NC/AR30/RBK/JM'.

1905   *9in (23cm) high*

£5,500-7,000   **DRA**

An early Newcomb College bulbous vase, by Marie de Hoa LeBlanc, with deeply incised jonquil blossoms, marked 'NC/JM/Q/DD52/MHLB', invisible repair to chip.

1909 7.5in (19cm) wide

£7,000-11,000   **DRA**

An early Newcomb College vase, carved and painted by Marie De Hoa LeBlanc, with blue wisteria and green leaves, marked 'NC', 'VV81' and artist's cipher.

1904   *9in (23cm) high*

£30,000-35,000   **DRA**

A Newcomb College early squat vase, by Marie Ross, with fruiting trees, and restoration to chip and line NC/AE85/MRoss.

1904   *6in (15cm) wide*

£2,000-3,000   **DRA**

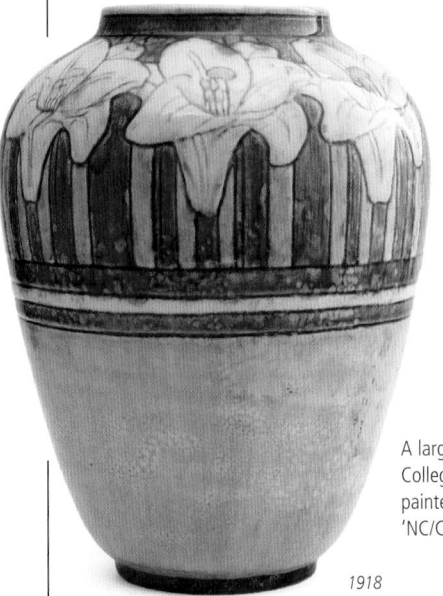

A large early Newcomb College vase, carved and painted with lilies, marked 'NC/C.L./188/KD9'.

1918   *10.25in (26cm) high*

£6,000-9,000   **DRA**

A Newcomb College Transitional vase, by Sadie Irvine, with tall pines under a full moon, marked 'NC/SI/JM/133/IZ63', restoration to opposing hairlines.

1917   *10.5in (26.5cm) high*

£3,000-4,000   **DRA**

A Newcomb College transitional vase, carved by A. F. Simpson, with paperwhites, marked 'NC/AFS/B/JM/250/JG66'.

1914   *8.25in (21cm) high*

£4,000-5,000   **DRA**

A rare Newcomb College plaque, carved by Henrietta Bailey, 'Pine Trees', with a cottage amid tall pines, carved 'NC/HB', paper label, in original frame.

12.25in (31cm) high

£6,500-8,000   DRA

A Newcomb College vase, carved by Sadie Irvine, with tall pine trees, marked 'NC/SI/JM/126/224/IB94'.

1916   *5in (12.5cm) high*

£1,800-2,300   DRA

A Newcomb College vase, carved by Sadie Irvine with a landscape.

Exhibited in 'American Art Pottery, 1875-1930,' at the Delaware Art Museum, Wilmington, 1978.

1927   *11in (28cm) high*

£6,000-7,000   CRA

A Newcomb College vase, carved by Sadie Irvine with trees and Spanish moss, marked 'NC/SI/JM/250/MW74'.

This is an unusual stylization of this moonlit landscape design.

1922   *8in (20cm) high*

£3,000-3,500   DRA

A tall Newcomb College vase, carved by A. F. Simpson, with a moonlit landscape of Spanish moss and live oak trees, incised 'NC/AFS/JM/150QC32'.

1927   *10.5in (26.5cm) high*

£6,000-9,000   DRA

A Newcomb College plaque, carved by A. F. Simpson, with live oaks and Spanish moss, mounted in original frame, signed 'NC/AFS'.

Given as a wedding gift to Josephine Dixon, niece of Brandt VB Dixon, the first president of Sophie Newcomb College.

8.25in (21cm) high

£6,000-9,000   DRA

A Newcomb College vase, carved by A. F. Simpson, with paperwhites, marked 'NC/AFS/JH/R020/77'.

1929   *6.75in (17cm) high*

£2,000-3,000   DRA

A Newcomb College bulbous vase, carved by A. F. Simpson, with a moonlit landscape of oak trees and Spanish moss, marked 'NC/AFS/SK26/JH500'.

1930   *6in (15cm) high*

£5,000-7,000   DRA

A Newcomb College tall vase, carved by A. F. Simpson, with a moonlit landscape of oak trees and Spanish moss, marked 'NC/AFS/JM/LM87/115', restored hairlines.

1921   *12.75in (32cm) high*

£3,000-4,000   DRA

A North Dakota School of Mines bulbous tapering vase, attributed to Edgar B. Everson, with excised lions in black on a mustard ground, with ink mark, incised 'EBE '36'.

1936   *6in (15cm) wide*

£3,500-4,000   **DRA**

A large North Dakota School of Mines bulbous vase, attributed to Marie Bentegeat Thormodsgard, the surface modelled with swimming fish, circular ink stamp, incised 'Marie'.

                                         8.5in (21.5cm) wide

£3,500-4,000   **DRA**

An unusual tall North Dakota School of Mines vase, incised and enamel-decorated with white blossoms on matte green ground, with indigo stamp 'DK1927'.

1927   *9.5in (24cm) high*

£9,000-11,000   **DRA**

A North Dakota School of Mines lidded vase, by Sonia Rimestad, with leaping gazelles and blossoming trees, with blue ink stamp, artist's mark and date.

1956   *10.5in (26.5cm) high*

£1,800-2,300   **DRA**

A North Dakota School of Mines bulbous vase, incised with fish under green and gunmetal glaze, with indigo stamp and incised 'Marie'.

                                         8.5in (21.5cm) high

£4,000-5,000   **DRA**

A George Ohr salt dish, mottled raspberry glaze with green drip, stamped 'G. E. OHR Biloxi Miss.', and signed 'Mobile clay 1899'.

1899   *3.5in (9cm) high*

£2,500-3,000   **CRA**

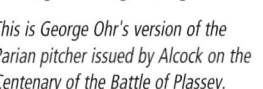

A George Ohr pitcher, with battle scene, gunmetal glaze, signed Biloxi.

This is George Ohr's version of the Parian pitcher issued by Alcock on the Centenary of the Battle of Plassey.

                                        10.25in (26cm) high

£1,500-2,500   **CRA**

A George Ohr oversized teapot, covered in green and brown flambé glaze with gunmetal sponging, the lid is original but not a match, stamped 'G, e. OHR Biloxi, Miss' twice.

When Ohr's pottery was stored in 1907, the lids were packed separately from the teapots. As a result, perhaps a third were mismatched. This pre-Carpentarian piece descended directly through the Ohr family.

                                          8in (20.5cm) wide

£6,000-9,000   **DRA**

A sculptural vessel, by George Ohr, marbleised clay, with script signature.

Ohr's experimental clays are even more remarkable than his skills as a thrower.

6in (15cm) wide

£7,000-9,000   **DRA**

A George Ohr corseted vessel, with two different ear-shaped handles, covered with mustard yellow, gunmetal, and green glaze, and stamped 'G.E. OHR, Biloxi, Miss.'.

                                          5in (12.5cm) wide

£3,500-4,000   **DRA**

A George Ohr vase, with ribbon handles, covered in mottled gunmetal and amber glaze, with raspberry and green flashes, stamped 'G.E. OHR, Biloxi, Miss.'.

                                         8.25in (21cm) high

£20,000-27,000   **DRA**

DECORATIVE ARTS

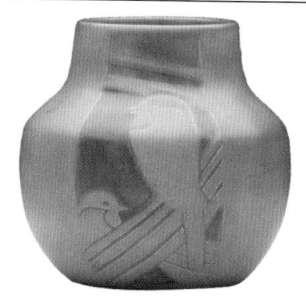

An Overbeck bulbous vase, excised with panels of stylised birds in green and brown, incised 'OBK E F'.

5.25in (13.5cm) high

£3,500-5,000   **DRA**

An Overbeck squat vessel, excised with elephants and birds in russet against a pale orange ground, incised 'OBK E F'.

5.5in (14cm) wide

£7,000-9,000   **DRA**

An Overbeck ovoid vase, covered in pink and white frothy glaze, incised 'OBK'.

8.25in (21cm) high

£700-1,000   **DRA**

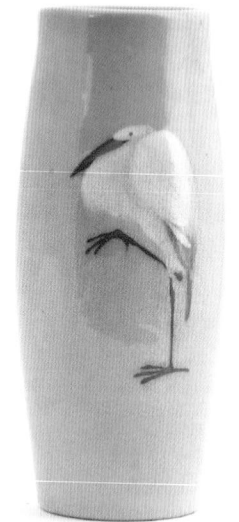

An Owens Lotus vase, finely painted by Charles Chilcote with an egret, and stamped 'OWENS 219'.

8in (20.5cm) high

£400-550   **DRA**

An Owens vase, painted by A. F. Best, 'Chief White Man-Kiowa', signed and titled, numbered '1073 5'.

10.5in (26.5cm) high

£900-1,200   **DRA**

A large Owens tile, decorated in cuenca with a cottage in a bucolic landscape, framed.

17.5in (44.5cm) wide

£2,000-3,000   **DRA**

A spectacular large and rare Pewabic squat vessel, covered in red, green, and opalescent lustered glaze, dripping over a matte blue ground, circular stamp 'PEWABIC DETROIT'.

11.5in (29cm) high

£13,000-17,000   **DRA**

A rare early Mary Chase Perry plate, painted in cobalt with a band of rabbits, signed 'Perry'.

The mark and technique of this plate dates it to the earliest work of Perry Pewabic.

10.5in (26.5cm) diam

£3,500-4,000   **DRA**

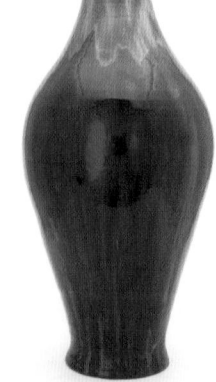

A Pewabic tall baluster vase in a lustered flambé glaze, restoration to chip to base, circular stamp.

20in high

£4,000-6,000   **DRA**

A Rookwood Standard Glaze 'Running Antelope Oncpapa', painted by Matt Daly, with portrait of an Indian chief, with flame mark, '581C', the title and 'M. A. Daly'.

Rookwood created a series of pieces with Native American portraits. Running Antelope, also known as Chief Tatokainyanka of the Oncpapa tribe in the Sioux Indian Nation, was born in 1821 in Grand Forks, South Dakota. He was known for his significant contributions in bridging the gap between European settlers and Native Americans. His picture appeared on the 1899 five-dollar silver certificate.

1897   *13.25in (33.5cm) high*

£12,000-15,000   **DRA**

A Rookwood Standard Glaze vase, painted by Grace Young after Thomas Lawrence's portrait of the 18thC British actress Sarah Siddons, with flame mark 'III/892C/GY'.

1903   *8.75in (22cm) high*

£1,800-2,300   **DRA**

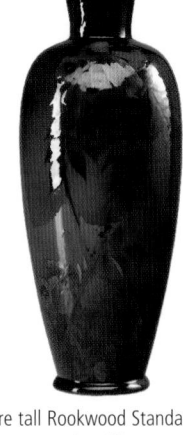

A rare tall Rookwood Standard Glaze vase, painted by Kataro Shirayamadani, with flame mark, '856B', artist's cipher and Paris Exposition label.

1899   *15.5in (39.5cm) high*

£4,000-5,000   **DRA**

A Rookwood Black Iris vase, painted by Sara Sax, with drilled base, overfired glaze (seconded), flame mark 'V/982C' and artist's cipher 'X'.

1905   *11.75in (30cm) high*

£2,000-2,500   **DRA**

A rare Rookwood 'Scenic Iris-glaze' vase, painted by Carl Schmidt, with swans and tall trees, and flame mark 'XII/1873V', artist's cipher.

1912   *5.25in (13.5cm) high*

£3,000-3,500   **DRA**

A rare Rookwood 'Iris Scenic' ovoid vase, painted by Harriet Wilcox, with tall trees by a stream, and flame mark '732C/H.E.W./X427X'.

1900   *6.75in (17cm) high*

£3,000-3,500   **DRA**

A Rookwood Jewel Porcelain footed vase, painted by Lorinda Epply in a Persian floral pattern, flame mark 'XXIII/784C/LE'.

1923   *10.75in (27cm) high*

£1,500-1,800   **DRA**

A Rookwood Jewel Porcelain plate, painted by William Hentschel in blue and white chinoiserie, flame mark 'XXIV/K2A', artist's cipher.

This plate was painted with the point of the brush in stipple technique, perhaps to impart a misty quality or to simulate craquelure. This is a modern take on the Wan-Li decorations of the late 17thC, as they appeared on Dutch Delft and German faience, Canton and Nanking.

1924   *10.25in (26cm) diam*

£900-1,200   **CRA**

A Rookwood Jewel Porcelain hemispherical vessel, painted by E. T. Hurley with large birds and blooming branches, and with flame mark 'XXIX/2254D/E.T.H.'

1929   *6.25in (16cm) wide*

£900-1,200   **DRA**

A Rookwood early Limoges-style pitcher, painted by Laura Fry, with a large scarab and insect, stamped 'ROOKWOOD 1884', kiln stamp '39' and artist cipher.

1884　　　*12in (30.5cm) high*

£700-1,200　　　　　**DRA**

A Rookwood Limoges-style pitcher, painted by Nat Hirshfield with reeds and bats, stamped 'Rookwood 1882/36/G/NJH/', with remnants of Rookwood paper label and Chicago retailer.

7.5in (19cm) high

£550-700　　　　　**DRA**

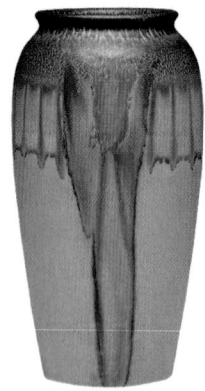

A tall Rookwood carved Matt vase, by William Hentschel, with stylised poppies, with flame mark and 'XII/917A/WEH'.

1912　　　*12in (30.5cm) high*

£3,000-3,500　　　　　**DRA**

A Rookwood Modeled Matt vase, by William Hentschell, with cattails, flame mark 'X/581E/WEH/X', seconded mark for light overglazing.

1910　　　*12.75in (32cm) high*

£1,200-1,500　　　　　**DRA**

A large Rookwood Later Matt/Matt Modern vase, by William Hentschel, with antelope, with flame mark, 'XXVII/2246C/WEH'.

14.5in (37cm) high

£2,000-2,500　　　　　**DRA**

A Rookwood Decorated Matt vase, painted by Jens Jensen, with bold yellow flowers on a grey-green ground, with flame mark, '904D/XXXI' and artist cipher.

1931　　　*8.25in (21cm) high*

£1,800-2,000　　　　　**DRA**

A tall Rookwood Decorated Matt vase, painted by Elizabeth Lincoln, with tall red tulips on a rose ground, with flame mark and 'XIX/892B/L.N.L'.

1919　　　*11in (28cm) high*

£1,200-1,800　　　　　**DRA**

A Rookwood Decorated Matt vase, painted by Elizabeth Lincoln, with wild flowers, with flame mark, 'XXX/614D/LNL'.

1930　　　*10.75in (27.5cm) high*

£1,200-1,500　　　　　**DRA**

A Rookwood painted Matt vase, by Olga G. Reed, with maple pods on a shaded ground, with flame mark and 'VI/O.G.R./907DD'.

1906　　　*10in (25.5cm) high*

£6,000-9,000　　　　　**DRA**

A Rookwood incised Matt tapered vase, decorated by Sara Sax, with peacock feathers in pink and green against a green ground, with flame mark, 'XIV/V/1655/E/V.' and artist's cipher, minor peppering.

1914　　　*8in (20.5cm) high*

£3,500-5,000　　　　　**DRA**

A Roseville 'Green Baneda' vase.

15.75in (40cm) high

£1,300-1,700   DRA

A Roseville 'Blackberry' jardinière and pedestal set.

28.5in (72.5cm) high

£1,800-2,300   DRA

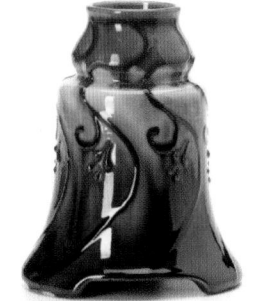

A rare Roseville 'Cremo' footed vase decorated with squeezebag floral design on a shaded red, yellow, blue and green ground, unmarked.

6.75in (17cm) high

£1,800-2,300   CRA

A large Roseville 'Crystalis' vase, covered in a fine golden crystalline glaze, post-factory drill hole to bottom.

25in (63.5cm) high

£2,000-3,000   DRA

A rare Roseville experimental 'Daffodil' vase, with a rich purple background, incised 'M' or 'W'.

8.75in (22cm) high

£2,000-3,000   DRA

A Roseville 'Della Robbia' gourd-shaped vase, with penguins and trees in celadon on blue-grey, Rozane medallion and 'EL', restoration to chips on rim and base.

8.25in (21cm) high

£1,800-2,300   DRA

A Roseville 'Della Robbia' vase, excised with lavender tulips and blue and green leaves on celadon ground, marked 'G', missing lid.

7.75in (19.5cm) high

£4,000-4,500   DRA

A tall Roseville 'Della Robbia' vase, with blossoms in apricot, yellow and blue on a celadon ground, restoration to base and rim.

15.75in (40cm) high

£12,000-15,000   DRA

An early rare Roseville Rozane 'Della Robbia' vase, carved with concentric rings of incised daisies, Rozane Ware medallion, 'M F', two chips to rim.

£7,000-11,000   DRA

A tall Roseville blue Falline vase, gold label, several small chips around foot ring.

15.25in (39cm) high

£1,200-1,500   DRA

A Roseville Red Ferella wall pocket, unmarked.

6.75in (17cm) high

£1,300-1,700   CRA

A Roseville Green Fuchsia jardinière and pedestal set, with faint impressed mark, some damage.

7.75in (19.5cm) high

£600-800   DRA

A Roseville 'Fudji' twisted four-sided vase, decorated with deep-blue poppies, with Rozane Ware seal, minor areas of wear on body.

9.5in (24cm) high

£1,200-1,800   DRA

DECORATIVE ARTS

A rare Roseville Futura 'Tank' vase, in blue to ivory shaded glaze.

These vases are rarely seen in such perfect condition, especially in his colour.

10in (25.5cm) high

£12,000-15,000   DRA

A rare large Roseville Imperial II floor vase, two chips to base.

22in (56cm) high

£3,000-4,000   DRA

A Roseville Imperial II ovoid vase, covered in a rich, mottled blue and yellow glaze over a ribbed body, with foil label, restoration to two drill holes.

11.25in (28.5cm) high

£550-700   DRA

A blue Roseville Wisteria jardinière and pedestal set, unmarked, and with restoration to rim and base of jardinière.

24in (61cm) high

£1,200-1,800   DRA

A Roseville blue Windsor ovoid two-handled vase, decorated with ferns, repair and chip to one handle, unmarked.

15.5in (39.5cm) high

£2,000-3,000   CRA

A Roseville fine experimental bulbous vase with ruffled rim, very slight overfiring at rim, raised mark '983-8', series of Experimental identification numbers.

8in (20.5cm) high

£1,500-2,000   CRA

A large and rare green Roseville Pine Cone urn, no. '912-15', with impressed mark.

£1,200-1,500   DRA

A Roseville Sunflower spherical vase, pin head-size fleck or burst to rim, very strong mould and colour.

7.25in (18.5cm) wide

£700-1,000   CRA

A rare Roseville experimental vase decorated with clusters of pink blossoms and leaves, marked to underside with a series of numbers in ink.

9.25in (23.5cm) high

£4,000-5,000   CRA

A Royal Dux bust of a woman, her hands clasped below her chin, raised on a canted square base, applied pink triangle mark.

£550-750   **L&T**

A Royal Dux 'Wedded' figure group, of a man and a woman embracing, on a shaped rectangular plinth, applied pink triangle mark.

22.75in (58cm) high

£300-500   **L&T**

A Royal Dux figure of a Spanish-style lady, in walking pose, hand-painted in bright polychrome colours all to a shaped elliptical base, applied lozenge and impressed marks.

The factory was founded at Dux (or Duchcov) in Bohemia in 1860. Dux became part of Czechoslovakia in 1918, but continued to use 'Bohemia' in the mark. The factory's porcelain figures were often copied from Royal Worcester, especially Worcester's matt ivory and bronze finishes. In the 1930s, Royal Dux created the Art Deco figures for which it is best known. It is still open today.

A Royal Dux Art Deco figural vase, the female figure with flowing hair and robe seated on a large shell, raised triangle mark to base.

9in (23cm) high

£400-500   **JA**

A Royal Dux figure of a running nude, with her Setter dog, pink triangle and printed mark to the base.

14.5in (37cm) high

£250-450   **DUK**

14.5in (37cm) high

£600-800   **FLD**

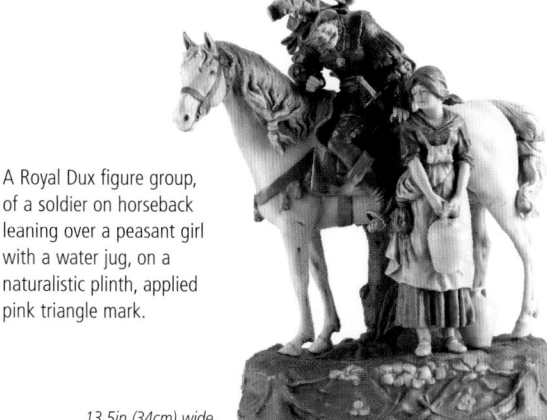

A Royal Dux figure group, of a soldier on horseback leaning over a peasant girl with a water jug, on a naturalistic plinth, applied pink triangle mark.

13.5in (34cm) wide

£400-600   **L&T**

A pair of Royal Dux figures, of a male and female water carrier, each with a pink triangle mark to the base and impressed numbers.

18.5in (47cm) high

£500-700   **DUK**

A large Ruskin Pottery Kingfisher lustre jar and cover, covered in an iridescent blue glaze, impressed 'Ruskin 1913', minor professional restoration to rim of cover.

Founded in 1901 in West Smethwick, England by William Howson Taylor (1876-1935), Ruskin Pottery was named in honour of the Arts and Crafts champion John Ruskin. Taylor was a glaze specialist, who perfected Soufflé, lustre, crystalline and high-fired glazes. The pottery closed in 1935.

1913   11.75in (30cm) high
£3,500-4,000   WW

A Ruskin Pottery high-fired stand, decorated in a mottled green and white bloom over a sang-de-boeuf ground, the rounded shoulders above pierced body falling to four scroll feet, with impressed marks.

4.75in (12cm) high
£600-800   FLD

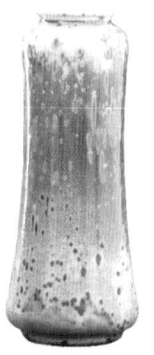

A Ruskin Pottery ovoid high-fired vase, mottled lavender, blue and green, with impressed mark.

1914   5.75in (14.5cm) high
£1,200-1,500   DN

A Ruskin Pottery high-fired vase, waisted cylindrical form, a lavender and sang-de-boeuf glaze over silver, speckled with mint green, impressed 'Ruskin Pottery West Smethwick'.

1906   9.5in (24cm) high
£2,200-2,800   WW

A Ruskin Pottery high-fired vase, mallet form with tall neck, a lavender and sang-de-boeuf glaze speckled with mint green, impressed 'Ruskin Pottery', indistinct date mark.

11.5in (29cm) high
£1,800-2,200   WW

A Ruskin high-fired stoneware vase, compressed form with silver-grey and purple snakeskin glaze, impressed marks, dated.

1923   7.75in (20cm) high
£2,200-2,800   WW

A Ruskin Pottery high-fired stoneware vase, carafe shape with everted rim, covered in a hare's-fur sang-de-boeuf, lavender over silver ground, impressed 'Ruskin Pottery West Smethwick'.

1906   10.5in (27cm) high
£1,500-2,000   WW

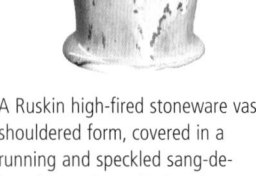

A Ruskin high-fired stoneware vase, shouldered form, covered in a running and speckled sang-de-boeuf lavender and mint glaze, impressed 'Ruskin Pottery'.

1910   10.5in (27cm) high
£1,800-2,200   WW

A rare 'Saturday Evening Girls' tile, marked 'HULL STREET GALLOUPE HOUSE', marked 'S.E.G. 12-12 SGB' in ink, with Paul Revere paper label.

3.75in (9.5cm) wide

£6,000-9,000   **DRA**

A Saturday Evening Girls mug, incised with roosters on a green ground, and 'THE EARLY BIRD', marked 'SEG', 'FR' and '26-5-09' in ink, minute glaze flake.

4in (10cm) high

£6,000-9,000   **DRA**

CLOSER LOOK – SATURDAY EVENING GIRLS

The Saturday Evening Girls (later Paul Revere Pottery) were a group of immigrant girls gathered weekly, from 1906 to 1942, to decorate pottery, which could then be sold in support of their settlement house activities.

This has a typically porous matte finish.

The vase is of a typically utilitarian form as it was intended for everyday use.

Banded decoration is typical of Saturday Evening Girls pieces.

A Saturday Evening Girls cylindrical vase, decorated in cuerda seca, with a village seen through tall trees, professional restoration to rim chip, signed '2?8.11.11.SEG IG'.

6.75in (17cm) high

£30,000-40,000   **DRA**

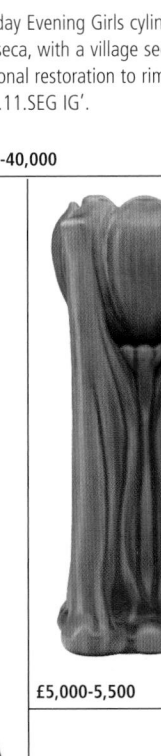

A Teco buttressed tulip vase, covered in smooth, finely charcoaled matte green glaze, stamped 'Teco' twice.

11.75in (30cm) high

£5,000-5,500   **DRA**

A Teco vase, with blades of grass, covered in smooth matte green glaze, stamped 'Teco', touch-ups to a few high points and base chip.

11.5in (29cm) high

£3,000-4,000   **DRA**

A large Teco architechtonic corseted vase, with four buttressed handles, covered in a smooth matte green glaze with charcoaling, three nicks and bruise to buttresses, stamped 'Teco 416'.

18in (46cm) high

£30,000-40,000   **DRA**

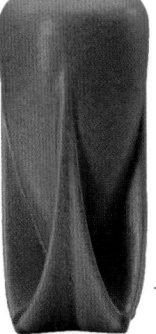

A Teco vase, with organic buttresses, covered in feathered matte green glaze, stamped 'Teco'.

9in (23cm) high

£6,000-7,000   **DRA**

A Teco vase, surrounded with reticulated handles of narrow leaves against a ribbed, flaring neck, covered in matte green glaze, stamped 'Teco'.

11.5in (29cm) high

£6,000-9,000   **DRA**

An early tall Van Briggle two-handled tapering vase, with hand-applied bronze overlay of stylised mistletoe, on an olive-green feathered ground, marked 'AA Van Briggle 1904 III 2311904'.

1904   *11in (28cm) high*
£45,000-60,000   **DRA**

An early tall Van Briggle vase, with heavily-embossed trefoils, the red clay showing through, under a flowing sky blue matte glaze, marked 'AA Van Briggle COLO SPRINGS 1906'.

1906   *12.5in (32cm) high*
£3,500-4,500   **DRA**

A 1920s Van Briggle bottle-shaped vase, with two climbing bears perched at rim, covered in Persian Rose glaze, marked 'AA Van Briggle U.S.A.'

          15.75in (40cm) high
£3,500-4,000   **DRA**

An early Van Briggle factory lamp base, with four buttressed handles, carved with tall flowers, atop a bronze foot, the glaze pooling at rim, small post-factory hole through bottom, marked 'AA Van Briggle 1904' with stamped numbers.

1904   *18in (46cm) high*
£9,000-12,000   **DRA**

An early Van Briggle vase, with heavily embossed poppies and pods under an organic matte burgundy glaze, marked 'AA Van Briggle 1902 III'.

1902   *8in (20.5cm) high*
£4,500-6,000   **DRA**

An unusual early Van Briggle vase, embossed with geese and covered in matte mustard glaze against a textured moss and mustard ground, incised 'AA Van Briggle 1902 III', crazing line at rim.

1902   *6.5in (16.5cm) high*
£12,000-15,000   **DRA**

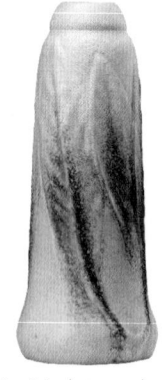

A tall Van Briggle tapered vase, embossed with tall leaves under a feathered pale blue and plum glaze, the clay showing through, mark obscured by glaze.

1902-03   *10in (25.5cm) high*
£3,000-3,500   **DRA**

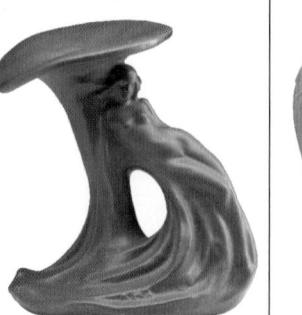

A 1920s Van Briggle 'Lady of the Lily' vase, in Persian Rose glaze, marked 'AA Van Briggle', long firing line to base.

          11.5in (29cm) wide
£1,200-1,500   **DRA**

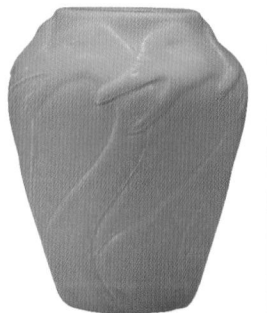

A rare early Van Briggle vase, carved with a gaggle of geese in profile, under a fine matte green glaze, incised 'AA Van Briggle 1902'.

1902   *6.25in (16cm) high*
£5,000-7,000   **DRA**

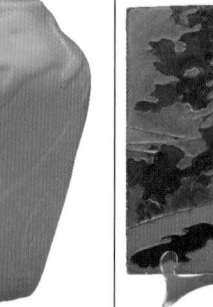

A large Van Briggle tile, decorated in cuenca with a tree against a mountainous landscape, three small nicks overall, chip to two corners, mounted in new Arts and Crafts frame.

          12.25in (31cm) wide
£9,000-12,000   **DRA**

A Van Briggle tile, decorated in cuenca with a blue jay on a branch, against a pale blue ground, a few flecks to high points, framed.

          6in (15cm) wide
£1,800-2,300   **DRA**

A Volkmar vase, carved with deep blue trillium and swirling leaves on mottled brown and green ground, incised 'V' mark.

8.25in (21cm) high

£1,500-1,800   **DRA**

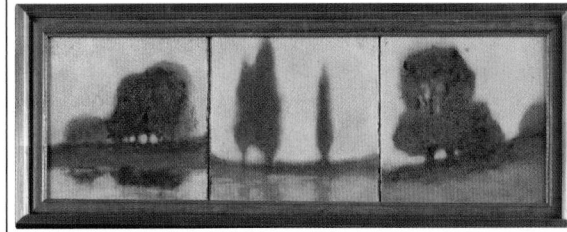

Three Volkmar tiles, matte-painted in the Impressionist style with a landscape in tones of green, framed together, each signed 'B'.

Each tile 8in (20.5cm) wide

£4,000-5,000   **DRA**

A tall vase, by W. J. Walley, covered in curdled semi-matte and lustrous green glaze, impressed 'WJW'.

16.5in (42cm) high

£3,000-3,500   **DRA**

A W. J. Walley bottle-shaped vase, covered in a fine feathered matte green glaze, and stamped 'WJW'.

4.75in (12cm) high

£600-900   **DRA**

A Studio pottery vase, by William J. Walley, the mottled green-brown glaze with leather skin texture at neck and shoulder over bulbous form with broad overlapping leaves, impressed 'WJW'.

1905   *6.75in (17cm) high*

£5,000-6,000   **SK**

A Walrath cylindrical vase, painted with a band of green pine boughs against a yellow and blue sky, on a matte green ground, incised 'Walrath Pottery'.

8.25in (21cm) high

£3,500-4,500   **DRA**

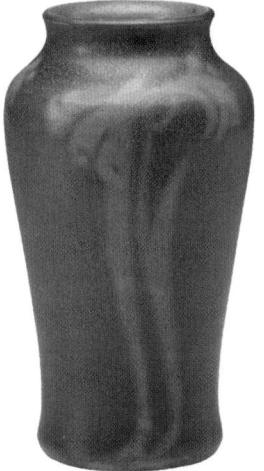

A Walrath vase, matte-painted with red lilies and green leaves on a deep green ground, incised 'Walrath Pottery'.

7.5in (19cm) high

£3,000-3,500   **DRA**

An unusual Walrath vase, with wooded landscape and cabin, incised 'Walrath Pottery'.

1915   *7.25in (18.5cm) high*

£9,000-12,000   **DRA**

A Walrath vase, matte-painted with a landscape, signed 'Walrath Pottery', a hairline from rim.

6.25in (16cm) high

£1,800-2,300   **DRA**

A large Wedgwood Fairyland Lustre octagonal bowl, 'Boxing Match' interior, 'Castle on a Road' exterior, with gold Wedgwood England stamp 'Z5125'.

11.5in (29cm) diam

£3,500-4,500   DRA

A Wedgwood Fairyland Lustre 'Butterfly Woman' trumpet vase, designed by Daisy Makeig-Jones, printed and painted in colours and gilt on a black lustre ground, printed and painted marks.

9.75in (24.5cm) high

£2,500-3,500   WW

A Wedgwood Fairyland Lustre 'Candlemas' vase, designed by Daisy Makeig-Jones, printed and painted in colours and gilt, printed factory mark.

8.5in (21.5cm) high

£4,000-4,500   WW

A Wedgwood Fairyland Lustre vase and cover, pattern Z4968, 'Ghostly Woods' under a pale blue-grey sky, printed mark.

Wedgwood's Fairyland Lustre range was designed by Daisy Makeig-Jones (1881-1945) in the 1920s. Her patterns of magical landscapes filled with fairies, goblins and pixies were then painted and printed in gold. These designs rarely bear Makeig-Jones's initials, but are sometimes numbered and prefixed with a 'Z'.

c1920   *15.5in (39.5cm) high*

£10,000-12,000   SK

A Wedgwood Fairyland Lustre 'Torches' vase, shape 3144, cylindrical form with flaring rim and foot, printed 'Z4968' mark.

c1920   *11.5in (29cm) high*

£1,500-1,800   SK

A Wedgwood Fairyland Lustre 'Woodland Bridge' pedestal bowl, designed by Daisy Makeig-Jones, printed factory marks, hairline crack.

8.75in (22.5cm) diam

£1,100-1,300   TEN

A Wedgwood Fairyland Lustre bowl, 'Woodland Bridge' and 'Picnic by a River' patterns, designed by Daisy Makeig-Jones, printed and painted in colours and gilt on a black lustre ground, printed and painted marks.

8.25in (21cm) diam

£2,800-3,200   WW

A Wedgwood black basalt centrepiece, designed by Paul Follot, modelled in low relief with sprays of fruit, impressed 'Wedgwood'.

14.25in (36cm) diam

£800-1,000   WW

A Wedgwood Fairyland Lustre 'Jewelled Tree' vase, designed by Daisy Makeig-Jones, printed and painted in colours and gilt on black lustre ground, printed and painted marks.

9.25in (23.5cm) high

£5,000-7,000   WW

A rare Wedgwood 'Garden Implements' lemonade jug and four beakers, designed by Eric Ravilious, printed in black and pink lustre, printed factory marks.

Jug 7.75in (20cm) high

£1,200-1,800   WW

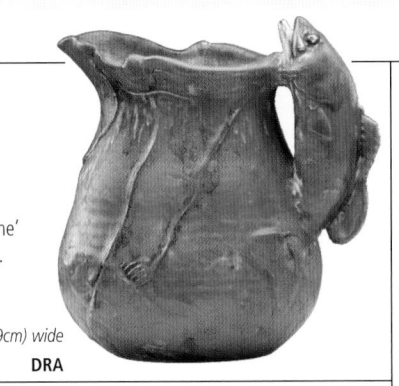

A rare Weller 'Coppertone' pitcher, with fish handle.

7.5in (19cm) wide

£1,500-1,800   **DRA**

A Weller 'Dickensware' ewer, decorated with an American Indian, 'Wolf Robein', with 'Dickensware' stamp, artist signed 'ELK' or 'ELH', stamped '176'.

11in (28cm) high

£550-700   **DRA**

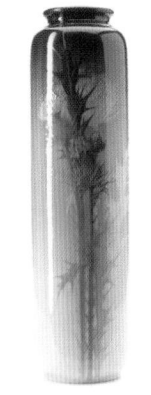

A Weller Eocean cylindrical vase, painted by Eugene Roberts with pink and ivory thistle, incised mark.

20.5in (52cm) high

£1,800-2,300   **CRA**

A large Weller 'Coppertone' frog sprinkler, includes fittings, short line to bottom at opening possibly caused in the firing.

10.25in (26cm) high

£1,500-2,000   **DRA**

A rare large Weller 'Gardenware' swan figure, marked in script, a chip to bottom tip of tail.

21in (53.5cm) wide

£6,000-7,000   **DRA**

A Weller 'Hudson' vase, by McLaughlin, with sailboats, kiln stamp with 'WELLER POTTERY' and artist's signature, opposing hairlines at rim.

8.75in (22cm) high

£900-1,200   **DRA**

A rare Weller 'Jap Birdimal' tall chocolate pot, carved and decorated in squeezebag with viking ships, impressed numbers, missing lid.

11.5in (29cm) high

£500-700   **DRA**

A rare tall Weller 'Jewell' vase, incised with fiddlehead ferns, and embossed with a band of birds against a purple ground, impressed 'Weller', post-factory drill-hole through bottom.

13in (33cm) high

£2,000-2,500   **DRA**

A Weller 'Knifewood' ovoid vase, with squirrels and oak branches, impressed mark, a few flecks to high points.

11in (28cm) high

£1,500-1,800   **DRA**

A Weller matt green vase, with reticulated poppy design around rim.

13.5in (34cm) wide

£2,000-3,000   DRA

A Weller Perfecto ovoid vase painted by Mae Timberlake with ivory and celadon thistles and leaves, stamped 'Weller', artist signed.

13.5in (34.25cm) high

£1,200-1,500   CRA

A tall Weller Sicard ovoid vase, painted with snails on a swirled ground in gold, green and purple, evenly fired, signed in script.

12.5in (32cm) high

£3,500-4,000   DRA

A Weller Sicard footed bowl, with green and gold iridescent butterflies and stars against a rusty-red iridescent background, signed on the side in gold iridescence 'Sicard Weller' and numbered on the underside '87'.

4.5in (11.5cm) high

£1,000-1,300   JDJ

A large rare Weller 'Woodcraft' vase, with owl perched on an apple tree branch, impressed mark, restoration to small area in hole, hairline to interior.

15.75in (40cm) high

£1,200-1,500   DRA

A rare Weller Zona jardinière and pedestal set, decorated with panels of cattails and kingfishers, with stamped mark and very minor hairline to both rim and base of jardinière.

30.5in (77.5cm) high

£1,200-1,500   DRA

A rare Wheatley vase, with four curled handles alternating with leaves, and covered in matte ochre glaze, with 'WP' and number.

12in (30.5cm) high

£1,800-2,300   DRA

A Wheatley lamp base, with buttressed feet and leaf and bud decoration under matte green glaze, incised 'WP 609'.

10in (30.5cm) high

£900-1,200   DRA

A Wheatley lamp base, in the Kendrick style, with buttressed feet, buds and full-height leaves, marked 'WP 6', factory hole to base, abrasion around rim, some chips to feet.

12.5in (32cm) high

£900-1,200   DRA

A Wheatley vase, modelled with leaves in the style of Grueby, covered in matte green glaze, the mark obscured by glaze.

8.5in (21.5cm) high

£900-1,200   DRA

ESSENTIAL REFERENCE – WEMYSS

The distinctive, brightly coloured, underglazed Wemyss ware was first made in 1882 at the Fife Pottery. The pottery was founded and run by Robert Methven Heron. Heron was assisted by his sister, Jessie, the firm's manager Robert McLaughlan, and master painter Karel Nekola. Wemyss ware was sold exclusively by the London firm Thomas Goode & Co.

- The pottery enjoyed the patronage of the nearby Wemyss family, after whom it named its wares. The wares were aimed at owners of country houses. Nekola died in 1915 and was succeeded by Staffordshire potter. Edwin Sandland.
- Wares include plates, biscuit barrels, ink wells, tea sets and animal figures, including the large ceramic pigs and cats for which the firm is best known. This multitude of forms was decorated with images inspired by nature, such as fruit and flowers, particularly the famous Wemyss cabbage roses, and the birds and animals of the British countryside.
- The brand moved to Bovey Tracey, Devon in 1930, where it was made until 1957.
- In 1985, Griselda Hill pottery began to make its modern Wemyss ware.

A Wemyss footbath, decorated by Karel Nekola with cabbage roses, painted and impressed marks, 'T. Goode & Co. London' painted retailer's marks.

c1900 20in (51cm) wide

£2,000-2,200 L&T

A large early 20thC Wemyss dog bowl, inscribed 'Plus je connais les hommes/ Plus j'admire les chiens', impressed mark 'Wemyss', 'T. Goode & Co.' retailer's mark.

8.25in (21cm) diam

£1,800-2,200 L&T

A large Wemyss ewer and basin, decorated with dog roses, shamrocks and thistles, impressed mark 'Wemyss Ware R. H. & S.' and 'T. Goode & Co.' retailer's mark on both, staining to base of ewer.

c1900 Ewer 9.75in (25cm) high

£3,000-3,500 L&T

A rare Wemyss sectional shaving set, decorated with cabbage roses, comprising a footed soap bowl, the interior with conical spiked prunts, a twin-handled water vessel and a chamber candlestick, minor restoration.

c1900 10in (25.5cm) high

£1,800-2,200 L&T

A Wemyss teapot, decorated with dog roses, impressed mark 'Wemyss'.

c1900 4.25in (11cm) high

£300-400 L&T

An early 20thC Wemyss coffee pot and cover, decorated with cabbage roses and bearing inscription to lid 'Coffee', impressed mark 'Wemyss'.

6.75in (17cm) high

£1,600-1,800 L&T

A tall early 20thC biscuit barrel and cover, decorated by Edwin Sandland with cabbage roses on black ground, cover inscribed 'Biscuits', painted and impressed marks 'Wemyss'.

6.25in (16cm) high

£550-750 L&T

A large Wemyss loving cup, decorated with cabbage roses, impressed mark 'Wemyss Ware R. H. & S.', minor restoration.

c1900 9.75in (24.5cm) diam

£1,000-1,500 L&T

A late 19thC Wemyss Victorian goblet, inscribed '1837' and '1897' to commemorate Queen Victoria's Diamond Jubilee, impressed mark 'Wemyss', minor paint flakes.

6in (15cm) high

£900-1,200 L&T

A Wemyss Kenmore vase, decorated by Karel Nekola, with cabbage roses, painted mark and impressed mark 'Wemyss', 'T. Goode & Co.' retailer's mark.

c1900   *14.5in (36.5cm) high*

£800-1,000   **L&T**

An early 20thC Wemyss bottle vase, decorated with cabbage roses, with green-painted neck, impressed mark 'Wemyss'.

9.75in (25cm) high

£1,100-1,300   **L&T**

An early 20thC Wemyss chamber stick, decorated by James Sharp with cabbage roses, painted mark 'Wemyss'.

5in (12.5cm) high

£1,800-2,000   **L&T**

An early 20thC Wemyss Kenmore vase, decorated with irises, impressed mark 'Wemyss', 'T. Goode & Co.' retailer's mark.

15in (38cm) high

£2,500-3,500   **L&T**

An early 20thC Wemyss 'Drummond' flowerpot, decorated with irises, impressed mark 'Wemyss', 'T. Goode & Co.' retailer's mark.

8.25in (21cm) high

£1,200-1,800   **L&T**

An early 20thC Wemyss comb tray, decorated with sweet peas, possibly by David Grinton, painted and impressed marks 'Wemyss', 'T. Goode & Co.' retailer's mark, restoration.

10.25in (26cm) wide

£400-500   **L&T**

An early 20thC Wemyss pin tray, decorated with thistles, inscribed 'I looked for something Scotch to send you/ And the Thistles asked if they would do.', painted and impressed mark 'Wemyss'.

5.75in (14.5cm) wide

£600-700   **L&T**

An early 20thC three-handled mug, decorated with thistles, impressed mark 'Wemyss'.

5.75in (14.5cm) high

£700-900   L&T

An early 20thC Wemyss 'Lincoln' flower pot, decorated by James Sharp, impressed and painted marks 'Wemyss', hairline cracks.

10.25in (26cm) high

£1,000-1,200   L&T

A set of three post-1930 Plichta cat figures, comprising large, medium and small figures, printed marks 'Plichta London England'.

Largest 10.25in (26cm) high

£900-1,200   L&T

A post-1930 Wemyss cat figure, decorated by Joe Nekola with shamrocks, painted mark 'Wemyss', restoration to foot.

13.5in (31cm) high Est

£2,000-3,000   L&T

A Wemyss 'Gordon' dessert plate, decorated with daffodils, with impressed mark 'Wemyss/ R. H. & S.', and printed 'T. Goode & Co.' retailer's mark, restored to rim.

8in (20.5cm) diam

£350-450   L&T

An early 20thC Wemyss three-handled mug, decorated with fuchsias, impressed mark 'Wemyss', restored handles.

5.25in (13.5cm) high

£500-700   L&T

A pair of tall Wemyss Kenmore candlesticks, decorated with lilacs, impressed mark 'Wemyss Ware', 'T. Goode & Co.' retailer's mark.

c1900   9.5in (24cm) high

£800-1,000   L&T

A large Wemyss mug, decorated with passion flowers, impressed mark 'Wemyss Ware R. H. & S.', hairline crack.

c1900   5.5in (14cm) high

£1,000-1,200   L&T

An early 20thC Wemyss biscuit barrel and cover, decorated with violets, painted and impressed marks 'Wemyss'.

4.25in (11cm) high

£1,300-1,500   L&T

DECORATIVE ARTS

An Art Nouveau Zsolnay plaque, painted with a maiden by a pond with swans, and 'framed' with three-dimensional gargoyles, entirely covered in blue and gold lustred glaze, five churches stamp with 'ZSOLNAY PECS', restored.

Zsolnay was established by Vilmos Zsolnay in Pécs, Hungary in c.1865. Until the 1890s, it mainly produced ornate ceramics inspired by Islamic pierced wares. The chemist Vincse Wartha became artistic director in 1893, and Zsolnay subsequently began to specialize in simple, organic Art Noveau forms. These often featured low-relief moulding, and were decorated with marbled, shaded and crystalline glazes. The most successful of these glazes was a lustrous, iridescent, greenish glaze known as 'Eosin'.

19in (48cm) high

£20,000-25,000   **DRA**

A Zsolnay vase, with six twisted buttresses, in red and nacreous gold-green to purple glaze, five churches medallion, marked '6204' and '23', minor scratches overall.

9.25in (23.5cm) high

£8,000-8,500   **DRA**

A Zsolnay organically-shaped vase with eight reticulated handles, covered in lustred blue-green glaze over a burgundy base, with five churches medallion.

7.5in (19cm) high

£6,500-7,000   **DRA**

A Zsolnay figural pitcher, with reticulated dragon under a blue Eosin glaze, five churches medallion '787 2 36 48', a few minor glaze flecks.

10.5in (26.5cm) high

£1,200-1,800   **DRA**

An unusual Zsolnay pelican-shaped pitcher, in polychrome Eosin glaze, five churches medallion, '1004', small chip to repaired area on base.

9.5in (24cm) high

£2,500-3,000   **DRA**

A Zsolnay baluster vase, painted in lustred glazes with birds in a Persian design, five churches medallion, marked 'Zsolnay Pecs 8767'.

8.75in (22cm) high

£1,500-2,000   **DRA**

A Zsolnay tapered vase, with snail handles, covered in mottled majolica glaze, five churches medallion, '6322 M', small fleck to raised point.

8.25in (21cm) high

£2,000-3,000   **DRA**

A Zsolnay Pecs figure of a crouching nude, no. 7991, red flambé glazed, on an oval base, with applied mark.

9.5in (24cm) long

£400-600   **DN**

An Art Nouveau Zsolnay pitcher, with four dancing muses under an Eosin glaze, five churches medallion, '7147 36 48', two minor glaze misses.

14in (35.5cm) high

£11,000-12,000   **DRA**

An Ault Pottery 'Propellor' vase, designed by Christopher Dresser, covered in a running green glaze.

5.5in (14cm) high

£200-250   WW

A tall Barum jardinière and pedestal, excised and enamel-glazed with stylised peacocks, complete with original stained-wood base, hand-incised 'C.H. Brannam, FB Barum, 1909, Ro. 44561', glaze flakes.

41in (104cm) high

£1,500-2,500   DRA

A small French vase, by Eugène Baudin, covered in turquoise glaze, and set into a hammered copper frame with dragonflies, signed.

3.75in (9.5cm) high

£900-1,200   DRA

A Boch Frères earthenware vase, enamelled in colours on a crackled glaze with exotic flowers, printed mark.

8.75in (22cm) high

£200-300   WW

A Bing & Grondahl white porcelain 'The Water Mother' sculpture, by Kai Nielsen, after his marble sculpture 'Vandmoderen', in the winter garden of Ny Carlsberg Glyptotek.

Originally made for display at the Paris Exhibition of 1925, which featured high-style Art Deco design.

c1925   19.25in (49cm) long

£1,500-2,500   SK

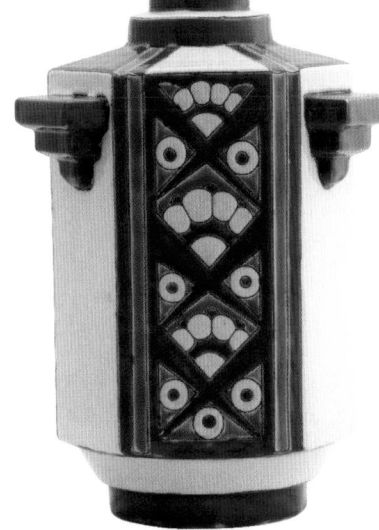

An Art Deco Boch Frères faceted faience vessel, decorated in cuerda seca with an abstracted floral pattern, with circular black ink stamp 'D. 1194, 1038'.

12.75in (32.5cm) high

£1,500-2,500   DRA

A C. H. Brannam pottery 'Galleon' centrepiece, by Reginald Pearce, modelled in low relief and glazed in shades of green, blue and brown, incised marks.

1913   12.25in (31cm) long

£300-400   WW

A C. H. Brannam Barnstaple basket, with a strap handle, each side modelled with a grotesque mask, with incised mark, unidentified artist's initials, dated, cracks.

1900   6.5in (16.5cm) high

£500-600   DN

A Burmantoft's Faïence 'Persian' vase, by Leonard King, design 91, painted with a mythical beast, in shades of blue and green on a white ground, impressed and painted marks, 'LK' monogram, minor damages.

9in (23cm) high

£700-900   WW

A massive Burmantoft's Faience 'Anglo Persian' vase, by Leonard King, shape no. 29, painted with a scrolling carnation design, impressed and painted marks, remains of a retail label.

The Burmantoft pottery was established in Yorkshire in 1858 by Wilcock & Co. It produced architectural bricks and ceramics, until it was acquired by the Leeds Fireclay Company in 1889. Burmantoft then began to produce ornamental earthenware fired at high temperatures, as well as single-glazed pieces in multi-coloured 'Isnic' that were similar to pieces by William de Morgan, and other wares in red, yellow and turquoise. It closed in the 1950s.

20in (51cm) high

£10,000-15,000   WW

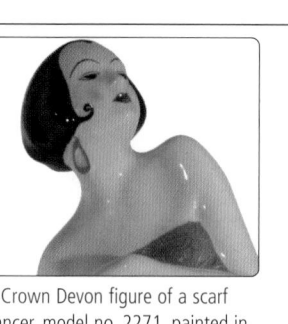

A Crown Devon figure of a scarf dancer, model no. 2271, painted in colours, highlighted in gilt, printed factory marks, hairline to base.

13.25in (33.5cm) high

£900-1,200   WW

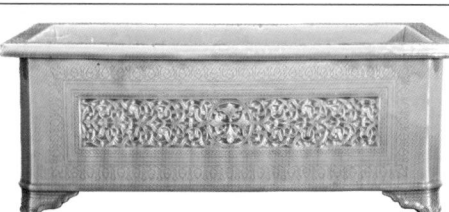

A Theodore Deck rectangular pottery planter, impressed with panels of foliage, glazed blue, impressed marks, damages.

16.5in (42cm) wide

£550-650   WW

A Theodore Deck charger, decorated by Albert Anker, with enamelled portrait of a lady, signed 'Anker', impressed 'TH. DECK'.

15.5in (39.5cm) diam

£4,000-5,000   DRA

A Della Robbia terracotta twin-handled vase, by Ruth Bare, incised and painted with waterlily flowers in shades of blue, yellow and green, incised marks, 'RB' monogram.

11.5in (29cm) high

£600-800   WW

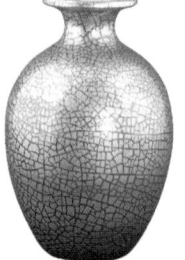

A Sunflower Pottery 'Gold Crackle' glaze vase, by Sir Edmund Elton.

Elton pieces in gold and silver are particularly collectable.

8.25in (21cm) high

£300-400   WW

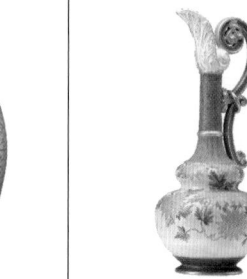

A tall Faience Manufacturing Co. ewer, by Edward Lycett, with gold daisies on a pale crackled ground, stamped 'FMCo. 324 650', some wear.

22.25in (56.5cm) high

£1,500-1,800   DRA

A Faience Manufacturing Co. vase on stand, by Edward Lycett, with pierced and gilded handles, stamped '659' on both vase and stand, small chips.

16.25in (41cm) high

£2,000-2,500   DRA

A Camille Faure enamel-decorated vase, on a rich red ground, signed 'Faure-Limoges/France'.

5.75in (14.5cm) high

£1,000-1,200   DRA

A large French organic jardinière, by Fives-Lille, with curled leaf-like handles under a dynamic and flowing white, blue, gold and pink crystalline glaze, die-stamp mark 'L'ISLE-ADAM', minor restoration.

12in (30.5cm) wide

£1,500-1,800   DRA

A Foley two-handled vase, by Frederick H. Rhead, decorated in squeezebag with yellow and orange flowers and tall brown leaves, stamped mark 'THE FOLEY 'URBATO' ENGLAND A 4014'.

6.25in (16cm) high

£400-500   DRA

A rare Emile Gallé ceramic vase, decorated with dianthus, butterflies and twigs, with gilded highlights, impressed 'Emile Gallé Nancy Depose', a few very minor flakes to glaze, bruise to rim.

8.25in (21cm) high

£1,200-1,500   DRA

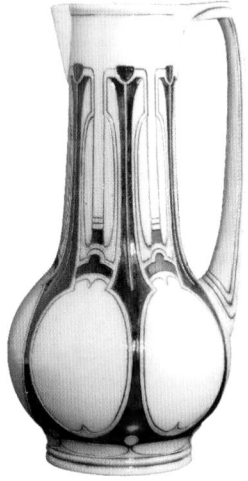

A Simon Gerz Art Nouveau stoneware ewer, model no. 1146, designed by Peter Behrens incised with vertical geometric repeat, glazed blue impressed marks.

13in (33cm) high

£500-600   WW

A rare large Gouda plaque, painted after Cornelis Springer (1817-91), 'Edam,' with a Dutch street scene, marked 'Made In Zuid Holland Gouda', titled and signed 'H. D. S. n CSpringer', in original gold-painted frame.

Plaque 21.25in (54cm) high

£1,800-2,200   DRA

A pair of tall Gouda vases, painted in a bold floral pattern, signed 'GOUDA PLAZUID HOLLAND 4425', paper label.

18.5in (47cm) high

£1,200-1,500   DRA

A Gray's Pottery 'Moon and Mountain' coffee set for six, designed by Susie Cooper, comprising coffee pot, milk-jug sugar basin, six cups and saucers, printed liner mark, painted '7960' mark.

Coffee pot 7.75in (20cm) high

£1,800-2,200   WW

DECORATIVE ARTS

A rare Shelley Pottery 'Shelley Girl' advertising figure, modelled seated holding a cup of tea, printed and painted in colours, printed mark to base.

12.25in (31cm) high

£4,500-5,500   **WW**

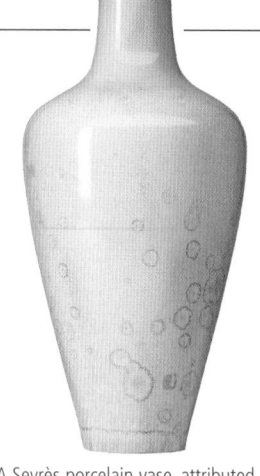

A Sevrès porcelain vase, attributed to Taxile Doat, with fully-blown gold and cream crystals on a feathered crystalline ground, stamped 'S 1900'.

1900   *14.5in (37cm) high*

£1,200-1,800   **DRA**

A Sevrès cabinet vase, by Taxile Doat, covered in French blue and plum flambé crystalline glaze in a star pattern, signed 'TDoat Sevres 1907'.

1907   *3.25in (8cm) high*

£2,000-2,200   **DRA**

A rare Charles Vyse lustre vase, painted with a figure riding a giant fish, in shades of blue and ruby lustre on sand, painted monogram, 'Chelsea 1923', minor professional restoration.

8.25in (21cm) high

£2,500-3,500   **WW**

A posy vase modelled as a bulldog, by Louis Wain, in standing pose, with abstract facial features, the body decorated with black swirls over yellow ground, painted signature to the rear leg, restored.

5.5in (14cm) long

£900-1,200   **FLD**

A posy vase modelled as a seated pig, by Louis Wain, with abstract facial features, the body decorated with black swirls over green ground, painted signature to the rear.

4.75in (12cm) high

£900-1,200   **FLD**

A Lord Haw Haw figural posy vase in the form of an abstract dog figure, by Louis Wain, with stylised features and body picked out in blue, green and red with black painted signature, printed and painted marks.

The British artist Louis Wain (1860-1939) was a successful illustrator, best known for his pictures of large-eyed anthropomorphic cats.

5in (13cm) high

£400-600   **FLD**

£2,500-3,000   **DRA**

A Wiener Werkstätte ceramic vase, by Koloman Moser, with swirled handles, covered in mirrored black and emerald green glaze, stamped 'KM' in block and '149 4, (..) MUSTER GESETZL GESCHZT', glaze flake to rim.

8in (20.5cm) high

A Watcombe Pottery terracotta jug, designed by Christopher Dresser, angular form with three serrated bands, printed 'Watcombe Torquay' and 'regd diamond'.

8in (20.5cm) high

£350-450   **WW**

An Austrian bottle-shaped vase, with applied, twisted ribbon-like designs, covered in a nacreous purple, blue, red and green glaze.

9.5in (24cm) high

£600-700   **DRA**

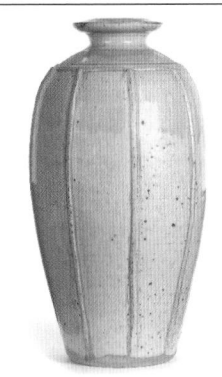

A Richard Batterham stoneware vase, ash glaze.

Batterham does not mark his work. He was at Leach Pottery, St Ives, 1957-8.

16.5in (42cm) high

£500-550   TEN

A Michael Ambrose Cardew stoneware bowl, the interior incised with chevrons and lines, the exterior with a blue brushwork wave within khaki bands, impressed 'MC' and 'Wenford Bridge' seals.

10.5in (27cm) diam

£600–700   TEN

A stoneware vase, by Hans Coper, of spade form with a cylindrical column base, with a rough-textured body picked out with a smeared matt manganese glaze, impressed circular 'HC' seal.

c1965-1970   8.5in (21.5cm) high

£4,000-6,000   FLD

ESSENTIAL REFERENCE – BERNARD LEACH

Bernard Leach (1991-2005) was born in Hong Kong to British parents and studied potting techniques in Japan.

- **He returned to England in 1920 and started the Leach Pottery in St Ives, Cornwall with Shoji Hamada.**
- **Leach's ceramics were traditional Eastern-style wares, deriving inspiration from Japanese Raku wares, but they used English techniques like slip decoration and salt glazing. He produced table wares and vases of simple, sturdy forms, decorated with subtle glazes and occasional boldly splashed or incised motifs.**
- **He believed strongly that 'pots, like all forms of art, are human expressions', and was largely responsible for the idea of the potter as an artist, rather than a craftsman. Leach also inspired the notion that the irregular texture of a hand-thrown pot is 'superior' to more highly-finished wares.**
- **Leach also trained many of the best British studio potters, including his son, David.**

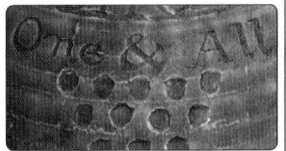

A rare Bernard Leach and Michael Ambrose Cardew earthenware pitcher, rich toffee-brown glaze with old Cornish inscription 'EVEUGH TOS DHO GERNOW TEG' and 'One & All', 'St Ives' seal.

c1926   9in (23cm) high

£1,000-1,500   TEN

A Bernard Leach stoneware vase, blue glaze with a tree design in khaki repeated front and back, unglazed foot rim, impressed 'England' and with 'BL' and 'St Ives Pottery' seals.

6.25in (16cm) high

£1,800-2,000   TEN

A Bernard Leach stoneware flat-sided bottle vase, tenmoku glaze, impressed 'BL' and 'St Ives Pottery' seals.

7.5in (19cm) high

£1,200-1,800   TEN

A Bernard Leach and Michael Ambrose Cardew earthenware jug, rich toffee-brown glaze with iron-painted decoration, 'St Ives' seal.

c1926   9in (23cm) high

£1,200-1,800   TEN

DECORATIVE ARTS

Two of a set of eight Aesthetic Movement walnut dining chairs, in the manner of Thomas Jekyll, with lattice framed splats on spirally reeded and channelled uprights, on turned and reeded tapering legs, stamped 'Maple & Co. Ltd'.

£1,500-2,000 SET   **L&T**

A pair of Aesthetic Movement oak hall chairs, the carved arched backs inset with a Minton Shakespeare series brown printed title, designed by John Moyr Smith, on ring turned front supports.

34.25in (87cm) high

£200-300   **DN**

An Aesthetic Movement side table, probably retailed by Goodyers, with rod and ball construction.

26.75in (68cm) high

£450-500   **WW**

An Aesthetic Movement walnut rectangular table, with ring turned and carved arcaded supports, a galleried undertier with flower-carved angle panels and ring turned feet, stamped 'LL 13006'.

27.25in (69cm) wide

£800-1,200   **DN**

An Aesthetic Movement tile-mounted and part-ebonized walnut library cabinet, the rectangular top and case with incised and scrolled supports, the frieze mounted with black and tan tiles, shelved interior.

c1880   *43.25in (110cm) wide*

£1,800-2,200   **SK**

An American Aesthetic Movement ebonised and parcel gilt Tabard Inn revolving library bookcase, on a four-legged stand.

The Tabard Inn Library was founded in 1902 by Seymour Eaton. The 'libraries' consisted of a revolving bookcase located in commercial outlets such as chemists or grocery stores throughout the United States. Each bookcase held 120 books, which were changed from a central location every week.

73in (185.5cm) high

£3,000-4,000   **SK**

A Victorian Aesthetic walnut side cabinet, by Gillow & Co., in the manner of Bruce James Talbert, with decorative gilding, ebony and boxwood-crossbanded borders to the drawers, the doors with painted panels, some faults.

75.5in (192cm) wide

£700-1,000   **TOV**

An Aesthetic Movement oak sideboard, the mirrored and shelved back with two carved foliate roundels, the base with a drawer flanked by panelled doors, on ring turned short supports.

60.25in (153cm) wide

£100-150   **DN**

A CLOSER LOOK – VIARDOT WRITING CABINET

A Japanese-style kingwood padouk, mahogany and rosewood writing cabinet, attributed to Gabriel Viardot, inlaid and banded with mother-of-pearl, ebony and strung in brass.

Beginning his career as a wood carver, Gabriel Viardot (1830–1906) took over the family firm from his father Charles in 1861. By 1870 he specialised in exotic furniture influenced by Chinese and Vietnamese styles, Vietnam being one of France's most important colonies. Around 1885 he employed about 100 workers. He exhibited widely, including at Crystal Palace in 1851, and was both participant and jury member for the 1867, 1878 and 1889 International Exhibitions in Paris. His major success was at the 1889 Paris Exposition Universelle where the firm was awarded a gold medal.

This dramatic piece is the perfect expression of the Aesthetic Movement that arose towards the end of the 19thC combining, as it does, European and Far Eastern elements.

The exotic pagoda-like top and the carved mythological dragons are features that make this piece particularly desirable. The dragons are vulnerable to knocks, and may show signs of damage or restoration.

The decoration to the front of this cabinet is exceptional, the mother-of-pearl and ebony inlays further reinforcing the influence from the Far East, while the mahogany and rosewood panels are traditionally more European.

c1880 108.25in (275cm) wide

£30,000-50,000 L&T

An Aesthetic Movement coromandel, amboyna crossbanded and ebonised canterbury, the pierced brass gallery above an inlaid frieze and four spindle turned divisions, the apron enclosing a drawer, on turned tapering legs.

30in (76cm) wide

£3,500-4,500 L&T

An early 20thC Aesthetic Movement style gilt-brass and copper gong stand, the frame cast naturalistically as branches.

36.5in (93cm) high

£400-500 DN

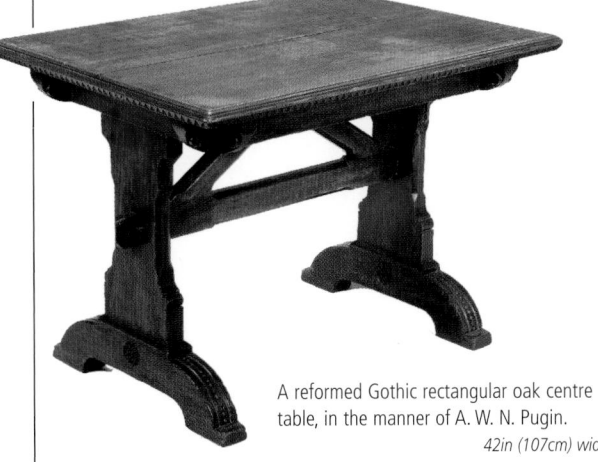

A reformed Gothic rectangular oak centre table, in the manner of A. W. N. Pugin.

42in (107cm) wide

£400-500 DN

A reformed Gothic oak and ebonised writing table, with a later baise lined top, with seven drawers with brass handles, spindle brackets and turned legs.

47.75in (121cm) wide

£700-800 DN

A carved oak day bed, in the style of John Moyr Smith, with architectural pillars and foliate capitals, inset with decorative copper panel.

63in (160cm) wide

£400-600　　　　**WW**

An Arts and Crafts stained oak centre table, in the manner of William Leiper, the reeded rectangular top above ring-turned legs linked by cross stretchers.

31in (79cm) high

£1,200-1,800　　**L&T**

An Arts and Crafts light oak refectory table, in the Cotswold School style, on chamfered X-frame base.

69in (175cm) wide

£600-700　　　　**DN**

A reclining armchair, in the manner of Morris & Co., with extending footrest and padded cushions.

67in (170cm) long

£250-350　　　　**WW**

An Arts and Crafts dining trestle table, with shoe feet and up-ended stretcher.

96in (73.5cm) wide

£3,500-4,500　　**DRA**

An Arts and Crafts oak low shaped circular table, in the manner of Lorimer, the five-piece pegged top, four moulded square twisted supports, with sled feet.

17.75in (45cm) diam

£800-1,000　　　**DN**

An Arts and Crafts mahogany and marquetry occasional table, the four fold down platforms with heart motifs.

23.5in (59.5cm) wide

£150-200　　　　**DN**

An inlaid mahogany wash stand, in the style of Charles Bevan, with veined marble top and black fruit tiles, probably Minton.

43.25in (110cm) wide

£300-400　　　　**WW**

An Arts and Crafts display cabinet, Shapland & Petter, inlaid with stylised mother-of-pearl foliage, the bowed base inset with blue enamel pewter drop handles, label for Dibb & Son, Otley.

46in (117cm) wide

£5,000-6,000 HT

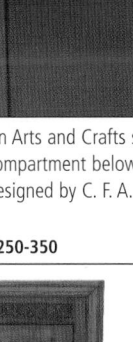

An Arts and Crafts leaded glass cabinet, with drop-front desk complete with gallery.

55in (140cm) wide

£3,000-4,000 DRA

An Arts and Crafts mahogany and inlaid display cabinet, with a pierced and carved foliate upstand, leaded and glazed doors, foliate carved brackets and on fluted square supports.

47.75in (121cm) wide

£2,500-3,000 DN

An Arts and Crafts stained mahogany escritoire, with fall front compartment below glazed doors, Elsley brass furniture designed by C. F. A. Voysey, with later cornice.

38.5in (98cm) wide

£250-350 WW

An Arts and Crafts rosewood and painted table casket, with chequered square inlay, the sides inset with six painted panels of youths in mediaeval dress and lines of verse, on bun feet.

19.75in (50.5cm) wide

£2,000-4,000 DN

A Keswick School of Industrial Art oak corner cupboard, the door inset with carved grape panels, impressed mark to back of door.

30.25in (77cm) high

£400-600 WW

ESSENTIAL REFERENCE – VOYSEY

Charles Francis Annesley Voysey (1857-1941) was a leading English architect and designer.

● **His early work is influenced by William Morris, A.H. Mackmurdo and the Arts and Craft movement, but Voysey soon evolved a personal style of greater lightness and elegance.**

● **He believed that wood should be left with its natural finish.**

● **Although he influenced the Art Nouveau movement and the functional, industrial designs of the early 20thC, he disowned both.**

A small Arts and Crafts hanging corner cupboard, the panel door painted with a titled figural scene 'The Pursuit of Beauty' with flower-painted sides.

18in (45.5cm) wide

£500-600 DN

An oak hall cupboard, by Earnest Archibald Taylor, White & Lochhead, stained, leaded glass panel, retailers label, stamped no. '116663'.

50.75in (129cm) wide

£1,500-2,500 L&T

A limed oak bookcase, designed by Charles Francis Annesley Voysey, for J. Horniman, with carved fluted panel and brass fittings by Elsey & Co., and with a photograph of the original plans.

£3,500-4,500 WW

A 1920s Robert 'Mouseman' Thompson oak monks' chair, with two carved monks' heads, three lattice panels, four octagonal legs joined by an X-stretcher, with carved mouse signature.

31.5in (80cm) high

£2,500-3,500   **TEN**

A Robert 'Mouseman' Thompson oak monk's chair, with two carved heads on the rail above two carved Yorkshire roses and a shield carved 'C.K. 1936', with carved mouse signature.

31.75in (80.5cm) high

£4,000-5,000   **TEN**

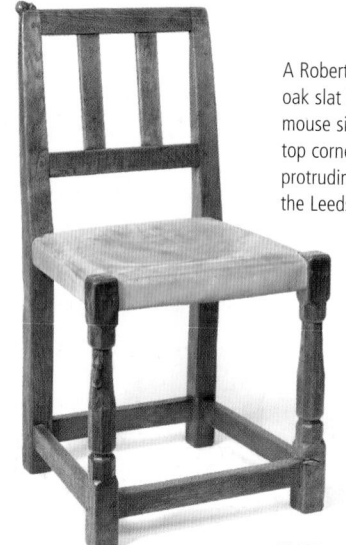

A Robert 'Mouseman' Thompson oak slat back chair, with carved mouse signature running along the top corner and a carved mouse protruding on the front leg, from the Leeds Girls' High School.

33.5in (85cm) high

£2,000-3,000   **TEN**

One of a pair of Robert 'Mouseman' Thompson smoking chairs, with hide panel backs and loose leather-covered seat cushions, the panel sides with inswept mouse-carved front legs.

c1950

£5,000-6,000 **PAIR**   **L&T**

A Robert 'Mouseman' Thompson oak stool, the dished adzed top on octagonal tapered supports joined by stretchers, mouse carved to one leg.

c1970   *15.75in (40cm) wide*

£800-1,000   **L&T**

A Mouseman refectory-style dining table, with adzed top on solid supports, painted with Rutherford College crest, on splay feet.

60in (152.5cm) wide

£800-1,200   **A&G**

A post-1955 Robert 'Mouseman' Thompson oak refectory table, on two octagonal legs joined by a solid stretcher, with carved mouse signature.

84.25in (214cm) wide

£2,500-3,500   **TEN**

A late 19thC French Art Nouveau fruitwood marquetry inlaid two-tier table, in the manner of Émile Gallé, with inlay of flower-filled landscape, on splayed legs.

29.5in (75cm) wide

£1,500-2,500   **SK**

CLOSER LOOK – BUGATTI CHAIRS

The style of, Italian designer, Carlo Bugatti, is idiosyncrantic, being a highly individual manifestation of the Art Nouveau style.

All of Bugatti's furniture was handmade, and this is evident in their construction and embellishment e.g. inlays with repeating patterns are not always uniform.

Elements seen here that are particularly associated with Bugatti include the ebonizing of the wood; the exotic inlays such as metal and bone; and the use of Middle-East-inspired script in the side panels.

The upholstery is not original on either chair. Although they may have been upholstered similarly originally, pieces upholstered in leather and vellum are likely to command higher prices.

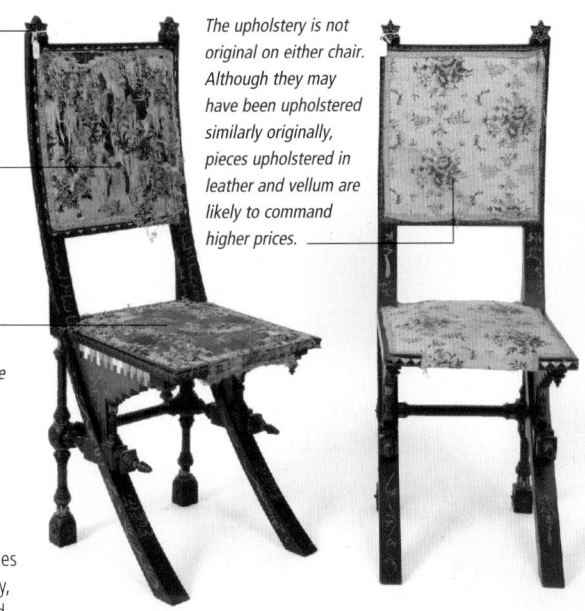

A pair of Carlo Bugatti Orientalism ebonised wood salon chairs, with walnut and bone inlay, the seat sides and legs decorated with metal inlay, the non-matching fabrics distressed.

c1900

38.5in (98cm) high

£10,000-15,000   **WEB**

An Art Nouveau Emile Gallé oak stand, the top and shelf inlaid with chestnut leaves, signed 'Gallé' on shelf.

45in (114.5cm) high

£3,000-4,000   **DRA**

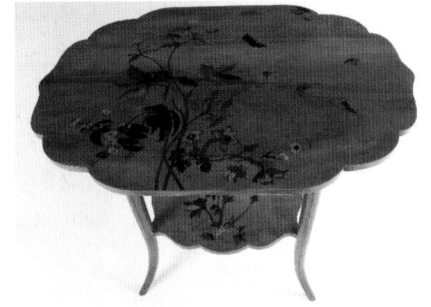

A Gallé occasional table, with scalloped top and lower shelf, both inlaid with wild flowers and butterflies, signed 'Emile Gallé France'.

34.25in (87cm) wide

£3,500-4,500   **DRA**

An Emile Gallé beachwood and nutwood étagère, with two rounded ledges, metal handles, floral inlay of different woods, marked 'Emile Gallé, Nancy'.

c1900   *32.25in (82cm) high*

£3,000-5,000   **WKA**

A French Art Noveau carved beech and marquetry jardinière stand, the top with rooks in a forest, the lower tier with a coastal verandah.

43in (109cm) high

£400-600   **DN**

An Edwardian mahogany and satinwood-crossbanded display cabinet, the astragal glazed doors applied with penwork marquetry plaquettes, on square tapering legs, with label to reverse 'From Charles Jenner & Compy., Edinburgh'.

49.5in (126cm) wide

£1,000-1,500   **L&T**

DECORATIVE ARTS

An Art Nouveau inlaid mahogany cabinet, with a stained glass door flanked by cupboard doors inlaid with mother of pearl, pewter, copper and harewood over three drawers and undertier, on plinth base.

45in (114.5cm) wide

£2,000-2,500   **GORL**

An Art Nouveau marquetry inlaid mahogany display cabinet, in the manner of Maple & Co., with raised back over two glazed doors with copper mounts and undertier on square legs and block feet.

48in (122cm) wide

£1,000-1,500   **GORL**

A Liberty & Co. mahogany stick stand, with a repoussé worked copper panel of stylised seed pod design to top, and lustre-glazed tiles below, lacking drip well, label on reverse.

28.25in (72cm) high

£800-1,200   **FLD**

A marquetry tray of twenty penguins, by Emile Gallé, in an icy landscape worked with maple, walnut, coromandel, kingwood and oak, signed lower left.

27.5in (70cm) wide

£1,200-1,800   **GORL**

A pair of J & J Kohn 'Fledermaus' red stained beech armchairs, designed by Josef Hoffmann.

J & J Kohn was an Austrian furniture company founded in 1868 by Jacob Kohn (1791-1868) and his son Josef Kohn (1814-1884). They made their reputation from bentwood furniture, and key architects such as Otto Wagner, Adolf Loos, Josef Hoffman and Koloman Moser designed for them.

29.25in (74cm) high

£400-500   **WW**

An early 20thC Austrian bentwood and upholstered bench, possibly Josef Hoffmann, with an ebonised frame with later upholstered seat.

47.25in (120cm) wide

£900-1,200   **SK**

A 'Knieschwimmer' armchair, by Adolf Loos, for F. O. Schmidt, Vienna, with oak feet and hardwood frame, with original inner spring upholstery, silk velvet renewed.

Used by Adolf Loos from 1906.

27.5in (70cm) wide

£5,000-10,000   **WKA**

A set of four armchairs, probably J. & J. Kohn, after a design by Josef Hoffmann.

33in (84cm) high

£500-600   **WW**

A beechwood armchair, by Josef Hoffmann, for J. & J. Kohn, Vienna, stained mahogany colour, aluminium studs all round, brass fittings, original leather upholstery with signs of wear.

1902   *30in (76cm) high*

£4,000-6,000   **WKA**

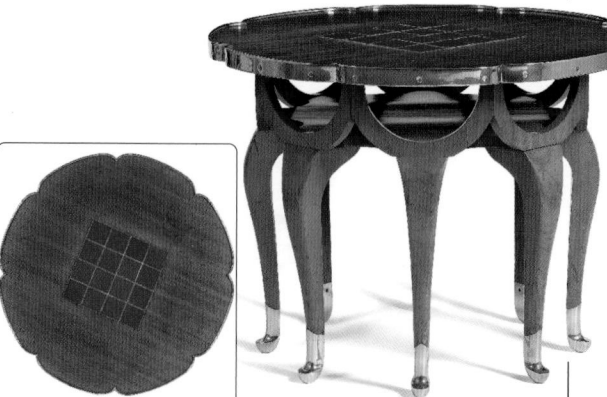

A rare 'Elephant's trunk' eight-legged solid oak table, by Adolf Loos, for F. O. Schmidt, with 16 red tiles by Bigot, Paris, and bronze detail.

Loos often used this table, initially in his designs for the Turnowsky apartment in 1900 and later in the Haberfeld apartment in 1902.

After 1900   *34.75in (88cm) diam*

£12,000-18,000   **WKA**

A yellow-varnished softwood buffet, by Dagobert Peche, for Wiener Werkstätte, with floral ornaments en relief and floral carvings relief with painted silver decoration, restoration on the side.

c1920   41.25in (105cm) wide

£15,000-30,000   WKA

A 'Model 7083' padouk cupboard, by Bruno Paul, for Vereinigte Werkstätten für Kunst im Handwerk, Munich and Berlin, marked 'M 7083, F 5288' on back.

This is probably identical to the furnishings in Bruno Paul's first apartment in Berlin.

1907   23.5in (60cm) wide

£5,000-10,000   WKA

ESSENTIAL REFERENCE – DAGOBERT PECHE

Austrian designer Dagobert Peche (1887-1923) trained as an architect. His style was similar to what is understood as Art Deco style, but Peche placed a greater emphasis on crafts, and his pieces had a hand-made look, and a whimsical sense of fantasy.

● He joined the Wiener Werkstätte in 1915, and became director of its Zürich branch in 1917. He gave up this position in 1919 when he returned to Vienna.

A gold-mounted carved limewood mirror, by Dagobert Peche, for Wiener Werkstätte, restored, with three original work drawings.

1922   20.5in (52cm) high

£35,000-45,000   WKA

A pair of oversized Art Deco walnut wingchairs, with burgundy cushions.

38.5in (98cm) high

£2,000-3,000   SDR

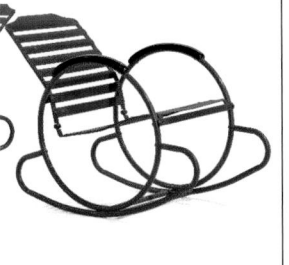

One of a pair of Art Deco enamelled tubular rocking chairs.

21in (53cm) wide

£2,000-3,000 PAIR   SDR

One of a pair of early 20thC oak and leatherette armchairs.

£500-700 PAIR   DN

Part of an Art Deco three-piece sitting suite, in satinwood veneer with ebonised panels, upholstered in pale blue and grey floral cut velvet.

66in (167.5cm) widest

£1,800-2,200 SET   HT

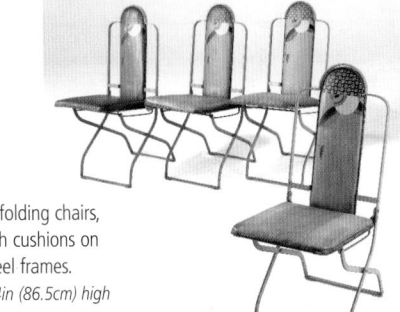

A set of six Art Deco folding chairs, with stencilled oilcloth cushions on orange enamelled steel frames.

34in (86.5cm) high

£2,000-3,000 SET   SDR

A Gustav Stickley set of four billiard V-back chairs, with oilcloth seats, unmarked.

Gustav Stickley (1857-1942) founded his company in 1898 to make furniture inspired by William Morris. His furniture is solid and comfortable and typically without ornament. Much of it was made from quarter-sawn oak with exposed mortise and tenon joints. Panel and frame construction was also used. His metalwork was bold and hand-wrought.

c1901   45.5in (115.5cm) high
£18,000-24,000   DRA

A Gustav Stickley early Morris chair, no. 2341, with loose seat cushion on a sling base, unmarked, new pillows.
c1901   38in (96.5cm) high
£6,000-8,000   CRA

A Gustav Stickley oversized ladder-back armchair, with drop-in seat, unmarked.
c1901   38.5in (97.5cm) high
£3,000-5,000   CRA

A Gustav Stickley U-back armchair, (no. 2616) with original rush seat, large red decal.
c1901   31.5in (80cm) high
£6,000-8,000   DRA

A Gustav Stickley spindled Morris chair, no. 368, with loose cushions, on sling base, small red decal.
c1905   37.5in (cm) high
£4,000-6,000   DRA

A large Gustav Stickley rocker, with a drop-in spring seat, loose back cushion covered in dark brown leather, and old refinish.
29in (73.5cm) wide
£1,500-2,500   DRA

A large Gustav Stickley rocker, with a drop-in spring cushion covered in brown leather, refinished, decal inside back seat rail.

29in (73.5cm) wide
£1,200-1,800   DRA

A Gustav Stickley even arm settle, variation on model no. 208, with a drop-in spring cushion covered in olive green vinyl, and original finish with overcoat.
66in (167.5cm) wide
£3,000-5,000   DRA

A massive Gustav Stickley custom-made sideboard, with butterfly joints, unmarked.

c1901   *100in (254cm) wide*
£40,000-45,000   **CRA**

A Gustav Stickley custom-made five drawer server, unmarked.

1901   *72in (183cm) wide*
£18,000-24,000   **CRA**

A Gustav Stickley rare drop-front desk and cabinet, with strap hinges, chamfered back, interior gallery, with early red decal.

38in (97.5cm) wide
£10,000-15,000   **DRA**

A Gustav Stickley drop-front desk, in two-over-two configuration, with an interior gallery and copper hardware with original key, branded on left drawer.

32in (81.5cm) wide
£1,800-2,400   **DRA**

A Gustav Stickley postcard desk, with two drawers, letter holders, partial lower shelf, original finish, and marked with red decal, some stains and wear.

39.5in (100.5cm) wide
£1,500-2,100   **DRA**

A Gustav Stickley Chalet writing desk, (no. 505) red decal.

46in (116.5cm) high
£1,800-2,400   **DRA**

A Gustav Stickley double-door no. 702 bookcase, designed by Harvey Ellis, with leaded glass, adjustable shelves, large red decal, professional heavy overcoat, factory misalignment of peg holes, one brass escutcheon missing.

48in (122cm) wide
£12,000-15,000   **DRA**

A Gustav Stickley cellarette, with pull-out copper surface, iron V-pulls, single drawer, and interior shelves complete with rotating bottle rack.

22in (56cm) wide
£1,500-2,100   **DRA**

A Gustav Stickley Harvey Ellis-designed single-door china cabinet, (no. 803) with three adjustable shelves, early Eastwood paper label and red decal.

36in (91.5cm) wide
£3,000-5,000   **DRA**

A Gustav Stickley shaving mirror, with shoe-feet and V-top, and branded mark.

23.5in (59.5cm) wide
£1,200-1,500   **DRA**

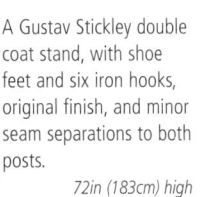

A Gustav Stickley double coat stand, with shoe feet and six iron hooks, original finish, and minor seam separations to both posts.

72in (183cm) high
£1,200-1,800   **DRA**

DECORATIVE ARTS

ESSENTIAL REFERENCE – ALBERT STICKLEY

Albert Stickley, like his brothers Gustav, Charles, Leo and John George, manufacturered US Arts and Crafts furniture.

● Albert Stickley's furniture is typically very rectilinear, and has conspicuously exposed structural elements such as through-tenoned stretchers and rails. His 'Quaint Furniture' trademark was also applied to more decorative items inspired by members of the Scottish School.

A Quaint Art Morris chair, with slatted sides and drop-in spring seat, reupholstered in chocolate brown leather, with paper label.

42in (106.5cm) high

£2,000-3,000   **DRA**

An armchair and rocker, by L. & J. G. Stickley, with drop-in spring cushions newly recovered, original finish, wear to colour on the arms, and 'The Work of...' decal under arms.

Tallest 39.25in (99.5cm) high

£1,500-2,100   **DRA**

A set of six Stickley Brothers ladder-back sidechairs, with drop-in seat cushions, newly recovered in leather, original finish, remnants of paper labels, and shadow of metal tag.

37.25in (94.5cm) high

£1,800-2,400   **DRA**

An L. & J. G. Stickley Morris rocker, with drop-in spring cushion covered in light linen-weave upholstery, refinished and replaced.

29.5in (75cm) wide

£1,000-1,500   **DRA**

A Stickley Brothers desk chair, with shaped and cut-out horizontal rails, shaped plank seat, original finish with overcoat, and metal tag.

15in (38cm) wide

£600-900   **DRA**

A drop-arm settee, by L. & J. G. Stickley, with a replacement drop-in spring cushion covered in dark brown leather, refinished.

77in (195.5cm) wide

£2,000-3,000   **DRA**

An L. & J. G. Stickley/Onondaga Shops even-arm settle, no. 738, with loose seat cushion and pillows, unmarked.

76.25in (193.5cm) wide

£3,000-4,000   **DRA**

An L. & J. G. Stickley tabouret, with flaring stretchers and legs mortised through the octagonal top, refinished.

15in (38cm) wide

£900-1,200   **DRA**

A Stickley Brothers stand, with rectangular overhanging top, slatted sides and broad lower stretcher, original finish, unmarked.

29.75in (75.5cm) high

£900-1,200   **DRA**

ESSENTIAL REFERENCE – CHARLES LIMBERT

Charles P. Limbert (1854-1923) produced pale oak furniture in Grand Rapids, Michigan, 1906-22.

- His forms were similar to those of Gustav Stickley, but many pieces show the direct influence of the Scottish designer, Charles Rennie Mackintosh, with cut-outs in their design. Dutch, Japanese, and American PrairieSchool influences are also evident.
- Limbert made a line of simpler inlaid furniture, called Ebon-Oak, with straight-line inlays of ebony with ebony squares at either end. These pieces often had cane inserts.
- Most pieces are marked with a large brand featuring a craftsman at work.

A Limbert double oval library table, no. 158, branded mark.

47.75in (121cm) wide

£6,000-9,000 DRA

A Limbert ebon-oak library table, with geometric inlay and square copper knobs, branded inside drawer.

42in (106.5cm) wide

£1,500-2,000 DRA

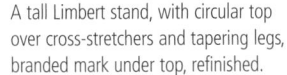

A tall Limbert stand, with circular top over cross-stretchers and tapering legs, branded mark under top, refinished.

26in (66cm) high

£900-1,200 DRA

A rare Limbert cut-out umbrella stand, no. 254, branded signature.

27in (68.5cm) high

£1,200-1,800 DRA

A Limbert three-door bookcase, no. 359, with three adjustable shelves per section, branded mark.

66.5in (169cm) wide

£5,000-8,000 DRA

A Limbert single-door bookcase, with three adjustable shelves, corbels under a shaped top, and an arched apron, branded on back.

29.5in (75cm) wide

£3,000-4,000 DRA

A Limbert trapezoidal magazine stand, with square cut-outs and five shelves, original finish, small holes in side, and branded under bottom shelf.

24in (61cm) wide

£1,500-2,200 DRA

A Limbert daybed, with spade shaped cut-outs and drop-in spring cushions covered in leather, original finish, edge nicks and wear, stenciled '351-'.

25.75in (65.5cm) wide

£1,800-2,500 DRA

DECORATIVE ARTS

A Roycroft bird's-eye maple vanity, with pivoting mirror, single-drawer, Macmurdo feet, and copper hardware, partially restored finish, branded and die-stamped 'R-O-35' to stretcher, together with a matching chair.

Vanity 39in (99cm) wide

£7,000-11,000   DRA

A Roycroft rocker, no. 107, with tacked-on red oil-cloth seat, carved 'Roycroft' on crest rail.

35in (89cm) high

£1,000-1,500   DRA

A Roycroft child's chair, with old tacked-on oil-cloth seat, the crest rail carved 'DAVID,' carved Orb & Cross mark.

25in (63.5cm) high

£1,500-2,200   DRA

A Roycroft 'Ali Baba' bench, no. 46, from the Roycroft Inn, carved Orb & Cross mark and production number for the Inn.

42in (106.5cm) wide

£7,000-11,000   DRA

A large Roycroft sideboard, with plate rack and leaded-glass doors, carved Orb & Cross mark.

Extremely rare, this sideboard descended through the family of Edwin and Katharine Van Berghen Knickerbocker.

45.5in (115.5cm) high

£7,000-11,000   DRA

A carved and polychrome armchair, in Native American motif with original textile.

45.5in (115.5cm) high

£3,500-4,500   DRA

A carved and polychrome armchair, in Native American motif.

46.25in (117cm) high

£5,000-7,000   DRA

A Byrdcliffe maple magazine stand, painted with lilies, complete with original drawing, signed and dated.

The Byrdcliffe Arts Colony was established in 1903 by Ralph Radcliffe Whitehead and his wife Jane Byrde McCall at their home near Woodstock, New York. Furniture was handmade on the site and sometimes painted by artists in the colony. It survives today as a multi-arts organisation called the Woodstock Byrdcliffe Guild.

1909   *30.25in (77cm) high*

£7,000-9,000   DRA

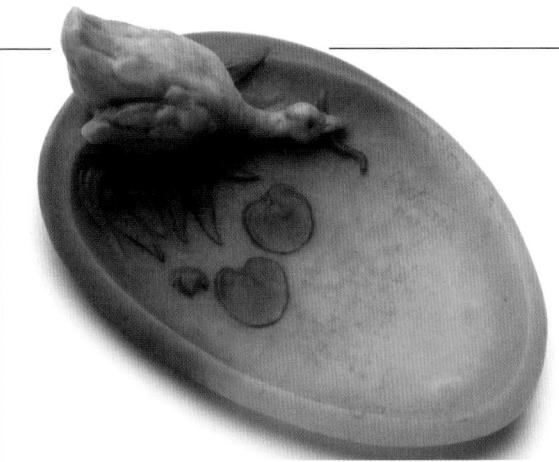

An Alméric Walter pâte-de-verre inkwell, decorated with colourful lizard and bee against an orange to mustard ground, signed 'A WALTER NANCY BERGC SC'.

An Alméric Walter pâte-de-verre vide-poche, with goose and worm, etched 'A WALTER NANCY' and 'G. MOUROT'.

Almeric Walter (1859-1942) was French Art Nouveau and Art Deco glassmaker. He specialised in opaque pate-de-verre pieces decorated with insects, small reptiles and sprays of berries. These included sculptural ornaments and small dishes turquoise, green, and yellow.

A vide-poche, meaning 'empty pocket', is a small dish for placing items such as keys, coins or cufflinks for safe-keeping after emptying out pockets.

4.25in (11cm) wide

6.5in (16.5cm) high

£6,000-7,000   DRA   £4,000-5,000   DRA

CLOSER LOOK – GABRIEL ARGY-ROUSSEAU VASE

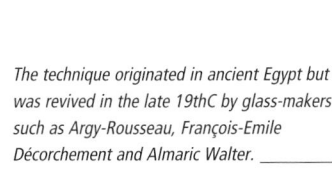

Joseph-Gabriel Argy-Rousseau was a leading exponent of pâte-de-verre in the 19thC, contributing to the high value of this piece.

The complex technique involved applying coloured glass paste to a mould and firing and then carving it.

The technique originated in ancient Egypt but was revived in the late 19thC by glass-makers such as Argy-Rousseau, François-Emile Décorchement and Almaric Walter.

A Gabriel Argy-Rousseau 'Flowered Medallions' pâte-de-verre vase, with a wide decorative band set against a cream coloured background with random mottling of purple, orange and green.

The attractive design is accurately executed and carved with great skill, appealing to glass collectors and lovers of Art Nouveau alike.

10.25in (26cm) high

£15,000-18,000   JDJ

DAUM

A miniature Daum bud vase, with wild orchid and spider web decoration on shaded purple to green background, signed in cameo on side.

A Daum vase, acid-etched and enamelled with strong blue cornflower decoration on shaded pink to deep blue mottled ground, with cameo signature on side.

4in (10cm) high

3.5in (9cm) high

£1,500-1,800   DRA   £1,200-1,800   DRA

DECORATIVE ARTS

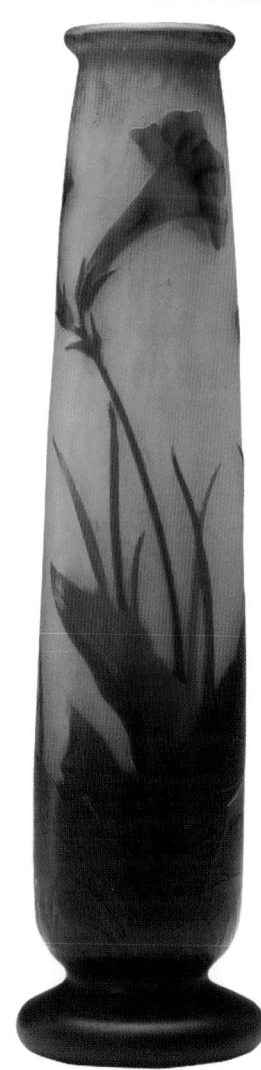

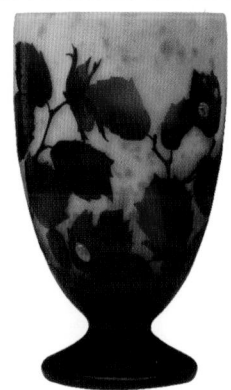

A large Daum coupe-shaped vase, acid-etched with leafy branches and colourful applied and wheel-carved cabochon scarabs, on mottled ground, signed 'DAUM NANCY FRANCE' and with Cross of Lorraine.

11.5in (29cm) high

£2,000-3,000   DRA

A Daum footed vase, acid-etched with deep red crocuses on a frosted to deep red wheel-carved martele ground, engraved 'DAUM NANCY' and with Cross of Lorraine.

5.5in (14cm) high

£1,800-2,200   DRA

A Daum bulbous vase, acid-etched with pink leafy vines against an opalescent, wheel-carved martele ground, acid-etched 'DAUM NANCY' and with Cross of Lorraine.

8.75in (22cm) high

£1,500-2,500   DRA

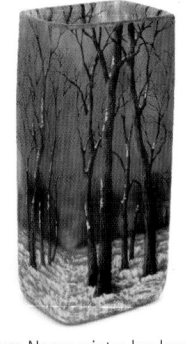

A Daum Nancy winter landscape vase, acid-etched and enamelled with snowy landscape, on a mottled orange and yellow ground, painted 'Daum Nancy' with a Cross of Lorraine.

c1900   7.5in (19cm) high

£1,500-2,500   JA

A narrow Daum vase, with tobacco flowers.

£1,500-2,000   DRA

A Daum cupped vase, wheel-carved with crocuses on frosted background, both the ground and foot with wheel-carved martele surface, signed 'DAUM NANCY' with the Cross of Lorraine.

In 1885, Jean-Louis Auguste and Jean Antonin Daum took over their father's glass factory and it became known as Daum Frères. They started producing Art Nouveau and cameo glass with designs inspired by nature and Eastern art. They used innovative techniques to enhance the naturalistic decoration, such as mottled or martelé backgrounds, enamel details, patterns at various depths, and applied foil-backed decoration. In the 1920s, they produced Art Deco pieces and the shapes became simpler with stylised geometric acid-etched patterns.

5.25in (13.5cm) high

£7,000-8,000   DRA

A miniature Daum etched and enamelled autumnal landscape glass vase, etched 'Daum Nancy' and Cross of Lorraine.

2.5in (6.5cm) high

£2,000-2,500   DRA

A Daum etched and enamelled scenic cabinet ewer, with applied handle and foot, and Dutch landscape with windmills in blue on white ground, engraved 'Daum Nancy' with Cross of Lorraine mark.

c1900   3.5in (9cm) high

£700-1,000   DRA

A pair of Durand orange 'Cluthra' urn-shaped vases, with black handles, both marked.

11in (28cm) high

£700-1,000   DRA

A pair of Durand footed vases, with blue-gold 'King Tut' decoration on green, with silver engraved signatures, and marked '2011-14'.

14in (35.5cm) high

£2,500-3,500   DRA

A Durand tapered vase with white hearts and vines on iridescent blue.

10in (25.5cm) high

£1,000-1,500   DRA

A Durand crackle decorated vase, in striped green and blue on white.

10.5in (26.5cm) high

£2,200-2,800   DRA

A pair of Durand vases, with white pulled-feather design on clear with flashed green tops, with silver engraved signature 'Durand V 1990-14'.

13.75in (35cm) high

£1,000-1,500   DRA

A tall Durand bottle, in white hearts-and-vine pattern on a lustred blue ground, area of bottle slightly flattened, etched 'Durand 19701-12'.

12.75in (32.5cm) high

£1,500-2,200   DRA

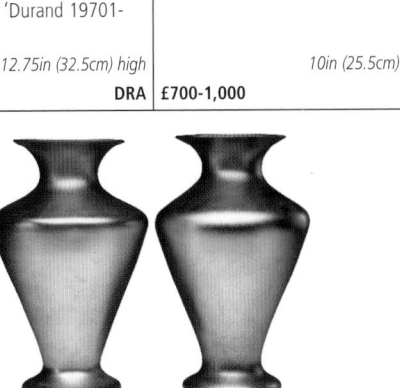

A Durand crackle vase, with green, white and gold iridescent decoration, a chip to pontil.

10in (25.5cm) high

£700-1,000   DRA

A pair of Durand gold iridescent bulbous vases, with silver engraved signatures '1710-10', a few scratches overall, one with a few flaws to surface in the making.

10in (25.5cm) high

£1,000-1,500   DRA

A pair of Durand gold iridescent large baluster vases, with silver engraved signatures '20139-14'.

14.5in (37cm) high

£1,800-2,400   DRA

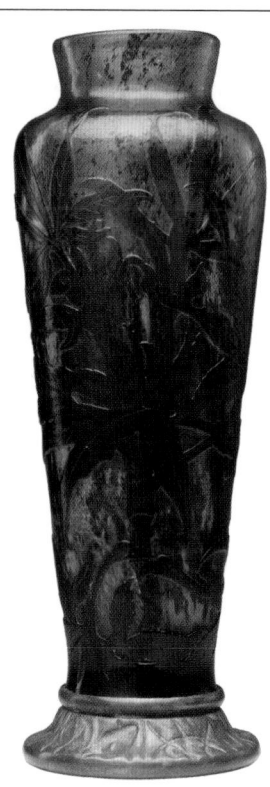

A tall Gallé vase, acid-etched with leafy plants in clear green against a highly textured green and amber ground, with metal foot affixed at later date, with cameo signature.

Emile Gallé (1864-1904) was a pioneer of the Art Nouveau style in France. He set up his first decorating workshop in Nancy in 1873 where he combined complicated cameo techniques with enamelling, mould casting, marquetry and inlay in designs inspired by nature. By 1900 his firm was the largest producer of luxury glassware in Europe, and although the highest quality items continued to be handcrafted, there was an increased use of acid-etching for mid-range pieces. Gallé died in 1904 but the factory remained open until 1936. A star by Gallé's signature indicates production after his death.

17in (43cm) high

£2,500-3,500   **DRA**

A Gallé bulbous vase, acid-etched with trees at sunset, in pink, green and brown, cameo signature 'Gallé'.

10.75in (27.5cm) high

£2,000-3,000   **DRA**

A Gallé vase, with wheel-polished light red cyclamen flowers on amber ground, acid-etched signature 'Gallé' on side of vase.

4.75in (12cm) high

£1,000-1,500   **DRA**

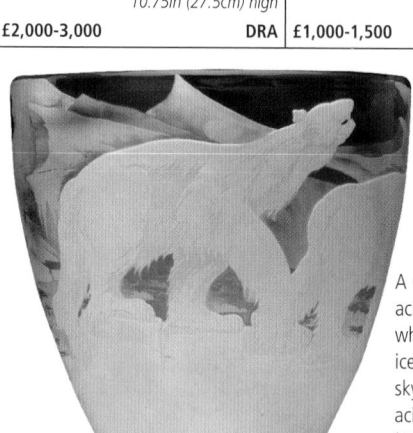

A Gallé coupe-shaped acid-etched vase, with white polar bear and iceberg decoration on sky blue ground, with acid-etched signature 'Gallé'.

11in (28cm) high

£1,500-2,500   **DRA**

A Gallé marquetry vase, with purple flowers, on original bronze foot, signed 'Etude' (study), foot signed 'Gallé'.

7in (18cm) high

£2,500-3,500   **DRA**

A Gallé blown-out glass vase, decorated with clematis branches, signed in cameo 'Gallé', circular stamp 'MADE IN FRANCE', small chip and minor acid burns from manufacturing.

9.5in (24cm) high

£5,500-6,500   **DRA**

A Gallé double gourd-shaped fire-polished vase, with cranberry-coloured flowers and leaves on a pale green ground, with fancy oriental cameo signature.

9in (23cm) high

£1,500-2,000   **DRA**

A Gallé cameo glass bud vase, with purple blossoms on amber ground, with cameo signature.

8.75in (22cm) high

£1,200-1,800   **DRA**

A Gallé 'Verrerie Parlante' fire-polished vase, with red flowers on an opal background with striping, as well as 'bonheur' (happiness) in cameo, with cameo signature.

9in (23cm) high

£800-1,200   **DRA**

CLOSER LOOK – GALLÉ VASE

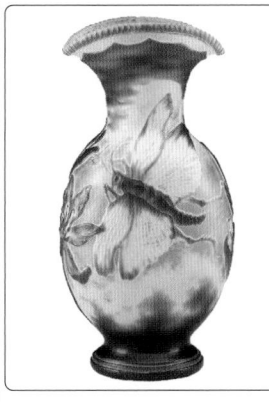

Adhering to Gallé's principle that nature should be accurately represented, the detail on the grasshopper is exquisite, utilising the most delicate carving to create diaphanous-looking wings.

Gallé was a major exponent of cameo glass and the first glassmaker to routinely sign his work.

The cameo technique, where two or more layers of differently coloured glass were fused together and the top one carved, allowed for shading and the illusion of light and shadow.

A Gallé wheel-carved vase, with flowers and an intricately carved grasshopper, engraved 'Dis aux petisque les etes sont couverts le colchique des alpes' below rim, engraved signature 'E. Gallé' with a matching wheel-carved flower and date.

1895

£15,000-18,000   **JDJ**

A Kralik 'Tortoiseshell' banded vase.

c1905

£180-220   **MDM**

A Kralik 'Sea Urchin' vase.

c1905

£350-450   **MDM**

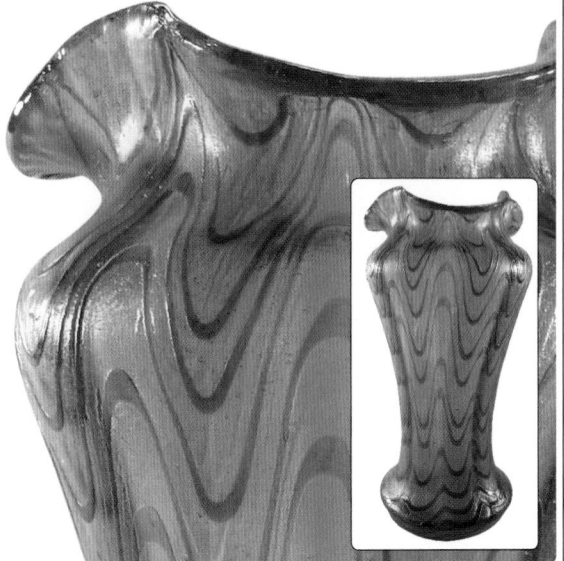

A Kralik green ribbon 'King Tut' vase.

c1905

£300-400   **MDM**

ESSENTIAL REFERENCE – LALIQUE

René Lalique (1860-1945), previously a master jeweller, began experimenting with glass in his jewellery designs in the 1880s. By the 1890s he had developed a serious interest in glass.

- He opened a shop in Paris in 1902, where he made perfume bottles and decorative wares for the commercial trade.
- In c1907 Lalique began producing Art Deco-style perfume bottles for François Coty. Soon most leading Parisian perfumeries followed suit.
- He established his own glasshouse at Combes-la-Ville in 1909 and another at Wingen-sur-Möder in 1921.
- At the Paris Exposition of 1925 he received critical acclaim for his Art Deco glassware.
- Between 1920 and 1930, Lalique produced designs for over 200 vases and 150 bowls. The crisply moulded details, and quality of moulding and design gives these mass-produced pieces a 'one off' feel.
- Lalique's famous pressed glass forms were produced in a variety of shapes. Many of his thinner vases are moulded. His pieces were primarily clear, opalescent or frosted, though some were produced in coloured glass.
- Virtually all pieces produced before Lalique's death in 1945 are marked "R. Lalique". Pieces made afterwards are marked "Lalique". The company is still operating today, under the name 'Cristallerie Lalique et Cie'.

A René Lalique 'Biskra' vase, M p. 455, no. 1078, of navy blue glass, stencilled 'R. LALIQUE FRANCE'.

c1932   *11in (28cm) high*

£15,000-18,000   **DRA**

A René Lalique 'Archers' vase, M p. 415, no. 893, of amber glass with white patina, engraved 'R. Lalique France'.

c1921   *10.25in (26cm) high*

£10,000-12,000   **DRA**

A René Lalique 'Canards' vase, M p. 437, no. 992, of cased opalescent butterscotch glass, white patina, stencilled 'R. LALIQUE FRANCE'.

c1927   *5.5in (14cm) high*

£3,000-3,500   **DRA**

A René Lalique 'Ceylan' vase, M p. 418, no. 905, of opalescent glass with blue patina, wheel-cut 'R. LALIQUE FRANCE'.

c1924   *9.5in (24cm) high*

£5,000-6,000   **DRA**

A René Lalique 'Courges' vase, M p. 417, no. 900, of electric blue glass, moulded 'R. LALIQUE'.

c1914   *7in (18cm) high*

£8,000-10,000   **DRA**

A Lalique 'Courlis' vase, yellow amber glass with whitish patina, stencilled 'R. LALIQUE FRANCE' mark.

c1931   *6.5in (16.5cm) high*

£4,500-5,000   **DRA**

A René Lalique 'Domremy' vase, M p. 434, no. 979, of amber glass, engraved 'R. Lalique France'.

c1926   *8in (20.5cm) high*

£3,000-4,000   **DRA**

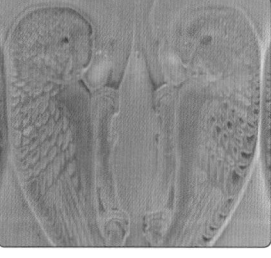

A rare René Lalique 'Inseparables' vase, M p. 414, no. 887, of frosted glass with blue-grey patina, moulded 'R. Lalique', engraved 'France'.

c1919   *13.5in (34cm) high*

£8,000-10,000   **DRA**

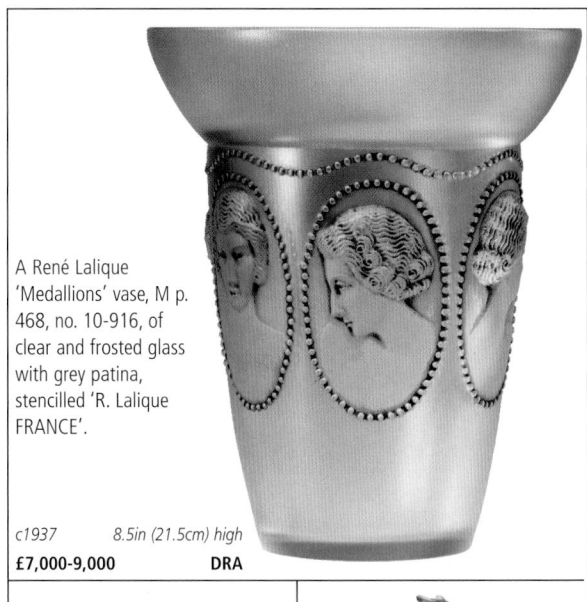

A René Lalique 'Medallions' vase, M p. 468, no. 10-916, of clear and frosted glass with grey patina, stencilled 'R. Lalique FRANCE'.

c1937   8.5in (21.5cm) high
£7,000-9,000   DRA

A René Lalique 'Le Mans' vase, M p. 454, no. 1074, of cased opalescent turquoise glass, stencilled 'R. LALIQUE FRANCE'.

c1931   3.75in (9.5cm) high
£2,500-3,500   DRA

A René Lalique 'Marguerites' vase, M p. 416, no. 897, of clear and frosted glass with sepia patina, stencilled 'R. LALIQUE FRANCE'.

c1914   9in (23cm) high
£5,500-6,500   DRA

A René Lalique 'Malesherbes' vase, M p. 442, no. 1014, of amber glass, engraved 'R. LALIQUE FRANCE'.

c1927   9.25in (23.5cm) high
£3,500-4,000   DRA

A René Lalique 'Amphitrite' perfume bottle, M p. 335, no. 514, of green glass, engraved 'R. Lalique France, no. 514'.

c1920   3.5in (9cm) high
£3,500-4,500   DRA

A René Lalique 'Le Baiser Du Faune' perfume bottle, for Molinard, M p. 945, no. 2, of clear and frosted glass, moulded 'R. Lalique', engraved 'Molinard Paris France'.

c1928   5.75in (14.5cm) high
£3,000-3,500   DRA

A René Lalique 'La Violette' perfume bottle, for Gabilla, M p. 940, no. 2, in clear and frosted glass with violet enamel, a small chip to tip of dauber, moulded 'R. LALIQUE'.

c1925   3.25in (8cm) high
£2,500-3,000   DRA

A René Lalique 'Ambre De Siam' perfume bottle, of frosted glass, raised mark 'R. LALIQUE'.

4.75in (12cm) high
£15,000-18,000   DRA

A René Lalique 'Petite Libellule' car mascot, M p. 501, no. 1144, of clear and frosted glass, moulded 'LALIQUE, FRANCE'.

c1928   *6.25in (16cm) long*

£7,000-9,000   **DRA**

A René Lalique 'Coq Nain' mascot hood ornament, M p. 381, no. 1135, smoky topaz, flake to top of head and to base, incised 'R. LALIQUE'.

c1928   *8in (20.5cm) high*

£1,200-1,800   **DRA**

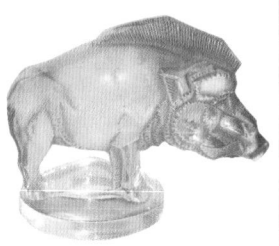

A René Lalique 'Sanglier' original grey stained car mascot.

c1929

£1,000-1,500   **MDM**

A René Lalique 'Longchamp' car mascot, M p. 502, no. 1152B, of clear and frosted glass, moulded 'R. LALIQUE', on original mount and black glass base, base stencilled 'R. LALIQUE FRANCE'.

c1929   *6.25in (16cm) wide*

£7,000-9,000   **DRA**

A René Lalique 'Chrysis' car mascot, M p. 505, no. 1183, in clear and frosted glass, in chrome mount, on contemporary wooden base, stencilled 'R. LALIQUE'.

c1931   *Glass 6.5in (16.5cm) high*

£2,000-3,000   **DRA**

A René Lalique 'Saint-Cristophe' car mascot, M p. 501, no. 1142, of clear and frosted glass, moulded 'R. LALIQUE'.

c1928   *4.5in (11.5cm) high*

£800-1,200   **DRA**

A René Lalique 'Archer' car mascot, M p. 498, no. 1126, of clear and frosted glass, moulded 'R. LALIQUE'.

c1926   *4.75in (12cm) high*

£1,800-2,200   **DRA**

A Lalique 'Grosses Feuilles' rocker blotter, clear and frosted glass with sepia patina, original metal rocker, moulded 'R. LALIQUE' mark.

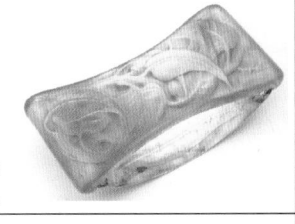

c1920   6.5in (16.5cm) long

£1,200-1,800   **DRA**

A René Lalique 'Feuilles D'Artichaut' rocker blotter, M p. 245, no. 155, of clear and frosted glass with green patina, moulded 'R. LALIQUE'.

c1920   6.5in (16.5cm) high

£1,000-1,200   **DRA**

A René Lalique 'Sirens et Grenouilles' bottle and stopper, M p. 737, no. 3150, in clear and frosted glass with green patina, engraved 'R. Lalique France'.

15in (38cm) high

£2,000-2,500   **DRA**

A René Lalique 'Satyre' carafe, M p. 741, no. 3167, of clear and frosted glass with sepia patina, complete with silvered port tag, engraved 'R. Lalique, pour Cusenier'.

c1923   9.75in (25cm) high

£2,000-2,500   **DRA**

A René Lalique 'Sirenes' statuette, of opalescent glass, M p. 497, no. 831, moulded 'R. Lalique'.

c1920   4in (10cm) high

£2,200-2,800   **DRA**

A René Lalique 'Six Figurines' decanter and single glass, M p. 738, no. 3158, of clear and frosted glass with sepia patina, engraved 'R. Lalique'.

c1914   14.25in (36cm) high

£1,500-2,000   **DRA**

René Lalique 'Jaffa' lemonade set, M p. 797, no. 3680, of butterscotch glass, comprising a pitcher, tray, and six glasses, stencilled 'R. LALIQUE'.

c1931 Pitcher 8.5in (21.5cm) high

£2,200-2,800   **DRA**

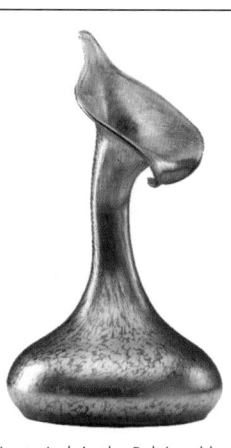

A Loetz Jack-in-the-Pulpit gold iridescent glass vase.

18in (46cm) high

£2,000-2,500   **DRA**

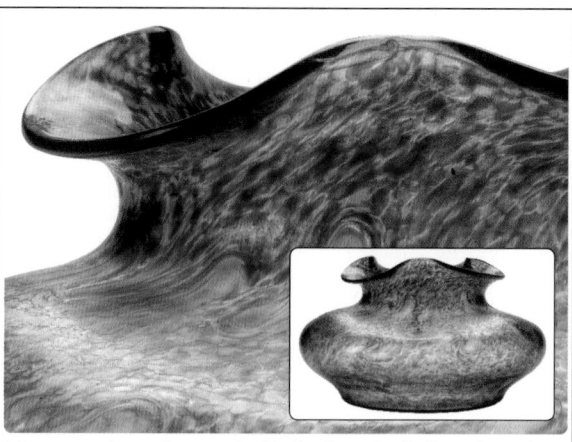

A large squat Loetz glass vessel, with dimples and a floriform rim, under a green and amber oil-spot finish.

12.5in (32cm) wide

£1,200-1,800   **DRA**

A Loetz 'Flamarion' green vase, no. 5239, of white opal glass, wound round with silvery threads over the entire surface, a broad band of green threads over the lower part.

1905   *9.75in (25cm) high*

£1,500-2,500   **WKA**

A Loetz vase, by Adolf Beckert, no. 5272, colourless glass with pink underlay, moss green overlay, etched decoration, fire polished and diamond cut, engraved 'Lötz'.

From 1909-1912 Adolf Beckert was artistic director at the Loetz glassworks. His designs from this period, described by Loetz as 'original pieces by Adolf Beckert', are often fine examples of particularly intricate glassmaking techniques.

1908   *7.75in (19.5cm) high*

£6,000-8,000   **WKA**

A Loetz 'Cytisus' silver-mounted vase, wound round with blue horizontal re-veined ribbons, irregularly spaced silver-yellow patches over them, mould-blown, covered with thin layer of iridescent glass.

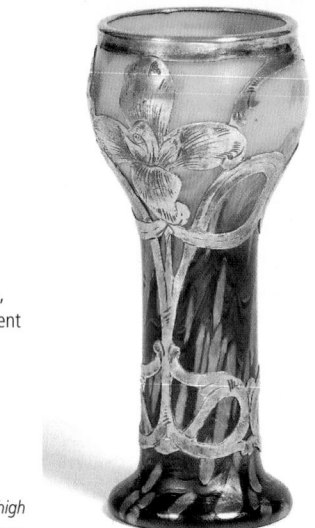

6in (15.5cm) high

£2,000-3,000   **WKA**

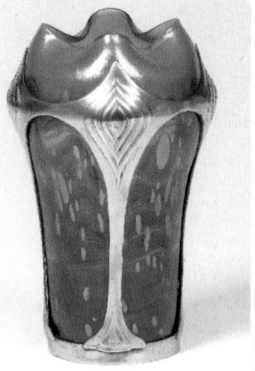

A Loetz 'Cytisus' tin-mounted vase, decorated with blue ribbons and sprinkled with silver-yellow patches, covered with a thin layer of iridescent glass.

c1900   *7.75in (19.5cm) high*

£4,000-5,000   **WKA**

A Loetz vase, by Marie Kirschner, for E. Bakolowits, no. 1090/238, purple glass preblown in an eight-part ribbed mould, turned diagonally, iridescent, base inscribed 'MK'.

5in (12.5cm) high

£2,500-3,500   **WKA**

A Loetz metallic yellow 'Phänomen Gre 356' vase, no. 357, by Franz Hofstötter, for the 1900 World Exhibition in Paris, mould-blown and formed, with 'Loetz Austria' engraved on base.

Hofstötter's designs are can be considered to be based on nature in an abstract form. Here, the soil is represented with a brown or brown-yellow base over which plants grow in a silvery, golden and bluish atmosphere into an imaginary sky.

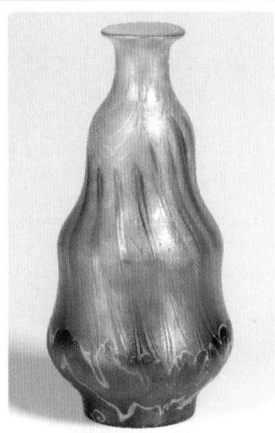

10.25in (26cm) high

£15,000-20,000   **WKA**

A Loetz opal 'Phänomen Gre 358' vase, attributed to Franz Hofstötter, no. 358, with thin opal glass underlay, wound round with veined silver-yellow, orange-red under the mouth, dark blue and silver-yellow at base, mould-blown and formed, iridescent, signed.

This form and décor was created for the 1900 World Exhibition in Paris.

12.75in (32.5cm) high

£10,000-12,000   **WKA**

CLOSER LOOK – A LOETZ VASE

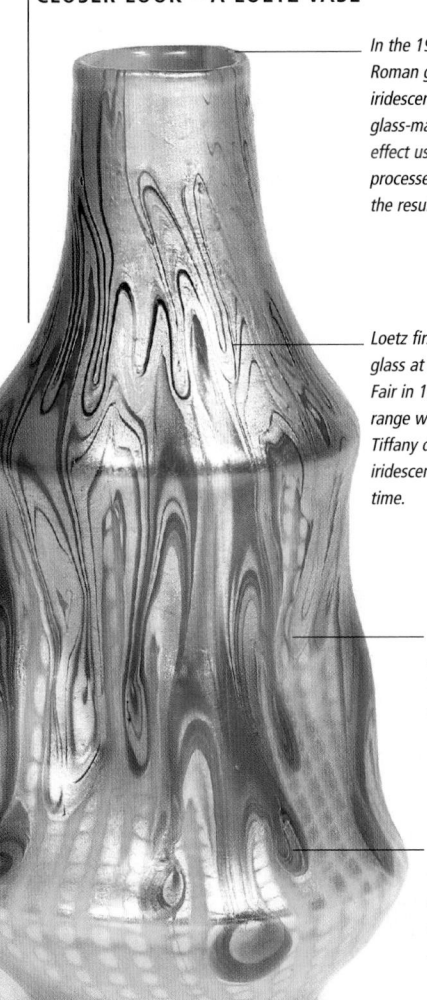

In the 19thC, the excavation of Roman glass which had become iridescent over time, inspired glass-makers to recreate the effect using metal oxides. The processes varied depending on the result required.

Loetz first exhibited iridescent glass at the Chicago World's Fair in 1893 and the Phänomen range was launched in 1897. Tiffany developed his 'Favrile' iridescent glass at the same time.

The rich yellow and blue, paired with silver threads are typical Loetz colours.

This piece is signed, an unusual feature in Loetz glass, which is usually unsigned and can be hard to identify.

A Loetz lemon yellow 'Phänomen Gre 353' vase, no. 691, colourless glass with yellow opal underlay, silver-yellow threads partially overlaid with blue and veined silver-yellow shaped into irregular drop-like tongues, mould-blown and formed, impressed four times, iridescent, signed.

1900   *10in (25.5cm) high*

£18,000-22,000   **WKA**

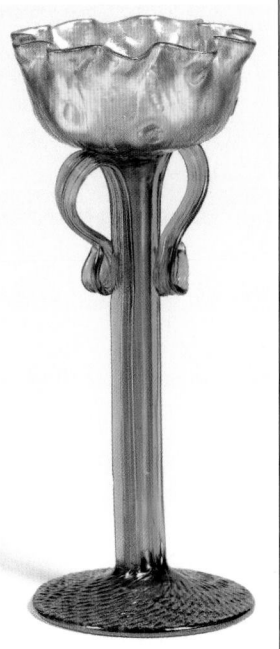

A Loetz 'Tulip' 'candia Rusticana' vase, optically preblown with gnarled structure, mould-blown and free formed.

c1903   *12.5in (32cm) high*

£3,000-4,000   **WKA**

A Loetz baluster lustred glass vase, in a feathered pattern, scratch to shoulder.

10in (25.5cm) high

£2,000-2,500   **DRA**

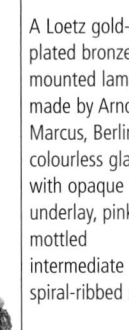

A Loetz gold-plated bronze-mounted lamp, made by Arndt & Marcus, Berlin, of colourless glass, with opaque white underlay, pink mottled intermediate layer, spiral-ribbed shaft.

1889   *59in (150cm) high*

£4,000-6,000   **WKA**

A tall Quezal Jack-in-the-Pulpit vase, with lustred gold blossom and purple to emerald stem, incised 'Quezal'.

14.75in (37.5cm) high

£2,000-3,000   **DRA**

A Quezal Jack-in-the-Pulpit vase, with a green and gold pulled-feather stem on gold ground, signed 'Quezal 533'.

6.5in (16.5cm) high

£2,200-2,800   **DRA**

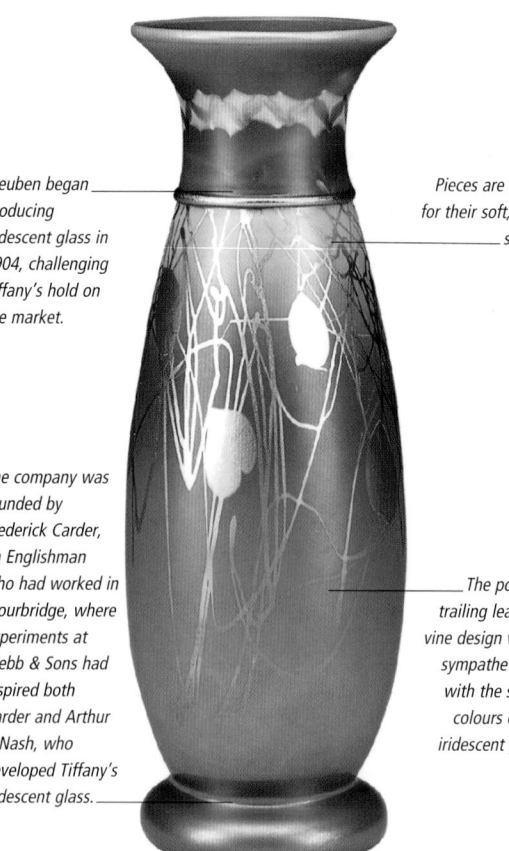

A Quezal decorated vase, with various gold feather designs on a background of opal shading to striped green, signed 'Quezal E286'.

7.25in (18.5cm) high

£3,000-5,000   **DRA**

A Steuben blue 'Aurene' vase, etched 'Steuben'.

7.75in (19.5cm) high

£800-1,200   **DRA**

A large Steuben blue 'Aurene' glass footed centrebowl, etched 'STEUBEN AURENE 6058'.

12.25in (31cm) diam

£1,500-2,200   **DRA**

CLOSER LOOK – STEUBEN VASE

A Steuben blue 'Aurene' tall twisted vase, etched 'STEUBEN AURENE 1030'.

9.75in (25cm) high

£1,800-2,400   **DRA**

A large Steuben 'Moss Agate' vase, with amber, brown, green and rust with random bubbles and internal crackling.

10.5in (26.5cm) high

£9,000-12,000   **JDJ**

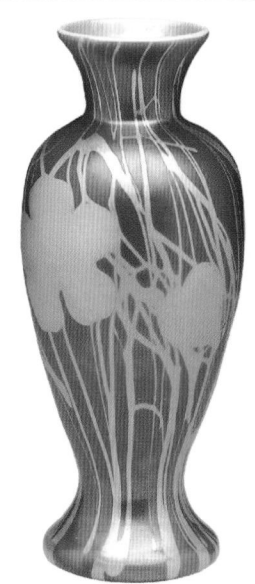

A rare Steuben red 'Aurene' decorated vase, with gold iridescent leaf flower and vine decoration, signed on the bottom 'Aurene 747'.

7.25in (18.5cm) high

£12,000-18,000   **JDJ**

Steuben began producing iridescent glass in 1904, challenging Tiffany's hold on the market.

Pieces are noted for their soft, even sheen.

The company was founded by Frederick Carder, an Englishman who had worked in Stourbridge, where experiments at Webb & Sons had inspired both Carder and Arthur J. Nash, who developed Tiffany's iridescent glass.

The popular trailing leaf and vine design works sympathetically with the subtle colours of the iridescent glass.

A Steuben 'Tyrian' vase, with rich gold iridescent leaf and vine design to body, with an applied neck with intarsia design and flaring rim, signed 'Tyrian' on the underside.

10in (25.5cm) high

£15,000-21,000   **JDJ**

A miniature Tiffany Studios Favrile two-handled glass vase, with pulled-feather decoration, etched 'L.C.T. N2011'.

3.25in (8cm) wide

£1,500-2,200   DRA

A large Tiffany Studios blue Favrile baluster vase, etched '1154 6163 J L.C.Tiffany Favrile', some burst bubbles near rim.

10.25in (26cm) high

£1,500-2,200   DRA

A miniature Tiffany Studios 'Tel El Amarna' blue Favrile glass vase, etched 'L.C.T. N2673', remnants of two paper labels.

2.5in (6.5cm) high

£1,500-2,200   DRA

A Tiffany Studios 'Tel El Amarna' vase, with a butterscotch applied band with silver decoration on blue body with platinum iridescence, matching applied foot, with engraved signature '738 L. C. Tiffany-Favrile'.

7.75in (19.5cm) high

£4,000-6,000   JDJ

ESSENTIAL REFERENCE – LOUIS COMFORT TIFFANY

Louis Comfort Tiffany (1848-1933) was the son of jewellery maker, Charles Tiffany. In 1878, he formed Louis Comfort Tiffany and Associated Artists, set up Tiffany Glass Co. in New York in 1885, Tiffany Furnaces in 1892, and Tiffany Studios in 1900.

● **Having first patented 'favrile' in 1880, Tiffany launched the Favrile range, the first iridescent art-glass range, in 1894 in the US. The decoration included the trademark 'peacock pattern', feathering, tooled threading, etc.**

● **Tiffany was fascinated by organic forms and used the fluidity of glass to suggest the growth and movement of plants.**

An early L. C. Tiffany decorated orange glass vase, with green pulled-feather decoration, marked 'L. C. T. F 1533', and early label.

6.5in (16.5cm) high

£4,000-6,000   DRA

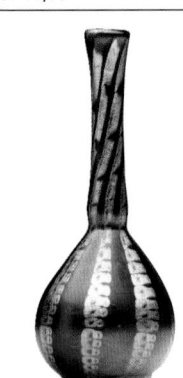

A Tiffany Studios 'Paperweight' glass vase, with tall brown and white leaves on a green to vermillion ground, etched '7798A'.

9in (23cm) high

£9,000-12,000   DRA

A Tiffany Studios 'Agate' glass cabinet vase, in amber, umber, and emerald, with four dimples, etched 'L.C.T. Favrile 0286'.

3in (7.5cm) high

£3,000-4,000   DRA

A miniature Tiffany Studios red Favrile glass 'Zipper' vase, with blue iridescent pattern, etched 'L.C.T. 0300'.

4.75in (12cm) high

£2,200-2,800   DRA

A rare Tiffany vase in red Favrile glass, signed '1043 K L. C. Tiffany-Favrile'.

5.75in (14.5cm) high

£3,000-4,000   DRA

DECORATIVE ARTS

A Monart C VII glass vase, mottled green with surface decoration.

7in (17.5cm) high

£300-400   **L&T**

A Monart glass vase, shape HF, size V, medium blue with air inclusions.

9.25in (23.5cm) high

£250-350   **DN**

A Monart QA VI glass vase, mottled pale green with aventurine inclusions, bears label.

Monart – free-blown shapes from coloured glass sandwiched between two layers of clear glass – was made by the Moncrieff Glassworks. It was made by Isobel, wife of John Moncrieff Jr, and Salvador Ysart and his sons from 1924–61. After World War II it was made by Paul Ysart, who specialized in paperweights.

10.25in (26cm) high

£350-450   **L&T**

A Monart KC VII glass vase, mottled pink with blue, aventurine inclusions.

8.5in (21.5cm) high

£250-350   **L&T**

A Monart PB V glass bowl and cover, mottled pale green with aventurine inclusions.

7in (18cm) high

£350-450   **L&T**

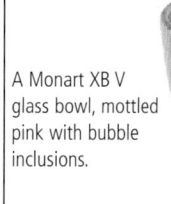

A Monart XB V glass bowl, mottled pink with bubble inclusions.

4.75in (12cm) high

£250-350   **L&T**

A small Thomas Webb footed vase, with scrolled handles and wheel-carved floral design in rose, the foot acid-etched.

4.25in (11cm) high

£1,200-1,800   **DRA**

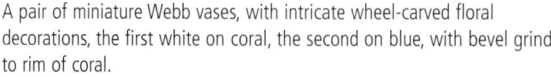

A pair of miniature Webb vases, with intricate wheel-carved floral decorations, the first white on coral, the second on blue, with bevel grind to rim of coral.

Thomas Webb & Sons was founded in 1837 by Thomas Webb (1804-1869). During the 19thC, it produced colour art glass and cameo ranges created from clear glass and at least one colour, such as red, blue or white. It became known for cut designs during the 1930s and 50s, before closing in 1990.

3in (7.5cm) high

£2,200-2,800   **DRA**

A 19thC Stourbridge cameo vase, by Thomas Webb, cased in opal over blue ground and cut with a spray of Arum lilies between banded and chevron borders.

5.75in (14.5cm) high

£900-1,200   **FLD**

A Burgin & Schverer vase, with acid-etched, wheel-carved, and gilded lavender poppies on frosted ground, with wheel-carved martele areas, elaborate gilded signature.

6.5in (16.5cm) high

£1,800-2,200　　　　　　**DRA**

A Burgin & Schverer multi-layered cameo glass vase, with carved decoration of poppies against a hammered surface, gilding to edges, stamped 'VERRERIE D'ART DE LORRAINE B S & Co. depose'.

6.75in (17cm) high

£3,000-4,000　　**DRA**

A miniature Burgin & Schverer martele vase, with acid-etched and wheel-carved white lilies on frosted lavender ground, with gilded details, elaborate gilded signature, some wear to gold.

4.75in (12cm) high

£2,200-2,800　　**DRA**

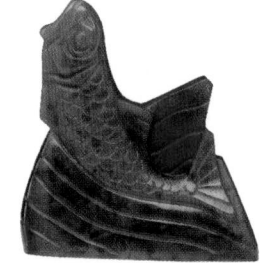

A Francois Décorchemont pâte-de-verre fish figure, in bright blue, orange and mottled green with amber, impressed mark.

7.25in (18.5cm) high

£1,500-2,000　　　　　　**DRA**

A Francois Décorchemont pâte-de-crystal vase, of pulverised polychrome glass, the upper edge of the plate re-cut and polished with three-dimensional, accentuated flowers, inscribed 'DECORCHMENT'.

1927

£4,500-6,500　　　　　　**WKA**

A panelled lilac glass decanter, by Josef Hoffmann.

8.25in (21cm) high

£1,500-2,500　　　　　　**DRA**

An early 20thC Cameo glass plafonnier, Muller Frères, Luneville, of dished circular form, the semi-translucent mottled body with red overlay glass in relief, signed on the rim.

15.75in (40cm) diam

£1,200-1,800　　　　　　**TEN**

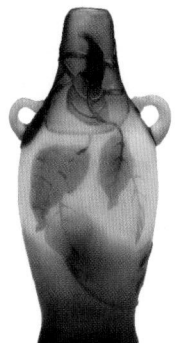

A Muller Frères Flurogravure glass vase, decorated with blooming vines in purple, green, orange and ivory, with cameo signature.

5.75in (14.5cm) high

£800-1,200　　**DRA**

A Muller Frères enamel-decorated flattened vase, with dragonflies in a lake landscape, signed 'Muller Fres Luneville', nick at rim.

6.5in (16.5cm) high

£1,500-2,000　　**DRA**

A large Schneider layered glass vase, with deep purple layer and fused orange 'handles', etched 'Schneider France'.

11in (28cm) wide

£1,200-1,800　　**DRA**

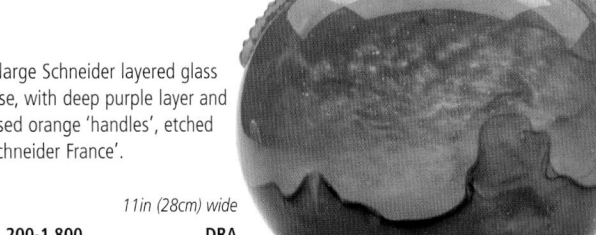

DECORATIVE ARTS

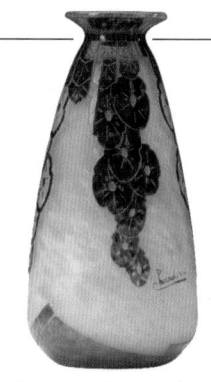

A Le Verre Français tapered cameo glass vase, decorated by Charles Schneider, with an Art Deco floral pattern , signed 'Charder Le Verre Francais'.

6.75in (17cm) high

£700-900   **DRA**

A 1920s Le Verre Français cameo vase, by Schneider, with tall bell-form body acid cut with a repeat graduated tessellating square design, bears small millefiori cane signature to the base.

10.5in (26.5cm) high

£900-1,200   **FLD**

A Teplitz vase, painted by Paul Dachsel with birch trees, purple stamp 'PD TURN TEPLITZ MADE IN AUSTRIA', loss to glaze on tree trunk.

8.75in (22cm) high

£1,000-1,500   **DRA**

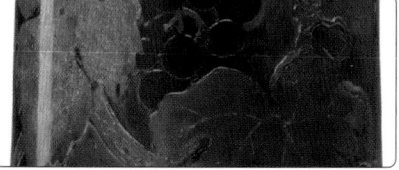

A Val St. Lambert corseted vase, with acid-etched grapevine design in iridised finish, engraved 'VSL'.

11.5in (29cm) high

£2,200-2,800   **DRA**

A rare Vallerysthal squat vase, acid-etched with intricate leaf design, against a frosted and gilded ground with floral etched design, with gilded signature and acid-etched, pressed mark.

5.5in (14cm) high

£1,500-2,000   **DRA**

A late Victorian stained glass panel, by Arthur Louis Moore, depicting the Greek goddess Thalia within a Classical interior, signed 'A. L. Moore, Glass Painter AKA 89 Southampton Row, London WC'.

Arthur Louis Moore was born in 1849 in Brixton, London. In 1868 he was apprenticed to J. T. Lyons, and about 1871 set up practice with S. Cibbs, first at 65 Great Russell Street and then 89 Southampton Row, London.

44in (112cm) high

£900-1,200   **TEN**

CLOSER LOOK – TIFFANY WINDOW

Louis Comfort Tiffany was inspired by the natural world and used it widely in his work, as reflected in the use of the arum lily, beloved by many Art Nouveau artists.

Tiffany trained as a painter and these skills are demonstrated in the use of perspective and framing to lend this landscape depth.

Stained glass panels, windows and doors became a feature of Art Nouveau decoration. Maxim's in Paris, The White House and Mark Twain's house in Hartford, CT, are amongst the best known examples of Tiffany's work.

A late 19thC stained glass panel, depicting St Michael in armour and a red dragon, with wood frame and illuminated back box.

The colours on certain areas, particularly the armour, have been achieved by double thickness glass.

57in (145cm) high

£900-1,200   **TEN**

A large Arts and Crafts leaded glass window, reverse painted with a courtship scene, secured in frame.

46in (117cm) high

£2,200-2,800   **DRA**

A Tiffany Studios 'Lily' window, plated with up to three layers and housed in an oak light box, signed in black enamel 'Tiffany Studios New York'.

Window 44in (112cm) high

£100,000-125,000   **JDJ**

A Victorian faceted red glass combined scent bottle-vinaigrette, by S. Mordan & Co., London, with foliate-engraved silver gilt mounts and a floral pierced grille, in fitted leather case.

1874   3.25in (8.5cm) long
£550-750   **DN**

A Coty set of three perfume bottles, 'La Rose', 'Jasmin de Corse', and 'L'Origan', in Coty crystal, sealed, with labels, in silk-lined leather case, stencilled 'CRISTAL COTY' marks.

c1923   2.25in (5.5cm) high
£1,200-1,500   **DRA**

A Coty 'L'Aimant' perfume bottle, clear and frosted glass, with sepia patina, sealed, with label, boxed, unwrapped for auction.

1920s   3.5in (9cm) high
£200-300   **DRA**

A DeVilbiss perfume atomiser, Cambridge Azurite glass with etched design and black patina, and special silvered-metal hardware.

c1922   8.5in (21.5cm) high
£500-800   **DRA**

A DeVilbiss perfume atomiser and bottle, glass with pink and black decoration, on twisted gilded glass stems, with dauber, marked 'DEVILBISS'.

c1926   7in (17.5cm) high
£1,000-1,500   **DRA**

A La Ducale 'Egizia' factice or cologne bottle, glazed ceramic, exotic head hung with brass earrings, lacking brass and cork stopper, marked 'CANOVA/CANOVA ITALY'.

c1936   11.75in (30cm) high
£400-500   **DRA**

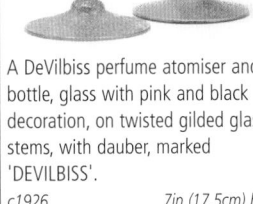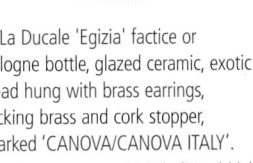

A Godet three perfume bottle set containing 'Cuir de Russie', 'Petite Fleur Bleue', and 'Sous-Bois', red and black glass, sealed, with labels, in presentation box.

1930s   3in (7.5cm) high
£500-800   **DRA**

A Hoffmann perfume bottle, purple crystal with unique jewelled metalwork, two putti stopper with dauber stub, metal 'CZECHOSLOVAKIA' tag.

1920s   6.75in (17cm) high
£900-1,200   **DRA**

A Langlois 'Duska' Art Deco perfume gift set, red and black glass with rouge and powder containers, with labels, in box.

1920s   *Tallest 4.5in (11.5cm) high*

£500-800   **DRA**

A Lanvin 'Scandal' perfume bottle, clear glass with gilded stopper and details, sealed, with label, boxed.

c1931   *2.25in (5.5cm) high*

£200-300   **DRA**

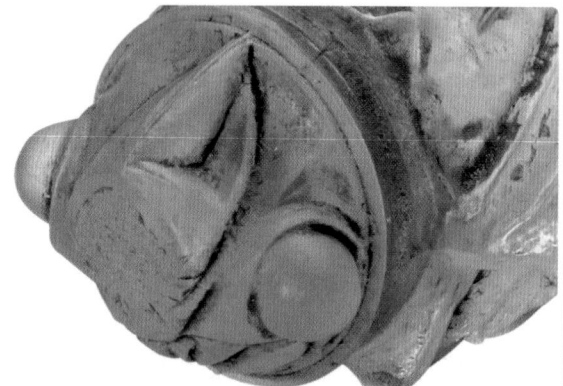

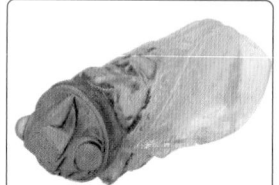

A Molinard Jeune 'Toute la Provence' perfume bottle, in clear glass with light green patina, with stopper, stamped 'Lousouleou Mon Amour'.

c1923   *2.5in (6.5cm) high*

£1,500-2,000   **DRA**

A Morlee crystal perfume bottle, with jewelled metalwork, putto stopper with dauber stub, stencilled oval 'MADE IN CZECHOSLOVAKIA' mark, foil 'MORLEE' label.

1920s   *3.75in (9.5cm) high*

£300-400   **DRA**

A Mury 'Notturno' Baccarat perfume bottle, black crystal with gilded detail, stencilled 'BACCARAT' mark.

c1926   *3.5in (8.5cm) high*

£350-450   **DRA**

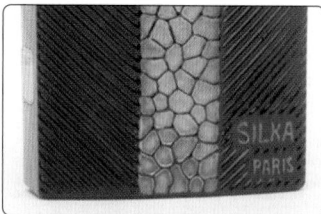

A Silka 'Ami' perfume bottle, black glass with frosted stopper, with gilded labels and faux eggshell decoration.

c1925   *7.75in (19.5cm) high*

£350-450   **DRA**

A La Valliere 'Jasmin D'Or' perfume bottle, clear glass with enamelled detail.

c1922   *2.25in (5.5cm) h*

£350-450   **DRA**

A yellow cameo glass and silver scent bottle, by Thomas Webb & Sons, in the form of a swan's head, with a silver top, Chester 1884.

Thomas Webb and Sons was a Victorian glass maker based in Stourbridge, England, who specialised in scent bottles, innovative both in technique and design.

9in (23cm) high

£8,000-10,000   **PART**

An Aesthetic Movement ebonised wood mantel clock, the rectangular frame set with painted panels, the brass dial cast with central radiating sun motif.

18.5in (47cm) high

£600-900   WW

A French giltwood sunburst wall timepiece, with eight-day movement, the dial within a carved bezel, with a repeating arrangement of radial sunbursts and leafy sprays to case.

c1900   *26.5in (67cm) diam*

£200-300   DN

An Art Nouveau mahogany and inlaid mantel clock, with a Japy Frères gong-striking eight-day movement, and 4in (10cm) Arabic numeral dial, the case with brass inlaid foliage, on brass ball feet.

10.75in (27.5cm) high

£400-500   DN

An Art Nouveau clock, by Alfred Daguet, in rocket-shaped hand-hammered brass-on-oak case with jewelled cabochons, signed on the front 'Alf. Daguet. 02' and on the reverse 'Les Cuivres S. Bing'.

Alfred Daguet was a metalworker employed by Siegfried 'Samuel' Bing producing goods for his gallery, Maison de L'Art Nouveau, in rue de Provence, Paris. Alfred Daguet created his objects in the studio above Bing's gallery.

16.25in (41cm) high

£3,500-4,500   TEN

A Duchess of Sutherland Cripples Guild copper mantel clock, model no. 2520, with applied silvered-metal foliate panels and feet, stamped number to base.

7in (17.5cm) wide

£500-600   WW

A hallmarked silver carriage clock, Chester, with embossed foliate decoration to whole and raised on four bun feet, with white enamelled dial with Roman numerals below arched carrying handle.

1907   *3.5in (9cm) high*

£400-500   FLD

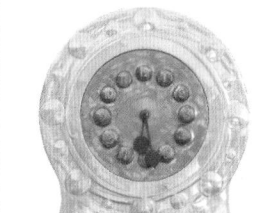

A Liberty & Co. Tudric pewter, copper and enamel clock, designed by Archibald Knox, model no. 0366, circular copper dial with enamelled circular numerals, stamped mark.

8in (20cm) high

£4,500-5,500   WW

A Liberty & Co. English pewter Tudric mantel clock, no. 01319, of rectangular section the domed case with circular enamelled copper dial, stamped marks.

13.5in (34cm) wide

£500-600   TEN

A cast bronze mantel clock, by Anton Puchegger, embossed with butterflies, with original patina, signed 'A PUCHEGGER 1139'.

8in (20.5cm) high

£1,000-1,500   DRA

An early 20thC French gilt-metal and steel framed carriage timepiece, panels of yellow translucent enamel on rayed grounds, ladybird motif.

3in (7.5cm) high

£600-700   WW

A large Handel table lamp, with 'Cattail' pattern octagonal shade, over a bulbous three-socket base in the style of William Grueby, both marked 'Handel'.

24in (61cm) high

£20,000-30,000   **DRA**

A large Handel table lamp, in the 'Cattail' pattern, over a fine bulbous three-socket Poppy base, stamped 'Handel', single panel replaced with original Handel glass.

26in (66cm) high

£9,000-12,000   **DRA**

A Handel table lamp, shade with 'Cattail' pattern against caramel slag glass, over a five-socket bronze base, original sockets, cap and chains, the base marked 'Handel 768?'.

30.5in (77.5cm) high

£30,000-40,000   **DRA**

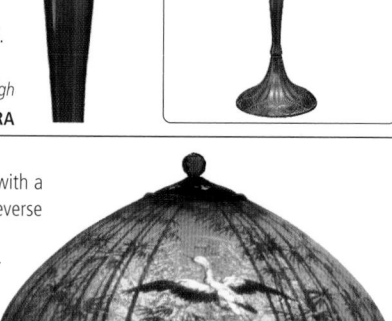

A Handel table lamp, the shade reverse and obverse painted with Mount Fuji and tall bamboo, over a three-socket base with floral design, shade ring marked 'Handel Lamps Pat'd No 979664'.

22in (56cm) high

£8,000-10,000   **DRA**

A Handel monumental table lamp, the three-socket bulbous poppy base topped by an octagonal filigree shade painted with pine trees, base marked 'Handel'.

25in (63.5cm) high

£15,000-20,000   **DRA**

A Handel table lamp, with a chipped-glass shade reverse painted with bamboo and cranes on a three-socket fluted bronzed base, base and shade stamped 'Handel'.

24in (61cm) high

£8,000-10,000   **DRA**

A Handel table lamp, the acid-etched shade reverse and obverse painted with an autumnal landscape, over a three-socket base, shade signed 'Handel 5209', artist signed 'R. Lockrow', stamped 'Handel' on base.

24.5in (62cm) high

£12,000-18,000   **DRA**

A large rare Handel 'Hollyhock' four-sided chandelier, complete with four sockets, original chain and ceiling cap, breaks to a few small glass pieces.

34in (86.5cm) wide

£20,000-30,000   **DRA**

A Handel hammered copper boudoir lamp, the conical shade suspended from hooks, pierced with stylised tulips and lined in caramel slag glass, on single-socket base, shade signed.

14in (35.5cm) high

£6,000-7,000   **DRA**

A Handel chandelier, with five leaded glass shades hanging from individual arms, fastened to a square brass ceiling plate.

33in (84cm) high

£6,000-7,000   **DRA**

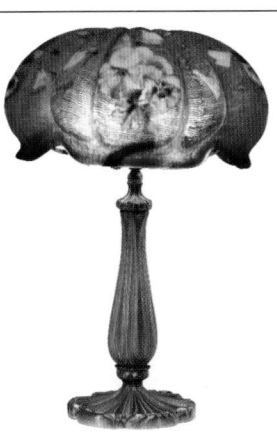

A Pairpoint table lamp, the two-socket base with stylised lotus blossoms, the lobed dome shade reverse painted, base stamped 'Pairpoint 53085'.

20in (51cm) high

£2,500-3,500　　　　**DRA**

A Pairpoint table lamp, the 'Puffy' shade decorated with hummingbirds and roses on a yellow and white plaid ground, over a two-socket gold-finish base stamped 'Pairpoint 63066', small nicks.

23in (58.5cm) high

£3,000-4,000　　　　**DRA**

A Pairpoint table lamp, the shade reverse painted with colourful landscape and stone wall, over a two-socket Classical silvered base, base stamped 'Pairpoint'.

22in (56cm) high

£3,000-4,000　　　　**DRA**

A Pairpoint 'Puffy' lamp, with tiger lilies in pink and white on a green ground, on its original pyramidal base, decorated with heavily embossed poppies, signed.

21in (53.5cm) high

£6,000-8,000　　　　**DRA**

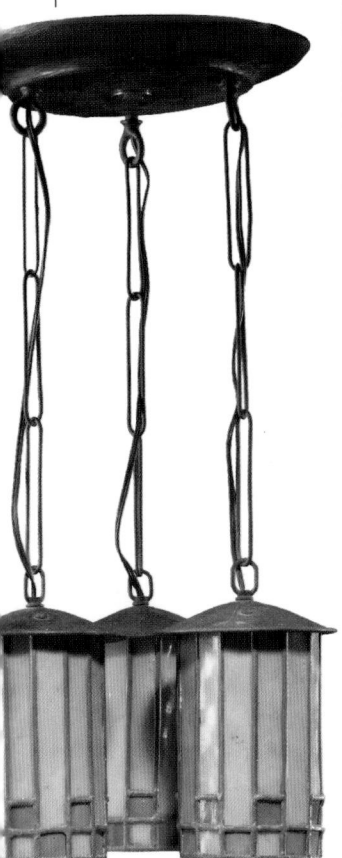

A Roycroft ceiling fixture, designed by Dard Hunter, with three leaded glass drops, complete with chains and ceiling cap, break to one piece of glass, missing finial and wear to patina on cap.

22in (56cm) high

£20,000-30,000　　　　**DRA**

A large Roycroft hammered copper table lamp, designed by Dard Hunter, the shade of leaded slag glass, over a three-socket base with original patina, original cap and finial, base with Orb and cross mark.

22.25in (56.5cm) high

£15,000-20,000　　　　**DRA**

A Roycroft flaring shade, designed by Dard Hunter, of bright green and purple leaded slag glass.

18in (45.5cm) wide

£7,000-9,000　　　　**DRA**

A Roycroft hammered copper chandelier, from the Roycroft Inn, with three reflective sockets, with original chains and ceiling cap, and original patina, Orb and Cross mark.

31in (79cm) high

£5,000-7,000　　　　**DRA**

A Roycroft table lamp, by Dard Hunter, the shade of hammered copper lined in green hammered glass, on single-socket oak base with copper fittings, glass replaced with Roycroft-type material.

23in (58.5cm) high

£8,000-10,000　　　　**DRA**

A Steuben boudoir lamp, the patinated candlestick base topped with ribbed shade, maker touch mark in fitter ring.

15.5in (39.5cm) high

£2,000-3,000　　　　**DRA**

An Arts and Crafts bronze chandelier, with four arms, suspending four Steuben shades.

35in (89cm) high

£3,000-4,000　　　　**DRA**

A Tiffany Studios table lamp, with an 'Acorn' pattern leaded glass shade over a converted bronze oil font base, shade signed.

22in (56cm) high

£12,000-18,000   **DRA**

CLOSER LOOK – TIFFANY LAMPSHADE

The development of the electric light inspired designers to think differently about lampshades and to use new forms.

Tiffany's designs began with the use of just a few colours but at the peak of production, he had 5,000 colours at his disposal.

Furthering his interest in stained glass windows, Louis Comfort Tiffany founded Tiffany Studios to create lamps in 1900, realising that the same effect could be created on a smaller scale, using artificial light.

Tiffany's legacy is his lampshades. He integrated the shade's design with the base, creating an organic whole.

A Tiffany Studios 'Red Poppy' table lamp, supported on a Tiffany Studios library base, with three sockets, both shade and base signed.

Overall 26in (66cm) high

£80,000-90,000   **JDJ**

A Tiffany Studios table lamp, with 'Acorn' glass shade, over three-socket faceted bronze base, base and shade signed.

23in (58.5cm) high

£9,000-12,000   **DRA**

A Tiffany 'Acorn' chandelier, of yellow and green slag glass in bronze mount, complete with original hanging chain, hook and ceiling plate.

14.75in (37.5cm) high

£25,000-30,000   **DRA**

A Tiffany Studios 'Black-eyed Susan' table lamp, on a three-socket fluted base, minor breaks to glass, with original bronze patina, stamped 'TIFFANY STUDIOS NEW YORK 370S182'.

22.5in (57cm) high

£30,000-40,000   **DRA**

A tall Tiffany Studios 'Dogwood' table lamp, on a four-socket elongated organic base, with original bronze patina, stamped 'TIFFANY STUDIOS NEW YORK 531'.

31in (79cm) high

£30,000-40,000   **DRA**

A Tiffany Studios 'Dogwood' lamp, using Tiffany patented glass techniques: confetti, striated, textured, library base, shade, base signed.

Shade 18in (45cm) diam

£25,000-35,000   **JDJ**

A Tiffany Studios 'Pomegranate' table lamp, over a two-socket fluted bronze base, base stamped 'TIFFANY STUDIOS NEW YORK 617', shade stamped 'TIFFANY STUDIOS NEW YORK 1561-15'.

18.25in (46.5cm) high

£8,000-9,000   **DRA**

A Tiffany Studios 'Poppy' table lamp, on a twisted vine three-socket bronze base, shade stamped 'TIFFANY STUDIOS NEW YORK 1531 – 14', base stamped 'TIFFANY STUDIOS NEW YORK 443'.

25.5in (64cm) high

£90,000-100,000   **DRA**

A Tiffany Studios 'Spider' lamp, with a six-sided leaded shade, over a three-socket base, base and shade marked 'TIFFANY STUDIOS NEW YORK 337'.

18in (45.5cm) high

£30,000-40,000   DRA

A Tiffany Studios 'Red Tulip' table lamp, the glass a combination of striated, cats paw, rippled and granular glass, on a three-socket mock turtleback base.

22.5in (57cm) high

£70,000-80,000   JDJ

A Tiffany Studios bronze and iridescent glass table lamp, shade with gold damascene decoration, shade unmarked, possibly attributed to Tiffany or Quezel, base signed 'Tiffany Studios, New York, 461'.

17.5in (44cm) high

£5,000-6,000   SK

A Tiffany Studios bronze counter-balance desk lamp, the ruffled gold Favrile glass shade in pulled-feather design, base stamped 'TIFFANY STUDIOS NEW YORK 416'.

15.5in (39.5cm) high

£3,000-5,000   DRA

A Tiffany Furnaces desk lamp, with a green and blue iridescent damascene shade signed 'L.C. Tiffany – Favrile', the enamel-decorated base signed 'Louis C. Tiffany Furnaces, Inc. 369'.

Overall 14in (35.5cm) high

£10,000-12,000   JDJ

A Tiffany Studios 'Scarab' lamp, with a heavy green and purple lustred Favrile glass scarab-shaped shade over a fluted bronze base, stamped 'TIFFANY STUDIOS NEW YORK 8018 5', original patina.

9in (23cm) high

£12,000-18,000   DRA

A tall Tiffany Studios four-light lamp, with twisted vine-like stems in original deep brown patina, and gold Favrile shades with diamond pattern and numbered 'L2857', base signed.

28in (71cm) high

£10,000-12,000   DRA

A Tiffany Studios three-light 'Lily' lamp, with a fluted base ending in a hook, complete with original switch, base stamped 'TIFFANY STUDIOS NEW YORK 306', shades etched 'L.C.T. Favrile', original patina.

17in (43cm) high

£6,000-8,000   DRA

A Tiffany Studios floor lamp, the shade composed of 10 linenfold glass panels in doré bronze framework, over single socket within harp, shade and base both signed.

1938   56in (142cm) high

£5,000-7,000   SK

A Tiffany Studios 'Fire Ball' lamp, the leaded orb shade with flame design made up of glass with different textures giving the effect of dancing flames, on a bronze base with single socket.

15in (38cm) high

£35,000-45,000   JDJ

A Tiffany Studios mosaic centrepiece, cast bronze base inset with gold Favrile mosaic, with a tall gold Favrile ribbed vase, leaves holding salt dishes, marked 'Tiffany Studios New York S31278', logo, vase, four dishes 'L.C.T. – Favrile'.

Favrile glass was patented by Louis Comfort Tiffany in 1894.

24in (61cm) diam

£40,000-50,000   JDJ

DECORATIVE ARTS

A hammered copper and mica table lamp, Dirk Van Erp, the shade atop a two-socket trumpet-shaped base, with original patina and mica, with open box windmill mark.

17in (43cm) wide

£10,000-12,000   **DRA**

A Dirk Van Erp hammered copper and mica table lamp, the shade over a two-socket base, windmill stamp with 'DIRKVANERP' and remnant of D'Arcy Gaw, repatinated, new mica.

20in (51cm) high

£6,000-8,000   **DRA**

An early table lamp, by Dirk Van Erp, the hammered copper two-socket base topped by a four-panel mica shade, with early closed box mark.

19in (48cm) high

£7,000-9,000   **DRA**

A rare Dirk Van Erp hammered copper and mica table lamp, the shade lined in mica flanking paper sheets pierced with a Japanese design of dragonflies, over a two-socket base, windmill stamp with 'DIRKVANEERP'.

17.5in (44.5cm) high

£8,000-10,000   **DRA**

An Argy Rousseau 'Fairy' lamp, the domed glass shade with floral design, over a wrought-iron base, marked 'ARGY-ROUSSEAU FRANCE'.

8.25in (21cm) wide

£5,000-6,000   **DRA**

A rare Bigelow, Kennard & Co. table lamp, with a leaded glass shade in a floral pattern over a three-socket bronze base, original patina.

23.25in (59cm) high

£8,500-10,500   **DRA**

A Daum Nancy 'Paysage-de-verre' table lamp, the thick-walled colourless overlaid glass with yellow dye powder meltings, and etched in red and purples in several steps, with engraved mark.

c1905   *19in (48cm) high*

£15,000-20,000   **WKA**

A crystal glass chandelier, by Leopold Bauer, for Atelier Engelhart, Vienna, for E. Bakalowits Söhne, with a central light and three arms fitted with five one-armed lamps, brass mounted, with original writing.

1902   *41.25in (105cm) high*

£8,000-10,000   **WKA**

A rare Albert Berry table lamp, the shade of pierced and hammered copper, with garland chain, over a single-socket mahogany base, with dark original patina, with break to one glass pane.

20in (51cm) high

£4,500-5,500   **DRA**

A Duffner & Kimberly leaded glass ceiling fixture, with four (replaced) sockets, brass rods and ceiling cap, one replaced glass piece.

25.75in (65.5cm) wide

£4,000-5,000   **DRA**

A Duffner & Kimberly 'Viking' table lamp, the shade leaded with six bronze bands ending in griffins, with intricate glass panels, signed 'The Duffner & Kimberley Co. New York', on original base.

Overall 27in (68.5cm) high

£50,000-60,000   **JDJ**

ESSENTIAL REFERENCE – DIRK VAN ERP

A native of Holland, Dirk Van Erp (1859-1933) emigrated to the USA in 1886 and settled in San Francisco, working as a coppersmith in the shipyards. Van Erp made small decorative copper items in his spare time, until this became his main activity in 1908.

- He produced items such as table lamps with mica shades, vases and writing-table equipment, which were simple in form and made decorative use of signs of handcrafting, such as exposed rivets and hammering marks. The first of his famous Van Erp copper lamps was designed with Eleanor D'arcy Gaw.
- Van Erp retired in 1929, and the Dirk van Erp Studio was subsequently run by his son, William, until 1944.

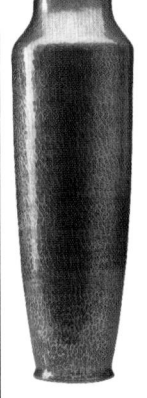

A tall rare Dirk Van Erp hammered-brass shell-casing vase, stamped windmill with 'DIRKVANERP', drilled base.

19.25in (49cm) high

£1,800-2,300   DRA

A large Native American Apache figural basket, attributed to Dirk Van Erp, with collar of riveted copper.

12in (30.5cm) high

£1,800-2,300   DRA

A large rare Dirk Van Erp red 'Warty' hammered-copper vase, with original patina, stamped windmill mark with open box, marked 'DIRKVANERP SAN FRANCISCO'.

15.5in (39.5cm) high

£30,000-36,000   DRA

A copper metalwork and wood box, Dirk Van Erp, California, with strapwork hinges and fitting, lined with wood, natural brown patina, impressed 'Dirk Van Erp' with windmill on base.

c1908   *10in (25.5cm) wide*

£1,500-2,000   SK

A Jarvie faceted sterling pitcher, attributed to George Elmslie, inscribed 'PRESENTED BY CHICAGO LIVE STOCK WORLD IOWA POLAND CHINA FUTURITY 1914', stamped 'STERLING JARVIE 2034'.

Robert Riddle Jarvie and his wife, Lillian Gray, started the Jarvie Shop in Chicago in 1904. They initially sold handmade copper and brass pieces, including the tall, graceful candlesticks for which Jarvie is best known, before moving in silver and gold hollowware in 1905. The shop closed in 1920.

9.5in (24cm) high

£13,000-17,000   DRA

A Jarvie 'Iota' brass candlestick, with bulbous top, some wear to patina, marked 'Jarvie' in script.

14in (35.5cm) high

£2,500-3,500   DRA

A Jarvie hammered sterling silver presentation cup by George Elmslie, 'Harbor Point Country Club', stamped 'JARVIE STERLING 2016', shallow dent.

1915   *7.75in (19.5cm) high*

£4,500-6,000   DRA

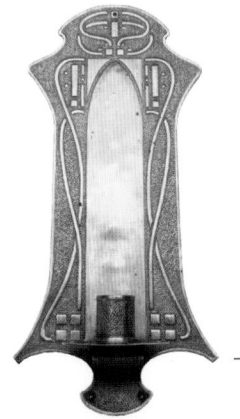

A Jarvie brass sconce, with tooled Arts and Crafts design, signed 'Jarvie' in script.

13.5in (34cm) high

£3,000-4,000   DRA

A large Georg Jensen silver bowl, designed by Georg Jensen, model no. 6, simple form on pierced foliate columns and domed foot, stamped marks.

5.5in (14cm) high

£800-1,000   WW

A Georg Jensen silver twin-handled bowl, model no. 456D, stamped marks.

3.25in (8cm) high

£350-550   WW

A silver tazza, by Georg Jensen, model no. 263B, the circular hammered bowl with bunches of grapes, stamped 'Georg Jensen Denmark Sterling GI 925 263B GI', London import marks.

1931   *7.75in (19.5cm) high*

£2,000-3,000   TEN

A Georg Jensen silver sauceboat, model no. 896, designed by Jørgen Jensen, with ebonised wood handle, stamped marks.

7in (18cm) wide

£400-600   WW

ESSENTIAL REFERENCE – JØRGEN JENSEN

Jørgen Jensen (1895-1960), second son of Georg Jensen, worked as a member of his father's firm from 1917 to 1923, and from 1936 to 1962.

● Jensen designed jewellery and hollowware for the Georg Jensen Silversmithy. His hollowware from the 1920s displays similarities with the earlier work of Johan Rohde (1856-1935), whereas in the 1930s, his work moved towards a more individual style, which dispensed with applied ornamentation in favour of incised parallel lines. After WWII, his sleek designs showed a more Modernist approach.

A Georg Jensen silver and ivory 'Blossom' coffee pot and cover, designed by Georg Jensen, model no. 2C, stamped marks.

8.75in (22cm) high

£1,500-2,000   WW

A five-piece sterling silver tea service, by Georg Jensen, comprising a coffee pot, teapot, cream jug, sugar bowl and tray.

c1925

£15,000-20,000   POOK

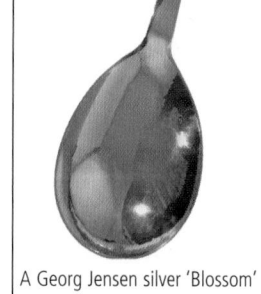

A Georg Jensen silver 'Blossom' serving spoon, model no. 84, stamped marks.

8.5in (21.5cm) long

£200-300   WW

A Liberty & Co. hammered-silver box, inset with colourful enamelled landscape, impressed 'MADE IN ENGLAND 'TUDRIC' 01021'.

3.5in (9cm) wide

£1,000-1,500   DRA

A small Liberty 'Cymric' covered sterling box, by Archibald Knox, the lid enamelled with a lyrical Arts and Craft motif, stamped 'L&C', anchor, lion rampant, and 'f, CYMRIC, 676C', minor dents.

2.25in (5.5cm) wide

£800-1,200   DRA

A Liberty & Co. 'Tudric' pewter biscuit box, by Archibald Knox, with stylised blossoms and leaves, stamped 'TUDRIC 0194'.

4.5in (11.5cm) high

£1,500-2,000   DRA

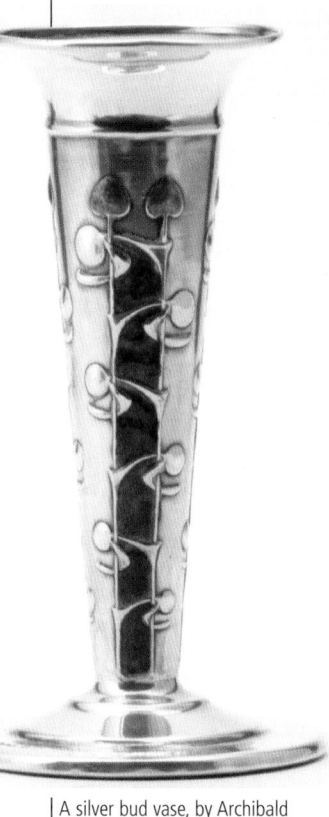

A silver bud vase, by Archibald Knox, for Liberty & Co., with stylised decoration in blue and green enamel, with 'RD467111 Hallmarks L & Co', anchor, lion rampant, 'K'.

5in (12.5cm) high

£5,000-6,000   DRA

An Art Nouveau Liberty & Co. 'Tudric' pewter clock, with stylised trees and enamelled blue and gold dial, stamped 'TUDRIC 0371'.

9in (23cm) high

£3,000-4,000   DRA

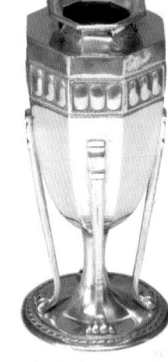

A Liberty 'Tudric' pewter faceted urn, on buttressed feet, stamped 'TUDRIC 01004'.

Liberty & Co., the famous London department store, introduced the 'Tudric' pewter range in 1901-02. Pieces in the range were designed by Archibald Knox, Bernard Cuzner, Oliver Baker, the Silver Studio and Jessie M. King.

8.25in (21cm) high

£1,000-1,500   DRA

A Liberty & Co. 'Tudric' pewter figural pitcher, of an owl with jade eyes, stamped 'TUDRIC 5 035', small, shallow dents.

8in (20.5cm) high

£900-1,200   DRA

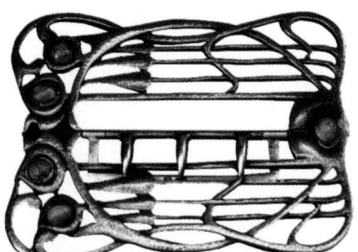

A Liberty & Co. silver belt buckle, inset with five turquoise stones, stamped 'CYMRIC L & CO' with hallmarks.

3in (7.5cm) wide

£2,000-2,500   DRA

A set of five Liberty & Co. enamelled silver hors d'oeuvres forks, with stylised leaf design in blue and green, in original box, impressed hallmarks.

Forks: 5in (12.5cm)

£1,500-2,000   DRA

ESSENTIAL REFERENCE – RAMSDEN

Omar Ramsden (1873-1939) and Alwyn Carr (1872-1940) were both born in Sheffield and studied at Sheffield School of Art and the Royal College of Art, London. Together they set up a workshop in London. It is likely that Ramsden was the entrepreneur, and Carr the designer. Carr joined the army in 1914 and Ramsden ran the workshop alone.

● Many pieces are engraved with a variation of 'OMAR RAMSDEN ET ALWYN CARR ME FECERUNT' ('Omar Ramsden and Alwyn Carr made me'). This trademark signature reinforced the perception of commissioning a piece of silver from a craftsman.

A silver tazza, Omar Ramsden, London, with a hammered finish, the bowl with a flange rim chased with a trailing tendril, the baluster pedestal with cast adornment, incised 'OMAR RAMSDEN – ME FECIT' on a mounted octagonal wooden plinth.

1927   10.5in (27cm) high excluding plinth 50oz (1,417g)

£15,000-20,000   **WW**

An Edwardian silver caddy spoon, Ramsden and Carr, London, with fig-shaped bowl, hammered finish, openwork stem, inset oval enamel cabochon.

1907   3.5in (78.5cm) long 1.2oz (34g)

£1,200-1,800   **WW**

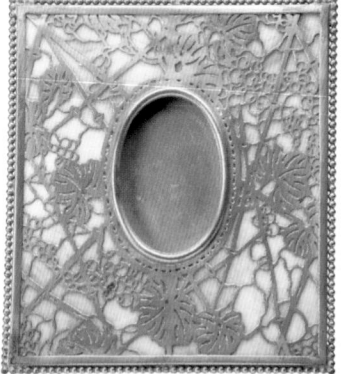

A Tiffany Studios table-top picture frame, in the 'Grapevine' pattern, gold doré finish and caramel slag-glass liner, stamped 'TIFFANY STUDIOS NEW YORK 949', original finish.

7.25in (18.5cm) high

£900-1,200   **DRA**

A Tiffany Studios table-top picture frame, in the 'Chinese' pattern, gold doré finish, stamped 'TIFFANY STUDIOS NEW YORK 1761', re-gilded.

9in (23cm) high

£1,500-2,000   **DRA**

A Tiffany Studios bronze rectangular picture frame, in the 'Pine Needle' pattern, lined in rich green mottled slag-glass, original green-brown patina, stamped 'TIFFANY STUDIOS NEW YORK'.

9.5in (24cm) high

£2,500-3,000   **DRA**

A Tiffany Studios table-top picture frame, in the 'Venetian' pattern, gold doré finish, original patina, stamped 'TIFFANY STUDIOS NEW YORK 1682'.

11.75in (30cm) high

£3,000-3,500   **DRA**

A Tiffany Studios six-piece bronze desk set, in the 'Venetian' pattern, comprising picture frame, double letter holder, stamp box, double inkwell and blotter ends, stamped 'TIFFANY STUDIOS NEW YORK' with numbers.

Letter holder 10in (25.5cm) wide

£1,200-1,800   **DRA**

A Tiffany Studios eleven-piece gold doré desk set, in the 'Bookmark' pattern, comprising cigar box, letter opener, inkwell, blotter ends, notebook holder, stamp box, rocker blotter, two letter holders and a calendar, stamped 'TIFFANY STUDIOS NEW YORK', and numbered.

Cigar box 6in (15cm) wide

£2,500-3,000   **DRA**

A Tiffany Studios bronze inkwell, in the 'Zodiac' pattern, stamped 'TIFFANY STUDIOS NEW YORK 1072'.

6.25in (16cm) wide

£400-500   DRA

A Tiffany Studios bronze paperweight, bust of a hound 'Shando', in gold doré finish, stamped 'TIFFANY STUDIOS NEW YORK'.

3.25in (8cm) wide

£1,200-1,800   DRA

A Tiffany & Co. sterling silver chamberstick of scalloped circular form with a loop handle, with floral and fauna repoussé decoration throughout.

c1877   *5.75in (13.5cm) diam*

£500-700   FRE

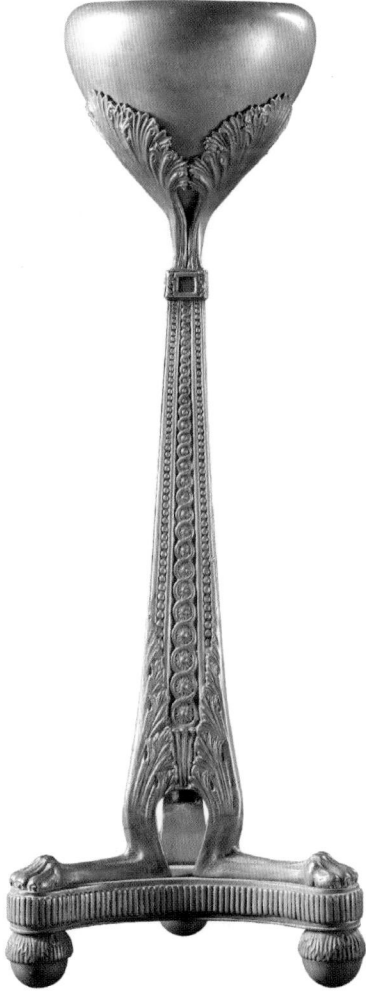

A Tiffany Studios Aesthetic Movement bronze planter, New York, the bowl on a decorated column with three paw feet on shaped platform, marked 'Tiffany Studios, New York' and logo, numbered '64871'.

c1900   *27in (68.5cm) high*

£4,000-5,000   SK

An early 20thC Tiffany Studios doré bronze vase, of bulbous form with flared lip and circular foot, marked 'Tiffany Studios, New York, 1862' on base.

6.25in (16cm) high

£600-800   SK

A Tiffany & Co. silver belt buckle, model no. 3225, decorated with floral roundels and wirework foliage, stamped marks.

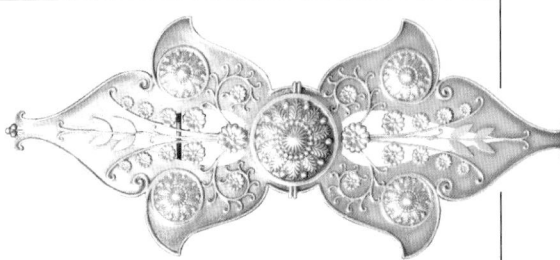

6.5in (16.5cm) wide

£900-1,200   WW

ESSENTIAL REFERENCE – TIFFANY & CO.

Unlike his son, Louis Comfort Tiffany, Charles Louis Tiffany (1812-1902) was a manufacturer and vendor, rather than a designer. He began dealing in 'fancy goods' in 1837 and was so successful that his company, Tiffany, Young and Ellis, set up a workshop for making jewellery. Tiffany took sole command of the firm in 1853.

- **In 1867 his display of silver was given an award at the Paris Exhibition.**
- **By the 1890s Tiffany had official appointments to Queen Victoria, the Tsar of Russia, the Shah of Persia, the Khedive of Egypt, among other royal and distinguished clients.**
- **In the late 19thC, the business expanded to include electroplating, so that Tiffany & Co. could complete with Reed & Barton, who had pioneered the technique in the USA in the 1850s.**
- **Tiffany pieces were made in a range of historic and exotic styles. From 1851, many were designed by Chandler Moore (1827-91).**
- **Tiffany also marketed some if the famous Art Nouveau lamps designed by his son, Louis Comfort Tiffany.**
- **On Charles Tiffany's death, Louis took over the management of Tiffany & Co.**
- **Tiffany & Co. currently flourishes in New York and London.**

DECORATIVE ARTS

A Roycroft copper bottle-shaped 'Ali Baba' vase, with Orb and Cross mark.

16in (40.5cm) high

£1,500-2,000   DRA

A Roycroft hammered copper bud vase, incised with tall leaves, with three buttress handles, Orb and Cross mark.

7.5in (19cm) high

£1,800-2,300   DRA

A pair of Roycroft hammered copper 'American Beauty' vases, Orb and Cross marks.

11.75in (30cm) high

£1,800-2,300   DRA

A Roycroft hammered copper vase, with four riveted buttressed handles, alternating with four small silver squares, against a woodgrain pattern ground, Orb and Cross mark.

8.25in (21cm) high

£2,500-3,000   DRA

A Roycroft hammered copper 'American Beauty' vase, for the Grove Park Inn, stamped.

Elbert Green Hubbard (1856-1915) founded the Roycroft community in 1895, at East Aurora, New York. The work of the Roycrofters was based on the principles of William Morris, whom Hubbard had met in 1894. They produced metalwork, leatherwork and simple furniture, marked with a cross with two horizontal bars and an R in a circle. Hubbard's son, Elbert Hubbard Jnr, took over the Roycrofters in 1915. The workshops closed in 1938.

21in (53.5cm) high

£3,500-4,500   DRA

A tall early Roycroft hammered copper 'American Beauty' vase, Orb and Cross mark.

21.75in (55cm) high

£1,500-2,000   DRA

A Roycroft hammered copper coffee pot, with Sheffield silver wash and mahogany handle, stamped with mid-period Orb and Cross mark.

9.5in (24cm) high

£1,800-2,100   DRA

A Roycroft hammered copper chafing dish, complete with burner, together with a circular tray with riveted handles, cleaned patina to chafing stand, Orb and Cross marks.

Chafing dish 10in (25.5cm) high

£900-1,300   DRA

A rare Roycroft chestnut log motto, carved 'PRODUCE GREAT PERSONS, THE REST FOLLOWS-WALT WHITMAN', hanging from original iron chains, original condition.

44.5in (113cm) wide

£3,300-4,500   DRA

A Roycroft hammered copper wall-hanging sign, 'TWILDO', with original, dark patina.

'TWILDO' is probably a shortened version of 'It will do'.

20in (51cm) wide

£4,000-5,500   DRA

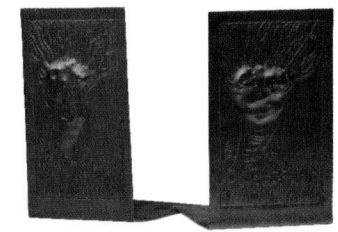

A pair of Roycroft copper bookends, embossed with large trees in a field of blossoms, with original patina, Orb and Cross marks.

6.5in (16.5cm) high

£4,000-5,500   DRA

One of three Samuel Yellin wrought-iron transom panels, two with birds and stylised trees, one with scrollwork.

These panels were part of thirteen room partitions built 1927-52 for the J. Walter Thompson Company, in the Greybar Building on Lexington Avenue, New York.

36.5in (92.5cm) high

£11,000-13,000 SET   DRA

One of four Samuel Yellin wrought-iron transom panels, each with fleurs-de-lys and scrollwork.

36.5in (82cm) high

£6,000-7,000 SET   DRA

A wrought iron tripod occasional table, by Samuel Yellin, with hammered copper tray.

21in (53.5cm) wide

£2,500-3,500   DRA

A sterling silver and enamel Old Newbury Crafters punch bowl and tray, retailed by Shreve, Crump & Low, bowl raised on silver-framed blue enamel bars joined to base, maker's and retailer's mark, sterling on base.

228 oz (6,470g)

£5,000-6,000   SK

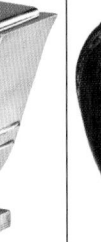

An Art Deco urn-shaped sterling-silver covered box, by Cardeilhac, with lapis lazuli handle, stamped with maker's marks and Minerva hallmark.

6in (15cm) high

£2,500-3,000   SDR

A George Kendrick lidded copper box, with banded floriform designs, stamped 'G. P. K.', with G. P. Kendrick paper label inside lid.

3.5in (9cm) wide

£3,000-4,000   DRA

DECORATIVE ARTS

A WMF silvered, patinated and inlaid brass covered jar, by Paul Haustein, with stamped mark.

Daniel Straub founded his company in Geislingen, Germany in 1853. In 1880, now an amalgamation of several firms, it was renamed WMF (Württembergische Metallwarenfabrik). It was famous for Art Nouveau metalware, particularly the maiden motif, which decorates some of the most popular pieces. It had similar success with Art Deco designs.

9.5in (24.5cm) high

£3,000-4,000   SDR

A silvered-gesso panel, cast from a model by Marcel Bouraine, framed.

21.25in (54cm) wide

£600-800   WW

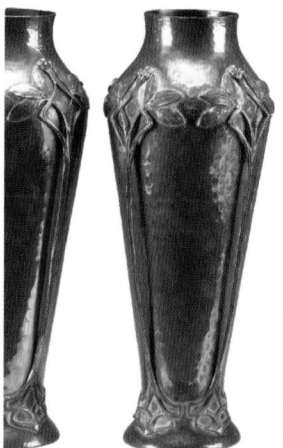

A pair of WMF beaten-copper tapered vases, with applied brass Art Nouveau berries and foliage, stamped Ostrich mark.

15.25in (39cm) high

£800–1,000   A&G

A WMF Art Nouveau pewter charger, decorated with a maiden and poppies and engraved presentation to bottom edge.

20in (51cm) diam

£500-700   GORL

A WMF Ikora metal pedestal vase, designed by Rudolf Rieger, in silver-and-black abstract patterns, on a circular base, stamped with the Oden Tower above WMF Ikora.

25.75in (65.5cm) high

£300-500   TEN

An Art Nouveau WMF electroplated dressing mirror, cast in relief with a maiden gazing at her reflection in the mirror, stamped marks.

14.5in (37cm) high

£800-1,000   WW

A James Fenton silver and enamel milk-jug and sugar basin, cast in low relief and enamelled with a flower spray, stamped marks.

1917   *3in (8cm) high*

£350-550   WW

An Art Nouveau silver bowl, Goldsmiths & Silversmiths Co. Ltd, London, the pedestal foot rising to a bowl chased with stylised irises with twin bifurcated tendril handles.

1909   *14in (35.5cm) wide 37oz (1,049g) 14dwt*

£1,000-1,500   TEN

A footed copper bowl, by Harry Dixon, with geometric designs around the exterior, stamped marks.

11in (28cm) diam

£900-1,200   DRA

A small Aesthetic Movement copper and white-metal-inlaid quatrefoil dish, by Gorham, hammered in lines and inset with two small plaques, stamped marks.

Gorham Manufacturing Co. (est. 1818) is the largest American silversmiths and amongst the largest in the world. Its impressed anchor trademark was introduced in 1848.

7.5in (19cm) wide

£300-500   DN

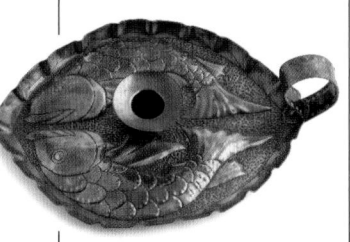

A copper and wrought iron 'Botanic' coal scuttle, attributed to Christopher Dresser, for Benham and Froud Ltd, stamped 'Rd 185919', modelled as a foliate form, with a detachable liner.

c1892   *22in (56cm) high*

£350-550   DN

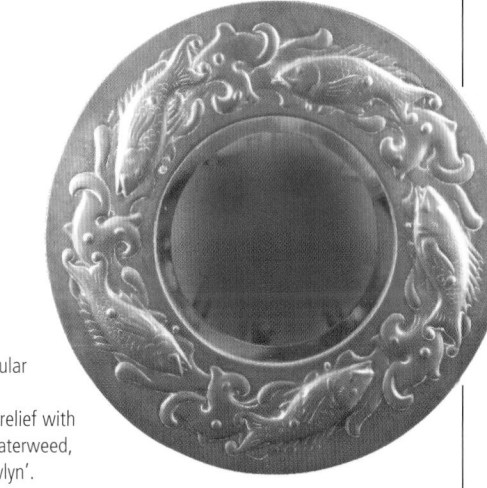

A Newlyn circular copper mirror, hammered in relief with fish among waterweed, stamped 'Newlyn'.

In the late 19thC, the village of Newlyn, Cornwall, became known for handmade copper wares in the Arts and Crafts style. Typical decoration includes hand-hammered, stylised repoussé foliate or marine design.

13.5in (34.5cm) diam

£800-1,000   WW

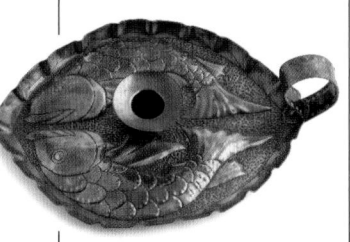

A Newlyn copper chamberstick, stamped in relief with scaly fish, unsigned.

10in (25cm)

£150-250   WW

A Newlyn copper picture frame, with easel back, hammered in relief with a frieze of fish and shells, stamped 'Newlyn' to the backplate.

8.75in (22cm) high

£700-900   WW

An Arts & Crafts silver-coloured metal, copper and enamel box, attributed to A. Edward Jones, with riveted straps and enamel roundels, with riveted corner pieces flaring to form the feet.

7.75in (20cm) wide

£600-800   DN

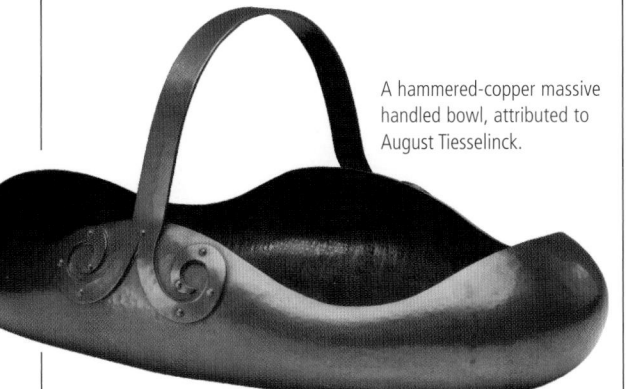

A hammered-copper massive handled bowl, attributed to August Tiesselinck.

20in (51cm) diam

£2,000-2,500   DRA

An Arts and Crafts copper, enamel and mother-of-pearl mounted box, the pull-off cover with a plaque in coloured enamels and foil, the body with copper decoration, mother-of-pearl and small plaques.

c1900   *5.75in (14.5cm) wide*

£2,500-3,500   TEN

A rare Guild of Handicrafts brass charger, by John Pearson, repoussé-decorated with birds amongst scrolling foliage, incised 'J Pearson 1891', no. 438.

15in (39cm) diam

£1,800-2,200   WW

A brass centrepiece, by Josef Hoffmann, for Wiener Werkstätte, hammer-tone finish, two screwed-in handles, marked on foot 'WIENER/WERK/STÄTTE, JH'.

The Wiener Werkstätte (1903-32) were founded in Vienna by Josef Hoffmann, Koloman Moser and Fritz Warndorfer, who wished to create an association of craftsmen based on C. R. Ashbee's Guild.

1924/25   6.75in (17.5cm) high

£15,000-20,000   WKA

A gold-plated brass vase, by Eduard Josef Wimmer, for Wiener Werkstätte, beaten with rosebud and rose leaf motif, pearl edging, signed on base, Rose mark and monogram of the metalworker Stanislaus Teyc.

1910-11   17.5in (44.5cm) high

£20,000-25,000   WKA

An Art Nouveau duet stand, the double-sided score-rest pierced with floral strapwork, supported on a gilt-metal bracket modelled as two winged bats with serpents' heads, with candle nozzles, raised on a part-gilt and painted carved pillar on a circular base.

60.5in (154cm) wide

£3,500-4,500   TEN

A Kayserzinn pewter photograph frame, designed by Hugo Leven, model no. 4313, easel back, cast in low relief with poppy seed heads, cast marks.

10.25in (26cm) high

£450-650   WW

An Orivit pewter casket, with hinged cover, cast in low relief with two peacocks below Art Nouveau maiden roundels.

9in (23cm) wide

£300-400   WW

An Arts & Crafts silver-coloured metal and enamel box and cover, the cover inset with an iridescent blue/green panel embossed decoration all over, on block feet.

7in (18cm) wide 12.5oz (354g)

£800-1,000   DN

A 19thC French bronze of a bacchante and two young satyrs, after Clodion, (1738-1814), signed 'Clodion'.

15.5in (39cm) high

£1,200-1,800   **L&T**

A bronze figure, 'L'Invasion', by Aristide-Onesime Croisy (French, 1840-99), medium-brown patina, signed 'Croisy', with Susse Frères, Paris foundry stamp, on a green-veined marble base.

Bronze 21.75in (55cm) high

£1,500-2,000   **FRE**

A bronze sculpture, 'La Science', by Marcel Debut (1865-1933), signed on base.

41in (104cm) high

£1,200-1,800   **POOK**

A bronze bust of Elsie Doncaster, by Alfred Drury (1856-1994), raised on a green marble square pedestal base, signed 'A. Drury'.

12.25in (31cm) high

£2,500-3,000   **L&T**

A pair of French bronze 'Peasant Children' statues, by Paul Dubois (1827-1905), with gold patina, on naturalistic circular plinths, bases inscribed 'P. Dubois'.

39.5in (100cm) high

£12,000–18,000   **L&T**

A bronze sculpture, 'Young Bacchus', by Beatrice Fenton (American, 1887-1983), bronze with brown patina, signed and dated 'Beatrice Fenton © 1930' on base.

28in (71cm) high

£9,000-10,000   **FRE**

A gilded bronze figure, 'Nil Virtuti Invium', by Henri Gauquie (French, 1858-1927), signed with foundry stamp.

c1885 23.5in (60cm) high

£7,000-8,000   **G&H**

A bronze bust of John Flaxman, by Samuel Joseph (1791-1850), cast by S. Parker, Argyll Place, inscribed 'JOHN FLAXMAN', signed and dated.

11.5in (29cm) high

£1,500-2,000   **L&T**

A bronze figure, 'Male Fencer', by Rudolf Kuchler (Austrian, 1867-?), dark-brown patina, signed 'R. Kuchler', foundry seal 'K VRAIS/BRONCE/DEPOSE'.

15in (38cm) high

£2,000-2,500   **L&T**

DECORATIVE ARTS

A French bronze model of a maiden, 'L'Aube', cast after Luca Madrassi (1848-1919), on a waisted circular marble socle, inscribed 'L. MADRASSI, PARIS'.
c1900   30.25in (77cm) high
£3,000-3,500   DN

A bronze figure of Theodore Roosevelt, by Vincenzo Miserendino (1876-1943), with inscription 'Aggressive Fight for the Right is the Noblest Sport the World Affords' on front, the back with inscription 'To my friend Martin Jenter', on a marble base.
c1923   8in (20.5cm) high
£1,500-2,000   FRE

A bronze figure, 'Mignon', by Hippolyte Moreau (1832-1927), signed.
c1900   25in (63.5cm) high
£5,500-6,500   G&H

A pair of bronze bookends, 'Hide and Seek', by Edith Barretto Parsons (American, 1878-1956), modelled as two naked children kneeling, medium-brown patina, both signed, dated '1913' and stamped 'Gorham Co. Founders'.
1913   Tallest 6.25in (16cm) high
£1,200-1,800   FRE

An gilded bronze figure, 'Clown Dance', Otto Poertzel (German 1876-1963), clown figure with coloured painted buttons, on octagonal marble base, signed 'PROFESSOR POERTZEL'.
c1925   13.75in (35cm) high
£1,200-1,800   VZ

A pair of bronze 'Nymphs', after Franz Rosse (1858-1900), brown patina, raised on marble pedestal bases, signed 'F. Rosse', one dated '93'.
            Tallest 14.5in (37cm) high
£1,500-2,000   FRE

A 19thC French School equestrian bronze group, of an officer of the Waterloo period on horseback, holding a military standard, upon an octagonal plinth base, indistinctly inscribed 'CN de Ruille', dark-brown patina.
            24.5in (62cm) high
£5,500-6,500   TEN

A large Italian bronze figure, by Luigi Secchi (1853-1921), cast as a nude boy seated on a cushioned stool with an artist's palette and brushes, raised on a mahogany plinth base, signed 'L. Secchi, Milano' and inscribed 'In Riposo'.
            49.25in (125cm) high
£10,000-12,000   L&T

An early 20thC bronze maquette of a war memorial, by Victor-Joseph Segoffin (1867-1925), modelled as an angel with outstretched wings standing on a rectangular plinth base, signed with monogram, inscribed 'Alex Rudier, Fondeur Paris', dated.
1914-18   13in (33cm) high
£1,800-2,200   L&T

A late 19thC French bronze bust of Esmeralda, cast from a model by Emmanuel Villanis (French, 1858-1914), the base inscribed 'ESMERALDA', signed 'E. Villanis, BRONZE GARANTI AU TITRE/LV/DEPOSE' foundry seal.
                23in (58.5cm)
£2,500-3,500   FRE

A bronze bust, 'Salammbo', by Emmanuel Villanis (French, 1858-1914), signed & stamped.
c1900   10.25in (26cm) high
£2,500- 3,500   G&H

A bronze sculpture, 'A Russian Couple on a Horse-Drawn Cart', by Albert Moritz Wolf (German, c1854-c1923), bronze with brown patina, signed in Cyrillic on base.
            9.5in (24cm) high
£6,000-7,000   FRE

A bronze figure of a bull, by Isidore Jules Bonheur (1827-1901), the walking figure with head lowered over an oval green marble plinth, likely a later casting.

13.5in (34cm) high

£700-900   **SK**

A bronze figure, 'Standing Bull', by Isidore Jules Bonheur (1827-1901), on a naturalistic oblong base, signed 'I. Bonheur'.

8.5in (21.5cm) wide

£900-1,200   **WW**

A pair of late 19thC patinated bronze and variegated red marble mounted models of recumbent lions, in the manner of Antonio Canova (1757-1822).

10.5in (27cm) wide

£800-900   **DN**

An early 20thC bronze group of a fox and a rabbit, cast after Clovis Edmond Masson (French 1838-1919), signed to the base.

7in (18cm) wide overall

£400-500   **DN**

A bronze figure of a setter, after Jule Moigniez (1835-94), alert and facing forwards with front right paw raised in anticipation, on rustic oval plinth, impressed 'J Moigniez' and engraved initials 'LA'.

11.5in (29cm) long

£600-700   **TEN**

A pair of large 20thC cast-bronze figures of seated whippets, after Pierre-Jules Mêne, each figure seated at attention, with octagonal socle and circular marble base.

41.5in (105.5cm) high

£4,500-5,500   **SK**

A French bronze figure of a roebuck, 'Chevreuil', by Pierre-Jules Mêne (1810-1879), the figure modelled drinking from a stream, on ovoid naturalistic base, incised signature.

9.5in (24cm) wide

£800-1,200   **SK**

A patinated bronze model of a racehorse, 'Eclipse', cast after James Osborne (1940-92), limited edition 26/30, on an oval veined-marble and mahogany base, signed.

Eclipse was a champion racehorse, who lived from 1764-1789. He sired over 340 foals, and it is thought that over 80 per cent of modern thoroughbreds have Eclipse in their breeding.

19.75in (50.5cm) long

£3,500-4,500   **DN**

A bronze sculpture, 'Baboon Group', by Joseph Franz Pallenberg (German, 1882-1946), bronze, brown patina, on a marble base, signed.

6in (15cm) high

£450-550   **FRE**

A 19thC bronze urn, with twin winged cherub and lion mask ring handles, with diaper work, lobed and beaded decoration, each side with a circular cartouche and a Masonic emblem, on a spreading foot with square plinth.

17.75in (45cm) high

£450-550   **L&T**

A bronze 'Stalking Wolf' statue, after Valton (French, 1851-1918), the naturalistic marble base with human footprints in the snow, signed 'VALTON' on bronze base.

14.25in (36cm) wide

£1,000-1,500   **L&T**

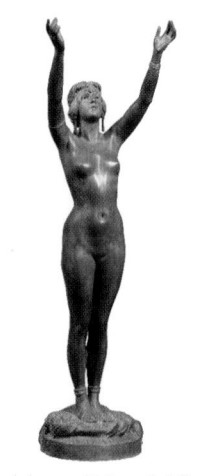

A French bronze 'Salammbo' figure of a nude slave girl, by Paul Eugène Breton (1868-1932), on titled ovoid base and marble plinth.

Figure 10.5in (26.5cm) high

£4,000-5,000 SK

A large bronze figure, 'The Egyptian Dancer', by Demêtre Chiparus (French, 1886-1947), on a stepped rectangular black marble plinth, unsigned.

24.5in (62.5cm) high

£6,000-7,000 FLD

CLOSER LOOK – CHIPARUS FIGURE

Demetre Haralamb Chiparus (1886-1947) was a Romanian sculptor who lived and worked in Paris. He is well known for his chryselephantine (ivory and bronze) figures

The well modelled face and fingers show that the workmanship is of the highest quality.

This dance has a long, slender, stylised appearance, typical of Chiparus.

Chiparus often used the photos of Russian and French dancers, and models from fashion magazines of his time.

A 1920s patinated bronze 'The Dancer' figure, by Demêtre Chiparus (French, 1886-1947), of a Ballet Russe-style dancer, with red-tinted patination and applied turquoise enamel, on a stepped base, engraved signature.

15.5in (39cm) high

£9,000-12,000 FLD

A gilt bronze 'Dance of the Daggers' figure, by Claire Jeanne Roberte Colinet (French 1880-1950), the dancer holding daggers, signed in the maquette 'C. J. R. Colinet'.

19.5in (49.5cm) high

£3,000-4,000 DN

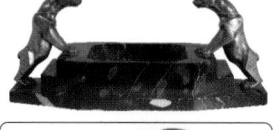

A silvered-bronze centrepiece of two bears, cast from a model by Gregoire, on striated marble base, signed in the bronze.

20.75in (53cm) wide

£900-1,200 WW

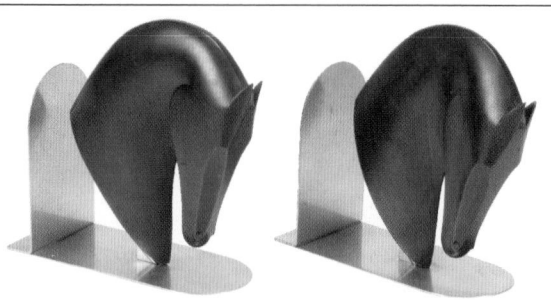

A pair of 1930s ebonised wood and polished steel bookends, by Atelier Hagenauer, modelled as stylised horse's heads, stamped marks 'Atelier Hagenauer Wien, Made in Vienna, Austria', small chips to ears.

8in (20.5cm) high

£2,200-2,800 DN

A heavy cast Art Deco patinated bronze figure, in the manner of Karl Hagenauer, of a stylised dog in standing pose, set to a plain rectangular base.

10.25in (26cm) high

£1,000-1,400 FLD

A gilt and patinated-bronze bust of Isis, cast from a model by Pierre-Eugène-Emile Hébert (French 1828-1893), signed in the bronze.

11.75in (30cm) high

£2,000-2,500 WW

A patinated bronze figure, 'Locomotion', cast from a model by Pierre Le Faguays (1892-1925), signed in the bronze.

26in (66cm) wide

£3,500-4,500 WW

A gilt-bronze study of a dancing female nude, by Josef Lorenzl, with left leg and right arm raised, mounted to a white marble domed base, signed 'Lenz'.

8.5in (22cm) high

£550-650   **FLD**

A bronze figure of a dancer with uplifted arms, by Josef Lorenzl, silvered with painted highlights, stamped 'Lorenzl', on a green-and-black onyx base.

12in (30.5cm) high

£1,500-2,000   **DN**

A bronze figure of a nude dancer with scarf, by Josef Lorenzl, signed 'LORENZL', on a green onyx cruciform base.

9.25in (23.5cm) high

£450-550   **DN**

An Art Nouveau cast-bronze figure of a semi-clad butterfly girl, her diaphanous drape spreading to form the base, green patina, with cast indistinct signature and date 'Renau 1901'.

10.25in (26cm) high

£2,200-2,800   **TOV**

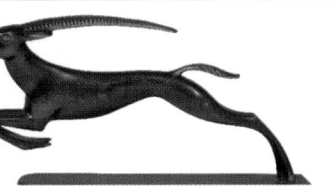

A patinated bronze model of a leaping gazelle, for retailer Rena Rosenthal, on shaped bronze base, stamped 'RR' mark.

9in (23cm) wide

£180-220   **WW**

An Art Deco silvered and painted bronze figure of an albatross, on a naturalistic base, the whole on a black marble plinth, signed C. Ruchot'.

28.25in (72cm) wide

£700-800   **L&T**

A large bronze figure of an archer, the naked male figure poised on a rocky outcrop pulling back the string of his bow, dated and with incised signature 'R. Schipke'.

1920   *39.75in (101cm) high*

£4,000-5,000   **SK**

A gilt-bronze figure of a nude woman, cast from a model by E. Soukonech, on square striated marble base, signed in the bronze.

10.5in (26.5cm) high

£700-1,000   **WW**

An Art Nouveau bronze figure of dancer balancing on a ball, on octagonal marble base, unsigned, base chipped.

13.75in (35cm) high

£250-350   **WW**

A group of three bronze garden figures of children, 'Story-telling', in whimsical poses, with verdigris patination.

27.5in (70cm) wide

£3,500-4,500   **L&T**

DECORATIVE ARTS

A French Art Deco bronze and ivory figure of a dancer, her attire with green and red patination, signed 'P. Philippe R.U.M', on a circular marble base, losses to both hands.

c1930   *22in (56cm) high*

£8,000-10,000   **JA**

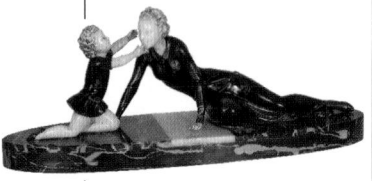

A patinated spelter and ivorine figure of a woman and child, cast from a model by Menneville, on striated black marble base, signed in the base.

                              25.5in (65cm) wide

£350-450   **6 WW**

A bronze and ivory group, by Etienne Watrin (French, ?-1915), of a girl in a cloak knitting, on a grassy base with a sheep and flowers, in mid-brown, light-brown and gilt, signed 'E. Watrin'.

                              11in (28cm) high

£800-1,200   **DN**

A small chryselephantine clown, by Demêtre Chiparus (French, 1886-1947), of patinated bronze and carved ivory, on a round marble pedestal, marked 'H. Chiparus, Etling Paris' on the back of the coat.

                              8.75in (22.5cm) high

£1,500-2,500   **WKA**

An Austrian bronze and ivory figure of a dancer, by Anton Endstorfer (Austrian, 1880-1960), with a hoop of flowers, signed in the maquette with a monogram, mid-brown patination, on marble base.

                              10.5in (27cm) high

£350-450   **DN**

Two cold-painted bronze and ivory figures, by Ferdinand Preiss (German, 1882-1943), of a page boy holding a casket and a girl with the key, signed in the maquette 'F. PRIESS', on marble plinths.

Boy 6.25in (16cm) high

£3,000-3,500   **DN**

A late 19th/early 20thC bronze and marble Art Nouveau female figure, modelled in marble, her gown of bronze, light-brown patina, signed 'Henry' with Schumacher foundry mark, raised on base.

                              19.5in (49.5cm) high

£6,000-8,000   **FRE**

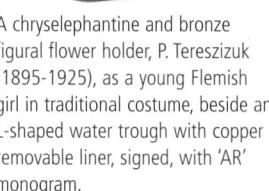

A chryselephantine and bronze figural flower holder, P. Tereszizuk (1895-1925), as a young Flemish girl in traditional costume, beside an L-shaped water trough with copper removable liner, signed, with 'AR' monogram.

c1900   *6.75in (17.5cm) high*

£300-500   **TEN**

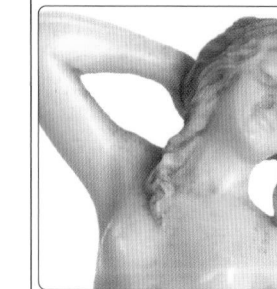

An Art Deco carved ivory figure of a nude maiden, a gold metal band on her left upper arm, on an octagonal onyx base.

c1925   *5in (13cm) high*

£1,500-2,000   **TEN**

An Art Deco bronze female figure, wearing a long gold-coloured evening dress, with carved ivory head, bust, amrs and hands, on marble base, signed 'R. Nannin'.

                              7in (18cm) high

£500-600   **A&G**

A William Morris style room-size rug, with a pattern of pods and acanthus leaves in ruby red and celadon on a black field, surrounded by a celadon floral border.

142in (360.5cm) wide

£600-800 DRA

One of three William Morris style runners, in the same floral and vine pattern, in cinnabar, ivory and forest green.

120in (305cm) long

£900-1,200 SET DRA

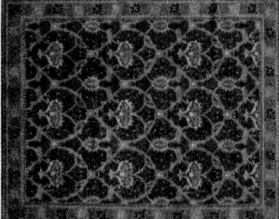

A William Morris style room-size rug, with a floral pattern in rich jewel tones.

141in (358cm) long

£1,000-1,500 DRA

A William Morris style room-size rug, with floral pattern on olive green ground.

165in (419cm) long

£1,000-1,500 DRA

An Arts and Crafts patterned runner, attributed to Gavin Morton, Donegal, reduced, some repairs.

126in (320cm) long

£1,000-1,500 DRA

An English Arts and Crafts room size carpet, hand-knotted, with a colourful floral and trellis border around a celadon green floral field, some staining, fading, and minor restoration.

216in (428.5cm) long

£6,500-8,500 DRA

A Liberty & Co. Donegal carpet, by Alexander Morton, in floral pattern in pink, lavender and emerald.

156in (396cm) long

£4,500-5,500 DRA

A Scottish Arts and Crafts area rug, with a floral vine pattern in rose and green, on an oatmeal ground, some repair and fraying to selvage.

84in (213.5cm) long

£650-850 DRA

A square Newcomb College table scarf, embroidered with stylised trees in amber and green.

15.25in (39cm) wide

£5,000-7,000 DRA

MODERN

The rise in prices for modern furniture and decorative accessories has been meteoric during the course of the last decade. Despite stumbling in the wake of the economic downturn and, in particular, following the crash of Lehman Brothers, there are still plenty of reasons for the continued interest in pieces produced after the Second World War.

It helps that this is a world-based market, consisting of furniture, glassware, ceramics, lighting, and more, made in Europe, North and South America and Japan. Whether the interest is in Danish Modern, Italian high-style work from the 1950s, or American organic furniture, there is ample stylish design for every taste. And, while buyers have shown most interest in the 'soft modernism' of the immediate postwar years – Charles and Ray Eames, Arne Jacobsen, Vladimir Kagan, for example – there are a growing number of people investing in later pieces – those exemplifying the 1960s plastics and Pop era or Postmodernism, such as Joe Colombo and Ettore Sottsass.

As always, pieces by recognisable designers command significantly higher (and rising) prices than their generic equivalent. There is increasing interest in the work of contemporary designers such as Ron Arad, and ceramics by European and American potters continue to lure buyers, in particular postwar pieces with unusual forms and glazes, such as the 'fat lava' ceramics produced in Germany during the 1960s and 1970s. Glass from the 20th century's major centres of excellence - the glasshouses of Scandinavia and Murano in Italy - continues to find willing buyers, especially for examples that combine vibrant colours with modern forms and for big names such as Barovier, Venini and Seguso or design classics such as the Pezzato range by Fulvio Bianconi for Venini. There are also signs that buyers are beginning to move away from production pieces in favour of one-off designs and prototypes that show the hand of the master. Similarly there is increasing demand for examples with provenance, such as a special commission.

The consumer base for 'modern' antiques is wider than most other fields, broadened by more than just die-hard collectors. With many 20th century pieces being found in greater numbers, and therefore still relatively affordable, a younger market continues to grow, while designers and decorators have been filling homes with a mix of eras and cultures, melding Powell with Ponti, and Wegner with Natzler. When it comes to price, it is worth pointing out that much Modern material can be considered a bargain when compared to the cost of buying brand new pieces of similar quality, and that the value of most new things tends to drop precipitously once purchased, while the resale prospects of period pieces are far more stable.

While the extent of the economic market's recovery have yet to be revealed, it is clear that people will need furniture for their homes. It seems a safe bet, therefore, that high quality pieces with long track records will continue to attract the interest of shrewd buyers.

Clockwise from top left: Natzler bowl, £4,000 at Sollo:Rago Auctions; 'pezzato' vase by Fulvio Bianconi £11,000 at Von Zezschwitz; Vladimir Kagan/Kagan Dreyfuss armchair and ottoman, £6,000 at Sollo:Rago.

ESSENTIAL REFERENCE – ALVAR AALTO

Finnish designer and architect, Hugo Alvar Henrik Aalto (1898-1976) was one of the leading figures in 20thC Modernist design. Rather than using typically Modern materials, such as tubular steel, Aalto favoured natural materials, such as laminated birch plywood, which he believed appealed to the psychological, as well as the physical needs, of man. He described this concept as 'psychophysical'.

- Aalto invented many new methods for bonding veneers and moulding plywood, and held numerous patents, such as his method of bending legs for stools.
- From 1929-33, he designed the Paimio Tuberculosis Sanitorium, Finland and its furniture. This included the model no.41 Paimio bentwood chair, which was designed to allow tuberculosis patients to breathe easily. Made from two hoops of laminated birch, which form the arms, legs, and floor runners, with a curving plywood seat in between, the Paimio chair's basic shape was an homage to Marcel Breuer's 'Wassily' chair.

- An exhibition of his furniture at Fortnum & Mason, London, in 1933, and his design for the Finnish Pavilion at the 1939 New York World's Fair, increased Aalto's popularity and launched his career in America.
- In 1935, Aalto, his wife Aino Marsio Aalto (1894-1949), Harry Gullichsen and Nils Hahl established Artek, a company for manufacturing and marketing furniture, fabrics and light-fittings made to Aalto's designs. Two further export companies followed: Finmar for exports to England, and Wohnbedarf, Switzerland for exports to other European markets
- The Savoy vase, widely considered to be Aalto's most iconic design, was created for a competition held by Karhula-Iittala glassworks to find pieces to exhibit at the 1937 Paris World's Fair. Originally entitled 'Eskimoerindens skinnbuxa' (Eskimo woman's leather trousers), it takes its current name from another Aalto architectural project, the Savoy restaurant in Helsinki, which placed the first major order for the vase in 1937.

An Alvar Aalto bent laminated birch and plywood armchair, model no. 31, retailed by Finmar Ltd., manufactured by Oy Huonekalu-ja Rakennustyotehdas AB, marked with ink stamp 'Aalto Design Made in Finland' and applied metal label 'Finmar Ltd'.

Designed 1932   25.75in (65.5cm) high

£1,500-2,500   L&T

An Alvar Aalto occasional table, model no. 915, retailed by Finmar, laminated birch sides bent into a closed curve with moulded plywood top, bears retailer's label, designed for the Paimio Sanatorium, Finland.

Designed 1931   23.5in (60cm) long

£550-750   L&T

A pair of Wassily chairs, model no. B3, designed by Marcel Breuer, bent chrome-plated tubular steel frame, brown leather seat and back sections.

Designed for Wassily Kandinsky's quarters at the Dessau Bauhaus, the no. B3 transformed the language of chair design, particularly in its method of manufacture.

c1969   28.75in (73cm) high

£1,000–1,500   TEN

A Marcel Breuer birch four-drawer single pedestal desk and wall-hanging bookshelves, designed for Rhoads Hall at Bryn Mawr College, desk stamped 'RHOADS'.

Desk 50in (19.5cm) wide

£2,500-3,500   SDR

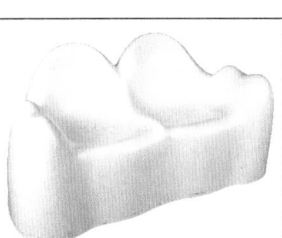

A white fiberglass 'Molar' sofa, Wendell Castle.

48in (122cm) wide

£2,000-3,000 DRA

A laminated wood pedestal, Wendell Castle, signed 'W.C. 73'.

1973   *20in (51cm) high*

£10,000-15,000 DRA

A Wendell Castle console table, with triangular maple top on flaring ebonised wood legs, signed 'Castle 92'.

1992   *38.5in (97.5cm) high*

£4,500-5,500 SDR

CLOSER LOOK – WENDELL CASTLE CHAIR

Wendell Castle's designs are simultaneously sculptural and functional. He has described himself as a 'furniture artist'.

This piece expertly combines the sleekness of American industrial design of the mid-20thC with the sensuous sculpted forms of studio furniture master Wharton Esherick. It defines a new language for American design.

The attractive grain of the wood is clearly visible. Castle liked to explore the aesthetic qualities of his material.

This piece, with its flowing lines, is typical of Wendell Castle's work during the 1960s, when he became known for his organically-shaped furniture.

An early Wendell Castle sculpted oak sleigh chair, with hard leather sling seat, signed 'WE 63'.

1963

34.5in (87.5cm) high

£120,000-180,000 SDR

A pair of Dunbar lounge chairs, upholstered in original tufted ochre wool, on dark-stained base with tapering legs, marked 'Dunbar' on decking, with detached fabric label.

31in (78.5cm) wide

£1,800-2,200 SDR

An upholstered sofa, by Dunbar, in eggshell white silk with tufted cushions on teak legs.

108in (274.5cm) wide

£2,000-3,000 DRA

A Dunbar bleached mahogany sideboard, with four drawers over four sliding doors, enclosing divided compartments and shelves, branded 'Dunbar' tag.

81.25in (206cm) wide

£1,800-2,200 SDR

A Dunbar mahogany and brass coffee table, with pull-out extensions at either end, inset with Murano glass tiles, with green 'Dunbar' tag.

69in (175cm) wide

£3,000-4,000 DRA

ESSENTIAL REFERENCE – CHARLES & RAY EAMES

Charles (1907-78) and Ray (1912-88) Eames were two of the most influential designers of the mid-20thC. They designed everything from house interiors to multimedia presentations, producing work that embodied the Modernist aim of marrying industry and art for social good.

- They favoured flexible and affordable materials, such as moulded plywood, plastic, fibreglass and aluminium.
- They were inspired by Modernism, Japanese architecture and Scandinavian design.
- Charles Eames's first notable design was a chair in moulded plywood and aluminium, designed in collaboration with Eero Saarinen (1910-61) in 1940.
- Designed in 1946, the classic 'Eames Chair' or DCM (short for Dining Chair Metal) chair consists of a seat and back made of curved plywood attached to a metal-rod frame.
- In 1947 the Eameses began a lifelong collaboration with the Herman Miller Furniture Company, which still manufactures Eames furniture today.
- Widely considered one of the most significant designs of the 20thC, the Eames lounge chair made its debut in 1956. Ray Eames stated it was popular precisely because it was 'comfortable and un-designy'.

An aluminium high-back armchair, designed by Charles and Ray Eames, with black channelled naugahyde upholstery.

Naugahyde is an artificial leather often used in upholstery.

39.5in (100cm) high

£400-500   WW

A rosewood lounge chair and ottoman, by Charles and Ray Eames, for Herman Miller, with black leather upholstery.

32in (81cm) high

£2,500-3,500   SDR

A moulded-ply LCW (Lounge Chair Wood) chair, designed by Charles and Ray Eames.

29in (74cm) high

£200-300   WW

A Charles and Ray Eames ash-veneered plywood CTW (Circular Table Wood) coffee table, the moulded circular top with slight indent, and raised on curved legs, refinished.

Designed 1946   34in (86.5cm) diam

£500-700   SK

A 'Surfboard' coffee table, by Charles Eames, for Herman Miller, with black laminate top on wire base, with oval Eames/Herman Miller metal tag.

89.5in (227.5cm) wide

£1,200-1,800   DRA

A first edition ESU (Eames Storage Unit) 201 desk, by Charles and Ray Eames, for Herman Miller.

c1952   47in (119.5cm) wide

£3,500-4,500   SDR

A Charles and Ray Eames ESU wall unit, in neutral colour and black finish plywood, with wire rod supports, some wear and delamination.

1955   65in (165cm) high

£5,000-7,000   SK

A six-fold bent-ply screen, designed by Charles Eames, probably manufactured by Herman Miller.

67.75in (172cm) wide

£650-850   WW

A Paul Evans sculpted bronze chair with orange crushed velvet upholstery.

31.75in (80.5cm) high

£9,000-12,000 **SDR**

A pair of Paul Evans verdigris-copper cube chairs, the cushions covered in blue leather patterned with Futurist designs.

These are one of only two pairs of cube chairs that Paul Evans ever finished in verdigris.

c1968 *30in (76cm) wide*

£20,000-30,000 PAIR **SDR**

A Paul Evans 'Skyscraper' glass-top coffee table, in sculpted steel painted in polychrome, signed 'Paul Evans 72'.

1972 *Base 47in (119.5cm) wide*

£20,000-30,000 **DRA**

A rare Paul Evans 'Argente' pedestal dining table, with circular top.

Of welded aluminium, this line is very represntative of the spirit of the 1960s.

48in (122cm) diam

£30,000-40,000 **SDR**

A Paul Evans sculpted bronze dining table with plate glass top resting on a serpentine 'stalagmite' base.

72in (183cm) wide

£7,000-10,000 **SDR**

A Paul Evans 'Argente' two-door cabinet, with biomorphic forms in sculpted aluminium, the interior with three shelves and antiqued finish, signed 'Paul Evans 68 S'.

1968 *36in (91.5cm) wide*

£40,000-50,000 **DRA**

A Paul Evans 'Double Stalagmite' sculptural room divider, of oxidised steel blades with welded geometric and swirling patterns.

c1965-66 *96in (244cm) high*

£9,000-12,000 **SDR**

CLOSER LOOK – PAUL EVANS CABINET

Paul Evans created a number of floor-standing and wall-mounted Sculpture Front cabinets. Highly sought after today, each has a unique decorative design.

Evans signed all of his pieces "Paul Evans"; those that were commissioned should also have a date.

Make sure all of the sculptural elements are present. There should be some kind of decorative detail in each individual panel.

The geometric sculptural panels are a key characteristic of these cabinets; look for brightly painted elements and gold leaf embellishment.

A Paul Evans sculpture-front cabinet, with natural cleft slate top.

74in (188cm) wide

£100,000-120,000 **SDR**

MODERN DESIGN

A Piero Fornasetti single-drawer red metal file cabinet, printed with gold sunburst motif.

19.75in (50cm) wide

£1,200-1,800   SDR

A Piero Fornasetti small four-panel screen, printed on front with columns and obelisks, marked bottom right 'No I-I-LXXXIX/NANE'.

53.5in (136cm) wide

£1,200-1,800   SDR

A Piero Fornasetti two-door Pompeian corner cabinet with two interior shelves, printed with an architectural facade with unique colouration in greys and black, signed on back panel 'Fornasetti '87'.

47in (199.5cm) wide

£6,500-8,500   DRA

A Finn Juhl sculpted teak settee, manufactured by Niels Vodder, upholstered in tan leather, with branded mark.

55in (140cm) wide

£5,000-7,000   SDR

An Arne Jacobsen 'Swan' chair, manufactured by Fritz Hansen, in blue upholstery on an adjustable four-prong aluminium base, with manufacturer's label and Danish control mark.

c1963   *33in (84cm) high*

£550–750   SK

A 1960s Arne Jacobsen Danish teak and aluminium coffee table, the circular top on an aluminium centre post with three prong feet, some dark areas on surface.

18.75in (47.5cm) high

£300-400   SK

A Finn Juhl 'Chieftain' chair, made by Niels Vodder, with reddish-brown leather cushions on teak frame, with branded mark.

40.5in (103cm) wide

£25,000-35,000   SDR

A Finn Juhl walnut credenza, for Baker Furniture, with wicker-panelled sliding doors concealing four drawers and single shelf, Baker metal tag.

78in (198cm) wide

£700-1,000   SDR

ESSENTIAL REFERENCE – VLADIMIR KAGAN

Vladimir Kagan (b1927) is a German-born furniture designer who emigrated to the United States in 1938. With a career spanning more than sixty years, he is one of the most enduring designers of modern furniture.

- In 1947, having studied architecture at Columbia University, Kagan joined his father, Illi Kagan, a master cabinet-maker, at his woodworking shop. There he learnt about the process of making furniture.
- From the late 1940s, Kagan focused primarily on sofas and lounge chairs, but also produced tables and other pieces of furniture. Many of his designs were upholstered in white, black, and red.
- Some of his earliest commissions included creating furniture for the cocktail lounges for delegates in the first United Nations headquarters in Lake Success, New York (1947-48), as well as furniture for the 'Monsanto House of the Future' at Disneyland.
- Kagan's first shop opened in New York on East 65th Street in 1948, and moved to fashionable 57th Street in 1950.
- His work is influenced by nature and architecture. Early studies in anatomy also created an 'ergonomic background' for his seating pieces.

An early 'Unicorn' chair, by Vladimir Kagan, with original fabric upholstery on V-shaped aluminium base.

29in (73.5cm) high

£25,000-35,000   DRA

A set of six Vladimir Kagan shield-back dining chairs, for Dreyfuss, with mottled amber vinyl upholstery on sculpted walnut frames, with 'Vladimir Kagan factory' tags.

37in (94cm) high

£6,500-8,500   SDR

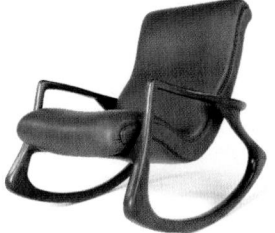

A Vladimir Kagan sculptured walnut rocking chair, upholstered in dark purple leather.

36.5in (93cm) high

£6,500-8,500   DRA

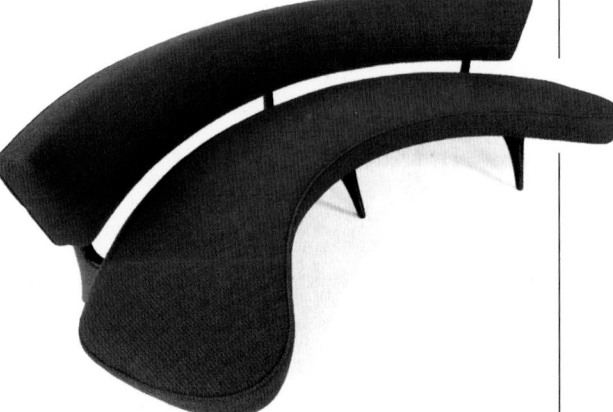

A Vladimir Kagan curved 'Floating Curve' sofa, upholstered in indigo wool, on sculpted walnut frame.

90in (228.5cm) wide

£15,000-25,000   SDR

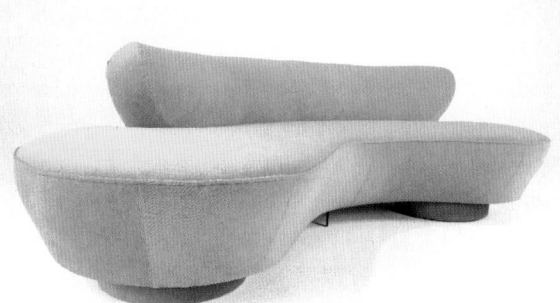

A Vladimir Kagan 'Cloud' sofa, retailed by Directional, upholstered in golden velvet on two covered circular bases and single lucite fin, with 'Directional' label.

95in (241.5cm) wide

£9,000-12,000   SDR

A Vladimir Kagan walnut extending dining table, for Dreyfuss, with two 24in (61cm) leaves, 'Kagan Dreyfuss' branded marks.

71.5in (181.5cm) wide

£5,000-7,000   SDR

A Vladimir Kagan extending dining table, covered in exotic veneer, with two leaves stored inside the pedestal base.

68in (173cm) wide closed

£800-1,200   DRA

A Florence Knoll multicoloured fabric-upholstered sofa, for Knoll, with an integrated two-drawer walnut end-table, on polished steel frame.

119.5in (303.5cm) wide

£700-1,000 DRA

A Florence Knoll six-drawer teak credenza, for Knoll, with black soapstone top, on steel base.

54.75in (139cm) wide

£1,000-2,000 DRA

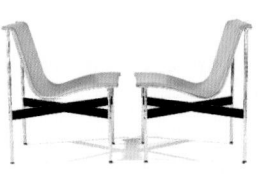

A pair of LaVerne side chairs, by Katavolos, Littell and Kelley, with tan hard leather sling seats on polished and enamelled steel frame.

23in (58.5cm) wide

£900-1,200 SDR

A Philip LaVerne 'Madame Pompadour' occasional table, with polychrome floral motif, with 'Philip LaVerne Gallery' paper tag.

30in (76cm) wide

£1,500-2,000 DRA

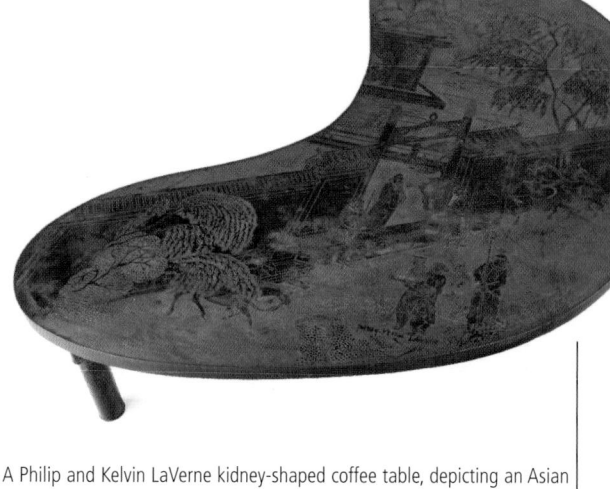

A Philip and Kelvin LaVerne kidney-shaped coffee table, depicting an Asian courtyard scene, on faux-bamboo legs, signed 'Philip Kelvin Laverne'.

Philip LaVerne and his son, Kelvin, are best known for their beautifully patinated bronze and pewter tables and cabinets. They coined the phrase 'functional sculpture' for their pieces, which were influenced by Chinese and Greek antiquities. Each piece is either unique or part of a limited series, and is signed by the artists.

62in (158cm)

£12,000-18,000 SDR

A large 1950s American wood, brass and lacquer cabinet, in the manner of James Mont, in the form of three stacked oriental chests.

During the 1950s, several noted designers, such as Paul Frankl and Tommi Parzinger, worked in an Oriental style, but this cabinet relates strongly to the works of James Mont for Kittinger.

51.25in (130cm) wide

£2,500-3,500 L&T

A set of eight James Mont dining side chairs, on ebonised frames with sateen-upholstered seats.

35.5in (90cm) high

£12,000-18,000 SDR

A James Mont upholstered settee, with ebonised fretwork frame, upholstered in patterned fabric.

54in (137cm) wide

£3,500-4,500 SDR

A set of six George Nakashima maple dining chairs, each impressed 'George Nakashima'

£6,500-8,500   POOK

A George Nakashima conoid cushion chair, in American black walnut with hickory spindles and leather webbing, with cushions upholstered in blue wool fabric.

1964   33.5in (86cm) high

£10,000-15,000   SK

A George Nakashima Widdicomb armchair, with brown and black boucle upholstery on walnut frame.

32in (81cm) wide

£5,000-7,000   SDR

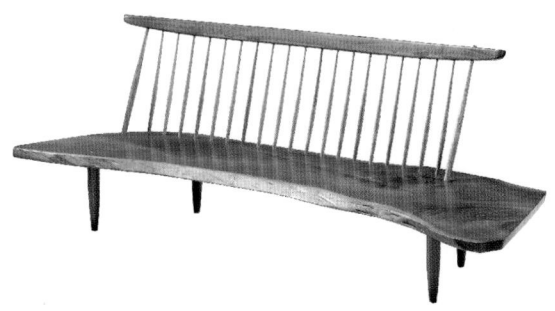

A George Nakashima walnut conoid bench, with free-edge seat and rosewood butterfly joint, and twenty-one hickory spindles, on cyclindrical tapering legs.

87in (221cm) long

£20,000-30,000   FRE

A George Nakashima walnut trestle table, signed with origianl owner's name.

85in (216cm) wide

£7,000-10,000   POOK

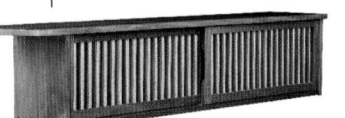

A George Nakashima walnut wall-hanging cabinet, with two sliding doors lined in pandanus cloth, enclosing interior shelves.

72in (183cm) wide

£10,000-15,000   SDR

A George Nakashima walnut chest-of-drawers, New Hope, Pennsylvania, free-edge top with dovetail joints at end, three sliding doors along front, fitted with nine drawers in banks of three.

1961   84in (213.5cm) long

£12,000–18,000   SK

A George Nakashima walnut desk, New Hope, Pennsylvania, the rectangular top above a single bank of drawers flanked by tapering legs.

48in (122cm) wide

£6,500-8,500   SK

CLOSER LOOK – GEORGE NAKASHIMA TABLE

The top of this coffee table is made from one single piece of English oak. The unfinished edges are a hallmark of Nakashima's work – an expression of his desire to preserve the natural shape of the tree.

Nakashima designs that combine 'un-tamed' wood like this tabletop, with machine-made elements, such as the geometric table base are particularly sought after

Made of oak, this table is relatively rare, as the majority of Nakashima's work tends to use walnut.

A George Nakashima 'Minguren I' coffee table, with English oak burl top on laurel base.

1969

£50,000-70,000

42.5in (108cm) wide

SDR

MODERN DESIGN

ESSENTIAL REFERENCE – GEORGE NELSON

George Nelson (1908-86) was one of the founders of American Modernism, along with Eliot Noyes, Charles Eames and Walter B. Ford, all of whom he collaborated with.

- Nelson studied architecture at Yale University, graduating in 1928. He received a bachelor degree in fine arts in 1931.
- Through his writing in 'Pencil Points', the highly influential architecture and design journal founded in 1920, Nelson introduced the work of Walter Gropius, Mies van der Rohe, Le Corbusier and Gio Ponti to North America.
- After reading Nelson's book 'Tomorrow's House', D.J. DePree, the founder of Herman Miller Inc., asked him to become the company's director of design, even though Nelson had yet to design any furniture of his own. Nelson was subsequently responsible for the emphasis on well-designed modern furniture that characterised Herman Miller's output after World War II (previously, the company had been known as a predominantly wood-based design house).
- Nelson's greatest innovation was the Comprehensive Storage System or CSS: the first domestic storage system and the forerunner of system furniture. Produced from 1959 to1973, the CSS consisted of 20 components, including cabinets, desks and shelves, that provided complete flexibility.

A George Nelson 'Coconut' chair, for Herman Miller, upholstered in black bouclé.

40in (101.5cm) wide

£1,200-1,800   SDR

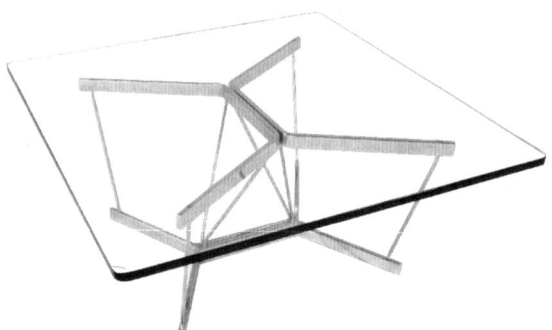

A George Nelson 'Catenary' coffee table, for Herman Miller, with plate-glass top on polished steel base.

36in (91.5cm) wide

£800-1,200   SDR

A George Nelson 'Thin-Edge' jewellery chest, for Herman Miller, with nine drawers and hourglass pulls, with circular Herman Miller tag.

23.5in (59.5cm) high

£5,500-7,500   DRA

A George Nelson swag-leg desk, for Herman Miller, with two shallow drawers.

39in (99cm) wide

£3,000-4,000   DRA

A George Nelson 'Home Office' desk, with tan leather covering to sliding doors and to writing surface, a lift-top storage compartment, and mesh Pendaflex file.

54.25in (138cm) wide

£5,000-7,000   DRA

A George Nelson 'Thin-Edge' four-drawer rosewood chest, for Herman Miller, with porcelain pulls, with Herman Miller foil label.

33in (84cm) wide

£2,500-3,500   DRA

A George Nelson 'Marshmallow' sofa, for Herman Miller, upholstered in burnt orange velvet on brushed and enamelled steel frame.

51.5in (131cm) wide

£7,000-10,000   DRA

A George Nelson and Charles Deaton CSS unit, accompanied by a Charles Deaton desk.

97in (246.5cm) wide

£4,000-5,000 SET   DRA

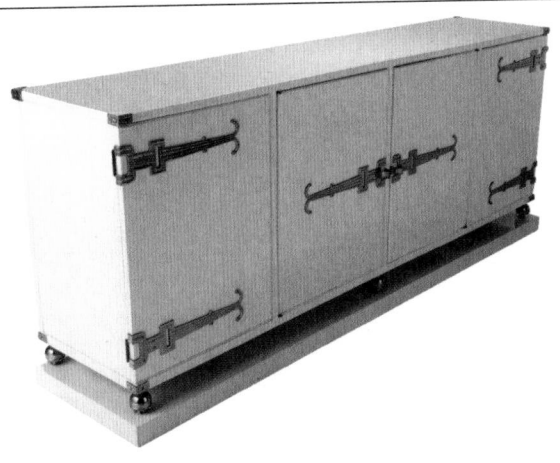

A Tommi Parzinger pale yellow enamelled wood cabinet, with interior shelves, brass strap hinges and ball feet, all raised on a platform.

Born in Germany, Tommi Parzinger (1903-81) settled in New York City in 1935, and opened his first showroom in 1939. Trained as a painter and as well as in metalwork, ceramics and furniture design, he made refined modern pieces with elegant detailing. At the height of his fame in the 1950s, his clients included the Rockefellers and Marilyn Monroe.

92.5in (235cm) wide

£15,000-20,000   **SDR**

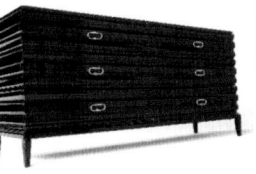

A Tommi Parzinger settee, upholstered in green leather on ebonised wood base.

55in (140cm) wide

£2,500-3,500   **SDR**

A Tommi Parzinger mahogany extending dining table, with bleached mahogany inlay and base, with two leaves.

72in (183cm) wide

£5,500-7,500   **DRA**

A Tommi Parzinger six-drawer mahogany dresser, with chromed metal drop-pulls.

72in (183cm) wide

£12,000-18,000   **DRA**

A Tommi Parzinger four-door sideboard, with black lacquered finish, silvered drop pulls, and silver-studded doors and sides, with two interior shelves.

72in (183cm) wide

£15,000-20,000   **DRA**

A rare Warren Platner prototype seven-piece copper dining set, for Knoll, consisting of six chairs upholstered in black wool, and a pedestal dining table.

Table 54in (137cm) wide

£6,500-8,500   **DRA**

A Warren Platner circular rosewood and steel dining table and four upholstered dining chairs, for Knoll, with wire frame, with 'Knoll Associates' tags.

Table 54in (137cm) diam

£4,000-5,000   **SDR**

A Warren Platner lounge chair and ottoman, for Knoll, upholstered in original Alexander Girard ochre fabric, on black wire frames, with 'Knoll Associates' tags.

39in (99cm) high

£3,500-4,500   **SDR**

A rare Warren Platner sofa, for Knoll, covered in terracotta bouclé.

One of only forty-five produced.

67in (94cm) wide

£2,000-3,000   **DRA**

A Phillip Lloyd Powell walnut 'New Hope' chair, with woven seat support and olive green velvet cushions.

28in (71cm) high

£12,000-18,000 SDR

A Phillip Lloyd Powell walnut bench, with woven ecru fabric cushions, with integrated marble top table.

100.5in (255cm) wide

£15,000-20,000 DRA

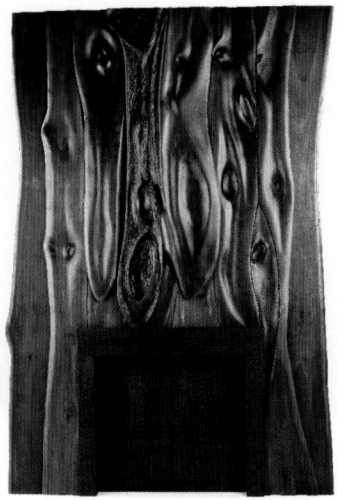

A Phillip Lloyd Powell carved and sculpted walnut fireplace, from the original showroom in New Hope, Pennsylvania.

A Phillip Lloyd Powell walnut freeform wall-hanging shelf, with ebony butterfly key.

80in (203cm) wide

£10,000-15,000 SDR

A Phillip Lloyd Powell and Paul Evans walnut wall-hanging stereo cabinet, with four sliding doors and single cabinet door fitted with patinated Paul Evans sculpted steel panel.

66in (167.5cm) wide

£30,000-40,000 DRA

Phillip Lloyd Powell (1919-2008) studied engineering, but after World War II he moved to New Hope, Pennsylvania, and started refurbishing antiques and making furniture. Subverting the cool, clean lines of mid-century Modernism, he favoured a naturalistic approach, showing the contour of grain and letting it dictate the shape of the piece. He often used atypical materials like metal and stone, and even found objects, such as antlers. He met Paul Evans in 1951, and later collaborated with him. Powell was particularly known for his cabinets. Working at a measured pace, he produced barely a thousand pieces in his lifetime. c1956-58.

67in (170cm) wide

£60,000-80,000 SDR

A set of six Philippe Starck mahogany 'Costes' chairs, for Driade Aleph, on black lacquered steel legs, with leather cushions, with 'ALEPH STARCK' labels.

31.5in (80cm) high

£1,800-2,200 SDR

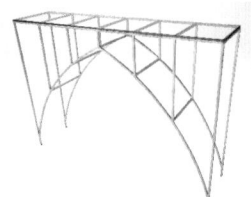

A Philippe Starck dining table, for Driade, with mahogany parquet top on sharply tapered aluminium legs, the legs marked 'ALEPH STARCK'.

82in (208cm) wide

£7,000-10,000 DRA

An 'M (Serie Lange)' frosted glass and aluminium dining table, by Philippe Starck, for Driade, with frosted glass top on cast aluminium legs, signed.

82.5in (209.5cm) wide

£1,500-2,000 SDR

A pair of Philippe Starck side tables, with elliptical plate-glass tops on cantilevered aluminium bases, signed 'P. Starck XO'.

19.5in (49.5cm) wide

£1,000-1,500 DRA

ESSENTIAL REFERENCE – HANS WEGNER

Innovative and prolific, Hans Wegner (1914-2007) was one of the Danish furniture designers who made mid-century Danish design internationally popular.

● Wegner specialised in elegant but comfortable furniture created from rounded forms that melt into each other, making his wooden pieces look as though they could have been moulded in plastic. His wooden furniture typically boasts an immaculate, satiny-smooth hand-finish, often reminiscent of Chinese hardwood furniture.

● He trained as a cabinet-maker, and worked out the prototype of each design at the workshop bench, as well as on paper.

● From 1938 to 1942, he worked as a furniture designer in Arne Jacobsen and Erik Moller's architectural practice.

● Wegner's chair designs were manufactured primarily by PP Møbler and Carl Hansen & Son.

● His two most famous chairs were both introduced in 1949. The 'Wishbone' chair has a Y-shaped back-split and a curved back and armrest suggested by a Chinese child's chair he had seen. 'The Chair', also known as the 'Round' chair, has a caned seat, with the back and armrests made of one continuous semicircle of wood. It was used in the televised Kennedy-Nixon presidential debates of 1960.

A Hans Wegner 'Peacock' chair, manufactured by Johannes Hansen, on ash frame with teak armrests and woven cord seat, with branded 'Johannes Hansen Copenhagen Denmark'.

42in (106.5cm)high

£900-1,500   SDR

A Hans Wegner teak valet chair, manufactured by Johannes Hansen, with hinged seat, with branded mark.

37.5in (95cm) high

£10,000-15,000   DRA

A Hans Wegner 'Ox' chair, manufactured by A. P. Stolen, with horns, covered in striped fabric over original slate grey fabric, with circular Danish Furnituremakers control tag.

38in (96.5cm) wide

£9,000-12,000   DRA

A Hans Wegner 'Papa Bear' chair and ottoman, on teak frames upholstered in plum-coloured fabric.

Chair 39in (99cm) high

£9,000-12,000   SDR

A Hans Wegner Danish oak, teak and cane chaise longue, manufactured by Johannes Hansen, Copenhagen, branded mark.

c.1950   *60in (152.5cm) diam*

£30,000-50,000   SDR

A Hans Wegner oak dropleaf table and two wishbone chairs, table with drop leaves on four tapered cylindrical legs, marked 'Hans Fabrikat Andr Tuck Arkitekt Hans J. Wegner, Made in Denmark', table wear, chairs with wear and loose joints.

This model of chair was designed in 1949.

c1960   *93.5in (237cm) wide*

£700-1,000   SK

A teak dropleaf dining table, by Hans Wegner, for Andreas Tuck, with brass supports.

52in (132cm) wide

£3,000-4,000   SDR

A Hans Wegner Danish oak credenza, manufactured by Ry Møbler, with sliding doors enclosing four sliding trays and four adjustable shelves, stamped 'RY'.

78.75in (200cm) wide

£2,000-3,000   SDR

A pair of Edward Wormley club chairs, for Dunbar, upholstered in original orange tweed fabric on swivel base, marked 'Dunbar' on upholstery.

32in (81cm) high

£3,500-4,500   DRA

A pair of Edward Wormley mahogany gueridon tables, for Dunbar, with faceted posts and tripod bases, with 'Dunbar' metal tags.

22in (56cm) diam

£2,000-3,000   SDR

One of a pair of corrugated cardboard 'Wiggle' chairs, designed by Frank O. Gehry, for Easy Edges.

33.5in (85cm) high

£2,000-3,000 PAIR   SDR

CLOSER LOOK – ESHERICK MUSIC STAND

The combination of the sculptural with the functional is a key characteristic of Esherick's later work; such pieces are particularly sought after.

This music stand, originally made in 1960, is one of 12 made in 1962. The majority of Esherick's designs were one-off commissions, and it is rare to find pieces produced in greater numbers.

Esherick favoured native woods, such as cherry and walnut, both of which are native to Pennsylvania where Esherick had his studio; they have a rich, warm colour that deepens with age.

Although Esherick was influencedby the Arts & Crafts movement and initially preferred to work with hand tools, he began to use power tools from the 1960s, and this may be evident in his later work.

A Wharton Esherick carved cherry music stand, on three legs, signed 'WE 1962'.

A pair of Eileen Gray 'E1027' height-adjustable glass and chrome tables.

This table design was named after E.1027, the cliff-top summer house that Eileen Gray built for herself and her collaborator, Jean Badovici, at Roquebrune-Cap Martin on the French Mediterranean coast. The name was developed from their initials: E is for Eileen, 10 is for Jean (J is the 10th letter of the alphabet), 2 for B(adovici) and 7 for G(ray). Eileen Gray designed this adjustable table to enable one of her sisters to indulge her love of eating breakfast in bed.

24.75in (63cm) high

£500-700   TEN

Wharton Esherick (1887-1970) was a sculptor best known for his work in wood. He began his career as a carpenter in his mid-thirties, carving functional forms that blurred the lines between furniture and sculpture. His early work is influenced by the heavy shapes of much Arts and Crafts furniture, but he gradually developed a tactile, free-form style of his own that was widely copied, resulting in his reputation as 'the Dean of American Craftsmen' amongst his colleagues.

1962   *44in (112cm) high*

£60,000-80,000   DRA

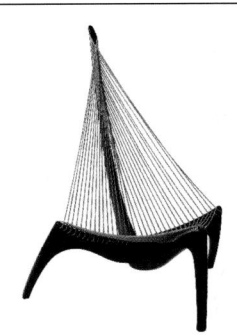

A 'Harp' chair, designed by Jorgen Hovelskov, on ebonised frame with flag line seat.

51.5in (131cm) high

£2,500-3,500   **SDR**

A pair of 'PK22' lounge chairs, designed by Poul Kjaerholm, and manufactured by E. Kold Christensen, covered in tan leather on steel bases, with impressed marks.

28in (71cm) high

£3,500-4,500   **SDR**

A three-drawer rosewood desk, by Knoll, with two slide-out shelves, on polished steel frame, with Knoll Associates label.

72in (183cm) wide

£1,200-1,800   **DRA**

A Memphis vanity mirror, designed by Michele de Lucci, in coloured laminate, with Memphis Milano metal tag stamped 'Michele de Lucci' and date.

1984.   *15.75in high*

£600-800   **SDR**

A Danish beech, upholstery and leather sofa, designed by Børge Mogensen, manufactured by Fritz Hansen, model no. 1798.

Mogensen helped on the interior design of the Stemann house in Oxfordshire and would have personally placed this piece within their collection.

1945

£700-1,000   **L&T**

A teak rocking stool, designed by Isamu Noguchi for Knoll, with steel wire frame.

c1954   *14in (35.5cm) wide*

£4,500-5,500   **DRA**

A forged and welded steel circular 'Dragon's Back' dining table, designed by Albert Paley, in black and contrasting patinated steel finish, with bevelled glass top on pedestal base, signed 'Albert Paley 1998'.

Born and raised in Rochester, New York, Albert Paley (b.1944) is a renowned American metalworker who has received many prestigious public and private commissions, including, for example, the entrance gates for the State Courthouse in San Francisco, and a sculpture and plaza for Adobe Systems in San Jose, California. He works primarily in milled steel, and produces monumental sculpture and architectural furniture as well as smaller pieces such as paperweights.

1998.   *64in (162.5cm) wide*

£25,000-35,000   **SDR**

A French fibreglass easy chair '300', designed by Pierre Paulin, manufactured by Artifort, with removable upholstered polyfoam pad.

1967

£200-300   **L&T**

A pine wardrobe, designed by Charlotte Perriand, with single sliding slatted door concealing four black tray drawers and storage compartments, on cylindrical black metal legs.

58in (147.5cm) wide

£2,000-3,000   **SDR**

An Italian 'I Feltri' chair, designed by Gaetano Pesce, manufactured by Cassina, Milan, the wool impregnated with thermosetting resin, stitched edges, early production.

1987

£1,800-2,200   **L&T**

A 'Jack' coffee table, designed by Gio Ponti, with plate-glass top on ebonised wood base.

36in (91.5cm) wide

£1,800-2,200   SDR

A double-seat school desk, designed by Jean Prouvé, with oak shelf and top, on green enamelled metal base.

45in (114.5cm) wide

£4,000-5,000   SDR

A hardwood veneer and paint two-piece Gilbert Rhode secretary, manufactured by Herman Miller, model no. 4160, fitted with shelves, letter slots, drawers and pull-out drop-down writing surface.

1941   Bottom 52in (123cm) wide

£700-1,000   SK

A pair of 'Barcelona' chairs, by Mies van der Rohe, for Knoll, with black leather cushions on polished steel frames, one Seagram label.

These were from the Seagram Building in New York City.

31in (79cm) wide

£4,000-5,000   DRA

A 'Grasshopper' chair, designed by Eero Saarinen, for Knoll, with corduroy upholstery.

34.5in (87.5cm) high

£1,500-2,500   DRA

A stainless steel cube lounge chair, designed by Jonathan Singleton, with upholstered cushions.

33in (84cm) wide

£1,200-1,800   SDR

A mahogany extending dining table, designed by Frank Lloyd Wright, for Henredon, in the 'Taliesin' pattern, with two leaves.

Closed 63in (160cm) wide

£2,000-3,000   SDR

A 'Taliesin' ten-drawer sideboard, by Frank Lloyd Wright, for Henredon, with recessed handles.

65.5in (166.5cm) wide

£1,500-2,500   DRA

A multicoloured and patterned laminate 'Carlton' bookcase unit, designed by Ettore Sottsass for Memphis.

Austrian-born Italian architect and designer Ettore Sottsass established his own office in Milan in 1947. His early designs, such as office machines for Olivetti (1958-69), embraced the Modern movement, but by the late 1970s he had abandoned the idea of 'good form', and was on the way to becoming one of the most influential members of the post-modern movement. He played a major part in the establishment of the Memphis group, for which he designed a variety of bizarre forms, including coloured plastic laminate MDF furniture (from 1981).

75in (190.5cm) wide

£6,500-8,500   SDR

A Minori Yamasaki chromed metal coffee table, with plate glass top.

Yamasaki (1912-86), the architect of the World Trade Centre, designed this table, using it in his Michigan home as well as in the Montgomery Ward Headquarters, both of which were completed in 1972.

36in (91.5cm) wide

£2,000-3,000   SDR

A New Hope school walnut armchair, with handwoven seat cover.

28.5in (72.5cm) high

£250-350   DRA

A pair of mid-20thC Italian exotic wood armchairs, upholstered in muslin.

24.5in (62cm) wide

£1,800-2,200   SDR

A pair of Italian-style armchairs, in mahogany with crimson velvet upholstery.

From a hotel in Buenos Aires, Argentina.

33.75in (86cm) high

£1,000-1,500   DRA

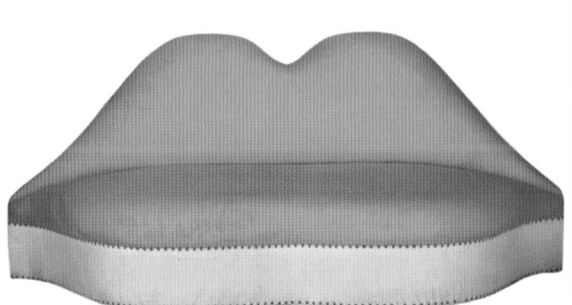

A sofa, after 'Mae West Lips' sofa, unmarked.

Inspired by a 1930s design by Salvador Dali that was originally executed by Green & Abbot, London, and Jean-Michel Frank, France.
1960-70   *87in (221cm) wide*

£2,000-3,000   SDR

A French curved sofa, upholstered in champagne chenille, on oak feet.

92in (233.5cm) wide

£5,000-7,000   SDR

A mid-1960s Italian rosewood and steel library table.

82.75in (210cm) wide

£1,800-2,200   L&T

A German enamelled wood and metal vanity, with flip-flop adjustable mirror and interior trays, together with stool with orange and white shag wool seat cover.

A Studio carved rosewood music stand with perforated panel.

45in (114.5cm) high

£1,500-2,000   SDR

Vanity 11.25in (28.5cm) wide

£1,200-1,800   SDR

MODERN DESIGN

A large porcelain teapot, by Tom Coleman, multi-fired with lithium-barium glazes.

23in (58.5cm) high

£10,000-15,000   DRA

A large earthenware vessel, Ralph Bacerra, carved and pierced with abstract and geometric patterns, the exterior covered in volcanic uranium glaze, the top in turquoise and black majolica glaze, with a gilded shoulder, signed 'Bacerra 98'.

1998   20in (51cm) wide

£7,000-10,000   DRA

A large stoneware 'Saalal' vessel, by Claude Conover, signed and titled.

18.5in (49.5cm) high

£7,000-10,000   SDR

A large stoneware 'Suhuy' vase, by Claude Conover, signed and titled.

23.5in (59.5cm) high

£10,000-15,000   SDR

A Giovanni Desimone earthenware vase, decorated with figures of a man and a woman in a colourful landscape on a stippled white ground, signed and dated on side.

An artist and writer, Giovanni Desimone was influenced by his close friend, Pablo Picasso.

1975   19.75in (50cm) high

£200-300   SK

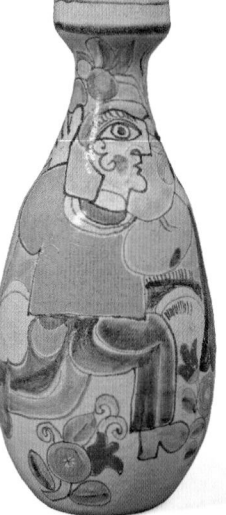

A Richard Devore stoneware vase, with asymmetrical rim and 'torn' edges under beige glaze, numbered '517' on base, accompanied by letter from the artist.

14in (35.5cm) high

£4,000-5,000   SDR

A tall glazed stoneware covered vessel, by Ken Ferguson, signed and dated.

1982.   21.5in (54.5cm) high

£2,000-3,000   SDR

A David Gilhooly ceramic sculpture, 'Breadfrog Making a Vegetable Stew of Himself'.

17in (43cm) high

£4,000-5,000   DRA

A large wheel-thrown vase, by Maija Grotell, covered in mottled glazes with copper lustre.

10in (25.5cm) wide

£4,500-5,500   SDR

An Otto Natzler ceramic sculpture, in the form of a hemisphere with two holes on a cylinder base, vibrant red iridescent glaze revealing blue veining, monogram, marked 'Otto Natzler, 1983, X301'.

1979   *13in (33cm) high*

£5,000-7,000   **SK**

An Otto Natzler ceramic sculpture box, with orange and black mottled glaze, geometric layers revealing two openings, signed monogram, marked 'Otto Natzler. 1978, X107'.

1978   *9.75in (25cm) wide*

£4,500-5,500   **SK**

A Madoura faience pitcher, by Pablo Picasso, with abstract animal design, signed 'EDITION PICASSO MADOURA', and numbered '165/200'.

Pablo Picasso (1881-1973) worked with potters George and Suzanne Ramie at the Madoura pottery in Vallauris, France from 1947 onwards, creating both one-off sculptures and limited edition ceramics such as plates and jugs. He did not throw the pieces himself, but was closely involved in the design of the forms. Picasso decorated his work with stylised designs reminiscent of his art.

11.5in (29cm) wide

£5,000-7,000   **DRA**

A Madoura faience pitcher, by Pablo Picasso, with abstract faces design, signed 'EDITION PICASSO MADOURA', numbered '84/300'.

9.25in (23.5cm) high

£5,000-7,000   **DRA**

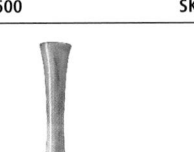

An unusually large Pillin tall vase, painted with ladies and fish, incised 'Pillin'.

22in (56cm) high

£2,500-3,500   **SDR**

A faience vase, by Gio Ponti, for Richard Ginori, with horses on green ribbed ground, stamped 'RICHARD-GINORI S.CRISTOFORO MILANO MADE IN ITALY 81.T 5911 M'.

8.5in (21.5cm) high

£6,000-8,000   **DRA**

An early large four-sided faience vase, by Henry Varnum Poor, decorated with Shakespearian scenes, incised 'HVP 32'.

1932   *14.5in (37cm) high*

£5,000-7,000   **DRA**

An Axel Salto hemispherical vessel, with prunts covered in matte tortoiseshell glaze, incised 'Salto 1935/3564/850'.

Because of its lack of association with Royal Copenhagen, this piece may be a unique studio effort.

1935   *2.25in (14.5cm) high*

£1,000-1,500   **SDR**

A Royal Copenhagen 'Budding' vessel, by Axel Salto, covered in reddish brown and grey flambé glaze, incised 'SALTO', stamped in green 'ROYAL COPENHAGEN DENMARK', numbered '660T' with triple wave mark.

7.75in (19.5cm) high

£5,000-7,000   **SDR**

An Edwin Scheier ceramic African fertility sculpture, depicting a wrapped figure cradled in a footed pod-like structure.

19in (48cm) high

£1,000-1,500   **SDR**

A late 20thC sectional cast 'Mini Totem No. 3' ceramic sculpture, by Ettore Sottsass, for Bitossi, in pastel shades and high-glazed finish.

From a limited edition of 150.

19.75in (50cm) high

£2,000-3,000   **FLD**

A glazed stoneware moonpot, by Toshiko Takaezu, signed.

1982   *10.5in (26.5cm) high*

£7,000-10,000   **SDR**

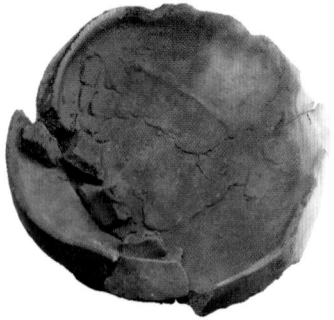

A Robert Turner glazed stoneware vessel, mottled red, amber and blue matte.

10.5in (26.5cm) high

£3,000-4,000   **DRA**

A large raku-fired plate, by Peter Voulkos, with torn chunks, signed and dated.

Peter Voulkos (1924-2002) was at the forefront of the so-called 'Revolution in Clay' in the United States in the 1950s, and his work celebrates the raw qualities inherent in unworked clay. Although they are based on functional forms, his pieces are torn, twisted and buckled – with no concern for function, but full of energy.

1995   *21in (53.5cm) wide*

£7,000-10,000   **DRA**

A glazed, wheel-formed stoneware vessel, by Peter Voulkos, with stylised Japanese motifs, signed 'Voulkos, 55'.

1955 8in (21cm) high

£5,000-7,000   **SDR**

An earthenware bowl, by Beatrice Wood covered in turquoise and lavender glazes, signed 'BEATO'.

7.25in (18.5cm) high

£4,000-5,000   **SDR**

A long elliptical bowl, by Betty Woodman, with sculpted spiral pattern, painted in coloured glazes.

27.5in (70cm) wide

£3,500-4,500   **SDR**

A red earthenware 'Pillow Pitcher', by Betty Woodman, stamped 'WOODMAN'.

22in (56cm) wide

£10,000-15,000   **DRA**

ESSENTIAL REFERENCE – MURANO GLASS

In the 13thC, glassmakers moved from Venice to the nearby island of Murano to protect the wealthy city from furnace fires. Murano was the world's leading glassmaking centre from the mid-15th until the17thC. The island's historic techniques remained in use throughout the radical changes the 1950s brought to glass design, with brighter colours used on abstract and sculptural forms, and new designers invited to the island.

- Influential designers include Paolo Venini, Fulvio Bianconi, Flavio Poli, Ercole Barovier and Dino Martens. Landmark designs, such as Dino Martens's 'Oriente' and Venini's 'fazzoletto' (handkerchief) vases, are particularly desirable.
- Venini (est. 1921) produced elegant, organic shapes, decorated with regular patterns of enamel-twist decoration.
- A.VE.M (est. 1932) used their own designs and commissioned others from Italian painters to create technically and artistically refined coloured glass.
- Barovier (est.1942) merged with Ferro Toso (est. 1901) in 1936, becoming known as Barovier & Toso from 1942. The new company used many different combinations of colour and pattern in vivid colours.
- Other notable factories include Seguso Vetri d'Art (1933-92), Salviati (1859-1988), and Veteria Vitosi (est. 1945).

An A.VE.M. vase designed by Ansolo Fuga, with a band of applied multicoloured pulled trails and green and blue dots.
c1955   *8.25in (21cm) high*
£1,200-1,800   QU

An A.VE.M. 'Anse Volante' handled vase by Giorgio Ferro, of cobalt blue and colourless glass with an iridescent finish.
1952   *12in (30.5cm) high*
£2,000-3,000   QU

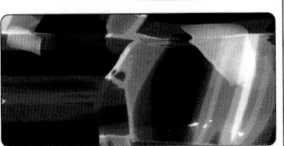

A Barovier & Toso glass vase.
c1958
£1,200-1,800   DOR

A Barovier & Toso 'Efeso' globe vase, by Angelo Barovier, the colourless body with powdered grey enamel inclusions and air bubbles.
c1964   *10.5in (26.5cm) high*
£600-800   QU

A Barovier & Toso 'Rotellato' glass vase.
10.5in (27cm) high
£1,500-2,000   DOR

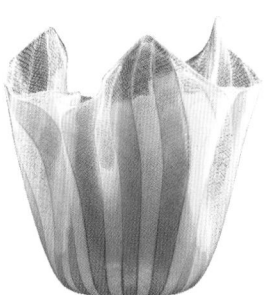

A large Venini 'fazzoletto' glass vase, in pink and white zanfirico, etched 'Venini Italia'.
11.5in (29cm) high
£600-800   DRA

A mid-1960s Venini crepuscolo lavender glass vase, by Toni Zuccheri, with blue insert.
12in (30.5cm) high
£1,200-1,800   SDR

A Venini stoppered bottle, by Paolo Venini, of blue incalmo glass with red mezza filigrana centre.
15in (38cm) high
£700-1,000   SDR

A Murano Vistosi glass vase, the design attributed to Vinicio Vianello, manufacturer's foil label.
1960   *10.25in (26cm) high*
£200-300   L&T

MODERN DESIGN

An Italian Alessandro Pianon glass and metal Pulcini Bird sculpture, for Vistosi Glassworks, the triangular-shaped blue glass body with internal red stripes and green-and-yellow murrine eyes, raised on copper legs.

c1960   6.75in (17cm) high

£2,500-3,500   SK

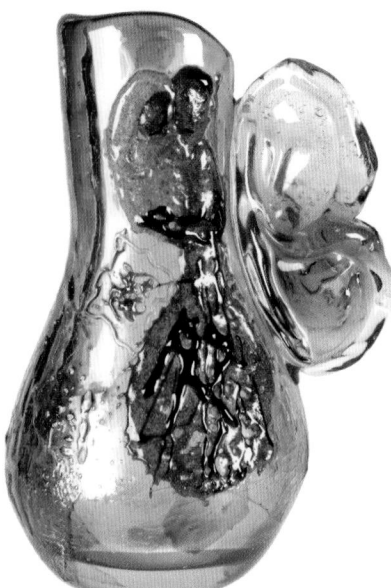

A handcrafted 'Anfora Sposi' glass vase, by Marc Chagall & Egidio Costantini, the rose-tinted body decorated in relief with two lovers and a clear glass violet-tinted handle depicting male and female faces, inscribed on the base 'M. Chagall – E Costantini, 1954, Fucina degli Angeli Venecia' and numbered '2', from a limited edition of three.

Egidio Costantini was born in Brindisi in 1912 and studied in Venice. After World War II, he embarked on a glassmaking career, creating sculptures based on drawings by contemporary artists. His work with a group of Venetian artists led to the founding of the Centro Studio Pittori nell'Arte del Vetro di Murano in 1950. After a successful collaboration with Oskar Kokoschka, he travelled to Paris to work with some of the most famous artists of the day, including Pablo Picasso, Max Ernst, Jean Arp, Gino Severini, Alexander Calder and Mark Chagall.

Chagall, already famous as a designer of stained glass, was fascinated by the mysterious chemistry of glass and fire. 'Costantini', he wrote, 'gave wealth to the range of colours of the painter, the violence of which is an agreement by moderate tone well differentiated'. From 1954 onwards, the two artists worked together, exhibiting their work at Costantini's studio gallery in Venice. After opening to initial success, the gallery was forced to shut in 1958, but re-opened in 1961 thanks to patronage from the famous American collector Peggy Guggenheim, who exhibited their work in her Venetian palace.

1954   15.5in (39.5cm) high

£12,000-18,000   A&G

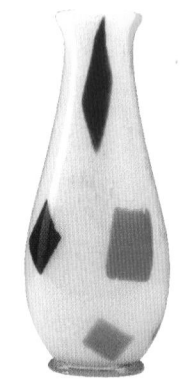

An early 1950s Aureliano Toso bulbous 'Oriente' glass vase, by Dino Martens.

8.25in (21cm) high

£1,500-2,000   DRA

An Aureliano Toso 'Pulegoso' glass vase, by Dino Martens, with random geometric patches in polychrome.

13in (33cm) high

£6,000-8,000   DRA

A Murano glass baluster vase, the opaque white-cased body overlaid with sections of red, purple or blue cased canes with opaque white cores, and similarly coloured panels.

c1965   11.5in (29cm) high

£1,500-2,000   QU

A 'Mizar' cobalt and clear glass vase, by Ettore Sottsass, for Compagnia Vetraria, with coloured loops, engraved 'Memphis Milano by Compagnia Vetraria Muranese'.

13.75in (5.5cm)

£1,500-2,000   SDR

A 'Clesitera' polychrome glass vase, by Ettore Sottsass, for Memphis, with forms suspended from two tiers, marked 'E. Sottsass for Memphis by Toso Vetri d'Arte'.

19.5in (49.5cm) high

£1,000-1,500   DRA

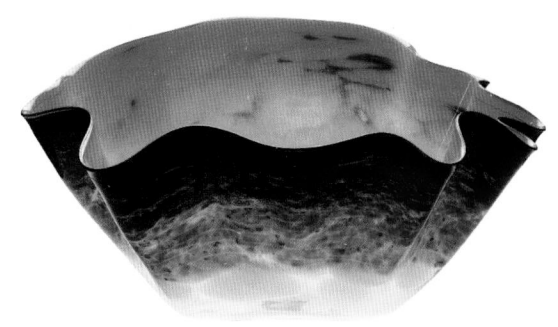

A large 'Macchia' vase, by Dale Chihuly, of cobalt, vermilion and white mottled glass, with acid-etched signature and date.

Seattle artist Dale Chihuly (b. 1941) works with a team of glass-blowers to create glass sculptures, often at a large scale, as works of installation or environmental art. His 'Macchia' series, named after the Italian for 'spot', referring to the spots of colour used in their production, is characteristic of his organic, colourful forms.

1988   31in (89cm) wide
£12,000-18,000   **SDR**

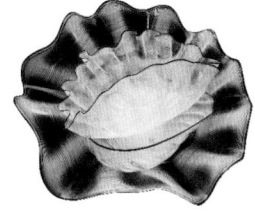

A three-piece clear glass 'Seaform' set, by Dale Chihuly, with opalescent swirls and black lip wraps, largest piece engraved 'Chihuly' and dated.

1984   Largest 18.5in (47cm) wide
£7,000-10,000   **SDR**

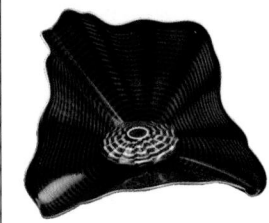

A studio edition 'Imperial Iris' two-piece Persian set, by Dale Chihuly, for Portland Press Group, with Chartreuse Lip Wraps, with plexiglass display box, signed 'Dale Chihuly 1234.PP2P.99.'

1999   Largest 13.25in (33.5cm) wide
£2,500-3,500   **DRA**

An American hand-blown cobalt glass sculpture, by Rik Allen, from the 'Cyclone' series.

2001   12.5in (32cm) high
£300–400   **RTC**

A large etched glass 'Chalice Root' vase, by Bernard Katz, in sunset salmon, ruby and amethyst, engraved 'Bernard Katz'.

22.5in (57cm) high
£500-700   **DRA**

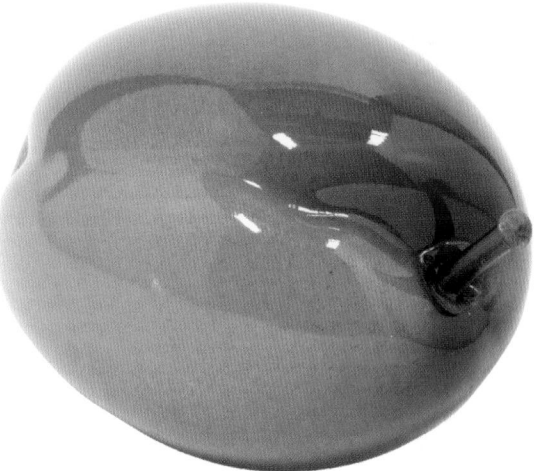

An American art glass 'Victorian Plum' sculpture, by Joey Kirkpatrick and Flora Mace.

2000   15.75in (40cm) long
£1,500-2,000   **RTC**

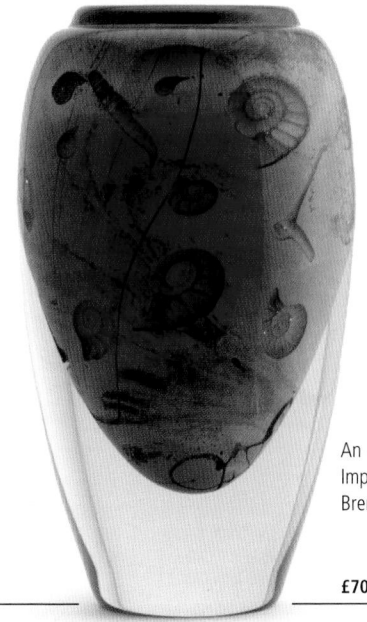

An American polychrome art glass vase, by Mark Russell Jr, from the 'Squares in Gray' series.

1985   5in (12.5cm) high
£150-250   **RTC**

An ovoid glass 'Minor Impressions V' vase, by Brent Kee Young.

10.75in (27.5cm) high
£700-1,000   **DRA**

A large Orrefors 'Graal' vase, by Eva Englund, depicting animals, engraved 'Orrefors Graal Nr.V 1215.7 Eva Englund'.

15in (38cm) high

£2,500-3,500   DRA

An Orrefors green-tinted circular tapered vase, with interior decoration of fish and seaweed, no. 2178D, signed 'Edward Hals'.

6.25in (16cm) high

£450-550   A&G

An Orrefors 'Tulpenglass' vase, by Nils Landberg, in rose glass, engraved 'Orrefors Expo Nu 312-57'.

1957   *17in (43cm) high*

£1,200-1,800   DRA

An Orrefors 'Ariel' glass vase, by Ingeborg Lundin, with geometric pattern, signed 'Orrefors Ariel Nr 476-63 Ingeborg Lundin'.

5.75in (14.5cm) high

£700-1,000   DRA

An Orrefors blown-glass 'Apple' vase, by Ingeborg Lundin, in green, 'engraved Orrefors Expo DU 32-57 Ingeborg Lundin'.

1957   *16.5in (42cm) high*

£3,500-4,500   DRA

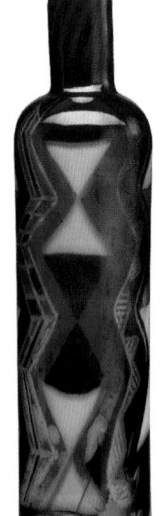

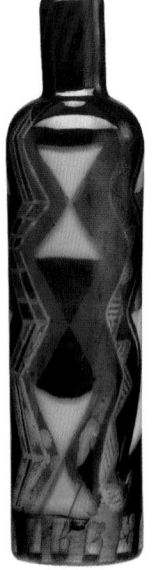

A tall bottle-shaped Graal glass vase, by Eva Englund, signed 'Eva Englund SBH Muraya Wilke Graal 42 11 90'.

1990   *17in (43cm) high*

£1,200-1,800   SDR

A Graal 'Slottsfroknar,' glass vase, by Eva Englund, signed 'Eva Englund Muraya Dorothy K. Wilke A. Graal 080990'.

1990   *12.5in (32cm) high*

£5,000-7,000   SDR

A blown-glass vase, by Sam Herman, for Val Saint Lambert, cylindrical form, signed in script 'Samuel Herman VAL 163'.

16.5in (42cm) high

£700-1,000   L&T

A Whitefriars willow-coloured glass banjo vase, pattern no. 9681, designed by Geoffrey Baxter.

c1967-73   *12.5in (31.5cm) high*

£600-800   TOV

A Gillies Jones 'Landscape Series' green glass globe vase, with carved decoration, signed 'Gillies Jones 1998 Landscape Series 01/40 Rosedale'.

6.75in (17.5cm) high

£250-350   TEN

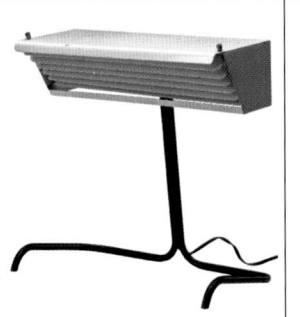

An enamelled metal table lamp, attributed to Jacques Biny, with perforated shade.

12in (30.5cm) high

£900-1,200   SDR

An Italian enamelled metal 'Lampiatta' table light, by Jonathan de Pas, Donato D'Urbino, Paolo Lomazzi, for Stilnovo.

14.25in (36cm) high

£300-400   L&T

A Desny nickelled-bronze and clear glass table lamp.

5.5in (14cm) high

£2,000-3,000   SDR

A Fontana Arte brushed nickel table lamp, with ribbed glass shade.

23in (55cm) high

£1,200-1,800   SDR

CLOSER LOOK – DESKEY LAMP

Donald Deskey (1894-1989) was an influential American designer who produced a wide variety of pioneering work, from household-product packaging to one-off luxury suites, in the streamlined modern style that became widespread in the US in the 1920s and 1930s.

This lamp is not in perfect condition, but in this case, the value is not affected because the piece is extremely rare. Only one other example of this lamp is known to exist, which is in a private collection.

The stepped design and chromed surface are typical of the Art Deco style. Deskey is best known for his Art Deco interiors for New York's Radio City Music Hall.

Deskey often used geometric patterns and new materials, such as chromium plate, as in this example.

A chrome-plated metal desk lamp, designed by Donald Deskey.

It is said that this lamp was bought at a house sale for £5. It sold at auction for £70,000, having been estimated at £1,000-2,000.

1927   *13.25in (33.5cm) high*

£80,000-120,000   SDR

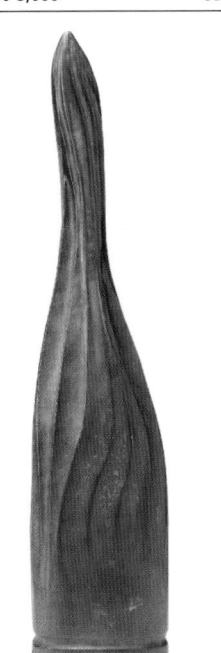

A Wharton Esherick carved walnut 'Flame' table lamp, carved 'WE 1933'.

1933   *19.25in (49cm) high*

£15,000-25,000   DRA

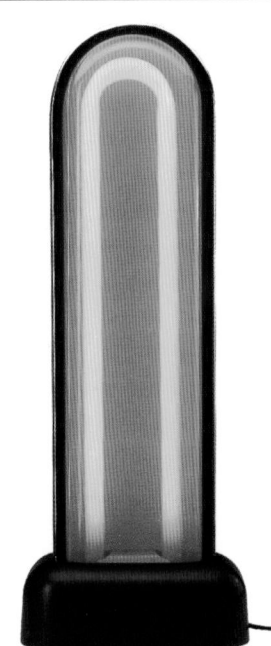

An 'Asteroid' lamp, Ettore Sottsass, with pink shade on blue base, with 'Design Centre Made in Italy' label.

28.75in (73cm) high

£3,000-4,000   SDR

A 'Mystery Science Lamp' #2, by Edward Zucca, signed and dated.

2002   *19in (48cm) high*

£2,000-3,000   SDR

A prototype 'Ashoka' table lamp, by Ettore Sottsass, for Memphis, dated and numbered '25'.

1981   *35in (89cm) high*

£2,000-3,000   DRA

A pair of Albert Paley Vulcan candleholders, stamped 'Albert Paley 1994'.

1994　　　*20.25in (51.5cm) high*

£3,000-4,000

SDR

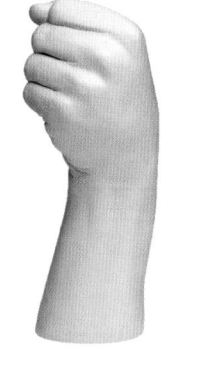

A pair of cast plaster candlesticks, Richard Etts, signed '1976 Richard Etts'.

1976　9.5in (24cm) high

£1,500-2,000　　SDR

A pair of Lino Sabattini candlesticks with spiral arms.

11.5in (29cm) high

£600-800　　　SDR

A polychrome glass candlestick, by Ettore Sottsass, for Memphis, signed 'E. Sotsass for Memphis by Toro Vetri D'Aria'.

20.25in (51.5cm) high

£900-1,200　　DRA

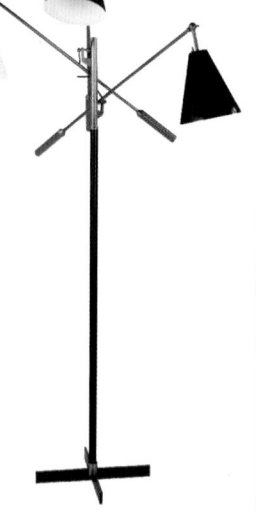

An Arredoluce 'Triennale' floor lamp, in brass and enamelled metal with three adjustable arms.

The Italian lighting firm Arredoluce was formed in the 1950s, originally producing chandeliers. The company quickly rose to international prominence, with a reputation for innovation and quality. The 'Triennale' lamp, combining stylish form with functionality, is one of Arredoluce's most successful designs.

59in (150cm) high

£6,000-8,000

SDR

A 'Cobra' table light, by Angelo Lelli, for Arredoluce, with magnetic adjustable metal shade, 'Arredoluce' label.

24.5in (62cm) high

£3,000-4,000　　SDR

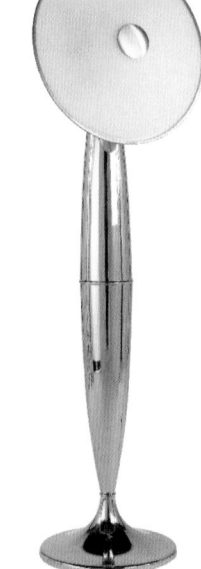

A large Italian polished brass floor lamp, the adjustable head with frosted glass diffuser.

80in (203cm) high

£7,000-10,000　　SDR

An Italian sheet-acrylic and steel 'Catasta' floor lamp sculpture, by Ugo la Pietra.

55in (140cm) high

£2,500-3,500 PAIR　L&T

An Arteluce chandelier, with twelve brass sockets radiating outward on a black enamelled metal frame.

34in (86.5cm) wide

£4,000-5,000   **SDR**

A Paul Evans banded and perforated copper hanging fixture, with verdigris patina.

22.25in (56.5cm) high

£12,000-18,000   **DRA**

A Fontana Arte glass chandelier, with partially etched cast glass prisms on brushed steel frame.

17in (43cm) high

£1,200-1,800   **SDR**

A Tommi Parzinger polished brass six-arm chandelier, with white perforated metal shades.

34in (86.5cm) diam

£3,000-4,000   **DRA**

A large eight-arm chandelier, by Karl Springer, of silvered Venetian glass, with polished chrome hardware and ceiling cap.

Accompanied by copy of the original invoice from Karl Springer Ltd., New York.

39in (99cm) wide

£4,000-5,000   **SDR**

A twelve-arm iron chandelier, by Erik Höglund, for Boda Afors, with drop crystals, and clear glass discs impressed with fish and primitive faces, includes four original hanging hooks.

Erik Höglund (1932-1998) was a Swedish painter, sculptor and graphic designer, who worked with glass, wrought-iron and bronze. He worked at Boda Glass Works from 1953-73.

Chandelier 39in (99cm) high

£15,000-20,000   **SDR**

A brass chandelier, by Paavo Tynell, for Taito-Idman, with perforated metal elements and yellow glass shades, stamped 'TAITO'.

31in (79cm) high

£4,000-5,000   **SDR**

An Italian eighteen-arm brass chandelier, with trumpeting floral arms.

40in (101.5cm) wide

£2,500-3,500   **DRA**

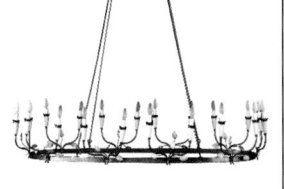

An Italian brass and enamelled metal elliptical chandelier, with floriform motif.

61.5in (156cm) diam

£5,000-7,000   **SDR**

A pair of large 'Stilnovo' spherical chrome hanging lamps.

68in (173cm) high

£800-1,200 PAIR   **DRA**

ESSENTIAL REFERENCE – PAUL EVANS

Paul Evans (1931-87) was an American furniture designer, sculptor and artist, who produced monumental work that was a mix of mid-century furniture design and mixed-metal sculpture in bronze, silver and gold.

- Evans studied both sculpture and jewellery design at the School for American Crafters in Rochester, New York and at Michigan's Cranbrook Academy of Art, but turned to furniture-making after a visit to Philip Lloyd Powell's store in New Hope, Pennsylvania. From 1954, he sold his work through Powell, and eventually they began to collaborate.
- Believing that it was still possible to make a profit from handmade furniture and sculpture, Evans made unique pieces that married hand-craftsmanship with the latest technological innovations.
- He typically used materials such as bronze, aluminium and copper on wooden bases.
- Evans exhibited in a group show in 1957 at the Museum of Contemporary Crafts in New York City.
- In 1964, he became the designer of furniture manufacturer Directional, where he introduced such highly collectable editions as the 'Argente' series, sculpted bronze pieces, and the popular 'Cityscape' collection. His relationship with Directional ended in 1980. In 1981, Evans opened a New York showroom, where he sold his own work.
- Most Paul Evans pieces are signed, and all the custom items bear a signature and a date.

A Paul Evans pewter pitcher, with rosewood handle.

Pitchers of this type are from a relatively small production, made while Evans was still working as a craftsman in Sturbridge Village, a 'living museum', before setting up shop in New Hope, Pennsylvania.

c1952   11in (28cm) high

£1,000-1,500   SDR

A Paul Evans 'Cityscape' hinged cigar box.

10in (25.5cm) wide

£400-500   SDR

A Paul Evans 'Argente' patchwork aluminium box, with antiqued interior.

Small items of this type were a common staple in Evans's shop. They were affordable and readily accessible to his customers.

16in (40.5cm) high

£15,000-20,000   SDR

A Paul Evans sculpted bronze lidded box, covered in circular designs.

10.25in (26cm) wide

£3,000-4,000   SDR

A small Paul Evans cast bronze ashtray, with freeform rim.

9in (23cm) wide

£2,000-3,000   SDR

A Paul Evans cast aluminium ashtray, with ribbed border.

This ashtray is a unique piece and represents one of Evans's experimentations with new styles and forms.

8in (20.5cm) wide

£1,500-2,000   SDR

A rare early Paul Evans welded and wrought steel fountain sculpture, with abstract floral and geometric elements.

c1956-57   43.25in (82cm) high

£25,000-35,000   DRA

A Paul Evans steel patchwork sculpture, signed and dated 'PE 1964'.

1964   76in (193cm) high

£90,000-120,000   DRA

A steel and bronze bell, by Paul Evans and Phillip Lloyd Powell, with walnut handle.

Evans and Powell collaborated on special Christmas gifts for their clients. Approximately 50 of these bells were produced.

11.5in (29cm) high

£2,000-3,000   SDR

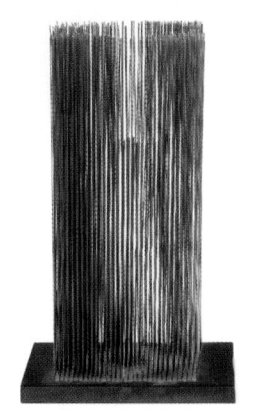

A 'sonambient' gold-plated stainless steel sound sculpture by Harry Bertoia, on brass base.

1965   *10.25in (26cm) high*

£12,000-18,000   **SDR**

A stainless steel 'Willow' sculpture by Harry Bertoia.

Harry Bertoia (1915-78) was born in Italy and moved to the US in 1930. He began his career experimenting with jewellery forms, exploring ideas that would later emerge in his sculptures. In 1943 he worked with Charles and Ray Eames and later established his own studio in Pennsylvania. In the 1950s he joined Knoll International, where he designed chairs that brought him wide acclaim. As well as working as a furniture designer and sculptor, he experimented in making sound sculptures and kinetic works of art.

66in (167.5cm) high

£25,000-35,000   **SDR**

A Hagenauer wood and brass model of a woman dancing, stylised form, with ribbon, stamped marks, remains of paper label.

21.25in (54cm) high

£1,800-2,200   **WW**

A Klaus Ihlenfeld phosphorous bronze, untitled.

7in (17.5cm) high

£2,500-3,500   **SDR**

A Philip and Kelvin Laverne bronze plaque, acid-etched and painted with figural scene, signed 'Philip Kelvin Laverne'.

35in (88cm) wide

£2,500-3,500   **SDR**

A unique painted metal 'model for Mobile I', by Kenneth Martin, for International Union of Architects.

9in (22.5cm) wide

£10,000-15,000   **L&T**

A Jan De Swart cast aluminium sculpture.

15.75in (40cm) high

£2,000-3,000   **SDR**

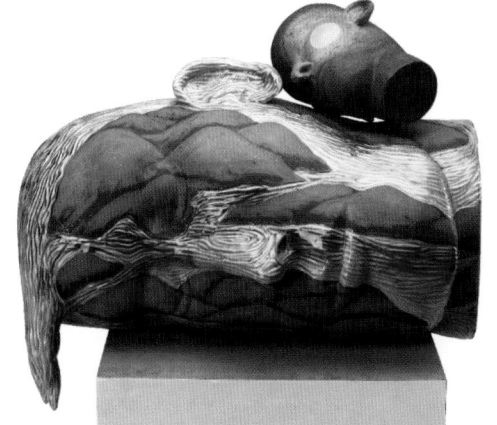

A hand-built carved and glazed ceramic sculpture, by Michael Lucero, 'Island Dreamer', with partially overhanging wood base, signed 'Michael Lucero 1983'.

1983   *27in (68.5cm) wide*

£9,000-12,000   **SDR**

A large glazed terracotta gourd-shaped sculpture, by Graham Marx.

30in (76cm) high

£10,000-15,000   **DRA**

A Carpet circular area rug, with radial burst pattern in blues and greens on a mustard ground.

142in (360cm) diam

£1,200-1,800 SDR

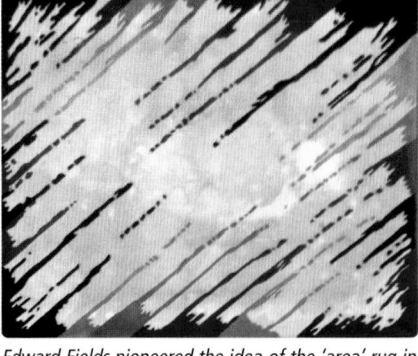

A rectangular wool rug, by Edward Fields, with minimalist design in blue, grey and black, signed and dated on selvage.

Edward Fields pioneered the idea of the 'area' rug in the 1950s – a portable rug that could move house with its owners, rather than a fitted carpet that could not. His rugs were a huge success and widely copied by other designers, although Fields remained a leader in terms of quality and design.

1988 *107in (272cm) long*

£500-700 DRA

A maguey fibre 'Balloons' tapestry, by Alexander Calder, with abstract design in navy, yellow, red, peach and black, Bon Art tag, signed with embroidered copyright, 'CA 74 57/100'.

1974 *8in (20.5cm) wide*

£4,500-5,500 DRA

A Wharton Esherick mahogany tray, carved 'WE 1967'.

1967. *23.75in (60.5cm) wide*

£3,000-4,000 DRA

A pair of walnut rectangular salt and pepper shakers, Paul Evans and Phillip Lloyd Powell, with pewter inlay.

These were original sample models and have never been used.

Tallest 4in (10cm) high

£1,800-2,200 SDR

A sculptural maple burl centrebowl, by Mark Lindquist, with natural occlusions, signed 'Mark Lindquist 1977 Maple Burl'.

17.5in (44.5cm) wide

£700-1,000 DRA

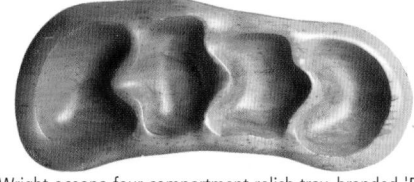

A Russel Wright oceana four-compartment relish tray, branded 'Russel Wright' in script.

17.5in (44cm) wide

£600-800 SDR

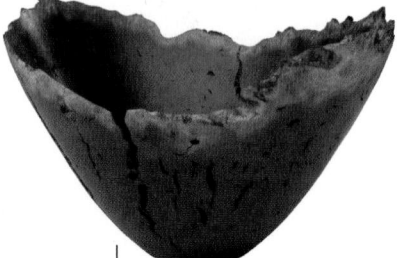

A 'Wild Lilac' burl bowl, by Hap Sakwa, engraved 'Hap Sakwa 3/81 Wild Lilac'.

6.25in (16cm) wide

£450-550 DRA

A Melvin Lindquist claro walnut burl-wood vessel, with natural occlusions, signed 'Mel Lindquist/Claro Walnut/Burl/3-86'.

1986 *3.5in (9cm) high*

£700-1,000 SDR

A walnut bottle, Paul Evans and Phillip Lloyd Powell, with pewter inlay, marked with 'Designer's Inc. Paul Evans' tag'.

Difficult to produce, only five of these bottles were made. This one belonged to Powell and is most likely the original example after which the others were patterned.

14.25in (36cm) high

£4,000-5,000 SDR

ADVERTISERS

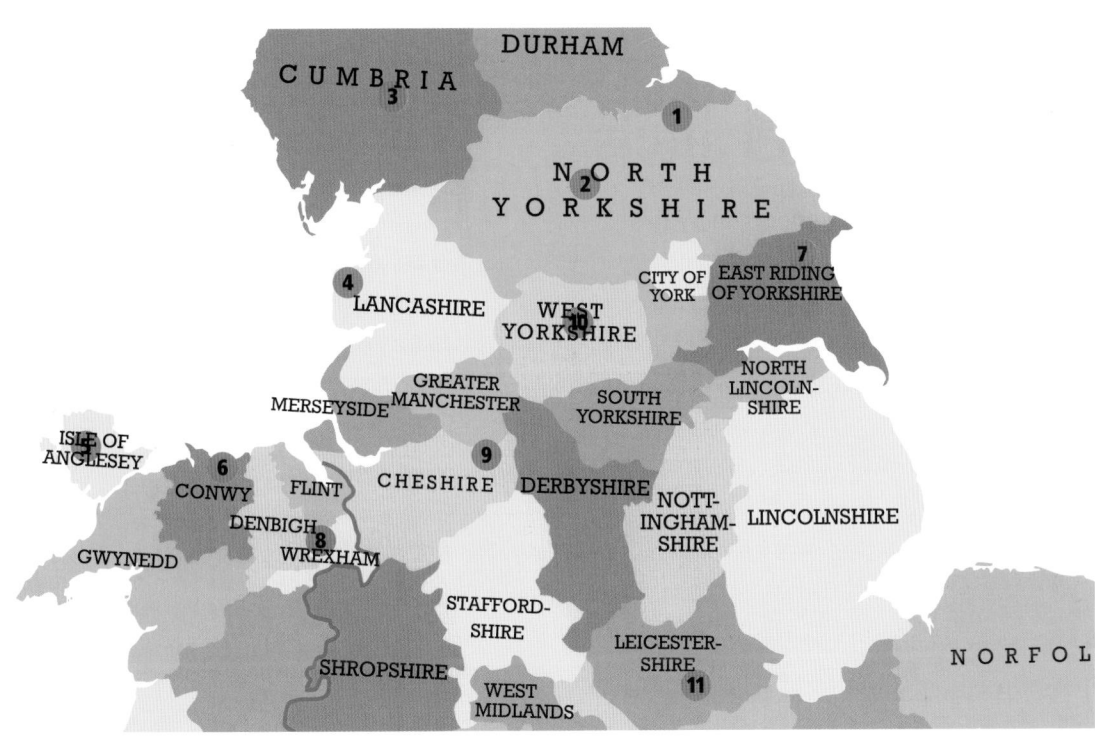

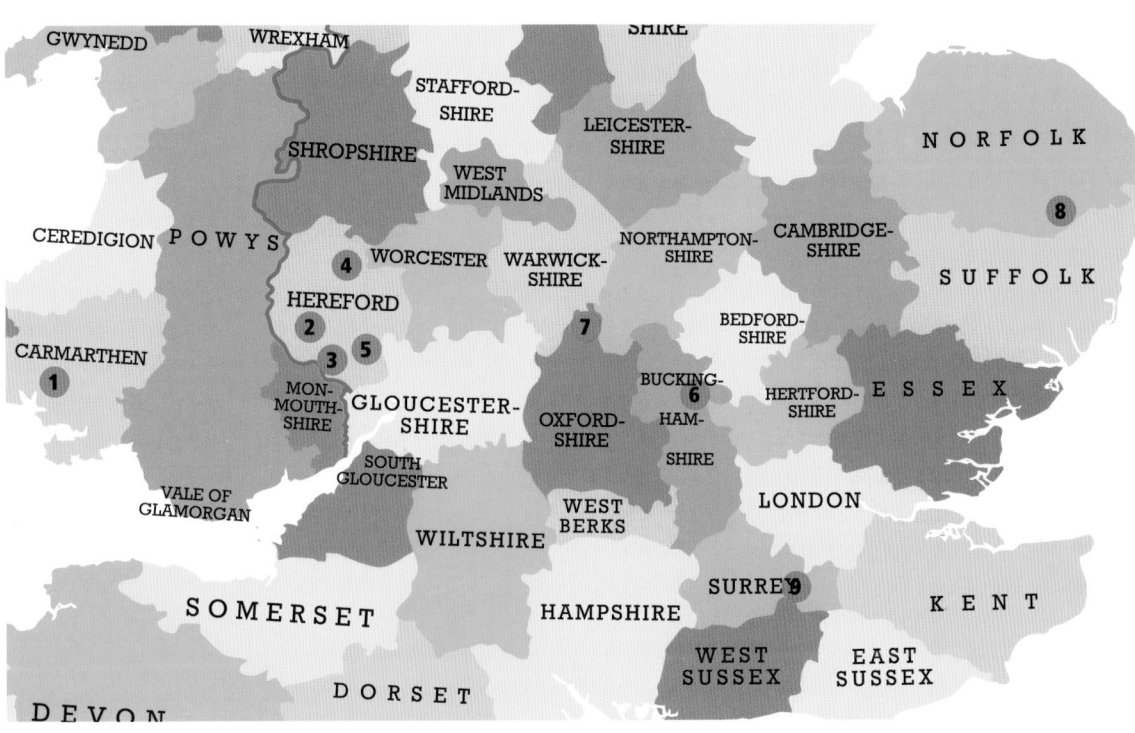

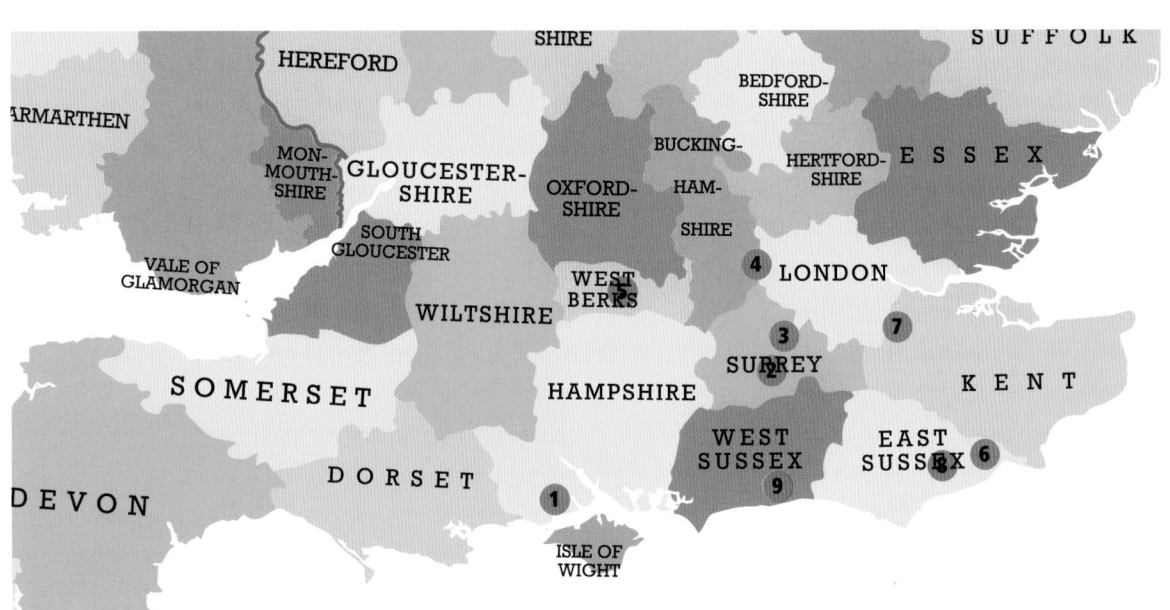

Every antique illustrated in Miller's Antiques has a letter code which identifies the dealer or auction house that sold it. The list below is a key to these codes. In the list, auction houses are shown by the letter A and dealers by the letter D. Some items may have come from a private collection, in which case the code in the list is accompanied by the letter P. Inclusion in this book in no way constitutes or implies a contract or a binding offer on the part of any of our contributors to supply or sell the goods illustrated, or similar items, at the prices stated.

A&G (A)
ANDERSON & GARLAND
Anderson House,
Crispin Court,
Newbiggin Lane,
Westerhope,
Newcastle upon Tyne,
NE5 1BF
Tel: 0191 430 3000
www.andersonandgarland.com

ADA (A)
ADAM'S
26 St Steven's Green, Dublin 2
Tel: 00 353 1 676 0261
www.adams.ie

ASC (D)
ALLAN SMITH CLOCKS
Tel: 01793 822977
www.allansmithantiqueclocks.
co.uk

BB (D)
BARBARA BLAU
South Street Antiques Market
615 South 6th Street,
Philadelphia,
PA 19147-2128 USA
Tel: 001 215 739 4995

BE (A)
BEARNES
St Edmund's Court,
Okehampton Street,
Exeter, Devon, EX4 1DU
Tel: 01392 413100
www.bearnes.co.uk

BEJ (D)
BÉBÉS ET JOUETS
c/o Lochend Post Office,
165 Restalrig Road,
Edinburgh EH7 6HW
Tel: 0131 332 5650
bebesetjouets@tiscali.co.uk

BER (A)
BERTOIA AUCTIONS
2141 Demarco Drive,
Vineland NJ 08360 USA
Tel: 001 856 692 1881
www.bertoiaauctions.com

BLNY (A)
BLOOMSBURY AUCTIONS
6 West 48th Street,
New York, NY 10036-1902
Tel: 001 212-719-1000
http://ny.bloomsburyauctions.com

BLO (A)
BLOOMSBURY AUCTIONS
Bloomsbury House,
24 Maddox Street,
London W1 S1PP
Tel: 020 7495 9494
www.bloomsburyauctions.com

BZ (P)
BASIA ZARZYCKA
52 Sloane Square,
London,
SW1W 8AX
Tel: 0207730 1660
www.basia-zarzycka.com

CANS (D)
CANDY SAYS
39 Elm Road,
Leigh-on-Sea,
Essex, SS9 1SW
Tel: 01277 212134
www.candysays.co.uk

CRA (A)
CRAFTSMAN AUCTIONS
333 North Main Street,
Lambertville, NJ 08530 USA
Tel: 001 609 397 9374
www.ragoarts.com

DA&H (A)
DEE, ATKINSON & HARRISON
The Exchange Saleroom,
Driffield, East Yorkshire
Tel : 01377 253151

DCP (D)
THE DUNLOP COLLECTION
PO Box 6269,
Statesville,
NC 28687 USA
Tel: 001 871 2626
dunloppaperweights@mac.com

DOR (A)
DOROTHEUM
Palais Dorotheum,
Dorotheergasse 17, 1010 Vienna,
Austria
Tel: 0043 1 515 600
www.dorotheum.com

DN (A)
DREWEATTS
Donnington Priory Salerooms,
Donnington, Newbury,
Berkshire RG14 2JE
Tel: 01635 553553
www.dnfa.com/donnington

DR (D)
DEREK ROBERTS FINE
ANTIQUE CLOCKS &
BAROMETERS
25 Shipbourne Road,
Tonbridge, Kent, TN10 3DN
Tel: 01732 358 986
www.quallityantiqueclocks.com

DRA (A)
DAVID RAGO AUCTIONS
333 North Main Street,
Lambertville, NJ 08530, USA
Tel: 001 609 397 9374
www.ragoarts.com

DUK (A)
HY DUKE & SON
The Dorchester Fine Art
Salerooms,
Weymouth Avenue,
Dorchester,
Dorset DT1 1QS
Tel: 01305 265 080
www.dukes-auctions.com

EAL (D)
EXETER ANTIQUE LIGHTING
43, The Quay, Exeter EX2 4AN
Tel: 01392 433604
www.antiquelightingcompany.com

FLD (A)
FIELDINGS AUCTIONEERS
Mill Race Lane, Stourbridge,
DY8 1JN
Tel: 01384 444140
www.fieldingsauctioneers.co.uk

FRE (A)
FREEMAN'S
1808 Chestnut Street,
Philadelphia, PA 19103, USA
Tel: 001 215 563 9275
www.freemansauction.com

G&H (D)
GARRET AND HURST
Tel: 01323 848824
www.garretandhurst.co.uk

GBA (A)
GRAHAM BUDD AUCTIONS
PO Box 47519,
London N14 6XD
Tel: 020 8366 2525
www.grahambuddauctions.co.uk

GCHI (D)
THE GIRL CAN'T HELP IT!
Grand Central Window,
Ground Floor,
Alfie's Antiques Market,
13-25 Church Street,
London NW8 8DT
Tel: 0207 724 8984
www.thegirlcanthelpit.com

GHOU (A)
GARDINER HOULGATE
Bath Auction Rooms,
9 Leafield Way,
Corsham, SN13 9SW
Tel: 01225 812 912
www.gardinerhoulgate.co.uk

GORL (A)
GORRINGES
15 North Street,
Lewes, East Sussex
BN7 2PD
Tel: 01273 472503
www.gorringes.co.uk

GVI (D)
GARTH VINCENT
The Old Manor House,
Allington,
Nr Grantham,
Lincolnshire, NG32 2DH
Tel: 01400 281358
www.guns.uk.com

H&G (D)
HOPE AND GLORY
131A Kensington Church Street,
London W8 7LP

HALL
HALLS FINE ART
Welsh Bridge, Shrewsbury,
SY3 8LA
Tel: 01743 284 777
www.hallsestateagents.co.uk

HT (D)
HARTLEY'S
Victoria Hall, Little Lane,
Ilkley, LS29 8EA
Tel: 01943 816363
www.hartleysauctions.co.uk

JA (A)
JOEL AUSTRALIA
333 Malvern Road,
South Yarra, 3141, Victoria,
Melbourne, Australia
www.leonardjoel.com.au

JDJ (D)
JAMES D JULIA INC
PO Box 830, Fairfield,
ME 04937, USA
Tel: 001 207 453 7125
www.juliaauctions.com

JH (D)
JEANETTE HAYHURST FINE
GLASS
32A Kensington Church St.,
London W8 4HA
Tel: 020 7938 1539
www.antiqueglass-london.com

KEMB (D)
STEPHEN T. P. KEMBER
3 The Corn Exchange,
The Pantiles,
Tunbridge Wells, Kent,
TN2 5TE
Tel: 01892 618200
www.antique-musicboxes.com

KT (A)
KERRY TAYLOR AUCTIONS
Unit C25
Parkhall Road Trading Estate,
40 Martell Road,
Dulwich, London SE21 8EN
Tel: 020 8676 4600
www.kerrytaylorauctions.com

L&T Ⓐ
LYON AND TURNBULL LTD.
33 Broughton Place,
Edinburgh, Midlothian EH1 3RR
Tel: 0131 557 8844
www.lyonandturnbull.com

LDY Ⓟ
LADY DOUBLE YOU
info@ladydoubleyou.com
www.ladydoubleyou.com

LOC Ⓐ
LOCKE & ENGLAND
18 Guy Street,
Leamington Spa, CV32 4RT
Tel: 01926 889100
www.leauction.co.uk

LOW Ⓐ
LOWESTOFT PORCELAIN
Surrey Street,
Lowestoft, NR32 1LJ
Tel: 01296892736
www.lowestoftchina.co.uk

LT Ⓐ
LOUIS TAYLOR
Britannia House,
10 Town Road, Hanley,
Stoke on Trent ST1 2QG
Tel: 01782 214111
www.louistaylorfineart.co.uk

MDM Ⓓ
M&D MOIR
www.manddmoir.co.uk

MEA Ⓓ
MEALY'S
The Square, Castlecomer,
County Kilkenny, Ireland
Tel: 00 353 56 41229
www.mealys.com

MGT Ⓓ
MARY & GEOFF TURVIL
Corner House,
116 Heath Road,
Petersfield, Hants GU31 4EL
Tel: 020 7629 0834
forest.antiques@virgin.net

ML Ⓓ
MARK LAINO
Mark of Time,
132 South 8th Street,
Philadelphia, PA 19107 USA
Tel: 001 215 922 1551
lecoultre@verizon.net

PART Ⓓ
PARTRIDGE FINE ARTS PLC
No longer trading.

PC Ⓟ Ⓒ
PRIVATE COLLECTION

POOK Ⓐ
POOK & POOK
463 East Lancaster Avenue,
Downington,
PA 19335, USA
Tel: 001 610 269 4040
www.pookandpook.com

QU Ⓐ
QUITTENBAUM
Theresienstrassebol, D-80333,
München, Germany
Tel: 0049 892 73702125
www.quittenbaum.de

RCC Ⓓ
**ROYAL COMMEMORATIVE
CHINA**
413 High Road,
Harrow Weald, Middlesex,
HA3 6EL
Tel: 020 8863 0625
royalcommemoratives
@hotmail.com

RGA Ⓓ
**RICHARD GARDNER
ANTIQUES**
Swan House,
Market Square,
Petworth, West Sussex
GU28 0AH
Tel: 01798 343 411
www.richardgardenerantiques.co.u
k

ROS Ⓐ
ROSEBERY'S
74-76 Knight's Hill,
West Norwood,
London SE27 0JD
Tel: 020 8761 2522
www.roseberys.co.uk

RTC Ⓐ
RITCHIES
No longer trading

SAS Ⓐ
SPECIAL AUCTION SERVICES
Kennetholme,
Midgham,
Nr. Reading, Berkshire RG7 5UX
Tel: 0118 971 2949
www.specialauctionservices.com

SBG Ⓓ
SWEETBRIAR GALLERY LTD
29 Beechview Road,
Kinglsey, Frodsham,
Cheshire WA6 8DF
Tel: 071913 458470
www.sweetbriar.co.uk

SDR Ⓐ
**SOLLO:RAGO MODERN
AUCTIONS**
333 North Main Street,
Lambertville, NJ 08530 USA
Tel: 001 609 397 9374
www.ragoarts.com

SK Ⓐ
SKINNER INC.
The Heritage on the Garden,
63 Park Plaza
Boston MA 02116, USA
Tel: 001 617 350 5400
www.skinnerinc.com

SOT Ⓐ
SOTHEBY'S (US)
1334 York Avenue,
New York, NY 10021, USA
Tel: 001 212 606-7000
www.sothebys.com

SOTA Ⓐ
SOTHEBY'S (AMSTERDAM)
De Boelelaan 30,
1083 HJ Amsterdam,
Netherlands
Tel: 0031 20 550 22 00
www.sothebys.com

SOTH Ⓐ
SOTHEBY'S (LONDON)
34-35 New Bond Street,
London, W1A 2AA
Tel: 020 7293 5000
www.sothebys.com

SOTP Ⓐ
SOTHEBY'S (PARIS)
Galerie Charpentier,
76 rue du Faubourg,
Saint Honoré, 75008 Paris,
France
Tel: 00 33 1 53 05 53 05
www.sothebys.com

SWO Ⓐ
SWORDERS
14 Cambridge Road,
Stansted Mountfitchet,
Essex CM24 8GE
Tel: 01279 817 778
www.sworder.co.uk

TOV Ⓐ
TOOVEY'S
Spring Gardens, Washington,
West Sussex, RH20 3BS
Tel: 01903 891955
www.tooveys.com

TDM Ⓐ
THOMAS DEL MAR LTD
25 Blythe Road,
London W14 0PD
Tel: 0207 602 4805
www.thomasdelmar.com

TEN Ⓐ
TENNANTS
The Auction Centre, Leyburn,
North Yorkshire, DL8 5SG
Tel: 01969 623 780
www.tennants.co.uk

VEC Ⓐ
VECTIS AUCTIONS
Fleck Way, Thornaby,
Stockton on Tees,
County Durham TS17 9JZ
Tel: 01642 750 616
www.vectis.co.uk

VZ Ⓐ
**VON ZEZSCHWITZ KUNST
UND DESIGN**
Friedrichstrasse 1a, 80801
Munich, Germany
Tel: 0049 89 38 98 930
www.von-zezschwitz.de

W&W Ⓐ
WALLIS AND WALLIS
West Street Auction Galleries,
Lewes, East Sussex BN7 2NJ
Tel: 01273 480 208
www.wallisandwallis.co.uk

WAD Ⓐ
WADDINGTON'S
111 Bathurst St., Toronto,
Ontario M5V 2R1, Canada
Tel: 001 416 504 9100
www.waddingtons.ca

WEB Ⓐ
WEBBS
18 Manukau Road, PO Box 99
251, Newmarket, Auckland 1000,
New Zealand
Tel: 09 524 6804
www.webbs.co.nz

WKA Ⓐ
**WIENER KUNST AUKTIONEN -
PALAIS KINSKY**
Freyung 4, 1010 Vienna,
Austria
Tel: 00 43 15 32 42 00
www.palais-kinsky.com

WW Ⓐ
WOOLLEY & WALLIS
51-61 Castle Street,
Salisbury,
Wiltshire SP13SU
Tel: 01722 424 500
www.woolleyandwallis.co.uk

NOTE

For valuations, it is advisable to contact the dealer or auction house in advance to confirm that they will perform this service and whether any charge is involved. Telephone valuations are not possible, so it will be necessary to send details, including a photograph, of the object, along with a stamped addressed envelope for response. While most dealers will be happy to help you, do remember that they are busy people. Please mention Miller's Antiques when making an enquiry.

This is a list of auctioneers that conduct regular sales. Auction houses that would like to be included in the next edition should contact us at info@millers.uk.com.

LONDON

Angling Auctions
PO Box 2095, W12 8RU
Tel: 020 8749 4175
angling-auctions.co.uk

Auction Atrium
101B Kensington Church Street, W8 7LN
Tel: 020 7792 9020
www.auctionatrium.com

Baldwins
11 Adelphi Terrace, WC2N 6BJ
Tel: 020 7930 6879
www.baldwin.co.uk

Bloomsbury
24 Maddox Street, W1 S1PP
Tel: 020 7495 9494
www.bloomsbury-book-auct.com

Bonhams
101 New Bond Street, W1S 1SR
Tel: 020 7447 7447
www.bonhams.com

Graham Budd Auctions Ltd.
P.O. Box 47519, London N14 6XD
Tel: 020 8366 2525
www.grahambuddauctions.co.uk

Chiswick Auctions
1 Colville Road, Acton, W3 8BL
Tel: 020 8992 4442
www.chiswickauctions.co.uk

Christie's
8 King Street, St. James's, SW1Y 6QT
Tel: 020 7839 9060
85 Old Brompton Road, SW7 3LD
Tel: 020 7930 6074
www.christies.com

Criterion Auctioneers
53 Essex Road, N1 2SF
Tel: 020 7359 5707
www.criterionauctions.co.uk

Dix-Noonan-Webb
16 Bolton Street, W1J 8BQ
Tel: 020 7016 1700
www.dnw.co.uk

Lots Road Galleries
71-73 Lots Road, SW10 0RN
Tel: 020 7376 6800
www.lotsroad.com

Rosebery's
74-76 Knights Hill, SE27 OJD
Tel: 020 8761 2522
www.roseberys.co.uk

Sotheby's
34-35 New Bond Street, W1A 2AA
Tel: 020 7293 5000
www.sothebys.com

Spink & Son Ltd.
69 Southampton Row, WC1B 4ET
Tel: 020 7563 4000
www.spink.com

Kerry Taylor Auctions
Unit C25 Parkhall Rd Trading Estate,
40 Martell Rd, Dulwich SE21 8EN
Tel: 020 8676 4600
www.kerrytaylorauctions.com

AVON

Aldridges of Bath
Newark House, 26-45 Cheltenham Street, Bath BA2 3EX
Tel: 01225 462830
www.aldridgesofbath.com

Gardiner Houlgate
9 Leafield Way, Corsham SN13 9SW
Tel: 01225 812912
www.gardinerhoulgate.co.uk

BEDFORDSHIRE

W. & H. Peacock
26 Newnham Street, Bedford MK40 3JR
Tel: 01234 266366
www.peacockauction.co.uk

BERKSHIRE

Cameo Auctions
Kennet Holme Farm, Bath Road, Midgham, Reading, RG7 5UX
Tel: 01189 713772
www.cameo-auctioneers.co.uk

Dreweatts
Donnington Priory, Donnington, Nr Newbury RG14 2JE
Tel: 01635 553553
www.dnfa.com

Special Auction Services
Kennetholme, Midgham,
Nr. Reading RG7 5UX
Tel: 0118 971 2949
www.specialauctionservices.com

BUCKINGHAMSHIRE

Amersham Auction Rooms
Station Road, Amersham, HP7 0AH
Tel: 01494 729292
www.amershamauctionrooms.co.uk

Bourne End Auction Rooms
Station Approach, Bourne End SL8 5QH
Tel: 01628 531500
www.bourneendauctionrooms.com

Dickins Auctioneers
Claydon House Park, Calvert Rd,
Middle Claydon MK18 2EZ
Tel: 01296 714 434
www.dickins-auctioneers.com

CAMBRIDGESHIRE

Cheffins
Clifton House, 1 & 2 Clifton Road,
Cambridge CB1 7EA
Tel: 01223 213 343
www.cheffins.co.uk

Hyperion Auctions Ltd
Station Road, St. Ives PE27 5BH
Tel: 01480 464140
www.hyperionauctions.co.uk

Rowley Fine Art Auctioneers
8 Downham Road, Ely CB6 1AH
Tel: 01353 653020
www.rowleyfineart.com

W & H Peacock, Ambrose and Locke & England Auctioneers
Bedford Auction Centre, 26 Newnham St, Bedford MK40 3JR
Tel: 01234 266366
www.peacockauction.co.uk

CHANNEL ISLANDS

Martel Maides
Martel Maides Auctions,
Cornet Street, St. Peter Port,
Guernsey GY1 1LF
Tel: 01481 722700
www.martelmaides.co.uk

CHESHIRE

Frank R. Marshall & Co.
Marshall House, Church Hill, Knutsford WA16 6DH
Tel: 01565 653284
www.frankmarshall.co.uk

Halls Fine Art Auctions
Booth Mansion, 30 Watergate Street, Chester CH1 2LA
Tel: 01244 312300
www.hallsestateagents.co.uk

Maxwells of Wilmslow
133A Woodford Road, Woodford, SK7 1QD
Tel: 01614 395182

Peter Wilson Auctioneers
Victoria Gallery, Market Street, Nantwich CW5 5DG
Tel: 01270 623878
www.peterwilson.co.uk

CORNWALL

W. H. Lane & Son
Jubilee House, Queen Street, Penzance TR18 4DF
Tel: 01736 361447
www.whlaneauctioneersandvaluers.co.uk

David Lay FRICS
The Penzance Auction House
Alverton, Penzance TR18 4RE
Tel: 01736 361414
www.davidlay.co.uk

CUMBRIA

Penrith Farmers' & Kidd's
Skirsgill Salesrooms, Penrith CA11 0DN
Tel: 01768 890781
www.pfkauctions.co.uk

Thomson, Roddick & Medcalf
Coleridge House, Shaddongate,
Carlisle CA2 5TU
Tel: 01228 528939
www.thomsonroddick.com

DERBYSHIRE

Bamfords Ltd
The Old Picture Palace, 133 Dale Road,
Matlock, Derbyshire DE4 3LU
www.bamfords-auctions.co.uk

DEVON

Bearnes Hampton & Littlewood
St Edmund's Court, Okehampton Street,
Exeter EX4 1DU
Tel: 01392 413100
www.bhandl.co.uk

Dreweatts
Honiton Saleroom, 205 High Street,
Honiton EX14 1LQ
Tel: 01404 42404
www.dnfa.com/honiton

S. J. Hales Auctioneers
Tracey House, Newton Road, Bovey
Tracey, Newton Abbot TQ13 9AZ
Tel: 01626 836 684
www.sjhales.com

The Plymouth Auction Rooms,
Faraday Mill Trade Park,
Cattedown, Plymouth,
Devon PL4 0SF
Tel: 01752 254 740
www.plymouthauctions.co.uk

DORSET

Charterhouse
The Long Street Salerooms,
Sherborne DT9 3BS
Tel: 01935 812277
www.charterhouse-auctions.co.uk

Cottees Auctions Ltd.
The Market, East Street, Wareham BH20 4NR
Tel: 01929 552826
www.auctionsatcottees.co.uk

Dalkeith Auctions
Dalkeith Hall, Dalkeith Steps, 81 Old Christchurch Rd, Bournemouth BH1 1EW
Tel: 01202 292905
www.dalkeith-auctions.co.uk

Hy. Duke & Son
The Dorchester Fine Art Saleroom,
Weymouth Avenue,Dorchester DT1 1QS
Tel: 01305 265080
www.dukes-auctions.com

Onslows
The Coach House, Manor Road,
Stourpaine DT11 8TQ
Tel: 01258 488 838
www.onslows.co.uk

Riddetts of Bournemouth
177 Holdenhurst Road, Bournemouth BH8 8DG
Tel: 01202 555686

DURHAM

Vectis Auctions Limited
Fleck Way, Thornaby, Stockton on Tees TS17 9JZ
Tel: 01642 750 616
www.vectis.co.uk

ESSEX

Mullucks Wells Inc.
The Old Town Hall, Great Dunmow CM6 1AU
Tel: 01371 873014
www.mullucks.co.uk

Sworders
14 Cambridge Road,
Stansted Mountfitchet CM24 8BZ
Tel: 01279 817778
www.sworder.co.uk

GLOUCESTERSHIRE

Clevedon Salerooms
The Auction Centre, Kenn Road, Kenn,
Clevedon, Bristol BS21 6TT
Tel: 01934 830111
www.clevedon-salerooms.com

The Cotswold Auction Co. Ltd.
4-6 Clarence St, Gloucester GL1 1DX
Tel: 01452 521177
Chapel Walk Saleroom,
Cheltenham GL50 3DS
Tel: 01242 256363
The Coach House, Swan Yard,
9-13 West Market Place,
Cirencester, GL7 2NH
Tel: 01285 642420
www.cotswoldauction.co.uk

Dreweatts
St. John's Place, Apsley Road, Clifton
Bristol BS8 2ST
Tel: 0117 973 7201
www.dnfa.com/bristol

Mallams Fine Art Auctioneers
26 Grosvenor Street, Cheltenham
GL52 2SG
Tel: 01242 235712
www.mallams.co.uk

Moore, Allen & Innocent
33 Castle St, Cirencester,
Gloucestershire GL7 1QD
Tel: 01285 646050
www.mooreallen.com/cat

Tayler & Fletcher
London House, High Street, Bourton-on-
the-Water, Cheltenham GL54 2AP
Tel: 01451 821666
www.taylerfletcher.com

Dominic Winter Book Auctions
Mallard House, Broadway Lane,
South Cerney GL7 5UQ
Tel: 01285 860006
www.dominicwinter.co.uk

Wotton Auction Rooms Ltd
Tabernacle Road,
Wotton-under-Edge GL12 7EB
Tel: 01453 844733
www.wottonauctionrooms.co.uk

HAMPSHIRE
Andrew Smith & Son
Manor Farm, Itchen Stoke SO24 0QT
Tel: 01962 735988
www.andrewsmithandson.com

George Kidner Auctioneers
The Lymington Saleroom, Emsworth
Road, Lymington SO41 9BL
Tel: 01590 670070
www.georgekidner.co.uk

Jacobs & Hunt Auctioneers
Lavant Street, Petersfield GU32 3EF
Tel: 01730 233933
www.jacobsandhunt.com

D.M. Nesbit & Co.
Southsea Salerooms, 7 Clarendon Road,
Southsea PO5 2ED
Tel: 02392 295568
www.nesbits.co.uk

HEREFORDSHIRE
Brightwells
The Fine Art Saleroom,
Easters Court, Leominster HR6 0DE
Tel: 01568 611122
www.brightwells.com

Morris Bricknell
Stroud House, 30 Gloucester Road,
Ross-on-Wye HR9 5LE
Tel: 01989 768320
www.morrisbricknell.com

Nigel Ward & Co.
The Border Property Centre, Pontrilas
HR2 0EH
Tel: 01981 240140
www.nigel-ward.co.uk

HERTFORDSHIRE
Sworders
42 St Andrew St, Hertford SG14 1JA
Tel: 01992 583508
www.sworder.co.uk

Tring Market Auctions
Brook Street, Tring HP23 5EF
Tel: 01442 826446
www.tringmarketauctions.co.uk

ISLE OF WIGHT
Shanklin Auction Rooms
79 Regent St, Shanklin PO37 7AP
Tel: 01983 863441
www.shanklinauctionrooms.co.uk

KENT
Bentley's Fine Art Auctioneers
The Old Granary, Waterloo Road,
Cranbrook TN17 3JQ
Tel: 01580 715857
www.bentleysfineartauctioneers.co.uk

Canterbury Auction Galleries
40 Station Rd, Canterbury CT2 8AN
Tel: 01227 763337
www.thecanterburyauctiongalleries.com

Dreweatts
10 Mount Ephraim, Tunbridge Wells,
TN4 8AS
Tel: 01892 544500
www.dnfa.com/tunbridgewells

Gorringes
85 Mount Pleasant Road, Tunbridge
Wells TN1 1PX
Tel: 01892 619670
www.gorringes.co.uk

Ibbett Mosely
125 High Street, Sevenoaks TN13 1UT
Tel: 01732 456731
www.ibbettmosely.co.uk

Lambert & Foster Auction
77 Commercial Road,
Paddock Wood, TN12 6DR
Tel: 01892 832325
www.lambertandfoster.co.uk

Mervyn Carey
Twysden Cottage, Benenden, Cranbrook
TN17 4LD
Tel: 01580 240283

LANCASHIRE
Capes Dunn & Co. Fine Art
The Auction Galleries, 38 Charles Street,
Manchester M1 7DB
Tel: 0161 273 1911

Smythes Fine Art
174 Victoria Road West, Cleveleys FY5
3NE
Tel: 01253 852184
www.smythes.net

LEICESTERSHIRE
Gilding's Auctioneers & Valuers
64 Roman Way, Market Harborough
LE16 7PQ
Tel: 01858 410414
www.gildings.co.uk

Tennants Auctioneers
Millhouse, South Street, Oakham,
Rutland LE15 6BG
Tel: 01572 724666
www.tennants.co.uk

LINCOLNSHIRE
Eleys Auctioneers
Old Wharf Road, Grantham, Lincolnshire
NG31 7AA
Tel: 01476 575202
www.eleys-auctions.co.uk

Marilyn Swain
Northend Farm, Long Street, Foston,
Grantham NG32 2LD
Tel: 01400 283377
www.marilynswainauctions.co.uk

MERSEYSIDE
Cato Crane & Co.
6 Stanhope St, Liverpool L8 5RF
Tel: 01517 095559
www.cato-crane.co.uk

NORFOLK
Garry M. Emms & Co. Ltd.
Beevor Road, Great Yarmouth NR30
3QQ
Tel: 01493 332668
www.greatyarmouthauctions.com

T.W. Gaze & Son
Roydon Road, Diss IP22 4LN
Tel: 01379 650306
www.twgaze.com

Holt's Auctioneers
Church Farm Barns, Walferton PE31
6HA
Tel: 01485 542822
www.holtandcompany.co.uk

Keys Auctioneers & Valuers
Aylsham Salerooms, Palmers Lane,
Aylsham, NR11 6JA
Tel: 01263 733195
www.keysauctions.co.uk

NOTTINGHAMSHIRE
Mellors & Kirk
Gregory Street, Nottingham,
Nottinghamshire NG7 2NL
Tel: 0115 979 0000
www.mellorsandkirk.com

Dreweatts
192 Mansfield Road,
Nottingham NG1 3HU
Tel: 0115 962 4141
www.dnfa.com/nottingham

John Pye & Sons
James Shipstone House,
Radford Rd, Nottingham NG7 7EA
Tel: 0870 910 9000
www.johnpye.co.uk

T Vennett-Smith Auctioneers
11 Nottingham Rd, Gotham NG11 0HE
Tel: 0115 9830541
www.vennett-smith.com

OXFORDSHIRE
Holloway's
49 Parsons Street, Banbury OX16 5NB
Tel: 01295 817777
www.hollowaysauctioneers.co.uk

Jones & Jacob Ltd.
Watcombe Manor Saleroom
Ingham Lane, Watlington OX49 5EJ
Tel 01491 612810
www.jonesandjacob.com

Mallams Fine Art Auctioneers
Bocardo House, 24a St. Michael's St,
Oxford OX1 2EB
Tel: 01865 241358
www.mallams.co.uk

SHROPSHIRE
Brettells Antiques & Fine Art
58 High Street, Newport TF10 7AQ
Tel: 01952 815925
www.brettells.com

Halls Fine Art
Welsh Bridge, Shrewsbury SY3 8LA
Tel: 01743 284777
www.hallsgb.com

Walker Barnett & Hill
Cosford Auction Rooms, Long Lane,
Cosford TF11 8PJ
Tel: 01902 375555

SOMERSET
Greenslade Taylor Hunt
The Priory Saleroom, Winchester St,
Taunton TA1 1QE
Tel: 01823 332525
www.gth.net

Lawrence's Fine Art Auctioneers
The Linen Yard, South Street, Crewkerne
TA18 8AB
Tel: 01460 73041
www.lawrences.co.uk

Dreweatts
St Johns Place, Apsley Rd, Clifton BS8 2ST
Tel: 01179 737201
www.dnfa.com/bristol

STAFFORDSHIRE
Louis Taylor Auctioneers
10 Town Road, Hanley ST1 2QG
Tel: 01782 214111
www.louistaylorfineart.co.uk

Potteries Specialist Auctions
271 Waterloo Road, Cobridge ST6 3HR
Tel: 01782 286622
www.potteriesauctions.com

Richard Winterton Auctioneers
Main Midland Saleroom, Hawkins Lane,
Burton-on-Trent DE14 1PT
Tel: 01283 511224
www.richardwinterton.co.uk

Wintertons
Uttoxeter Auction Centre, Short St,
Uttoxeter ST14 7LH
Tel: 01889 564385
www.wintertons.co.uk

SUFFOLK
Lacy Scott and Knight Fine Art
10 Risbygate Street, Bury St. Edmunds
IP33 3AA
Tel: 01284 748600
www.lsk.co.uk

Neal Sons & Fletcher
26 Church Street, Woodbridge IP12
1DP
Tel: 01394 382263
www.nsf.co.uk

Sworders
The Saleroom, Burkitts Lane, Sudbury
CO10 1HB
Tel: 01787 880305
www.sworder.co.uk

SURREY
Clarke Gammon Wellers
4 Quarry St, Guildford, Surrey GU1 3TY
Tel: 01483 880900
www.clarkegammon.co.uk

Crows Auction Gallery
Reigate Road, Dorking RH4 1SG
Tel: 01306 740382
www.crowsauctions.co.uk

Ewbank Auctioneers
Burnt Common Auction Rooms, London Rd, Send, Woking GU23 7LN
Tel: 01483 223101
www.ewbankauctions.co.uk

Dreweatts
Baverstock House, 93 High Street, Godalming GU7 1AL
Tel: 01483 423 567
www.dnfa.com/godalming

John Nicholson
Longfield, Midhurst Road, Haslemere GU27 3HA
Tel: 01428 653727
www.johnnicholsons.com

Lawrences' Auctioneers Ltd.
Norfolk House, 80 High Street, Bletchingley RH1 4PA
Tel: 01883 743323
www.lawrencesbletchingley.co.uk

P.F. Windibank Auctioneers
Dorking Halls, Reigate Road, Dorking RH4 1SG
Tel: 01306 884556/876280
www.windibank.co.uk

EAST SUSSEX
Burstow & Hewett
Lower Lake, Battle, East Sussex TN33 0AT
Tel: 01424 772374
www.burstowandhewett.co.uk

Dreweatts
46-50 South Street, Eastbourne BN21 4XB
Tel: 01323 410419
www.dnfa.com/eastbourne

Eastbourne Auction Rooms
Auction House, Finmere Road, Eastbourne BN22 8QL
Tel: 01323 431444
www.eastbourneauction.com

Gorringes Auction Galleries
Terminus Road, Bexhill-on-Sea TN39 3LR
Tel: 01424 212994
15 North Street, Lewes BN7 2PD
Tel: 01273 472503
www.gorringes.co.uk

Raymond P. Inman
The Auction Galleries, 98A Coleridge Street, Hove BN3 5 AA
Tel: 01273 774777
www.invaluable.com/raymondinman

Rye Auction Galleries
Rock Channel, Rye TN31 7HL
Tel: 01797 222124
www.ryeauctiongalleries.co.uk

Wallis & Wallis
West Street Auction Galleries, Lewes BN7 2NJ
Tel: 01273 480208
www.wallisandwallis.co.uk

WEST SUSSEX
Henry Adams Fine Art
Baffins Hall, Baffins Lane, Chichester PO19 1UA
Tel: 01243 532223
www.henryadamsfineart.co.uk

John Bellman Ltd.
New Pound, Wisborough Green, Billinghurst RH14 0AZ
Tel: 01403 700858
www.bellmans.co.uk

Sotheby's Sussex
Summers Place, Billinghurst RH14 9AD
Tel: 01403 833500
www.sothebys.com

Toovey's
Spring Gdns, Washington RH20 3BS
Tel: 01903 891955
www.tooveys.com

TYNE AND WEAR
Anderson & Garland
Anderson House, Crispin Court, Newbiggin Lane, Westerhope, Newcastle upon Tyne NE5 1BF
Tel: 0191 430 3000
www.andersonandgarland.com

WARWICKSHIRE
Bigwood Auctioneers Ltd
The Old School, Tiddington CV37 7AW
Tel: 01789 269415
www.bigwoodauctioneers.co.uk

Locke & England
18 Guy Street, Leamington Spa CV32 4RT
Tel: 01926 889100
www.leauction.co.uk

WEST MIDLANDS
Biddle & Webb
Ladywood, Middleway, Birmingham B16 0PP
Tel: 0121 455 8042
www.biddleandwebb.co.uk

Bonhams
101 New Bond St, London W1S 1SR
Tel: 0207 447 7447
www.bonhams.com

Fellows & Sons
Augusta House, 19 Augusta Street, Hockley, Birmingham B18 6JA
Tel: 0121 212 2131
www.fellows.co.uk

WILTSHIRE
Henry Aldridge & Son
Unit 1 Bath Road Business Centre Bath Road, Devizes SN10 1XA
Tel: 01380 729199
www.henry-aldridge.co.uk

Woolley & Wallis
51-61 Castle Street, Salisbury SP1 3SU
Tel: 01722 424500
www.woolleyandwallis.co.uk

WORCESTERSHIRE
Andrew Grant Auctioneers
5 New Road, Bromsgrove, B60 2HX
Tel: 01527 579977
www.andrew-grant.co.uk

Philip Serrell Auctioneers
Barnards Green Road, Malvern WR14 3LW
Tel: 01684 892314
www.serrell.com

EAST YORKSHIRE
Dee Atkinson & Harrison
The Exchange Saleroom, Driffield YO25 7LJ
Tel: 01377 253151
www.dee-atkinson-harrison.co.uk

NORTH YORKSHIRE
Boulton & Cooper
St Michael's House, Market Place, Malton YO17 7LR
Tel: 01653 696151
www.boultoncooper.co.uk

David Duggleby Fine Art
The Vine Street Salerooms, Scarborough YO11 1XN
Tel: 01723 507111
www.davidduggleby.com

Malcolm's No. 1 Auctioneers
Tel: 01977 684 971
www.malcolmsno1auctions.co.uk

Morphets of Harrogate
6 Albert Street, Harrogate HG1 1JL
Tel: 01423 530030
www.morphets.co.uk

Tennants
The Auction Centre, Leyburn DL8 5SG
Tel: 01969 623780
www.tennants.co.uk

SOUTH YORKSHIRE
BBR Auctions
Elsecar Heritage Centre, Barnsley S74 8HJ
Tel: 01226 745156
www.onlinebbr.com

ELR Auctions Ltd.
The Sheffield Saleroom, The Nichols Building, Shalesmoor, Sheffield S3 8UJ
Tel: 0114 281 6161
www.elrauctions.com

WEST YORKSHIRE
Andrew Hartley Fine Arts
Victoria Hall Salerooms, Little Lane, Ilkley LS29 8EA
Tel: 01943 816363
www.andrewhartleyfinearts.co.uk

John Walsh & Co. Auctioneers
55 Jenkin Road, Horbury, Wakefield, West Yorkshire WF4 6DP
Tel: 01924 271710
www.john-walsh.co.uk

SCOTLAND
Auction Rooms Ltd.
Castle Laurie, Bankside, Falkirk, Sterlingshire FK2 7XF
Tel: 01324 623000
www.auctionroomsfalkirk.co.uk

Bonhams
22 Queen St, Edinburgh EH2 2JL
Tel: 0131 225 2266
www.bonhams.com

Loves Auction Rooms
Arran House, Arran Road, Perth PH1 3DZ
Tel: 01738 633337

Lyon & Turnbull Ltd.
33 Broughton Place,
Edinburgh EH1 3RR
Tel: 0131 557 8844

182 Bath St, Glasgow G2 4HG
Tel: 0141 333 1992
www.lyonandturnbull.com

D.J. Manning Auctioneers
Bridgeness Road, Bo'ness, West Lothian EH51 9SF
Tel: 01506 827693
www.djmanning.co.uk

McTear's
Meiklewood Gate, 31 Meiklewood Road, Glasgow G51 4EU
Tel: 0141 810 2886
www.mctears.co.uk

Sotheby's
7 Howe Street, Edinburgh EH3 6TE
Tel: 0131 558 7799
www.sothebys.com

Thomson, Roddick & Medcalf
Carnethie St, Rosewell, Edinburgh EH24 9AL
Tel: 0131 440 2448
Irongray Road, Dumfries DG2 0JE
Tel: 01387 721635
www.thomsonroddick.com

WALES
Anthemion Auctions
15 Norwich Road, Cardiff CF23 9AB
Tel: 029 2047 2444
www.anthemionauctions.com

Bonhams
9-10 Park Place, Cardiff, CF10 3DP
Tel: 02920 727980
13 Spilman Street, Carmarthen SA31 1JY
Tel: 01267 238231
www.bonhams.com

Morgan Evans
28-30 Church Street, Llangefni, Isle of Anglesey LL77 7DU
Tel: 01248 723303/421582
www.morganevans.com

Peter Francis
Towyside Salerooms, Old Station Road, Carmarthen, SA31 1JN
Tel: 01267 233456
www.peterfrancis.co.uk

Welsh Country Auctions
2 Carmarthen Road, Cross Hands, Llanelli, Carmarthenshire SA14 6SP
Tel: 01269 844428
www.welshcountryauctions.co.uk

Wingetts Auction Gallery
29 Holt Street, Wrexham, Clwyd LL13 8DH
Tel: 01978 353553
www.wingetts.co.uk

AUSTRALIA
Bonhams & Goodman
7 Anderson Street, Double Bay, 2028
Tel: 0061 2 9327 9900
www.bonhamsandgoodman.com.au

Deutscher-Menzies
12 Todman Avenue, Kensington, 2033
Tel: 0061 2 8344 5454
www.deutschermenzies.com

Lawsons
1A The Crescent, Annadale 2038
Tel: 02 9566 2377
www.lawsons.com.au

Menzies
12 Todman Avenue, Kensington 2033
Tel: 02 8344 5404
www.menziesartbrands.com

Shapiro
162 Queen Street, Woollahra, New South Wales 2025
Tel: 0061 2 9326 1588
www.shapiroauctioneers.com.au

NEW ZEALAND
Webb's
18 Manukau Road, PO Box 99 251, Newmarket, Auckland 1000
Tel: 0064 9 524 6804
www.webbs.co.nz

Specialists who would like to be listed in the next edition, or have a new address or telephone number, should contact us at info@millers.uk.com. Readers should contact dealers before visiting to avoid a wasted journey.

ANTIQUITIES
Ancient Art
85 The Vale, London N14 6AT
Tel: 020 8882 1509
www.ancientart.co.uk

Finch & Co.
Suite No 744, 2 Old Brompton Rd,
London SW7 3DQ
Tel: 020 7413 9937
www.finch-and-co.co.uk

John A. Pearson
Horton Lodge, Horton Rd, Horton, Near
Slough, Berkshire SL3 9NU
Tel: 01753 682136

Rupert Wace Ancient Art Ltd.
14 Old Bond St, London W1S 4PP
Tel: 020 7495 1623
www.rupertwace.co.uk

Ancient & Gothic
PO Box 5390, Bournemouth, BH7 6XR
Tel: 01202 431721

ARCHITECTURAL
Joanna Booth
P.O. Box 50886, London SW3 5YH
Tel: 020 7352 8998
www.joannabooth.co.uk

Drummonds
The Kirkpatrick Buildings, 25 London
Road, Hindhead, Surrey GU26 6AB
Tel: 01428 609444
www.drummonds-arch.co.uk

LASSCO
30 Wandsworth Rd, London SW8 2LG
Tel: 0207 394 2100
www.lassco.co.uk

Sweerts de Landas
Dunsborough Park, Ripley, Surrey GU23
6AL
Tel: 01483 225366
www.sweerts.com

Robert Mills Ltd.
Narroways Rd, Eastville, Bristol BS2 9XB
Tel: 0117 955 6542
www.rmills.co.uk

ARMS & MILITARIA
Q&C Militaria
22 Suffolk Road, Cheltenham, GL50
2AQ
Tel: 01242 519815
www.qcmilitaria.com

Garth Vincent
The Old Manner House, Allington,
Nr Grantham, NG32 2DH
Tel: 01400 281358
www.guns.uk.com

West Street Antiques
63 West Street, Dorking, RH4 1BS
Tel: 01306 883487
www.antiquearmsandarmour.com

BAROGRAPHS
Richard Twort
Tel: 01934 612439
walls@mirage-interiors.com

CARPETS & RUGS
Gallery Yacou
127 Fulham Rd, London SW3 6RT
Tel: 020 7584 2929
www.galleryyacou.com

Gideon Hatch
21 Lambourn Rd, London SW4 0LS Tel:
0207 720 7543
www.gideonhatch.co.uk

John Eskenazi Ltd.
P.O. Box 55621, London W9 2XA
Tel: 020 7409 3001
www.john-eskenazi.com

Karel Weijand
Lion & Lamb Courtyard, Farnham,
Surrey GU9 7LL
Tel: 01252 726215
www.karelweijand.com

Lindfield Galleries
62 High Street, Lindfield, West Sussex
RH16 2HL
Tel: 01444 483817
david@orientalandantiquerugs.com

Wadsworth's
Marehill, Pulborough, West Sussex RH20
2DY
Tel: 01798 873 555
www.wadsworthsrugs.com

BOOKS
Biblion
1/7 Davies Mews, London W1K 5AB
Tel: 020 7629 1374
www.biblionmayfair.co.uk

Barter Books
Alnwick Station, Alnwick NE66 2NP
Tel: 01665 604888
www.barterbooks.co.uk

George Bayntun
Manvers Street, Bath BA1 1JW
Tel: 01225 466000
www.georgebayntun.com

David Aldous-Cook
PO Box 413, Sutton SM3 8SZ
Tel: 020 8642 4842
www.ukbookworld.com/members/aldousco
ok

BOXES
Alan & Kathy Stacey
www.antiqueboxes.uk.com

Mostly Boxes
93 High Street, Eton,
Windsor, Berkshire SL4 6AF
Tel: 01753 858 470

CERAMICS
Albert Amor Ltd.
7 Bury Street, London SW1Y 6AU
Tel: 020 7930 2444
www.albertamor.co.uk

Andrew Dando
34 Market Street, Bradford-on-Avon,
Wiltshire BA15 1LL
Tel: 01225 865444
www.andrewdando.co.uk

Brian & Angela Downes
PO Box 431, Chippenham,
Wiltshire SN14 6SZ
Tel/Fax: 01454 238134

Clive & Lynne Jackson
Cheltenham, Gloucestershire
Open by appointment only
Tel: 01242 254 3751

Davies Antiques
c/o Cadogan Tate, Unit 6, 6-12 Ponton
Road, London SW8 5BA
Tel: 020 8947 1902
www.antique-meissen.com

E & H Manners
66A Kensington Church Street, London
W8 4BY
Tel: 020 7229 5516
www.europeanporcelain.com

Garry Atkins
P.O. Box 50415, London W8 7XY
Tel: 020 7727 8737
www.englishpottery.com

Hope & Glory
131A Kensington Church Street,
London W8 7LP
Tel: 020 7727 8424

John Howard at Heritage
6 Market Place, Woodstock, Oxon OX20
1TA
Tel: 01993 812580
www.antiquepottery.co.uk

Jonathan Horne Antiques Ltd.
22 Brook's Mews, London W1K 4DY
Tel: 020 7409 1799
www.jonathanhorne.co.uk

**Mary Wise and Grosvenor
Antiques**
58 Kensington Church Street, London
W8 4DB
Tel: 020 7937 8649
www.wiseantiques.com

Roderick Jellicoe
PO. Box No. 50732 London NW6 6XW
Tel: 020 7624 6471
www.englishporcelain.com

Rogers de Rin
76 Royal Hospital Road, Paradise Walk,
Chelsea,London SW3 4HN
Tel: 020 7352 9007
www.rogersderin.co.uk

Roy W. Bunn Antiques
Tel: 01282 813703
www.roywbunnantiques.co.uk

Steppes Hill Farm Antiques
Steppes Hill Farm, Stockbury,
Sittingbourne, Kent ME9 7RB
Tel: 01795 842205
www.steppeshillfarm.com

Stockspring Antiques
114 Kensington Church Street, London
W8 4BH
Tel: 020 7727 7995
www.antique-porcelain.co.uk

T.C.S. Brooke
The Grange, 57 Norwich Road,
Wroxham, Norfolk NR12 8RX
Tel: 01603 782644

Valerie Main
PO Box 92, Carlisle, Cumbria CA5 7GD
Tel: 01228 711342
www.valeriemain.co.uk

W.W. Warner Antiques
The Green, High Street,
Brasted, Kent TN16 1JL
Tel: 01959 563698

Yvonne Adams Antiques
The Coffee House, 3 & 4 Church St,
Stow on the Wold, Glos. GL54 1BB
Tel: 01451 832 015
www.antiquemeissen.co.uk

Julian Eade
Tel: 07973 542971
julian.eade@cbre.com

Barling Porcelain
Tel: 01621 890058

Tony Horsley
PO Box 3127, Brighton BN1 5SS
Tel: 01273 550770
www.tonyhorsley.co.uk

Greystoke Antiques
4 Swan Yard, Sherborne DT9 3AX
Tel: 01935 812833

Winson Antiques
Unit 11, Langston Priory Workshops,
Kingham OX7 6UP
Tel: 01608 658856 / 07764 476776
www.clivepayne.co.uk

Judi Bland Antiques
Tel: 01276 857576

CLOCKS, WATCHES & BAROMETERS
P.A. Oxley
The Old Rectory, Cherhill, Calne,
SN11 8UX
Tel: 01249 816227
www.britishantiqueclocks.com

Coppelia Antiques
Holford Lodge, Plumley, Moor Rd,
Nr Knutsford, Plumley, WA16 9RS
Tel: 01565 722197
www.coppeliaantiques.co.uk

The Grandfather Clock Shop
Sheep St, Stow-on-the-Wold, GL54 1JS
Tel: 01451 830455
www.stylesofstow.co.uk

Woodward Antique Clocks
21 Suffolk Parade,
Cheltenham GL50 2AE
Tel: 01242 245667
www.woodwardclocks.co.uk

Northern Clocks
Boothsbank Farm, Worsley,
Manchester M28 1LL
Tel: 0161 790 8414
www.northernclocks.co.uk

The Clock-Work-Shop
6A Parchment Street
Winchester S023 8AT
Tel: 01962 842331
ww.clock-work-shop.co.uk

The Clock Clinic Ltd.
85 Lower Richmond Road,
Putney, SW15 1EU
Tel: 020 8788 1407
www.clockclinic.co.uk

Roderick Antique Clocks
23 Vicarage Gate, London W8 4AA
Tel: 020 79378517
www.roderickantiqueclocks.com

Allan Smith Clocks
Amity Cottage, 162 Beechcroft Rd,
Upper Stratton, Swindon SN2 7QE
Tel: 01793 822977
www.allansmithantiqueclocks.co.uk

Brian Loomes
Calf Haugh Farm, Pateley Bridge,
Yorkshire HG3 5HW
Tel: 01423 711163
www.brianloomes.com

Alan Walker
Halfway Manor, Halfway, Nr. Newbury,
Berkshire RG20 8NR
Tel: 01488 657670
www.alanwalker-barometers.com

Baskerville Antiques
Saddlers House, Saddlers Row,
Petworth, West Sussex GU28 0AN
Tel: 01798 342067
brianbaskerville@aol.com

Derek and Tina Rayment
Orchard House, Barton Rd, Barton,
Nr. Farndon, Cheshire SY14 7HT
Tel: 01829 270429
www.antique-barometers.com

Derek Roberts
25 Shipbourne Road,
Tonbridge, Kent TN10 3DN
Tel: 01732 358986
www.qualityantiqueclocks.com

Pendulum of Mayfair
51 Maddox St, London W1S 2PJ
Tel: 020 7629 6606
www.pendulumofmayfair.co.uk

Raffety & Walwyn Ltd.
79 Kensington Church Street,
London W8 4BG
Tel: 020 7938 1100
www.raffetyantiqueclocks.com

Somlo Antiques
35-36 Burlington Arcade, London
N1J 0QB
Tel: 020 7499 6526   www.somlo.com

Styles of Stow
The Grandfather Clock Shop,
Sheep Street, Stow-on-the-Wold,
Gloucestershire GL54 1JS
Tel: 01451 830455
www.stylesofstow.co.uk

The Watch Gallery
129 Fulham Rd, London SW3 6RT
Tel: 020 7581 3239
www.thewatchgallery.co.uk

Anthony Woodburn Ltd.
PO Box 2669, Lewes,
East Sussex BN7 3JE
Tel: 01273 486666
www.anthonywoodburn.com

Horological Workshops
204 Worplesdon Road, Guildford,
Surrey GU2 6UY
Tel: 01483 576496
www.horologicalworkshops.com

COSTUME JEWELLERY & ACCESSORIES
Cristobal
26 Church St, London NW8 8EP
Tel: 020 7724 7230
www.cristobal.co.uk

Linda Bee
Grays Antique Dealers, 58 Davies St &
1-7 Davies Mews, London W1K 5AB
Tel: 020 7493 9344
www.graysantiques.com

Lynn & Brian Holmes
By appointment
Tel: 020 7368 6412

Richard Gibbon
neljeweluk@aol.com

William Wain at Antiquarius
Stand J6, Antiquarius, 135 Kings Road,
Chelsea, London SW3 4PW
Tel: 020 7351 4905
williamwain@btopenworld.com

DECORATIVE ARTS
Adrian Sassoon
14 Rutland Gate, London SW7 1BB
Tel: 020 7581 9888
www.adriansassoon.com

Aesthetics
Stand V2, Antiquarius, 131-141 Kings
Road, London SW3 4PW
Tel: 020 7352 0395

Arenski Fine Arts Ltd.
The Coach House, Ledbury Mews North,
London W11 2AF
Tel: 020 8202 3075
www.arenski.com

Art Deco Etc.
73 Upper Gloucester Road, Brighton,
Sussex BN1 3LQ
Tel: 01273 202 937
decojohn@hotmail.com

Art Nouveau Originals c.1900
The Bindery Gallery, 69 High St,
Broadway, Worcestershire WR12 7DP
Tel: 01386 854645

Beth
Stand G043/46, Alfies Antiques Market,
13-25 Church St, London NW8 8DT
Mob: 07776 136 003

Beverley
Stand G028-30, Alfies Antiques
Market, 13-25 Church St,
London NW8 8DT
Tel: 07776 136 003

Circa 1900
6 Camden Passage, London N1 8ED
Mob: 0771 370 9211
www.circa1900.org

Fay Lucas Art Metal
Christie's Fine Art Security,
42 Ponton Rd, London SW8 5RA
Tel: 020 7371 4404
www.faylucas.com

**Gallery 1930/Susie Cooper
Ceramics**
18 Church St, London NW8 8EP
Tel: 020 7723 1555
www.susiecooperceramics.com

Halcyon Days Ltd.
14 Brook St, London W1S 1BD
Tel: 020 7629 8811
www.halcyondays.co.uk

Hall-Bakker at Heritage
6 Market Place, Woodstock, Oxon OX20
1TA
Tel: 01993 811 332
www.hallbakker.co.uk

Mike Weedon
7 Camden Passage, Islington,
London N1 8EA
Tel: 020 7226 5319
www.mikeweedonantiques.com

Richard Gardner Antiques
Swan House, Market Square,
Petworth, West Sussex GU28 0AH
Tel: 01798 343 411
www.richardgardnerantiques.co.uk

Robert Bowman Ltd.
34 Duke Street, St James's,
London SW1Y 6DF
Tel: 020 7930 8003
www.robertbowman.com

Rumours
4 The Mall Antiques Arcade,
359 Upper St, London N1 0PD
Tel: 020 7704 6549

Spencer Swaffer Antiques
30 High Street, Arundel, West Sussex
BN18 9AB
Tel: 01903 882132
www.spencerswaffer.co.uk

Style Gallery
10 Camden Passage, London N1 8ED
Tel: 020 7359 7867
www.styleantiques.co.uk

Tadema Gallery
10 Charlton Place, Camden Passage,
London N1 8AJ
Tel: 020 7359 1055
www.tademagallery.com

The Country Seat
Huntercombe Manor Barn, Nr. Henley
on Thames, Oxon RG9 5RY
Tel: 01491 641349
www.thecountryseat.com

The Design Gallery
5 The Green, Westerham,
Kent TN16 1AS
Tel: 01959 561234
www.designgallery.co.uk

The Red House
Duncombe Place, York, North Yorkshire
YO1 7ED
Tel: 01904 637 000
www.redhouseyork.co.uk

Titus Omega
Tel: 020 7688 1295
www.titusomega.com

Van Den Bosch
123 Grays, 58 Davies St,
London W1K 5LP
Tel: 020 7629 1900
www.vandenbosch.co.uk

Clarion Antiques & Fine Art
Ground Floor, 2 St Georges Sq,
Lytham St Anns, FY8 2NY
Tel: 01253 721903

Crafts Noveau
112 Alexandra Park Road,
Muswell Hill, N10 2AE
Tel: 0208 444 3300
www.craftsnoveau.co.uk

Mitofsky Antiques
8 Rathfarnham Road,
Terenure, Dublin 6
Tel: +353 1 4920033
www.mitofskyantiques.com

Garret & Hurst Sculpture
PO Box 658,
East Grinstead, RH19 3GH
Tel: 01342 311729
www.garretandhurst.co.uk

DOLLS AND TOYS
Bébés et Jouets
Tel: 0131 332 5650
bebesetjouets@tiscali.co.uk

Collectors Old Toy Shop & Antiques
89 Northgate, Halifax,
West Yorkshire HX1 1XF
Tel: 01422 360434
www.collectorsoldtoyshop.com

Sue Pearson
147 High St, Lewes, East Sussex
BN7 1XT
Tel: 01273 442677
www.suepearson.co.uk

Victoriana Dolls
101 Portobello Road,
London W11 2BQ
Tel: 01737 249 525
heather.bond@homecall.co.uk

Teddy Bears of Whitney
99 High St, Witney, OX28 6HY
Tel: 01993 706616
www.teddybears.co.uk

FISHING
The Old Tackle Box
PO Box 55, High Street,
Cranbrook, TN17 3ZU
Tel: 01580 713979
www.oldtacklebox.com

FURNITURE
Alistair Sampson Antiques
120 Mount St, London W1K 3NN
Tel: 020 7409 1799
www.alistairsampson.com

Anthemion
Cartmel, Grange-over-Sands, Cumbria
LA11 6QB
Tel: 015395 36295
www.anthemionantiques.co.uk

The Antiques Warehouse
25 Lightwood Road, Buxton,
Derbyshire SK17 7BJ
Tel: 01298 72967

Antony Preston Antiques Ltd.
The Square, Stow-on-the-Wold,
Cheltenam, Glos GL54 1AB
Tel: 01451 831586
www.antonypreston.com

Avon Antiques
25-27 Market Street, Bradford-on-Avon,
Wilts BA15 1LL
Tel: 01225 862052
www.avon-antiques.co.uk

Baggott Church Street Ltd.
Church Street, Stow-on-the-Wold,
Gloucestershire GL54 1BB
Tel: 01451 831392
www.baggottantiques.com

Blanchard Ltd.
86/88 Pimlico Road, London SW1W 8PL
Tel: 020 7823 6310
piers@jwblanchard.com

Charles Lumb & Sons Ltd.
1 Montpellier Gardens, Harrogate,
North Yorkshire HG1 2TF
Tel: 01423 504118
www.harrogateantiques.com

Cheverons Antiques Ltd
Unit 8, New Place, Blackboys Road,
Framfield, East Sussex TN22 5EQ
Tel: 01825 891 223
www.chevertons.com

Christopher Buck Antiques
56-60 Sandgate High St, Sandgate,
Folkestone, Kent CT20 3AP
Tel: 01303 221229
chrisbuck@throwley.freeserve.co.uk

Country Antiques (Wales) Ltd.
Castle Mill, Kidwelly Carmarthenshire,
SA17 5AJ
Tel: 01554 890534
www.welshantiques.com

David Love
10 Royal Parade, Harrogate,
North Yorkshire HG1 2SZ
Tel: 01423 565797
david.love@btconnect.com

Denzil Grant
Green Farm Gallery, Thurston, Bury St
Edmunds, Suffolk IP31 35N
Tel: 01359 230888
www.denzilgrant.com

Elaine Phillips Antiques Ltd.
1 & 2 Royal Parade, Harrogate,
North Yorkshire HG1 2SZ
Tel: 01423 569 745
www.elainephillipsantiques.co.uk

Freeman & Lloyd
44 Sandgate High St, Sandgate,
Folkestone, Kent CT20 3AP
Tel: 01303 248986
www.freemanandlloyd.com

Georgian Antiques
10 Pattison St, Leith Links, Edinburgh,
EH6 7HF, Scotland
Tel: 0131 553 7286

John Bly
By appointment London SW1Y 6AL
Tel: 01442 823030
Showroom:
The Swan at Tetsworth, 5 High St,
Tetsworth, Oxon OX9 7AB
www.johnbly.com

John Hobbs Ltd.
107A Pimlico Road, London SW1W 8PH
Tel: 020 7730 8369
www.johnhobbs.co.uk

Lennox Cato Antiques
1 The Square, Church Street,
Edenbridge, Kent TN8 5BD
Tel: 01732 865 988
www.lennoxcato.com

Lucy Johnson
PO Box 84, Carterton, Burford,
Oxfordshire OX18 4AT
Tel: 07071 881232
www.lucy-johnson.com

Mac Humble Antiques
7-9 Woolley Street, Bradford-on-Avon,
Wiltshire BA15 1AD
Tel: 01225 866329
www.machumbleantiques.co.uk

Michael Norman Antiques
61 Holland Road, Hove,
East Sussex BN3 1JN
Tel: 01273 326712

Oswald Simpson
Hall St, Long Malford, Suffolk
CO10 9JL
Tel: 01787 377523

Owen Humble Antiques
By appointment only
Newcastle Upon Tyne, NE2 4RP
Tel: 01912 812100

Patrick Sandberg Antiques
150-152 Kensington Church Street,
London W8 4BN
Tel: 020 7229 0373
www.antiquefurniture.net

Paul Hopwell Antiques
30 High Street, West Haddon,
Northamptonshire NN6 7AP
Tel: 01788 510636
www.antiqueoak.co.uk

Peter Bunting
Harthill Hall, Alport, Bakewell,
Derbyshire DE45 1LH
Tel: 01629 636203
www.countryoak.co.uk

Peter Foyle Hunwick
The Old Malthouse,
15 Bridge Street, Hungerford, Berkshire
RG17 0EG
Tel/Fax: 01488 682209

Phillips of Hitchin (Antiques)
The Manor House, Hitchin, Hertfordshire
SG5 1JW
Tel: 01462 432067

R G Cave & Sons Ltd.
Walcote House, 17 Broad Street,
Ludlow, Shropshire SY8 1NG
Tel: 01584 873568

R N Myers & Son Ltd.
Endsleigh House, High Street, Gargrave,
Skipton, North Yorkshire BD23 3LX
Tel: 01756 749587
rnmyersson@aol.com

Reindeer Antiques Ltd.
81 Kensington Church Street, London
W8 4BG
Tel: 020 7937 3754
43 Watling Street, Potterspury,
Northamptonshire NN12 7QD
Tel: 01908 542407
www.reindeerantiques.co.uk

Robert Young Antiques
68 Battersea Bridge Road,
London SW11 3AG
Tel: 020 7228 7847
www.robertyoungantiques.com

Roderick Butler
Marwood House, Honiton,
Devon EX14 1PY
Tel: 01404 42169

Thomas Coulborn & Sons
Vesey Manor, 64 Birmingham Road,
Sutton Coldfield B72 1QP
Tel: 0121 354 3974
www.coulborn.com

Tobias Jellinek Antiques
20 Park Road, East Twickenham,
Middlesex TW1 2PX
Tel: 020 8892 6892
toby@jellinek.com

W A Pinn & Sons
124 Swan Street, Sible Hedingham,
Essex CO9 3HP
Tel: 01787 461127

W R Harvey & Co Ltd.
86 Corn Street, Witney,
Oxfordshire OX8 7BU
Tel: 01993 706501
www.wrharvey.co.uk

Wakelin & Linfield
PO Box 48, Billingshurst,
West Sussex RH14 0YZ
Tel: 01403 700004
www.wakelin-linfield.com

Witney Antiques
96-100 Corn Street, Witney, Oxfordshire
OX28 6BU
Tel: 01993 703902
www.witneyantiques.com

Pugh's Antiques
Portley House, North Road,
Leominster, H36 0AA
Tel: 01568 616546
www.pughsantiques.com

Lorraine Spooner Antiques
211 Watling Street West,
Towcester, NN12 6BX
Tel: 01327 358777
www.lsantiques.com

Destiny Antiques, Art & Design
Perth Airport,
Scone, Perthshire, PH2 6PL
Tel: 01738 553273
www.destinyantiques.co.uk

Cross Hayes Antiques
Unit 6, Westbrook Farm, Draycot,
Chippenham, Wiltshire SN15 5LH
Tel: 01249 720033
www.crosshayes.co.uk

S.W. Antiques
Abbey Showrooms,
Newlands Road, Pershore,
WR10 1BP
Tel: 01386 555580
www.sw-antiques.co.uk

GENERAL
Alfies Antique Market
13-25 Church Street, Marylebone,
London NW8 8DT
Tel: 020 7723 6066
www.alfiesantiques.com

Antiquarius
131-141 Kings Road London SW3 4PW
Tel: 020 7823 3900
www.antiquarius.co.uk

Grays Antiques Markets
1-7 Davies Mews & 58 Davies St,
London W1K 5AB
Tel: 020 7629 7034
www.graysantiques.com

Heritage
6 Market Place, Woodstock,
Oxfordshire OX20 1TA
Tel: 01993 811332
www.atheritage.co.uk

Otford Antiques & Collectors Centre
26-28 High Street, Otford, Kent TN14
5PQ
Tel: 01959 522025
www.otfordantiques.co.uk

Pantiles Spa Antiques
4-6 Union House, The Pantiles,
Tunbridge Wells, Kent TN4 8HE
Tel: 01892 541377
www.pantiles-spa-antiques.co.uk

The Ginnel Antiques Centre
Off Parliament Street,
Harrogate, North Yorkshire HG1 2RB
Tel: 01423 508 857
www.theginnel.co.uk

The Swan at Tetsworth
5 High St, Tetsworth, Oxon
OX9 7AB

Woburn Abbey Antiques Centre
Woburn Abbey, Woburn,
Bedfordshire, MK17 9WA
www.woburn.co.uk/antiques

GLASS
Andrew Lineham Fine Glass
PO Box 465, Chichester, West Sussex
PO18 8WZ.
Tel: 01243 576 241
www.antiquecolouredglass.com

Frank Dux Antiques
33 Belvedere, Lansdown Road
Bath BA1 5HR
Tel: 01225 312367
www.antique-glass.co.uk

Christine Bridge Antiques
78 Castelnau, London SW13 9EX Tel:
0208 741 5501
www.bridge-antiques.com

Delomosne & Son Ltd.
Court Close, North Wraxall,
Chippenham, Wiltshire SN14 7AD
Tel: 01225 891505
www.delomosne.co.uk

Jeanette Hayhurst Fine Glass
32A Kensington Church St, London W8
4HA
Tel: 020 7938 1539
www.antiqueglasslondon.com

JEWELLERY
N. Bloom & Son (1912) Ltd.
Tel: 020 7629 5060
www.nbloom.com

J H Bonnar
72 Thistle Street, Edinburgh, EH2 1EN
Tel: 0131 226 2811

MODERN
Fragile Design
14-15 The Custard Factory, Digbeth,
Birmingham, West Midlands B9 4AA
Tel: 0121 224 7378
www.fragiledesign.com

Francesca Martire
1st Floor, Alfies Antique Market, 13-25
Church Street, London NW8 8DT
Tel: 020 7724 4802
www.francescamartire.com

Rennies Seaside Modern
47 The Old High St
Folkestone, Kent CT20 2RN
Tel: 01303 242427
www.rennart.co.uk

Twentieth Century Marks
Whitegates, Rectory Rd, Little Burstead,
Nr Billericay, Essex CM12 9TR
Tel: 01474 872460
www.20thcenturymarks.co.uk

MUSIC
Stephen T. P. Kember Ltd,
3 The Corn Exchange, The Pantiles,
Tunbridge Wells, Kent, TN2 5TE
Tel: 01959 574067/07850 358067
www.antique-musicboxes.co.uk

Turner Violins
1-5 Lily Grove, Beeston, NG9 1QL
Tel: 0115 943 0333
www.turnerviolins.co.uk

ORIENTAL AND ASIAN
Guest & Gray
1-7 Davies Mews, London W1K 5AB
Tel: 020 7408 1252
www.chinese-porcelain-art.com

Roger Bradbury
Church Street, Coltishall, Norwich,
Norfolk NR12 7DJ
Tel: 01603 737 444

R & G McPherson Antiques
40 Kensington Church Street,
London W8 4BX
Tel: 020 7937 0812
www.orientalceramics.com

PAPERWEIGHTS
Sweetbriar Gallery Ltd
Tel: 01805 990024
www.sweetbriar.co.uk

SCIENTIFIC INSTRUMENTS
Charles Tomlinson
Chester
Tel: 01244 318395
charlestomlinson@tiscali.co.uk

SILVER
B. Silverman
4 Campden Street, Off Kensington
Church Street, London W8 7EP
Tel: 020 7985 0555
www.silverman-london.com

Didier Antiques
58-60 Kensington Church Street,
London W8 4DB
Tel: 020 7938 2537
www.didierantiques.com

Fay Lucas Artmetal
Christies Fine Art Securities
42 Ponton Road, London SW9 5RA
Tel: 020 7371 4404
www.faylucas.com

Goodwins Antiques Ltd
15 & 16 Queensferry Street,
Edinburgh EH2 4QW
Tel: 0131 225 4717
www.goodwinsantiques.com

Mary Cooke Antiques
12 The Old Power Station, 121 Mortlake
High Street, London SW14 8SN
Tel: 020 8876 5777
www.marycooke.co.uk

Nicholas Shaw Antiques
Virginia Cottage, Lombard Street,
Petworth, West Sussex GU28 0AG
Tel: 01798 345 146
www.nicholas-shaw.com

Paul Bennett
48a George Street, London W1U 7DY
Tel: 020 7935 1555
www.paulbennettonline.com

Payne & Son (Goldsmiths) Ltd
131 High Street
Oxford, Oxfordshire OX1 4DH
Tel: 01865 243 787
www.goldandsilverjewellery.co.uk

Peter Cameron Antique Silver
PO Box LB739, London W1A 9LB
petercameron@idnet.co.uk

Peter Szuhay
302-303 Grays Antiques Market,
58 Davies Street, London W1Y 2LB
Tel: 020 7408 0154
pgszuhay@aol.com
www.peterszuhay.co.uk

Sanda Lipton
28a Devonshire Street, London W1G
6PS
Tel: 020 7431 0688
www.antique-silver.com

S & J Stodel
Vault 24, London Silver Vaults,
Chancery Lane, London WC2A 1QS
Tel: 020 7405 7009
www.chinesesilver.com

Shapiro & Company
380 Grays Antiques Markets,
58 Davies Street, London W1K 5LP
Tel: 020 7491 2710

Smith & Robinson
101 Portobello Road, London W11 2QB
Tel: 020 7371 0552
www.smithandrobinson.com

Steppes Hill Farm Antiques
Steppes Hill Farm, Stockbury,
Sittingbourne, Kent ME9 7RB
Tel: 01795 842205
www.steppeshillfarm.com

Van Den Bosch
123 Grays, 58 Davies St, London W1K
3LP
Tel: 020 7629 1900
www.vandenbosch.co.uk

William Walter Antiques Ltd
London Silver Vaults, Chancery House,
Chancery Lane, London, WC2A 1QS
Tel:020 7242 3248
www.williamwalter.co.uk

Daniel Bexfield Antiques
26 Burlington Arcade, W1J 0PU
Tel: 020 7491 1720
www.bexfield.co.uk

TEXTILES
Antique Textiles and Lighting
34 Belvedere, Lansdowne Road, Bath,
Avon BA1 5HR
Tel: 01225 310 795/443884
www.antiquesofbath.com

Esther Fitzgerald Rare Textiles
28 Church Row, London NW3 6UP
Tel: 020 7431 3076
www.estherfitzgerald.co.uk

Junnaa & Thomi Wroblewski
78 Marylebone High Street,
Box 39, London W1U 5AP
Tel: 020 7499 7793
junnaa@wroblewski.eu.com
thomi@wroblewski.eu.com

Rellick
8 Golborne Road,
London W10 5NW
Tel: 020 8962 0089

Vintage to Vogue
28 Milsom Street, Bath,
Avon BA1 1DG
Tel: 01225 337 323

Erna Hiscock & John Shepherd
Barn Owls, Finn Farm Road, Kings
North, Ashford, Kent TN23 3EX
Tel: 01233 661407
www.ernahiscockantiques.com

TRIBAL ART
Jean-Baptiste Bacquart
62 Gloucester Place, London W1U 8HW
Tel: 020 7224 0282
www.AfricanAndOceanicArt.com

Michael Graham Stewart
173 New Bond Street
London W1S 4RF
Tel: 020 7495 4001

Owen Hargreaves & Jasmine Dahl
9 Corsham Street
London N1 6DP
Tel: 020 7253 2669
www.owenhargreaves.com

SPORTING
Manfred Schotten Antiques
109 High Street, Burford, Oxfordshire
OX18 4RG
Tel: 01993 822302
www.schotten.com

WINE ANTIQUES
Christopher Sykes
The Old Parsonage
Woburn, Milton Keynes,
Buckinghamshire MK17 9QL
Tel: 01525 290259

INDEX TO ADVERTISERS

INDEX

INDEX